SOCIAL STUDIES CURRICULUM RESOURCE HANDBOOK

A Practical Guide for K-12 Social Studies Curriculum

KRAUS INTERNATIONAL PUBLICATIONS
A Division of The Kraus Organization Limited
Millwood, New York

Consulting editors:

Dennis W. Cheek
*Coordinator, Curriculum Development, New York Science,
Technology and Society Education Project,
New York State Education Department, Albany, New York*

Sylvester Kohut, Jr.
*Dean, College of Education and Behavioral Science, Morehead
State University, Morehead, Kentucky*

First Printing 1992

Printed in the United States of America

Library of Congress Cataloging-in-Publication Data

Social studies curriculum resources handbook : a practical
  guide for K-12 social studies curriculum.
     p.   cm.
  Includes bibliographical references and index.
  ISBN 0-527-20805-1 : $19.95
  1. Social sciences--Study and teaching (Elementary)--United
States--Handbooks, manuals, etc. 2. Social sciences--Study and
teaching (Secondary)--United States--Handbooks, manuals,
etc. 3. Curriculum planning--United States. I. Kraus International Publications
LB1585.S6375 1992
300.71'73--dc20   92-20365

CONTENTS

PART III: TEXTBOOKS, CLASSROOM MATERIALS, AND OTHER RESOURCES

PUBLISHER'S FOREWORD

THE *Social Studies Curriculum Resource Handbook* is one of a new series of practical references for curriculum developers, education faculty, veteran teachers, and student teachers. The handbook is designed to provide basic information on the background of social studies curriculum, as well as current information on publications, standards, and special materials for K-12 social studies. Think of this handbook as the first place to look when you are revising or developing your social studies curriculum--or if you need basic resource information on social studies any time of the year.

This handbook does not seek to prescribe any particular form of curriculum, nor does it follow any set of standards or guidelines. Instead, the book provides a general grounding in social studies curriculum, so that you can use this information and then proceed in the direction best suited for your budget, your school, and your district. What this handbook gives you is a sense of the numerous *options* that are available--it is up to you to use the information to develop the appropriate curriculum or program for your situation.

How to Use This Handbook

There are various ways to use this resource handbook. If you are revising or creating a social studies curriculum, you should read the Introduction (for an overall sense of the different philosophies of curriculum--and how this will affect the program you develop), Chapter 1 (for basic background on the trends and research in K-12 social studies), and Chapter 2 (for a how-to guide to developing curriculum materials). With this background, you can go through the other chap-

ters for the specific information you need-- ranging from topics to be covered at various grade levels (Chapter 4), to state requirements (Chapter 5), to publishers and producers (Chapter 11).

If you know what type of information you need, then you should check the Table of Contents for the most appropriate chapter, or check the Index to see where this material is covered. For instance:

1. If you are looking for materials for use in special social studies projects, turn to Chapter 9.
2. If you are looking for a new textbook or new supplementary material (book, video, or software), turn to Chapter 11.
3. If you need to contact state departments of education for curriculum documents, check the list provided in Chapter 6.

What's in the Handbook

The *Introduction* provides an overview of the ideologies and philosophies that have affected American curriculum through the years. This section will acquaint you with the various ideologies, so that you can determine whether your school is following one such philosophy (or a combination), and how this might influence the development of your curriculum. The Introduction is generic by design, since these ideologies pertain to all subject areas.

Chapter 1 provides an overview of *Trends and Issues* in social studies curriculum. This chapter discusses the development of present-day curriculum, and looks at the directions social studies curriculum is taking. The major research works are cited, so that you can get more detailed information on particular topics.

Chapter 2 is a step-by-step description of *Curriculum Process and Design.* It is meant to be a practical guide to creating or revising social studies curriculum guides. An Appendix to this chapter, *Funding the Project,* gives information on grants for program development.

Chapter 3, *Funding the Curriculum Project,* lists funding programs that are studying or developing curriculum. Along with addresses and phone numbers, the names of contact persons are provided, wherever possible, to expedite your gathering of information.

Chapter 4 provides an *Overview and Outline of Important Topics* in K-12 social studies. This is not meant to be a pattern to follow, but instead is a reflection of what most schools cover and what current research recommends.

Chapter 5, *State-Level Curriculum Guidelines: An Analysis,* describes the curriculum materials and includes the similarities among states and within regions, plus differences and gaps in coverage.

Chapter 6, *State-Level Curriculum Guidelines: A Listing,* supplements the previous chapter by listing addresses of state departments of education and publication titles.

Chapter 7 is an annotated list of *Recommended Curriculum Guides* for social studies.

Chapter 8 reprints sections of two social studies curriculum guides, to use as examples in creating your own curriculum materials.

Chapter 9 is a *Source List for Ideas and Materials* for special projects in social studies. This list provides the names and addresses of organizations that sponsor special programs, as well as publications that provide ideas for these projects.

Chapter 10 gives information on children's *Trade Books* that can be used as supplementary texts in social studies classrooms. This chapter discusses the bibliographic tools to use in finding these trade books; it also cites the various published lists of children's books for social studies.

Chapter 11 is an annotated list of *Curriculum Material Producers* and textbook publishers. It lists, by publisher/producer, textbooks, videos, software, and other materials for use in K-12 social studies.

Chapter 12 describes *Statewide Text Adoption,* with lists of the textbooks adopted by each state.

Chapter 13 is an *Index to Reviews* of social studies textbooks and supplementary materials. Since these items are reviewed in a wide variety of publications, we have assembled the citations of appropriate reviews in index form (cited by title, author, publisher/distributor, subject, and grade level).

Chapter 14 provides a list of *Kraus Curriculum Development Library* (KCDL) subscribers; KCDL is a good source for models of curriculum guides in all K-12 subject areas.

Acknowledgements

The content of this handbook is based on numerous meetings and discussions with educators and curriculum specialists across the country. Our thanks go to the curriculum supervisors in schools across the United States; the faculty at education departments in the colleges and universities we visited; and curriculum librarians. Special thanks go to the members of the Curriculum Materials Committee (CMC) and the Problems of Access and Control of Education Materials (PACEM) committee of the Association of College and Research Libraries' Education and Behavioral Science Section (ACRL/EBSS). Our meetings with the committees during American Library Association Conferences continue to provide Kraus with valuable ideas for the handbooks and for future curriculum projects.

We also acknowledge with thanks the assistance of Anne Isner, Marjorie Miller Kaplan, Carrie Lesh, Paula Martin, Barbara Meyers, Jean Russo, and the indexers at AEIOU.

Your Feedback

We have a final request of our readers. At the back of this handbook is a user survey that asks your opinions about the book, its coverage, and its contents. Once you have used this book, please fill out the questionnaire--it should only take a minute or so--and mail it back to us. If the form has already been removed, please just send us a letter with your opinions. We want to keep improving this new series of handbooks, and we can only do this with your help!

Please send questionnaires or other responses to:

Kraus International Publications
358 Saw Mill River Road
Millwood, NY 10546-1035
(914) 762-2200 / (800) 223-8323
Fax: (914) 762-1195

SERIES INTRODUCTION

P. Bruce Uhrmacher
Assistant Professor of Education
School of Education, University of Denver, Denver, Colorado

W HEN I travel by airplane and desire conversation, I inform the person sitting next to me that I'm in education. Everyone has an opinion about education. I hear stories about teachers (both good and bad), subject matter ("The problem with the new math is . . ."), and tests ("I should have gotten an A on that exam in seventh grade"). Many people want to tell me about the problems with education today ("Schools aren't what they used to be"). Few people are apathetic about schooling. When I do not wish to be disturbed in flight, however, I avoid admitting I'm in education. "So, what do you do?" someone trying to draw me out asks. I reply matter-of-factly, "I'm a curriculum theorist." Unless they persist, my retort usually signals the end of the dialogue. Unlike the job titles *farmer*, *stockbroker*, or even *computer analyst*, for many people *curriculum theorist* conjures few images.

What do curriculum theorists do? The answer to this question depends in part on the way curriculum theorists conceive of curriculum and theory. The term *curriculum* has over 150 definitions. With so many different ways of thinking about it, no wonder many curriculum theorists see their task differently. In this introduction, I point out that curriculum theorists have a useful function to serve, despite the fact that we can't agree on what to do. In short, like economists who analyze trends and make recommendations about the economy (and, incidentally, who also agree on very little), curriculum theorists generate a

constructive dialogue about curriculum decisions and practices. Although curricularists originally fought over the word *curriculum*, trying to achieve conceptual clarity in order to eliminate the various differences, in time educators recognized that the fight over the term was unproductive (Zais 1976, 93). However, the problem was not simply an academic disagreement. Instead, curricularists focused on different aspects of the educational enterprise. At stake in the definition of curriculum was a conceptual framework that included the nature of the role of the curricularist and the relationships among students, teachers, subject matter, and educational environments. Today, most curricularists place adjectives before the term to specify what type of curriculum they're discussing. Thus, one often reads about the intended, the operational, the hidden, the explicit, the implicit, the enacted, the delivered, the experienced, the received, and the null curriculum (see glossary at the end of this chapter). Distinctions also can be made with regard to curricularist, curriculum planner, curriculum worker, and curriculum specialist. I use the terms *curricularist* and *curriculum theorist* to refer to individuals, usually at the college level, who worry about issues regarding curriculum theory. I use the other terms to refer to people who actually take part in the planning or the implementation of curriculum in schools.

In order to trace the development that has brought the field of curriculum to its present state,

I will begin with a brief overview of the progression of curriculum development in the United States. First, I examine issues facing the Committee of Ten, a group of educators who convened in 1892 to draft a major document regarding what schools should teach. Next, I focus on the perennial question of who should decide what schools teach. Curriculum was not a field of study until the 1920s. How were curriculum decisions made before there were curriculum specialists? How did curriculum become a field of study? We learn that the profession began, in part, as a scientific endeavor; whether the field should still be seen as a scientific one is a question of debate. Finally, I provide a conceptual framework that examines six curriculum "ideologies" (Eisner 1992). By understanding these ideologies, educators will discern the assumptions underlying various conceptions of curriculum. Then they should be able to decide which ideology they wish to pursue and to recognize its educational implications.

What Should Schools Teach?

In the nineteenth century, curriculum usually meant "the course of study," and what many educators worried about was what schools should teach. Under the theoretical influence of "mental discipline" (derived from the ideas of faculty psychologists), many educators believed that certain subjects strengthened the brain, much like certain exercises strengthened body muscles. Greek, Latin, and mathematics were important because they were difficult subjects and thus, presumably, exercised the brain. By the 1890s, however, with the great influx of Italian, Irish, Jewish, and Russian immigrants, and with the steady increase of students attending secondary schools, a concern grew over the relevance and value of such subjects as Greek and Latin. Why should German or French be any less worthy than Greek or Latin? In addition, students and parents raised further questions regarding the merits of vocational education. They wanted curricula that met their more practical needs.

While parents pressed for their concerns, secondary school principals worried about preparing students for college, since colleges had different entrance requirements. In 1892 the National Education Association (NEA) appointed the Committee of Ten to remedy this problem. Headed by Charles W. Eliot, president of Harvard University, the committee debated and evaluated the extent to which a single curriculum could work for a large number of students who came from many different backgrounds with many different needs. In its final report, the committee suggested that colleges consider of equal value and accept students who attended not only the classical curriculum program, but also the Latin scientific, the modern language, and the English programs.

By eliminating the requirement of Greek for two of the programs and by reducing the number of required Latin courses, the committee broke with the traditional nineteenth-century curriculum to some degree. Yet, they were alert to the possibility that different kinds of curriculum programs taught in different ways could lead to a stratified society. Eliot had argued that the European system of classifying children into "future peasants, mechanics, trades-people, merchants, and professional people" was unacceptable in a democratic society (Tanner and Tanner 1975, 186). The committee believed all should have the opportunity for further studies under a "rational humanist" orientation to curriculum, a viewpoint that prizes the power of reason and the relevance and importance of learning about the best that Western culture has to offer.

The committee's report met with mixed reviews when it came out. One of its foremost opponents was G. Stanley Hall, a "developmentalist," who argued that the "natural order of development in the child was the most significant and scientifically defensible basis for determining what should be taught" (Kliebard 1986, 13). According to Hall, who had scientifically observed children's behavior at various stages of development, the committee did not take into account children's wide-ranging capabilities, and it promulgated a college-bound curriculum for everyone, even though many high school students would not go to college. Rather than approaching curriculum as the pursuit of a standard academic experience for all students, Hall and other developmentalists believed that knowledge of human development could contribute to creating a curriculum in harmony with the child's stage of interest and needs.

Thus far I have indicated two orientations to curriculum: the rational humanist and the developmentalist. We should understand, however, that at any given time a number of interest groups struggle for power over the curriculum. Historian Herbert Kliebard observes:

> We do not find a monolithic supremacy
> exercised by one interest group; rather we

find different interest groups competing for dominance over the curriculum and, at different times, achieving some measure of control depending on local as well as general social conditions. Each of these interest groups, then, represents a force for a different selection of knowledge and values from the culture and hence a kind of lobby for a different curriculum. (Kliebard 1986, 8)

Who Should Decide What Schools Teach?

Thinking about curriculum dates back in Western culture to at least the ancient Greeks. Plato and Aristotle, as well as Cicero, Plutarch, and Rousseau, all thought about curriculum matters in that they debated the questions of what should be taught to whom, in what way, and for what purposes. But it wasn't until 1918 that curriculum work was placed in the professional domain with the publication of *The Curriculum* by Franklin Bobbitt, a professor at the University of Chicago. Although supervisors and administrators had written courses of study on a piecemeal basis, "Professor Bobbitt took the major step of dealing with the curriculum in all subjects and grades on a unified and comprehensive basis" (Gress 1978, 27). The term *curriculum theory* came into use in the 1920s, and the first department of curriculum was founded at Teachers College, Columbia University, in 1937. Of course, the question arises: If curricularists (a.k.a. curriculum specialists, curriculum theorists, and curriculum workers) were not making decisions about what should be taught in schools prior to the 1920s, then who was?

As we have seen, national commissions made some of the curricular decisions. The NEA appointed the Committee of Ten to address college-high school articulation in 1892 and the Committee of Fifteen to address elementary school curriculum in 1895. In the early 1900s the NEA appointed another committee to develop fundamental principles for the reorganization of secondary education. Thus, university professors, school superintendents, and teachers made some curricular decisions as they acted in the role of acknowledged authorities on national commissions.

Along with commissions, forces such as tradition have shaped the curriculum. One longtime student of curriculum, Philip Jackson, observes:

One reason why certain subjects remain in the curriculum is simply that they have been there for such a long time. Indeed, some portions of the curriculum have been in place for so long that the question of how they got there or who decided to put them there in the first place has no answer, or at least not one that anyone except a historian would be able to give. As far as most people are concerned, they have just "always" been there, or so it seems. (Jackson 1992, 22)

Jackson also notes here that subjects such as the three R's are so "obviously useful that they need no further justification"--or, at least, so it seems.

Texts and published materials have also been factors in shaping the curriculum. Whether it was the old *McGuffey Readers* or the modern textbooks found in almost any classroom in the United States, these books have influenced the curriculum by virtue of their content and their widespread use. According to some estimates, text materials dominate 75 percent of the time elementary and secondary students are in classrooms and 90 percent of their time on homework (Apple 1986, 85). Textbook writers are de facto curriculum specialists.

National Commission committees, tradition, textbooks, instructional materials, and the influence from numerous philosophers (e.g., Herbart and Dewey) were focal in deciding what schools should teach. Of course, parents, state boards of education, and teachers had their own convictions as to what should be in the curriculum. However, as the United States moved toward urbanization (30 percent of 63 million lived in cities in 1890; over 50 percent of 106 million lived in cities in 1920 [Cremin 1977, 93]), new factors influenced schooling. In particular, the industrial and scientific revolutions commingled in the minds of some to produce new ways of thinking about work. Franklin Bobbitt applied these new ideas to education. Influenced by Frederick Winslow Taylor, the father of the scientific management movement, Bobbitt assumed that the kinds of accomplishments that had been made in business and industry could be made in education. What was needed was the application of scientific principles to curriculum.

Briefly, Bobbitt believed that "educational engineers" or "curriculum-discoverers," as he called them, could make curriculum by surveying the array of life's endeavors and by grouping this broad range of human experience into major fields. Bobbitt wrote:

The curriculum-discoverer will first be an analyst of human nature and of human affairs. . . . His first task . . . is to discover the total range of habits, skills, abilities, forms of thought . . . etc., that its members need for the effective performance of their vocational labors; likewise the total range needed for their civic activities; their health activities; their recreations, their language; their parental, religious, and general social activities. The program of analysis will be no narrow one. It will be as wide as life itself. (Bobbitt 1918, 43)

Thus, according to Bobbitt, curriculum workers would articulate educational goals by examining the array of life's activities. Next, in the same way one can analyze the tasks involved in making a tangible object and eliminate waste in producing it, Bobbitt believed one could streamline education by task analysis, by forming objectives for each task, and by teaching skills as discrete units.

Bobbitt's push for the professionalization of curriculum did not replace other factors so much as it added a new dimension. By arguing that schools needed stated objectives and that curricularists should be chosen for the task since they were trained in the science of curriculum, Bobbitt opened up a new line of work. He and his students would be of direct help to practitioners because they would know how to proceed scientifically (analyze the range of human experience, divide it into activities, create objectives) in the making of curriculum, and this knowledge gave curricularists authority and power. The world was rapidly changing in communications, in agriculture, in industry, and most of all in medicine. Who could argue with the benefits of science?

If Franklin Bobbitt created the field of professional curriculum activities, Ralph Tyler defined it. In his short monograph, *Basic Principles of Curriculum and Instruction* (1949), Tyler offered a way of viewing educational institutions. He began his book by asking four fundamental questions that he believed must be answered in developing curriculum:

1. What educational purposes should the school seek to attain?
2. What educational experiences can be provided that are likely to attain those purposes?
3. How can these educational experiences be effectively organized?
4. How can we determine whether these purposes are being attained? (Tyler 1949, 1)

Tyler devoted one chapter to each question.

Unlike some curricularists, Tyler did not say what purposes a school should seek to attain. He recognized that a school in rural Idaho has different needs from an urban one in Boston. Rather, Tyler suggested that schools themselves determine their own purposes from three sources: studies of the learners themselves, studies of contemporary life, and studies from subject matter specialists.

Tyler, like Bobbitt before him, wished to bring order to the complex field of education. Although there are differences between the two men, both believed there was work to be done by professional curricularists. Both men trained students in the field of curriculum, and both believed in the liberal ideals of rationality and progress. Curricularist Decker Walker summarizes the tradition that Bobbitt and Tyler started as follows:

Since Bobbitt's day, planning by objectives (PBO) had developed into a family of widely used approaches to curriculum improvement. As a method of curriculum materials design, PBO focuses early attention on developing precise statements of the objectives to be sought. If the process is to be fully scientific, the selection of objectives must be rationally justifiable and not arbitrary. (Walker 1990, 469)

While Bobbitt and Tyler taught students how to become professional curricularists and encouraged them to conduct research, to write, and to attain university positions, differences of opinion on what curricularists should be doing soon mounted. At issue was not only the utility of scientific curriculum making, but also the specific endeavors many curricularists pursued.

A Framework for Thinking about Curriculum

Tyler produced a seminal work that provided curriculum workers with a way of thinking about curriculum. While some elaborated on his ideas (Taba 1962), others wondered whether indeed Tyler provided the best questions for curricularists to think about. During the 1970s, numerous educators began to seek other ways of thinking about curriculum work. William Pinar, for example, asked, "Are Tyler's questions . . . no longer pertinent or possible? Are they simply cul-de-sacs?" (Pinar 1975, 397). Reconceptualizing the term *curriculum* (race course) from the verb of the Latin root, *currere* (to run a race), Pinar goes on to argue:

> The questions of *currere* are not Tyler's; they are ones like these: Why do I identify with Mrs. Dalloway and not with Mrs. Brown? What psychic dark spots does the one light, and what is the nature of "dark spots," and "light spots"? Why do I read Lessing and not Murdoch? Why do I read such works at all? Why not biology or ecology? Why are some drawn to the study of literature, some to physics, and some to law? (402)

More will be said about Pinar's work later. My point here is that curriculum theorists do not necessarily agree on how one should approach thinking about curriculum. By trying to redefine curriculum entirely, Pinar drew attention to different aspects of the educational process.

Out of this continuing discussion among curricularists, various ideologies--beliefs about what schools should teach, for what ends, and for what reasons--have developed (Eisner 1992). In this section, I present six prominent curriculum ideologies that should prove useful in thinking about developing, adapting, or implementing curriculum. While these ideologies are important, they are not the only ones. Elliot Eisner writes of religious orthodoxy and progressivism and excludes multiculturalism and developmentalism. Some authors may include constructivism rather than developmentalism.

I remind the reader that few people actually wear the labels I describe. These conceptualizations are useful in helping one better articulate a set of assumptions and core values. They help us see the implications of a particular viewpoint. They also help us understand issues and concerns that may otherwise be neglected. Sometimes ideologies are specified in mission statements or some other kind of manifesto; at other times, ideologies are embedded in educational practice but are not made explicit. Rarely does a school adhere to one curriculum ideology--though some do. More often, because public schools are made up of people who have different ideas about what schools should teach, a given school is more likely to embrace an array of curricular ideas. While some readers may resonate strongly with a particular ideology because it expresses their inclinations, some readers may appreciate particular ideas from various ideologies. In either case, it may be a good idea to examine the strengths and weaknesses of each one. Later in this chapter I argue that one does not need to be ideologically pure in order to do good curriculum work.

Rational Humanism

We have already seen, in the historical example of Charles Eliot and the Committee of Ten, an early exemplar of rational humanism. During Eliot's day, rational humanists embraced the theory of mental discipline, which provided a handy rationale for traditional studies. Why study Greek and Latin? Because these subjects exercised the mind in ways that other subjects did not. While mental discipline fell by the wayside, rational humanism did not. From the 1930s through the 1950s, Robert Maynard Hutchins and Mortimer Adler championed the rational humanistic tradition, in part by editing *The Great Books of the Western World*. Hutchins argued that the "great books" offer the best that human beings have thought and written. Thus, rather than reading textbooks on democracy, science, and math, one ought to read Jefferson, Newton, and Euclid.

Today, one may find the rational humanist ideology in some private schools and in those public schools that have adopted Adler's ideas as represented in the *Paideia Proposal* (Eisner 1992, 310). In short, the Paideia plan provides a common curriculum for all students. Except for the choosing of a foreign language, there are no electives. All students learn language, literature, fine arts, mathematics, natural science, history, geography, and social studies.

While Adler endorses lecturing and coaching as two important teaching methods, the aspect of teaching Adler found most engaging was maieutic or Socratic questioning and active participation. In essence, maieutic teaching consists of a seminar situation in which learners converse in a group. The teacher serves as a facilitator who moves the conversation along, asks leading questions, and helps students develop, examine, or refine their thinking as they espouse particular viewpoints. This process, according to Adler, "teaches participants how to analyze their own minds as well as the thought of others, which is to say it engages students in disciplined conversation about ideas and values" (Adler 1982, 30).

Another important educational feature of these seminars is that one discusses books and art but not textbooks. In a follow-up book to *The Paideia Proposal*, Adler (1984) provides a K-12 recommended reading list in which he recommends for kindergarten to fourth grade Aesop, William Blake, Shel Silverstein, Alice Walker, Jose Marie Sanchez-Silva, Langston Hughes, and Dr. Seuss, among other authors. I indicate these authors in particular because the charge that

Adler's program embraces only the Western European heritage is not entirely accurate. While Adler would argue that some books are better than others, and that, in school, students should be reading the better ones, one can see that Adler includes authors who are not elitist and who are from culturally diverse backgrounds.

Developmentalism

Another approach to curriculum theory, which was discussed briefly in the historical section of this chapter, is developmentalism. Although a range of scholars falls under this heading, the basic point is that, rather than fitting the child to the curriculum, students would be better served if the curriculum were fitted to the child's stage of development. Why? One argument is that doing otherwise is inefficient or even detrimental to the child's development. It would be ridiculous to try to teach the Pythagorean theorem to a first grader, and it could be harmful (to use a fairly noncontroversial example) to teach a fourth grader to master throwing a curve ball. By understanding the range of abilities children have at various ages, one can provide a curriculum that meets the needs and interests of students. Of course, while the stage concept cannot pinpoint the development of a particular child at a given age, it serves as a general guide.

One might also pay attention to the idea of development when creating or adapting curriculum because of the issue of "readiness for learning." There are two ways of thinking about readiness. Some educators, in their interest to hurry development, believe that encouraging learners to perform approximations of desired behaviors can hasten academic skills. In this case, one tries to intervene in apparently natural development by manipulating the child's readiness at younger and younger ages. The research findings on whether one can greatly enhance one's learning processes are somewhat mixed, but, in my opinion, they favor the side that says "speed learning" is inefficient (Duckworth 1987, Good and Brophy 1986, Tietze 1987). I also think the more important question, as Piaget noted, is "not how fast we can help intelligence grow, but how far we can help it grow" (Duckworth 1987, 38).

A different way of thinking about readiness for learning concerns not how to speed it up, but how to work with it effectively. Eleanor Duckworth, who studied with Piaget, believes the idea of readiness means placing children in developmentally appropriate problem situations where students are allowed to have their own "wonderful ideas." She believes that asking "the right question at the right time can move children to peaks in their thinking that result in significant steps forward and real intellectual excitement" (Duckworth 1987, 5). The challenges for teachers are to provide environmentally rich classrooms where students have the opportunity to "mess about" with things, and to try to understand children's thought processes. Students should have the opportunity to experiment with materials likely to afford intellectual growth, and teachers should learn how their students think. In this approach to curriculum, mistakes are not problems; they are opportunities for growth.

The developmental approach to curriculum teaches us to pay attention to the ways humans grow and learn. One basic idea underlying the various theories of human development in regard to curriculum is that the curriculum planner ought to understand children's abilities and capabilities because such knowledge enables one to provide worthwhile educational activities for students.

Reconceptualism

As noted earlier with Pinar's use of the term *currere*, during the 1970s numerous individuals criticized the technical aspects and linear progression of steps of the Tyler rationale. Loosely labelled as reconceptualists, some educators felt the following:

> What is missing from American schools . . . is a deep respect for personal purpose, lived experience, the life of imagination, and those forms of understanding that resist dissection and measurement. What is wrong with schools, among other things, is their industrialized format, their mechanistic attitudes toward students, their indifference to personal experience, and their emphasis on the instrumental and the out of reach. (Pinar 1975, 316)

Reconceptualists have focused on Dewey's observation that one learns through experience. Given this assertion, some important questions arise. For example, how can teachers, teacher educators, or educational researchers better understand the kinds of experiences individual students are having? To answer this question, reconceptualists employ ideas, concepts, and theories from psychoanalysis, philosophy, and literature.

Another question that arises when one reflects on understanding experience is, How can teachers provide worthwhile conditions for students to undergo educational experiences? Maxine Greene divides educational experiences into two types: "an education for having" and "an education for being." Education for having is utilitarian--for example, one may learn to read in order to get a job. Some students need this kind of experience. Education for being is soulful--one may learn to read for the sensual qualities it can provide. All students, she says, need the latter kind of experience. One problem is that the latter has often been neglected or, if not, often provided for the talented or gifted at the expense of others (Green, 1988a).

In their effort to reperceive education, reconceptualists such as Maxine Greene, Madeleine Grumet, and William Pinar do not usually offer specific educational ideas that are easily implemented. In part, this is because the kind of education with which they are concerned is not easy to quantify or measure. In general, reconceptualists do not believe their theories and ideas need quick utilization in schools in order to validate their worth. If in reading their writings you think more deeply about educational issues, then I think they would be satisfied.

Nevertheless, I can think of two practical challenges for education that stem from their writing. First, how could you write a rigorous and tough-minded lesson plan without using objectives? What would such a lesson plan look like? Second, if you wanted to teach students a concept such as citizenship, how would you do it? Rational humanists would have students read Thomas Jefferson or Martin Luther King, Jr. Reconceptualists, however, would wonder how teachers can place students in problematic situations (i.e., in the classroom or on the playground) where students would grapple with real issues concerning citizenship.

Critical Theory

The idea of critical theory originated at the Institute for Social Research in Frankfurt ("the Frankfurt school") in the 1920s. Today, scholars who continue to recognize the value and importance of Marxist critiques of society and culture draw from and build on ideas from critical theory. In education they reveal, among other things, that schooling comprises a value-laden enterprise where issues of power are always at play.

For instance, while many people perceive schools as neutral institutions, places that will help any hard-working student to get ahead in life, critical theorists suggest that, on the contrary,

schools do not operate that way. Michael Apple points out, "Just as our dominant economic institutions are structured so that those who inherit or already have economic capital do better, so too does cultural capital act in the same way" (Apple 1986, 33). According to Apple, schools reflect the general inequities in the larger society. Rather than changing society through cultural transformation (teaching students to question or to be independent thinkers), schools actually maintain the status quo through cultural reproduction.

Unlike some curricularists who try to appear neutral in exercising judgments about curriculum matters, Apple's values are well known. He believes in John Rawls's insight that "for a society to be truly just, it must maximize the advantage of the least advantaged" (Apple 1979, 32). Apple encourages curricularists to take advocacy positions within and outside of education. While critical theory makes for a powerful theoretical tool, one question frequently asked of critical theorists is how this information can be used in the classroom. Teachers point out that they may not be able to change the school structure, the kinds of material they must cover, or the kinds of tests that must be given. Although admittedly application is difficult, one high school English educator in Boston who employs the ideas of critical theory is Ira Shor.

In an activity called "prereading," for example, Shor tells students the theme of a book they are about to read and has them generate hypothetical questions the book may answer. At first students are reluctant to respond, but after a while they do. Shor believes this kind of exercise has numerous functions. First, it provides a bridge for students to decelerate from the "rush of mass culture" into the slow medium of the printed word. Habituated to rock music and MTV, students need a slow-down time. Also, after creating a list of questions, students are curious how many will actually be addressed. Students may still reject the text, says Shor, but now it won't be a result of alienation. Perhaps most importantly, prereading demystifies the power of the written word. Rather than approaching the text as some kind of untouchable authority, "students' own thoughts and words on the reading topic are the starting points for the coordinated material. The text will be absorbed into the field of their language rather than they being ruled by it" (Shor 1987, 117).

Critical theory offers a radical way of thinking

about schooling. Particularly concerned with students who are disenfranchised and who, without the critical theorists, would have no voice to speak for them, critical theory provides incisive analyses of educational problems.

Multiculturalism

In some ways, multiculturalists are in affinity with the critical theorists. Though critical theory traditionally is more concerned with class, most critical theorists have included race and gender in their analyses and discussions. Multiculturalism, however, deserves its own category as a curriculum ideology because it is rooted in the ethnic revival movements of the 1960s. Whether the purpose is to correct racist and bigoted views of the larger community, to raise children's self-esteem, to help children see themselves from other viewpoints, or to reach the child's psychological world, the multicultural ideology reminds educators that ethnicity must be dealt with by educators.

One major approach to multicultural education has been termed "multiethnic ideology" by James Banks (1988). According to Banks, Americans participate in several cultures--the mainstream along with various ethnic subcultures. Therefore, students ought to have cross-cultural competency. In addition to being able to participate in various cultures, Banks also suggests that when one learns about various cultures, one begins to see oneself from other viewpoints. The multiethnic ideology provides greater self-understanding.

When teaching from a multiethnic perspective, Banks advises that an issue not be taught from a dominant mainstream perspective with other points of view added on. This kind of teaching still suggests that one perspective is the "right one," though others also have their own points of view. Rather, one should approach the concept or theme from various viewpoints. In this case, the mainstream perspective becomes one of several ways of approaching the topic; it is not superior or inferior to other ethnic perspectives. In addition to what takes place in the classroom, Banks also argues that a successful multiethnic school must have system-wide reform. School staff, school policy, the counseling program, assessment, and testing are all affected by the multiethnic ideology.

Cognitive Pluralism

According to Eisner, the idea of cognitive plural-

ism goes back at least to Aristotle; however, only in the last several decades has a conception of the plurality of knowledge and intelligence been advanced in the field of curriculum (Eisner 1992, 317). In short, cognitive pluralists expand our traditional notions of knowledge and intelligence. Whereas some scientists and educators believe that people possess a single intelligence (often called a "g factor") or that all knowledge can ultimately be written in propositional language, cognitive pluralists believe that people possess numerous intelligences and that knowledge exists in many forms of representation.

As a conception of knowledge, cognitive pluralists argue that symbol systems provide a way to encode visual, auditory, kinesthetic, olfactory, gustatory, and tactile experiences. If, for example, one wants to teach students about the Civil War, cognitive pluralists would want students not only to have knowledge about factual material (names, dates, and battles), but also to have knowledge about how people felt during the war. To know that slavery means by definition the owning of another person appears quite shallow to knowing how it feels to be powerless. Cognitive pluralists suggest students should be able to learn through a variety of forms of representation (e.g., narratives, poetry, film, pictures) and be able to express themselves through a variety of forms as well. The latter point about expression means that most tests, which rely on propositional language, are too limiting. Some students may better express themselves through painting or poetry.

One may also think about cognitive pluralism from the point of view of intelligence. As I mentioned, some scholars suggest that intelligence may be better thought of as multiple rather than singular. Howard Gardner, a leading advocate of this position (1983), argues that, according to his own research and to reviews of a wide array of studies, a theory of multiple intelligences is more viable than a theory about a "g factor." He defines intelligence as follows:

> To my mind, a human intellectual competence must entail a set of skills of problem-solving-- enabling the individual to resolve genuine problems or difficulties that he or she encounters and, when appropriate, to create an effective product--and must also entail the potential for finding or creating problems-- thereby laying the groundwork for the acquisition of new knowledge. (Gardner 1983, 60-61)

Gardner argues that there are at least seven distinct kinds of human intelligence: linguistic, musical, logical-mathematical, spatial, bodily-kinesthetic, interpersonal, and intrapersonal. If schools aim to enhance cognitive development, then they ought to teach students to be knowledgeable of, and to practice being fluent in, numerous kinds of intelligences. To limit the kinds of knowledge or intelligences students experience indicates an institutional deficiency.

Applying Curriculum Ideologies

While some teachers or schools draw heavily on one particular curriculum ideology (e.g., Ira Shor's use of critical theory in his classroom or Mortimer Adler's ideas in Paideia schools), more often than not, a mixture of various ideologies pervade educational settings. I don't believe this is a problem. What Joseph Schwab said in the late 1960s about theory also applies to ideologies. He argued that theories are partial and incomplete, and that, as something rooted in one's mind rather than in the state of affairs, theories cannot provide a complete guide for classroom practice (1970). In other words, a theory about child development may tell you something about ten year olds in general, but not about a particular ten year old standing in front of you. Child development cannot tell you, for example, whether or how to reprimand a given child for failing to do his homework. Schwab suggested one become eclectic and deliberative when working in the practical world. In simpler terms, one should know about various theories and use them when applicable. One does not need to be ideologically pure. One should also reflect upon one's decisions and talk about them with other people. Through deliberation one makes new decisions which lead to new actions which then cycle around again to reflection, decision, and action.

To understand this eclectic approach to using curriculum ideologies, let's take as an example the use of computers in the classroom. Imagine you are about to be given several computers for your class. How could knowledge of the various curriculum ideologies inform your use of them?

Given this particular challenge, some ideologies will prove to be more useful than others. For example, the rational humanists would probably have little to contribute to this discussion because, with their interests in the cultivation of reason and the seminar process of teaching, computers are not central (though one of my students noted, that, perhaps in time, rational humanists will want to create a "great software" program).

Some developmentalists would consider the issue of when it would be most appropriate to introduce computers to students. Waldorf educators, who base their developmental ideas on the writings of philosopher Rudolf Steiner (1861-1925), do not believe one should teach students about computers at an early age. They would not only take into account students' cognitive development (at what age could students understand computers?), but they would also consider students' social, physical, and emotional development. At what age are students really excited about computers? When are their fingers large enough to work the keyboard? What skills and habits might children lose if they learned computers at too early an age? Is there an optimum age at which one ought to learn computers? Waldorf educators would ask these kinds of developmental questions.

Developmentalists following the ideas of Eleanor Duckworth may also ask the above questions, but whatever the age of the student they are working with, these educators would try to teach the computer to children through engaging interactive activities. Rather than telling students about the computer, teachers would set up activities where students can interact with them. In this orientation, teachers would continue to set up challenges for students to push their thinking. Sustaining students' sense of wonder and curiosity is equally important. In addition to setting new challenges for students, teachers would also monitor student growth by trying to understand student thought processes. In short, rather than fitting the child to the curriculum, the curriculum is fitted to the child.

Reconceptualists' first impulse would be to consider the educational, social, or cultural meaning of computers before worrying about their utility. Of course, one should remember that there isn't one party line for any given ideological perspective. Some reconceptualists may be optimistic about computers and some may not. Although I don't know William Pinar's or Madeleine Grumet's thoughts on computers, I imagine they would reflect on the way computers bring information to people. Pinar observes that place plays a role in the way one sees the world (Pinar 1991). The same machine with the same software can be placed in every school room, but even if students learn the same information, their relationship to this new knowledge will vary. Thus, to understand the impact of computers one needs to know a great deal about the people who will learn from and use them. Having students write autobiographies provides one way to attain this understanding. Students could write about or dramatize their encounters with technology. After such an understanding, teachers can tailor lessons to meet student needs.

Critical theorist Michael Apple has examined the issue of computers in schools. Though he points out that many teachers are delighted with the new technology, he worries about an uncritical acceptance of it. Many teachers, he notes, do not receive substantial information about computers before they are implemented. Consequently, they must rely on a few experts or pre-packaged sets of material. The effects of this situation are serious. With their reliance on purchased material combined with the lack of time to properly review and evaluate it, teachers lose control over the curriculum development process. They become implementers of someone else's plans and procedures and become deskilled and disempowered because of that (Apple 1986, 163).

Apple also worries about the kind of thinking students learn from computers. While students concentrate on manipulating machines, they are concerned with issues of "how" more than "why." Consequently, Apple argues, computers enhance technical but not substantive thinking. Crucial political and ethical understanding atrophies while students are engaged in computer proficiency. Apple does not suggest one avoid computers because of these problems. Rather, he wants teachers and students to engage in social, political, and ethical discussions while they use the new technology.

Multiculturalists would be concerned that all students have equal access to computers. Early research on computer implementation revealed that many minority students did not have the opportunity to use computers, and when they did, their interaction with computers often consisted of computer-assisted instruction programs that exercised low-level skills (Anderson, Welch, Harris 1984). In addition to raising the issue that all students should have equal access to computers, multiculturalists would also investigate whether software programs were sending biased or racist viewpoints.

Finally, cognitive pluralists, such as Elliot Eisner, would probably focus on the kinds of knowledge made available by computers. If computers were used too narrowly so that students had the opportunity to interact only with words and numbers, Eisner would be concerned.

He would point out, I believe, that students could be learning that "real" knowledge exists in two forms. If, however, computers enhance cognitive understanding by providing multiple forms of representation, then I think Eisner would approve of the use of this new technology in the classroom. For example, in the latest videodisc technology, when students look up the definition of a word, they find a written statement as well as a picture. How much more meaningful a picture of a castle is to a young child than the comment, "a fortified residence as of a noble in feudal times" (*Random House Dictionary* 1980, 142).

In addition to learning through a variety of sensory forms, Eisner would also want students to have the opportunity to express themselves in a variety of ways. Computers could be useful in allowing students to reveal their knowledge in visual and musical as well as narrative forms. Students should not be limited in the ways they can express what they know.

Each curriculum ideology offers a unique perspective by virtue of the kinds of values and theories embedded within it. By reflecting on some of the ideas from the various curriculum ideologies and applying them to an educational issue, I believe educators can have a more informed, constructive, and creative dialogue. Moreover, as I said earlier, I do not think one needs to remain ideologically pure. Teachers and curricularists would do well to borrow ideas from the various perspectives as long as they make sure they are not proposing contradictory ideas.

The following chart summarizes the major proponents, major writings, educational priorities, and philosophical beliefs of each curriculum ideology covered in this chapter. (Of course, this chart is not comprehensive. I encourage the reader to examine the recommended reading list for further works in each of these areas.) In the fifth column, "Teachers, Curriculum, or Schools Expressing Curriculum Ideology," I indicate places or texts where readers may learn more. One could visit a Paideia school, Carini's Prospect School, or the Key School in Indianapolis. One may read about reconceptualism, critical theory, and multiculturalism in the listed texts. Finally, in the sixth column, "Suggestions for Curriculum Development," I also include interesting points found in the literature but not necessarily contained in this chapter.

CURRICULUM IDEOLOGIES

Ideology	Major Proponent	Major Writings	Educational Priorities	Philosophical Beliefs	Teachers, Curriculum, or Schools Expressing Curriculum Ideology	Suggestions for Curriculum Development
Rational Humanism	R.M. Hutchins M. Adler	The Paideia Proposal (Adler 1982) Paideia Problems and Possibilities (Adler 1983) The Paideia Program (Adler 1984)	Teaching through Socratic method. The use of primary texts. No electives.	The best education for the best is the best education for all. Since time in school is short, expose students to the best of Western culture.	Paideia Schools. See Adler (1983) for a list of schools.	Teach students how to facilitate good seminars. Use secondary texts sparingly.
Developmentalism	E. Duckworth R. Steiner	Young Children Reinvent Arithmetic (Kamii 1985) "The Having of Wonderful Ideas" and Other Essays (Duckworth 1987) Rudolf Steiner Education and the Developing Child (Aeppli 1986)	Fit curriculum to child's needs and interests. Inquiry-oriented teaching.	Cognitive structures develop as naturally as walking. If the setting is right, students will raise questions to push their own thinking.	Pat Carini's Prospect School in Burlington, VT.	Allow teachers the opportunity to be surprised. Rather than writing a curriculum manual, prepare a curriculum giude.
Reconceptualism	W. Pinar M. Grumet	Bitter Milk (Grumet 1988) Curriculum Theorizing (Pinar 1975) Curriculum and Instruction (Giroux, Penna, Pinar 1981)	Use philosophy, psychology, and literature to understand the human experience. Provide an "education for having" and an "education for being."	One learns through experience. We can learn to understand experience through phenomenology, psychoanalysis, and literature.	See Oliver (1990) for a curriculum in accordance with reconceptualist thinking.	Write lesson plans without the use of objectives. Curriculum writers ought to reveal their individual subjectivities.
Critical Theory	M. Apple I. Shor P. Freire	Ideology and Curriculum (Apple 1979) Teachers and Texts (Apple 1986) Pedagogy of the Oppressed (Freire 1970) Freire for the Classroom (Shor 1987)	Equal opportunities for all students. Teaching should entail critical reflection.	A just society maximizes the advantage for the least advantaged. Schools are part of the larger community and must be analyzed as such.	See Shor's edited text (1987) for a number of ideas on implementing critical theory.	Curriculum writers ought to examine their own working assumptions critically and ought to respect the integrity of teachers and students.
Multiculturalism	J. Banks E. King	Multiethnic Education (Banks 1988) Multicultural Education (Banks and Banks 1989)	Students should learn to participate in various cultures. Approach concept or theme from various viewpoints.	Students need to feel good about their ethnic identities. All people participate in various cultures and subcultures.	See King (1990) for a workbook of activities teaching ethnic and gender awareness.	Make sure that text and pictures represent a variety of cultures.
Cognitive Pluralism	E. Eisner H. Gardner	"Curriculum Ideologies" (Eisner 1992) The Educational Imagination (Eisner 1985) Frames of Mind (Gardner 1983)	Teach, and allow students to express themselves, through a variety of forms of representation. Allow students to develop numerous intelligences.	Our senses cue into and pick up different aspects of the world. Combined with our individual history and general schemata, our senses allow us to construct meaning.	The Key School in Indianapolis.	Curriculum lesson plans and units ought to be aesthetically pleasing in appearance. Curriculum ought to represent a variety of ways of knowing

Recommended Reading

The following is a concise list of recommended reading in many of the areas discussed in this chapter. Full bibliographic citations are provided under *References*.

Some general **curriculum textbooks** that are invaluable are John D. McNeil's *Curriculum: A Comprehensive Introduction* (1990); William H. Schubert's *Curriculum: Perspective, Paradigm, and Possibility* (1986); Decker Walker's *Fundamentals of Curriculum* (1990); and Robert S. Zais's *Curriculum: Principles and Foundations* (1976). These books provide wonderful introductions to the field.

The recently published *Handbook of Research on Curriculum* (Jackson 1992) includes thirty-four articles by leading curricularists. This book is a must for anyone interested in research in curriculum.

For a discussion of **objectives** in education, Tyler (1949) is seminal. Also see Kapfer (1972) and Mager (1962). Bloom refines educational objectives into a taxonomy (1956). Eisner's (1985) critique of educational objectives and his notion of expressive outcomes will be welcomed by those who are skeptical of the objectives movement.

Good books on the **history of curriculum** include Kliebard (1986), Schubert (1980), and Tanner and Tanner (1975). Seguel (1966), who discusses the McMurry brothers, Dewey, Bobbitt, and Rugg, among others, is also very good.

Some excellent books on the **history of education** include the following: Lawrence Cremin's definitive book on progressive education, *The Transformation of the School: Progressivism in American Education, 1876-1957* (1961). David Tyack's *The One Best System* (1974) portrays the evolution of schools into their modern formation; and Larry Cuban's *How Teachers Taught: Constancy and Change in American Classrooms, 1890-1980* (1984) examines what actually happened in classrooms during a century of reform efforts. Philip Jackson's "Conceptions of Curriculum and Curriculum Specialists" (1992) provides an excellent summary of the evolution of curriculum thought from Bobbitt and Tyler to Schwab.

For works in each of the ideologies I recommend the following:

To help one understand the **rational humanist** approach, there are Mortimer Adler's three books on the **Paideia school**: *The Paideia Proposal: An Educational Manifesto* (1982), *Paideia Prob-lems and Possibilities* (1983), and *The Paideia Program: An Educational Syllabus* (1984). Seven critical reviews of the Paideia proposal comprise "The Paideia Proposal: A Symposium" (1983).

For works in **developmentalism** based on Piaget's ideas see Duckworth (1987, 1991) and Kamii (1985). Among Piaget's many works you may want to read *The Origins of Intelligence* (1966). If you are interested in Waldorf education see Robert McDermott's *The Essential Steiner* (1984) and P. Bruce Uhrmacher's "Waldorf Schools Marching Quietly Unheard" (1991). Willi Aeppli's *Rudolf Steiner Education and the Developing Child* (1986), Francis Edmunds's *Rudolf Steiner Education* (1982), and Marjorie Spock's *Teaching as a Lively Art* (1985) are also quite good.

A general overview of the developmental approach to curriculum can be found on pages 49-52 of Linda Darling-Hammond and Jon Snyder's "Curriculum Studies and the Traditions of Inquiry: The Scientific Tradition" (1922).

Two books are essential for examining **reconceptualist** writings: William Pinar's *Curriculum Theorizing: The Reconceptualists* (1975) and Henry Giroux, Anthony N. Penna, and William F. Pinar's *Curriculum and Instruction* (1981). Recent books in reconceptualism include William Pinar and William Reynolds's *Understanding Curriculum as Phenomenological and Deconstructed Text* (1992), and William Pinar and Joe L. Kincheloe's *Curriculum as Social Psychoanalysis: The Significance of Place* (1991).

Some excellent works in **critical theory** include Paulo Freire's *Pedagogy of the Oppressed* (1970) and *The Politics of Education* (1985). Apple's works are also excellent; see *Ideology and Curriculum* (1979) and *Teachers and Texts* (1986). For an overview of the Frankfurt School and the application of Jürgen Habermas's ideas, see Robert Young's *A Critical Theory of Education: Habermas and Our Children's Future* (1990).

For an application of critical theory to classrooms see the Ira Shor-edited book, *Freire for the Classroom* (1987) with an afterword by Paulo Freire.

In **multicultural education** I recommend James Banks's *Multiethnic Education: Theory and Practice* (1988) and Banks and Banks's *Multicultural Education: Issues and Perspectives* (1989). Also see Gibson (1984) for an account of five different approaches to multicultural education. Nicholas Appleton (1983), Saracho and Spodek (1983), and Simonson and Walker (1988) are also important. Edith King's *Teaching Ethnic and*

Gender Awareness: Methods and Materials for the Elementary School (1990) provides useful ideas about multicultural education that could be used in the classroom. John Ogbu's work (1987) on comparing immigrant populations to involuntary minorities is also an important work with serious educational implications.

Important works in the field of **cognitive pluralism** include Elliot Eisner (1982, 1985, 1992) and Howard Gardner (1983, 1991). Some philosophical texts that influenced both of these men include Dewey (1934), Goodman (1978), and Langer (1976).

For $20.00, the Key School Option Program will send you an interdisciplinary theme-based curriculum report. For more information write Indianapolis Public Schools, 1401 East Tenth Street, Indianapolis, Indiana 46201.

Glossary of Some Common Usages of Curriculum

delivered curriculum: what teachers deliver in the classroom. This is opposed to Intended curriculum. Same as operational curriculum.

enacted curriculum: actual class offerings by a school, as opposed to courses listed in books or guides. *See* official curriculum.

experienced curriculum: what students actually learn. Same as received curriculum.

explicit curriculum: stated aims and goals of a classroom or school.

hidden curriculum: unintended, unwritten, tacit, or latent aspects of messages given to students by teachers, school structures, textbooks, and other school resources. For example, while students learn writing or math, they may also learn about punctuality, neatness, competition, and conformity. Concealed messages may be intended or unintended by the school or teacher.

implicit curriculum: similar to the hidden curriculum in the sense that something is implied rather than expressly stated. Whereas the hidden curriculum usually refers to something unfavorable, negative, or sinister, the implicit curriculum also takes into account unstated qualities that are positive.

intended curriculum: that which is planned by the teacher or school.

null curriculum: that which does not take place in the school or classroom. What is not offered cannot be learned. Curricular exclusion tells a great deal about a school's values.

official curriculum: courses listed in the school catalogue or course bulletin. Although these classes are listed, they may not be taught. *See* enacted curriculum.

operational curriculum: events that take place in the classroom. Same as delivered curriculum.

received curriculum: what students acquire as a result of classroom activity. Same as experienced curriculum.

References

Adler, Mortimer J. 1982. *The Paideia Proposal: An Educational Manifesto*. New York: Collier Books.

——. 1983. *Paideia Problems and Possibilities*. New York: Collier Books.

——. 1984. *The Paideia Program: An Educational Syllabus*. New York: Collier Books.

Aeppli, Willi. 1986. *Rudolf Steiner Education and the Developing Child*. Hudson, NY: Anthroposophic Press.

Anderson, Ronald E., Wayne W. Welch, and Linda J. Harris. 1984. "Inequities in Opportunities for Computer Literacy." *The Computing Teacher: The Journal of the International Council for Computers in Education* 11(8): 10-12.

Apple, Michael W. 1979. *Ideology and Curriculum*. Boston: Routledge and Kegan Paul.

——. 1986. *Teachers and Texts: A Political Economy of Class and Gender Relations in Education*. New York: Routledge and Kegan Paul.

Appleton, Nicholas. 1983. *Cultural Pluralism in Education*. White Plains, NY: Longman.

Banks, James A. 1988. *Multiethnic Education: Theory and Practice*. 2d ed. Boston: Allyn and Bacon.

Banks, James A., and Cherry A. McGee Banks, eds. 1989. *Multicultural Education: Issues and Perspectives*. Boston: Allyn and Bacon.

Bloom, Benjamin S., ed. 1956. *Taxonomy of Educational Objectives: The Classification of*

Educational Goals, Handbook 1: Cognitive Domain. New York: McKay.

Bobbitt, Franklin. 1918. *The Curriculum*. Boston: Houghton Mifflin.

Cremin, Lawrence A. 1961. *The Transformation of the School: Progressivism in American Education, 1876-1957*. New York: Vintage Books.

———. 1977. *Traditions of American Education*. New York: Basic Books.

Cuban, Larry. 1984. *How Teachers Taught: Constancy and Change in American Classrooms 1890-1980*. White Plains, NY: Longman.

Darling-Hammond, Linda, and Jon Snyder. 1992. "Curriculum Studies and the Traditions of Inquiry: The Scientific Tradition." In *Handbook of Research on Curriculum: A Project of the American Educational Research Association*, ed. Philip W. Jackson, 41-78. New York: Macmillan.

Dewey, John. 1934. *Art as Experience*. New York: Minton, Balch.

Duckworth, Eleanor. 1987. *"The Having of Wonderful Ideas" and Other Essays on Teaching and Learning*. New York: Teachers College Press.

———. 1991. "Twenty-four, Forty-two, and I Love You: Keeping It Complex. *Harvard Educational Review* 61(1): 1-24.

Edmunds, L. Francis. 1982. *Rudolf Steiner Education*. 2d ed. London: Rudolf Steiner Press.

Eisner, Elliot W. 1982. *Cognition and Curriculum: A Basis for Deciding What to Teach*. White Plains, NY: Longman.

———. 1985. *The Educational Imagination*. 2d ed. New York: Macmillan.

———. 1992. "Curriculum Ideologies." In *Handbook of Research on Curriculum: A Project of the American Educational Research Association*, ed. Philip W. Jackson, 302-26. New York: Macmillan.

Freire, Paulo. 1970. *Pedagogy of the Oppressed*. Trans. Myra Bergman Ramos. New York: Seabury Press.

———. 1985. *The Politics of Education*. Trans. Donaldo Macedo. South Hadley, MA: Bergin and Garvey.

Gardner, Howard. 1983. *Frames of Mind*. New York: Basic Books.

———. 1991. *The Unschooled Mind: How Children Think and How Schools Should Teach*. New York: Basic Books.

Gibson, Margaret Alison. 1984. "Approaches to Multicultural Education in the United States: Some Concepts and Assumptions." *Anthropol-*

ogy and Education Quarterly 15: 94-119.

Giroux, Henry, Anthony N. Penna, and William F. Pinar. 1981. *Curriculum and Instruction: Alternatives in Education*. Berkeley: McCutchan.

Good, Thomas S., and Jere E. Brophy. 1986. *Educational Psychology*. 3d ed. White Plains, NY: Longman.

Goodman, Nelson. 1978. *Ways of Worldmaking*. Indianapolis: Hackett.

Greene, Maxine. 1988a. "Vocation and Care: Obsessions about Teacher Education." Panel discussion at the Annual Meeting of the American Educational Research Association, 5-9 April, New Orleans.

———. 1988b. *The Dialectic of Freedom*. New York: Teachers College Press.

Gress, James R. 1978. *Curriculum: An Introduction to the Field*. Berkeley: McCutchan.

Grumet, Madeleine R. 1988. *Bitter Milk: Women and Teaching*. Amherst: Univ. of Massachusetts Press.

Jackson, Philip W. 1992. "Conceptions of Curriculum and Curriculum Specialists." In *Handbook of Research on Curriculum: A Project of the American Educational Research Association*, ed. Philip W. Jackson, 3-40. New York: Macmillan.

Kamii, Constance Kazuko, with Georgia DeClark. 1985. *Young Children Reinvent Arithmetic: Implications of Piaget's Theory*. New York: Teachers College Press.

Kapfer, Miriam B. 1972. *Behavioral Objectives in Curriculum Development: Selected Readings and Bibliography*. Englewood Cliffs, NJ: Educational Technology.

King, Edith W. 1990. *Teaching Ethnic and Gender Awareness: Methods and Materials for the Elementary School*. Dubuque, IA: Kendall/ Hunt.

Kliebard, Herbert M. 1986. *The Struggle for the American Curriculum, 1893-1958*. Boston: Routledge and Kegan Paul.

Langer, Susanne. 1976. *Problems of Art*. New York: Scribners.

McDermott, Robert A., ed. 1984. *The Essential Steiner*. San Francisco: Harper & Row.

McLaren, Peter. 1986. *Schooling as a Ritual Performance: Towards a Political Economy of Educational Symbols and Gestures*. London: Routledge and Kegan Paul.

McNeil, John D. 1990. *Curriculum: A Comprehensive Introduction*. 4th ed. Glenview, IL: Scott, Foresman/Little, Brown Higher Education.

Mager, Robert. 1962. *Preparing Instructional Objectives*. Palo Alto, CA: Fearon.

Ogbu, John. 1987. "Variability in Minority School Performance: A Problem in Search of an Explanation." *Anthropology and Education Quarterly* 18(4): 312-34.

Oliver, Donald W. 1990. "Grounded Knowing: A Postmodern Perspective on Teaching and Learning." *Educational Leadership* 48(1): 64-69.

"The Paideia Proposal: A Symposium." 1983. *Harvard Educational Review* 53 (4): 377-411.

Piaget, Jean. 1962. *Play, Dreams and Imitation in Childhood*. New York: Norton.

———. 1966. *Origins of Intelligence*. New York: Norton.

Pinar, William F., ed. 1975. *Curriculum Theorizing: The Reconceptualists*. Berkeley: McCutchan.

Pinar, William F., and Joe L. Kincheloe, eds. 1991. *Curriculum as Social Psychoanalysis: The Significance of Place*. Albany: State Univ. of New York Press.

Pinar, William F., and William M. Reynolds, eds. 1992. *Understanding Curriculum as Phenomenological and Deconstructed Text*. New York: Teachers College Press.

The Random House Dictionary. 1980. New York: Ballantine.

Saracho, Olivia N., and Bernard Spodek. 1983. *Understanding the Multicultural Experience in Early Childhood Education*. Washington, DC: National Association for the Education of Young Children.

Schubert, William H. 1980. *Curriculum Books: The First Eight Years*. Lanham, MD: Univ. Press of America.

———. 1986. *Curriculum: Perspective, Paradigm, and Possibility*. New York: Macmillan.

Schwab, Joseph J. 1970. *The Practical: A Language for Curriculum*. Washington, DC: National Education Association.

Seguel, M. L. 1966. *The Curriculum Field: Its Formative Years*. New York: Teachers College Press.

Shor, Ira, ed. 1987. *Freire for the Classroom: A Sourcebook for Liberatory Teaching*. Portsmouth, NH: Heinemann.

Simonson, Rick, and Scott Walker, eds. 1988. *The Graywolf Annual Five: Multi-Cultural Literacy*. St. Paul, MN: Graywolf Press.

Spock, Marjorie. 1985. *Teaching as a Lively Art*. Hudson, NY: Anthroposophic Press.

Taba, Hilda. 1962. *Curriculum Development: Theory and Practice*. New York: Harcourt Brace Jovanovich.

Tanner, Daniel, and Laurel N. Tanner. 1975. *Curriculum Development: Theory into Practice*. New York: Macmillan.

Tietze, Wolfgang. 1987. "A Structural Model for the Evaluation of Preschool Effects." *Early Childhood Research Quarterly* 2(2): 133-59.

Tyack, David B. 1974. *The One Best System: A History of American Urban Education*. Cambridge: Harvard Univ. Press.

Tyler, Ralph W. 1949. *Basic Principles of Curriculum and Instruction*. Chicago: Univ. of Chicago Press.

Uhrmacher, P. Bruce. 1991. "Waldorf Schools Marching Quietly Unheard." Ph.D. diss., Stanford University.

Walker, Decker. 1990. *Fundamentals of Curriculum*. New York: Harcourt Brace Jovanovich.

Young, Robert. 1990. *A Critical Theory of Education: Habermas and Our Children's Future*. New York: Teachers College Press.

Zais, Robert S. 1976. *Curriculum: Principles and Foundations*. New York: Thomas Y. Crowell.

TRENDS AND ISSUES
IN SOCIAL STUDIES CURRICULUM

by Stephen J. Thornton
Associate Professor of Social Studies and Education
Teachers College, Columbia University, New York, New York

SOCIAL studies education poses special challenges for the curriculum developer. In practice, social studies incorporates content drawn from history, geography, and the social sciences (anthropology, economics, political science, psychology, sociology), and less commonly from other areas such as law, the humanities, and interdisciplinary fields such as American studies and ethnic or gender studies. There is longstanding disagreement, however, concerning both the educational purposes this content should serve and how the curriculum should be organized: Should social studies, for example, need no rationale beyond its intrinsic importance and mean no more than the simplification of the disciplines for instructional purposes, as Diane Ravitch (1989) has argued? Or is social studies properly understood as a fusion of knowledge from the disciplines to foster informed decision making by the citizens of a democratic society in an increasingly interdependent world (Engle and Ochoa 1988)? These two models of social studies admittedly define the extremities of the debate, but they underscore the sharply different views about what constitutes "good" curriculum. Moreover, these conflicting conceptions of social studies aims and consequent curricular organization reflect underlying value

conflicts in United States society.

The structure of this chapter reflects the continuing debates about what should be taught and how the curriculum should be organized. In practice, for example, social studies curriculum is usually a compromise--that is, more than the disciplines simplified for pedagogical purposes and less than a fusion of them. This compromise pleases strong advocates of neither side.

I also emphasize in this chapter persistent value conflicts over issues such as gender, multiculturalism, poverty, abortion, AIDS education, censorship, and gun control in American society, because they too are a source of the continuing debate about the proper aims of social studies education. Although space limitations have required that I largely restrict my discussion to value conflicts over gender and multiculturalism, issues such as the others mentioned above also clearly remain major sources of curriculum disputes. It is unlikely that any of these divisive issues can be addressed in social studies education in a way that entirely satisfies all interested parties.

My aim in this chapter is to provide an overview of social studies curriculum and some of the major factors that influence it. More specifically, I shall first outline the origins of the dominant scope and sequence (what is taught and in what order) that is often considered the de facto national curriculum. Second, I shall describe some of the major current influences on social studies curriculum policy making. Third, I will examine the implications of available research on curriculum change, as well as on teaching and learning, insofar as they are informative in developing curriculum. Finally, I shall turn to some trends in social studies that appear to be harbingers of curriculum changes to come.

Evolution of the Social Studies Curriculum

The beginnings of the modern social studies curriculum roughly coincided with the rise of mass schooling in the United States during the late nineteenth and early twentieth centuries. During this period, educational policymakers were attempting to adjust schools to the needs of a new urban-industrial reality (Lagemann 1989; Wiebe 1967). Moreover, the public schools were increasingly given the charge to "Americanize" the offspring of "new" immigrants from eastern and southern Europe (Tyack 1974). How the policymakers of the Progressive Era addressed these issues, as we shall see, has had an enduring influence on the social studies curriculum.

Before the rise of mass education, there was no widely accepted or authoritative curriculum in social studies. Indeed, although some geography, history, and civics may have been taught, the term *social studies* was not widely used to designate a school subject. Nevertheless, in the years after the Civil War, as a larger proportion of youngsters enrolled in schools and students' years of attendance also increased, social studies instruction increasingly supplemented the rudimentary three Rs and moralistic tales (Elson 1964) of the earlier common school.

The first two important steps toward standardizing what was taught under the rubric of social studies came in 1893 and 1899, when groups of university-based historians, educators, and schoolteachers issued reports on the place of "history and allied subjects" in the school curriculum (Hertzberg 1981). They suggested a scope and sequence consisting mostly of history. This emphasis reflected the history backgrounds of most committee members and the nascent state of the social sciences in the late nineteenth century. Underlying these two reports were two significant

assumptions: (1) that social studies courses should be taught to all secondary-school students and should resemble the courses already offered in private academies to prepare students for college, and (2) that the European roots of the United States should be underscored in both the elementary and secondary grades.

The reports of 1893 and 1899 established precedents for a de facto national framework for social studies, but it was a later, more influential report issued by the National Education Association (NEA) that established what is essentially still the secondary-level scope and sequence: *The Social Studies in Secondary Education* (1916). The ferment of progressive thought was then at high tide in the United States, and in the same year John Dewey's fullest statement on education, *Democracy and Education* (1916/1966), was also published. It had clearer implications for secondary education than had Dewey's earlier work, which had been much more focused on elementary education. Although he did not use the term *social studies*, in *Democracy and Education* Dewey argued that history and geography "are the two great school resources for bringing about the enlargement of the significance of a direct personal experience" (Dewey 1916/1966, 217-18).

Although Dewey did not serve on the 1916 committee, its report is consistent in most respects with his thinking (see Hertzberg 1988). One of the most influential members of the 1916 committee was Dewey's colleague at Columbia University, the historian James Harvey Robinson. Just as Dewey underscored the importance of linking the curriculum to students' experiences, Robinson's conception of the "new history" stressed the relationships of the past to the present (Whelan 1991). Both Dewey and Robinson believed that history and other social studies courses should be harnessed to the task of addressing current problems. In brief, both scholars argued that the rationale for social studies was its role in preparing citizens for a democratic society.

This spirit pervaded the recommendations of the 1916 committee members. For example, they advocated that United States history be taught with an eye to current problems, and they recommended the creation of a capstone course in the twelfth grade that would address current "problems of democracy." Moreover, they significantly decreased the amount of European history recommended and increased emphasis on the United States past and present. The resultant scope and sequence was a combination of disciplinary courses and courses that fused content from several disciplines. (See chapters 4-6 for a full treatment of current curriculum frameworks.)

The elementary social studies scope and sequence familiar today--the expanding environments or expanding horizons model (fig. 1)--was not widely adopted until a generation after the Progressive Era. This model first gained national attention when Paul Hanna was one of the leaders of a Virginia curriculum revision project in 1934 (LeRiche 1992; Ravitch 1987). The basic assumption underlying the expanding environments model is that children should begin in the primary grades (K-3) with familiar subject matter such as themselves, their families, and the local community. In the upper elementary grades (4-6), the

scope of the curriculum is broadened to incorporate U.S. states and regions, the nation as a whole, and the world beyond the United States. Hanna's rationale broadly followed in the tradition of the 1916 report, with its citizenship-oriented emphasis on real-life problem solving.

The expanding environments model was widely adopted and by the 1940s was the standard elementary-level scope and sequence throughout the United States. Over the years, however, there seems to have been some broadening of the primary grades sequence, insofar as topics such as families and communities now often include comparisons with families and communities abroad.

Expanding environments remains the dominant scope and sequence today, despite charges

FIG. 1. THE EXPANDING ENVIRONMENTS MODEL

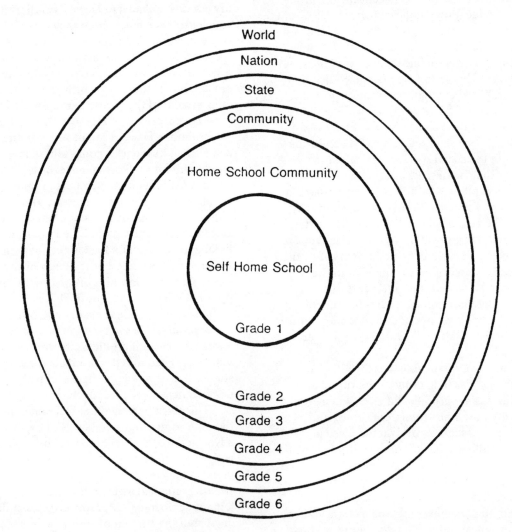

Source: Texas Education Agency, *Social Studies Framework, Kindergarten-Grade 12*
(Austin: Texas Education Agency, 1986), 15. Reproduced with permission

from critics that it devotes too much time to relatively trivial subject matter that children already know and too little time to less familiar and more imaginative subjects such as folklore and historical tales in which children are said to be very interested (e.g., Larkins, Hawkins, and Gilmore 1987; Ravitch 1987). There may be some basis to these criticisms. Linda S. Levstik (1986) has demonstrated, for example, the rich opportunities for engaging learning provided by the use of historical fiction (which also has the advantage of being readily integrated with "whole language" programs). Moreover, the primary grades may be a propitious time to introduce subject matter outside children's direct experiences because they seem to be more open and interested in things perceived as "other" prior to fourth grade, when stereotypes and prejudices begin to harden (Stone 1986). However, even when critics of expanding environments have been prominent in subsequent curriculum development efforts, such as Ravitch with the recent California framework (1988), there has not been a complete break with the expanding environments approach. While the California framework incorporates more history than has been traditional in expanding environments, the sequence of moving from the local to the more distant in time and space has not been entirely discarded.

While there has seldom been a shortage of critics of the de facto national curriculum, it has been remarkably resistant to change. No doubt this is partly explained because radical departures from the de facto national scope and sequence present difficulties for would-be reformers. For example, most instructional materials are designed with a particular grade level and associated subject matter in mind. Thus, moving world history from one grade level to another may mean that no suitable materials are available. The status quo is also reinforced because the resources--time, energy, and money--needed for curriculum revision are usually in short supply in most school systems.

Despite the factors reinforcing the status quo, social studies has sometimes been affected by curriculum reform movements. Some of these movements have sought directly to change social studies curriculum; other movements have indirectly affected social studies. Two reform movements are illustrative of these two kinds of effects. First, I shall consider the most striking and ambitious example of a direct change effort: the New Social Studies (NSS) of the 1960s.

The NSS reformers were part of a broader curriculum reform movement that began around the time of *Sputnik* and at first concerned mainly mathematics and science education. The most prominent spokesperson for this movement was a Harvard University psychologist, Jerome Bruner. In his highly influential *The Process of Education* (1960), which summarized the proceedings of a conference where most of the attendees were psychologists, scientists, and mathematicians, Bruner called for curricula that would foster inquiry or discovery learning. Bruner wanted to break with traditional pedagogy, which emphasized recitation and recall of information. Rather, he favored giving students opportunities to "learn how to learn" (Bruner 1960, 6). This type of learning was possible, Bruner argued, because each of the academic disciplines has a structure: "To learn structure, in short, is to learn how things are related" (1960, 7).

Generally, NSS reformers followed in the spirit of Bruner's thinking (e.g., Fenton 1967). There was a rash of calls for teaching structure, concepts, and inquiry in social studies (e.g., Beyer and Penna 1971; Hebert and Murphy 1968). Altogether, more than one hundred curriculum projects were produced, though fewer than half of these found publishers (Fenton c. 1981). There was a heavy emphasis on the disciplines, especially the social sciences, where the reformers were more successful in identifying subjects' structures than they were with history.

Most important for my purposes here, there was a poor fit between the interests of most curriculum reformers, many of whom were based in universities and had little (if any) experience in the schools, and the interests of teachers. As Hazel Hertzberg later put it, the reformers "were strangely oblivious to school and classroom realities" (1981, 165). It has been estimated that possibly only 5 percent of social studies classrooms were affected by the NSS materials (Haas 1977, 79). In retrospect, there are lessons about curriculum change to be learned from the failure of the NSS movement, and I shall return to them below.

It is ironic that the NSS reformers set out to change social studies curricula and failed, while the reformers to whom we shall now turn did change social studies even though they had no interest in doing so. These new reformers were most interested in improving the elementary-level teaching and learning of the "basics"--which they usually defined in practice as reading and math.

In the aftermath of the curriculum reform movements of the 1960s and early 1970s, which included the NSS as well as other movements such as "values clarification" and "open education," there was widespread concern that standards in the schools had fallen. In particular, there were charges that too few children were mastering reading and computational skills. "Back-to-basics" proponents contended that these skills were needed as a foundation for virtually all subsequent learning. The growing use of norm-referenced tests to assess students' skills in reading comprehension and math computation reinforced the trend towards greater emphasis in elementary curriculum on math and reading--leaving less time and resources for subjects such as social studies, the fine arts, and science.

By the late 1970s, the time allocated to social studies in the primary grades had decreased; indeed, it was not even taught in some schools (Lengel and Superka 1982). Meanwhile, in grades 4-6, social studies also suffered relative to the basics, though less severely than in the lower grades. Even though social studies continued to be taught in the upper elementary grades, it was increasingly shortchanged. For example, social studies received less time than the basics. It was also scheduled later in the day, when students' energies are at their lowest and when sundry disruptions to the school schedule, such as special events and pull-out programs, often occur (see Thornton and Wenger 1990).

Although it is unclear at the time of writing whether the greater emphasis given to history in the recent California framework (1988) will spread to other states, the 1990s began with expanding environments and the 1916 NEA report still forming the basic curriculum framework in nearly all states. Recent proposals for national curriculum standards and national content-based tests also may portend change--particularly since a number of recent proposals such as *America 2000* (U.S. Department of Education 1991) have stressed history and geography, rather than a more unitary conception of social studies.

Sources of Social Studies Curriculum Policy

There are a number of major sources of policy on what should be taught in social studies. As should be apparent by now, not all social studies policy-

makers agree. I use the term *policymaker* broadly to include all those who influence the curriculum that actually finds its way into the classroom. Because of space limitations, only three main groups will be discussed: (1) state and federal governments, (2) university-based scholars and professional organizations, and (3) educational practitioners at the local level.

According to the United States Constitution, education is a responsibility reserved to the states. Traditionally, local school districts provided most of their own funding and enjoyed considerable autonomy. By the 1970s, however, the often great inequalities of funding across districts were increasingly held by the courts to be denials of constitutional guarantees for an equal education (James 1992, 188-89). This and other factors contributed to a decline in local control of school financing. As local control of funding diminished, local control of school policies also waned. The states increasingly specified what should be taught. It is entirely possible, given these developments, that substantial local control of curriculum will pass into history just as the one-room school-house did.

The states, of course, had always exercised some control over social studies in local school districts. Among the principal ways in which states have exercised this power is by mandating the teaching of certain subject matters and by testing. The amount of state control, however, varied widely from state to state. New York, for example, has long had a statewide system of content-based examinations, and these have to a considerable degree driven the curriculum. In contrast, California in the early 1980s had social studies guidelines that were merely advisory and could easily be ignored by practitioners. Until the last few years, however, there were two main effects of state regulation of social studies curriculum.

First, states have long mandated the teaching of certain courses. U.S. history has been, and remains, a required course in virtually all states; in 1988, for instance, forty-seven states and the District of Columbia required the teaching of U.S. history. Most states also require the teaching of the state constitution or government and state history (Jenness 1990, 36). Various other courses, such as economics, are required by many states as well.

The second major traditional instrument of state power over social studies curriculum is textbook adoption (which is discussed at length in chapter 12 of this volume). Textbook adoption means different things in different states, but its ultimate effect is to limit and standardize the types of textbooks that are available. This tendency greatly influences social studies curriculum because the textbook is a key influence on what teachers decide to teach (Thornton 1991).

About one-half of the states have some form of statewide adoption process (Tyson-Bernstein 1988). All are sunbelt states in the South and the West. California and Texas, the two most populous adoption states, can account for almost 20 percent of a textbook's sales. What will sell in California and Texas, to a considerable extent, determines what gets published and is therefore available in nonadoption states as well (Apple 1985).

Presumably, statewide adoption is supposed to assure that the books adopted are of sufficient quality and appropriateness. As presently conducted, however, the adoption process is used by many interest groups to assure that their viewpoints are represented in textbooks. This influence typically results in a great deal of "mentioning" and, given space limitations, little elaboration of what the "mentionings" mean. Thus, the coherence of textbooks is undermined, and students' opportunities to understand complex subjects are likewise undermined. The adoption process is also highly politicized in another sense: It has often been used to censor unpopular or controversial views (see Nelson and Stanley 1985). Recent media accounts of the sometimes bitter disputes on the Los Angeles and Oakland school boards about California's newly adopted social studies textbooks underscore the difficulties of reaching consensus in the adoption process (Reinhold 1991).

Like the states, the federal government has taken an active role in social studies curriculum policy. Although the federal government has retreated from funding large-scale curriculum development projects such as *Man: A Course of Study* (1970), leading federal officials such as former Secretary of Education William Bennett, current Secretary of Education Lamar Alexander, and Assistant Secretary Diane Ravitch have expressed strong views on what should be taught in social studies. In particular, they have argued for a change from the 1916 NEA report and its replacement by a history and geography core (e.g., Bennett 1986; 1987). Furthermore, the federally funded National Center for History in the Schools, based at the University of California at Los Angeles, has recently announced a 311-page

document specifying the "lessons from history" that students should acquire (National Center for History in the Schools 1992). Although lacking constitutional authority over curriculum, the federal government can still influence social studies curriculum through such means as funding for grants, proposals for national testing, and curriculum standards, and, more generally, by its power to lead public opinion.

State and federal policies tend to be cast in broad terms open to various interpretations at the local level. Social studies professional organizations provide leadership in the interpretation and dissemination of policy initiatives, as well as in formulating policies themselves. State mandates requiring courses in U.S. history, for example, may not indicate what should be taught under that label or how material should be organized and evaluated.

The largest and most influential professional organization in the field is the National Council for the Social Studies (NCSS). NCSS publishes in its official journal, *Social Education*, recommended scope and sequence frameworks, and position statements on current curriculum issues such as the Columbus quincentenary and early childhood education. NCSS publications and meetings (at national, regional, and local levels) can provide both a good starting point and a rich repository of materials for local curriculum development projects.

In addition to NCSS, there are many other more specialized professional organizations in social studies education. These more specialized organizations generally aim to promote the teaching of some part of social studies. For example, the Bradley Commission (1988) recommended guidelines for increasing the amount of history taught in social studies by changing the de facto national curriculum. Other groups, such as the proponents of law-related education, have placed more emphasis on infusing their topics and perspectives into the existing scope and sequence and on changing teacher education (see Anderson and Naylor 1991).

Professional organizations in the disciplines, such as the American Historical Association and the Association of American Geographers, would seem at first glance another obvious place to look for guidance in curriculum development efforts. Although obviously social studies education must be informed by new scholarship in the disciplines, disciplinary organizations have shown only limited and fluctuating interest in school social studies.

For a useful summary of the curricular perspectives of the American Anthropological Association, American Economic Association, American Historical Association, American Psychological Association, American Sociological Association, Association of American Geographers, Joint Council on Economic Education, National Council for Geographic Education, and Organization of American Historians, see *Charting a Course: Social Studies for the 21st Century* (National Commission on Social Studies in the Schools 1989, 31-77).

Involvement in school social studies by university-based historians and social scientists was more common prior to the 1940s. The divergent interests encouraged by increasing academic specialization in the disciplines, versus educators' necessary interest in broad syntheses suitable for children and adolescents, contributed to a decline in collaboration between social studies educators and their colleagues in the disciplines (Hertzberg 1980).

A growing number of disciplinary scholars, however, did express concern about social studies in the schools in the 1980s. Geographers, for example, claimed that their discipline was being neglected in the schools (e.g., Joint Committee on Geographic Education 1984). Historians said the same of history (e.g., Bradley Commission 1988).

Unfortunately, too often this new interest by disciplinary scholars has resulted in fragmentation of effort, rather than joint efforts with existing social studies groups. Disciplinary scholars have shown greatest interest in promoting the teaching of their own discipline, while social studies educators have argued that the disciplines are a necessary but insufficient focus for social studies education (e.g., Muessig 1987). Even when scholars in the disciplines have become more deeply involved in formulating an overall scope and sequence framework, such as the one presented by the National Commission on Social Studies in the Schools, there was scant reference to relevant social studies research. For example, the commission's claim that "the history-geography matrix has proved a powerful approach in the past" (National Commission on Social Studies in the Schools 1989, 26) is unsupported by research findings yet is used to justify a chronological approach to history (Levstik 1990).

In an important sense, though, disputes over the role of the disciplines in social studies may have distracted attention from a more pressing issue: the curriculum that is taught in classrooms (Thornton 1990). As I have argued at length elsewhere, teachers are in many ways the crucial social studies policymakers. They are curricular-instructional gatekeepers (Thornton 1991). Since there is no "teacherproof" curriculum, what teachers choose to emphasize and how they organize instruction, evaluation, and expectations are the "key" determinants of what is actually taught (Shaver, Davis, and Helburn 1980).

Given that many students report that the social studies instruction they receive is dull, unmemorable, and irrelevant to their lives (Shaver, Davis, and Helburn 1980, 9-10), whether the disciplines are given increased weight in social studies programs may not be the most pressing issue facing social studies education. Put simply, the central problems associated with the curriculum enacted in the classroom, the best evidence suggests, will be only marginally influenced by scholarly disputes about curriculum policy.

Despite the urgency of the problems facing social studies, the tensions between disciplinary advocates and social studies advocates seem nowhere near to being settled. The unfortunate outcome has been a fragmentation of efforts in a field already short on needed resources and expertise (Hertzberg 1988).

Although it has seldom been achieved in the past half-century, genuine collaboration between disciplinary specialists, social studies educators, and school practitioners is still worth aiming for because each group has a distinctive contribution to make to curriculum development projects. In addition to scholars' disciplinary knowledge and practitioners' practical knowledge of schools and classrooms, social studies research adds perspectives that may not be familiar to either disciplinary specialists or social studies teachers.

Curriculum, Teaching, and Learning

The history of social studies reform efforts holds lessons for today's would-be reformers. Advocates of change must confront two apparently contradictory forces. On the one hand, teachers frequently complain about the lack of specificity in the curriculum frameworks provided to them (Gross and Dynneson 1983, 44-47). Moreover, teachers seldom have the necessary combination of time, resources, interest, and expertise to develop curriculum frameworks for themselves. On the other hand, successful adoption of a new curriculum will not occur without teachers' understanding and agreement.

Teachers' lack of understanding and interest was evident with many of the NSS projects, even though the same projects were enthusiastically received by academics and professional organizations. For example, Bruner's own elementary curriculum package, *Man: A Course of Study,* or *MACOS* (1970), received favorable notices from the American Educational Research Association and NCSS (Shaver 1987). However, it received a lukewarm reception in most schools. MACOS was built around the nature of "man" as a species and the forces that have shaped human history. It features illustrative, inquiry-oriented case studies of many human societies and included studies of other primates, such as baboons (Bruner 1966). While this content and approach represented much of what was best in social science scholarship, many teachers saw it as a sharp break with familiar pedagogy and content. Moreover, in many communities, traditionalists and Christian fundamentalists denounced MACOS for teaching moral relativism (Shaver 1987). The replacement of familiar textbooks with films and a curriculum kit, as well as MACOS's lack of fit with the traditional expanding environments model, may also have contributed to its unenthusiastic reception in the schools.

It is plain that some form of meaningful involvement by teachers is indispensable, since even innovative curricula with proven impact on student learning, such as the Harvard Social Studies Project (Oliver and Shaver 1966), were "quietly ignored" because of their incompatibility with traditional instruction (Shaver 1987, 117). Even when school districts are forced to comply with state mandates, "the imposed curriculum should allow for some degree of local participation in order to relieve tensions and resentments and to achieve the support of the classroom teacher" (Gross and Dynneson 1983, 46).

While adoption of curricula developed outside local school districts may face teachers' resistance to change and may not fit the needs of a particular district, local curriculum development remains a formidable task. Moreover, it sometimes runs the risk of reinventing the wheel. Nevertheless, local curriculum development projects can be beneficial for the professional growth of teachers and can give teachers a personal stake in adoption. It should be emphasized, however, that local curriculum development projects will fail unless they are undertaken with adequate time, leadership, resources, and expertise (Parker 1991).

The ultimate purpose of curriculum planning is, of course, to facilitate teaching and learning. It would make no sense to design a curriculum that students are incapable of learning. The scope and sequence of the curriculum, however, has been only partially examined from a developmental perspective (Hertzberg 1982, 8-9). The scarcity of evidence about students' learning in social studies is unfortunate, since it seems that the way students learn in social studies is different from the way they learn in other school subjects (Stodolsky 1988).

Although the available evidence about students' learning is limited, it can still be instructive for curriculum developers. For example, chronology is the typical organizing device for history curricula. It has long been appreciated, however, that children and many adolescents find historical time difficult or even impossible to understand (e.g, Oakden and Sturt 1922). Indeed, a number of British researchers in the 1960s and 1970s concluded that historical understanding was not possible until children reached what Piaget called the "stage of formal operations" (e.g., Hallam 1979).

There is no necessity, however, for history curriculum to adhere always to the chronological model. More recently, researchers in both Britain and the United States have suggested that a different approach to history may result in dramatically improved outcomes (Downey and Levstik 1991; Knight 1989; Levstik 1990; Thornton and Vukelich 1988). For example, encouraging outcomes have been reported from using a more topical or thematic approach (e.g., Shelmit 1980), from trying different genres of historical literature such as historical fiction (e.g., Levstik and Pappas, 1987), and from exposing students to primary sources (e.g., Holt 1990). Furthermore, there seems to be a potentially powerful relationship between history and what Erik Erickson claimed is the central task of adolescence, the individual's quest for personal identity. Several researchers have suggested that interweaving adolescents' personal autobiographies with formal history leads to "a sense of the past in which" they have woven their "own existence[s] into the mainstream of societal history" (Sleeper 1973, 274; see also Hertzberg 1980; Holt 1990).

These examples drawn from research on the learning of history also underscore a broader concern: Scope and sequence should be attuned to the kinds of teaching and learning we hope to foster in the schools. It is increasingly apparent, for example, that current prevalent emphases on breadth of coverage, rather than depth, impede meaningful learning (see Newmann 1991). If we are serious about teaching the young to think for themselves and not just to recite information, then the extensive coverage specified in curriculum guidelines in states such as New York sends the wrong message to both teachers and students.

Recent Trends in Social Studies

Because social studies is so closely aligned with disputes about values in American society, it is often strongly affected by trends in the broader society. No issue better illustrates this point than current controversies about inclusion and perspective-taking. In social studies, these entail a more multicultural conceptualization of the United States, past and present, as well as a move away from a Eurocentric perspective on the rest of the globe.

Although the United States has always been a pluralistic society, this fact was largely ignored in social studies curriculum until the past generation. History courses usually focused on the experiences of white males in the United States and on the influence of the West on the rest of the world. The perspectives and experiences of women, people of color, and the powerless in the United States, as well as the perspectives of peoples of Africa, Asia, the Pacific, and Latin America were mostly absent (Banks 1988; FitzGerald 1980; Garcia 1990; Tetreault 1986). For example, Africa figured in world history courses merely as an episode in European imperialism, while the experiences of American women were hardly mentioned in United States history courses.

Understandably, inclusion and perspective-taking are considered no more than equal treatment by the previously excluded. Moreover, it is undeniable that the United States is growing more pluralistic and more interdependent with the rest of the world. These facts are acknowledged by virtually everyone except fringe groups such as the Ku Klux Klan. Still, at least some forms of inclusion have attracted heated criticism. Ravitch (1990), for example, while acknowledging that attention must be paid to diversity, has condemned "Afrocentric" curricula that are intended to build African-American youngsters' self-esteem through exposure to a positive portrayal of their heritage. She contends that such an approach not

only is bad history but will actually increase racial intolerance. In contrast, Molefi Kete Asante, Professor of African-American Studies at Temple University, has argued that "empowering" African-American youngsters requires dealing with their heritage. He contends that the current program in most schools is a "white self-esteem curriculum" (Asante 1991/1992, 29).

Conflicts over the proper meaning of *multiculturalism* also surfaced during disputes over New York State's recent review of the social studies curriculum, *One Nation, Many Peoples*. According to the report, social studies is

> the primary avenue through which the school addresses our cultural diversity and interdependence.... *If the United States is to continue to prosper in the 21st century, then all of its citizens, whatever their race or ethnicity, must believe that they and their ancestors have shared in the building of the country and have a stake in its success.* (New York State Social Studies Review and Development Committee 1991, 3-4 [their italics])

Some prominent members of the committee vigorously dissented from the report. The historian Arthur M. Schlesinger, Jr., for example, noted in the report that "students should learn more about the rich variety of peoples and cultures that have forged this new American identity . . . but we should also be alert to the danger of a society divided into distinct and immutable ethnic and racial groups, each taught to cherish its own apartness from the rest" (89).

Whatever meaning is attached to the concept of multiculturalism, it is clear that urban school districts have taken a leading role in its implementation. Although a multicultural perspective is essential in rural, suburban, and urban schools, pluralistic student populations are most common in the cities. In New York City, the nation's largest school district, fully 80 percent of the students are from racial, ethnic, and linguistic minority groups (Saravia-Shore and Arvizu 1992, 497). Some urban districts have experimented with core curricula with a theme to which the various disciplines and skills can be related. The aim here is that less curricular fragmentation will help culturally diverse classes learn more effectively (Saravia-Shore and Arvizu 1992, 502-503). For example, at Central Park East, a public alternative school in East Harlem, social studies and English are taught together and are centered around a common theme. Using teacher teams who jointly plan curriculum, pedagogy, and assessment procedures, the Central Park East approach has had considerable success, as measured by dropout rates and college admissions (Meier 1992).

It is important to note, however, that while much has been written about urban education in general, much less is known about how social studies is faring in particular. In the 1970s, NCSS sponsored case studies comparing social studies (Jarolimek 1977) in urban, suburban, and rural settings (Branson 1977; Clegg 1977; Diem 1977; Huber 1977; Lahnston and Nevins 1977; Ort 1977). It would be timely to repeat the exercise, especially since dwindling funding, most notably at the federal level under the Reagan and Bush administrations, has apparently harmed the ability of urban schools to address the needs of their students (Kozol 1991).

The meaning of inclusion of women's experience in the social studies curriculum is also currently in dispute. Although much more space is now devoted to women in social studies textbooks and curricula than was true a generation ago, critics charge that the dominant organization of social studies remains masculine in orientation. For example, feminist scholars have argued that simply adding more information about women in United States history courses does not change the fact that the mainstay of the story is still about wars, diplomacy, business, and politics--areas traditionally dominated by men. Domains in which women have usually been in the forefront-- such as childcare, homemaking, and often peace- making (see Reardon 1988)--remain marginal topics in most social studies programs (Noddings 1992; Tetreault 1986).

Counter to the feminist critique, the American Textbook Council has bluntly labeled appeals for gender equity as "astonishing" (American Textbook Council 1992, 3). The council claims that feminists are trying to substitute their equity agenda for what the council says is "the crucial and unending question: by what means does a commonwealth organize itself in the realms of governance and production?" (American Textbook Council 1992, 5).

While the ultimate curricular effects of inclusion and perspective-taking remain to be seen, it seems safe to say that the issues will not simply go away. Given these circumstances, three conclusions seem warranted. First, although the American political tradition is mainly Western and masculine in origin, U.S. history and government courses must also incorporate the experiences of those long denied a voice in that tradi-

tion; these neglected voices include those of African Americans, Native Americans, Latinos, and women. Second, as David Jenness observes, world history courses have "reflected largely . . . what Americans need to know about the rest of the world in order to understand their own situation" (Jenness 1990, 298). World history, world geography, global studies, and related courses must also include the perspectives of peoples in other parts of the globe and the reality of United States interdependence with other nations. Finally, the first two conclusions do not mean that the traditional focus on powerful elites in the United States and abroad should be entirely abandoned. For better or worse, the powerful have done a great deal to make the world what it is. There remains a correspondingly great need for the young to understand who has power, how it has been used, and to what effects, if they are to be knowledgeable and participating citizens. It would be a grave mistake to assume that ignoring power will make it go away--such would be a recipe for helplessness.

It is more difficult to draw firm conclusions about some more contentious areas of inclusion. For example, there is no widespread agreement about the desirability and efficacy of using curricula to build the self-esteem of particular groups. This debate involves issues unresolved in U.S. politics, and, further, I am aware of no conclusive evidence of the efficacy of such programs (even if all parties could agree on their desirability). School districts can make prudent decisions on this issue only by carefully weighing the evidence.

In addition to inclusion, the question of whether we should be teaching more history is the other major current debate about social studies curriculum. As I have already mentioned when discussing professional associations, some historians and educational policymakers have called for a history core in social studies. A number of the proposals for including more history are based on the assumption that the content of history is intrinsically more worthwhile than the content of other social studies courses (e.g., Bradley Commission 1988). Thus, these proposals advocate replacing some existing courses with history courses. This appeal is based also on the claim that not as much history is taught as was once the case.

Although I strongly believe in the educational importance of history for all students, the claims above require close scrutiny. First, there is scant evidence, if any, to support the view that less history is taught today than a generation or two ago (Jenness 1990, 255-258). Second, history courses are taught throughout the nation already, yet students seem indifferent to them; why would more history courses necessarily be better? Third, requiring more history seems to understate what the history advocates are after. Upon examination of their curriculum frameworks (e.g., National Commission on Social Studies in the Schools 1989), it seems that they are advocating not only more history but also history that is chronologically organized. As I noted earlier, there is no empirical evidence to support the superiority of a chronological organization.

In states such as California, a history-dominated social studies curriculum has already been mandated. History is also a prominent component of other reform proposals such as *Education 2000* (U.S. Department of Education 1991). It may be that more history, and less of some other courses, will become a national reality. It is important to remember, however, whichever way it ends up, that the problems traditionally associated with the enacted curriculum in classrooms will not simply vanish with the teaching of more or less history.

Conclusion

At the beginning of this chapter, I warned of the special challenges facing social studies curriculum developers. The proper scope and sequence of social studies is more disputed than that of any other subject and is likely to remain so. Moreover, despite generations of reform efforts, relatively few reforms have had great and lasting impact on practices in the schools (Cuban 1991; Hertzberg 1981).

The trends and issues discussed in this chapter represent important developments in social studies. They are discussed in broader terms than are necessary for curriculum decision making at the local level, which must take account of the constraints and possibilities of a particular context and particular students. Nevertheless, this overview should provide perspective to local curriculum development efforts and help curriculum planners to avoid the errors of past reformers.

References

American Textbook Council. 1992. "Do Textbooks Shortchange Girls?" *Social Studies Review* 11: 3-5.

Anderson, C. C., and D. T. Naylor, eds. 1991. *Law-related Education and the Preservice Teacher*. N.p.: American Bar Association.

Apple, M. W. 1985. "Making Knowledge Legitimate: Power, Profit, and the Textbook." In *Current Thought on Curriculum*, ed. A. Molnar, 73-89. Alexandria, VA: Association for Supervision and Curriculum Development.

Asante, M. K. 1991/1992. "Afrocentric Curriculum." *Educational Leadership* 49(4): 28-31.

Banks, J. A. 1988. *Multiethnic Education*. 2d ed. Boston: Allyn & Bacon.

Bennett, W. J. 1986. *First Lessons: A Report on Elementary Education in America*. Washington, DC: U.S. Department of Education.

———. 1987. *James Madison High School: A Curriculum for American Students*. Washington, DC: U.S. Department of Education.

Beyer, B. K., and A. N. Penna, eds. 1971. *Concepts in the Social Studies*. Washington, DC: National Council for the Social Studies.

Bradley Commission on History in Schools. 1988. *Building a History Curriculum: Guidelines for Teaching History in Schools*. Washington, DC: Educational Excellence Network.

Branson, M. S. 1977. "The Status of Social Studies Education: Marin County." *Social Education* 41: 591-94.

Bruner, J. S. 1960. *The Process of Education*. Cambridge, MA: Harvard Univ. Press.

———. 1966. *Toward a Theory of Instruction*. Cambridge, MA: Harvard Univ. Press, Belknap Press.

California Department of Education. 1988. *History-Social Science Framework for California Public Schools Kindergarten through Grade Twelve*. Sacramento.

Clegg, A. A., Jr. 1977. "The Status of Social Studies Education: Three Midwest Cities." *Social Education* 41: 585-87, 601.

Cuban, L. 1991. "History of Teaching in Social Studies." In *Handbook of Research on Social Studies Teaching and Learning,* ed. J. P. Shaver, 197-209. New York: Macmillan.

Dewey, J. 1916/1966. *Democracy and Education*. New York: Free Press.

Diem, R. A. 1977. "The Status of Social Studies Education: San Antonio." *Social Education* 41: 595-97.

Downey, M. T., and L. S. Levstik. 1991. "Teaching and Learning History." In *Handbook of Research on Social Studies Teaching and Learning,* ed. J. P. Shaver, 400-10. New York: Macmillan.

Elson, R. M. 1964. *Guardians of Tradition.* Lincoln: Univ. of Nebraska Press.

Engle, S. H., and A. S. Ochoa. 1988. *Education for Democratic Citizenship.* New York: Teachers College Press.

Fenton, E. 1967. *The New Social Studies.* New York: Holt, Rinehart and Winston.

———. c. 1981. *What Happened to the New Social Studies: A Case Study in Curriculum Reform.* Unpublished manuscript, Carnegie-Mellon Univ.

FitzGerald, F. 1980. *America Revised: History Schoolbooks in the Twentieth Century.* New York: Vintage.

Garcia, J. 1990. "Does *Charting a Course* Include a Multiethnic Perspective?" *Social Education* 54: 444-46.

Gross, R. E., and T. L. Dynneson. 1983. *What Should We Be Teaching in the Social Studies?* Bloomington, IN: Phi Delta Kappa Educational Foundation.

Haas, J. D. 1977. *The Era of the New Social Studies.* Boulder, CO: ERIC Clearinghouse for Social Studies/Social Science Education and Social Science Education Consortium.

Hallam, R. N. 1979. "Attempting to Improve Logical Thinking in School History." *Research in Education* 21: 1-24.

Hebert, L. J., and W. Murphy, eds. 1968. *Structure in the Social Studies.* Washington, DC: National Council for the Social Studies.

Hertzberg, H. W. 1980. "The Teaching of History." In *The Past Before Us,* ed. M. Kammen, 474-504. Ithaca, NY: Cornell Univ. Press.

———. 1981. *Social Studies Reform, 1880-1980.* Boulder, CO: Social Science Education Consortium.

———. 1982. "Social Studies Reform: The Lessons of History." In *Social Studies in the 1980s,* ed. I. Morrissett, 2-14. Alexandria, VA: Association for Supervision and Curriculum Development.

———. 1988. "Are Method and Content Enemies?" In *History in the Schools,* ed. B. R. Gifford, 13-40. New York: Macmillan.

Holt, T. 1990. *Thinking Historically.* New York: College Entrance Examination Board.

Huber, J. D. 1977. "The Status of Social Studies Education: Mid-America." *Social Education* 41: 588-90, 601.

James, T. 1991. "State Authority and the Politics of Educational Change." In *Review of Research in Education* 17, ed. G. Grant, 169-224. Washington, DC: American Educational Research Association.

Jarolimek, J. 1977. "The Status of Social Studies Education: Six Case Studies." *Social Education* 41: 574-79.

Jenness, D. 1990. *Making Sense of Social Studies.* New York: Macmillan.

Joint Committee on Geographic Education, National Council for Geographic Education, and Association of American Geographers. 1984. *Guidelines for Geographic Education: Elementary and Secondary Schools.* Washington, DC: Association of American Geographers; Macomb, IL: National Council for Geographic Education.

Knight, P. T. 1989. "Research on Teaching and Learning History: A Perspective from Afar." *Social Education* 53: 306-9.

Kozol, J. 1991. *Savage Inequalities.* New York: Crown.

Lagemann, E. C. 1989. *The Politics of Knowledge.* Middletown, CT: Wesleyan Univ. Press.

Lahnston, A. T., and P. Nevins. 1977. "The Status of Social Studies Education: Boston." *Social Education* 41: 580-84.

Larkins, A. G., M. L. Hawkins, and A. Gilmore. 1987. "Trivial and Noninformative Content of Elementary Social Studies: A Review of Primary Texts in Four Series." *Theory and Research in Social Education* 15: 299-311.

Lengel, J. G., and D. P. Superka. 1982. "Curriculum Patterns." In *Social Studies in the 1980s,* ed. I. Morrissett, 32-38. Alexandria, VA: Association for Supervision and Curriculum Development.

LeRiche, L. 1992. "The Political Socialization of Children in the Expanding Environments Sequence." *Theory and Research in Social Education* 20: 126-40.

Levstik, L. S. 1986. "Teaching History: A Definitional and Developmental Dilemma." In *Elementary School Social Studies: Research as a Guide to Practice,* ed. V. A. Atwood, 68-84. Washington, DC: National Council for the Social Studies.

———. 1990. "The Research Base for Curriculum Choice: A Response." *Social Education* 54: 442-44.

Levstik, L. S., and C. C. Pappas. 1987. "Exploring the Development of Historical Understanding." *Journal of Research and Development in Education* 21: 1-15.

Man: A Course of Study. 1970. New York: Curriculum Development Associates.

Meier, D. 1992. "Reinventing Teaching." *Teachers College Record* 93: 594-609.

Muessig, R. H. 1987. "An Analysis of Developments in Geographic Education." *Elementary School Journal* 87: 519-30.

National Center for History in the Schools. 1992. *Lessons from History: Essential Understandings and Historical Perspectives Students Should Acquire*. Los Angeles.

National Commission on Social Studies in the Schools. 1989. *Charting a Course: Social Studies for the 21st Century*. Washington, DC

National Education Association. 1916. *The Social Studies in Secondary Education*. Washington, DC: Government Printing Office.

Nelson, J. L., and W. B. Stanley. 1985. "Academic Freedom: 50 Years Standing Still." *Social Education* 49: 662-64, 666.

Newmann, F. M. 1991. "Classroom Thoughtfulness and Students' Higher Order Thinking: Common Indicators and Diverse Social Studies Courses." *Theory and Research in Social Education* 19: 410-33.

New York State Social Studies Review and Development Committee. 1991. *One Nation, Many Peoples: A Declaration of Cultural Interdependence*. Albany: New York State Education Department.

Noddings, N. 1992. "Social Studies and Feminism." *Theory and Research in Social Education* 20: 230-41.

Oakden, E. C., and M. Sturt. 1922. "The Development of Knowledge of Time in Children." *British Journal of Psychology* 12: 309-36.

Oliver, D. W., and J. P. Shaver. 1966. *Teaching Public Issues in the High School*. Boston: Houghton Mifflin.

Ort, E. P. 1977. "The Status of Social Studies Education: Birmingham." *Social Education* 41: 598-601

Parker, W. C. 1991. *Renewing the Social Studies Curriculum*. Alexandria, VA: Association for Supervision and Curriculum Development.

Ravitch, D. 1987. "Tot Sociology." *American Scholar* (Summer): 343-54.

——. 1989. "The Plight of History in American Schools." In *Historical Literacy: The Case for History in American Education*, ed. P. Gagnon and The Bradley Commission on History in Schools, 51-68. New York: Macmillan.

——. 1990. Multiculturalism. *American Scholar* (Summer): 337-54.

Reardon, B. A., ed. 1988. *Educating for Global Responsibility: Teacher Designed Curricula for Peace Education, K-12*. New York: Teachers College Press.

Reinhold, Robert. 1991. "Class Struggle: Cowgirls in the Bantu Migration." *New York Times Magazine*, 29 September.

Saravia-Shore, M., and S. F. Arvizu. 1992. "Implications for Policy and Practice." In *Cross-Cultural Literacy: Ethnographies of Communication in Multicultural Classrooms*, ed. M. Saravia-Shore and S. F. Arvizu, 491-510. New York: Garland.

Shaver, J. P. 1987. "Implications from Research: What Should Be Taught in Social Studies?" In *Educators' Handbook: A Research Perspective*, ed. V. Richardson-Koehler, 112-138. New York: Longman.

Shaver, J. P., O. L. Davis, Jr., and S. W. Helburn. 1980. "An Interpretive Report on the Status of Precollege Social Studies Education Based on Three NSF-Funded Studies." In *What Are the Needs in Precollege Science, Mathematics, and Social Science Education? Views From the Field*. Washington, DC: Government Printing Office.

Shelmit, D. 1980. *History 13-16 Evaluation Study*. Edinburgh: Holmes McDougall.

Sleeper, M. 1973. "The Uses of History in Adolescence." *Youth and Society* 4: 259-74.

Stodolsky, S. S. 1988. *The Subject Matters*. Chicago: Univ. of Chicago Press.

Stone, L. 1986. "International and Multicultural Education." In *Elementary School Social Studies: Research as a Guide to Practice*, ed. V. A. Atwood, 34-54. Washington, DC: National Council for the Social Studies.

Tetreault, M.K.T. 1986. "Integrating Women's History: The Case of United States History High School Textbooks." *History Teacher* 19: 211-62.

Texas Education Agency. 1986. *Social Studies Framework: Kindergarten-Grade 12*. Austin.

Thornton, S. J. 1990. "Should We Be Teaching More History?" *Theory and Research in Social Education* 18: 53-60.

——. 1991. "Teacher as Curricular-Instructional Gatekeeper in Social Studies." In *Handbook of Research on Social Studies Teaching and Learning*, ed. J. P. Shaver, 237-48. New York: Macmillan.

Thornton, S. J., and R. Vukelich. 1988. "Effects of Children's Understanding of Time Concepts on Historical Understanding." *Theory and Research in Social Education* 16: 69-82.

Thornton, S. J., and R. N. Wenger. 1990. "Geography Curriculum and Instruction in Three Fourth-Grade Classrooms." *Elementary School Journal* 90: 515-531.

Tyack, D. B. 1974. *The One Best System: A History of American Urban Education*. Cambridge, MA: Harvard Univ. Press.

Tyson-Bernstein, H. 1988. *A Conspiracy of Good Intentions: America's Textbook Fiasco*. Washington, DC: Council for Basic Education.

U.S. Department of Education. 1991. *America 2000: An Education Strategy*. Washington, DC.

Whelan, M. 1991. "James Harvey Robinson, the New History, and the 1916 Social Studies Report." *History Teacher* 24: 191-202.

Wiebe, R. H. 1967. *The Search for Order, 1877-1920*. New York: Hill and Wang.

Acknowledgments

I am grateful to Linda S. Levstik and Michael Whelan for their helpful suggestions on an earlier draft of this chapter.

CURRICULUM GUIDES: PROCESS AND DESIGN

by Jurg Jenzer

Director of Curriculum, Supervision, and Instruction
Lamoille North Supervisory Union, Hyde Park, Vermont

D ESIGNERS of curriculum guides face complex decisions in developing a quality social studies program. The stakes are high, with judgments being made for years to come about what teachers should teach and what students should learn. Many factors are involved: district size, geographic location, funding capability, philosophy, state statutes, and demographic characteristics. Many are affected by these curricular decisions, and therefore, many should participate in deciding on a course of action.

A curriculum guide often shapes the development of social studies lessons in classrooms and schools. Since classroom teachers are the primary users of social studies curriculum guides, it is important that teachers participate in developing these materials.

Textbooks still drive the curriculum in many districts. In social studies, textbooks offer a scope of topics, as well as the sequence in which they are to be taught and learned. As a result, textbooks are a powerful influence on the curriculum materials developed by states or by single school districts. It is not surprising to see textbook language and design reflected in many locally developed social studies curricula.

Numerous critics have argued that the textbook has eroded the need to train teachers to design and evaluate curriculum guides (Apple 1979; Aronowitz and Giroux 1985; Giroux 1983). Designing curriculum materials at the district level challenges both the textbook industry and the dependency teachers have on textbooks. A curriculum process, moreover, allows teachers to discover some surprising facts. Alternatives to textbook-style scope and sequence programs in social studies not only are possible, but can offer interesting instructional alternatives as well.

Veteran teachers are already curriculum designers by practice. They tend to use textbooks eclectically, identifying strengths and weaknesses in each book and picking and choosing from all available resources. A formal, district-level curriculum guide fosters this development and is at odds with any single textbook series, unless the structure of the text is directly copied into the curriculum.

A curriculum development process with and for teachers provides insight into the decision-making process that generates both textbooks and curriculum guides. It is the process, rather than the document, which provides an exciting opportunity: time to examine one's own assumptions and practices, an environment to discuss and test new assumptions and practices, and a reasonable incentive to get involved.

Curriculum is not so much a document as it is

instruction. At its best, it teaches all those involved with its development and implementation. The actual curriculum in social studies--or in any other subject--is the one being taught. The taught curriculum may or may not resemble the planned curriculum (the adopted textbook or the curriculum guide). This point is crucial. The curriculum development process that is organized as a challenging learning opportunity will affect instruction far more than the document alone. A local curriculum process challenges the separation of planning and implementation, an issue all too often obscured by arguments for state or national curriculum initiatives. Unless teachers understand the process and decisions that generate a curriculum guide, implementation may be in jeopardy.

In general, the total process of curriculum design and implementation can be divided into numerous steps that curriculum designers and committees may need to deal with when developing or revising elementary, middle, and/or high school social studies programs. These steps can be outlined as follows:

- Performing a needs assessment
- Defining the mission statement
- Choosing the participants
- Scheduling the project
- Forming a curriculum committee
- Budgeting
- Looking at standards
- Examining key topics in social studies
- Choosing curriculum features and design options
- Population analysis (target students)
- Field testing
- Public input
- Editing, ratification, production, and dissemination
- Adoption process
- Staff development and support
- Monitoring and supervision
- Evaluation and revision

Note that the steps described here are only *typical* of the process involved. The actual steps may differ in your district--there may be more steps or fewer ones, and some steps may occur in a different order. At some stage in the process, you will probably encounter many of these steps, and this chapter is meant to acquaint you with them and many of the related decisions.

Before a curriculum guide can be written and implemented, curriculum designers plan and organize a process.[1] Just as importantly, these designers must set realistic expectations for the teachers who will ultimately be required to turn these blueprints into meaningful experiences for children and young adults.

Performing a Needs Assessment

The needs assessment of the social studies program is an important part of curriculum planning, in that it provides a direction for the curriculum. The assessment defines the priorities of the curriculum (under local and state standards and in view of recommendations from national organizations), the goals of curriculum development in social studies, and the gaps that exist in the current curriculum.

In order to get a clearer picture of the school's needs in social studies, curriculum planners may wish to compare their current and planned curriculum program with those of other states and districts (for further discussion on sources of curriculum materials, see below under *Examining Key Topics in Social Studies* and *Choosing Curriculum Features and Design Options*).

Defining the Mission Statement

Closely related to the needs assessment is the creation of the school or district mission statement. While curriculum implementation may be the province of teachers and school administrators, the mission statement should be developed with members of the school board, teachers, parents, students, state education officials, the private sector, and others within the community. A widely shared understanding of the mission of the school district in curricular and programmatic terms greatly enhances the odds for successful implementation. Formulating a new curriculum is expected to do the following:

- Establish a relationship between district goals and instructional programs and methods
- Establish a relationship between local programs, state and national standards, laws, and policies
- Link curriculum and educational programs with important policy and budgetary decisions
- Inform communities about the schools' direction and programs
- Ensure a coordinated and planned educational program

Choosing the Participants

Curriculum affects a teacher's behavior and decision making. The teacher's understanding, acceptance, and implementation of a social studies curriculum are the most important and, oddly enough, the most commonly missed factor in the curriculum process.

All schools and school districts employ teachers of varying degrees of ability, from novice teachers to seasoned veterans. Their growth as professional educators will define their relationship with the curriculum.[2] Gaining insight into the quality and dynamics of the teaching staff for whom the curriculum is written is of critical importance. Some of the more important questions to be asked are:
- How many teachers will be charged with implementation? What are their experiences specifically with curriculum development? Have they worked with districtwide curricula before?
- What are the teachers' attitudes regarding the current curriculum? How well or to what extent are current curricula implemented?
- Can the school district support a curriculum process in which teachers have leverage over the curriculum?
- How many building administrators have experience specifically with curriculum development?

Interviewing prospective participants and reviewing appropriate records allows curriculum designers to recruit teachers best suited for the task ahead.

Scheduling the Project

When developing a reasonable timetable for a curriculum process, numerous factors must be considered. The following is a list of some of the more common concerns:
- Scope of the project (e.g., K-4, 5-8, 9-12, K-12)
- Mission of the project (complete revision, partial revision, etc.)
- Number of employees and students affected by the curriculum
- How the project fits into the participants' work schedules
- Staff development time that will be required to implement the new curriculum
- Available resources (also see below under *Budgeting*)

- Deadlines (from the state, from local education agency, from federal agency mandates)
- Meeting times (see below)

Since teachers have relatively inflexible classroom schedules, a method must be chosen that will ensure their participation. Three of the more common methods used are *pullout projects*, *after-school projects*, and *course projects*. Each method offers significant fiscal and procedural advantages.

Pulling teachers out of the classrooms for full-day work sessions allows them to concentrate on the project. Typically, this reduces the number of meetings necessary to complete the project. On the other hand, this method requires substitute teachers, with the resulting cost. Teachers who leave their classrooms for entire days must devote considerable effort to preparing substitutes. In addition, the frequency with which teachers are pulled out of the classroom must be calculated to eliminate any potentially negative impact on students.

After-school projects avoid most of the negative implications of the pullout project. Some costs remain if contracts require compensation of personnel for extra duty. The most significant problem with this method, however, is that teachers are often tired after spending a day in the classroom; this minimizes their energy level and the quality of their work. This method also increases the number of meetings needed, because after-school meeting time is limited.

Course projects are usually planned in collaboration with institutions of higher education. The strength of this method is its scheduling flexibility. Course projects can be organized as evening courses or as intensive two- or three-week work sessions during school vacations. Graduate credits issued by the cooperating college or university can be an attractive incentive for teachers who apply credits toward graduate degrees and/or salary schedules. One well-known problem with this method lies in potential conflicts between school district personnel and higher education faculty over controlling the project, the mission, and the curriculum itself.

Forming a Curriculum Committee

Curriculum designers, whether they be administrators, classroom teachers, or education professors, must be able to work effectively with others. In addition, curriculum designers must have an excellent grasp of the subject, have classroom experience, and communicate effectively in order to be accepted and respected by teachers.

In forming a curriculum committee, curriculum designers encounter such questions as these:
- Who wants to participate? Who should be recruited?
- Which teachers can play leadership roles? Who will chair the committee?
- Should all affected schools and grade levels be represented?
- What are the advantages of small versus large committees?
- Should elementary-level committees work separately from middle-level or secondary-level committees? How will they coordinate transitions between levels?
- What types of incentives are available to recruit quality committees?
- How committed are the school board and the administration to the committee's work?
- Are department heads, administrators, program specialists, guidance counselors, parents, students, board members, and business and community representatives on the committee?

The First Committee Meeting: Checklist
The importance of the first meeting cannot be overstated. Curriculum designers should carefully plan and orchestrate this meeting in order to develop team spirit and a sense of purpose within the committee itself.

Scheduling: If the first meeting is held during the school year, check with building principals about events or meetings. If the meeting occurs after school, limit it to setting the agenda, getting to know one another, and starting a checklist of current topics and issues in social studies.

Committee Structure: Identify the committee's mission, meeting schedule, political conditions (level of administrative or school board support, etc.), and preliminary activities (conducting needs assessment, obtaining copies of state statutes and regulations, important articles or resources gathered, etc.).

Meeting Environment: If possible, meet outside the schools in a suitable room equipped with comfortable chairs, large tables, climate controls, chalkboard or overhead projector, and a steady supply of coffee and juice. In all-day meetings, do not skimp on lunch.

Budgeting

Resource Checklist
There are numerous factors to be considered when deciding about resources. The budget[3] and other logistical problems deserve careful consideration. Some of these factors are:

Logistics
- Secretarial assistance
- Access to computers
- Access to databases and other forms of information (i.e., ERIC, KCDL, libraries, etc.)
- A place for the committee to meet
- Possible collaboration with a local college or university
- Access to production facilities (i.e., graphics, desktop publishing, printing, copying, editing, etc.)

Budgetary Considerations
- Hiring substitutes
- Consultant(s)
- Computer
- Secretarial
- Production (layout, paper, printing, copying, distribution, binders, graphics, etc.)
- Administrative
- Legal (reviews for compliance with state and federal laws)
- Other costs

Curriculum developers might want to explore the possibilities of outside funding to help support the extra costs involved in the project. Some national foundations provide grants for the development of particular curricula; these organizations often have regional restrictions or will fund only certain types of curricula. In addition, some corporations fund educational projects in their state or region. The appendix to this chapter provides a listing of foundations that offer grants for education projects; this list gives some idea of the types of funding available.

Looking at Standards

It is essential to consult standards--and to keep track of emerging standards--when designing or adopting curriculum guides. As arguments over national curriculum and testing systems fly back and forth, curriculum designers are first and foremost concerned with understanding and dealing with the present trends relating to social studies (see chapter 1 for an overview of these trends). Undoubtedly, national standards will make a difference, but major curriculum decisions reside at the local level.

Every school district has standards that emerge from (*a*) community values, (*b*) the successes and failures of local reform and restructuring efforts in response to pressures from state and federal agencies, and (*c*) the curriculum in use. Curriculum designers must decide on standards with these factors in mind.

Even the best curriculum documents become outdated as soon as new standards and trends emerge across the nation. Teachers in school districts with an ongoing curriculum development process will be better equipped to adapt to new standards from any source.

State and Local Standards

Copies of all state statutes, regulations, and policies regulating curriculum development or revision should be made available to all parties participating in, or affected by, the curriculum process.

Under the United States Constitution, the state has the ultimate responsibility for education, and state education agencies define standards and conditions under which schools operate. This is where the commonality ends, however, because the degree to which states regulate curriculum varies widely. In some cases, the state sets standards for social studies and defines acceptable instructional resources for implementing that curriculum. In other cases, the curriculum process is largely controlled by local educational agencies (LEAs). Curriculum designers need to ascertain the nature and scope of these standards as well as the degree of flexibility LEAs have in interpreting and implementing these standards (for details regarding particular states, see chapter 5).

When state regulations are mostly generic, they allow for significant local variation. This opens the door to local emphases on issues such as global studies or multiethnic/multicultural studies.

In addition to state regulations, there are other factors that may have resulted in de facto standards in school districts. For instance, the district may have adopted a particular way of teaching history which unifies instruction in some way (e.g., a common textbook series, the adoption of activity-oriented civics). Just as importantly,

when teachers "import" new ideas, materials, or methods into the school, they act as role models for other teachers. In fact, this is the most common way in which social studies can be transformed at the classroom level, and is an excellent indicator of what can be termed "local standards."

National Standards

The nation's concern over education has ignited a demand for leadership and change. For example, the publication of mathematics standards by the National Council for Teachers of Mathematics (1989) demonstrates the importance of a national consensus which supplies direction and focus to local curriculum efforts. However, national standards do not necessarily suggest a national curriculum, although this option is supported by some in the United States.

There is no equivalent to the NCTM standards in K-12 social studies, but there are numerous reports, documents, and model curricula that embody high standards and are considered exemplary.

Two recent reports deal with the nature and content of history education. In 1992 the National Center for History in the Schools (based at the University of California at Los Angeles) released its report *Lessons from History: Essential Understandings and Historical Perspectives Students Should Acquire.* The report stresses four major themes in history education:

1. The changing character of human societies
2. The economic and technological development of societies
3. People's understanding of themselves and their place in the universe and different societies' representations of these beliefs
4. Political theories and organizations

A second document, The Bradley Commission's report *Building a History Curriculum* (1988), warns that "history should never be reduced to a thin recital of successive dates and facts, but carry what has been called 'thick narrative,' which combines lively storytelling and biography with concepts drawn from every relevant discipline." The report delineates six vital themes for the study of history (10-11):

1. Conflict and cooperation
2. Comparative history and major developments
3. Patterns of social and political interaction
4. Civilization, cultural diffusion, and innovation

5. Human interaction with the environment
6. Values, beliefs, political ideas, and institutions

Another report covers general guidelines for geography: A joint effort by the National Council for Geographic Education, the Association of American Geographers, and the Joint Committee on Geographic Education produced *Guidelines for Geographic Education--Elementary and Secondary Schools* (1984), which provided meaningful direction for geography curricula by outlining five fundamental themes:

1. Location: Position on Earth's surface
2. Place: Physical and human characteristics
3. Relationships within places: Humans and environments
4. Movement: Humans interacting on the Earth
5. Regions: How they form and change

Charting a Course: Social Studies for the 21st Century (1989), prepared by the National Commission on Social Studies in the Schools, picked up where the Bradley Commission and the geographers left off--that is, assisting local school districts in making responsible choices. This report suggests a number of conceptual standards, which are listed below.

Characteristics of a Social Studies Curriculum for the 21st Century

1. A well-developed social studies curriculum must instill a clear understanding of the roles of citizens in a democracy and provide opportunities for active, engaged participation in civic, cultural and volunteer activities designed to enhance the quality of life in the community and in the nation.

2. A complete social studies curriculum provides for *consistent* and *cumulative* learning from *kindergarten* through *12th grade*. At each grade level, students should build upon knowledge and skills already learned and should receive preparation for the levels yet to come. Redundant, superficial coverage should be replaced with carefully articulated in-depth studies.

3. Because they offer the perspectives of time and place, history and geography should provide the matrix or framework for social studies; yet concepts and understandings from political science, economics and the other social sciences must be integrated throughout all social studies courses so that by the end of 12th grade, students will have a firm under-standing of their principles and methodologies.

4. *Selective* studies of the history, geography, government and economic systems of the major civilizations and societies should together receive attention at least equal to the study of the history, geography, government, economics and society of the United States. A curriculum that focuses on only one or two major civilizations or geographic areas while ignoring others is neither adequate nor complete.

5. Social studies provides the obvious connection between the humanities and the natural and physical sciences. To assist students to see the interrelationships among branches of knowledge, integration of other subject matter with social studies should be encouraged whenever possible.

6. Content knowledge from the social studies should not be treated merely as received knowledge to be accepted and memorized, but as the means through which open and vital questions may be explored and confronted. Students must be made aware that just as contemporary events have been shaped by actions taken by people in the past, they themselves have the capacity to shape the future.

7. Reading, writing, observing, debating, role-play, or simulations, working with statistical data and using appropriate critical thinking skills should be an integral part of social studies instruction. Teaching strategies should help students to become both independent and cooperative learners who develop skills of problem solving, decision making, negotiation and conflict resolution.

8. Learning materials must incorporate a rich mix of written matter, including original sources, literature and expository writing; a variety of audiovisual materials including films, television and interactive media; a collection of items of material culture including artifacts, photographs, census records and historical maps; and computer programs for writing and analyzing social, economic and geographic data. Social studies coursework should teach students to evaluate the reliability of all such sources of information and to be aware of the ways in which various media select, shape, and constrain information.

9. A complete social studies curriculum for students can only be provided through the support of school boards, school administrators and the community. Teachers must be granted appropriate in-service opportunities

for enhancing their content knowledge and their abilities to use appropriate teaching strategies. Above all, teachers must be provided substantial blocks of time in which to prepare course outlines, teaching guides and lesson plans.

10. The core of essential knowlege to be incorporated in the instructional program at every level must be selective enough to provide time for extended in-depth study and must be directed toward the end goals of social studies education--the development of thoughtful Americans who have the capacities for living effective personal and public lives.

Source: National Commission on Social Studies in the Schools, *Charting a Course: Social Studies for the 21st Century*, 1989, 3-4. Reproduced with permission.

Examining Key Topics in Social Studies

The literature regarding elementary and secondary social studies is rich, and it can be somewhat overwhelming (for a basic introduction to the literature, see chapter 1). However, curriculum designers cannot afford to ignore it. The most critical decision to be made here deals with time. Should teachers be involved in reviewing and discussing this literature, or should the facilitator conduct a review and then brief the participants? This review allows participants to gain a critical perspective on current controversies in social studies, as well as on their own assumptions regarding what a social studies curriculum is and will be in the future.

An alternative approach is to review other school districts' curricula or current textbooks (an annotated list of outstanding social studies curriculum guides is provided in chapter 7, and a discussion of state curriculum guides is given in chapter 5). On the one hand, this review yields a great deal of practical comparisons between districts as well as a sense of security (commonality) in the decision-making process. However, if the committee members are not fully knowledgeable about current trends and methods, this method could lead to the continued use of potentially obsolete curriculum design features and instructional topics.

Reviewing three types of information--the publishing sector (textbooks), the school sector (current curriculum guides), and the academic sector (research)--will provide a balanced data

collection. The following examples are a selection of topics under discussion at the time of publication (chapters 1 and 4 provide more detailed information on current controversies):

· The search for national standards
· Time versus demand: picking from the pile of "important" knowledge
· Global education
· Multicultural education: developing tolerance and diversity
· Cultural, racial, and gender bias in social studies materials
· Columbus: hero or villain?
· Appropriate choice and use of software in social studies
· Developing activity-based civics courses
· The role of authentic information: biographies, letters, photographs, etc.
· AIDS/HIV programs
· Geographic literacy
· Integrating social studies with other subjects: searching for model programs

Curriculum designers are advised to develop their own checklists with the curriculum committee. These checklists will allow teachers to share questions linked directly to social studies instruction, topics and controversies they are interested in, personal positions or philosophies, and an exploration of their colleagues' positions.

The next step could be the most difficult in the curriculum development and design procedures. The committee must make choices regarding the organization of the guide, including the identification of strands or domains (e.g., history, geography, sociology, economics), the relationship between strands (e.g., Should "global studies" be integrated into history and geography or be separated as a discrete strand?), and the specific topics to be covered at each grade level, grade cluster, or developmental level. *Charting a Course* (1989) provides one starting point, as summarized below.

TOPICS FOR K-12 SOCIAL STUDIES (SUMMARY OF TOPICS GIVEN IN *CHARTING A COURSE*)

Kindergarten to Grade 3
1. Provide a balance of local, national, and global information so that students begin to recognize how details fit into a larger whole.
2. Stress the importance of following school and community rules.
3. Continual development of students' sense of

time and place; present such concepts as change, diversity, justice, power, and trade-offs in concrete terms.

4. Present equal amount of information on the United States and other times and places.
5. Examine how children and their families are the same and how they differ, and how also rules for behavior change with time.
6. Use songs, stories, pictures, artifacts, role playing, map making, model building, etc., to excite students' imaginations.
7. Expand the concept of community as it existed throughout the world in the past and exists today.
8. Broaden students' horizons with stories and descriptions of people living in various places and under different conditions.
9. Use maps and globes to introduce geographic skills.
10. Cut across lines of sex, race, and ethnicity to identify a variety of heroes and heroines as models for admiration and emulation as well as a variety of common people.
11. Integrate social studies into language arts, mathematics, science, art, etc.
12. National and religious holidays, as celebrated here and around the world, can teach important concepts (if used to inform, not to indoctrinate).
13. Establish a basic understanding of world geography, continents, major countries, climate zones, and maps.

Grades 4 through 6
United States History
1. Civic and political systems should be stressed, with emphasis on Native Americans, early European explorers and settlers, the nation's founders, later immigrants and pioneers, abolitionists, populists, suffragists, inventors, artists, business and labor leaders, etc.
2. Highlight basic documents of the United States government, such as the The Declaration of Independence, the Constitution and the Bill of Rights.
3. Investigate the role of individuals and groups in the struggle for democracy.

World History
4. Identify the major economic, cultural, and political patterns of history, including: Paleolithic hunting and gathering; Neolithic villages; early urban civilizations in Eastern

and Western hemispheres, including Africa and Latin America; and worldwide industrialization.

Geography (Physical and Cultural)
5. An exploration of world geography should include: global patterns of atmospheric and oceanic circulation as they affect climate in different parts of the world; varied physical landscapes and plate tectonics (drifting continents); topography, soils, vegetation, and water resources; and how climatic patterns relate to the tilt of the Earth's axis and affect earth-sun relationships.
6. Examination of regional patterns of human land use, agriculture, economic activity and environment, with focus on the impact these have on such global conditions as ozone depletion, global warming, acid rain, etc.
7. Students should be able to relate their knowledge of history, geography, government, and economics to the national and the global scenes. Students should be able to utilize time lines, charts, graphs, and maps, and have a firm grasp of the concept of chronology.

Grades 7 and 8
Local Community
1. This should include a longitudinal study of the neighborhood and the municipality in which the school is located; may include state history and geography, where mandated.
2. Local and community relationships (socioeconomic, cultural, gender-based, etc.) should be explored, as well as public issues such as housing, sanitation, and transportation.
3. A variety of information should be used in this exploration such as the study of old buildings, oral interviews with the elderly in the community, census data, old photographs, newspaper files, historical archives and maps, church and civic records of life cycle events; also, information should be made availble from local historical and geographical societies.

The United States
4. Students further examine and increase their understanding of the Constitiution and the amendments as these have related to social and economic factors in the nineteenth and twentieth centuries. Students should also examine how the judicial, executive, and legislative branches have worked together to

develop a democratic form of government as it exists in America today.

5. A comparative study of capitalism, socialism, and communism should be undertaken so that students may begin to understand the impact that political and ecomomic systems have on international events.

Grades 9 through 12
World and American History and Geography to 1750

1. Such characteristics of classical civilizations as caste, Confucian family, natural law, and democracy are studied; also, such themes as gender roles, technological innovation, the evolution of social classes, transformation of the environment, growth of bureaucracy, codification of law, and the structure and types of govermnment are explored.
2. Major religions (Cristianity, Confucianism, Hinduism, Islam and Judaism) are examined as are cultural achievements of the past in art, architecture, music, and literature, etc.
3. Students explore the influence that individual cultures bring to bear on each other, including the various ways in which the African nations, Native American societies, as well as the English and European heritages have contributed to shaping the United States.

World and American History and Geography, 1750-1900

1. The impact of three transformations of modern times should be emphasized: the democratic revolution, the industrial and technological revolution, and population growth and mobility.
2. Key elements in the study of this period should include: the American Revolution; the French and industrial revolutions in Europe; the South American revolutions of Bolivar's time; Bismarck's Germany; westward expansion; the Civil War and Reconstruction in the United States; the opening of Japan and its new government; and the rise of European colonial empires.

World and American History and Geography Since 1900

1. Emphasis should be placed on how three dominant movements of the 19th century were resolved in the twentieth century: the spread of liberal democratic ideals and

practice beyond the western world; the rise of Marxism and Fascism; and the collapse of European colonial empires.
2. Students should also focus on the diverse forms of democracy throughout the world: the industrial-technological transformation and its impact on life everywhere; demographic shifts brought about by the triumphs of modern medicine; transportation technology; and changes in family dynamics.

Grade 12
Government/Economics (These may be taught together or separately)

1. Government issues should include: more detailed examination of the Declaration of Independence, United States Constitution, Bill of Rights, and Federalist Papers; and a clear understanding should be given of constitutional principles and the tensions between liberty and order, market capitalism and political equality.
2. Students should critically study newspapers, political speeches, debates, news programs, political films, etc.
3. Economics issues should include how markets for services and products solve conflicts regarding what and how something is produced, and for whom it is produced. How incentives (for producers, consumers, and workers) affect decisions, should also be examined. Students need to understand what markets and how they work, as these markets are affected by governmental decisions.

Source: National Commission on
Social Studies in the Schools, *Charting a Course: Social Studies for the 21st Century*,
Washington, DC, 1989, 7-20.
Reproduced with permission.

Choosing Curriculum Features and Design Options

When considering design and content of the curriculum, a developer must analyze the teachers as an audience as well as what type of curriculum guide the teachers would find most attractive (besides being useful in the functional sense). This brings developers back to an earlier step ("Choosing the Participants") and the expansion of the user analysis begun there. In general, the larger the audience (number of future users) for a social studies curriculum, the more difficult the search is for an appropriate design and content selection. The curriculum designer's own classroom experience and interaction with teachers will greatly facilitate the assessment of what teachers need and/or want.

Do some curriculum designs and content options work better than others? This depends upon the use of the guide and the audience. Here are some factors to consider:

· Which topics should be taught at certain grade levels in order to secure a high degree of achievement for most learners?
· How should these topics be described in the curriculum? Should they be described as "skills" students should master, or as discrete "content" areas which teachers ought to cover?
· Should a curriculum be much like a textbook and describe all aspects of instructional work and implement state or local goals and objectives?
· Should a curriculum be brief and merely outline instructional scope and sequence in "blueprint fashion," thus leaving most curriculum decision making to teachers?
· Should curriculum guides contain one feature or multiple features or types of information?
· Does the actual curriculum content or design make any difference to teachers?
· Can curriculum guides be attractive to teachers and thus shift the incentive for implementation from top-down mandates to the inherent benefits of the document itself?
· If teachers have greatly varied professional needs and practices, should the curriculum in fact consist of multiple documents with varied content?

Social studies curriculum guides offer different choices of content features; some emphasize one feature above others, while other guides vary both the number and the combination of features. One of the best ways to examine the different features of curriculum guides is to use actual guides as examples and models.

One source for curriculum models is the Kraus Curriculum Development Library (KCDL). This annual program offers a large number of curriculum guides (commercial and noncommercial), all reproduced on microfiche. Of interest here are the two subject areas of "History/ Geography" and "Social Studies/Social Sciences."

Chapter 14 lists current KCDL customers, whose fiche collection can be viewed.

Another good source for information on current guides is the Association for Supervision and Curriculum Development (ASCD). For many years, ASCD has organized an exhibit of noncommercial curriculum materials, for display at its annual conference. Most of these displays have included curriculum guides on history, geography, and social studies in general. In more recent years, ASCD has published a directory of the documents on display (the newer editions of this directory will be included in a CD-ROM package being planned by ASCD). Contact ASCD for information on the annual conference and for the availability of directories for the noncommercial curriculum materials display.

In addition, the School of Education at California State University, Sacramento, has been collecting and cataloguing the guides that were on display at the ASCD Conference. Once the cataloguing is completed, the guides themnselves will be available on interlibrary loan.

The following list describes common curriculum features; examples for some of these features are shown in full-page reproductions from published guides (figures 1 through 6):

A. Objectives/Instructional Strategies

Instructional objectives are written as specific topics that teachers must cover, described as specific knowledge areas (see figure 1).

B. Student Activities

Most often expressed in terms of student projects, games, or specific behaviors, this feature often translates instructional objectives into desired or proven methodologies which focus on engaging the student in the learning process as actively as possible.

C. Skills/Competencies

This feature is by far the most common type of information in curriculum guides (see figure 2). The national agenda for accountability in education has clearly left its mark on guides published during the past decade. The focus on outcomes of instruction sets a baseline for testing or measurement of achievement, giving the teacher the result rather than the "what" or "how." Many curriculum documents actually code skills in reference to standardized testing instruments.

FIGURE 1. EXAMPLE OF OBJECTIVES/INSTRUCTIONAL STRATEGIES

WORLD HISTORY, C

Objectives (priority items circled)	Suggested teaching activities
The Western Europeans	
(15.) Identifying the motivations of Western European leaders' sponsorship of exploration.	15. Discuss attempts by Columbus and other explorers to get money from Italian leaders. Explain why they were refused.
(16.) Defining European nationalism and economic competition.	16. Role play a European ruler attempting to make his/her country a leader in exploration. Give a "speech" describing goals.
(17.) Identifying the advances made by the 15th century which permitted exploration to take place.	17. Show drawings of European ocean-going vessels. Compare them to the Venetian vessels.
(18.) Characterizing the accomplishments of significant explorers.	18. On a world map, trace the routes of Columbus, Vespucci, Magellan, and others.
The Songhay Empire	
(19.) Describing the geographical advantages and mineral resources which aided the development of Songhay.	19. Locate Songhay on a map of Africa. Trace gold trade routes from West Africa to the Mediterranean.
(20.) Describing the rise of the Songhay monarchy and its relationship to the spread of Islam.	20. Pick one of the Songhay kings. Read about how he came to power using religion to gain supporters.
(21.) Identifying the impact of Portuguese demand for gold along the coast of Songhay.	21. Show on a map where new trading centers developed after trade with Portugal began. Show how the population of Timbuctu and Jenne declined as a result.
22. Defining the concepts of civil war and secession in order to explain the decline of Songhay.	22. Define the terms civil war and secession. Apply these concepts to Songhay.

Source: Boston Public Schools, *High School Curriculum Objectives*
(Boston: Boston Public Schools, 1987), 95. Reproduced with permission.

FIGURE 2. EXAMPLE OF A SKILLS/COMPETENCIES LIST

SOCIAL STUDIES SCOPE AND SEQUENCE K-12

GENERAL COGNITIVE DOMAIN

Prior to graduation, a student should:

1. Understand the various relationships between people and their social physical environments, past and present.

2. Understand how beliefs, values and behavior patterns originate, interrelate, and affect people.

3. Apply the above understandings to new situations and data.

I – Introduce   D – Development
X – Mainstream Focus
X – Focus Mainstream & Special Ed.
D – Development for Mainstream &
    Focus Special Ed.

Goal 10100.00

Students will demonstrate knowledge and understanding of various social organizations.

Objective
The student should:

	K	1	2	3	4	5	6	7	8	9	10	11	12
10101.00 identify some groups that human beings form and indicate why and how those groups form.	I	X	X	X	X	D	X	X	D	X	X	X	D
10102.00 identify some preferences among people that lead to group identification.	I	X	X	D	D	D	D	D	D	D	X	D	X
10103.00 describe some of the functions of groups such as family, peer, community, professional, national, and international groups in various cultures and indicate how and why these functions change; give explanations of the consequences of these changing functions.	I	X	X	X	D	D	X	D	D	X	X	X	X
10104.00 describe some of the functions of basic institutions.	I	D	D	D	D	D	D	X	D	X	X	X	X
10105.00 identify "cultural universals" such as shelter, food, communications, socialization, family organization, and religion; recognize that these "cultural universals" take different forms in various cultures and that these forms change over time.	I	X	X	D	D	D	X	X	D	D	D	X	D

Source: Bloomington Public Schools, *Social Studies Scope and Sequence* (Bloomington, MN: Bloomington Public Schools, 1984), 27. Reproduced with permission.

D. Subject Information

This is perhaps the oldest feature found in curriculum guides. Its use dates back to the days when textbooks were the primary source for curriculum, focusing on the legitimacy and preponderance of certain areas of knowledge over others. In some cases, excerpts from textbooks are copied directly into the guide.

E. Resources

This feature is prevalent in school district guides where the state establishes the legitimacy of certain textbooks or instructional resources (see figures 3 through 5).

F. Evaluation/Testing

Again, this feature is commonly found in curriculum guides, often in conjunction with Skills/Concepts, which are then cross-referenced with specific testing instruments. A similar feature is the curriculum map (see below).

G. Curriculum Maps

The chief purpose of curriculum maps (see figure 6) is to give teachers information regarding where and how single units, chapters, or topics fit into the overall (i.e., K-12) program. Maps may also include cues regarding students' previous learning experiences which may be of consequence to the teacher's instructional style (e.g., introduce, reinforce, test, and evaluate).

H. Document Size and Number of Features

Some school districts wish to increase both the number of features (e.g., to meet different types of needs) and the amount of detail. Some schools deliberately limit the number of content features (e.g., to provide emphasis or direction) as well as the size of the curriculum guides (e.g., to make the guides more manageable or to increase individual teachers' control over the curriculum). There is little evidence, if any, suggesting that one format or selection of features works better than another. Much is based on the characteristics of each school district, the mission of the curriculum project, administrative agendas to empower teachers or increase centralized control, and other decisive factors.

While these curriculum designs clearly rule the landscape in social studies, there is no compelling reason to limit curriculum guides to these formats. In fact, educators and textbook publishers alike have challenged this tradition, including the assumption that a curriculum guide must be limited to one subject.

Through the years, curriculum designers have searched for alternatives to these standard features. School districts have experimented with integrated or interdisciplinary designs.[4] In doing so, they have challenged many fundamental assumptions about the nature of curriculum as well as about the nature of schooling.

The key challenge issued within all interdisciplinary designs is directed toward the very organization of school schedules. The artificial segregation of academic disciplines may have served to develop a specialized workforce rather than the current agenda of versatile and broadly educated children and young adults. For most public school graduates, the world of work does not revolve around forty-five minutes of history followed by forty-five minutes of music. Their world presents problems that must be handled with knowledge and skills borrowed from mathematics, social studies, medical science, and other disciplines. The majority of designers using interdisciplinary models argue that the curriculum ought to reflect those realities and provide similar learning situations.[5]

Most alternative designs result from locally developed experiments, often in conjunction with more traditional subject-based guides. Two possible designs, the thematic curriculum and the interdisciplinary curriculum, are described below.

I. The Thematic Curriculum

An instructional unit or theme--chosen by teachers, administrators, students, parents, or a combination of these groups--serves as a focus for study and investigation for a given period of time. The theme is then examined from a variety of perspectives or traditional disciplines, such as mathematics, art, science, home economics, and physical education. For example, labor history can be taught through the works of Sinclair Lewis (literature), immigrants' journals (social history), samples of factory budgets and employees' salaries (math), and an examination of assembly-line technology from the late nineteenth century to the current day (physical science/business).

J. The Interdisciplinary Curriculum

This design model can focus on skills that are considered essential for the students' future work or study, such as reading, collaborative skills, problem-solving techniques, test-taking skills, numeracy, research techniques, interpreting information, and others. Subject areas such as geography, language arts, or physics serve as diverse contexts in which those skills are acquired and practiced.

Population Analysis (Target Students)

While teachers are the audience for whom curriculum guides are written, it is really the students who are the beneficiaries of high-quality guides. The demographic characteristics of the student population are a key factor in defining curriculum content and in choosing features, scope, resource specifications, and so on. For example, curriculum developed in an affluent Los Angeles suburb may work well there, but it could fail completely when implemented in a Detroit inner-city school.

This consideration is particularly important for districts with diverse student populations and for schools in districts with diverse cultural and economic settings.

The characteristics of a given student population determine the teacher's ability to implement a curriculum guide. While such materials are usually formatted to outline performance expectations or specific topics for, say, *all* ninth graders or fifth graders, such generic design assumptions about student populations may simply be ignoring realities teachers must deal with on a daily basis. In fact, any given grade-level classroom will include students above and below grade level. Some classes may have up to 25 percent of the students on IEP's, requiring the teacher to make drastic adaptions to curriculum expectations. In this light, the blame for "failing to implement" may rest not with the teacher but with the designer. It also explains the surging interest in curriculum guides designed not for grade levels but for developmental levels.

Field Testing

There is no need to separate the drafting process from the field testing of a new curriculum guide; indeed, it may be counterproductive. The best field testing involves a limited number of teachers who are either participants or who have been experimenting with changing a current social studies program (curriculum in use). Such tests should be conducted in cooperation with the department chair and faculty.

There are numerous reasons to conduct field tests during the drafting stage. First, it allows all building-level teachers an early look at upcoming changes in the social studies program. If that new program, for example, heavily builds upon NCSS standards, the transition from a traditional curriculum to an NCSS-type curriculum will require time for extensive staff development activities. Building ownership for a new social studies program throughout the design process will greatly facilitate successful implementation.

The final stage of field testing should be conducted with a completed curriculum at a building or district level. One or two years of a district-level field test may be required for a gradual transition; teachers should be asked to provide feedback to the curriculum committee in order to provide practical information for final editing work. This should include, if possible, one-on-one interviews with each teacher who participated in the field test, preferably conducted by curriculum committee participants. Some of the more important questions that can be posed are:

· Have you found the curriculum useful? How?
· Do you have any reservation or concerns you would like to share?
· Are suggested activities useful for implementation?
· What do you need to implement this curriculum?
· Is there anything else you would like the curriculum committee to know?

Public Input

Schools--and curriculum development--can benefit a great deal from collaborating with parents, community-based organizations and agencies, the private sector, and institutions of higher education. The question for the curriculum designer is, How can this be organized and what do we do with the information?

There are a number of critical factors to consider in organizing public input:

1. Should public input be sought at the beginning of the curriculum process in order to avoid the impression that such input amounts to mere formality after educators have made all the decisions?
2. Should public input be sought after field testing in order to give the curriculum an opportunity to prove itself?
3. Should public input be conducted through an open forum (public meetings, curriculum or parent nights at the school, press reports,

FIGURES 3-5. EXAMPLES OF RESOURCE INFORMATION

<u>Developmental Activities</u>

1. To help the students identify rules that are needed at school, plan some of the following activities:

    ● Show the pictures in I Like School (Crabtree), pp. 6-7, 10-11, 13, 15, 19, 22, and 25. Ask the students to describe the pictures and tell what rules are being followed in each setting.

    Record the rules on a chart such as the following:

Rules in School			
Classroom	Music Room	Library	Playground

    Elicit the definition of a rule. A <u>rule</u> tells what you can and cannot do.

    ● To further reinforce the definition of <u>rule</u>, show the videotape, <u>Behave</u>, <u>Bernard</u>! Discuss Bernard's actions and what made him a better dog. Select one of the following as a follow-up activity:

    < Ask the students to draw a picture of Bernard following a rule. Share the drawings with the class.

    > Have the students draw a picture of Bernard following a rule and write a sentence describing the rule.

    ● Have the students examine pictures in People (Holt), pp. 98-99, and Families and Friends (Macmillan), pp. 68-70, to name important school rules. List the rules on chart paper. Discuss the reason for each one. Elicit additional school rules that need to be followed. Illustrate what could happen if a rule is not followed.

    ===

    < Read the poem from Resource Sheet 4, "Mary's Lamb," to the students. Ask the students questions such as the following:

    1. What was the rule that Mary broke?

Source: Baltimore County Public Schools, *Families, Friends and Me: A Social Studies Program for the First Grade* (Towson, MD: Baltimore County Public Schools, 1986), 32. Reproduced with permission.

FIGURE 4. EXAMPLES OF RESOURCE INFORMATION (*continued*)

Question 3:   What values affect us in school?

Values are those principles which become part of the belief systems of groups and individuals and which guide their respective behaviors. Values are developed through a variety of experiences with people and ideas. The values addressed in this question are directly related to the ability to work successfully within the school environment toward the goal of effective citizenship. These values are courtesy, honesty, tolerance, compassion, responsible citizenship, and patriotism.

Values education is an ongoing process which is merely initiated in this question. The activities presented here represent just one part of a consistent program of values education which will extend throughout the students' school program. The activities used to develop this topic should be selected according to the students' needs. It is recommended that the question be read thoroughly and the choices made prior to beginning the question with the students.

Alternate activities may be incorporated as the year progresses, both according to situational needs and as part of the regular program for opening exercises.

Suggested time: 1 week

Objectives

Knowledge

Students should be able to:

Become aware of specific values

Understand the importance of developing positive attitudes

Become aware of cooperative behavior in the classroom.

Skills

Students should be able to:

Express points of view and support these statements

Participate in group activities

Gain information by listening and observing

Interpret pictures.

49

Source: Baltimore County Public Schools, *Families, Friends and Me; A Social Studies Program for the First Grade* (Towson, MD: Baltimore County Public Schools, 1986), 49. Reproduced with permission.

FIGURE 5. EXAMPLES OF RESOURCE INFORMATION (*continued*)

BEING A GROUP MEMBER

Directions: Match the rule to the picture.

A. I follow rules.   B. I help others.

C. I listen.   D. I share.

Source: Baltimore County Public Schools, *Families, Friends and Me; A Social Studies Program for the First Grade* (Towson, MD: Baltimore County Public Schools, 1986), 263. Reproduced with permission.

FIGURE 6. EXAMPLE OF A CURRICULUM MAP

SOCIAL SCIENCES – SKILLS CONTINUUM

R = Reinforce
P = Proficiency

	K	1	2	3	4	5	6	7	8
14. Explain the value of competing political ideas and interest groups.							I	R	R
15. Talk about major civic problems.			I	R	R				
16. Discuss instances where economic power usually brings political power and vice-versa.			I	R	R	R	R	R	R
17. Describe how public exposure via mass media is an important source of power.							I	R	R
18. Discuss ways man is trying to alleviate his most serious problems: war, poverty, overpopulation, and pollution.							I	R	R
19. Describe ways the federal government shares some of the state and local functions: foreign affairs, national security and defense, interstate affairs and problems.					I	R	R	R	R
20. Understand that citizens can write to or talk with public officials about a problem or an idea to solve a problem.							I	R	R
21. Name some major Presidents and explain their contributions.						I	R	R	R
22. Describe the functions of each branch of government. Tell how each limits the power of the other.							I	R	R
B. Structure									
1. Compare the state and federal branches of government with local government.						I	R	R	R
2. Describe responsibilities of students, teachers, administrators, and the school board.						I	R	R	R
3. Discuss ways that governmental powers are limited by the people through the Constitution.						I	R	R	R

Source: Cupertino Union School District, *Social Sciences/Scope and Sequence Curriculum K-6* (Cupertino, CA: Cupertino Union School District, 1986), 12. Reproduced with permission.

Table 1. Sample Evaluation of K-5 Social Studies Curriculum		
Rationale	**Participants**	**Goals**
The evaluation will identify strengths and weaknesses in the K-5 social studies program.	Curriculum committee members; supervisory personnel; consultant	Quantity of document (design, format, volume, type of information); effectiveness of staff development; effectiveness of supervision; quality of achievement
Mission	**Revision**	**Content**
To what degree has the curriculum been implemented? Have adopted standards and goals been achieved? Have social studies achievement scores been raised? Have teachers adopted the curriculum?	K section on community studies; revise 4th-grade program (sequence); redesign 4-6 staff development program; incorporate NCSS standards for 3rd grade	Is the information in the document accurate, verifiable, measurable, "teachable," developmentally appropriate?
Needs Assessment	**Assessment**	**Instruction**
The K teachers must be involved in redesigning the community studies section. The grade 4 curriculum is too demanding, geared to advanced students. Staff development efforts for 4-6 teachers ineffective. Grade 3 goals do not meet intent of NCSS standards.	Does the testing program cover this curriculum? Have teachers changed their assessment tools and strategies effectively to accommodate the curriculum? Have achievement scores changed with the implementation of this curriculum?	Do teachers have sufficient time to teach the curriculum? Have teachers changed instructional methods? Have teachers used the curriculum in planning instruction? Are instructional resources (textbooks, filmstrips, software, etc.) available?

etc.), or should such input be targeted by inviting feedback from specific individuals, constituencies, or organizations which are most likely to understand social studies?

Public input, particularly when obtained in an open forum, can often yield contradictory opinions and requests. It is critical for the implementation process, however, to combine public input with feedback received from future users. Regardless of the nature of public feedback, or of whether or not all such input translates into actual changes in the social studies curriculum, experienced curriculum designers (or school districts) must respond to those who have answered the invitation to participate.

Editing, Ratification, Production, and Dissemination

Editing

Editing a curriculum has two major purposes. First, it should minimize jargon and technical language without eliminating the technical detail that teachers need for clarity. Whenever possible, a school district should hire an outside curriculum specialist or auditor when editing new guides or curricula in use (English 1988).

Second, the curriculum committee edits the drafted curriculum guide in order to fix weaknesses or missing parts identified in the interviews with future users (discussed above, under *Field Testing*) and the public (see above, under *Public Input*).

Ratification

Curriculum designers need to discuss ratification procedures with the administration in order to comply with state statutes, regulations, and local school board policies. Such procedures often involve local school board action. If that is the case, it is important to plan this event carefully.

School boards and communities should be informed about curriculum changes on an ongoing basis rather than being confronted with finalized documents; they may choose to review the document themselves before granting final approval. When a board is ready to vote on the matter, the curriculum designer (or the appropriate administrator) should make a formal presentation. This gives the district as a whole an opportunity to celebrate its achievement, to congratulate all participants for their efforts (including recognition ceremonies), and to confirm the importance of curriculum and instruction matters publicly (Carr and Harris in press). This event should include participants and citizens and be publicized in the local media.

Production

Curriculum designers should consider ways to make a new curriculum guide attractive as well as high quality in terms of content. A well-designed and well-printed document reveals care and commitment to the curriculum on the part of the district--and it may facilitate implementation.

Three-ring binders of various sizes offer significant advantages: (*a*) the name of the district, titles, and graphic designs can be silk-screened on binders at reasonable prices; (*b*) binders allow users to add new sections of the curriculum during revisions, remove outdated sections, or add their own instructional plans to it; (*c*) binders tend to have a longer life than cardboard covers or spiral-bound documents.

Curriculum production involves numerous decisions leading to printing and publication:

· Should the social studies curriculum be published in its entirety (K-12) in order to demonstrate a comprehensive approach to social studies?
· Should the social studies curriculum be published in sections or as separate documents (e.g., K-3, 4-6, 7-8, 9-12) to accommodate varying user needs and/or to save paper?
· Should the curriculum be prepared by a layout artist in order to prepare an attractive document (typeface, graphics, etc.)?
· Does the district have desktop publishing capability, and can the district develop its own layout?
· Should the document be bound in book fashion (may prolong cohesion), be bound with plastic spirals (may save production costs), or be placed in three-ring binders?
· Who should be given authorship for the final document? (Note: It is recommended that the school district retain all rights; the district can issue letters or certificates to participating committee members to affirm their contribution.)

Production efforts should be entirely planned and coordinated by the curriculum designer or administrative staff. Production may involve the contracted services of a printing company (unless administrative staff can handle the job). The process for purchasing binders (or an alternative) may follow a similar route.

Dissemination

The timing of dissemination should be carefully planned. Summer break and other vacations offer teachers an opportunity to read the documents and incorporate curriculum objectives into plans for upcoming quarters or semesters. An additional concern regarding dissemination addresses district plans for staff development or in-service training. It can be helpful to disseminate new curricula during staff development time; this provides time for reading and discussion among teachers or for carefully targeted workshops which address the new curriculum.

Adoption Process

By far the most challenging phase of the curriculum process is the adoption of a curriculum at the building level, along with the assurance that teachers plan instruction with the curriculum in hand. In this phase, curriculum is translated into instruction. The complexity of the curriculum, the degree to which assumptions about social studies are spelled out or hidden, the volume of the curriculum, and the teacher's disposition toward the curriculum guide are all factors that affect adoption.

In facing a mandatory curriculum, teachers must first decide whether or not they will work with that curriculum. This is a decision that can be mandated but not necessarily implemented. Because curriculum adoption at the classroom level is, at least in part, a personal decision, curriculum designers must take several factors into consideration which influence that decision:

- The degree to which teachers "own" the curriculum
- Level of experience working with district curriculum
- The degree to which the teacher depends on the textbook
- The teacher's flexibility and willingness to change
- The administrator's willingness and ability to support teachers
- Availability of necessary resources and materials
- Level of support from community, school board, state officials, etc.
- Availability and quality of staff development opportunities

Staff Development and Support

Staff development can be an effective implementation strategy, a fact that is voiced by many writers (Fullan 1990; Joyce and Showers 1988; Goodlad 1990; Holmes Group 1990; Loucks-Horsely et al. 1987; Schon 1987). From this standpoint, the teachers charged with implementing the curriculum may require specific training. Curriculum designers often see multiple training needs. To assess those needs as accurately as possible, administrators need to examine several factors:

1. Who are the users of the new curriculum? This information will determine the scale of training which will have to be provided to the district (e.g., How many classroom teachers per grade level? How many specialists?).
2. Which local, state, or national goals and standards are being adopted? This information must be included in order to effectively train and inform staff about adopted standards or goals effectively.
3. Has a timetable been adopted? This information defines the curriculum implementation timetable. Ideally, staff development targeted to facilitate curriculum implementation should be planned over several years and linked with a clear message to teachers that adoption is a longitudinal learning process.
4. What types of resources are needed/available? Available resources, such as trainers and staff development consultants, must be identified and included in the district's staff development budget.

5. Who has served on the curriculum committee? Educators who have participated in the curriculum design process can be used as discussion leaders or to model implementation in their own classrooms.
6. What are current topics in K-12 social studies? Current topics, controversies, or problems in K-12 social studies should have been identified in the review of the literature; this information can be helpful in defining topics for staff development workshops. In addition, authors and researchers may be available to serve as trainers or lecturers.
7. Which design format has been adopted? If the chosen format differs significantly from that previously used in district curricula, some staff development time may be required to instruct teachers in using the new materials.
8. What are the results from the field test? Teachers will often reveal staff development needs and topics when interviewed anonymously during the pilot testing process.

Monitoring and Supervision

Supervisors who observe teachers play a key role in supporting the implementation process; these supervisors provide opportunities for teachers to share and discuss problems and uncertainties with regard to their implementation efforts. In order for supervisors to be effective in this role, they must consider the following guidelines:

- Prove to teachers that supervision aims to support the teacher's many tasks; teachers are invited to share implementation issues without fearing that this sharing process will have a negative impact on performance evaluations. In fact, separating supervision from evaluation roles may be necessary.
- Be familiar with the curriculum and the teacher's stage of professional development; focus on issues, students, lesson plans, and instructional techniques in reference to, and appropriate for, his/her classroom.
- Provide feedback to the curriculum designer or committee that deals with staff development plans or curriculum revision.

Evaluation and Revision

Evaluation

After all the dust has settled, all the decisions have been made, and, at long last, a new social studies guide has been adopted for implementation, all participants surely deserve a rest. For the curriculum designer, however, the greatest challenge still lies ahead.

Social studies curriculum documents that are more than four or five years old require a thorough evaluation. Changes in the field, new research information, new standards, and better instructional methods appear quickly, making ongoing curricular adjustments necessary. This explains the need for school districts to have a curriculum process rather than merely a document. Curriculum designers should communicate this issue to all educators, parents, and policymakers.

Traditionally, achievement scores are held to be indicators of the quality of a social studies curriculum. Such scores, however, are but one source of curriculum evaluation data, and they are useful only insofar as the tested curriculum correlates with both the planned and the taught curriculum (English 1980).

Again, curriculum designers face some critical decisions:

1. What is the purpose of evaluating the curriculum? Is it a tool to evaluate teachers, students, or schools?
2. Who will participate in evaluating the curriculum? Should the same curriculum committee be used, or would a different perspective, and therefore a fresh committee, serve better?

The curriculum evaluation committee should be empowered to investigate the strengths and weaknesses of an implemented curriculum in full pursuit of the truth. This committee should not feel that the administration, for instance, has already invested four years into the project and will not react kindly to a report suggesting that the curriculum has not affected past classroom practices. Similarly, teachers who are asked to comment or submit grade sheets to the evaluation committee should do so without fear of negative consequences. While these examples appear overly dramatized, vested interests can have a negative impact on efforts to assess the quality of a curriculum.

Curriculum designers should clarify the evaluation process in advance. Included in this process is a clarification of the following:

· Who the evaluation committee *participants* will be
· To what degree curriculum process *goals* have been achieved

· Whether the overall *mission* of the curriculum project has been reached
· Whether curriculum *content* is appropriate in light of district characteristics and mission objectives
· Whether *instruction* is based on the curriculum
· Whether the *assessment* process measured the taught curriculum against the planned curriculum

Table 1 provides a sampling of the goals and questions that may be addressed during evaluation of a curriculum.

The evaluation, then, will yield a *needs assessment* to clarify what types of resources, time demands, training and workshops, and supervision strategies must be in place in order for successful implementation to continue. In addition, a *revision plan* should be issued for the curriculum guide itself, giving specifics for additions or deletions.

Revision

Planning for the next generation of social studies programs begins now. The first step consists of educating the school board, the staff, and the community that implementation will yield a variety of positive experiences as well as numerous problems. Information of this sort must be collected and organized in view of future revisions of the curriculum. Any curriculum has room for improvement and must be dynamic enough to incorporate upcoming changes in the field of social studies.

Curriculum designers should therefore present a *curriculum development process,* if not at the outset, then certainly at the time of adoption and implementation. This will clarify the ground rules for all concerned. A development process at the district level should incorporate all curriculum areas. However, in order to remain manageable, the district should avoid revising all curricula during the same year. Revising a social studies curriculum can be as complex as designing it in the first place. Numerous decisions must be made and numerous sources of information considered:

· Is a revision necessary in view of available information, or should the revision cycle be changed (to revise sooner or later than planned)?
· Should a committee be established to carry out the revision?
· Have conditions changed since the social

studies curriculum was first implemented (new standards, new testing systems, new staffing patterns, significant changes in enrollment, budget crises, etc.)?

Curriculum designers often battle the assumption that completed curriculum guides finalize the curriculum process--in reality, a curriculum guide marks the *beginning* of a curriculum. A curriculum guide that looks the same five years after it was written will most likely be outdated. Teachers tend to leave them on the shelf, and for good reason.

Each school or district must have a process in place for curriculum development and revision. The schools and districts that have an ongoing curriculum revision process are best equipped to react to new standards and methods in social studies and in all other K-12 subjects--and these are the schools that can best serve their students and prepare them for the world beyond graduation.

Notes

1. Other practical guidebooks are available to supplement this handbook. See Carr and Harris 1992, in press; Frey et al. 1989; Bradley 1985; National Commission on Social Studies in the Schools 1989; California Department of Education 1988; National Council for Geographic Education, Association of American Geographers, and Joint Committee on Geographic Education 1984; Geographic Education National Implementation Project 1985, 1985a; New York State Education Department 1984; Wisconsin Department of Public Instruction 1986.

2. Among the numerous outstanding resources which discuss the issue of teachers as adult learners in detail are L. Thies-Sprinthall 1986; Sprinthall and Thies-Sprinthall 1983; McNergney and Carrier 1981; Oja and Ham 1987.

3. Budget models based on curricular or programmatic priorities are discussed in Wood 1986.

4. For a historical perspective on the interdisciplinary curriculum, see Vars 1991.

5. For a comprehensive review of interdisciplinary curriculum models and procedures, see Palmer 1991; Jacobs 1989; Miller, Cassie, and Drake 1990; Drake 1991.

References

Anderson, S. A., et al. 1987. *Curriculum Process: Yale Public Schools*. Yale, MI.

Apple, M. W. 1979. *Ideology and Curriculum*. Boston: Routledge and Kegan Paul.

Argyris, C. 1982. *Reading, Learning, and Action: Individual and Organizational*. San Francisco: Jossey-Bass.

Aronowitz, S., and H. A. Giroux. 1985. *Education under Siege*. South Hadley, MA: Bergin and Garvey.

Bradley Commission on History in Schools. 1988. *Building a History Curriculum*. Washington, DC: Educational Excellence Network.

Bradley, L. H. 1985. *Curriculum Leadership and Development Handbook*. Englewood Cliffs, NJ: Prentice Hall.

Butts, F. R. 1980. *The Revival of Civic Learning*. Bloomington, IN: Phi Delta Kappa Educational Foundation.

Caine, R. N., and G. Caine. 1991. *Making Connections--Teaching and the Human Brain*. Alexandria, VA: Association for Supervision and Curriculum Development.

California Department of Education. 1988. *History-Social Science Framework, K-12*. Sacramento.

Campbell, M., et al. 1989. "Board Members Needn't Be Experts to Play a Vital Role in Curriculum." *American School Board Journal* 176 (April 1989): 30-32.

Carr, J. F., and D. E. Harris. In press. *Getting It Together: A Process Workbook for Curriculum Development, Implementation, and Assessment*. Boston: Allyn & Bacon.

Connelly, F. M., and D. J. Clandinin. 1988. *Teachers as Curriculum Planners: Narratives of Experience*. New York: Teachers College Press.

Crutchfield, M. A. 1978. *Elementary Social Studies: An Interdisciplinary Approach*. Columbus, OH: Merrill.

Doll, R. C. 1989. *Curriculum Improvement: Decision Making and Process*. 7th ed. Boston: Allyn & Bacon.

Drake, S. M. 1991. "How Our Team Dissolved the Boundaries." *Educational Leadership* 49 (October): 20-22.

English, F. W. 1988. *Curriculum Auditing*. Lancaster, PA: Technomic.

——. 1980. "Improving Curriculum Management in the Schools." Occasional Paper 30. Washington, DC: Council for Basic Education.

Frey, K., et al. 1989. "Do Curriculum Development Models Really Influence the Curriculum?" *Journal of Curriculum Studies* 21 (November-December): 553-59.

Fullan, M. G. 1990. "Staff Development, Innovation, and Institutional Development." In *ASCD Yearbook*, 3-25. Alexandria, VA: Association for Supervision and Curriculum Development.

Geographic Education National Implementation Project. 1985a. *K-6 Geography--Themes, Key Ideas, and Learning Opportunities.* Skokie, IL: Rand McNally.

——. 1985b. *7-12 Geography--Themes, Key Ideas, and Learning Opportunities.* Skokie, IL: Rand McNally.

Giroux, H. A. 1983. *Theory and Resistance in Education.* South Hadley, MA: Bergin and Garvey.

Glatthorn, A. A. 1987. *Curriculum Leadership.* Glenview, IL: Scott, Foresman.

Glickman, C. 1990. *Supervision of Instruction: A Developmental Approach.* 2d ed. Boston: Allyn & Bacon.

Goodlad, J. I. 1990. *Teachers for Our Nation's Schools.* San Francisco: Jossey-Bass.

Hanna, P. R. 1987. *Assuring Quality for the Social Studies in Our Schools.* Stanford, CA: Hoover Institution Press.

Harris, D. E., and Jenzer, J. 1990. "The Search for Quality Curriculum Design: Four Models for School Districts." Paper presented at National Association of Supervision and Curriculum Development Conference, San Antonio, TX.

Holmes Group. 1990. *Tomorrow's Schools: Principles for the Design of Professional Development Schools.* East Lansing, MI.

Jacobs, H. H. 1989. *Interdisciplinary Curriculum--Design and Implementation.* Alexandria, VA: Association for Supervision and Curriculum Development.

Joyce, B., and B. Showers. 1988. *Student Achievement through Staff Development.* White Plains, NY: Longman.

Kanpol, B., and E. Weisz. 1990. "The Effective Principal and the Curriculum--A Focus on Leadership." *NASSP Bulletin* 74 (April): 15-18.

Loucks-Horsely, S., et al. 1987. *Continuing to Learn: A Guidebook for Teacher Development.* Andover, MA: Regional Laboratory for Educational Improvement of the Northeast and the Islands.

Maxim, G. W. 1991. *Social Studies and the Elementary School Child.* New York: Macmillan.

McNeil, J. D. 1985. *Curriculum--A Comprehensive Introduction.* 3d ed. Boston: Little, Brown.

McNergney, R., and C. Carrier. 1981. *Teacher Development.* New York: Macmillan.

Miller, J., B. Cassie, and S. M. Drake. 1990. *Holistic Learning: A Teacher's Guide to Integrated Studies.* Toronto: Ontario Institute for Studies in Education.

Montana State Office of the Superintendent of Public Instruction. 1990. *The Curriculum Process Guide: Developing Curriculum in the 1990's.* Helena, MT.

National Center for History in the Schools. 1992. *Lessons from History: Essential Understandings and Historical Perspectives Students Should Acquire.* Los Angeles.

National Commission on Social Studies in the Schools. 1989. *Charting a Course: Social Studies for the 21st Century.* Washington, DC

National Council for Geographic Education, Association of American Geographers, and Joint Committee on Geographic Education. 1984. *Guidelines for Geographic Education--Elementary and Secondary Schools.* Indiana, PA: Indiana Univ. of Pennsylvania.

National Council for Teachers of Mathematics. 1989. *Curriculum and Evaluation Standards for School Mathematics.* Reston, VA.

New York State Education Department. 1984. *Curriculum Development: A Handbook for School Districts.* Albany, NY.

Oja, S. N., and M. Ham. 1987. *A Collaborative Approach to Leadership in Supervision.* Project funded by U.S. Department of Education (OERI). ED. no. 400-85-1056. Washington, DC

Page, R., and L. Valli. 1990. *Curriculum Differentiation: Interpretive Studies in U.S. Secondary Schools.* Albany, NY: State University of New York Press.

Palmer, J. M. 1991. "Planning Wheels Turn Curriculum Around." *Educational Leadership* 49 (October): 57-60.

Schon, D. 1987. *Educating the Reflective Practitioner.* New York: Basic Books.

Sprinthall, N. A., and L. Thies-Sprinthall. 1983. "The Teacher as an Adult Learner: A Cognitive-Developmental View." In *Eighty-second Yearbook of the National Society for the Study of Education*, 13-35. Chicago, IL: National Society for the Study of Education.

Thies-Sprinthall, L. 1986. "A Collaborative Approach to Mentor Training: A Working Model." *Journal of Teacher Education* 19 (November-December): 13-20.

United States Department of Education. 1983. *A Nation at Risk: The Imperative for Educational Reform*. Washington, DC

Vars, G. F. 1991. "Integrated Curriculum in Historical Perspective." *Educational Leadership* 49 (October): 14-15.

Wisconsin Department of Public Instruction. 1986. *A Guide to Curriculum Planning in Social Studies*. Madison, WI.

Wood, R. C., ed. 1986. *Principles of School Business Management*. Reston, VA: Association of School Business Officials International.

Wulf, K. M., and B. Schave. 1984. *Curriculum Design*. Glenview, IL: Scott, Foresman.

Young, H. J. 1990. "Curriculum Implementation: An Organizational Perspective." *Journal of Curriculum and Supervision* 5 (Winter): 132-49.

FUNDING CURRICULUM PROJECTS

THE greatest challenge curriculum developers often face is locating money to finance their projects. We hear that money is available for such projects, but are at a loss as to how it can be accessed. Frequently, it requires as much creativity to locate financing as to generate the curriculum. This chapter includes information on three types of funding that are available for education projects:

1. Federal programs providing money for special school projects
2. Foundations and organizations that have recently endowed social studies and general education projects
3. Foundations and organizations that provide state funds for education, including special projects, as a mission.

When seeking a potential funding source for the project, first review any information that is available about the organization. Specifically look at the following areas:

- Purpose: Is providing money for education a mission of the foundation?
- Limitations: Are there specific geographic requirements? Are there some regions that are disqualified?
- Supported areas: Does the organization provide funding for special projects?
- Grants: After a review of the education projects that have been funded, does it appear that the organizations and projects are similar to yours?

Your search will be most useful if you also keep these questions in mind:

- Has the foundation funded projects in your subject area?
- Does your location meet the geographic requirements of the organization?
- Is the amount of money you are requesting within the grant's range?
- Are there foundation policies that prohibit grants for the type of support you are requesting?
- Will the organization make grants to cover the full cost of a project? Does it require costs of a project to be shared with other foundations or funding sources?
- What types of educational groups have been supported? Are they similar to yours?
- Are there specific application deadlines and procedures, or are proposals accepted continuously?

This information can be found in the annual report of the foundation or in *Source Book Profiles*. Many of the larger public libraries maintain current foundation directories. If yours does not, there are Foundation Center Libraries located at:

79 Fifth Avenue
New York, NY 10003-3050
(212) 620-4230

312 Sutter Street
San Francisco, CA 94180
(415) 397-0902

1001 Connecticut Avenue, NW
Suite 938
Washington, DC 20036
(202) 331-1400

1442 Hanna Building
1442 Euclid Avenue
Cleveland, OH 44115
(216) 861-1934

Identifying appropriate foundations is the first step in your quest for money. The next step is initiating contact with the foundation, either by telephone or by letter. It is a good idea to direct your inquiry to the person in charge of giving; otherwise, you run the risk of your letter going astray. A phone call to the foundation will provide you with this information.

Federal Programs Providing Money for Special School Projects

Jacob B. Javits Gifted and Talented Students
Research Applications Division
Programs for the Improvement of Practice
Department of Education
555 New Jersey Avenue, NW
Washington, DC 20202-5643
(202) 219-2187
Provides grants for establishing and operating model projects to identify and educate gifted and talented students.

Technology Education Demonstration
Division of National Programs
Office of Vocational and Adult Education
Department of Education
400 Maryland Avenue, SW
Washington, DC 20202-7242
(202) 732-2428
Funding to establish model demonstration programs for technology education in secondary schools, vocational education centers, and community colleges.

The Secretary's Fund for Innovation in Education
Department of Education
FIRST
Office of Educational Research and Improvement
Washington, DC 20208-5524
(202) 219-1496
Funding for educational programs and projects that identify innovative educational approaches.

Foundations and Organizations that Have Recently Endowed Social Studies and General Education Projects

The Blandin Foundation
100 Pokegama Avenue, North
Grand Rapids, MN 55744
(218) 326-0523
Contact: Paul M. Olson, President
Limited to MN, with an emphasis on rural areas.
· $125,500 to Grand Rapids Independent School District 318, Rapids Quest Program, Grand Rapids, MN, to continue imaginative enrichment programs for Grand Rapids students.
· $25,000 to Independent School District 317, Deer River, MN, to produce Ojibwe K-12 curriculum.
· $50,000 to Mahnomen School District 432, Mahnomen, MN, for their Ojibwe curriculum.

The Cleveland Foundation
1422 Euclid Avenue, Suite 1400
Cleveland, OH 44115-2001
(216) 861-3810
Initial approach should be through a letter.
· $50,000 to Cleveland Board of Education, Cleveland, OH, for citizenship curriculum to be introduced into the Cleveland Public Schools Social Studies program.

Du Pont Community Initiatives Fund
Du Pont External Affairs
Wilmington, DE 19898
Matching-grant program for projects to encourage company sites to develop or adopt programs in their communities that will upgrade the quality of public education and increase public understanding of environmental matters.

James Irvine Foundation
One Market Plaza
Spear Street Tower, Suite 1715
San Francisco, CA 94105
· $85,000 (over two years) to the Junior Statesman Foundation, Redwood City, CA, for expansion of a peer civics education program in inner-city Los Angeles.

W. Alton Jones Foundation, Inc.
232 East High Street
Charlottesville, VA 22901
(804) 295-2134
· $70,000 to Episcopal School of New York
City, New York, NY, for general school
development and teacher professional
development.

Knight Foundation
One Biscayne Tower, Suite 3800
Two Biscayne Boulevard
Miami, FL 33131
(305) 539-2610
Limited to areas where Knight-Ridder newspa-
pers are published.
· $15,000 to the First Amendment Congress,
Denver, CO, for a project to develop a First
Amendment Social Studies curriculum for K-
12.

The Nellie Mae Fund for Education
50 Braintree Hill Park, Suite 300
Braintree, MA 02184
(617) 849-1325
Generally limited to the six New England states.
· $10,000 to Volunteers in Providence Schools,
Providence, RI, for after-school study centers
at eleven sites throughout Providence
· $12,000 to Winthrop School Department,
Winthrop, MA, to develop Modeling for
Success project (positive role models for at-
risk middle school students).

The Medtronic Foundation
7000 Central Avenue, NE
Minneapolis, MN 55432
(612) 574-3029
Giving primarily in areas of company operations.
· $12,500 to Minneapolis Public Schools,
Minneapolis, MN to work with the community on general curriculum development.

National Council for the Social Studies
F.A.S.S.E. General Grant
3501 Newark Street, NW
Washington, DC 20016
(202) 966-7840
Fund for the Advancement of Social-Studies
Education (F.A.S.S.E.) General Grant for teachers in categories of K-5, 6-9, 10-12, and collegiate/
university (teacher education) categories.

The Reader's Digest Foundation
Pleasantville, NY 10570
One hundred minigrants of up to $500 each to
fund innovative-teaching programs for schools in
Westchester and Putnam counties, NY.

The Spencer Foundation
900 North Michigan Avenue, Suite 2800
Chicago, IL 60611
Grants for various research projects related to
cultural variations, high school teaching, school
choice, and so forth.

Steelcase Foundation
P.O. Box 1967
Grand Rapids, MI 49507
(616) 246-4695
Limited to areas of company operations.
· $20,000 to Forest Hills Education Foundation,
Grand Rapids, MI, for development of
science curriculum for special education
students.

The Tandy Corporation
1800 One Tandy Center
Fort Worth, TX 76102
·   Tandy Educational Grants to 11 schools and
colleges/universities for using microcomputers
for classroom management to increase
student/teacher productivity.

Foundations and Organizations that Provide Funds for Education, Including Special Projects, as a Mission

Aetna Foundation, Inc.
151 Farmington Avenue
Hartford, CT 06156-3180
(203) 273-6382
Contact: Diana Kinosh, Management Information
Supervisor

The Ahmanson Foundation
9215 Wilshire Boulevard
Beverly Hills, CA 90210
(213) 278-0770
Contact: Lee E. Walcott, Vice President &
Managing Director
Giving primarily in southern California.

Alcoa Foundation
1501 Alcoa Building
Pittsburgh, PA 15219-1850
(412) 553-2348
Contact: F. Worth Hobbs, President
Giving primarily in areas of company operation.

The Allstate Foundation
Allstate Plaza North
Northbrook, IL 60062
(708) 402-5502
Contacts: Alan Benedict, Executive Director;
    Allen Goldhamer, Manager; Dawn Bougart,
    Administrative Assistant

American Express Minnesota Foundation
c/o IDS Financial Services
IDS Tower Ten
Minneapolis, MN 55440
(612) 372-2643
Contacts: Sue Gethin, Manager of Public Affairs,
    IDS; Marie Tobin, Community Relations
    Specialist
Giving primarily in Minnesota.

American National Bank & Trust Co. of Chicago
Foundation
33 North La Salle Street
Chicago, IL 60690
(312) 661-6115
Contact: Joan M. Klaus, Director
Giving limited to six-county Chicago, IL, metro-
politan area.

Anderson Foundation
c/o Anderson Corp.
Bayport, MN 55003
(612) 439-5150
Contact: Lisa Carlstrom, Assistant Secretary

The Annenberg Foundation
St. Davids Center
150 Radnor-Chester Rd., Suite A-200
St. Davids, PA 19087
Contact: Dr. Mary Ann Meyers, President

AON Foundation
123 North Wacker Drive
Chicago, IL 60606
(312) 701-3000
Contact: Wallace J. Buya, Vice President
No support for secondary educational institutions
or vocational schools.

Atherton Family Foundation
c/o Hawaiian Trust Co., Ltd.
P.O. Box 3170
Honolulu, HI 96802
(808) 537-6333
Fax: (808) 521-6286
Contact: Charlie Medeiros
Limited to Hawaii.

Ball Brothers Foundation
222 South Mulberry Street
Muncie, IN 47308
(317) 741-5500
Fax: (317) 741-5518
Contact: Douglas A. Bakken, Executive Director
Limited to Indiana.

Baltimore Gas & Electric Foundation, Inc.
Box 1475
Baltimore, MD 21203
(301) 234-5312
Contact: Gary R. Fuhronan
Giving primarily in Maryland, with emphasis on
Baltimore.

Bell Atlantic Charitable Foundation
1310 North Courthouse Road, 10th Floor
Arlington, VA 22201
(703) 974-5440
Contact: Ruth P. Caine, Director
Giving primarily in areas of company operations.

Benwood Foundation, Inc.
1600 American National Bank Building
736 Market Street
Chattanooga, TN 37402
(615) 267-4311
Contact: Jean R. McDaniel, Executive Director
Giving primarily in the Chattanooga, TN, area.

Robert M. Beren Foundation, Inc.
970 Fourth Financial Center
Wichita, KS 67202
Giving primarily to Jewish organizations.

The Frank Stanley Beveridge Foundation, Inc.
1515 Ringling Boulevard, Suite 340
P.O. Box 4097
Sarasota, FL 34230-4097
(813) 955-7575
(800) 356-9779
Contact: Philip Coswell, President
Giving primarily to Hampden County, MA,
organizations that are not tax-supported.

F.R. Bigelow Foundation
1120 Norwest Center
St. Paul, MN 55101
(612) 224-5463
Contact: Paul A. Verret, Secretary-Treasurer
Support includes secondary education in greater
St. Paul, MN, metropolitan area.

Borden Foundation, Inc.
180 East Broad Street, 34th Floor
Columbus, OH 43215
(614) 225-4340
Contact: Judy Barker, President
Emphasis on programs to benefit disadvantaged
children in areas of company operations.

The Boston Globe Foundation II, Inc.
135 Morrissey Boulevard
Boston, MA 02107
(617) 929-3194
Contact: Suzanne Watkin, Executive Director
Giving primarily in greater Boston, MA, area.

The JS Bridwell Foundation
500 City National Building
Wichita Falls, TX 76303
(817) 322-4436
Support includes secondary education in Texas.

The Buchanan Family Foundation
222 East Wisconsin Avenue
Lake Forest, IL 60045
Contact: Huntington Eldridge, Jr., Treasurer
Giving primarily in Chicago, IL.

The Buhl Foundation
Four Gateway Center, Room 1522
Pittsburgh, PA 15222
(412) 566-2711
Contact: Dr. Doreen E. Boyce,
   Executive Director
Giving primarily in southwestern Pennsylvania,
particularly the Pittsburgh area.

Edyth Bush Charitable Foundation, Inc.
199 East Welbourne Avenue
P.O. Box 1967
Winter Park, FL 32790-1967
(407) 647-4322
Contact: H. Clifford Lee, President
Giving has specific geographic and facility limita-
tions.

California Community Foundation
606 South Olive Street, Suite 2400
Los Angeles, CA 90014
(213) 413-4042
Contact: Jack Shakley, President
Orange County:
13252 Garden Grove Boulevard, Suite 195
Garden Grove, CA 92643
(714) 750-7794
Giving limited to Los Angeles, Orange, Riverside,
San Bernadino, and Ventura counties, CA.

The Cargill Foundation
P.O. Box 9300
Minneapolis, MN 55440
(612) 475-6122
Contact: Audrey Tulberg, Program and Adminis-
   trative Director
Giving primarily in the seven-county Minneapolis-
St. Paul, MN, metropolitan area.

H.A. & Mary K. Chapman Charitable Trust
One Warren Place, Suite 1816
6100 South Yale
Tulsa, OK 74136
(918) 496-7882
Contacts: Ralph L. Abercrombie, Trustee;
   Donne Pitman, Trustee
Giving primarily in Tulsa, OK.

Liz Claiborne Foundation
119 West 40th Street, 4th Floor
New York, NY 10018
(212) 536-6424
Limited to Hudson County, NJ, and the metropolitan New York area.

The Coca-Cola Foundation, Inc.
P.O. Drawer 1734
Atlanta, GA 30301
(404) 676-2568

The Columbus Foundation
1234 East Broad Street
Columbus, OH 43205
(614) 251-4000
Contact: James I. Luck, President
Giving limited to central Ohio.

Cowles Media Foundation
329 Portland Avenue
Minneapolis, MN 55415
(612) 375-7051
Contact: Janet L. Schwichtenberg
Limited to Minneapolis, MN, area.

Dade Community Foundation
200 South Biscayne Boulevard, Suite 4770
Miami, FL 33131-2343
(305) 371-2711
Contact: Ruth Shack, President
Funding limited to Dade County, FL.

Dewitt Families Conduit Foundation
8300 96th Avenue
Zelland, MI 49464
Giving for Christian organizations.

Dodge Jones Foundation
P.O. Box 176
Abilene, TX 79604
(915) 673-6429
Contact: Lawrence E. Gill, Vice President, Grants
    Administration
Giving primarily in Abilene, TX.

Carrie Estelle Doheny Foundation
911 Wiltshire Boulevard, Suite 1750
Los Angeles, CA 90017
(213) 488-1122
Contact: Robert A. Smith III, President
Giving primarily in the Los Angeles, CA, area for
non-tax-supported organizations.

The Educational Foundation of America
23161 Ventura Boulevard, Suite 201
Woodland Hill, CA 91364
(818) 999-0921

The Charles Engelhard Foundation
P.O. Box 427
Far Hills, NJ 07931
(201) 766-7224
Contact: Elaine Catterall, Secretary

The William Stamps Farish Fund
1100 Louisiana, Suite 1250
Houston, TX 77002
(713) 757-7313
Contact: W. S. Farish, President
Giving primarily in Texas.

Joseph & Bessie Feinberg Foundation
5245 West Lawrence Avenue
Chicago, IL 60630
(312) 777-8600
Contact: June Blossom
Giving primarily in Illinois, to Jewish organizations.

The 1525 Foundation
1525 National City Bank Building
Cleveland, OH 44114
(216) 696-4200
Contact: Bernadette Walsh, Assistant Secretary
Giving primarily in Ohio, with emphasis on
Cuyahoga County.

The Edward E. Ford Foundation
297 Wickenden Street
Providence, RI 02903
(401) 751-2966
Contact: Philip V. Havens, Executive Director
Funding to independent secondary schools.

George F. & Sybil H. Fuller Foundation
105 Madison Street
Worcester, MA 01610
(508) 756-5111
Contact: Russell E. Fuller, Chairman
Giving primarily in Massachusetts, with emphasis
in Worcester.

The B. C. Gamble & P. W. Skogmo Foundation
500 Foshay Tower
Minneapolis, MN 55402
(612) 339-7343
Contact: Patricia A. Cummings, Manager of
    Supporting Organizations
Giving primarily for disadvantaged youth, handi-
capped, and secondary educational institutions in
the Minneapolis-St. Paul, MN, metropolitan area.

The Gold Family Foundation
159 Conant Street
Hillside, NJ 07205
(908) 353-6269
Contact: Meyer Gold, Manager
Support primarily for Jewish organizations.

The George Gund Foundation
1845 Guildhall Building
45 Prospect Avenue West
Cleveland, OH 44115
(216) 241-3114
Fax: (216) 241-6560
Contact: David Bergholz, Executive Director
Giving primarily in northeastern Ohio.

The Haggar Foundation
6113 Lemmon Avenue
Dallas, TX 75209
(214) 956-0241
Contact: Rosemary Haggar Vaughan, Executive

Director
Limited to areas of company operations in Dallas and south Texas.

Gladys & Roland Harriman Foundation
63 Wall Street, 23rd Floor
New York, NY 10005
(212) 493-8182
Contact: William F. Hibberd, Secretary

Hasbro Children's Foundation
32 West 23rd Street
New York, NY 10010
(212) 645-2400
Contact: Eve Weiss, Executive Director
Funding for children with special needs, under the age of 12.

The Humana Foundation, Inc.
The Humana Building
500 West Main Street
P.O. Box 1438
Louisville, KY 40201
(502) 580-3920
Contact: Jay L. Foley, Contribution Manager
Giving primarily in Kentucky.

International Paper Company Foundation
Two Manhattanville Road
Purchase, NY 10577
(914) 397-1581
Contact: Sandra Wilson, Vice President
Giving primarily in communities where there are company plants and mills.

The Martha Holden Jennings Foundation
710 Halle Building
1228 Euclid Avenue
Cleveland, OH 44115
(216) 589-5700
Contact: Dr. Richard A. Boyd, Executive Director
Limited to Ohio.

Walter S. Johnson Foundation
525 Middlefield Road, Suite 110
Menlo Park, CA 94025
(415) 326-0485
Contact: Donna Terman, Executive Director
Giving primarily in Alameda, Contra Costa, San Francisco, San Mateo, and Santa Clara counties in CA and in Washoe, NV; no support to private schools.

Donald P. & Byrd M. Kelly Foundation
701 Harger Road, No. 150
Oak Brook, IL 60521
Contact: Laura K. McGrath, Treasurer
Primarily in Illinois, with emphasis on Chicago.

Carl B. & Florence E. King Foundation
5956 Sherry Lane, Suite 620
Dallas, TX 75225
Contact: Carl Yeckel, Vice President
Giving primarily in Dallas, TX, area.

Thomas & Dorothy Leavey Foundation
4680 Wiltshire Boulevard
Los Angeles, CA 90010
(213) 930-4252
Contact: J. Thomas McCarthy, Trustee
Primarily in southern California, to Catholic organizations.

Levi Strauss Foundation
1155 Battery Street
San Francisco, CA 94111
(415) 544-2194
Contacts: Bay Area: Judy Belk, Director of Contributions; Mid-South Region: Myra Chow, Director of Contributions; Western Region: Mario Griffin, Director of Contributions; Rio Grande: Elvira Chavaria, Director of Contributions; Eastern Region: Mary Ellen McLoughlin, Director of Contributions
Generally limited to areas of company operations.

Lyndhurst Foundation
Suite 701, Tallan Building
100 West Martin Luther King Boulevard
Chattanooga, TN 37402-2561
(615) 756-0767
Contact: Jack E. Murrah, President
Limited to southeastern United States, especially Chattanooga, TN.

McDonnell Douglas Foundation
c/o McDonnell Douglas Corp.
P.O. Box 516, Mail Code 1001440
St. Louis, MO 63166
(314) 232-8464
Contact: Walter E. Diggs, Jr., President
Giving primarily in Arizona, California, Florida, Missouri, Oklahoma, and Texas.

Meadows Foundation, Inc.
Wilson Historic Block
2922 Swiss Avenue
Dallas, TX 75204-5928
(214) 826-9431
Contact: Dr. Sally R. Lancaster, Executive Vice
President
Limited to Texas.

Metropolitan Atlanta Community Foundation,
Inc.
The Hurt Building, Suite 449
Atlanta, GA 30303
(404) 688-5525
Contact: Alicia Philipp, Executive Director
Limited to metropolitan area of Atlanta, GA, and
surrounding regions.

The Milken Family Foundation
c/o Foundation of the Milken Families
15250 Ventura Boulevard, 2nd Floor
Sherman Oaks, CA 91403
Contact: Dr. Jules Lesner, Executive Director
Giving limited to the Los Angeles, CA, area.

The New Hampshire Charitable Fund
One South Street
P.O. Box 1335
Concord, NH 03302-1335
(603) 225-6641
Contact: Deborah Cowan, Associate Director
Limited to New Hampshire.

The New Haven Foundation
70 Audubon Street
New Haven, CT 06510
(203) 777-2386
Contact: Helmer N. Ekstrom, Director
Giving primarily in greater New Haven, CT, and
lower Naugatuck River Valley.

Dellora A. & Lester J. Norris Foundation
P.O. Box 1081
St. Charles, IL 60174
(312) 377-4111
Contact: Eugene Butler, Treasurer
Funding includes secondary education.

The Northern Trust Company Charitable Trust
c/o The Northern Trust Co., Corp. Affairs Div.
50 South LaSalle Street
Chicago, IL 60675
(312) 444-3538

Contact: Marjorie W. Lundy, Vice President
Limited to the metropolitan Chicago, IL, area.

The Principal Financial Group Foundation, Inc.
711 High Street
Des Moines, IA 50392-0150
(515) 247-5209
Contact: Debra J. Jensen, Secretary
Primarily in Iowa, with emphasis on the Des
Moines area.

Sid W. Richardson Foundation
309 Main Street
Fort Worth, TX 76102
(817) 336-0497
Contact: Valleau Wilkie, Jr., Executive Vice
President
Limited to Texas.

R.J.R. Nabisco Foundation
1455 Pennsylvania Avenue, NW, Suite 525
Washington, DC 20004
(202) 626-7200
Contact: Jaynie M. Grant, Executive Director

The Winthrop Rockefeller Foundation
308 East Eighth Street
Little Rock, AR 72202
(501) 376-6854
Contact: Mahlon Martin, President
Funding primarily in Arkansas or for projects that
will benefit Arkansas.

The San Francisco Foundation
685 Market Street, Suite 910
San Francisco, CA 94105-9716
(415) 495-3100
Contact: Robert M. Fisher, Director
Giving limited to Bay Area and the counties of
Alameda, Contra Costa, Marin, San Francisco,
and San Mateo, CA

Community Foundation of Santa Clara County
960 West Hedding, Suite 220
San Jose, CA 95126-1215
(408) 241-2666
Contact: Winnie Chu, Program Officer
Limited to Santa Clara County, CA.

John & Dorothy Shea Foundation
655 Brea Canyon Road
Walnut, CA 91789
Giving primarily in California.

Harold Simmons Foundation
Three Lincoln Center
5430 LBJ Freeway, Suite 1700
Dallas, TX 75240-2697
(214) 233-1700
Contact: Lisa K. Simmons, President
Limited to Dallas, TX, area.

Sonart Family Foundation
15 Benders Drive
Greenwich, CT 06831
(203) 531-1474
Contact: Raymond Sonart, President

The Sosland Foundation
4800 Main Street, Suite 100
Kansas City, MO 64112-2510
(816) 756-1000
Fax: (816) 756-0494
Contact: Debbie Sosland-Edelman, Ph.D.
Limited to Kansas City, MO, and KS areas.

Community Foundation for Southeastern
   Michigan
333 West Fort Street, Suite 2010
Detroit, MI 48226
(313) 961-6675
Contact: C. David Campbell, Vice President of
   Programs
Giving limited to southeastern Michigan.

Springs Foundation, Inc.
P.O. Drawer 460
Lancaster, SC 29720
(803) 286-2196
Contact: Charles A. Bundy, President
Limited to Lancaster County and/or the town-
ships of Ft. Mill and Chester, SC.

Strauss Foundation
c/o Fidelity Bank, N.A.
Broad & Walnut Streets
Philadelphia, PA 19109
(215) 985-7717
Contact: Richard Irvin, Jr.
Giving primarily in Pennsylvania.

Stuart Foundations
425 Market Street, Suite 2835
San Francisco, CA 94105
(415) 495-1144
Contact: Theodore E. Lobman, President
Primarily in California; applications from Washington will be considered.

T.L.L. Tempee Foundation
109 Tempee Boulevard
Lufkin, TX 75901
(409) 639-5197
Contact: M. F. Buddy Zeagler, Assistant Executive Director and Controller
Giving primarily in counties in Texas constituting
the East Texas Pine Timber Belt.

Travelers Companies Foundation
One Tower Square
Hartford, CT 06183-1060
(203) 277-4070/4079
Funding for school programs limited to Hartford,
CT.

Turrell Fund
111 Northfield Avenue
West Orange, NJ 07052
(201) 325-5108
Contact: E. Belvin Williams, Executive Director
Giving limited to New Jersey, particularly the
northern urban areas centered in Essex County;
also giving in Vermont.

U.S. West Foundation
7800 East Orchard Road, Suite 300
Englewood, CO 80111
(303) 793-6661
Contact: Larry J. Nash, Director of
   Administration
Limited to states served by US WEST calling
areas. Address applications to local US WEST
Public Relations Office or Community Relations
Team.

Philip L. Van Every Foundation
c/o Lance, Inc.
P.O. Box 32368
Charlotte, NC 28232
(704) 554-1421
Primarily in North Carolina and South Carolina.

Joseph B. Whitehead Foundation
1400 Peachtree Center Tower
230 Peachtree Street, NW
Atlanta, GA 30303
(404) 522-6755
Contact: Charles H. McTier, President
Giving limited to metropolitan Atlanta, GA.

Winn-Dixie Stores Foundation
5050 Edgewood Court
Jacksonville, FL 32205
(904) 783-5000
Contact: Jack P. Jones, President
Limited to areas of company operation.

The Zellerbach Family Fund
120 Montgomery Street, Suite 2125
San Francisco, CA 94104
(415) 421-2629
Contact: Edward A. Nathan, Executive Director
Giving primarily in the San Francisco Bay area,
CA.

This chapter includes a sampling of foundations
that can be contacted for funding your curriculum
project. By no means are these all the resources
that can be tapped. Remember, think creatively!
Are there any community service organizations--
such as the Jaycees, Lions Club, or Rotary
International--that can be contacted? Is there a
local community fund that supports education
projects? Ask friends and neighbors about the
organizations they support. Ask if you can use
their names as references--and be sure to get the
names of the people to contact. Make many initial

contacts and don't be discouraged by rejections.
The money is there for you; all you need is be
persistent!

References

Catalogue of Federal Domestic Assistance. 1991.
Washington, DC: Government Printing Office.
Directory of Research Grants. 1992. Phoenix: Oryx
Press.
Information on a wide variety of funding
organizations; index includes terms for
elementary education, secondary education,
teacher education, and so on.
The Foundation Grants Index. 1992. New York:
Foundation Center.
Provides funding patterns and other informa-
tion about the most influential foundations in
the United States.
Source Book Profiles. 1992. New York: Foundation
Center.
Information on the one thousand largest
United States foundations.

TOPICS IN THE SOCIAL STUDIES CURRICULUM, GRADES K-12

by John J. Patrick
Professor and Director of the Social Studies Development Center,
Indiana University, Bloomington, Indiana

SINCE the early years of the 1980s, there has been a lively public debate about the content of the social studies curriculum in elementary and secondary schools. Central questions in the curriculum reform literature have pertained to selection, organization, and presentation of academic subject matter for all students as part of their general education for citizenship in a constitutional democracy. What subjects and topics should be taught to all students? In what sequence should subject matter be taught, from grades kindergarten through twelve, within and among the different courses in the curriculum? What should be the connections between different courses and topics of the social studies, and between the social studies subjects and topics and the content of other subjects of the K-12 curriculum, such as science, mathematics, and English?

This chapter is a summary of current common responses to these questions about the scope and sequence of subjects and topics in the social studies curriculum of grades K-12. This summary of curriculum patterns and trends is descriptive, not prescriptive. There is a grade-by-grade description of subjects and topics commonly offered to students of the social studies from kindergarten through the twelfth grade.

This treatment of topical patterns and trends in the social studies curriculum portrays both nationwide similarities and notable variations from traditional patterns in new state-level curriculum frameworks. However, the synopses of topics which follow treat only one dimension of the social studies curriculum--the subject matter or knowledge domain. Other dimensions of standard social studies curricula pertain to cognitive processes and skills, participation skills, and attitudes about citizenship. Of course, these skills and attitudinal dimensions of the curriculum are pervasively integrated with and based on the substantive content, and the scope and sequence, of academic subjects and topics.

The grade-by-grade descriptions and listings of topics in this chapter are presented as examples of widespread curriculum practices, or notable variations from them. They are not offered as ideal programs; however, they may provide useful examples for curriculum specialists and teachers in their ongoing efforts to improve social studies programs.

This chapter has three main parts. Part 1 treats the traditional patterns of subjects and topics, which prevailed in 1980 and remain in use, partially or fully, in many areas of the country. Part 2 presents the subjects and topics of the

California *History-Social Science Framework*, which has attracted national attention and influenced local school district curriculum development projects throughout the United States. The California framework is a significant departure from the traditional curriculum patterns, especially in the K-7 part of the curriculum. Part 3 describes the subjects and topics, from kindergarten through grade 12, of the Florida curriculum framework, which is an interesting blend of traditional subject-matter patterns and variations from these common themes. This presentation also includes examples of connections of topics between the social studies and other subjects of the school curriculum, such as science, mathematics, language arts, foreign languages, and the fine arts.

Traditional Curriculum Patterns

During the 1980s, there was a dominant social studies curriculum pattern, which can be traced directly to an influential 1916 report, *The Social Studies in Secondary Schools*.[1] Curriculum surveys revealed the following topical patterns during the first half of the 1980s (Haley et al. 1990, 3-5).

TABLE 1

TRADITIONAL CURRICULUM PATTERNS

Grade	Topic
K	Self, School, Community, Home
1	Families and the Home
2	Neighborhoods
3	Communities
4	State History/Geographic Regions
5	American History
6	World Cultures/Western Hemisphere
7	World History/Geography/World CulturesEastern Hemisphere
8	American History
9	Civics/World Cultures/ Geography
10	World History
11	American History
12	American Government/ Economics/Sociology/Psychology

There are numerous variations from this dominant curriculum pattern, and these common themes have been treated variously in different frameworks of state and local school systems. However, by the beginning of the 1990s, curriculum frameworks throughout the country reflected, more or less, the themes and sequence of this traditional pattern of topics and courses. A 1991 survey by the Council of State Social Studies Specialists revealed only slight deviations from the long-standing curriculum pattern in more than half of the fifty states' reports on course offerings and requirements (Svengalis 1992).

A grade-by-grade descriptive listing of typical topics of the traditional curriculum pattern, a composite list derived from several sources, is presented below.[2] This synopsis of topics does not represent a standard curriculum; rather, it reflects long-standing common practices, carried into the 1990s, from which there are many variations.

Kindergarten

The main theme of the kindergarten program is to develop awareness and knowledge of the self in relationship to places with which the child is most familiar: the home, the school, and the local community. Socialization of the child to school rules and procedures, as they fit family and community expectations, is a primary concern. Examples of major topics are:

· Similarities and differences of people in the home, school, and community
· The meaning and purposes of rules
· Wants and needs of people and how they are met through the family, the school, and the local community
· Special holidays, how and why we celebrate them
· Roles of different persons in the family, the school, and the local community

First Grade

The focus of the traditional first-grade program is on families and the home in relationship to the neighborhood. Socialization to the school, started in kindergarten, is continued and expanded. Examples of major topics are:

· Kinds of families
· Families around the world
· How people are alike and different in the United States and around the world
· Using resources to meet human needs in the United States and around the world
· The neighborhood as a community

· The school as a community
· The need for and use of rules in the family, the school, and the neighborhood community
· Jobs and work in the community
· Cooperation in achievement of goals as an important part of life in the home, school, and community
· Important holidays in the community
· Geographic relationships in the community
· Introduction to maps and globes

Second Grade

The central theme of second-grade social studies is how people interact to form, maintain, and change the groups in which they live. Human relationships are emphasized and examined. Examples of major topics are:

· Living in groups
· Kinds of groups people form
· Groups in the community
· Different kinds of communities in the United States and around the world
· How people cooperate in groups of the community
· Rules and laws in groups and communities
· Rights, responsibilities, and duties of members of groups
· Communities of the past in North America
· How and why people celebrate holidays in their communities
· How people work in groups and communities to meet human needs
· How groups and communities continue and change over time
· Using maps and globes to locate communities and describe geographic characteristics of communities

Third Grade

In grade three, various kinds of communities, especially the city, are emphasized, in comparative, historical, and global terms. Political, economic, and social functions of urban, suburban, and rural communities are examined. Examples of major topics are:

· Communities of different kinds and sizes, such as the city, the town, the village, and the metropolis
· Communities in American history
· Comparison of cities in the United States and in other parts of the world
· Government and citizenship in cities and in other types of communities
· Working in urban and rural communities to

produce goods and services; the economic life of communities
· Cultural and social diversity and unity in cities and in other kinds of communities in America and other parts of the world
· Continuity and change in the cultures of cities and other kinds of communities
· Comparison of human and natural characteristics of cities in North America and around the world
· Interactions of people in communities with their natural environments
· Maintaining community traditions through celebration of holidays and the use of symbols

Fourth Grade

A geography-based study of states and regions of the United States and of selected world regions is the core of fourth-grade social studies. In addition, students are required to study the history of their state. Examples of major topics are:

· Introduction to the geographic study of regions
· Geography of the northeastern region of the United States
· Geography of the southern region of the United States
· Geography of the midwestern region of the United States
· Geography of the western region of the United States
· Comparison of selected world regions with regions of the United States
· Examination of historical examples to show how regions of the United States have changed from one time to another
· Studies of state history that emphasize key events, people, and places that have shaped the political, economic, and social development of the state
· History of the state in the context of regional and national history
· The peopling of the state and the cultural unity and diversity in the historical development and contemporary society of the state
· Current governmental institutions of the state in historical perspective
· Responsibilities and rights of citizenship in the states

Fifth Grade

American history, from the arrival of the first people to the present, is the content of social studies in grade five. There tends to be an emphasis on pre-twentieth-century history. These historical studies are linked to a geographic context and perspective. Some curricula also include studies of the contemporary societies of regions of North America. Examples of major topics are:

· The land of North America: the spatial context of American history
· The first people of North America
· Similarities and differences of Native American cultures in different regions of North America
· The European discovery and explorations of America, from the Vikings to Columbus to Cabot, Cartier, and others
· European settlements in North America-- Spanish, French, and English
· Development of the English colonies of North America--New England Colonies, Middle Colonies, and Southern Colonies--including the coming of various people to North America from Europe and Africa
· The American Revolution and achievement of independence as the United States of America
· Founding a new American nation and framing a constitutional government for the United States of America
· The movement of people west of the Appalachian Mountains and across the Mississippi River in the periods before the Civil War
· Development of a national culture and regional culture varieties in the North, South, and West
· Sectional conflict about the nature of the federal union and slavery
· Civil War and Reconstruction
· Settlement of the last western frontier
· Industrial development and the growth of cities as a result of internal migration and immigration
· The United States becomes a world leader in industrial production, commerce, and military power
· Causes and consequences of American involvement in World War I
· Great Depression and New Deal
· Causes and consequences of American involvement in World War II
· Challenges and changes of the United States in modern times

Sixth Grade

The focus of sixth-grade social studies is on peoples and cultures in different world regions, such as regions of North and South America, Europe, and Australia and New Zealand. Many curricula treat only regions of the Western Hemisphere. Examples of major topics pertaining to the study of regions of the Western Hemisphere are:

· Natural environments of the Americas, the spatial context of the history and cultures of different regions of the Western Hemisphere
· How people use their natural environments to meet needs and make a living
· First peoples and cultures of the Americas
· Comparative study of selected Native American cultures, such as the Maya, Aztec, Inca, and Iroquois ways of life
· History, geography, and contemporary life of Canada
· History, geography, and contemporary life of Mexico
· History, geography, and contemporary life of Central American peoples and countries
· History, geography, and contemporary life of Caribbean peoples and countries
· History, geography, and contemporary life of peoples and countries in different regions of South America

Seventh Grade

Social studies in the seventh grade tends to involve a continuation and extension of the world culture/studies initiated in the sixth grade. In addition, there is often an emphasis on world history, from ancient civilizations through studies of selected civilizations and periods of world history, to an examination of the state of the world in modern times. Programs that treat primarily the Western Hemisphere in grade six usually focus on the Eastern Hemisphere in grade seven. Examples of major topics pertaining to the study of regions of the Eastern Hemisphere are:

· Natural environments of world regions
· Ancient civilizations in Mesopotamia and Egypt
· Early civilizations of India and China
· Ancient and classical civilizations of Greece and Rome
· The rise of European civilizations from the fall of Rome through the Middle Ages to the Renaissance
· Origins and development of European nation-states (e.g., France, England, and Spain)

- The global reach of Western European civilization during and after the period of exploration and discovery
- Industrial and political revolutions transform civilization in Western Europe and have worldwide influence
- Land, peoples, and cultures of European regions in the present, including Eastern Europe and Russia
- History and geography of Southwest Asia and North Africa from the origins and spread of Islam until the present
- Land, peoples, and cultures of Southwest Asia and North Africa in the present
- History and geography of Africa south of the Sahara, with emphasis on early African kingdoms, European colonies in Africa, and achievement of independence in the twentieth century
- Land, peoples, and cultures of African regions in the present
- History and geography of South Asia and East Asia, with emphasis on the historical development of India, China, and Japan
- Land, peoples, and cultures of South Asia and East Asia in the present
- History and geography of Australia, New Zealand, and Oceania
- Land, peoples, and cultures of Australia, New Zealand, and Oceania in the present

Eighth Grade

The history of the United States tends to be the course requirement in social studies at the eighth grade. This course is offered at the seventh grade in a few states, such as Virginia. The emphasis tends to be on periods before the twentieth century. In some states and school districts, such as Indiana, the eighth-grade U.S. history course only includes pre-twentieth-century history. Examples of major periods and topics are:

- The first peoples of the Americas (beginnings to 1500)
- European explorations and first settlements in the Americas (1000-1600)
- Meeting and interactions of peoples and cultures of Europe, Africa, and the Americas 1492-1620)
- Colonization of North America by Spain, France, and England (1600-1763)
- **American Revolution and Independence** of the United States of America (1763-1783)
- Founding a new nation, framing a constitution, and initiating national development

under a new federal government (1783-1815)
- Growth of a national culture and development of sectional cultural variations (1800-1860)
- National expansion and westward movement of people (1800-1860)
- Development of democracy and movements for social and economic reforms, especially the abolition of slavery and achievement of rights for women (1820-1860)
- Sectional conflict and the beginning of Civil War (1850-1861)
- The Civil War and Reconstruction, with emphasis on consequences for nationalism, federalism, and the rights of individuals and groups (1861-1877)
- Settlement of the last frontier (1865-1900)
- Industrial and commercial development and urbanization of the United States (1865-1900)
- Movement of protest and reform in response to the post-Civil War transformation of American society (1865-1900)
- The Progressive Reform Movement (1900-1920)
- Advancement of international involvement and world power of the United States, exemplified by victory in the war with Spain and construction of the Panama Canal (1880-1914)
- Causes and consequences of American participation in World War I and the Versailles peace settlement (1914-1921)
- Boom times and hard times in post-World War I American society (1918-1929)
- Great Depression, New Deal, and the presidency of Franklin Roosevelt (1929-1945)
- Causes and consequences of American participation in World War II (1939-1945)
- Origins and consequences of American involvement in the Cold War, including the military engagements in Korea and Vietnam (1945-1990)
- Domestic issues, programs, and reforms of post-World War II America, including the black civil rights movement and the women's rights movement (1945-1990)

Ninth Grade

There is no single dominant course offering at the ninth grade. The most commonly offered courses tend to be civics, world studies, and world geography. However, many school districts offer their required U.S. history course at this grade. Many school districts also offer a world history course at the ninth grade. The topical examples presented below, however, pertain to world geography, because world history topics are listed for grade ten and civics/government topics are listed for grade twelve. Examples of major topics in world geography are:

· Nature of geography; what it is and why it is useful
· Tools of geographic inquiry
· Landscapes of the earth
· Weather, climate, and vegetation
· Resources of the earth
· Waterways of the earth
· Population distribution patterns of our world
· Cultural patterns of our world, including languages, religions, economic development, and urban development
· Physical and cultural geography of the United States and Canada
· Physical and cultural geography of Mexico and Central America
· Physical and cultural geography of the Caribbean islands
· Physical and cultural geography of South American regions and countries
· Physical and cultural geography of western European countries
· Physical and cultural geography of central and eastern European countries
· Physical and cultural geography of North African and middle eastern countries
· Physical and cultural geography of African countries south of the Sahara
· Physical and cultural geography of south Asian countries
· Physical and cultural geography of east Asian countries
· Physical and cultural geography of Australia, New Zealand, Oceania, and Antarctica

Tenth Grade

The tenth-grade world history course provides for study of selected civilizations and cultures of the world from ancient times until the present. The course tends to emphasize the antecedents, origins, development, and global influence of western civilization. However, there also is substantial treatment of east Asian, south Asian, and Middle Eastern civilizations, especially the histories of Arabian, Indian, Chinese, and Japanese civilizations. Examples of major topics and periods are:

· Human origins and the agricultural revolution (beginnings to 500 B.C.)
· Ancient civilizations of Mesopotamia and Egypt (4000-500 B.C.)
· Ancient civilizations of South Asia and East Asia (2500-500 B.C.)
· Classical civilizations of Greece and its diffusion through the Hellenistic period (2000-31 B.C.)
· Classical civilization of Rome and diffusion through the Roman Empire (1000 B.C.-476 A.D.)
· Classical civilization of India (500 B.C.-500 A.D.)
· Classical civilization of China (500 B.C.-500 A.D.)
· Origins, development, and demise of Byzantine civilization (500-1453)
· Origins and development of western European civilization in the Middle Ages (500-1500)
· The rise of Islamic civilization and its worldwide impact, especially the influence of Arabian and Islamic people in Europe and Africa (622-1500)
· East Asian civilization of China and Japan (500-1750)
· The impact of Mongol invasion of China and Eurasia, especially on the border lands of Europe, and its influence on communication between Europe and central and east Asia
· Civilizations of East and West Africa (500-1750)
· Mayan, Aztec, and Inca civilizations of the Americas (500-1500)
· European Renaissance and Reformation (1400-1650)
· European voyages of exploration and discovery and subsequent expansion into overseas territories (1400-1800)
· Europe's scientific revolution (1600-1800)
· Europe's industrial and commercial revolution (1750-1914)
· Democratic political revolution in Western civilization (1689-1815)
· The development of nationalism in Europe and its global diffusion (1815-1914)
· European colonization and imperialism in Latin America (1500-1945)
· European imperialism in North Africa and the Middle East (1750-1945)
· European imperialism in sub-Saharan Africa (1750-1945)
· European imperialism in Asia (1750-1945)
· Westernization of Russia and its subsequent imperial domination of Central Asia and Siberia (1700-1945)

· Adaptation of western civilization and technology by Japan and its subsequent imperialism in South and East Asia (1850-1945)

· Two world wars and a changing world order (1914-1950)

· The conflict and challenge of the modern world (1950-1990)

Eleventh Grade

U.S. history is a required high school course in nearly all school districts throughout the country. This course tends to be offered at grade eleven. In recent years, there has been a tendency to emphasize periods following the Civil War and Reconstruction in the high school U.S. history course. In some states (Indiana, for example), the high school course mainly treats twentieth-century U.S. history, following a quick review of earlier periods. This high school course builds upon ideas and themes presented in preceding courses on American history, usually offered at grades five and eight. Major topics and periods of the twentieth-century version of the high school American history course are:

· Founding a new nation; the Revolutionary War, the Constitutional Convention, and the establishment of the federal government (1763-1800)

· National development and divisive issues of the new American republic (1801-1860)

· Civil War and Reconstruction of a divided union of states to establish the foundation for a unified nation (1861-1877)

· Development of industries, businesses, cities, transportation networks, and western settlements that transformed the United States into a world power commercially and militarily (1865-1900)

· The Progressive reform movement, its cause and consequences (1900-1920)

· The presidency during the Progressive era (1900-1920)

· Military and commercial domination of Latin American countries by the United States (1900-1920)

· American involvement in World War I and the peacemaking process (1914-1920)

· The expansion of business, prospering of society, and politics of normalcy (1921-1929)

· Onset of the Great Depression and hard times for Americans (1929-1933)

· The New Deal and the struggle to revive economic life (1933-1939)

· The world in crisis and war (1931-1941)

· American involvement in World War II, the military front (1941-1945)

· Americans at war, the home front during World War II (1941-1945)

· Domestic issues, policies, and reforms of the Truman and Eisenhower presidencies (1945-1960)

· The cold war crisis and super power rivalry in international affairs (1945-1970)

· Movement for civil rights (1955-1970)

· The Vietnam War and a divided America (1955-1975)

· The hopes, achievements, and failures of the Nixon presidency to its termination in the Watergate scandal (1969-1974)

· Domestic and world affairs during the presidencies of Ford and Carter (1974-1980)

· Domestic and world affairs during the presidencies of Reagan and Bush (1981-1992)

· American involvement in the decline and demise of the Soviet Union and international communism (1981-1992)

· A changing America faces a challenging future at home and abroad (1990-1992)

Twelfth Grade

A one-semester high school civics or government course is required for graduation in most school districts across the country. In most schools, this course is offered at grade twelve, but it is also often found at grades nine or ten. A one-semester course in economics or in another social or behavioral science (e.g., sociology or psychology) also tends to be offered at the twelfth grade. However, since a government or civics course is the most prevalent offering, examples of major topics included in this course are:

· Purposes, principles, and common types of government

· Origins and establishment of constitutional government in the United States

· Principles of the U.S. Constitution

· Theory and practice of federalism in the United States

· Citizenship rights and responsibilities

· Civil liberties and rights under the U.S. Constitution

· Political parties, voting in elections, and the election process

· Participation in interest groups to influence government

· Public opinion and the mass media in a democracy

· The U.S. Congress: its organization, powers, duties, and processes
· The federal bureaucracy: its organization, powers, duties, and processes
· The federal judiciary: its organization, powers, duties, and processes
· Public policy making and provision of services by the federal government
· Taxing and budgeting in the federal government: how the government pays for services it provides
· State constitutions and government in the federal system
· Organization, institutions, officers, and processes of state governments
· Organization, institutions, officers, and processes of local governments
· Paying for state and local governments: taxes, budgets, and expenditures
· Relationships of government policies to the economic system
· Comparing different systems of government

The California History-Social Science Framework

In 1988, the California State Board of Education published the *History-Social Science Framework for California Public Schools, Kindergarten Through Grade Twelve*. This document has attracted national attention because it is a significant departure from traditional social studies curriculum patterns.

In particular, the California framework departs emphatically from the "expanding environment" design, which has dominated the elementary school social studies curriculum for most of the twentieth century. This expanding environment curriculum is often portrayed as a set of concentric circles that begins with the child in the center and moves outward to the family, neighborhood, community, region, nation-state, and the world. By the 1940s, the expanding environment curriculum prevailed in American elementary schools. History was practically pushed out of the primary grades in favor of content drawn from sociology, psychology, civics, and economics, and it was de-emphasized in grades four through six.

During the 1980s, the expanding environment curriculum still dominated the social studies program, but it faced formidable challenges.

Charlotte Crabtree, Director of the National Center for History in the Schools at UCLA, pointed out that there is no foundation in research on child development and learning for the tenets of the expanding environment framework (Crabtree 1989). Further, Professor Crabtree writes: "Returning history to the elementary school curriculum [to replace traditional content of the expanding environment framework] is one of the decade's [1980s] major movements for school reform" (173).

The twenty-member team (including Professor Crabtree) that created the California *History-Social Science Framework* designed a new curriculum that put history and geography at the center of the elementary and secondary school curriculum. The document reflects the input of over 1700 field reviewers and was unanimously adopted by the California Curriculum Commission and the State Board of Education. And the subjects of the primary and intermediate grade programs include interrelated topics in history, geography, literature, and the arts from various historical periods and diverse cultures and places around the world. So students do not have to wait until the higher grades to seriously study events of the past and diverse peoples and places of various parts of the world. They can be exposed to these more enriching and challenging subjects in the primary grades to set the terms and tone of more complex learning experiences later on. The framework offers this explanation:

> The goals of this *History-Social Science Framework* fall into three broad categories: Knowledge and Cultural Understanding, incorporating learnings from history and other humanities, geography, and the social sciences; Democratic Understanding and Civic Values, incorporating an under-standing of our national identity, constitutional heritage, civic values, and rights and responsibilities; and Skills Attainment and Social Participation, including basic study skills, critical thinking skills, and participation skills that are essential for effective citizenship.
>
> None of these goals is developed wholly independent of the rest. All interact within this curriculum. Study skills and critical thinking skills, for example, are developed through challenging studies in history and other humanities, geography, and the social sciences. Democratic understandings and civic values are enriched through an understanding of the history of the nation's institutions and ideals. Civic participation requires political knowledge and incurs ethical choice.

The learnings contained in this curriculum can be enriched in countless ways. However, teachers and curriculum developers should be aware that for each of the three major goals, some essential learnings are integral to the development of this history-social science curriculum. These basic learnings serve as curriculum strands, unifying this curriculum across all grades, kindergarten through grade twelve. These basic learnings are first introduced in the primary grades, in simple terms that young children understand, and then regularly reappear in succeeding years, each time deepened, enriched, and extended.

These curriculum strands are a constant in every grade, not options to be added or dropped from one year to the next. In every grade teachers will be expected to integrate and correlate these strands as part of their teaching of the history-social science curriculum. (California State Board of Education 1988, 10-12)

The scope and sequence of subjects and topics of the California framework, from kindergarten through grade twelve, are presented below (Svengalis 1990, 5; California State Board of Education 1988, iii-iv).

TABLE 2
CALIFORNIA HISTORY-SOCIAL SCIENCE FRAMEWORK

Grade	Topics or Subjects
K	Working and Learning Now and Long Ago
1	A Child's Place in Time and Space
2	People Who Make a Difference
3	Continuity and Change
4	California: A Changing State
5	United States History and Geography: Making a New Nation
6	World History and Geography: Ancient Civilizations
7	World History and Geography: Medieval and Early Modern Times
8	United States History and Geography: Growth and Conflict
9	Elective Courses in History-Social Science (chosen from modern state history, physical or world-regional geography, comparative world religions, the humanities, area studies, women's studies, ethnic studies, law-related education, anthropology, sociology, and psychology)
10	World History, Culture, and Geography: The Modern World
11	United States History and Geography: Continuity and Change in the Twentieth Century
12	Principles of American Democracy and Economics

A grade-by-grade descriptive listing of topics of each course in the California curriculum is presented below.[3] Note the similarities and differences of the California *History-Social Science Framework* in comparison with the traditional curriculum patterns presented in Part 1 of this chapter.

Kindergarten
The main theme of the kindergarten program of the California framework is Learning and Working Now and Long Ago. The program initiates the process of building upon learnings and cognitive capacities the child brings to school from preschool experiences and development. In kindergarten, the child is expected to learn how to participate with others as learners in the classroom and school. In addition, the child is expected to develop a sense of personal identity and self-worth. Major topics of the kindergarten program are:
· Learning to work together
· Working together: exploring, creating, and communicating
· Reaching out to times past

First Grade
The main theme in this grade is A Child's Place in Time and Space. Content is drawn from history, geography, economics, and literature to treat these three main topics:
· Developing social skills and responsibilities
· Expanding children's geographic and economic worlds
· Developing awareness of cultural diversity, now and long ago

Second Grade

The main theme of the second grade is People Who Make a Difference. The focus is on significant individuals who care for the young learner, who provide goods and services to meet human needs, and who have "made a difference" through extraordinary achievements in the history of our country and our world. Three major topics are treated:

· People who supply our needs
· Our parents, grandparents, and ancestors
· People from many cultures, now and long ago

Third Grade

Continuity and Change is the central theme of the third grade program. Children begin to learn how some things change and others remain the same with reference to their local community and the United States. Subjects are drawn from local history, national history, and biographies. Dramatic stories in historical literature and fiction are used to teach about continuity and change. Two main topics are emphasized:

· Our local history: discovering our past and our traditions
· Our nation's history: meeting people, ordinary and extraordinary, through biography, story, folktale, and legend

Fourth Grade

The subject of grade four is the history of the state of California. A geographic perspective is brought to this historical study through an examination of human-environmental interactions in different regions of California during different periods of the state's history. Seven major topics are treated:

· The physical setting: California and beyond
· Pre-Columbian settlements and people
· Exploration and colonial history
· Missions, ranches, and the Mexican War for Independence
· Gold rush, statehood, and the westward movement
· The period of rapid population growth, large-scale agriculture, and linkage to the rest of the United States
· Modern California: immigration, technology, and cities

Fifth Grade

The subject for the fifth grade is United States History and Geography: Making a New Nation. The focus is on early American history, from the beginnings through the founding and early development of the United States of America. Geography is linked to the events and developments of each historical period of this course. Major topics are:

· Land and people before Columbus
· Age of exploration
· Settling the colonies: the Virginia settlement, life in New England, the middle colonies
· Settling the Trans-Appalachian West
· The War for Independence
· Life in the young republic
· The nation's westward expansion
· Linking past to present: the American people then and now

Sixth Grade

The subject for the sixth grade is World History and Geography: Ancient Civilizations. The focus is on those ancient civilizations that had the greatest impact on the development of subsequent civilizations around the world. As in historical studies at other grades, a geographic perspective is involved in this study of ancient civilizations. Major topics are:

· Early humankind and the development of human societies
· Beginning of civilization in the Near East and Africa: Mesopotamia, Egypt, and Kush
· Foundation of western ideas: the ancient Hebrews and Greeks
· West meets East: the early civilizations of India and China
· East meets West: Rome

Seventh Grade

World History and Geography: Medieval and Early Modern Times is the subject matter of grade seven, and is a continuation of the studies of world history and geography of the preceding grade. The geographic context of world history involves all the continents, and the time span is from 500 A.D. to 1789. Major topics are:

· Connecting with past learnings: uncovering the remote past
· Connecting with past learnings: the fall of Rome
· Growth of Islam
· African states in the middle ages and early modern times: Ghana, Mali, and Songhay
· Civilizations of the Americas: Mayans, Aztecs, and Incas
· Chinese civilization from the T'ang dynasty through the Mongol conquest to the Ming

dynasty
· Japan during the reign of Prince Shotoku (592-632)
· Medieval societies: Europe and Japan
· Europe during the Renaissance and Reformation
· Early modern Europe: the Age of Exploration to the Enlightenment and the political revolutions in England, America, and France
· Linking past to present

Eighth Grade

The subject matter at this grade is United States History and Geography: Growth and Conflict. The focus of the course is on the critical events from the creation and implementation of the U.S. Constitution to World War I. Geographic themes are connected to the events and development of each period of U.S. history treated in this course. Major topics are:

· Connecting with past learnings: our colonial heritage
· Connecting with past learnings: a new nation
· The Constitution of the United States
· Launching the Ship of State
· The divergent paths of the American people: the West, the Northeast, the South, 1800-1850
· Toward a more perfect union, 1850-1879
· Rise of Industrial America, 1877-1914
· Linking past to present

Ninth Grade

In grade nine, the California framework offers numerous courses from which students can choose: (1) Our State in the Twentieth Century, (2) Physical Geography, (3) World Regional Geography, (4) The Humanities, (5) Comparative World Religions, (6) Area Studies: Cultures, (7) Anthropology, (8) Psychology, (9) Sociology, (10) Women in Our History, (11) Ethnic Studies, and (12) Law-Related Education. One of these electives, Comparative World Religions, is of particular interest because it is an innovative attempt to treat a long-neglected subject in accordance with Supreme Court decisions about how to include religion in the school curriculum. Therefore, this elective course teaches about religious beliefs and practices comparatively and within the context of historical periods pertaining to the origins and developments of these beliefs and practices. Preferential preaching of doctrine is avoided. The major topics of Comparative World Religions are (California State Board of Education 1988, 80-81):

· Judaism's basis in ethical monotheism; its historic covenant between God and the Jewish people; the Torah as the source of Judaism's beliefs, rituals, and laws; and the Torah's ethical injunction, "Do justice, love mercy, and walk humbly with thy God."
· Christianity's continuity with Judaism; its belief that Jesus of Nazareth fulfilled Old Testament expectations of the Messiah; and its faith that in his Crucifixion and Resurrection, Jesus Christ reconciled the world to God so that, through forgiveness of sin, the eternal life of God could flow into the lives of human beings
· Islam's continuity with Judaism and Christianity in its proclamation of belief in one God; its belief that God's will has been given final expression in the Koran in words revealed to the last and the greatest of the prophets, Mohammed; and its observances of the "Five Pillars of Islam"
· Buddhism's origins in the Buddha or Enlightened One; its path of enlightenment through meditation; its ethical mandate to inflict no suffering; and its acceptance of the transmigration of the soul, of Karma, and of Nirvana, the ultimate state of all being
· Hinduism's belief in monism, the oneness of all gods and all living things in the Divine One, Brahma; in pure and unchanging spirit behind the impermanence of the material world; in the peace found only in union with the eternal spirit of Brahma; and in reincarnation, Karma, and Hindu ethics
· The explanations given by different religions for the origin of mankind
· The present-day numbers, influence, and geographic distribution of followers of each faith
· The differences between the original tenets of these religions; their historical development; and the major variations in beliefs, sects, or interpretations presently associated with each

Tenth Grade

The subject matter of the required tenth-grade course is World History, Culture, and Geography: The Modern World. The emphasis is on major turning points in development of the modern world, from the late 1700s until our own times. There is a continual interrelationship of major themes of geography with major turning points of world history. The major themes of this course are:

· Unresolved problems of the modern world
· Connecting with past learnings: the rise of
  democratic ideas
· The Industrial Revolution
· The rise of imperialism and colonialism: a
  case study of India
· World War I and its consequences
· Totalitarianism in the modern world: Nazi
  Germany and Stalinist Russia
· World War II: its causes and consequences
· Nationalism in the contemporary world: case
  studies of the Soviet Union and China, the
  Middle East, Sub-Saharan Africa, and Latin
  America.

Eleventh Grade

At this grade, there is the required course in
United States History and Geography: Continuity
and Change in the Twentieth Century. This
course emphasizes major turning points in U.S.
history in the twentieth century. The turning
points are presented in geographic perspective to
show the close connections of geography and
history. Major topics of this course are:
· Connecting with past learnings: the nation's
  beginnings
· Connecting with past learnings: the United
  States to 1900
· The Progressive Era and its movements for
  social and political reforms
· The jazz age and social change
· The Great Depression
· World War II
· The cold war
· Hemispheric relationships in the postwar era
· The civil rights movement in the postwar era
· American society in the postwar era
· The United States in recent times

Twelfth Grade

At grade twelve there is a required two-course
sequence for the year: (1) a one-semester course
of Principles of American Democracy and (2) a
one-semester course of Economics. The first
course emphasizes political ideas and issues,
institutions and practices of government and
politics, and the rights and responsibilities of
citizenship. Major topics in Principles of American Democracy are:
· The Constitution and the Bill of Rights
· The courts and the governmental process
· Our government today: the legislative and
  executive branches
· Federalism: state and local government

· Comparative governments with an emphasis
  on comparisons between democracies and
  dictatorships of the right and of the left
· Contemporary issues of international politics
  in the world today

The major topics in Economics are:
· Fundamental economic concepts
· Comparative economic systems
· Microeconomics
· Macroeconomics
· International economic concepts

The Florida Curriculum Framework: Major Social Studies Topics and Curriculum Connections

In 1990, the Florida Commission on Social
Studies Education issued a report, *Connections,
Challenges, Choices*, which presents the objectives,
subjects, topics, and rationale for the state of
Florida's new social studies program of study for
K-12. A central theme of the rationale is this
statement: "We recommend the adoption of a K-
12 social studies program of study that . . . emphasizes history and geography" (Florida Department
of Education 1990, 3). Thus, the Florida Commission on Social Studies Education joined the
authors of the *History-Social Science Framework
for California Public Schools* in placing the
synthesizing and integrating subjects of history
and geography at the center of the K-12 social
studies curriculum. Like the California framework, the Florida program also departs from the
expanding environments design in the elementary
grades.

However, there are interesting differences
between the new Florida and California curriculum frameworks which can be discerned by
examining the grade-by-grade listing of topics in
this part of the chapter and comparing them with
the listings for the California Framework, in Part
2. In addition, a distinctive strength of the new
Florida document is its specifications of curriculum connections between the social studies topics
and other subject areas, such as science, mathematics, the fine arts, language arts, and foreign
languages.

The sequence of courses and topics of the
Florida social studies curriculum is presented in
Table 3.

TABLE 3
FLORIDA CURRICULUM FRAMEWORK

Grade	Course of Study
K	My Family and Others
1	Families Near and Far
2	Our Cultures: Past and Present: Unity and Diversity in the United States
3	Beginnings: People, Places and Events: Studies of Turning Points in World History
4	United States and Florida History and Geography to 1880
5	United States and Florida History and Geography since 1880
6	Geography: Asia, Oceania, and Africa
7	Geography: Europe and the Americas
8	Florida: Challenges and Choices
9	Eastern and Western Heritage: World History to 1750
10	United States History to 1920
11	U.S. History in the Cotext of World History, 1848 to the Present
12	American Political System and American Economic System

Grade-by-grade listings of major courses of study and topics for each course are presented below. In addition, examples of curriculum connections are presented for each grade level which show linkages of major topics to other subject areas, such as science, mathematics, and language arts.[4]

Kindergarten

The theme of social studies in kindergarten is an examination of self in relationship to one's family and in comparison to other families in the world. Students examine life in families with reference to (1) human diversity, social interactions, and human needs, (2) geographic influences, (3) personal responsibilities and role models, and (4) kinds of celebrations and expressions of creativity. Families are studied in these areas of the world:

· North America (United States)
· Asia (Japan)
· Africa (Nigeria)
· Australia

Connections to other subjects:
· Science: Seasonal change, plants and animals from other parts of the world
· Mathematics: Currency and numbers
· Language Arts: Stories, poems, songs, biographies, folktales from lands and peoples around the world

First Grade

In the first grade, there is a continuation of studies of the self and the family started in kindergarten. This course of study, Families Near and Far, treats once again the themes that were introduced in kindergarten: human variations, social interactions, basic needs, geographic influences, personal responsibilities, role models, and celebrations and expressions of creativity. Families are studied in the following places:
· North America (United States)
· North America (Canada)
· North America (Mexico)
· South America (Brazil)
· Europe (Germany)

Connections to other subjects:
· Science: Use of natural resources to meet human needs
· Mathematics: Currency and numbers
· Language Arts: Oral and written poems and stories
· Foreign Languages: Common vocabulary words and greetings

Second Grade

The main theme of the second grade is the "ethnicity, customs, traditions, and values of the United States." This course of study, Our Cultures: Past and Present, treats the diversity of cultural heritage and the common values of the United States. Major topics are:
· Personal history--heritage of parents, grandparents, and their respective customs, beliefs, and traditions
· Native populations--culture, art, and traditions of selected groups of Native Americans
· Immigrant populations--European, African, Asian, and Hispanic people who have had an impact on the development of the United States

· Local communities--contributions of many ethnic groups to the texture of the local community

Connections to other subjects:
· Science: Technological innovations
· Mathematics: Currency, charts, calendars
· Language Arts: Folklore, biographies, stories, poems, autobiographies
· Foreign Languages: Common vocabulary words and common greetings

Third Grade

The main theme of the third-grade course is Critical Events of the Past that Helped Shape the Present. This course treats important people, places, and events from the earliest civilizations through the Renaissance. Major topics of this course are:

· Early civilizations--fire, wheel, tools, language, art, agriculture, early trade, alphabet, writing, telling time, number system
· Ancient civilizations--democracy, love of beauty, art, architecture, Olympics, concrete roads, compass, astronomy
· The Middle Ages--rise of cities, guilds, commerce, universities, church, gunpowder, moveable type, paper money, exploration
· The Renaissance--art, music, literacy, and scientific discoveries and inventions, such as the telescope, printing press, and mechanical clock.

Connections to other subjects:
· Science: Early scientific discoveries, inventions
· Mathematics: History of mathematics and number system
· Language Arts: All forms of written and oral expression
· Foreign Languages: Words of Arabic, Hebrew, and French associated with number systems

Fourth Grade

The course of study is United States and Florida History and Geography to 1880. The course treats main themes of geography and the history of Florida within the context of U.S. history. Major topics of this course are:

· Explorers and Native Americans of early Florida
· Colonial America/revolution, government/ imperial Florida

· Growth and expansion/pioneer Florida
· States' rights/Civil War/Reconstruction/Civil War and Reconstruction in Florida

Connections to other subjects:
· Science: Inventions, technological growth and their impact on society
· Mathematics: Time lines, charts, graphs
· Language Arts: All forms of American prose and poetry
· Foreign Languages: Spanish and French names and phrases

Fifth Grade

This course of study is United States and Florida History and Geography Since 1880. This course is a continuation of the fourth grade course. Major topics are:

· Railroads/highways/cities in the United States and Florida
· Becoming a world power/from rural Florida to modern Florida
· Suffrage/civil rights/feminist movement/civil rights in Florida
· Government/economy/immigration/growth/ education/Florida problems of today and tomorrow

Connections to other subjects:
· Science: Impact of technology on society
· Mathematics: Timelines, graphs, charts, distance, scale
· Language Arts: All forms of American prose and poetry; use of written and oral communication to express ideas
· Foreign Languages: Influence of other languages on everyday vocabulary of the United States

Sixth Grade

This course of study is Geography: Asia, Oceania, and Africa. The course involves analysis of human behavior and societies in terms of five fundamental themes of geography: location, place, human-environment interactions, movement, and regions. Major topics are:

· The Indian Subcontinent--rivers, landforms, climate, British colonialism, social classes, economic change, traditions, and religions
· The Orient (East Asia)--population, urban versus rural, revolution, nature and human behavior, changing social roles, economic activity, climate
· Australia--islands and continent, migration,

urbanization, federalism, acculturation, political geography
· Micronesia, Melanesia, and Polynesia--islands, acculturation, urbanization, federalism (island nations), migration, political geography
· Sub-Saharan Africa--uneven economic development, colonialism and nationalism, apartheid and tribal conflict, savannas and rain forests, artistic expression, ethnic diversity, desertification (sahel)
· North Africa and Southwest Asia--location (crossroads), ethnic diversity, monotheistic religions, climate, consequences of colonialism, family and social customs, economic activity

Connections to other subjects:
· Science: Application of the scientific method, as used in geology and biology, to inquiries in cultural geography
· Mathematics: Interpretation of statistical data through charts, graphs, maps, and other graphic representations
· Language Arts: Recognition of the interaction between literature and cultural norms
· Foreign Languages: Exploration of words and phrases of diverse languages of the people of each region and the interaction of language and culture

Seventh Grade
This course of study is Geography: Europe and the Americas. This course completes the study, begun in the sixth grade, of the world's major land areas. The five major themes of geography are used: location, place, human-environment interactions, movement, and region. Major topics are:
· Eastern Europe and Russia--location, nationalism, ethnic diversity, environmental problems, trends in political thought, economic activity, religion
· Western Europe--location, emigration, nationalism, industrialization, physical diversity, art and thought, economic unity, European community
· Anglo-America (Canada and the United States)--physical diversity, urbanization, cultural pluralism, federalism, mobility, regionalism
· Latin America--varied environments, ethnic diversity, social structure, uneven economic development, religion, urban migration,

revolution, immigration
· Caribbean--coastlines and islands, ethnic diversity, political instability, island economies, out-migration

Connections to other subjects:
· Science: Applications of scientific method and concepts of science associated with understanding of critical ecological problems
· Mathematics: Interpretation of statistical data
· Language Arts: Relationship of language and culture and exploration of words and phrases of the diverse languages of the regions studied in this course

Eighth Grade
This course of study is Florida: Challenges and Choices. The course involves "systematic analysis of contemporary Florida people and issues." Major topics are:
· The environment--physical characteristics, renewable and nonrenewable resources, land use, urban growth and developing rural areas, the environmental movement, environmental concerns of the region
· The people--demographics, cultural pluralism, ethnic polarization, migration, public service, people and the law
· Economic development--allocating public and private resources, poverty and the affluent economy, the growth of international trade, economic leadership in the Caribbean region

Connections to other subjects:
· Science: Ecological studies of environmental issues and problems
· Mathematics: Making comparisons using statistical data
· Language Arts: Development of skills in written and oral communication
· Foreign Languages: Exploring the incorporation of foreign words into the English language as spoken in Florida

Ninth Grade
This course of study is world history from the beginning of civilization to the Renaissance, Reformation, Scientific Revolution, and Age of Enlightenment. Major topics are:
· Birth of civilizations throughout the world--origins of civilized societies (Mesopotamia, Africa, China, Indian, and Meso-American) from the perspective of cultural geography
· Four classic civilizations--development of

India, China, Greece, and Rome (growth, dissemination, and decline)
· Emerging civilizations--the role of isolation and interaction in the development of the Byzantine Empire, African and Meso-American civilizations, India, China, Japan, and Europe
· Transitions--Renaissance, Reformation, and revolutions in science and other areas of thinking and doing (emergence of new social, political, economic, and religious institutions and ideas)

Connections to other subjects:
· Science: Comprehension of origins and the methods of modern science in Europe's Scientific Revolution
· Mathematics: Development of data interpretation skills and computational skills
· Language Arts: Examination of literature of peoples and civilizations covered in this course and development of writing and speaking skills
· Foreign Languages: Words and phrases of peoples and civilizations covered in this course
· Fine Arts: Appreciation and comprehension of the paintings, sculpture, architecture, and music of various periods and civilizations in world history

Tenth Grade
This course treats United States history from the period of European explorations and settlement through World War I. The major topics are:
· Colonizations--a consideration of the foundations and early development of the United States as organized by the visions of the Anglo-Americans, who participated in the colonizations
· Revolutions--a study of the multiple revolutions leading to the establishment and early successes of the United States, including political, social, cultural, intellectual, and technological revolutions
· Federalism and nationalism--an examination of the structure and function of political decisions, especially of the federal constitution and the development of the federal government
· Reforms and reactions--an analysis of the impact of economic, social and political changes on traditional American values, the various reactions, the growth of sectionalism,

and the Civil War
· Transformations--the emergence of an industrial, urban, and pluralistic society

Connections to other subjects:
· Science: Influence of scientific advances on social development and political issues
· Mathematics: Comparing, interpreting, and manipulating statistical data about economic development and demography
· Language Arts: Reading literature related to events in history; writing essays based on interpretation of primary sources
· Fine Arts: Appreciation for music, sculpture, and paintings of the period of history treated in this course

Eleventh Grade
The course of study is U.S. History in the Context of World History, 1848 to the Present. This course continues both the course on world history of grade nine and the course on U.S. history in grade ten. A geographic perspective is applied to the study of events in history. Major topics are:
· European revolutions and imperialism--use the ideas of revolution, nationalism, and imperialism to study European history from 1848 through 1914
· European wars: regional struggles and the destruction of colonialism--thematic and chronological study of international politics from 1914 to 1945, emphasizing the two world wars, postwar Europe, the reappearance of independent cultures, and the development of communism
· Domestic policies--thematic and chronological examination of domestic issues facing the United States from 1880 to the present
· International relations--thematic study of U.S. economic, political, and social policies and their effects on the world from 1898 to the present

Connections to other subjects:
· Science: Analysis of science-related social issues
· Mathematics: Analysis of statistical data in graphs, charts, diagrams
· Language Arts: Analysis of literature from the different periods of history of this course of study
· Fine Arts: Interpretation and appreciation of works of art that reflect different cultures represented in this course of study

Twelfth Grade

Government, politics, and economics are treated at grade twelve in two one-semester courses: (1) The American Political System: Process and Power and (2) The American Economic System: Scarcity and Choice. Major topics for the political system course:

- Nature of political behavior--defining political behavior, defining power, and the acquisition, maintenance, and extension of power
- Origins of political thought--classical and modern political theorists and thought, comparative political systems, evaluation of democratic political systems
- American political system--sources, structure, and function of government, constitutional framework, federalism, separation of powers, American government as a system
- The individual in the political process--political socialization, public opinion, interest groups, political parties, elections and political efficacy, majority/minority conflict, elitism versus pluralism, public policy formation, media influence, rights and responsibilities of citizenship, civil liberties, conflict and compromise, ethical behavior, and effective decision making

Major topics for the economic system course:

- Nature of economic behavior--importance of economics and economic behavior, relationship of power to economic and political behavior, scarcity, factors of production, basic economic questions, circular flow, opportunity costs, and trade offs
- Origins of economic thought--contributions of individuals such as Adam Smith, Karl Marx, and John Kenneth Galbraith; their impact on the growth and change of economic activity throughout the world
- American economic system--mixed-market system, federalism and economic responsibility, media and public opinion, the role of government, macroeconomics and politics, and international influences
- The individual in the economic process--consumers and producers, unions, supply and demand, economic decision making, macroeconomics, economic problems, equal economic opportunity, compromise, ethics of economic behavior, and problem solving

Connections to other subjects:

- Science: Application of the scientific method to problems of political science and economics
- Mathematics: Interpretation of graphic representations of statistical data and creation of graphic representations of data
- Language Arts: Development of skills in writing and speaking about policy issues in government and economics

Notes

1. *The Social Studies in Secondary Education*, published in 1916, was the report of the Committee on Social Studies of the National Education Association. The contents of this report are discussed insightfully in Hertzberg 1981.

2. This listing was derived from examination of Banks 1990, 10-16; Haley et al. 1990, 19-35; Scott, Foresman 1990; Silver Burdett & Ginn 1990. In addition, the current state-level curriculum frameworks of Idaho, Indiana, and Virginia were examined.

3. The topics listed in this section are quoted directly from California State Board of Education 1988, 32-111. Copyright 1988; reproduced with permission. The complete book is available for $6.00 from the Bureau of Publications, California Department of Education, P.O. Box 271, Sacramento, CA 95812-0271.

4. The theme statements and topics listed in the grade-by-grade descriptions are quoted from Florida Commission on Social Studies Education 1990, 25-161. Reproduced with permission.

References

Banks, James A. 1990. *Teaching Strategies for the Social Studies*. White Plains: Longman.

California State Board of Education. 1988. *History-Social Science Framework for California Public Schools Kindergarten Through Grade Twelve*. Sacramento.

Crabtree, Charlotte. 1989. "Returning History to the Elementary Schools." In *Historical Literacy: The Case for History in American Education*, ed. Paul Gagnon, 173-187. New York: Macmillan.

Florida Commission on Social Studies Education. 1990. *Connections, Challenges, Choices: Florida K-12 Social Studies Program of Study*. Tallahassee: Florida Department of Education.

Haley, Frances, et al., eds. 1990. *Social Studies Curriculum Planning Resources*. Washington, DC: National Council for the Social Studies.

Hertzberg, Hazel. 1981. *Social Studies Reform, 1880-1980*. Boulder, CO: Social Science Education Consortium.

Scott, Foresman Social Studies, K-7. 1990. Glenview, IL: Scott, Foresman.

Silver Burdett & Ginn Social Studies, Grades K-7. 1990. Morristown, NJ: Silver Burdett & Ginn.

Svengalis, Cordell M. 1992. *National Survey of Course Offerings in Social Studies, Kindergarten-Grade 12, 1991-1992*. Washington, DC: Council of State Social Studies Specialists.

STATE-LEVEL CURRICULUM GUIDELINES: AN ANALYSIS

by Bruce Frazee
Associate Professor
Department of Education, Trinity University, San Antonio, Texas

T HE intent of this chapter is to provide a comprehensive and practical analysis of state social studies guidelines for assisting school districts, administrators, and classroom teachers who are organizing and writing local curriculum documents. Historically, state curriculum guides have very little influence on classroom teachers or instruction. Current educational reform efforts and testing movements have influenced the use of state curriculum guides as important references for district curriculum alignment, continuity, and accountability. State curriculum documents suggest frameworks and broad goals to assist districts in organizing systematic, comprehensive, and affective social studies scope and sequence. Local curriculum guides can serve as indicators of how successful are state and district curriculum mandates in changing classroom instruction and learning. There are increasing numbers of states that test students at various levels to assess the impact that state mandates and district curriculum guides have on student outcomes and performance based learning.

How to Use a State Curriculum Guide

An initial step in developing local social studies curriculum guides is to analyze the district's program for grades K-12. This can be done through a needs assessment or curriculum mapping. Determining needs enables curriculum writers to realize the status of the social studies program. Once a district determines current conditions, decisions need to be made regarding the direction and goals of the social studies curriculum in relationship to state curriculum documents, mandates, and regulations. Most state curriculum documents encourage a reflective process to help form a defensible rationale and philosophy for a social studies program. Taking time to align the curriculum with testing programs and learner outcomes or competencies increases teacher awareness and understanding of a holistic social studies program.

Having a sense of where the social studies program has been, where it is, and where it needs to be is beneficial to the development of a coherent and thoughtfully sequenced curriculum. Many scholars and practitioners believe that the process of curriculum analysis is far more beneficial than the final product. Once the opportunity to reflect and analyze social studies documents is complete, a solid and defensible philosophy can be established so curriculum writers can proceed in developing curriculum guides that satisfy state standards.

All state curriculum guides analyzed in this chapter provide various degrees of goals and learner outcomes related to knowledge, skills, and values. The intent of state documents is not to dictate daily lesson plans but to provide a set of flexible standards to assist in developing a comprehensive social studies scope and sequence for all grades. All states delegate responsibility to the local level for designing, planning, and implementing knowledge, skills, and values goals. States appear to be more interested in student outcomes than in how a social studies program will be implemented in a local classroom.

Common Features in State Curriculum Guides

All states that provide social studies curriculum guides list broad goals in terms of knowledge, skills, and values. Many states also encourage local interpretation for organizing social studies curriculum guides. There are increasing numbers of states that mandate assessment of student learning for determining the success of state and local goals. Most states emphasize student mastery of basic goals over the methods of attaining these goals. Much flexibility is given to districts to determine how they approach the teaching of knowledge, skills, and values goals. Most states cover the basic social sciences in their recommendations. These social sciences typically include anthropology, economics, geography, government, history, philosophy, political science, psychology, and sociology. Some argument exists in professional literature for and against the teaching of the social sciences, especially in high school. Some theorists argue that history and geography should dominate the social studies curriculum with little or no emphasis on social sciences. Some states resolve this dilemma by suggesting that history and geography be integrated with social science themes or strands. The integrated curriculum enriches and extends student understanding by interrelating the humanities while stressing global interdependence.

The dominant organization scheme in the social studies is the expanding environments

approach, which follows this approximate grade sequence:

K. Self, School, Home
1. Families
2. Neighborhood
3. Communities
4. State History, Geographic Regions
5. U.S. History
6. World Culture
7. World History or Geography
8. American History
9. Civics
10. World History
11. American History
12. American Government

This format sequences topics closest to the child and then moves through environments that are progressively more distant. Developed primarily for the elementary grades, the expanded horizons approach as a pattern of organizing the scope and sequence of social studies curriculum is questionable. Several state documents provide alternatives to this organizational scheme.

Textbook publishers, however, still organize content around the expanding horizons approach. Local districts should consider a flexible curriculum that focuses on conceptual learning. Most states do not impose a standardized format, and most encourage development-appropriate knowledge, processes, and beliefs for responsible, participatory citizenship. Most states are increasing flexibility for organizing social studies curriculum around themes and strands that connect and interrelate knowledge, skills, and values.

Some state documents suggest activities and supplementary material to assist curriculum-writing teams. The worthiness and usefulness of pedagogical models at the state level are questionable. The vast array of features found in state guidelines should be analyzed to develop a comprehensive and usable curriculum guide that improves social studies instruction and learning.

Criteria Used for Evaluating State Curriculum Guides

The criteria used to analyze state curriculum guides was based on knowledge, skills, and values goals. How these goals fit into the social science disciplines, expanding environment, learner outcomes, activities, and supplementary materials provides useful insights for curriculum development teams. The degree of support and suggestions for program development and evaluation in state documents vary so dramatically that there is little basis for comparison. Social studies curriculum must include multicultural, global, and technological concepts. These topics are analyzed in this chapter for each state that provided a social studies document.

Organization of the Chapter

Most state curriculum documents are lengthy and bulky resources that contain commonalities as well as creative deviations. To analyze and organize the material according to the above established criteria, the fifty states are divided into seven regions. These regions and states are:

1. **New England Region**
   Connecticut
   Maine
   Massachusetts
   New Hampshire
   Rhode Island
   Vermont

2. **Middle Atlantic Region**
   Delaware
   Maryland
   New Jersey
   New York
   Pennsylvania

3. **Southeast Region**
   Alabama
   Florida
   Georgia
   Kentucky
   Mississippi
   North Carolina
   South Carolina
   Tennessee
   Virginia
   West Virginia

4. **South Central Region**
   Arkansas
   Louisiana
   Oklahoma
   Texas

5. **North Central Region**
   Illinois
   Indiana
   Iowa
   Kansas
   Michigan
   Minnesota
   Missouri
   Nebraska
   North Dakota
   Ohio
   South Dakota
   Wisconsin

6. **Mountain West Region**
   Arizona
   Colorado
   Idaho
   Montana
   Nevada
   New Mexico
   Utah
   Wyoming

7. **Pacific States Region**
   Alaska
   California
   Hawaii
   Oregon
   Washington

Each state within a region appears in a chart indicating the following common ingredients: social science disciplines, expanding horizons, learner outcomes, activities, and supplementary materials. Each state that provided a social studies document for this analysis is summarized in outline form according to knowledge, skills, values, global perspective, multiculturalism, and technology. The chapter concludes with regional and state comparisons, recommended state guides, and future implications.

See chapter 6 for publication information on the state curriculum documents, as well as the addresses and phone numbers for all state departments of education.

New England Region

State	Covers Social Science Disciplines	Follows Expanded Horizons Approach	Specifies Learner Outcomes	Suggests Activities	Lists Supplem. Materials
CT (1989)	yes	modified	yes	yes	yes
ME	no state social studies document provided				
MA	no state social studies document provided				
NH (1987)	yes	no	yes	no	no
RI	no state social studies document provided				
VT (1986)	yes	yes	yes	no	no

I. Connecticut (K-12 social studies document)

A. Knowledge
1. Provides extensive background information, including a history of social studies
2. Describes process tasks and timelines for curriculum committees
3. Provides models and outlines for writing local social studies curriculum
4. Summarizes National Council for the Social Studies guidelines
5. Lists guidelines for knowledge outcomes in three broad areas--United States studies, global studies, and social science disciplines-- to determine local district cognitive goals.
6. Follows recommendations of professional organizations such as the National Council for Geographic Education and the Joint Council on Economic Education
7. Recommends that knowledge be organized around themes

B. Skills
1. Lists steps for teaching thinking skills
2. Provides various decision-making models
3. Emphasizes critical thinking skills
4. Provides a framework for sequential development of skills
5. Indicates themes for integrating geography skills

C. Values
1. Supports sanctity of the classroom for free exchange of ideas
2. Shows how values are to be applied to subject matter
3. Lists appropriate attributes and attitudes for the social studies curriculum
4. Declares that local boards should develop written policies to support teaching of controversial issues
5. Lists affective objectives for student participation

D. Global Perspective
1. Enlarges the meaning of citizenship from community to world
2. Stresses pluralism, interdependence, and change
3. Provides a K-12 model that is based upon four essential elements and is organized around five conceptual themes and four persistent problem themes

E. Multiculturalism
1. Encourages development of local approaches to diversify material and rid inaccuracies and stereotypes that still persist in commercially prepared materials
2. Provides guidelines and criteria to evaluate multiethnic materials
3. Provides guidelines and criteria to evaluate sexual stereotyping

F. Technology
1. Acknowledges importance of technology to social studies knowledge base
2. Extends technology beyond the computer
3. Provides criteria for evaluating nonprint materials

II. New Hampshire (K-8 and 9-12 general curriculum set of guidelines)
A. Knowledge
  1. Emphasizes understanding of democratic beliefs in the elementary schools
  2. Encourages many organizational patterns based on thematic or topical approach in the middle schools
  3. States general program goals for high schools
B. Skills
  1. Mentions decision making, data gathering, and critical thinking for the elementary schools
  2. Emphasizes a skills continuum of broadly defined skills for middle schools
  3. States general program goals for high school
C. Values
  1. Describes little about attitudes in the elementary school
  2. Encourages development of attitudes, citizenship, and group participation in the middle and high schools
D. Global perspective
  1. Mentions international studies and global awareness at all levels
  2. Proposes few goals
E. Multiculturalism
  1. Relates no direct reference to this term or concept
F. Technology
  1. Offers no technology goals for social studies at any level

III. Vermont (K-8 and 9-12 social studies documents)
A. Knowledge
  1. Provides suggestions and concepts through specific lists of learner outcomes for grades K-3, 4-6, 7-8, 9-12
  2. Emphasizes content for each social science discipline
B. Skills
  1. Integrates with content of each social science discipline
C. Values
  1. Integrates with content of each social science discipline

D. Global
  1. Mentions study of another country and world cultures only
E. Multiculturalism
  1. Provides no direct reference to this term or concept
F. Technology
  1. Offers no technology goals for social studies at any level

Summary of the Region

Maine, Massachusetts, and Rhode Island have no state-mandated guidelines for social studies. Each district is expected to produce its own local social studies curriculum guide.

The states in this region have an enormous amount of latitude in developing local social studies guidelines. Connecticut provides a thoughtful and comprehensive framework that is extremely valuable to educators engaged in curriculum writing or revision in social studies at any level. The format, suggestions, and supplementary material will strengthen the thoroughness of a local curriculum guide and provide a defensible document for many diverse social studies factors. The Connecticut guide follows current professional organization recommendations and provides numerous examples, tables, and checklists that would be valuable to a curriculum-writing team. The New Hampshire standards are general, with few guidelines to assist educators in writing or revising curriculum. Vermont's framework provides suggestions for concepts, skills, and content to help local districts revise course scope and sequence in order to meet approved general standards and specific learner outcomes.

The parameters for social studies curriculum and development in this region are rather flexible. The clear exception is Connecticut's comprehensive and contemporary guide, a unique resource that adequately covers crucial theoretical and practical aspects of social studies curriculum for all grade levels.

Middle Atlantic Region

State	Covers Social Science Disciplines	Follows Expanded Horizons Approach	Specifies Learner Outcomes	Suggests Activities	Lists Supplem. Materials
DE	yes	no	yes	no	no
MD (1988)	yes	yes	yes	yes	yes
NJ	no state social studies document provided				
NY	yes	yes	yes	yes	yes
PA	no state social studies document provided				

I. Delaware (1-12 social studies document)
A. Knowledge
   1. Lists twenty-five elementary goals with subelement for each goal
   2. Lists few goals and subgoals for secondary subjects
B. Skills
   1. Describes skills and applications
   2. Lacks sequential development of skills except for goal and subgoal statements
C. Values
   1. Incorporates values throughout goals and subgoals
D. Global perspective
   1. Cites several goal and subgoal concepts
   2. Uses term throughout document
E. Multiculturalism
   1. Lacks depth, use of term, and conceptual development
F. Technology
   1. Offers no suggestions or guidelines for use of technology

II. Maryland (K-12 document)
A. Knowledge
   1. Offers a system to organize content around seven goals and respective subgoals
   2. Suggests themes for elementary grades
   3. Emphasizes citizenship in democratic society
   4. Shares common theme of people relating to and interacting with other people in their environments
B. Skills
   1. Mentions study skills to encourage further learning
   2. Lacks clarity and direction for skill development in scope and sequence
   3. Limits skills to a few broad subgoal statements
C. Values
   1. Describes minimal needs of positive self-concept, strong set of personal values, and experiences with personal meaning
   2. Indicates that value should be reflected in local curriculum
D. Global perspective
   1. Mentions understanding and appreciation of world cultures, the reality of interdependence, and the need for world cooperation when planning social studies curriculum
   2. Neglects use of term
E. Multiculturalism
   1. Expresses a need to accept others and the contribution of ethnic, racial, religious, and other diverse groups
   2. Neglects use of term
F. Technology
   1. States no technological goals for social studies at any level
   2. Offers no guidelines or suggestions for classroom use.

III. New York (A social studies curriculum program is provided for each grade or subject level.)
A. Knowledge
   1. Begins with helpful background information for teachers at every grade level
   2. Provides content outlines for each grade level
   3. Correlates to competency exams
   4. Provides guides for selecting specific factual

content from available texts and resources

B. Skills
1. Provides skill development sequence for each grade level
2. Suggests procedures for systematic skill development in teaching and diagnosing
3. Encourage development as a planned part of each lesson and activity
4. Furnishes extensive theoretical and practical information for each grade level

C. Values
1. Expresses specific attitude objectives for each grade level and skill category
2. Directs teachers toward developing students' self-management attitudes
3. Links process to affect skills development in each lesson

D. Global perspective
1. Describes global understanding for each grade level
2. Presents techniques and activities to promote global awareness
3. Recommends literature and resources
4. Labels ninth and tenth grades as global studies
5. Promotes comprehensive coverage throughout all grade levels

E. Multiculturalism
1. Identifies key concepts and strategies throughout
2. Elaborates on multicultural and multiethnic experiences
3. Recommends a large variety of literature, resources, and activities

F. Technology
1. Provides technology as a key concept goal in K-6 curriculum
2. Defines technology as a tool and method used by people to get what they need and want

3. Offers no suggestions or guidelines for technology in the classroom
4. Limits educational technology resources to films, filmstrips, and video resources

Summary of Region

New Jersey and Pennsylvania have no specific social studies curriculum guides. Each district is expected to produce and seek approval for its own local social studies curriculum guide.

Maryland's succinct social studies guide provides a broad outline from which local systems can write comprehensive social studies programs. The guide's four parts--philosophy, goals and strategies, illustrative objectives, and the curriculum development process--successfully assist curriculum developers and writers in designing curriculum to meet regulations.

New York syllabi books for each grade level comprise a well-designed and comprehensive program. Each syllabus has background theoretical information and very specific content that is to be taught at each level. All levels provide content, skill attitude, evaluation, activities, and resources. The lesson plan format outlines an entire program while encouraging teacher modification. This structured approach is meant to insure basic program coverage throughout the state, and it is tested to assess student social studies learning. Because of the comprehensiveness of the New York curriculum, little if any work is needed to develop local curriculum guides. Teachers could teach their social studies program from the grade level curriculum books provided for each level of instruction. New York is presently considering a complete revision of its syllabi in light of state concerns over inaccurate or insufficient emphases on multiculturalism. The state may also be moving toward an outcome-based structure.

Southeast Region

State	Covers Social Science Disciplines	Follows Expanded Horizons Approach	Specifies Learner Outcomes	Suggests Activities	Lists Supplem. Materials
AL (1986)	yes	yes	yes	no	yes
FL (1990)	see summary				
GA (1990)	yes	modified	yes	no	no
KY	see summary				
MS (1986)	yes	no	yes	no	no
NC (1985)	yes	yes	yes	no	no
SC	see summary				
TN (1991)	yes	modified	yes	no	no
VA (1989)	yes	yes	yes	no	no
WV (1990)	yes	modified	yes	no	no

I. Alabama (K-12 social studies document)
A. Knowledge
   1. Underscores democratic traditions with a map and globe stand emphasis at each level K-7
   2. Provides a course description outline and skills column at the elementary level
   3. Provides course description, instructional objectives, skill development, and course outline with suggested time allocation at the secondary level
B. Skills
   1. Describes skills through content
   2. Lists comprehensive skills in appendix
C. Values
   1. Integrates values into content throughout all grade levels
   2. Contains an appendix to promote value of responsibility through study habits and homework
   3. Encourages development of a local plan for responsible behavior
D. Global perspective
   1. States specific global understandings
   2. Describes high school option for contemporary world issues course
E. Multiculturalism
   1. Acknowledges investigation of diverse multicultural experiences at the local, regional, national, and international levels
F. Technology
   1. Acknowledges use of nonprint material and use of computers when appropriate
   2. Offers no technology goals or guidelines

II. Georgia (available on computer disk)
A. Knowledge
   1. Follows a Quality Core Curriculum that is

correlated to criteria-referenced test objectives for writing, reading, mathematics, and 76 Quality Basic Education Act competencies
   2. Lists series of competencies through concepts for each grade level
B. Skills
   1. Incorporates skills into content, concepts, guidance, and support documentation for local curriculum development
C. Values
   1. Incorporated into content/concepts
   2. Lacks guidance and support documentation for local curriculum development
D. Global perspective
   1. Refers indirectly to global understanding
   2. Neglects use of term in objectives
E. Multiculturalism
   1. Lacks comprehensive and systematic incorporation of terms or concepts in objectives
F. Technology
   1. Expects use of multiple sources but cites only printed material
   2. Offers no goals or guidance

III. Mississippi (K-12 social studies document)
A. Knowledge
   1. Lists 823 competencies with prescribed levels for when concept is to be taught and when the concept is expected to be introduced or mastered
   2. Mentions NCSS (1983) guidelines before listing of competencies
B. Skills
   1. Incorporates in the concept list
   2. Lacks guidance and support documentation for local curriculum development
C. Values
   1. Incorporates in the concept list
   2. Lacks guidance and support documentation for local curriculum development
D. Global perspective
   1. Shows GLB abbreviation on concept list to indicate when it is taught
   2. Lacks global perspective throughout grade levels
E. Multiculturalism
   1. Offers direct reference to this term and concept
   2. Limits coverage to minority studies
F. Technology
   1. Offers no technology goals or guidance

IV. North Carolina (K-12 social studies document)
A. Knowledge
   1. Explores relationship with others in the elementary grades
   2. Provides a major emphasis for each grade level K-12
   3. States general competencies, specific objectives, and measures for each grade or subject level
   4. Provides detailed statements for assessment through competency-based curriculum
B. Skills
   1. Promotes a sequential program to systematically practice, apply, and refine skills
   2. Identifies academic self-management and social participation skills
   3. Provides comprehensive information and references about skill teaching
C. Values
   1. Supports integration of affect throughout the curriculum
   2. Avoids support and emphasis on values
D. Global perspective
   1. Neglects use of the term in the competencies
   2. Lacks in-depth global perspective
E. Multiculturalism
   1. Lacks comprehensive or deliberate incorporation of term or concept in competencies
F. Technology
   1. Mentions that the competency-based curriculum is entered on the computer at the State Department of Public Instruction
   2. Offers no technological goals or suggestions

V. Tennessee (draft, K-6; 7-8; 9-12)
A. Knowledge
   1. Lists goals, subject disciplines, and terminal objectives
   2. Provides little or no background information
   3. Contains minimum required for each course with broadly stated objectives to allow for varied learning levels and environments at local level
B. Skills
   1. Acknowledges skills on minimum objectives
   2. Offers no guidance or suggestion for structured skill development at any level
C. Values
   1. Incorporates into minimum objectives
   2. Lacks support or detail for values curriculum
D. Global perspective
   1. Describes some global understanding in high school objectives

2. Provides a global strand for each level in the elementary framework

E. Multiculturalism
   1. Incorporates these understandings through-out the curriculum at a minimum level
F. Technology
   1. Offers no goals or guidance specifically for social studies

VI. Virginia (K-12 document)
A. Knowledge
   1. Emphasizes the history and culture of the nation and world, physical and cultural geography theories, systems and processes of government, and economics
   2. Lists learning objectives and descriptive statements for each grade level
B. Skills
   1. Emphasizes map, globe, time, date, chart, graph, picture, cartoon, and study and inquiry skills
   2. Skills are broadly stated throughout, with skills list at end of document
C. Values
   1. Emphasizes democratic beliefs
   2. Describes affect in broad objectives
D. Global perspective
   1. Recognizes world theory through several broad objectives
   2. Lacks direct emphasis on global concepts or term
E. Multiculturalism
   1. Promotes respect and understanding throughout objectives
   2. Lacks comprehensive and systematic multicultural emphasis in objectives
F. Technology
   1. Refers to student study of influence and impact but suggests no goals or guidance for teacher use in social studies curriculum

VII. West Virginia (K-12 social studies document)
A. Knowledge
   1. Approaches K-4 with modified organization pattern where learners have multiple oppor-tunities to develop a child's self- and group management, study skills, place in time, space, and society, and needs and wants
   2. Provides interdisciplinary topics in grades 5-12 in broadly stated terms
   3. Establishes a sound rationale for entire

curriculum while suggesting sample instruc-tional objectives
B. Skills
   1. Emphasizes throughout sample objectives
C. Values
   1. Acknowledges throughout each grade level through responsibilities of citizenship
D. Global perspective
   1. States several sample global objectives
E. Multiculturalism
   1. Lacks use of term
   2. Encourages acceptance and appreciation of cultural diversity
F. Technology
   1. Refers to its influence and impact on society and behavior to the point of use of technology and refusal to use technology
   2. Lacks goals and objectives for educational technology implementation into the social studies curriculum

Summary of the Region

Florida provides social studies curriculum guides for local use at grades 6-12. The guides are written for each course at these levels. They list major content and concepts and state individual out-comes for each course. There is no suggested content or goals for elementary grades. Each local district is expected to devise its own curriculum. Kentucky lists eight broad goals for use at all levels in local district curriculum development. South Carolina is in the process of revising its social studies curriculum, which will not be available until 1993. Within this region, there is much diversity in the content and organization of state curriculum guides. Most states in this region rely on competencies and listings of minimum standards.

North Carolina has an in-depth and bulky publication that promotes extensive coverage. Alabama's, North Carolina's, West Virginia's, and Virginia's documents allow far more flexibility at the local level. Each of these states provides extra guidance with rationale statements that are useful in developing local frameworks. West Virginia's guide is contemporary in the way it organized its elementary school program; it is thoughtful of future needs. However, all states in this region lack a comprehensive approach to include global perspective, multiculturalism, and technology in their social studies programs.

South Central Region

State	Covers Social Science Disciplines	Follows Expanded Horizons Approach	Specifies Learner Outcomes	Suggests Activities	Suggests Supplem. Materials
AR (1990)	yes slightly modified	yes	yes	yes	yes
LA (dates vary by grade)	yes	modified at grade 6	yes	yes	yes
OK (1991)	yes	no	yes	no	no
TX (1986)	yes	yes	yes	no	no

I. Arkansas (grades 4-8 document; high school document)
A. Knowledge
  1. Provides outline of general goals and under-standings for K-3 in a 4-8 document
  2. Uses five themes to structure social studies curriculum for all schools: history, geography, culture, government, and economics
  3. Organizes content around strands of basic skills, developmental skills, and strategies in lines of competencies for grade levels 4-12
B. Skills
  1. Encourages use of thinking skills
  2. Stresses information gathering, inquiry, communication, participation, and decision making skills
  3. Suggests no lists of skills for grades K-3
C. Values
  1. Describes values throughout the three strands
  2. Offers many open-ended situations in strategies strand
D. Global perspective
  1. Stresses global perspective in grades K-3
  2. Uses term and comprehensive coverage throughout course content guide
E. Multiculturalism
  1. Uses term rarely but all strands include conceptual coverage due in part to culture theme
F. Technology
  1. Includes understanding and competencies about how technology affects life

  2. Offers no guidelines or suggestions for use of technology in the classroom

II. Louisiana (K-6 document; six lengthy high school guides)
A. Knowledge
  1. Provides grade level themes, conceptual strands, and numerous activities at all grade levels
  2. Formats elementary social studies differently than junior and senior high school guides
  3. Formats junior and senior high school with content outline, concepts, generalizations, and objectives
  4. Organizes activities into three levels--slow, average, and above average--to gear learning of content to different abilities
  5. Provides an abundance of supplementary materials
B. Skills
  1. Stresses learner outcomes from introduction, ongoing mastery, and continuing use for each grade level based on NCSS skill chart
  2. Prescribes skills and sequence for student proficiency
  3. Provides skill chart at end of each guide
C. Values
  1. Examines values as a major curriculum goal
  2. Suggests value concepts and strategies through activities
D. Global perspective
  1. Lacks use of term and comprehensive coverage

2. Some global concepts covered through activities and study of culture conceptual strand

E. Multiculturalism
  1. Lists several goals and objectives that lead to study of culture; however, no direct acknowledgment of the multicultural component is stated
  2. Suggests activities that are multicultural

F. Technology
  1. Notes impact and effect of technology on society
  2. Offers no guidelines or suggestions for use of educational technology in the classroom

III. Oklahoma (documents for grade 1, grade 2, and grades 6-12; no guidelines provided for grades 3-5)

A. Knowledge
  1. Follows NCSS 1979 guidelines
  2. Provides four basic learner outcomes
  3. Stresses interdependence of content, skills, and beliefs

B. Skills
  1. Emphasizes use of language for social and intellectual growth
  2. Stresses thinking, problem solving, and decision making

C. Values
  1. Presents values as beliefs
  2. Encourages analyzing fundamental democratic beliefs

D. Global perspective
  1. Emphasizes interdependence and interrelationships throughout basic learner outcomes and suboutcomes
  2. Uses terms frequently for past and current issues

E. Multiculturalism
  1. Provides outcomes and concepts throughout the program

F. Technology
  1. Presents learner outcomes to determine impact of technology in a variety of outcomes

2. Offers no specific guidelines for classroom use

IV. Texas (K-12 document)

A. Knowledge
  1. Lists essential elements and subelements for each grade level
  2. Urges extension of essential elements
  3. Provides background information about the process of local curriculum guide writing

B. Skills
  1. Articulates a skills program throughout each grade level or course of study
  2. Develops skills and processes as a major goal of the social studies program

C. Values
  1. Stresses decision making through personal, social, and civic settings
  2. Develops values as a major goal of the social studies program

D. Global perspective
  1. Includes elements about world perspectives but lacks specific use of terms or concepts

E. Multiculturalism
  1. Lists elements that address culture and different beliefs
  2. Uses term and reflects coverage of multicultural concepts

F. Technology
  1. Offers no specific guidelines for the use of educational technology
  2. Encourages modification of material through use of multimedia materials

Summary of Region

Arkansas and Louisiana neglect specific content for early elementary grades. General outlines of goals provide for a wide range of early childhood social studies experiences. Texas offers specific essential elements for all levels. Louisiana provides a variety of numerous activities and lessons that offer a bulky array of materials to provide activity and experience in all levels of social studies education.

North Central Region

State	Covers Social Science Disciplines	Follows Expand-ed Horizons Approach	Specifies Learner Outcomes	Suggests Activities	Suggests Supplem. Materials
MO (1991)	yes	no	yes--grades 3-10 only	samples for assess-ment only	no
NB	no state social studies document provided				
ND (1991 draft)	yes	no	no	yes	yes
OH	no state social studies document provided				
SD (1981)	yes	no	yes	guidelines for teachers	yes
WI (1986)	yes	yes	no	yes	yes
IL (1986)	yes	no	yes--grades 3, 6, 8, 10, & 12 only	no	
IN (1987)	yes	yes	yes	no	reference only
IA (1986)	yes	yes	no	yes	yes
KS	no state social studies document provided				
MI (1991)	yes	not organized by topics	yes	no	no
MN (1991)	yes	no	yes	yes, for local curriculum development	yes

I.   Illinois (social science document)
A. Knowledge
  1. Expresses five broad terminal goals with sample set of district-level objectives for social studies
  2. Presents eight intentions for local districts to follow
B. Skills
  1. Organizes skills throughout goals-encoded sample objectives
  2. Gives no specific sequence
C. Values
  1. Describes values indirectly in broad goals
D. Global perspective
  1. Lacks global perspective
E. Multiculturalism
  1. Lacks development throughout the curriculum
F. Technology
  1. Offers no goals or guidelines

II. Indiana (K-12 social studies document)
A. Knowledge

  1. Tests proficiency statements and sample indicators
  2. Presents an integrated and interdisciplinary approach
  3. Encourages interrelated development of themes and concepts at various developmental levels
B. Skills
  1. Develops thinking and decision-making skills systematically through grade levels and proficiency statements
  2. Encourages readiness, active practice, and instruction in skills
C. Values
  1. Presents experiences throughout grade levels and proficiency statements
  2. Emphasizes the importance of values and beliefs
D. Global perspective
  1. Contains proficiency statement and sample indicators to cover major concepts
E. Multiculturalism
  1. Contains proficiency statements and sample

indicators to cover major concepts
2. Offers no guidelines or suggestions for technology in the classroom
F. Technology
1. Offers no guidelines or suggestions for the use of educational technology in the classroom

III. Iowa (K-12 social studies document)
A. Knowledge
1. Contains samples of scope, sequence, strands, organization, effective strategies, lesson formats, and course description
2. Stresses concepts and topics and notes the importance of factor
3. Uses NCSS 1984 task force suggestions
B. Skills
1. Recommends teaching in situations that require use of skills
2. Stresses the developments of sequential skill strands.
3. Provides scope and sequence of essential skills with suggested strengths of instructional effort
C. Values
1. Emphasizes democratic beliefs and values
2. Provides background and suggestion for a value and attitude strand
D. Global perspective
1. Uses term throughout document
2. Stresses importance of global affairs and concepts at end grade level
E. Multiculturalism
1. Emphasizes development of concepts
2. Suggests strategies, activities, strands, and format to assist local writers
F. Technology
1. Provides some background for selectivity using other nonprint resources with sample rating instruments
2. Contains background information for computer technology, software, and an abstract of available computer software programs

IV. Michigan (document covers all educational outcomes K-12)
A. Knowledge
1. Organizes core curriculum outcomes in topics for both context and process at elementary, middle/junior high, and high school levels
2. Develops social studies topics assuming a multicultural and interdependent global

society whose citizens make rational decisions and participate in society
3. Emphasizes integrated interdisciplinary and developmental approach to social studies
B. Skills
1. States topic outcomes for each of the three levels
C. Values
1. States democratic values and civic participation topics for each of the three levels
D. Global perspective
1. Uses term and concept throughout core curriculum topics
E. Multiculturalism
1. Uses term and concept throughout core curriculum topics
F. Technology
1. Contains an entire educational outcome on technology
2. Provides guidelines and outcomes for integrating at each level using these topics: problem solving, knowledge and technology, social and ethical issues, and technological applications
3. Requires development in local curriculum delivery

V. Minnesota (K-12 social studies document)
A. Knowledge
1. Lists thirteen learner goal statements based on current and future intellectual, social, emotional, physical, and career/vocational needs in contemporary society
2. Stresses an informed, participating, and empowered citizen
3. Offers three fundamental perspectives: pluralist, global, and participatory
B. Skills
1. Emphasizes skills throughout learner outcomes
2. Stresses participatory, thinking, and decision-making skills
C. Values
1. Emphasizes values throughout learner outcomes and three perspectives
2. Stresses human dignity as the core around which values are constituted
D. Global perspective
1. Requires concepts at local level
2. Suggests specific perspective in learner outcomes
3. Uses term consistently
E. Multiculturalism
1. Requires concepts at local level

2. Suggests specific perspective in learner outcomes
3. Uses term consistently

F. Technology
1. Requires integration of technology into the curriculum
2. Lacks specific guidelines to assist implementation at local level in the social studies

VI. Missouri (documents for grade 3, grade 4, grade 5, grade 6, and grades 7-10)

A. Knowledge
1. Divides core competencies into areas at designated grade levels: geography, history, government, economics, and other social studies
2. Provides concept analysis for each competency
3. Specifies test content with sample test items

B. Skills
1. Lists component skills for each competency
2. Specifies test content for skills component

C. Values
1. Contains value competencies throughout core
2. Lacks emphasis but includes information in concept analysis for relevant competencies

D. Global perspective
1. Lacks global perspective

E. Multiculturalism
1. Lacks comprehensive coverage although some concepts are presented in competencies

F. Technology
1. Acknowledges effects of technology in competencies
2. Offers no guidelines or suggestions for use of educational technology in the classroom

VII. North Dakota (K-12 social studies document)

A. Knowledge
1. Offers three major goals and twelve strands
2. Presents knowledge in strands of cultural literacy and social sciences
3. Describes goals and concepts through narrative and example lists

B. Skills
1. Presents skills through acquiring information using and organizing information, interpersonal relationships, and social participation
2. Provides essential-skills chart with suggested strengths of instructional effort

C. Values
1. Stresses democratic beliefs and civic responsibility
2. Presents values, strands of American identity, constitutional heritage, and participation
3. Provides skill scope and sequence

D. Global perspective
1. Uses term in narrative concept description
2. Offers global view course at grade seven

E. Multiculturalism
1. Provides concept development as major goal

F. Technology
1. Offers no guidelines or suggestions for use of educational technology in the classroom

VIII. South Dakota (K-12 social studies document)

A. Knowledge
1. Provides nineteen areas to focus goals organized around themes
2. Suggests grade level placement where goal is introduced, reinforced, and mastered

B. Skills
1. Integrates skills throughout the curriculum
2. Emphasizes problem solving and critical thinking skills

C. Values
1. Infuses values throughout instructional goals and skills

D. Global
1. Of nineteen areas, the fifth presents the use of the term and concepts for K-12 curriculum development

E. Multiculturalism
1. Of nineteen areas, the thirteenth presents the use of the term and concepts for K-12 curriculum development

F. Technology
1. Offers no guidelines or suggestions for use of educational technology in the classroom

IX. Wisconsin (K-12 social studies document)

A. Knowledge
1. Uses concepts for organizing curriculum around fifteen major themes
2. Suggests methods and activities to implement topics and concepts in grades K-12
3. Provides course and grade level description with illustrative objectives

B. Skills
1. Provides systematic practice throughout social curriculum
2. Emphasizes thinking and reasoning skills

C. Values
1. Encourages students to be active and critical and to participate in society

2. Stresses democratic principles and beliefs
D. Global perspective
    1. Develops concepts through several themes
E. Multiculturalism
    1. Develops concepts through several themes
F. Technology
    1. Provides guidelines for computers, computer software, and database management
    2. Presents abstract of available social studies computer software programs

Summary of Region

This region contains some of the most innovative and interesting social studies curriculum guidelines. Missouri is organized specifically around assessment. Indiana lists proficiency statements while maintaining that its dynamic document reflects the most recent and best thought-out social studies research. Illinois provides samples of learner outcomes to encourage strong local development as well.

Iowa provides a traditional guide that is filled with a wealth of supplementary and background information. The guide is comprehensive in the coverage of suggestions and strategies. There are eleven useful appendices for those who want a potpourri of ideas for general social studies curriculum development.

The Dakotas and Wisconsin organize curriculum around general themes and topics with fewer competency statements. The emphasis is on goals and concepts. Wisconsin topics offer a unique way of presenting concepts through questions.

Michigan and Minnesota provide contemporary documents that inspire future perspectives. Minnesota has distinctive sections that are extremely useful in assisting local districts to reform and develop curriculum. The suggestions and material provided by Minnesota lead curriculum writers through essential steps to reflect and formulate stages of social studies program development. Michigan offers a common core of standards, presenting a wide range of perspectives that connects subjects in the three levels of schools in a dramatic and new vision of curriculum organization. Noteworthy is the organization pattern for including educational technology in social studies and all newly defined areas of the Michigan curriculum. When combined, Minnesota and Michigan provide exemplary working documents that should be valuable resources for local district curriculum development.

Mountain West Region

State	Covers Social Science Disciplines	Follows Expanded Horizons Approach	Specifies Learner Outcomes	Suggests Activities	Suggests Supplem. Materials
AZ (1989)	yes	no	yes	yes	no
CO	no state social studies document provided				
ID (1988)	yes	yes	yes	no	no
WY	no state social studies document provided				
NV (1984)	yes	no	yes	no	no
NM (1990)	no	no	yes	no	no
UT (1992)	modified	yes	yes	no	no
MT (1989)	yes	no	yes	no	no

I.   Arizona (K-12 social studies document)
A.   Knowledge
  1. Cites fourteen premises embodied in its
     social studies framework
  2. Lists four basic goals and sixteen strands
     related to the four major goals for each grade
     level to unify the curriculum
  3. Stresses historical literacy and participatory
     citizenship
B.   Skills
  1. Lists skills as one of the major goals
  2. Relates as a fundamental for effective
     citizenship
  3. Stresses critical thinking and problem solving
     skills
C.   Values
  1. Lists civic values and responsibilities as one
     of the major goals
  2. Stresses democratic process for change
D.   Global perspective
  1. Lists several strands to assist coverage of
     global concepts
  2. Develops civil responsibilities to include
     international obligations
E.   Multiculturalism
  1. Lists several strands to assist coverage of
     multiculturalism
  2. Defines multiculturalism in the third premise
  3. Covers concepts throughout basic learning
     statements
F.   Technology
  1. Defines social studies to include use of
     technology to contribute to instruction in the
     tenth premise
  2. Provides criteria and guidelines for technol-
     ogy in appendix

II.   Idaho (elementary and 21-page secondary
social studies documents)
A.   Knowledge
  1. States broad goals to help students under-
     stand human affairs and the human condition
  2. Describes thirteen components in a well-
     designed social studies curriculum
  3. Avoids reliance on the expanding horizon
     approach
B.   Skills
  1. Promotes skill development throughout all
     levels of its curriculum
  2. Stresses critical, creative, and decision
     making skills through participation
C.   Values
  1. Lists eight topics to develop throughout the
     curriculum

  2. Encourages teacher modeling and reflection
     in the schools' operation
D.   Global perspective
  1. States that subject matter at all grade levels
     needs to be taught from a global perspective
E.   Multiculturalism
  1. Lacks a strong emphasis
  2. Covers some concepts in goal statements
F.   Technology
  1. Provides some concepts on the impact of
     technology
  2. Offers no specific guidelines for the use of
     educational technology

III.   Nevada (social studies K-8 section in state
course-of-study document)
A.   Knowledge
  1. Emphasizes the development of citizenship
  2. Lists seven basic essential elements
B.   Skills
  1. Identifies skills as one of the major essential
     elements to be developed throughout the
     curriculum
C.   Values
  1. Identifies values as one of the major essen-
     tial elements to be developed throughout the
     curriculum
D.   Global perspective
  1. Identifies global issues as one of the major
     essential elements to be developed through-
     out the curriculum
E.   Multiculturalism
  1. Lacks development throughout the curricu-
     lum
F.   Technology
  1. Offers no goals or guidelines

IV.   New Mexico (1-8 state competency guide)
A.   Knowledge
  1. States there is no generally accepted se-
     quence for developing a social studies
     program
  2. Presents broad competencies focused on
     United States history, government, economy,
     and geography
  3. Integrates all subjects into state competen-
     cies
B.   Skills
  1. Lacks continuity or development
C.   Values
  1. Lacks continuity or development
D.   Global perspective
  1. Lacks continuity or development
  2. Provides a few general competency state-

ments related to global issues
E. Multiculturalism
    1. Lacks development of this term or concept
F. Technology
    1. Offers no goals or guidelines

V. Utah (K-6 and 7-12 documents)
A. Knowledge
    1. Provides core standards with objectives for all grade levels
    2. Describes course description for each level course
    3. Emphasizes an interdisciplinary approach with understanding of concepts and processes over acquisition of isolated facts
B. Skills
    1. Presents a strong skills strand and continuum
    2. Emphasizes higher-level thinking and process skills
    3. Provides for global awareness and geographic skills
C. Values
    1. Promotes basic American values
    2. Encourages social participation to explore values
    3. Emphasizes citizenship and character practices and principles
D. Global perspective
    1. Stresses the importance of global interdependence at all levels
    2. Provides key concepts to promote global education and awareness
E. Multiculturalism
    1. Incorporates concepts throughout core standards
    2. Encourages multicultural participation
F. Technology
    1. Acknowledges technology standards for middle and high school core curriculum by integration or special classes
    2. Requires plans for integrating educational technology into the core curriculum

VI. Montana (K-12 standard and procedures manual)
A. Knowledge
    1. Lists broad model learner goals for the primary, intermediate, and graduation requirements
B. Skills
    1. Presents skills throughout model learner goals
C. Values
    1. Presents values throughout model learner goals
D. Global perspective
    1. Lacks use of term and development of this concept
E. Multiculturalism
    1. Lacks use of term and development of this concept
F. Technology
    1. Offers no guidelines or suggestions for the use of educational technology in the classroom
    2. Acknowledges the impact of technology upon society through several model learner subgoals

Summary of Region

This region provides little support to assist teachers in developing curriculum. Most states have suggested broadly stated social studies learner outcomes listed in state policy documents. There appears to be more flexibility at the local level throughout the region. The most helpful document is from Arizona. This state provides philosophical and pedagogical information to assist teachers in the development of social studies curriculum beyond lists of outcomes. The Nevada elementary social studies course of study also provides helpful background information for curriculum writing committees.

Pacific States Region

State	Covers Social Science Disciplines	Follows Expanded Horizons Approach	Specifies Learner Outcomes	Suggests Activities	Suggests Supplem. Materials
AK (1985)	yes	no	yes	yes	yes
CA (1987)	yes	no	no	no	no
OR (1990)	no	no	yes	no	no
WA	yes	no	yes	yes	yes

I. Alaska (K general and 1-12 social studies documents)
A. Knowledge
   1. Recognizes three critical components of knowledge, democratic beliefs, and skill development
   2. Organizes content around themes for grades 1-8
   3. Promotes interrelated interdisciplinary approach
B. Skills
   1. Stresses critical thinking and problem solving
   2. Identifies three categories: acquiring information, organizing information, and social participation
C. Values
   1. Integrates development throughout the curriculum
   2. Stresses democratic beliefs and citizenship
D. Global perspective
   1. Acknowledges concepts and content of global society throughout the curriculum
E. Multiculturalism
   1. Addresses diversity of ethnic and racial origins
   2. Lacks strong emphasis on multicultural concepts
F. Technology
   1. Provides section on use of social studies and the computer
   2. Encourages development and use of educational technology

II. California (K-12 history-social science document)
A. Knowledge

   1. Centers around importance of in-depth chronological study of history
   2. Stresses familiarity with literature of the period and about the period throughout all grade levels
   3. Provides content and background for teaching history and social sciences without emphasizing learner outcome
   4. Promotes three basic goals with twelve interrelated strands
B. Skills
   1. Emphasizes skills throughout all grade levels
   2. Provides three strands: study, critical thinking, and participation skills
C. Values
   1. Emphasizes values throughout all grade levels
   2. Provides three strands: national identity, constitutional heritage, civic values, rights and responsibilities
D. Global perspectives
   1. Emphasizes global learning for the twenty-first century
E. Multiculturalism
   1. Develops a perspective that respects the dignity and worth of all people
   2. Stresses the development of cultural literacy
F. Technology
   1. Provides guidelines for use of technology-related material
   2. References guidelines for educational software

III. Oregon (social studies documents for grades 3, 5, 8, and 12)
A. Knowledge

1. Prescribes common curriculum goals and essential learning skills for the end of the four grade levels
2. Provides common strands to organize concepts at the four grade levels
3. Allows for spiraling development of concepts embodied in the goals

B. Skills
1. Emphasizes three strands of skills: communication/study, thinking/decision making, and interpersonal/participation
2. Encourages development throughout the curriculum

C. Values
1. Provides two strands: civic values/responsibility and constitutional/democratic heritage
2. Focuses the context for study generally on the United States

D. Global perspective
1. Encourages the development in the philosophy and rationale
2. Provides coverage in the essential learning skills concepts

E. Multiculturalism
1. Encourages its development in the philosophy and rationale
2. Provides coverage in the essential learning skills

F. Technology
1. Offers no suggestions or guidelines for use in local social studies frameworks

IV. Washington (K-12 social studies document)
A. Knowledge
1. Lists twelve outcomes in question form to assist local curriculum developers in self-study
2. Suggests activities and teacher implications for each grade level to suggest and question good social studies teaching
3. Uses the NCSS Task Force Report on Scope and Sequence as a study document

B. Skills
1. Encourages development throughout each grade level
2. Suggests modification for local needs of NCSS skill development sequence

C. Values
1. Covers values through activities and questions

D. Global perspective
1. Lacks emphasis and use of term in the twelve principal outcomes

E. Multiculturalism
1. Provides coverage and use of term in the twelve principal outcomes
2. Suggests activities to promote multicultural concepts

F. Technology
1. Offers no suggestions or guidelines for classroom use

Summary of Region

This region depends less on the expanded horizon approach to organizing a social studies scope and sequence. Each state document is unique in how each provides a sound rationale with general goals for local districts to write their curriculum frameworks. Washington's use of questioning to stimulate curriculum writers to reflect on social studies scope and sequence is helpful for reflection.

By far, the California framework deviates the most from documents in this region and within the United States. Its narrative approach attempts to teach educators chronological history, as opposed to stating minimum learner outcomes. This lengthy text provides a rationale for each grade level and subject. The framework attempts to make teachers and students literate in history and related historical literature. The design and nature of the California framework makes it an interesting document to compare to traditional state curriculum guides.

Conclusion

State social studies curriculum documents describe standards and regulations for district curriculum development. The descriptions contain goals and student outcomes by which school districts are to incorporate minimum state standards. The overall purpose of state social studies curriculum documents is to assist local schools in developing a thoughtful and coherent scope and sequence to improve social studies instruction at the local level. The documents analyzed in this chapter set forth a wide variety of guidelines at different depths and levels, in an attempt to provide useful material and information to local schools and districts.

Some states produce documents that contain broad statements for each district to devise and write local and district plans. Other states provide documents that contain a variety of materials and resources that attempt to help local districts understand more about social studies teaching, learning, and curriculum writing. Many other states develop extensive materials, sample lessons, supplementary materials, checklists, need assessments, and appendices that contain a wealth of background information. Several states provide no particular social studies documents but list broad legislative statements, leaving complete development up to a local district. The majority of states list goals, outcomes, competencies, or essential elements to provide a base of common knowledge, skills, and values that all students should experience in a comprehensive social studies curriculum.

There is no correlation between the different social studies documents within regions. In the United States and within these regions, there is a need to clarify and unify expectations for social studies curriculum. A clear set of standards for the nation, states, and regions would be beneficial for developing local social studies documents. Therefore, local committees should obtain standards from the various social science professional organizations, such as the National Council for Social Studies, the National Council for Geographic Education, the American Historical Association, the Organization of American Historians, the National Council on Economic Education, and so forth. These organizations have specific content, skills, and values criteria that are useful for producing intelligent, coherent, comprehensive, and challenging social studies curriculum.

Overall, there are some basic steps and procedures that local districts should follow when writing social studies scope and sequence (see chapter 2 for a more detailed discussion of this):

1. Know and study the recommendations of professional organizations that represent the social sciences.
2. Clarify various roles and responsibilities of curriculum writers.
3. Know the state regulations and specific legislative requirements for your state as well as your district.
4. Assess the current social studies situation and know where your program has been, where it is now, and where you believe you would like it to be.
5. Review trends and issues surrounding social studies curriculum and instruction.
6. Develop a clear vision and a succinct rationale focused on local needs.
7. Form a vision and rationale while developing clear and concise goals for each grade level K-12.

8. Organize a structure and format for a scope and sequence that chronologically builds and connects concepts and core knowledge that is meaningful to the developmental level of the students.
9. Choose relevant facts and concepts to build upon each other that show a thoughtful, coherent, and defensible pattern for challenging and involving children in the content, skills, values, and process of social studies instruction.
10. Select literature, books, technology, and other useful resources that will provide for the various learning styles of students in your local district.
11. Develop a comprehensive, performance-based system of evaluating student outcomes as well as the impact of the social studies scope and sequence.
12. Implement the program, allowing time for staff development, reflection, and constant review of the social studies program.
13. Continually revise and review the social studies program to insure that it constantly meets the ever-changing demands of society within the context of local and global awareness.

The task of developing social studies curriculum is not the domain of the state. It is the role and the responsibility of the local school district to carefully develop a social studies scope sequence that will impact the lives of the students through the use of a curriculum that has utility for the classroom teacher. The following state curriculum guides are recommended as useful to district curriculum writers; however, there is no one state document that by itself provides districts with an entire process of developing a thoughtful, chronological, comprehensive, and organized social studies scope and sequence.

New England Region

Connecticut
This document provides a meaningful definition and process for developing local guidelines. It shows ways of evaluating existing curriculum, developing rationales, and establishing specific objectives around thoughtful goals. It suggests guidelines for instructional techniques as well as instructional materials. It deals with technology and includes criteria for selecting print and nonprint material. This document also describes

background information and specific materials for social studies curriculum implementation and evaluation. It lists frameworks, guidelines, and numerous appendices that would be helpful for curriculum writers. This particular document does not have overwhelming lists of student outcomes, but it is organized around useful material to assist local districts in guiding the curriculum development process in social studies.

Middle Atlantic Region

Maryland

This state provides a short, concise structure that emphasizes strategies for initiating curriculum development. It contains a definition of social studies and describes the impact of social studies on the learner. The guide shows four different models for developing alternative scope and sequence models. The variety of examples shows how creative structures can successfully meet state goals within local districts.

North Central Region

Michigan

This state offers a curriculum model that takes a contemporary approach to connecting all areas of a core curriculum, with an emphasis on disciplinary and interdisciplinary outcomes. The guide emphasizes process skills, problem solving, critical thinking, team building, decision making, and technological skills. The ways subject areas are linked to the core curriculum makes this document a good one for providing alternative structures for an integrated school curriculum. One of the major strands of core knowledge is technology. This document provides an excellent overview of ways to incorporate technology into all curriculum subject areas; Michigan has one of the best technological models of all the state documents.

Minnesota

This state provides a document that is beneficial to curriculum-writing teams because of the excellent information in the front matter. The initial part of this guide helps curriculum groups to understand missions, visions, definitions, and contemporary perspectives within the social studies curriculum. A four-step model helps local writing teams produce a scope and sequence through a set of philosophical phases. In addition,

a worksheet leads local developers through specific tasks to assist in the incorporation of knowledge, skills, and values. The guide also presents a good perspective for multicultural and global education.

Mountain West Region

Arizona

This state provides a series of distinguishing characteristics that should be discussed whenever writing a social studies scope sequence. There are fourteen suggested points to help develop a rationale for a social studies program. A visual model shows a web of literacy achievement, participation, and understanding within the context of sixteen strands. This visual provides a good model for establishing a framework for a K-12 social studies program. Its emphasis on various modes of literacy, democracy, social and political participation, and critical thinking and problem solving skills develops excellent background for reflection and incorporation of a thoughtful and organized social studies curriculum.

Pacific States Region

California

This is a document that is unlike any other within the United States. The narrative format prescribes a system for aligning a social studies framework within a chronology of historical fact and concepts. This framework provides historical background and rationale that present a body of knowledge for those involved in curriculum reform and curriculum writing. The numerous literature selections correlate to the historical chronology and are extremely beneficial in providing a useful bibliography.

Washington

The Washington guideline is helpful because it asks teachers specific questions to encourage reflection. It provides implications and featured activities to stimulate curriculum development. It encourages looking at alternative means of providing scope and sequence for social studies.

These state documents provide a variety of insights into social studies philosophy, content, process, and organization. Referring to these documents would help local committees develop coherent, interdisciplinary curriculum for social studies in their schools or school districts.

Implications

There are several implications that need to be considered for the future of social studies curriculum documents in grades K-12. Three crucial areas can be strengthened at the national, state, and local level. The first implication is the multicultural dimension: Many states' documents do not have a comprehensive development of such concepts. They do not provide adequate information for local districts to develop curriculum that represents multicultural concepts, skills, and values. It is imperative that local school districts understand multicultural content and suggest goals and objectives to meet the emerging needs of a multicultural society.

A second implication which is essential to the development of a comprehensive social studies program is global interdependence. Certainly, knowing the impact of our community, our state, and our nation is vitally important, but to ignore the interdependence and the need to work, live, and cooperate within a global perspective is an area which needs much improvement and consistent development in order for citizens to actively participate in the twenty-first century.

A third implication is technology. As the students in our schools move throughout their grade levels, technology is going to play an important and influential role in their lives. A social studies curriculum must reflect, not simply the impact of technology upon the lives of people and their community, state, world, and workplace, but the implication and use of technology in accessing and compiling information. Technology is a relatively new area within the schooling process, and social studies educators need to begin to provide guidelines, suggestions, and materials to help

teachers develop a complete technological strand within their social studies scope and sequence.

The last implication is assessment and evaluation. States and citizens are demanding more accountability for student learning in all subject areas, and social studies is no exception. Growing numbers of states mandate statewide testing for learner outcomes. Some states specify competencies that must be tested at certain grade levels where mastery is expected. However, the growing trend for testing and assessment is in student performance outcomes. Assessing these in social studies is a difficult task because it involves demonstrating and participating in concepts as opposed to memorizing a specified body of facts. Concepts, performance, and social studies processes are hard to assess through traditional testing procedures. Therefore, states, districts, and local schools must develop alternative means of assessing student learning in social studies programs. Participatory summaries, student artifacts, and portfolio documents are several ways that districts can provide accountability.

When looking at the state of the art of social studies through the state curriculum guides, it is apparent that the expanded horizons curriculum is becoming outmoded. State and local districts need to look at alternative means of organizing a curriculum that is going to deal with a chronological set of an explicit body of knowledge. These concepts need to be built upon throughout the school years in order to make an impact towards knowledgeable, participating, productive members of society who can function within the global arena of the twenty-first century.

STATE-LEVEL CURRICULUM GUIDELINES: A LISTING

THIS chapter provides bibliographic information on the state curriculum documents discussed in chapter 5. The publications are organized by state; for each state, we have provided the full address for that state's department of education, including the office to contact regarding curriculum publications (if such an office has been specified by the state department). The phone number shown is the best number to use for ordering the publications or for getting further information on the publications. We have also provided the addresses and phone numbers for states whose departments of education do not publish statewide curriculum frameworks. These states may produce curriculum materials on specific topics in social studies and in other disciplines, but they are not statewide guides as described in chapter 5.

For each publication, the listing provides the full title, document number and/or ISBN (if available), number of pages, year of publication (or reprinting), and price. Pricing is given on those publications for which Kraus had information; note that the prices shown are taken from the department's order form. Shipping and handling are often extra, and some states offer discounts for purchases of multiple copies. If a document is listed in ERIC, its ED number is shown as well.

Alabama

State Department of Education
Gordon Persons Office Building
50 North Ripley Street
Montgomery, AL 36130-3901

Division of Student Instructional Services
Coordinator, Curriculum Development/Courses
of Study
(205) 242-8059

Alabama Course of Study: Social Studies
Bulletin 1986, No 31, 193 p., 1986. $6.00.

Alaska

State Department of Education
Goldbelt Building
P.O. Box F
Juneau, AK 99811

Division of Education Program Support
Administrator, Office of Basic Education
(907) 465-2841

Alaska Curriculum Guide: Social Studies
Second ed., 258 p., n.d. $6.00 in-state, $10.00 out-of-state.

Arizona

State Department of Education
1535 West Jefferson
Phoenix, AZ 85007

Education Services
Instructional Technology
(602) 542-2147
Arizona Essential Skills: Social Studies
NKA960, 55 p., 1989. $1.55.

Arkansas

Department of Education
Four State Capitol Mall
Room 304 A
Little Rock, AR 72201-1071

Instructional Services
Coordinator, Curriculum and Assessment
(501) 682-4558

Social Studies, Grades 4-8 Arkansas Public School Course Content Guide
ACT-6471, 112 p., 1990. ED 322 061.

High School Social Studies [grades 9-12] *Arkansas Public School Course Content Guide*
100 p., n.d.

California

State Department of Education
P.O. Box 944272
721 Capitol Mall
Sacramento, CA 95814

California Department of Education
Bureau of Publications
(916) 445-1260

History-Social Sciences Framework for California Public Schools: Kindergarten through Grade Twelve
ISBN 0-8011-0712-1, 122 p., 1988. $6.00. ED 293 779.

Colorado

State Department of Education
201 East Colfax Avenue
Denver, CO 80203-1705

The Colorado State Department of Education does not produce statewide frameworks.

Connecticut

State Department of Education
P.O. Box 2219
165 Capitol Avenue
State Office Building
Hartford, CT 06106-1630

Program and Support Services
Division of Curriculum and Professional Development
(203) 566-8113

A Guide to Curriculum Development in Social Studies
110 p., 1989.

A Guide to Curriculum Development: Purpose, Practices and Procedures
72 p., 1981.

Delaware

State Department of Public Information
P.O. Box 1402
Townsend Building, #279
Dover, DE 19903

Instructional Services Branch
State Director, Instruction Division
(302) 739-4647

Content Standards for Delaware Public Schools
233 p., 1986. Includes content standards for social studies.

District of Columbia

District of Columbia Public Schools
The Presidential Building
415 12th Street, N.W.
Washington, DC 20004

Office of the Vice-Superintendent
Assistant Superintendent, Curriculum Development and Educational Technology
(202) 576-6580

Social Studies Scope and Sequence: Grades 1-6
84-IP734, 41 p., 1984, reprinted 1990.

District of Columbia (cont'd)
Social Studies Scope and Sequence: Grades 7-12
84-IP734, 100 p., 1984, reprinted 1990.

Florida

State Department of Education
Capitol Building, Room PL 116
Tallahassee, FL 32301

Curriculum Support Services
Bureau of Elementary and Secondary Education
(904) 488-6547

Curriculum Frameworks for Grades 9-12 Basic and Adult Secondary Programs. Volume VIII: Social Studies
116 p., 1990.

Curriculum Frameworks for Grades 6-8 Basic Programs. Volume VIII: Social Studies
29 p., 1990.

Georgia

State Department of Education
2066 Twin Towers East
205 Butler Street
Atlanta, GA 30334

Office of Instructional Programs
Director, General Instruction Division
(404) 656-2412

The Georgia State Department of Education issues its statewide frameworks only on diskette.

Georgia's Quality Core Curriculum (K-12)
AppleWorks version 25-diskette set ($100.00) or IBM WordStar version 17-diskette set ($68.00), 1989. Includes 87 pages on social studies curriculum.

Georgia Studies (8th Grade). Teacher Resource Guide
AppleWorks version 6-diskette set ($24.00) or IBM WordStar version 2-diskette set ($8.00).

Social Science Fair. Teacher Resource Guide
AppleWorks version or IBM WordStar version, 1 diskette ($4.00 each).

Hawaii

Department of Education
1390 Miller Street, #307
Honolulu, HI 96813

Office of Instructional Services
Director, General Education Branch
(808) 396-2502

The Hawaii Department of Education is currently revising its statewide frameworks; the new publications will be available in 1993.

Idaho

State Department of Education
Len B. Jordan Office Building
650 West State Street
Boise, ID 83720

Chief, Bureau of Instruction/School Effectiveness
(208) 334-2165

Social Studies: Elementary Course of Study
51 p., 1988.

Social Studies: Secondary Course of Study
22 p., 1988.

Illinois

State Board of Education
100 North First Street
Springfield, IL 62777

School Improvement Administration
Curriculum Improvement
(217) 782-2826

State Goals for Learning and Sample Learning Objectives. Social Sciences: Grades 3, 6, 8, 10, 12
4M 7-476B-26 No. 238, 65 p., 1986. ED 277 605.

Indiana

State Department of Education
Room 229, State House
100 North Capitol Street
Indianapolis, IN 46024-2798

Center for School Improvement and Performance
Manager, Office of Program Development
(317) 232-9157

Social Studies Proficiency Guide
64 p., 1987.

Iowa

State Department of Education
Grimes State Office Building
East 14th and Grand Streets
Des Moines, IA 50319-0146

Division of Instructional Services
Bureau Chief, Instruction and Curriculum
(515) 281-8141

*A Guide to Curriculum Development in Social
Studies. Curriculum Coordinating Committee
Report*
184 p., 1986. ED 280 783.

Kansas

State Department of Education
120 East Tenth Street
Topeka, KS 66612

The Kansas State Department of Education does
not produce statewide frameworks.

Kentucky

State Department of Education
1725 Capitol Plaza Tower
Frankfort, KY 40601

Office of Instruction
Division of Curriculum and Staff Development
(502) 564-2106

*A List of Valued Outcomes for Kentucky's Six
Learning Goals. Council on School Performance
Standards*
6 p., n.d. The Kentucky State Department of
Education does not produce other statewide
frameworks.

Louisiana

State Department of Education
P.O. Box 94064
626 North 4th Street, 12th Floor
Baton Rouge, LA 70804-9064

Office of Academic Programs
Secondary Education (504) 342-3404
Elementary Education (504) 342-3366

Social Studies Curriculum Guide, Grades K-6
Bulletin 1601, 274 p., 1981. $6.00

*World Geography Curriculum Guide: Secondary
Social Studies*
Bulletin 1727, 640 p., 1985. $6.75. ED 295 884.

American Studies Curriculum Guide, Grade 7
Bulletin 1604, 117 p., 1981. $4.50.

Louisiana Studies Curriculum Guide, Grade 8
Bulletin 1605, 215 p., revised 1990. $5.00.

American History Guide
Bulletin 1599, 290 p., revised 1989. $11.00. ED 295
885.

Western Civilization Curriculum Guide
Bulletin 1759, 166 p., 1987. $7.00.

World History Curriculum Guide
Bulletin 1758, 355 p., 1987. $8.00. ED 296 921.

Maine

State Department of Education
State House Station No. 23
Augusta, ME 04333

Bureau of Instruction
Director, Division of Curriculum
(207) 289-5928

The Maine State Department of Education does
not produce statewide frameworks.

Maryland

State Department of Education
200 West Baltimore Street
Baltimore, MD 21201

Bureau of Educational Development
Division of Instruction, Branch Chief,
Arts and Sciences
(410) 333-2307

Social Studies. A Maryland Curricular Framework
40-637 12/84, 46 p., 1983. ED 237 433.

Massachusetts

State Department of Education
Quincy Center Plaza
1385 Hancock Street
Quincy, MA 02169

School Programs Division
(617) 770-7540

The Massachusetts State Department of Education does not produce statewide frameworks.

Michigan

State Board of Education
P.O. Box 30008
608 West Allegan Street
Lansing, MI 48909

Instructional Specialists Program
(517) 373-7248

Model Core Curriculum Outcomes [working document].
73 p., 1991. Contains educational outcomes on K-12 subjects, including outcomes for world studies and for cultural and aesthetic awareness.

Minnesota

State Department of Education
712 Capitol Square Building
550 Cedar Street
St. Paul, MN 55101

Minnesota Curriculum Services Center
(612) 483-4442

Model Learner Outcomes for Social Studies Education
E727, 137 p., 1991. $5.50.

Mississippi

State Department of Education
P.O. Box 771
550 High Street, Room 501
Jackson, MS 39205-0771

Bureau of Instructional Services
(601) 359-3778

Mississippi Curriculum Structure: Social Studies
106 p., 1986.

Missouri

Department of Elementary and Secondary Education
P.O. Box 480
205 Jefferson Street, 6th Floor
Jefferson City, MO 65102

Center for Educational Assessment (University of Missouri--Columbia)
(314) 882-4694

Core Competencies and Key Skills for Missouri Schools. Grade 2: Social Studies/Civics
40 p., 1991. $10.00 for grade 2 guide, all subjects.

Core Competencies and Key Skills for Missouri Schools. Grade 3: Social Studies/Civics
50 p., 1991. $10..00 for grade 3 guide, all subjects.

Core Competencies and Key Skills for Missouri Schools. Grade 4: Social Studies/Civics
75 p., 1991. $10.00 for grade 4 guide, all subjects.

Core Competencies and Key Skills for Missouri Schools. Grade 5: Social Studies/Civics
90 p., 1991. $10.00 for grade 5 guide, all subjects.

Core Competencies and Key Skills for Missouri Schools. Grade 6: Social Studies/Civics
91 p., 1991. $10.00 for grade 6 guide, all subjects

Montana

Office of Public Instruction
106 State Capitol
Helena, MT 59620

Department of Curriculum Services
Curriculum Assistance and Instructional
Alternatives
(406) 444-5541

Montana School Accreditation: Standards and Procedures Manual
34 p., 1989. The Montana Office of Public Instruction does not produce other statewide frameworks for social studies.

Nebraska

State Department of Education
301 Centennial Mall, South
P. O. Box 94987
Lincoln, NE 68509

The Nebraska State Department of Education does not produce statewide frameworks.

Nevada

State Department of Education
Capitol Complex
400 West King Street
Carson City, NV 89710

Instructional Services Division
Director, Basic Education Branch
(702) 687-3136

Elementary Course of Study
65 p., 1984. Includes scope and sequence for social studies. ED 278 511.

Nevada Secondary Course of Study. Volume 1: Academic Subjects
0-5282, 72 p., n.d. Includes information on required courses and elective courses in social studies.

New Hampshire

State Department of Education
101 Pleasant Street
State Office Park South
Concord, NH 03301

Division of Instructional Services
General Instructional Services Administrator
(603) 271-2632

Minimum Standards for New Hampshire Public Elementary School Approval, Kindergarten-Grade 8: Working Together
36 p., 1987. Includes elementary school curriculum, K-8.

Standards & Guidelines for Middle/Junior High Schools
101 p., 1978. Includes information on social studies.

Standards for Approval of New Hampshire Public High Schools, Grades 9-12
53 p., 1984.

New Jersey

Department of Education
225 West State Street, CN 500
Trenton, NJ 08625-0500

Division of General Academic Education
(609) 984-1971

New Jersey High School Graduation Requirements
1 p., 1988.

World History/Cultures Curriculum Guide
53 p., 1988. Social Studies Curriculum Committee. ED 312 169.

The New Jersey Department of Education does not produce other statewide frameworks.

New Mexico

State Department of Education
Education Building
300 Don Gaspar
Santa Fe, NM 87501-2786

Learning Services Division
Instructional Materials (505) 827-6504

An Elementary Competency Guide for Grades 1-8
88 p., 1987, revised ed. 1990. Provides "Competencies by Subject Area," including social studies.

Graduation Requirements
SBE Regulation No. 90-2, section A.4.3, 12 p., 1990. High school graduation requirements.

New York

State Education Department
111 Education Building
Washington Avenue
Albany, NY 12234

The University of the State of New York
The State Education Department
Publications Sales Desk
(518) 474-3806

Handbook on Requirements for Elementary and Secondary Schools. Education Law, Rules of the Board of Regents, and Regulations of the Commissioner of Education
140 p., second ed. 1989.

Social Studies Program, Kindergarten
156 p., updated ed. 1988. ED 299 205.

Social Studies Program 1
87-9051, 058700, 73 p., 1982, updated ed. 1987. $3.00. ED 287 788.

Social Studies Program 2
90-9290, 089000, 95 p., revised ed. 1987, reprinted 1990. $3.00. ED 292 742.

Social Studies Program 3
89-9241, 088900, 89 p., updated ed. 1988, reprinted 1989. $3.00. ED 304 378.

Social Studies Program 4
89-9240, 088900, 85 p., updated ed. 1987, reprinted 1989. $3.00. ED 295 882.

Social Studies Program 5
89-9242, 088900, 93 p., updated ed. 1987, reprinted 1989. $3.00. ED 290 682.

Social Studies Program 6
223 p., updated ed. 1987. ED 292 743.

Social Studies 7-8: United States and New York State History [tentative syllabus]
86-8073, 134 p., 1987. $2.00.

Social Studies 9-10: Global Studies [tentative syllabus]
90-9300, 089000, 202 p., reprinted 1990. $2.00. ED 290 681.

Social Studies 11: United States History and Government [tentative syllabus]
87-6539, 109 p., 1987. $2.00. ED 288 797.

Social Studies 12: Participation in Government [tentative syllabus]
88-7757, 128800, 51 p., 1987. $2.00. ED 302 467.

Social Studies 12: Economics and Economic Decision Making [tentative syllabus]
90-7248, 63 p., 1990. $2.00.

North Carolina

Department of Public Instruction
Education Building
116 West Edenton Street
Raleigh, NC 27603-1712

Publications Sales Desk
(919) 733-4258

North Carolina Standard Course of Study and Introduction to the Competency-Based Curriculum
530 p., 1985. $7.50. ED 264 640.

Teacher Handbook: Social Studies, Grades K-12. North Carolina Competency-Based Curriculum
710 p., 1985. $12.00.

North Dakota

State Department of Public Instruction
State Capitol Building, 11th Floor
600 Boulevard Avenue East
Bismarck, ND 58505-0440

Office of Instruction, Supplies
(701) 224-2272

*North Dakota Social Studies Curriculum Guide,
K-12* [draft]
64 p., n.d.

Ohio

State Department of Education
65 South Front Street, Room 808
Columbus, OH 43266-0308

At the current time, the Ohio State Department
of Education does not produce statewide frameworks for social studies.

Oklahoma

Department of Education
Oliver Hodge Memorial Education Building
2500 North Lincoln Boulevard
Oklahoma City, OK 73105-4599

Instructional Services Division
Curriculum/Instructional Computers
(405) 521-3361

*Learner Outcomes. Oklahoma State Competencies,
Grade One*
100 p., 1992. Includes learner outcomes for social
studies.

*Learner Outcomes. Oklahoma State Competencies,
Grade Two*
95 p., 1992. Includes learner outcomes for social
studies.

*Learner Outcomes. Oklahoma State Competencies,
Grades Six-Twelve*
347 p., 1992. Includes learner outcomes for social
studies: civics, government, economics, Oklahoma
history, world geography, United States history,
and world history.

Oregon

State Department of Education
700 Pringle Parkway, S.E.
Salem, OR 97310

Publications Sales Clerk
(503) 378-3589

Social Studies: Common Curriculum Goals
10 p., 1990. ED 323 157.

Pennsylvania

Department of Education
333 Market Street, 10th Floor
Harrisburg, PA 17126-0333

Office of Basic Education
Director, Bureau of Curriculum and Instruction
(717) 787-8913

*Chapter 5 Curriculum Regulations of the Pennsylva-
nia State Board of Education. Guidelines for
Interpretation and Implementation*
32 p., 1990. The Pennsylvania Department of
Education does not produce statewide frameworks.

Rhode Island

Department of Education
22 Hayes Street
Providence, RI 02908

Division of School and Teacher Accreditation
(401) 277-2617

The Rhode Island Department of Education does
not produce statewide frameworks for social
studies.

South Carolina

State Department of Education
1006 Rutledge Building
1429 Senate Street
Columbia, SC 29201

The South Carolina State Department of Education is revising its statewide frameworks; the
revised publications will be issued in 1993.

South Dakota

Department of Education and Cultural Affairs
435 South Chapelle
Pierre, SD 57501

Division of Elementary and Secondary Education
Office of Curriculum and Instruction
(605) 773-3261 and (605) 773-4670

*South Dakota Social Studies Curriculum Guide,
Kindergarten-Twelve*
110 p., 1981. $2.50.

Tennessee

State Department of Education
100 Cordell Hull Building
Nashville, TN 37219

Curriculum and Instruction
(615) 741-0878

Tennessee K-8 Curriculum Frameworks
10 p., 1991. Includes frameworks for language
arts, music, art, physical education, technology,
mathematics.

Texas

Texas Education Agency
William B. Travis Building
1701 North Congress Avenue
Austin, TX 78701-1494

Publications Distribution Office
(512) 463-9744

Social Studies Framework, Kindergarten-Grade 12
CU637011, 84 p., 1986. $2.00. ED 277 620.

Utah

State Office of Education
250 East 500 South
Salt Lake City, UT 84111

Division of Operations
Coordinator, Curriculum
(801) 538-7774

Social Studies Core Curriculum, Grades K-6
39 p., revised ed. 1991. $1.25.

Social Studies Core Curriculum, Grade 7-12
75 p., revised ed. 1991. $2.00.

Vermont

State Department of Education
120 State Street
Montpelier, VT 05602-2703

Basic Education
Chief, Curriculum and Instruction Unit
(802) 828-3111

*Framework for the Development of a Social Studies
Scope and Sequence* [grades K-6]
17 in. x 22 in. folded sheet, n.d.

*Framework for the Development of a Social Studies
Scope and Sequence* [grades 9-12]
17 in. x 22 in. folded sheet, n.d.

Virginia

Department of Education
P.O. Box 6-Q, James Monroe Building
Fourteenth and Franklin Streets
Richmond, VA 23216-2060

Instruction and Personnel
Administrative Director of General Education
(804) 225-2730

*Standards of Learning Objectives for Virginia Public
Schools: Social Studies*
38 p., revised ed. 1989. ED 316 466.

Washington

Superintendent of Public Instruction
Old Capitol Building
Washington and Legion
Olympia, WA 98504

Curriculum, Instruction Support and Special
Services Unit
Director, Curriculum Support
(206) 753-6727

Guidelines for K-12 Social Studies Education Curriculum Development
IPS-629-91, 150 p., n.d.

International Education Curriculum Guidelines
IPS-652-88, 86 p., 1988.

West Virginia

State Department of Education
1900 Washington Street
Building B, Room 358
Charleston, WV 25305

Bureau of General, Special, and Professional Education
Director, General Education
(304) 348-7805

Social Studies Program of Study
35 p., 1991.

Wisconsin

State Department of Public Instruction
General Executive Facility 3
125 South Webster Street
P. O. Box 7841
Madison, WI 53707-7841

Publication Sales
(608) 266-2188

A Guide to Curriculum Planning in Social Studies
Bulletin No. 6251, 216 p., 1986, revised ed. 1990.
$20.00.

Wyoming

State Department of Education
2300 Capital Avenue, 2nd Floor
Hathaway Building
Cheyenne, WY 82002

Division of Certification, Accreditation, and Program Services
Accreditation/Special Services Unit
(307) 777-6808

School Accreditation
6 p., n.d. The Wyoming State Department of Education does not produce other statewide frameworks.

RECOMMENDED CURRICULUM GUIDES

by John J. Patrick
Professor and Director of the Social Studies Development Center
Indiana University, Bloomington, Indiana

I N recent years, there has been a lively debate about the content of school curricula, about priorities in the teaching and learning of core knowledge. Numerous curriculum study projects have been conducted in the social studies, and in other fields of knowledge, to assess teaching and learning in core subjects and to recommend improvements in widely distributed reports. Various proposals for curriculum improvement have led to renewed interest in development of curriculum frameworks for the social studies and other fields of subject matter.

The select, annotated bibliography of this chapter highlights for social studies practitioners--curriculum specialists, elementary and secondary school teachers, and teacher educators--the key documents of the current curriculum reform efforts. The types of documents in this bibliography are social studies curriculum frameworks of state-level departments of education, curriculum reform reports on the social studies, national assessment reports of student achievement in core subjects of the social studies, curriculum materials on specific subjects in the social studies (e.g., American history, world history, geography, government, civics, economics, and international studies), and exemplary multimedia materials.

The documents in this annotated bibliography are *not* an exhaustive listing of the available curriculum materials. Rather, they are representa-

tive of the best available materials, which meet the following criteria:
- These curriculum documents pertain to teaching and learning of social studies subjects in grades K-12.
- The materials are current and reflective of trends and issues in the social studies today; with few exceptions, all documents in this bibliography have been produced and distributed since 1988.
- All items in this bibliography can be obtained by contacting the sources listed at the end of each citation.
- These curriculum materials are relevant to the work of social studies practitioners--curriculum supervisors, curriculum developers, classroom teachers, teacher educators, school administrators, and educational policymakers.
- With a few exceptions, these curriculum materials have been developed and distributed by noncommercial publishers and nonprofit educational agencies.

The following bibliography is organized according to three categories: (1) Comprehensive Curriculum Frameworks and Reports, (2) Curriculum Materials on Core Subjects, and (3) Exemplary Multimedia Materials. Part 1 includes documents that pertain generally to the social studies, such as the report of the National Commission on Social Studies in the Schools. Part 2 includes materials on specific core subjects of the social studies, such as history, geography, civics, government, economics, law-related education, and international studies. Part 3 involves multimedia materials, such as video programs, computer programs, and related print materials.

An ED number is included in the citation for most of the items in this bibliography, which indicates that these documents can be found in the database of the Educational Resources Information Center (ERIC). ERIC is an information system sponsored by the Office of Educational Research and Improvement, within the U.S. Department of Education. These ERIC documents are available in microfiche and paper copies from the ERIC Document Reproduction Service (EDRS). For information about prices, contact EDRS, 7420 Fullerton Road, Suite 110, Springfield, VA 22153-2852; telephone numbers are 703-440-1400 and 800-443-3742. Use the ED numbers in this bibliography to identify and order documents from the EDRS. Overnight delivery and fax services are provided by EDRS for customers who need to obtain ERIC documents quickly. The annotation for each item in the ERIC database is quoted from *Resources in Education*, a monthly publication of the U.S. Department of Education.

Comprehensive Curriculum Frameworks and Reports

Adams, Ron, et al. 1990. *Social Studies in the Nineties: An NHCSS Statement*. Littleton, NH: New Hampshire Council for the Social Studies. ED number will be assigned.
A guide to the basic goals, structure, and methods of the social studies for New Hampshire is outlined. Recommendations on instructions, scope and sequence, assessment, minimum requirements, alternative learning experiences, teacher's preparation, and funding are included. A six-item bibliography of selected resources concludes the document.

Alberta Department of Education. 1990. *Social Studies: Teacher Resource Manual, Senior High*. Edmonton, Alberta, Canada: Alberta Department of Education. ED 330 603.
Developed to help Alberta, Canada, teachers implement a new sequence of social studies courses, this teacher resource manual offers suggestions for organizing, teaching, and evaluat-

ing the new program, and supplies additional information about the program. It is organized into the following sections and subsections: (1) Teaching Social Studies: social studies program objectives, fundamental goals, responsible citizenship, teaching strategies, meeting students' needs, and technology in the social studies classroom; (2) Planning for Instruction: evaluation and planning for the course; (3) Instruction/ Evaluation Strategies; (4) Organizational Models and Activities: Social Studies 13--Canada in the modern world, Social Studies 23--the growth of the global perspective, and Social Studies 33--the contemporary world; and (5) Learning Resources. Six appendices also are included.

Albuquerque Board of Education. 1992. *Resource Guide for Elementary Social Studies*. Albuquerque, NM: Albuquerque Public Schools. ED number will be assigned. This document also is available from Albuquerque Public Schools, Instructional Services and Support, 220 Monroe St., SE, Albuquerque, NM 87106.
Objectives, course content, skills, and teaching strategies are specified for social studies at grades K-5. Relationships of course specifications to the state curriculum framework are described. Background information and curriculum resources are suggested so that users of this guide can strengthen their programs according to their individual needs.

Allen, Michael G. 1990. *Middle Level Social Studies: Teaching for Transition to Active and Responsible Citizenship*. Rowley, MA: New England League of Middle Schools. ED number will be assigned. This document also is available from the New England League of Middle Schools, 15 Summer St., Rowley, MA 01969. $10.00.
This publication considers some of the salient issues in the field of social studies, explores ways to gain a more comprehensive understanding of the important developmental stage of early adolescence, and discusses how to recognize the importance of developing and implementing sound social studies programs based on this knowledge. Section 1 discusses the developmental realities of early adolescence, with an emphasis on implications for social studies instruction. Section 2 considers social studies specifically with a definition and analysis of the objectives of social studies and guidelines for enhancing instruction. Section 3 contains selected resources useful to

social studies educators. Section 4 offers selected conclusions and recommendations regarding middle-level social studies curriculum and instruction. Section 5, the final section of the publication, contains "resources for additional reading" and provides a wide variety of suggested sources for those wishing to go beyond the scope of the publication.

American Federation of Teachers. 1987. *Education for Democracy: A Statement of Principles. Guidelines for Strengthening the Teaching of Democratic Values*. Washington, DC: American Federation of Teachers. ED 313 217. Paper copy also is available from the American Federation of Teachers, 555 New Jersey Ave., NW, Washington, DC 20001. First copy free; additional copies $2.50 each.
Based on the premise that democracy's values will not survive if they are not purposefully transmitted to successive generations, this booklet proposes that U.S. schools increase efforts to improve citizenship education. The featured issues are the reasons improvements are needed, what citizens need to know, and the role of humanities and history instruction as the core of democratic education. The booklet concludes that there is a need for (1) the teaching of a more demanding social studies curriculum; (2) a reordering of curricula around history and geography; (3) the using of enhanced imagination in history instruction; (4) increasing global studies; and (5) offering more humanities instruction, especially in literature, ideas, and biography. A major curriculum reform effort will require more effective textbooks and resource materials, collaboration between schools and universities, and new approaches to teacher education. A model social studies curriculum is presented at the end of this booklet.

Arizona State Department of Education. 1989. *Arizona Social Studies Essential Skills*. Phoenix: Arizona State Department of Education. ED 324 259.
The Arizona Social Studies Framework formulates goals for student competency in four broad categories: knowledge and cultural understanding, understanding of democratic principles, individual and group participation in social political affairs, and fundamental skill attainment for effective citizenship. Under each social studies goal are listed the basic learnings that comprise the K-12 social studies program. These curriculum strands

are constant in every grade level; no options are to be dropped or added from one year to the next. The strands under Goal 1 (knowledge and cultural understanding), for example, are historical literacy, geographic literacy, economic literacy, social-political literacy, cultural literacy, and ethical literacy. For each of four grade levels (K-3, 4-6, 7-8, 9-12) there is a four-column presentation of essential skills under the following headings: goals and strands; essential/exit skills; content and descriptors; and instructional strategies/related concepts. The essential skills column is identified as the critical component of this document. An appendix outlining criteria for evaluating instructional materials is included.

Arkansas State Department of Education. 1990. *Social Studies, Grades 4-8: Arkansas Public School Course Content Guide*. Little Rock: Arkansas State Department of Education. ED 322 061.
This course content guide identifies the objectives that form the basis for social studies in grades 4-8 in Arkansas schools. Classroom teachers, curriculum specialists, administrators, professors, and the Department of Education personnel participated in the guide's development. The information for each grade is presented in three columns. The first column lists basic skills; the second, developmental skills; and the third suggests teaching strategies. It is stated that although all of the skills should be taught, the basic skills are those on which the Minimum Performance Test (MPT) items are based. The strategies are offered as recommendations and may be used in any way a teacher or staff deems relevant. An outline of the scope and sequence of the social studies recommended for grades K-8 is included.

California State Department of Education. 1988. *History-Social Science Framework for California Public Schools*. Sacramento: California State Department of Education. ED 293 779. Paper copy is available only from Bureau of Educational Sales, California State Department of Education, P.O. Box 271, Sacramento, CA 95802-0271. $6.00.
This framework, centered in the chronological study of history, proposes an integrated and correlated approach to the teaching of history and the social sciences. The framework is structured around three major goals, each comprising several curriculum strands which are to be developed for grades K-12. The three goals are knowledge and

cultural understanding, democratic understanding and cultural values, and skills attainment and social participation. The programs for grades K-3 are "Learning and Working Now and Long Ago," "A Child's Place in Time and Space," "People Who Make a Difference," and "Continuity and Change." State history is taught in the fourth grade. Fifth graders study U.S. history from the pre-Columbian period through 1850. The sixth-grade program is developed around the ancient world to A.D. 500. The medieval and early modern world through 1789 are presented in grade seven, setting the context for the study of U.S. history from 1783 to 1914 in grade eight. The modern world from 1789 to the present is studied in grade ten. The eleventh grade provides an in-depth study of the United States from 1900 to the present. Students choose electives in grade nine from a variety of courses. The culminating courses are principles of U.S. democracy and economics in grade twelve. Criteria for evaluating instructional materials are provided.

California State Department of Education. 1991. *Literature for History-Social Science, Kindergarten Through Grade Eight.* Sacramento: California Department of Education. ED number will be assigned. This publication also is available from the Bureau of Publications, Sales Unit, California Department of Education, P.O. Box 271, Sacramento, CA 95802-0271. $5.25.

The use of literature in the history-social science curriculum has been found to be an effective means of generating students' interest, enhancing their understanding, and enriching the curriculum. This annotated guide contains listings of books to be used in teaching students in grades K-8 that have been selected as particularly helpful in the study of history and geography. The use of literature of the historical period being studied, as well as literature about that period, is emphasized. This guide is offered as a resource of titles for use by curriculum specialists, teachers, librarians, and resource personnel when planning a curriculum. While produced specifically for California teachers, the guide should be useful to teachers everywhere. A wide variety of books are listed in the guide, including historical fiction, biography, fables, myths and legends, folktales and fairy tales, nonfiction, poetry, plays, and songs.

Curriculum Task Force of the National Commission on Social Studies in the Schools. 1989. *Charting a Course: Social Studies for the 21st*

Century. Washington, DC: National Commission on Social Studies in the Schools. ED 317 450. This document also is available from the National Council for the Social Studies, 3501 Newark St., NW, Washington, DC 20016. $7.00 plus $2.00 postage and handling.

Part 1 of this report covers the recommended social studies curriculum for grades K-12. Part 2 discusses the research basis for curriculum choice. Part 3 contains essays prepared by representatives of the professional associations holding membership in the Social Science Association's Task Force for Pre-College Education. These essays provide perspectives from the fields of anthropology, economics, U.S. history, world history, political science, psychology, and sociology. The characteristics of a social studies curriculum for the twenty-first century, as set forth in this report, include eight points: (1) It must instill a clear understanding of the roles of citizens in a democracy and provide opportunities for active, engaged participation in civic, cultural, and volunteer activities. (2) It must provide consistent and cumulative learning throughout grades K-12. (3) History and geography should provide the matrix for social studies with concepts from political science, economics, and other social sciences integrated throughout the curriculum. (4) A global approach should be taken, for a curriculum that focuses on one or two major civilizations is neither adequate nor complete. (5) Integration of other subject matter with social studies should be encouraged. (6) Students must be made aware that they have the capacity to shape the future. (7) Teaching strategies should help students become both independent and cooperative learners who develop skills of problem solving, decision making, negotiation, and conflict resolution. (8) Learning materials must incorporate a rich mix of written matter, audiovisual materials, computer programs, and items of material culture.

Florida Commission on Social Studies Education. 1990. *Connections, Challenges, Choices.* Tallahassee: Florida Department of Education. ED number will be assigned. This document also is available from Instructional Support Section, Division of Public Schools, Florida Department of Education, Tallahassee, FL 32399.

This report includes recommendations for the Florida K-12 social studies program of study. It also specifies intended outcomes, course content, and teaching strategies for social studies in the elementary and secondary schools of Florida. Finally, the report sets forth a vision of the social studies that emphasizes common learnings based on the subject matter of history and geography.

Florida Department of Education. 1990. *Curriculum Frameworks for Grades 6-8 Basic Programs: Social Studies*. Tallahassee: Florida Department of Education. ED number will be assigned. This document also is available from Instructional Support Section, Division of Public Schools, Florida Department of Education, Tallahassee, FL 32399.

This curriculum framework specifies intended outcomes and major concepts for social studies courses at grades 6-8. Courses include United States history, geography, civics, law studies, and world cultures. There are specifications for basic and advanced treatments of each course at each grade.

Florida Department of Education. 1990. *Curriculum Frameworks for Grades 9-12 Basic and Adult Secondary Programs: Social Studies*. Tallahassee: Florida Department of Education. ED number will be assigned. This document also is available from Instructional Support Section, Division of Public Schools, Florida Department of Education, Tallahassee, FL 32399.

Curriculum frameworks for grades 9-12 are descriptions of the courses offered at the high school grades. Intended outcomes and major concepts are specified for each course in the curriculum. Courses treated include American government, civics, law studies, world history, American history, economics, and philosophy.

Huffman, Lewis E. 1990. *Social Studies Curriculum Standards, K-12*. Dover: Delaware State Department of Public Instruction. ED number will be assigned.

This guide contains social studies curriculum standards for grades K-12 and is meant to be used by school district administrators and teachers in Delaware to develop their local social studies program. The guide is not meant to offer day-to-day lesson plans; rather, it is intended to be used by administrators and teachers as a guide to the selection of strategies and materials to achieve the included goals and objectives. Standards are included for grades K-3; grades 4-6; grades 7-8; grades 7-12; consumer education; and for grades 9-12 economics, psychology, sociology, world

history, and U.S. history, civics, and government. For each grade grouping or curriculum subject, lists are given of what the program should provide in instruction and what students will be expected to learn or do.

Massachusetts Council for the Social Studies. 1989. *Excellence in Social Studies Education: The Foundation of Active Citizenship*. Boston: Massachusetts State Department of Education. ED 310 977.

Social studies programs have not received the attention they deserve in the last decade. This document is meant to help Massachusetts school districts strengthen the teaching of social studies at all grade levels. The rationale section offers direction about the need for and the primary purpose of social studies education, namely, citizen education. The section on teaching social studies at different grade levels clarifies the purpose and scope of social studies education at the elementary, middle, and high school levels. Elementary instruction should attempt to develop students' understanding of themselves and their immediate environment. Middle school instruction should expand on what was learned in the elementary grades and demonstrate principles of democracy. High school instruction should attempt to teach students the concepts, understandings, attitudes, skills, generalizations, and specific knowledge necessary for an individual to function in a positive and contributory fashion in a democratic society. The section on subject areas reviews the key concepts and principles of each of the social studies disciplines. The section on effective teaching strategies offers definitions and rationales for several alternative teaching strategies such as critical thinking, guest speakers, independent study, oral history, and student government. These strategies are important because too much emphasis is placed on lectures and textbooks. The resource section is a directory of noncommercial resources that might be useful to teachers.

Michigan Council for the Social Studies. 1991. *Core Curriculum Outcomes for Elementary Social Studies*. Grades K-3. East Lansing: Michigan Council for the Social Studies. ED number will be assigned.

These outlines of core curriculum outcomes for elementary social studies in grades K-3 include the following for each grade level: core curriculum knowledge outcomes, core curriculum skill outcomes, core curriculum democratic values outcomes, and core curriculum civic participation outcomes. For each individual outcome, several examples of learning activities designed to foster the specific outcome are given.

Michigan State Board of Education. 1989. *Defining Social Studies Education in Michigan, K-12.* Lansing: Michigan State Board of Education. ED 312 201.
This document begins by providing some introductory guidelines on constructing a K-12 social studies program and conducting a curriculum program review and then goes on to focus on the goals and objectives for social studies education in Michigan. These are divided into three groups: knowledge, democratic values, and skills. For each of these areas, specific goals and objectives are set out, with a discussion of how they apply to the various grade levels. The last quarter of the document contains definitions, illustrative concepts, and topics for various courses. This material is designed to help teachers and curriculum specialists enhance their understanding of the scope and structure of the social sciences, the humanities, and related areas of study. Appendices contain education codes for Michigan that relate to social studies education, a list of documents approved by the Michigan State Board of Education that contain recommendations specifically related to social studies education, and a textbook evaluation form.

New Mexico State Department of Education. 1991. *New Mexico Social Studies Framework/ Student Essential Competencies.* Albuquerque: New Mexico State Department of Education. ED number will be assigned.
This curriculum framework specifies objectives and competencies for social studies in grades K-12. Each school district is required to develop social studies curricula based on three interrelated strands: (1) knowledge and cultural understandings, (2) democratic understandings and civic values, and (3) skill attainment and social participation.

New York State Social Studies Review and Development Committee. 1991. *One Nation, Many Peoples: A Declaration of Cultural Interdependence.* Albany: New York State Education Department. ED number will be assigned.
The committee that produced this report was asked to review existing New York State social

studies syllabi and to make recommendations to the Commissioner of Education designed to increase students' understanding of U.S. culture and its history; the cultures, identities, and histories of the diverse groups that comprise U.S. society today; and the cultures, identities, and histories of other people throughout the world. A review of the existing syllabi respecting these concerns found them to be inadequate. The syllabi were found to contain insensitive language, to draw upon too narrow a range of culturally diverse contexts, and to omit content specific to some groups and areas of the world felt to be essential. Among the committee's overall recommendations was that the present New York State social studies syllabi be subjected to detailed analysis and revision in order to provide more opportunities for students to learn from multiple perspectives and in order to remove language that is insensitive or may be interpreted as racist or sexist. The committee also makes recommendations concerning the specific areas of teaching and learning, the State Syllabi, and guidelines for implementation. The report concludes with reflective commentaries by several members of the committee, in which some dissents are registered and in which others expand upon positions that are held by specific committee members.

Oregon State Department of Education. 1990. *Social Studies: Common Curriculum Goals.* Salem: Oregon State Department of Education. ED 323 157.
This document defines and provides common curriculum goals in social studies for Oregon public school students. The goals were designed to define what should be taught, while allowing local schools and districts to decide the specific context of instruction. The contents include design, organization, building and implementing a local program, a district-level implementation chart, and common curriculum goals. Ten strands of knowledge are outlined: (1) economic understandings, (2) political understandings, (3) geographic understandings, (4) historical understandings, (5) cultural and social understandings, (6) communications and study skills, (7) thinking/decision-making skills, (8) interpersonal/participation skills, (9) constitutional/democratic heritage, and (10) civic values and responsibilities. An evaluation form for the guide concludes the document.

Parker, Walter C. 1991. *Renewing the Social Studies Curriculum*. Alexandria, VA: Association for Supervision and Curriculum Development. ED 334 114. This publication also is available from ASCD Publications, 1250 N. Pitt St., Alexandria, VA 22314. $13.95.

This book concerns the art of curriculum deliberation in the field of social studies. Its audience is the local curriculum planning committee. Its themes are democratic education in a multicultural society and challenging lessons on essential learnings. The first chapter discusses the first theme and suggests five essential learnings. The second places curriculum planning in its social settings: school organization, the community, and, broadly, the present North American milieux. The third presents a case study of two curriculum renewal meetings of a school district curriculum planning committee. The fourth presents three general principles to guide curriculum renewal in social studies, an eight-part renewal model, and pitfalls to be avoided. The fifth describes the typical social studies curriculum in the U.S. today along with alternatives, issues, and trends. The final chapter advocates and examines two trends: authentic assessments and in-depth study on a limited number of essential topics.

Ravitch, Diane. 1990. *The Changing History-Social Science Curriculum: A Booklet for Parents*. Sacramento: California State Department of Education. ED 328 468. Paper copy also is available from the Bureau of Publications, Sales Unit, California Department of Education, P.O. Box 271, Sacramento, CA 95802-0271. $5.00 for 10 copies.

The lack of U.S. students' knowledge of history and geography has been portrayed on television and in the newspapers as a national problem. California's public schools are taking significant steps to ensure that all students have a well developed understanding of their society and the world. This guide for parents answers some of the most commonly asked questions about the 1987 California History-Social Science Framework (for K-12) and suggests concrete ways in which parents can help their children succeed in school. A literature list for parents and children (K-12) is included.

Staten, Theresa, et al. 1988. *Curriculum Review Handbook for Social Studies Education in Michigan*. Lansing: Michigan State Board of

Education. ED 307 197.

This document presents a ten-step action plan to guide educators through a review process designed to aid them in the improvement and enhancement of the social studies curriculum for grades K-12. Curriculum review and development are continuous tasks which extend over a span of several years and should be continuous processes. Step 1 involves the organization of a K-12 social studies curriculum committee. In Step 2 the committee produces a needs assessment and an evaluation of the current success in meeting those needs. Step 3 establishes a statement of philosophy within the social studies program. Step 4 involves the development of program goals designed to carry out that philosophy. Steps 5 and 6 identify the sequences of instruction and the range, instructional emphases, and course descriptions for various grade level clusters. In Step 7, the actual curriculum guides are drawn up. Step 8 involves the selection, development, and evaluation of instructional materials. Step 9 consists of the actual implementation of the program, and Step 10 is an evaluation and assessment of student achievement procedures. Six appendices offer models and procedures for implementation of the steps, as well as a policy on teaching controversial issues.

Svengalis, Cordell M. 1992. *National Survey of Course Offerings and Testing in Social Studies, Kindergarten-Grade 12*. Washington, DC: Council of State Social Studies Specialists. ED number will be assigned.

This survey presents the curriculum patterns in social studies in each of the fifty states and the District of Columbia. Required courses and popular electives are listed for each state. Statewide testing programs also are described. The key social studies contact person for each state is identified.

Task Force on Social Studies in the Middle School. 1990. *Social Studies in the Middle School*. Washington, DC: National Council for the Social Studies. ED number will be assigned.

This task force report is designed to focus attention on the young adolescent learner and provide direction for developing appropriate and meaningful social studies instruction for the middle school. Schools at the middle level characteristically focus on the unique developmental needs of young adolescents. A number of these needs are listed, in physical, social-emotional, and intellectual categories. It is recommended that the social studies curriculum be designed and implemented with the characteristics of middle-level learners in mind. These characteristics are organized into four basic themes: (1) concern with self: development of self-esteem and a strong sense of identity; (2) concern for right and wrong: development of ethics; (3) concern for others: development of groups and other-centeredness; and (4) concern for the world: development of a global perspective. Coming under an overall model curriculum entitled "Social Studies for Citizens of a Strong and Free Nation," the following scope and sequence options for grades 5-8 are recommended: Grade 5--People of the Americas: The United States and its Close Neighbors; Grade 6--People and Cultures: Representative World Regions; Grade 7--A Changing World of Many Nations: A Global View; and Grade 8--Building a Strong and Free Nation: The United States. A number of social studies instructional practices also are recommended as appropriate for middle-level social studies: experiential learning, interdisciplinary instruction, cooperative learning, heterogeneous grouping, addressing controversial issues, and performance-based assessment. A list of selected resources that feature organizations and publications is included.

Virginia State Department of Education. 1989. *Social Studies Standards of Learning: Objectives for Virginia Public Schools*. Richmond: Virginia State Department of Education. ED 316 466.
The standards in this document resulted from a statewide effort to identify a scope and sequence of content, concepts, skills, and attitudes in social studies for grades K-12. The goals embodied in the standards include (1) providing experiences that enable students to participate in society effectively and responsibly; (2) assisting students in understanding basic democratic ideals and values that affect decision making in public and private life; (3) offering a framework of knowledge and skills to assist students in understanding themselves and society and to serve as a basis for continuous learning in history and the social sciences; and (4) assisting students in acquiring concepts and problem-solving skills that foster rational solutions to problems encountered in everyday life. A program description is presented for each grade level and represents the major emphasis of the program. Learning objectives also are listed for each grade level that represent a

framework for instruction that is believed necessary for further education and employment. Paralleling learning objectives with current events or contemporary societal issues is an integral part of the program at each grade level.

Curriculum Guides, Reports, Resource Books, and Assessment of Learning on Core Subjects

Allen, Russell, et al. 1990. *The Geographic Learning of High School Seniors*. Princeton, NJ: National Assessment of Educational Progress, Educational Testing Service. ED 313 317. Paper copy also is available from the National Assessment of Educational Progress, Educational Testing Service, Rosedale Rd., Princeton, NJ 08541-0001. $15.00.
This report presents results of the 1988 National Assessment of Educational Progress (NAEP) survey of the geographic knowledge and skills of high school seniors. A national stratified sample of more than three thousand twelfth graders from three hundred public and private schools responded to seventy-six multiple-choice questions about four topics in geography: (1) knowing locations, such as countries, cities, and physical places; (2) using the skills and tools of geography, such as map and globe symbols and longitude and latitude; (3) understanding cultural geography, including human-environment relationships and cultural change; and (4) understanding physical geography, including climate, weather, tectonics, and erosion. The results indicate that students generally are deficient in geographic knowledge and skills. This problem may be associated with inadequate treatment of geography in the high school curriculum. Much of the geography presented to high school students is integrated with courses in history and science. Less than two-thirds of these respondents had taken a high school course in geography. There was no relationship, however, between taking geography coursework and better performance on this test. But students who studied geography in a U.S. history course performed better than those without this academic experience. Better performance on this test was linked to certain background factors, such as well-educated parents, both parents living at home, availability of many reading materials, limited viewing of television, and time spent doing homework.

Anderson, Lee, et al. 1990. *The Civics Report Card: Trends in Achievement from 1976 to 1988 at Ages 13 and 17; Achievement in 1988 at Grades 4, 8, and 12*. Princeton, NJ: National Assessment of Educational Progress, Educational Testing Service. ED 315 376. Paper copy also is available from NAEP, Educational Testing Service, Rosedale Rd., Princeton, NJ 08541-0001. $15.00.

This report summarizes findings from two national surveys of U.S. civics achievement conducted by the National Assessment of Educational Progress. Part 1 reports on a trend assessment of students at ages thirteen and seventeen, carried out during the 1975-76, 1981-82, and 1987-88 school years. Chapter 1 summarizes national trends, trends for demographic subpopulations, trends in students' ability to define democracy, and trends in students' ability to identify the value of multiple newspaper publishers. Part 2 reports on patterns of achievement of fourth-, eighth-, and twelfth-grade students in 1988. Chapter 2 summarizes the levels of civics proficiency across the grades. Chapter 3 compares civics proficiency across subpopulations defined by gender, race and ethnicity, region, and other characteristics. Chapter 4 explores students' performances in specific content areas such as democratic principles and the purpose of government, political processes, and rights, responsibilities, and the law. Chapter 5 describes the amount of instruction students reported receiving in civics, while chapter 6 discusses the topics studied and the instructional approaches used in these classes. Appendices contain procedural information and tables of statistical data that supplement the information in the text.

Bradley Commission on History in Schools. 1988. *Building a History Curriculum: Guidelines for Teaching History in the Schools*. Washington, DC: Educational Excellence Network. ED 310 008. Paper copy is available from the Bradley Commission on History in Schools, 29615 Westwood Rd., Suite A-2, Westlake, OH 44145; and the Educational Excellence Network, 1112 Sixteenth St., NW, Suite 500, Washington, DC 20036. $3.00.

The Bradley Commission on History in Schools was created in 1987 in response to concern over the inadequacy of the history taught in U.S. elementary and secondary classrooms. These history curriculum guidelines were designed by the Bradley Commission to help those responsible for making curriculum decisions realize the manifest importance of developing and maintaining a vigorous history curriculum. The Commission recommends that (1) historical studies focus on thematic context and chronological perspective to develop critical judgment capabilities; (2) the curricular time required to develop genuine understanding in history programs be considerably greater than that currently allowed; (3) the K-6 social studies curriculum be history-centered; (4) no fewer than four years of history be required between grades seven and twelve; (5) this curriculum include the historical experiences of peoples from all parts of the world and all constituent parts of those societies; and (6) a substantial program of history, with suitable structure and content, be required for certification of social studies teachers in middle and high schools. Thirty-two topics are suggested for the study of U.S. history, world civilization, and western civilization. Curricular patterns or course sequences are presented for both K-6 (three patterns) and middle and high schools (four patterns). Criteria are also given for the examination of the structure, priority, and content of courses.

Butts, R. Freeman. 1988. *The Morality of Democratic Citizenship: Goals for Civic Education in the Republic's Third Century*. Calabasas, CA: Center for Civic Education. ED number will be assigned. This book also is available from the Center for Civic Education, 5146 Douglas Fir Rd., Calabasas, CA 91302. $10.00.

In recent years, a number of political and educational leaders and groups have urged the nation's public schools to place a greater emphasis on teaching civic values and on educating students to become citizens. This book puts forth the civic values and ideas that schools should be teaching. The volume is not a handbook or curriculum guide, but is designed to broaden the perspective of curriculum specialists, textbook authors, teachers, and educational policymakers. In the first three chapters of this four-chapter book, the study of and learning about history, the study of and learning about constitutional principles, and the study of and learning about conceptions of citizenship are examined. The final chapter offers a set of twelve ideas and civic values that should suffuse teaching and learning in the schools. These twelve values are justice, equality, authority, participation, truth, patriotism, freedom, diversity, privacy, due process, property, and human rights.

California State Department of Education. 1990. *Readings for Teachers of United States History and Government*. Sacramento: California State Department of Education. ED number will be assigned. This document also is available from the Bureau of Publications, Sales Unit, California Department of Education, P.O. Box 271, Sacramento, CA 95802-0271. $3.25.

An annotated list of readings is suggested for high school teachers of U.S. history and geography at grade eleven and for teachers of courses in the principals of democracy at grade twelve. The list was designed for use in California, where the eleventh grade curriculum emphasizes twentieth century U.S. history and the twelfth grade concentrates on the institution of U.S. government and the comparison of different styles of government in the world today. Although the bibliography was prepared for use by California teachers, teachers from around the U.S. and other parts of the world might find it a useful resource. Principles of selection for the list include the following: Each book must be germane to the subject at hand, each must deal with a significant aspect of the subject, and each must be interesting and readable. The reading list has six sections: historical fiction, biography and autobiography, contemporary public affairs, books about education, U.S. history, and European and world history.

Clow, John E., et al. 1991. *Economics and Entrepreneurship, Teaching Strategies: Master Curriculum Guide*. New York: Joint Council on Economic Education. ED 326 653. This book also is available from the Joint Council on Economic Education, 432 Park Ave. S., New York, NY 10016. $21.95.

Designed for high school teachers of economics, social studies, and business education, this teaching package provides materials for a course that combines study of basic economic concepts with an understanding of entrepreneurship. The teacher resource manual consists of three parts. Part 1 is an overview of the relationship between economics and entrepreneurship education. Part 2 contains seventeen lessons: entrepreneurs; characteristics of entrepreneurs; human capital; scarcity; economic systems; markets; entrepreneurial innovation; interdependence of entrepreneurial activities; demand; supply; market equilibrium; profits; business organization; borrowing;

competitive markets; demand for labor; and government intervention. Contents of each lesson include time required, concepts, instructional objectives, rationale, required materials, vocabulary (terms with definitions), procedures (suggestions for adapting activities for students of different ability levels), and evaluation (tests or activities to assess students' understanding). Reduced-print pages of student activities follow each lesson. Part 3 describes instructional practices that foster entrepreneurial behavior on the part of students. A complete set of blackline masters for student activities completes the package.

Cooperman, Saul, and Joel Bloom. 1990. *Education for an Effective Citizenry: Civics Curriculum Guide*. Trenton: New Jersey State Department of Education. ED 323 158.

Civic education in a democracy is a central goal of the public schools. The purpose of civics education is to educate youth to enable them to participate in a democracy. This guide highlights the components of a K-12 civics curriculum which features knowledge, democratic ideals, skills, and social participation. Sample lessons, state goals and objectives, a list of resources and programs, and a twenty-item bibliography is included.

Gagnon, Paul. 1989. *Democracy's Half-told Story: What American History Textbooks Should Add*. Washington, DC: American Federation of Teachers. ED 313 305. A paper copy also is available from the Education for Democracy Project, American Federation of Teachers, 555 New Jersey Ave., NW, Washington, DC 20001. $7.00 each for 1-10 copies; additional copies $5.00.

The first purpose of a high school course in U.S. history must be to help students understand the essence of democracy and those events, institutions, and forces that have either promoted or obstructed it. This review examines five textbooks and analyzes how useful they are in aiding that process, and how they might be made more helpful. The five texts are *A History of the United States* (D. Boorstin and B. Kelley), *History of a Free People* (H. Bragdon and S. McCutchen), *The United States: A History of the Republic* (J. Davidson and M. Lytle), *People and Our Country* (N. Risjord and T. Haywoode), and *Triumph of the American Nation* (L. Todd and M. Curti). The texts are reviewed using topic divisions such as "History's Role in Civic Education," "Old World

Backgrounds," "Civil War and Emancipation," "Change and Reform Before World War I," and "Depression, New Deal, and War Again." The textbooks under review are at the same time over-detailed and under-detailed: over-detailed, because they try to mention something about everything; under-detailed, because they fail to develop major themes in depth. They labor too hard to balance affirmation and negation of U.S. history, and the result is a detached neutrality, passionless about both the ugly and the beautiful moments in that history. The texts should convey the complication, drama, suspense, and the paradox of comedy and tragedy found in history. The Education for Democracy Project's Statement of Principles and its signatories are given in the appendix.

Gagnon, Paul. 1987. *Democracy's Untold Story: What World History Textbooks Neglect.* Washington, DC: American Federation of Teachers. ED 313 268. A paper copy also is available from the Education for Democracy Project, American Federation of Teachers, 555 New Jersey Ave., NW, Washington, DC 20001. $4.98.

Content weakness in textbooks is a major obstacle to effective social studies teaching. Chapters 1-3 of this book provide the Education for Democracy Project's Statement of Principles, a consideration of history's role as the core of social studies education, and the role of textbooks in teaching world history. Chapters 4-14 examine five selected world history textbooks in terms of included information about and treatment of the purpose of history instruction; the Greek legacy; Rome's fall and legacy; Judaism's and Christianity's basic ideas; the Middle Ages as a source of representative government; the seventeenth-century English Parliament; ideas from the Enlightenment; the American and French revolutions; major ideas of the nineteenth century; nation-states, nationalism, and imperialism; World War I; totalitarianism; U.S. foreign policy; and democracy in the world since 1945. This book concludes that these world history textbooks tend to neglect democracy's ideas, principles, origins, needs, and significance and that, when included, these concepts are not systematically presented. Teachers may not be able to rely on world history textbooks to convey and teach the concepts of struggles for freedom, self-government, and justice.

Geographic Education National Implementation Project. 1989. *Geography in Grades 7-12:*

Themes, Key Ideas, and Learning Opportunities. Indiana, PA: National Council for Geographic Education. ED 322 028. This document also is available from the National Council for Geographic Education, 16A Leonard Hall, Indiana University of Pennsylvania, Indiana, PA 15705. $6.00.

This volume presents a framework for developing courses of study in geography at grade levels 7-12. Several sample courses illustrate how the framework may be used. Five fundamental themes in geographic education provide the basis for the framework. The suggested learning opportunities are designed to incorporate various levels of thinking and direct attention to the knowledge, skills, and attitudes that result in a total geography course. The fundamental themes for geographic education are as follows: (1) Location: position on the earth's surface; (2) Place: physical and human characteristics; (3) Relationships within places: humans and environments; (4) Movement: humans interacting on the earth; and (5) Regions: how they form and change. The cognitive skills that are developed in these courses are grouped as follows: asking geographic questions; acquiring geographic information; presenting geographic data; interpreting and analyzing geographic information; developing and testing hypotheses and geographic generalizations. A glossary of selected terms and a list of references are included.

Hammack, David C., et al. 1990. *The U.S. History Report Card: The Achievement of Fourth, Eighth, and Twelfth-grade Students in 1988 and Trends from 1986 to 1988 in the Factual Knowledge of High School Juniors.* Princeton, NJ: National Assessment of Educational Progress, Educational Testing Service. ED 315 377. A paper copy also is available from NAEP, Educational Testing Service, Rosedale Rd., Princeton, NJ 08541-0001. $15.00.

Each of the three parts of this report provides a somewhat different perspective on U.S. students' knowledge and understanding of U.S. history. Part 1 summarizes the assessment performance of fourth-, eighth-, and twelfth-grade students based on the National Assessment of Educational Progress history proficiency scale. Chapter 1 uses this measure to summarize the levels of proficiency displayed by students in the 1988 assessment, offering an overview and examples of their knowledge and understandings. Chapter 2 compares U.S. history proficiency across the grades and across subpopulations defined by race and ethnicity, gender, region, and other characteristics. Part 2 of the report takes a closer look at the assessment results. The chapters in this section provide information not only on the results of the assessment of students in grades four, eight, and twelve, but also on trends in the performance of eleventh-grade students, based on a special study conducted in 1986 and 1988. Chapter 3 explores students' knowledge of historical periods, chronology, documents, and persons, while chapter 4 summarizes their familiarity with the historical contexts of political and economic life as well as of cultural, social, and family life. Part 3 describes the amount and nature of social studies and U.S. history instruction reported by students who participated in the 1988 assessment and in the special trend assessment. Chapter 5 summarizes the extent of students' instruction in these subjects, and chapter 6 reports on various aspects of this instruction-- particularly the topics studied and the relevance of various instructional activities. Many tables of statistical data are included.

Haynes, Charles C. 1990. *Religion in American History: What To Teach and How*. Alexandria, VA: Association for Supervision and Curriculum Development. ED 320 843. This publication also is available from the Association for Supervision and Curriculum Development, 1250 N. Pitt St., Alexandria, VA 22314. $10.95.
It is clear that there is a new consensus in this country supporting teaching about religion and religious liberty in public schools. For too long educators have misunderstood the distinction between teaching religion, which is unconstitutional, and teaching about religion, which is not only constitutional but necessary for a sound education. This book is a guide for social studies teachers who wish to teach about the influence of religion and religious events in U.S. history. Part 1 of the book provides a comprehensive list of the significant religious influences in the history of the nation. Part 2 describes a practical method for natural inclusion of religious influences using original source documents. Teachers are urged to copy and use the thirteen facsimiles in the book and the background information that accompanies each one to help students interpret history based on their own reading of the documents. Part 3 contains consensus statements and general guidelines for teaching about religion in a public school setting.

Holt, Tom. 1990. *Thinking Historically: Narrative Imagination and Understanding*. New York: College Board. ED number will be assigned. This publication also is available from College Board Publications, Box 886, New York, NY 10101. $8.95.
In this book, a professional historian provides a personal narrative of how he thinks about teaching history. While the historian's experience seems, at first glance, to be removed from that of secondary teachers, it is to such teachers that his account is directed. The historian stresses that the essential questions about teaching history are the same at all levels. The document opens the practice of a historian to view and, in so doing, asks teachers to examine their assumptions about their work. The historian's own assumptions about teaching history include the following: Student misconceptions must be explored, not ignored; teachers must be models of mindfulness; strong teaching includes values and choices; a "basic skills" approach postpones learning; the meaning of "higher order skills" must be reexamined; authentic materials prompt thinking; and students know more than educators think. A twenty-nine-item list of references is included.

Hunter, Kathleen, ed. 1990. *Heritage Education Resource Guide*. Washington, DC: National Trust for Historic Preservation. ED number will be assigned. This document also is available from the National Trust for Historic Preservation, 1755 Massachusetts Ave., NW, Washington, DC 20036. $15.00.
Heritage education is defined as teaching and learning about U.S. history and culture. It is an interdisciplinary approach to education that encompasses subjects like architecture, art, community planning, social history, politics, conservation, and transportation. This guide is intended to help persons identify information about heritage education programs and materials. Listing over three hundred resources, the information highlights are available through museums, historic sites, and national, state, city, and town organizations, as well as through consultants and authors. The guide can be used to network among current practitioners in heritage education. It also can introduce educators from many disciplines to the values and principles of heritage education and can direct them to the various kinds of programs and educational materials.

Joint Committee on Geographic Education. 1984. *Guidelines for Geographic Education: Elementary and Secondary Schools*. Washington, DC: Association of American Geographers. ED 252 453. A paper copy also is available from the Association of American Geographers, 1710 Sixteenth St., NW, Washington, DC 20009; or the National Council for Geographic Education, Indiana University of Pennsylvania, 1-B Leonard Hall, Indiana, PA 15705. $3.00.

Intended as a current statement for improving geographic education, these guidelines suggest major changes needed to counteract a prevailing illiteracy in geography among U.S. citizens. A preface and problem statement provide a rationale for including geography education as a subject of study in the schools and as a scientific mode of inquiry. A section on the content and process of geographic education (1) demonstrates how geographic education focuses on five central themes (location, place, relationships within places, movement, and regions), how these themes recur and are amplified throughout the curriculum, and how they should be represented in the various levels of our schools; (2) suggests how schools can integrate these themes; (3) identifies the knowledge, skills, and perspectives students should gain from a systematic program in geographic education; and (4) suggests a variety of approaches to geography that each theme might imply. The following section, "The Place of Geography in the Curriculum," deals with the value of geographic inquiry, geography's relationship to other subjects, and geography as preparation for a career. In the next section, a chart depicting the role and sequence of geography education in the elementary school presents central foci and suggested learning outcomes by grade level. A suggested pattern of course offerings and sequence for geographic education in the secondary school is followed by an outline of skills to be included in high school geography courses and a list of learning outcomes arranged according to the five basic themes identified earlier in the guidelines.

Kemball, Walter G., et al. 1987. *K-6 Geography: Themes, Key Ideas, and Learning Opportunities*. Indiana, PA: National Council for Geographic Education. ED 288 807. This document also is available from the National Council for Geographic Education, 16A Leonard Hall, Indiana University of Pennsylvania, Indiana, PA 15705. $5.50.

This implementation guide is based upon the themes, geographic concepts, and suggested learning outcomes contained in *Guidelines for Geographic Education: Elementary and Secondary Schools*. The central themes for geographic education are location (position on the earth's surface); place (physical and human characteristics); relationships within places (humans and environments); movement (humans interacting on the earth); and regions (how they form and change). Resources are given for preparing daily lesson plans, curriculum guidelines, and resource materials. Key ideas and learning opportunities for each grade level are developed around the five themes. Each learning opportunity statement is designed to include various levels of thinking and to direct attention to the knowledge, skills, and attitudes of geographic education. The central focus progresses from the study of self in space in kindergarten to the study of world regions at the sixth grade. The document can be used to evaluate existing programs or to develop new ones. A list of selected terms in geographic education is included.

Louisiana State Department of Education. 1989. *American History Guide*. Baton Rouge: Louisiana State Department of Education. ED 328 469.

The state of Louisiana's curriculum guide for the American history course is presented. Subdivided into four to seven units, the six sections of the course are (1) Toward a New Nation; (2) Conflict and Reunion; (3) Emergence of Modern America; (4) Conflict and International Power; (5) Global Change and Conflict; and (6) Problem and Prospects. For each part of the course content outlined, an objective, concepts, generalizations, and activities are listed. The Louisiana Social Studies Program Rationale and Curriculum Goals are included, as are a bibliography and a section on evaluative techniques. A two part appendix contains (1) skills that are a major responsibility of social studies and (2) skills that are a definite, but shared, responsibility of social studies.

Maryland Geographic Alliance. 1990. *Geography in the Middle School: A Compendium of Lesson Plans for Social Studies and Other Subject Areas*. Baltimore, MD: Maryland Geographic Alliance. ED 322 065. This document also is available from the Geography Department, University of Maryland Baltimore Campus,

5401 Wilkens Ave., Baltimore, MD 21228. $5.00.

The geography lesson plans included in this packet of materials were prepared for middle school students. Lessons are divided into three categories according to the present school social studies curriculum: world cultures, United States history, and interdisciplinary focus. The lesson plans incorporate the five fundamental themes of location, place, human/environmental interaction, movement, and region. They are designed to provide the student with the skills necessary to prepare maps, tables, graphs, and an organized, coherent written or oral presentation. In addition, the lessons teach interpretation of trends portrayed on a line graph and the analysis of the relationships between information on two or more maps. The students also learn to develop and test hypotheses and make geographic generalizations. Maps, graphs, charts, and other reproducible visual aids are included.

New Jersey State Department of Education. 1988. *World History/Cultures Guide*. Trenton, NJ: New Jersey State Department of Education. ED 312 169. A paper copy also is available from New Jersey State Department of Education, 225 W. State St., CN 500, Trenton, NJ 08625. $3.25.

In 1988-89, a one-year course in world history/cultures was added to the list of courses required for graduation in the state of New Jersey, becoming the third required course in social studies. The course is intended to provide students with historical knowledge to better meet the demands of the world and to make the informed decisions that are so crucial to a democratic way of life. This curriculum guide is designed to stimulate multiple perspectives in the development, modification, and evaluation of such a course. The guide includes a statement of philosophy; a rationale for a world history/cultures course; curriculum guidelines; course objectives; five curriculum approaches; a twenty-seven-item resource list of agencies and organizations that could provide more information; an eight-item bibliography; and a feedback form. Course objectives are discussed in terms of knowledge, skills, attitudes, and social participation; each of the objectives is broken down into additional goals and objectives. The five curriculum approaches (two examples of each approach are given) are world history, world cultures, world geography, global studies, and international relations.

Patrick, John J. 1991. *Ideas of the Founders on Constitutional Government: Resources for Teachers of History and Government*. Washington, DC: Project '87 of the American Historical Association and the American Political Science Association. ED 335 285. This book also is available from the Director of Educational Activities, American Political Science Association, 1527 New Hampshire Ave., NW, Washington, DC 20036. $12.00.

The political ideas of John Adams, Alexander Hamilton, John Jay, Thomas Jefferson, James Madison, and other founders of the United States have been a rich civic legacy for successive generations of citizens. An important means of ensuring that these ideas on constitutional government continue to inspire and guide people in the twenty-first century lies in the curricula of secondary schools. Students need exposure to the constitutional thought of the founders, and the documents that contain the founders' ideas, if they are to be expected to think critically about these ideas in order to identify and maintain the best of them and to modify and improve upon the rest of them. Current secondary school curricula are flawed by neglect of core ideas in the political thought of the founders. This volume is designed to address this flaw; its contents highlight the constitutional thought of important founders in scholarly essays and teaching plans for high school history and government teachers and in document-based learning materials for students. The volume contains nine units, each of which is based on the ideas and primary sources found in essays originally published in *This Constitution: A Bicentennial Chronicle*. Each of the nine units includes four elements: (1) an introduction that announces the topic and main ideas of the constitutional government unit; (2) an essay written by a scholar that highlights primary sources on political ideas of one or more of the founders of the United States (3) a teaching plan for high school history and government teachers to guide their use of learning materials for students based upon the essay; and (4) a lesson for high school students of history and government designed to teach ideas in primary sources featured in the scholarly essay.

Patrick, John J., and Robert S. Leming, eds. 1991. *Resources for Teachers on the Bill of Rights*. Bloomington, IN: ERIC Clearinghouse for Social Studies/Social Science Education. ED 329 489. This document also is available from the Social Studies Development Center, Indiana University, 2805 E. Tenth St., Bloomington, IN 47408. $15.00; $8.00 per copy for orders of 10 or more copies.

Ideas and information that can enhance education about the constitutional rights of individuals in U.S. history and the current system of government in the United States are included in this book. The resource guide contains nine distinct parts dealing with aspects of learning and teaching about the Bill of Rights in both elementary and secondary schools. Part I, "Background Papers," features four essays for teachers on the origins, enactment, and development of the federal Bill of Rights. A fifth paper discusses the substance and strategies for teaching Bill of Rights topics and issues. Part II, "A Bill of Rights Chronology," is a timetable of key dates and events in the making of the federal Bill of Rights. Part III, "Documents," includes eleven primary sources about the origins, enactment, and substance of the federal Bill of Rights. Part IV, "Lessons on the Bill of Rights," consists of nine exemplary lessons. The remaining five parts include "Papers in ERIC on Constitutional Rights," "Select Annotated Bibliography of Curriculum Materials," "Periodical Literature on Teaching the Bill of Rights," "Bill of Rights Bookshelf for Teachers," and "Directory of Key Organizations and Persons."

Quigley, Charles N., et al. 1991. *CIVITAS: A Framework for Civic Education*. Calabasas, CA: Center for Civic Education. ED 340 654. This book also is available from NCSS Publications, Maxway Data Corporation, Suite 1105, 225 W. 34th St., New York, NY 10001. $50 per copy; orders of 10 or more copies are eligible for a 20% discount.

CIVITAS is a curriculum framework that sets forth a set of national goals to be achieved in a civic education curriculum, primarily for K-12 public and private schools. It is a framework that proposes to specify the knowledge and skills needed by citizens to perform their roles in U.S. democracy. There are two major sections in the framework. It begins with a rationale that explains the basic philosophy, purpose, and nature of the framework. The other major section is a statement of goals and objectives that civic education should foster. This section is divided into three parts: Civic Virtue, Civic Participation, and Civic Knowledge and Intellectual Skills. Parts 2 and 3 contain model scope and sequence statements that suggest what aspects of the subjects in the

framework can be taught at varying grade levels and how they may be taught. The part on Civic Knowledge and Intellectual Skills comprises by far the largest portion of the framework. It organizes summaries of numerous topics into three main groupings: the nature of politics and government, public government in the United States, and the role of the citizen.

Reinhartz, Dennis, and Judy Reinhartz. 1990. *Geography Across the Curriculum*. Washington, DC: National Education Association. ED 332 885. This publication also is available from the National Education Association, P.O. Box 509, West Haven, CT 06516. $9.95.

Geography should be infused into existing elementary and secondary school curricula rather than added as another separate subject at various levels. That is the thrust of this monograph, which suggests ways to integrate relevant geographic knowledge, concepts, and skills into specific elementary and secondary subjects. The relationship between geography and history, social studies, foreign languages, English/language arts, the arts, science, mathematics, business, and computer-based instruction is examined. A fifty-five-item bibliography is included, as is an extensive resource list.

Saunders, Phillip, et al. 1984. *Master Curriculum Guide in Economics: A Framework for Teaching the Basic Concepts*. 2d ed. New York: Joint Council on Economic Education. ED 247 198. Paper copy is available only from the Joint Council on Economic Education, 432 Park Ave. S., New York, NY 10016. $5.00.

Intended for curriculum developers, this revised Framework presents a set of basic concepts for teaching K-12 economics. The revision reflects the change and development which the field of economics has undergone and includes improvements suggested by users of the first edition. The purpose of teaching economics is to impart a general understanding of how our economy works and to improve economic decision making by students through the use of an orderly, reasoned approach. Chapters I, II, and III provide a brief introduction to the publication, discuss the elements of economic understanding, and list and describe some basic economic concepts. Chapter IV discusses the broad social goals that seem most important in the United States today, the problem of trade-offs among goals, and the role of self-interest and personal values. Chapter V illustrates the use of a decision-making model with two economic issues involving public policy. The concluding chapter, chapter VI, discusses the grade placement of the economic concepts.

Stoltman, Joseph P. 1990. *Geography Education for Citizenship*. Bloomington, IN: ERIC Clearinghouse for Social Studies/Social Science Education. ED 322 081. This publication also is available from the Social Studies Development Center, Indiana University, 2805 E. Tenth St., Bloomington, IN 47408-2698. $10.00.
Through its approach to knowledge and issues, geography education makes a significant contribution to the development of citizenship and citizenship competencies. The ways that geography education has contributed to citizenship education as the two have developed during this century are examined. It is argued that students who study geography should develop competencies in three areas: (1) literacy in the subject matter of geography; (2) the ability to apply geography, its fundamental themes, skills, and perspectives to a wide range of political, economic, social, and environmental issues; and (3) knowledge to help students actively participate as citizens in their local communities, the nation, and the world. Each of the seven chapters concludes with a list of references.

Study Commission on Global Education. 1987. *The United States Prepares for Its Future: Global Perspectives in Education*. New York: Global Perspectives in Education, Inc. ED 283 758. A paper copy also is available from The American Forum, 45 John St., Suite 1200, New York, NY 10038. $10.00 plus postage.
This report addresses the question of what knowledge and skills should be taught to citizens whose judgment is the ultimate source of policy in a democratic nation. The report recommends the adoption of new goals for school programs, changes in curriculum offerings and in teacher education, creation of curriculum development centers, greater cooperation among schools and universities, and increased support and cooperation from the private sector. The report further recommends that every subject area in primary and secondary schools be approached from a global perspective, and that four curricular areas be emphasized: (1) an understanding of the world as a series of interrelated systems; (2) increased attention to the development of world civilizations as they relate to the history of the United States; (3) greater attention to diversity of cultural patterns; and (4) more training in domestic and international policy analysis. To initiate a global studies program, school districts and states should emphasize existing goals pertaining to citizenship education and global understanding, and teachers should be involved in the planning and implementation of the process. Finally, the report outlines a scope and sequence of courses leading to global awareness by students and recommends appropriate materials for the courses. Appendices include a summary of recommendations of related reports, some statistical data on interdependence, an outline of the kinds of global education courses offered or required in selected states, a selected materials list, and a list of relevant curriculum development centers.

Task Force on International Education. 1989. *America in Transition: The International Frontier*. Washington, DC: National Governors' Association. ED number will be assigned. A paper copy is available only from the National Governors' Association, 444 N. Capitol St., NW, Suite 250, Washington, DC 20001. $10.95.
More than ever, U.S. economic well-being is intertwined with that of other countries through expanding international trade, financial markets, and investments. National security, and even world stability, depend upon U.S. understanding of and communication with other countries. Therefore, international education must be an integral part of the education of every student. This report highlights individual examples of worthy international education programs at all levels from across the country. These pockets of progress must be nurtured and expanded until they grow into a national commitment to international education. State governors must take the lead in creating an international focus for the U.S. educational system at all levels. Critical to the success of this effort will be the involvement of a broad coalition including teachers, school administrators and board members, legislators, university/college presidents and faculty, and the business community. The following objectives for state action are recommended: (1) International education must become part of the basic education for all students; (2) more students must gain proficiency in foreign languages; (3) teachers must know more about international issues; (4) schools and teachers must be aware of the wealth of resources and materials that are available for international education; (5) all college/university

graduates must be knowledgeable about the broader world and conversant in another language; (6) business and community support of international education should be increased; and (7) the business community must have access to international education, particularly information about export markets, trade regulations, and overseas cultures. A fifty-item bibliography is included.

Virginia State Board of Education. 1991. *Voter Education Program: A Guidebook of Teaching Strategies and Resources*. Richmond: Virginia State Board of Education. ED 334 095.
This document is a guidebook containing a sequence of learning strategies to teach facts and concepts of voter education. Strategies are grouped into four grade divisions: primary (K-3), intermediate (4-6), secondary (7-9), and high school (10-12). Each grade section is organized into the following order: introduction, strategy, major idea, learning objectives, teaching strategies, evaluation, teaching aids, vocabulary, lesson critique, and summary. A concluding section contains a bibliography; materials available from the State Board of Elections; a resource list; maps of congressional, senatorial, and Virginia house of delegates districts along with their locations; and a guide to voting in Virginia.

Walstad, William, and John C. Soper. 1988. *A Report Card on the Economic Literacy of U.S. High School Students*. New York: Joint Council on Economic Education. ED 310 055.
A study of over three thousand U.S. high school students who took the Test of Economic Literacy (TEL) in 1986 reveals a lack of basic understanding in the four basic TEL concept clusters (fundamental economics, microeconomics, macroeconomics, and international economics). The TEL was administered pre- and posttest where students were enrolled in one of four types of courses: basic economics, "consumer economics," social studies with economics, and social studies without economics. Students in the economics courses did show significant improvement (+7.5 percent) after the TEL posttest examination while the others did not. Regression analysis was used to identify the effects of variables such as student background and environment or teacher and course preparation. Students in districts that participated in the Developmental Economic Education Program (DEEP), sponsored by the Joint Council on Economic Educa-

tion, scored higher than other students. The amount of college coursework in economics taken by the teachers themselves was directly related to increased student performance in the classroom. A significant amount of ignorance was displayed in basic concepts and relationships in macroeconomics and international economics. Three tables of TEL data and twelve references are included in the report.

Walstad, William B., and John C. Soper, eds. 1991. *Effective Economic Education in the Schools*. New York: Joint Council on Economic Education. ED 332 904. This publication also is available from the National Education Association, P.O. Box 509, West Haven, CT 06516. $21.95.
The Developmental Economic Education Program (DEEP) was launched in 1964 by the Joint Council on Economic Education as an experimental program in three school districts. By 1989 there were 1,836 school districts enrolled in DEEP, covering some 39 percent of the precollege student population. This book tells the story of DEEP, an effort to improve the economics education curriculum by involving teachers, administrators, universities, and businesses in a curriculum change partnership. This current look at the DEEP experience is divided into five major parts. Part I consists of four chapters that give a rationale for economic education and explain in more detail the features of the DEEP model. Part II focuses on the research and evaluation that have been conducted over the twenty-five-year history of DEEP and on related studies of economic understanding among students in secondary and elementary grades. The next two parts offer case studies of how DEEP works. Part III looks at DEEP operations and issues in four diverse states. Part IV shows how the DEEP process works in six different school districts. In Part V the focus shifts from the present to the future; these chapters discuss the future of DEEP in the context of educational reform, requirements for new curriculum materials, needs of school districts, and leadership from the Joint Council on Economic Education.

Exemplary Multimedia Materials

Backler, Alan L. 1988. *Global Geography: A Teacher's Guide*. Bloomington, IN: Agency for Instructional Technology. ED 316 491. This publication and ten 15-minute video programs are available from AIT, Box A, Bloomington, IN 47402. Information about prices is provided by AIT.

Intended for use with grades 6-9, "Global Geography" is a series of ten 15-minute video programs that help students think their way through important issues and increase their understanding of world geography. The programs fit easily into normal classroom schedules and support the content of most existing course sequences. This guide is designed to help teachers use the video programs for their fullest possible instructional value. Each of the lessons, keyed to the video programs, contains a summary of the conceptual and thematic foundations of the video program, a summary of what appears on the screen, a glossary of key terms, and suggestions for activities before and during the program to help students understand the issues that have been introduced. In addition, each lesson includes discussion questions for use after viewing and ideas for activities with local application, so teachers can help students understand how the fundamental themes of world geography have relevance in their own communities. A list of supplementary readings and video materials is included, as are reproducible handouts to go with the lessons. A fold-out correlation matrix relates each "Global Geography" program to chapters in the geography textbooks most commonly used in middle and junior high schools. Black and white photographs are included.

CCA High School Social Science Curriculum Project. 1990. *U.S. Government, U.S. History, and Introductory Economics: Instructor's Guide.* Urbana: University of Illinois. ED 335 287. This publication and related computer programs are available from Computer-Based Education Research Laboratory, 103 S. Matthews Ave., Urbana, IL 61801. Information about prices is available from the distributor.

Descriptions of lessons within each of three computer-based curricula for high school students (U.S. government, U.S. history, and introductory economics) are presented in this instructor's manual. Each curriculum is divided into lesson units and covers basic concepts. The reading level is approximately tenth grade. Each unit consists of a pretest and computer instruction. If students do not pass a pretest, they are assigned the appropriate lesson. Posttests are not given because the lessons are mastery-based and give students

intensive review drills. The U.S. history curriculum is composed of fifteen units and fifteen lessons. The introductory economics curriculum is composed of five units and five lessons. This manual is intended only as a supplementary guide to the computer programs containing the lessons to be used in the classroom.

C-Span Classroom Project. 1990. *C-Span in the American Government Classroom.* Washington, DC: National Cable Satellite Corporation. ED 328 477. This publication is available from C-Span in the Classroom, 400 N. Capitol St., NW, Washington, DC 20001.

Encouraging educators' use of live and unedited television coverage of the functions of government, this publication contains seven lessons for the high school social studies curriculum. C-Span has no time or space constraints and broadcasts all events in their entirety; unedited lessons teach concepts and objectives, and emphasis is on the process of government. Lessons cover congressional hearings, how a bill becomes law, negotiating and compromising, congressional leadership, qualifications for Congress, Congress and the executive branch, and types of persuasion. Each lesson has an overview, list of objectives procedure, follow-up activities, and worksheets.

Erickson, Roy. 1991. *Macintosh Education Software Correlation Guide to the History-Social Science Framework for California Public Schools.* Cupertino, CA: Apple Computer, Inc. ED number will be assigned. This guide also is available from Apple Computer, Inc., 20525 Mariani Ave., Cupertino, CA 95014.

This guide is an annotated list of computer software programs dealing with various subjects of the social studies. Programs on geography and history are emphasized. Information about the availability of all materials, including prices, is presented.

Fleet, Jim, and John J. Patrick. 1987. *America Past: Teacher's Guide.* Bloomington, IN: Agency for Instructional Technology. ED 286 819. This publication and sixteen 15-minute video programs are available from AIT, Box A, Bloomington, IN 47402. Information about prices is available from AIT.

This teacher's guide was designed to accompany sixteen video programs that trace the social and cultural development of the United States and show that today's society is the result of diverse historical events, ideas, and people. The guide provides program summaries, ideas for discussion, review questions, and extra credit projects. Spanish, French, and English cultural contributions and their impact on U.S. society are detailed. The distinct social cultures that developed in the southern and New England colonies and their effect are emphasized. The development of transportation unified parts of the nation and gave impetus to the westward movement and industrialization of the north. These events are presented in several programs. The many reform movements (abolition, women's rights, utopian reform) that changed the nation and gave it its character are all part of the series. The way in which artists and writers contributed to the culture and helped to preserve it is also explored.

Grewar, Melinda. 1991. *Common Issues in World Regions: Teacher's Guide*. Bloomington, IN: Agency for Instructional Technology. ED number will be assigned. This publication and eight 30-minute video programs are available from AIT, Box A, Bloomington, IN 47402. Information about prices is available from AIT. This teacher's guide is designed to supplement eight 30-minute video programs, each of which presents two case studies that explore an issue from North American (United States and Canada) and Western European perspectives. The series of programs is intended to strengthen what junior and senior high school students in the United States and Canada learn about Western Europe as well as about their own countries. It is hoped that the series will help students learn how certain issues affect people, especially children their own age, and enable them to explore similarities and differences in the ways people of these regions respond to the issues. The video programs are constructed along basic geographic themes: location, place, human/environmental interaction, and movement. Each program explores now an issue related to these themes affects target-age students and their families in North America and Western Europe. The program topics are "Urban Renewal in Canada and Scotland," "Suburbanization in the United States and Italy," "Industrial Change in the United States and Germany," "Immigration to the United States and France," "Impact of Tourism in the United States and Spain," "Survival of the Family Farm in the United States and the Netherlands," "Environmental Problems in the United States and Norway," and "Isolation in Canada

and Switzerland." This teacher's guide provides program summaries, glossaries, suggested lesson plans, follow-up activities, reproducible maps, and a list of additional resources.

National Geographic Society. 1990. *GTV: A Geographic Perspective on American History*. Washington, DC: National Geographic Society. This product is distributed by Optical Data Corporation, 30 Technology Dr., Warren, NJ 07059. $995.00.
Computers and laser discs present a visual journey through American history, with a special focus on geography. Each segment treats a different topic. Software allows rearrangement of maps and pictures to create individualized presentations. This interactive video program includes two double-sided discs and accompanying HyperCard stacks. Three types of information are presented: (1) surveys of themes in American history, (2) primary documents, and (3) population data for particular periods of American history. The HyperCard stacks enable users to locate and organize particular historical or geographic information, maps, and graphs. A HyperCard stack in "Music" provides access to each piece of music used to accompany different parts of the video. The final part of the HyperCard stacks enables users to make their own programs from information on the videodiscs.

Nelson, Elizabeth, and Edward Nelson. 1990. *Social Science Instructional Modules Workshop*. Los Angeles: UCLA. ED 330 304.
The five instructional packages in this collection were created by faculty members in the California state universities to introduce students--and even faculty--to the easy steps involved in working with computers in instructional settings. Designed for students and faculty in entry-level courses who have little or no background in quantitative data analysis or computer use, the learning modules can also be made part of more advanced courses. They use actual, current data sets from the 1980s and are designed to be incorporated either as principal or supplemental instructional materials in the social sciences, political science, history, ethnic studies, women's studies, and quantitative methods courses. The modules can be used with the California central cyber system and SPSS or with an IBM/PC and SPSS/PC+. Each manual provides background information on the specific topic, an introduction to sampling and quantitative analysis, a codebook, instructions for use with

the main frame and microcomputers, and a series of graduated exercises that lead students into progressively more complex processes. This document contains summaries of the instructional modules; ordering information; instructions for getting started with the modules and integrating them into the classroom; using SPSS on campus; using SPSSX on the central cyber; and using SPSSONL on the central cyber. Also included are lists of project participants and campus representatives. Abstracts for each of the five modules are provided at the end of the document.

Patrick, John J. 1987. *The U.S. Constitution: A Teacher's Guide*. Bloomington, IN: Agency for Instructional Technology. ED 286 820. This publication and six 30-minute video programs are available from AIT, Box A, Bloomington, IN 47402. Information about prices is provided by AIT.

This teacher's guide was designed to accompany six 30-minute video programs on the fundamental constitutional principles that form this nation's foundation. Each lesson in the guide contains an introduction to the main ideas of the program, a program summary, and suggested activities to carry out before and after the program. The topics emphasized in the series are (1) limited government and the rule of law, (2) federalism, (3) separation of powers with checks and balances, (4) freedom of expression, (5) equal protection of the laws, and (6) the U.S Constitution and the economy. A copy of the constitution is appended.

Patrick, John J., and Joseph P. Stoltman. 1991. *Geography in American History: A Teacher's Guide*. Bloomington, IN: Agency for Instructional Technology. ED 337 386. This publication and ten 20-minute video programs are

available from AIT, Box A, Bloomington, IN 47401. Information about prices is provided by AIT.

Designed to accompany a series of ten video programs, this teaching guide helps students to use geographical principles and concepts in order to better understand major historical developments. The series uses the five basic geographic themes to enhance student understanding of significant events in U.S. history: location, place, human/environment relationships, movement, and regions. The ten programs in the series are (1) North vs. South in the Founding of the U.S.A., 1787-1796; (2) Jefferson Decides to Purchase Louisiana, 1801-1813; (3) Civil War and Social Change in Georgia, 1865-1890; (4) Clash of Cultures on the Great Plains, 1865-1890; (5) An Industrial Revolution in Pittsburgh, 1865-1900; (6) Americans Build the Panama Canal, 1901-1914; (7) A Nation of Immigrants: The Chinese-American Experience, 1850-1990; (8) Moving North to Chicago, 1900-1945; (9) New Deal for the Dust Bowl, 1931-1945; and (10) The Origin and Development of NATO, 1945-1991. This guide includes materials for teachers to help them utilize the videos in their classrooms. The discussion of each program in this guide features the following sections: curriculum connection, objectives, geographic theme, program summary, before the program, during the program, after the program, follow-up activities, and suggested readings. Handouts and documents accompany each program.

CURRICULUM GUIDE REPRINTS

CURRICULUM developers can often find ideas and models through the study of curriculum guides from state departments of education and school districts. In this chapter, we have reprinted the following materials:

I. *China Mosaic: Multidisciplinary Units for the Middle Grades.* 1988 (reprinted 1990). Olympia, WA: Office of the Superintendent of Public Instruction. Reproduced with permission.
This chapter reproduces the following parts of this curriculum guide: introductory matter, units on the Qin Dynasty and Confucius, and the three appendices: a pronunciation guide, a weights and measures guide, and a curriculum materials list. These extracts comprise just a portion of this 142-page guide. The guide provides a wide range of lessons and activities on China, including lesson objectives, background for the teacher, student readings, and worksheets. *China Mosaic* offers numerous ideas on developing a multidisciplinary course, as well as a variety of lessons. For complete copies of this guide, please contact the Office of the Superintendent of Public Instruction, P.O. Box 47200, Olympia, WA 98504-7200.

II. *American Heritage: A Curriculum for 5th Grade Social Studies.* 1990. Grand Junction, CO: Mesa County Valley School District No. 51. Reproduced with permission.
The introductory matter and the Native Americans unit of this guide have been reprinted here on pages 177-247. The introductory matter includes the district's social studies mission statement, as well as information on curriculum goals, scope and sequence, and skills in social studies. The Native Americans unit provides (among other material) unit outcomes, topic outline, and activities/resources for each lesson. This unit offers ideas on ways to develop a similar unit on Native Americans, or on other social studies topics.

While we have not reprinted this guide in its entirety, we do provide the table of contents so that readers can see what other topics are covered. (The reprinted sections are designated in the table of contents.) For a complete copy of *American Heritage,* contact the Mesa County Valley School District No. 51, 2523 Patterson Road, Grand Junction, CO 81501.

CHINA MOSAIC:

Multidisciplinary Units for the Middle Grades

CHINA MOSAIC:
MULTIDISCIPLINARY UNITS FOR THE MIDDLE GRADES

Judith A. Billings
Superintendent

Bridge L. Cullerton
Administrator
Curriculum, Instructional Support
and Special Education Services

Gene Liddell
Director
Curriculum

Nancy R. Motomatsu
Supervisor
International Education

Editor:

Mary Hammond Bernson

East Asia Resource Center
Jackson School of International Studies
Thomson DR-5
University of Washington
Seattle, Washington   98195

July, 1988
Reprinted: November, 1988
March, 1989
February, 1990

CHINA MOSAIC:
MULTIDISCIPLINARY UNITS
FOR THE MIDDLE GRADES

A NOTE TO TEACHERS

The authors of the lessons in China Mosaic are committed to the idea that students in American classrooms must learn about the rest of the world, and that upper elementary and middle school grades are ideal times to explore this world we live in. The teachers who wrote the lessons share an interest in China and a strong belief that information about other countries and cultures should be integrated into all subjects across the curriculum. These lessons show how it can be done, incorporating skills and knowledge taught not only in social studies and language arts but also in art, science and math. In this way, China can come alive for students, even when the curriculum does not officially include it as a topic.

These lessons were written by Sam Hayes, Tarry Lindquist, Elaine Magnusson, Marte Peet, and Theresa Ralph with additional suggestions and comments from Robert Blair, Barbara Guilfoil, Vincent Hagel, Roger Malfait, and Bonnie Whitman. They are the elementary and middle school teachers who participated in a 1986 Fulbright Group Project Abroad sponsored by the East Asia Resource Center, at the Jackson School of International Studies, University of Washington. Directors of the project were Professor Jack Dull, Director of the East Asia Center; Mary Hammond Bernson, Outreach Director of the Center; and Dru Gladney, an anthropologist.

Both in China and after their return, the group members worked as a team, sharing ideas and observations. All of them contributed to this book and to the success of the project. The teachers and their schools at the time of the project were: Robert Blair, McKnight Middle School, Renton; James Campbell, Hanford High School, Richland; David Carpentier, Marysville-Pilchuck High School, Marysville; Keith Forest, Decatur High School, Federal Way; Barbara Guilfoil, Lockwood Elementary School, Bothell; Vincent Hagel, Oak Harbor Middle School, Oak Harbor; Sam Hayes, Washington Middle School, Olympia; Tarry Lindquist, Lakeridge Elementary School, Mercer Island; Elaine Magnusson, Northshore Public Schools, Bothell; Roger Malfait, North Kitsap High School, Poulsbo; Richard Moulden, Chinook Middle School, Bellevue; Jack Parcell, Marysville Junior High School, Marysville; Marte Peet, Gause Intermediate School, Washougal; Theresa Ralph, Assumption School, Seattle; Bert Reese, Lynnwood High School, Lynnwood; Chuck Wade, Kent-Meridian High School, Kent; and Bonnie Whiteman, Kenroy Elementary School, East Wenatchee.

Our deepest gratitude is due to all the people who reviewed individual lessons, including Ding Xiang Warner, Warren Burton, Gina May, Jan Graves, and Larry Strickland. Many University of Washington faculty members contributed their expertise as well. Suzi Berard deserves special thanks; without her perseverance and dedication this book would not have reached its final form.

Mary Hammond Bernson, Outreach Director
East Asia Resource Center
Jackson School of International Studies DR-05
University of Washington
Seattle, Washington 98195

CHINA MOSAIC:
MULTIDISCIPLINARY UNITS
FOR THE MIDDLE GRADES

TABLE OF CONTENTS

1

THE QIN DYNASTY

GRADE LEVEL: 3rd through 6th grade

TIME: 1-5 days; depending upon the number of activities

OBJECTIVES: The students will:

1. recognize the accomplishments of China's first emperor.

2. understand the importance of these accomplishments in the development of Chinese history.

3. utilize reading, art, and math skills to help them appreciate ancient accomplishments.

MATERIALS:

1. student reading on the Qin Dynasty

2. student worksheets and vocabulary sheets

3. Materials for the follow-up activities are listed under each activity.

TEACHER BACKGROUND:

Qin Shihuangdi is a good emperor to teach about if you choose just one. He is extremely important in Chinese history, although the Chinese have argued for well over 1,000 years about how to judge his deeds. In modern times, Chairman Mao labeled him bad but later revised his estimation to good. Nowadays students study him in history classes and are taught that the Great Wall is his greatest contribution to Chinese civilization.

Because of his recently excavated burial site, Qin Shihuangdi has received extensive coverage in the western press and students can find many articles about him. Some of his tomb figures can be seen in traveling exhibits.

2

DAY 1:

PROCEDURE:

1. Hand out the student reading on "The Qin Dynasty."

2. Instruct the students to make vocabulary cards of underlined and unfamiliar words.

3. With older students, point out that there are various ways of romanizing Chinese (writing it in our alphabet system.) As they learn about this dynasty they may encounter Qin or Ch'in and Qin Shihuangdi or Ch'in Shih Huang-ti. The literal translation of the title is "First Emperor of Chin."

3

STUDENT READING:

STUDENT READING:

THE QIN DYNASTY
(221b.c. - 207b.c.)

THE EMPIRE BEGINS

The man who was to become China's first emperor was crowned king in 246 b.c. at the age of thirteen. Since he was too young to rule, a powerful <u>chancellor</u>, Lu Buwei, ruled until the king was 21 years old.

Through the use of spies and military might the king began to fulfill his dream of uniting the six <u>separate</u> kingdoms that made up China at this time into one empire. By the time he was 38 years old he had succeeded in creating a new kingdom ten times the size of the old one.

Since this was such a <u>spectacular</u> <u>accomplishment</u> the king decided he needed a new title. So the created the title First Sovereign Emperor of Qin, in Chinese, Qin Shihuangdi. It was from this emperor that China obtained its western name.

Although the Emperor Qin was well known for cruelty and hated by many of his subjects, many reforms he established lasted until the fall of the last <u>dynasty</u> in 1912.

ACCOMPLISHMENTS

STANDARDIZED WEIGHTS AND MEASURES

Before the Qin Dynasty, China was divided into many different kingdoms, each with its own language, writing, laws and measurements. To ensure that all kingdoms would be the same, the emperor standardized all systems of weights and measurements. He even standardized the axle widths of wagons, making transportation on rutted dirt roads easier. The laws for the whole empire were also made the same, as were the cruel punishments for disobedience.

4

LANGUAGE AND WRITING

Perhaps the most important accomplishment was the development of a single form of writing. Now the people from different parts of the empire could <u>communicate</u> even though they spoke different versions of the Chinese language.

Emperor Qin made these reforms not because he wanted everyone to be able to read and write but to <u>ensure</u> that his laws were obeyed. In fact, he hated teachers and ordered all books to be burned, except those on what he called "useful" subjects like farming, medicine and ancient history. He believed that uneducated people would not <u>criticize</u> his rule.

THE GREAT WALL

It was during Qin Shihuangdi's rule that the separate walls of many different kingdoms were joined together to create the Great Wall of China. The Great Wall stretched 1400 miles across north and northwest China. The wall was wide with watch towers built every 100 yards.

The Great Wall was built with forced labor. Some laborers were criminals but others were enemies of the Emperor and peasants taken from their land and forced to work. They worked in <u>remote</u> areas with little food or shelter, while one quarter of a million soldiers kept watch over them. Thousands died from starvation and <u>exhaustion</u>.

The Chinese say that every stone in the wall cost one human life. However, the wall protected China's northern frontier from the nomadic peoples, later called Tartars, who frequently came south to raid the Chinese settlements.

5

The original building which housed the warriors
collapsed thousands of years ago crushing the soldiers
inside. Today the archaeologists number these pieces and
carefully <u>reconstruct</u> them into their original form.
Sometimes this takes as long as two years. The completed
warriors are then placed in their original position in the
pit.

Qin Shihuangdi's tomb stands where the original capital
was, a few miles from Xi'an, in the Yellow River basin. He
was a cruel and heartless ruler but he left a monument that
amazes all who come to view it. Some people even consider
the army of terracotta warriors to be the eighth wonder of
the world.

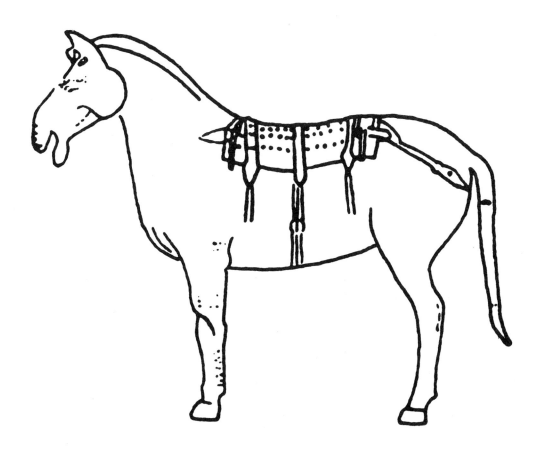

6

QIN SHIHUANGDI'S TOMB

It is not surprising that toward the end of his life the Emperor began to become fearful of being killed. He had a huge tomb and army built to protect him even after his death.

It is the Emperor's tomb that fascinates the modern world. Built by thousands of slaves, this tomb was to be the empire he expected to rule over after death. His actual tomb has not been <u>excavated</u> but early writings tell what might be inside.

"The slaves dug underground chambers and painted replicas of the sun, moon, and stars. On the floor was a map of Qin's Empire. The Yangzi and Yellow Rivers were filled with liquid <u>mercury</u>. Simple machines made the rivers flow. Finally, mechanically triggered crossbows were set to shoot anyone who entered."

To the east of this tomb, for its protection, lies an army of lifesized clay soldiers. This army of terracotta soldiers was first discovered in 1974 by peasants digging for a well. Several different pits were dig and the <u>archaeologists</u> began to put the pieces of the army together.

In pit number one, 1,000 warriors and 24 horses have been <u>excavated.</u> It is estimated that the pit contains over 6,000 warriors and horses. The bronze swords carried by some of the soldiers are still sharp after being buried for over 2,000 years.

Pit number two contains about 1,000 warriors and 80 chariots pulled by 400 horses. Many are infantrymen and charioteers as well as archers and cavalrymen. The archers carry either longbows or crossbows. The cavalrymen are leading their saddled horses.

Pit number three is the smallest. It contains 68 warriors and one chariot with 4 horses. Archaeologists believe that this was the commander's headquarters.

The warriors range in size from about five feet to over six feet tall. They were made from shaped coils of clay, covered with a clay slip (clay wash), then baked and painted.

The basic warrior's head was made from several molds. Then the ears, facial features and hair were added on, giving each warrior a <u>personality</u> uniquely his. The neck was long and just slipped into the body of the warrior.

7

STUDENT WORKSHEET

VOCABULARY

Write each of the underlined words in the article on a vocabulary card. Look them up in the dictionary and write the correct definition on the vocabulary card. Make sure that the definition makes sense in the context of the sentence. Keep the cards to use in your writing.

COMPREHENSION QUESTIONS

1. How did China obtain its western name?

_____

2. How many years did Emperor Qin need to create his empire?

_____

3. Describe the accomplishments of the Qin Dynasty. Tell why they were important.

_____

_____

_____

_____

_____

_____

4. Many people are amazed by the terracotta warriors. Why do you think some people consider them the eighth wonder of the world?

_____

5. Some people consider the terracotta warriors to be the eighth wonder of the world. Become an explorer and search for the original seven wonders of the world. Make a list of the seven wonders of the world and where they are located. Explain why they are considered to be so important.

8

Vocabulary

Word:

Definition:

Vocabulary

Word:

Definition:

Vocabulary

Word:

Definition:

Vocabulary

Word:

Definition:

9

DAY TWO: SIMULATION OF TRADE

OBJECTIVES: The students will:

1. understand the importance of the standardization of
    weights and measurements.

MATERIALS:

1. trade cards

PROCEDURE:

1. Divide the students into six teams called kingdoms.

2. Each kingdom picks an item to trade.

3. The kingdoms then make up a name and amount for the
    weight or measurement of their item.

4. Explain that their task is to trade their item to
    another kingdom for that kingdom's trade item.
    Their trade must be fair, keeping in mind the
    measurement and weight as well as the value of
    the item.

    Kingdom A decides to trade a "ping" of wheat.
    Kingdom B wants to trade a "gilp" of silk. They
    must get together and decide how many "gilps" they
    will trade for a "ping" or vice versa.

    This is not a true simulation of the situation that
    existed during the Qin Empire and before. In
    reality the people from the different kingdoms
    would have been speaking different languages,
    further complicating the trade.

5. After the activity, discuss with the students the
    problems they encountered.

    a. What problems did you have?
    b. Were they solved? If so, how?
    c. How would you change the situation so that the
        trading would be easier?
    d. Do you feel that you received a fair trade?
        Why/Why not?

10

EXTENSION ACTIVITIES:

1. Repeat the activity using a standard system of
    weights and measurements such as American or
    European. Ask the students:

    a. How did the trading change?
    b. Was it easier to trade? Why/Why not?
    c. Imagine what problems would exist if every
        state in the United States had a different
        system of measurement.
    d. Do you know of any comparable situations
        between modern nations?

Animals	Fruits
Silk	Pottery
Wheat	Millet
Weapons	Cloth

12

DAY THREE: TERRACOTTA WARRIORS

OBJECTIVES: The students will:

1.   gain an understanding of the size and scope of the terracotta army by creating a small replica of the archaeological dig.

MATERIALS:

1.   paper doll pattern

2.   large cardboard box and dirt (optional)

3.   brown paper and toilet paper rolls

4.   glue and scissors

PROCEDURE:

1.   Each student colors and cuts out one or two warriors and pastes them to toilet paper rolls.

2.   Stand the warriors in columns inside a large cardboard box lined with brown paper.

3.   In the back of the box, mound dirt to simulate the unexcavated soldiers.

4.   Have the students write a paragraph describing the tomb and its importance.

5.   Ask the students to calculate how many warriors each of their warriors represents, i.e. if the class makes 60 warriors then each warrior represents 100 warriors in pit #1.

ALTERNATE ACTIVITY:

MATERIALS:

1.   cut out paper dolls

2.   box filled with dirt, sand, or small pieces of styrofoam

PROCEDURE:

1.   Cut out some paper dolls. Then cut them into pieces and place them in a box of dirt.

2.   The children dig for the pieces and number them as they find them.

14

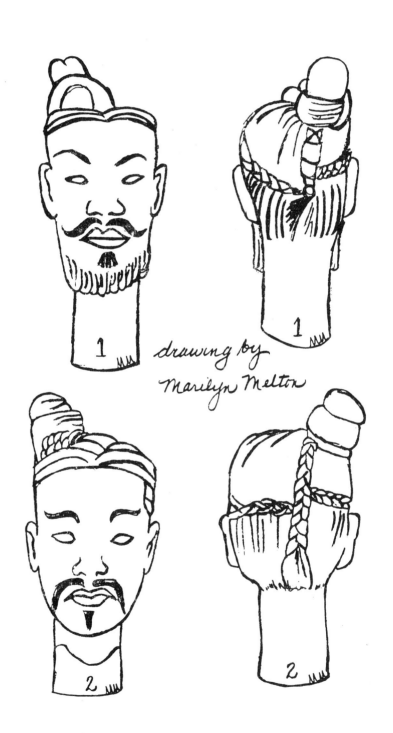

drawing by
Marilyn Melton

13

3. They then reconstruct the pieces into a warrior.

ALTERNATE ACTIVITY:

MATERIALS:

1. overhead projector

2. paper doll pattern

3. colored felt tip markers

4. large sheet of paper

PROCEDURE:

1. Project a warrior on the overhead onto a large
    sheet of paper.

2. Have the students trace a large six foot
    tall warrior.

3. Color the warrior and post him outside the
    classroom door.

ALTERNATE ACTIVITY:

MATERIALS:

1. plain paper doll pattern

PROCEDURE:

1. Using the plain head and body have the students
    create their own warrior.

2. The students write a brief description of who
    this person is. What is his job in the army? How
    does he feel about his job and his country? What
    are his feelings about the emperor?

15

16

CUT LINE FOR
HEAD INSERT

17

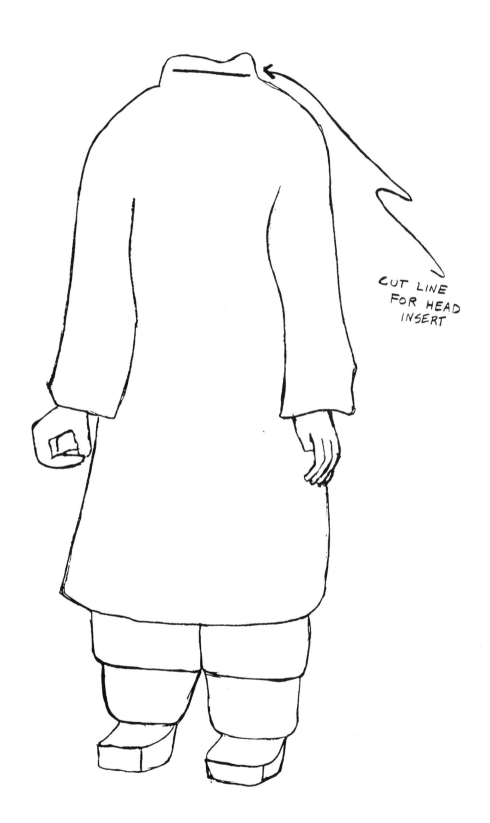

CUT LINE
FOR HEAD
INSERT

18

20

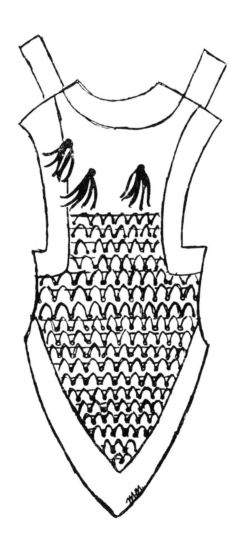

19

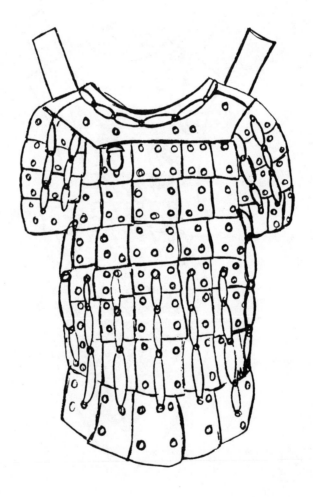

21

DAY FOUR: The Great Wall

OBJECTIVES: The students will:

1. recognize the size and scope of the construction of the Great Wall.

2. become acquainted with Chinese systems of measurement.

MATERIALS:

1. books or encyclopedias

PROCEDURE:

1. Find a chart of the Chinese system of measurements.* Note that the Chinese use the metric system for international trade. Traditional Chinese units of measurements are used for domestic transactions.

2. Calculate the length, height and width of the Great wall using Chinese measurements.

3. Calculate the above measurements of the Great Wall using the metric system.

ALTERNATE ACTIVITY:

MATERIALS:

1. The Great Wall by Leonard Everett Fisher.

PROCEDURE:

1. Make a diorama or model of the Great Wall using the book as a reference.

2. Label specific parts of the model with the appropriate Chinese characters.

3. Write a story about the construction of the Great Wall from the perspective of a particular character, such as a laborer, an advisor, a soldier, the Emperor, or a nomad outside the wall.

* see appendix

22

REFERENCES:

TEACHER AND STUDENT RESOURCES:

1. <u>Ancient China</u>*, by G.W. Barrett. Essex, England: Longman House, 1969.

2. <u>China</u>. Alexandria, Virginia: Time-Life Books, 1986.

3. <u>China: A History to 1949</u>, by Valjean McLenighan. Chicago: Childrens Press, 1983.

4. <u>The Underground Terracotta Army of Emperor Qin Shi Huang</u>, edited by Fu Tianchou. Beijing, China: New World Press, 1983.

STUDENT RESOURCES:

1. <u>The Ancient Chinese</u>, by Lai Po Kan. Silver Burdett.

2. <u>An Ancient Chinese Town</u> edited by R.J. Unstead. Barnes and Noble, 1986.

3. <u>The Great Wall</u>, by Leonard Everett Fisher. New York: Macmillan, 1986.

MEDIA

1. <u>The Heart of the Dragon</u>, "Remembering."

*These books are available through "China Books & Periodicals", 2929 2nd St., San Francisco, CA 94110 or "China in the Classroom, The Center for Teaching about China", 2025 Eye St., N.W., Suite 715, Washington, D.C. 2006.

23

<u>CONFUCIUS</u>

<u>GRADE LEVEL</u>: 3rd through 6th grade

<u>TIME</u>: 2 forty-minute sessions

<u>OBJECTIVES</u>: The students will:

   1. be introduced to China's greatest traditional
      philosopher.

   2. find parallels between Confucian and Western
      sayings.

   3. create original sayings about Western behavior.

<u>MATERIALS</u>:

   1. student readings (masters included)

<u>PROCEDURE</u>:

   1. Ask students what, if anything, they have heard
      about Confucius. Ask if they know any "Confucian
      sayings," either authentic or humorous. Point out
      that the influence of Confucius has been so
      enormous that people still quote his sayings now,
      almost 2500 years after his death.

   2. Distribute copies of the student reading and ask
      students to read them and fill in the blanks at
      the end. Ask students to share their own sayings,
      identifying the Confucian saying theirs most
      resembles.

   3. Ask students to identify differences and
      similarities between Confucian and Western
      ideal behavior, reminding them that people, past
      and present, are not perfect or ideal.

   4. Ask them to identify sources of Western behavioral
      rules and customs, such as religious teachings,
      hygiene, or desire for status.

   5. Have students create original sayings about
      Western ideal behavior and write them on the
      bottom of the worksheet.

   6. Collect worksheets and share original sayings via
      discussions or bulletin boards.

24

STUDENT READING:

CONFUCIUS
(551-479 b.c.)

Confucius lived during the Zhou dynasty (1028 b.c. - 256 b.c.), called by historians "The Warring States Period." Civil war between parts of China was common. Confucius looked to China's past history as a time of happiness and peace. He believed, after studying ancient history, that the perfect society could again exist if people followed certain rules of conduct.

Confucius was not very famous during his lifetime. It was long after his death, during the Han dynasty (206 b.c.- 220 a.d.), that Confucius became famous as a great teacher. His writings, in time, became an important part of the Chinese educational and governmental systems. His teaching also formed the basis of how an educated person lived in society.

Confucius believed that everyone must show good manners and behave properly, so he developed a long list of guidelines for proper conduct in every situation.

CONFUCIAN RULES

DRESS AND FOOD

Clothes must be dark; bright colors were for the uneducated. People must not eat or drink too much and the food must be prepared to perfection.

MEETING PEOPLE

The most important rule was "be polite," showing no anger or silliness. Bowing when greeting someone became an important way to show respect. The older and more important the person the deeper the bow. In the presence of the king one performed the "three kneelings and nine knockings," which means kneeling and bowing three times with each kneel.

FAMILY RULES

The guiding rule in a Confucian home was filial piety, showing respect to one's parents. Old age was a sign of wisdom and the most important member of the family was the oldest male. The second most important member was the oldest woman, if she was the mother of the oldest son. Everyone had a place in the family order and rules to govern their behavior. Children were expected to obey their father and to honor and serve him. If the children disobeyed their parents they would bring dishonor to the whole family.

25

WOMEN'S ROLE

The Confucian society was a man's world. When a woman married she went to live with her husband's family and that family became her new home. Her role was to obey her husband and raise his children. A Confucian rule said: "Women and people of low birth are very hard to deal with. If you are friendly with them they get out of hand, and if you keep them at a distance they resent it."

SUMMARY

Confucius' philosophy was taught generation after generation. His ideas became such a basic part of Chinese thinking that they were sometimes not even labeled as his. An example of their importance is the fact that all government officials until the beginning of this century had to pass a test about Confucius' writings.

China has been through great changes since the Revolution and Chinese leaders have attacked Confucius' ideas as wrong and old-fashioned. Although students nowadays do not study Confucius in school, many of his teachings live on as basic Chinese beliefs.

Although Confucius lived thousands of years ago, many of his sayings may sound familiar. See if you can find a Confucian version of "Mind your own business" and "The Golden Rule".

CONFUCIAN SAYINGS

"Attack the evil that is within yourself, not the evil that is in others."

"Never do to others what you would not like them to do to you."

"Always changing yourself to suit others keeps you from excellence."

"Set a good example, then ask others to follow it."

"Let the other man do his job without your interference."

"A man who thinks only of himself will make many enemies."

"Love your fellow man."

26

TO THE STUDENTS:

Read over the Confucian sayings. Think of western sayings that are similar to the ones above. Write your sayings on the lines below.

SAYING 1: _____

_____

_____

_____

SAYING 2: _____

_____

_____

_____

SAYING 3: _____

_____

_____

_____

27

REFERENCES:

1. <u>Ancient China</u> by G.W. Barrell. Essex, England:
   Longman House, 1969.

2. <u>The Foolish Old Man Who Moved Mountains</u>
   by Marie-Louise Gebhardt. New York: Friendship
   Press, 1969.

3. <u>What Did Confucius Say</u> by the East Asian Curriculum
   Project New York: East Asian Institute,
   Columbia University.

APPENDIX 1:

PRONUNCIATION GUIDE

Chinese words in this book are written in the Pinyin romanization system, which is the one most commonly used to write the Chinese language in a Roman alphabet. Until recently, names were more often written in the Wade-Giles romanization system. This has caused changes such as Zhou instead of Chou for that dynasty and Qin Shihuangdi instead of Ch'in Shih-huang ti for the First Emperor. Mao Tse-t'ung is now written Mao Zedong.

Most Pinyin symbols are pronounced more or less as English-speakers would expect, with the exception of:

c	is pronounced like the ts in it's
q	is pronounced like the ch in cheap
x	is pronounced like the sh in sheen
zh	is pronounced like the j in jump
z	is pronounced like the ds in lids
e	is pronounced like the e in talent or the uh in huh
e	before ng is pronounced like the u in rung
o	is pronounced like the aw in law
ou	is pronounced like the o in go

Chinese is a tonal language, with the standard dialect using four tones. Using the syllable "ma" as an example, the tones are:

ma	first tone:	relatively high-pitched, does not rise or fall
ma	second tone:	mid-range, rises rapidly
ma	third tone:	starts mid-range, dips to a low pitch and then rises
ma	fourth tone:	starts high and falls rapidly

Since tones are essential to the meaning of the syllables in Chinese, the four examples of "ma" can mean, among other things:

mā	mother
má	hemp
mǎ	horse
mà	scold

<u>APPENDIX 2</u>:

<u>WEIGHTS AND MEASURES</u>

LENGTH:

     1 <u>li</u> = 0.31 mile = 0.5 kilometer
     1 <u>chi</u> = 1.09 feet = 0.33 meter

     1 mile = 3.22 <u>li</u> = 1.61 kilometers
     1 foot = 0.91 <u>chi</u> = 0.31 meter

     1 <u>chi</u> = 10 <u>cun</u>
     1 <u>cun</u> = 1.2 inches

AREA:

     1 <u>mu</u> = 0.16 acre = 6.67 hectares
     1 acre = 6.07 <u>mu</u> = 0.41 hectare
     1 hectare = 15 <u>mu</u> = 2.47 acres

WEIGHT:

     1 <u>jin</u> = 1.1 pounds = 0.5 kilogram
     1 pound = 0.91 <u>jin</u> = 0.45 kilogram

141

APPENDIX 3:

CURRICULUM MATERIALS ABOUT CHINA

Sources for good teaching materials about China include:

CTIR PRESS, Center for Teaching International Relations, University of Denver, Denver, Colorado 80208. CTIR distributes a variety of useful materials, including Changing Images of China and Demystifying the Chinese Language, both of which use creative activities to further cultural awareness. Suitable for a wide range of grade levels.

CHINA BOOKS AND PERIODICALS, 2929 Twenty-fourth Street, San Francisco, California 94110. This is the best single source for English-language materials from and about China. The free catalog includes craft items and children's books.

EAST ASIA RESOURCE CENTER, Jackson School of International Studies, Thomson DR-05, University of Washington, Seattle, Washington 98195. Telephone: (206) 543-1921. This book is one of a series of curriculum materials about China, Japan, and Korea developed by the EARC. Letters from Chengdu, Letters from Korea, Modern Japan: An Idea Book for K-12 Educators, and Teaching about Japan through the Arts are others. Write to the EARC to receive a free quarterly newsletter announcing programs, institutes, and curriculum materials.

EAST ASIAN CURRICULUM PROJECT, East Asia Institute, Columbia University, 420 East 118th Street, New York, New York 10027. This project has published two comprehensive curriculum supplements on China and Japan. China: A Teaching Workbook covers a wide range of topics and includes charts, maps, and audiovisual suggestions. The second edition, published in 1982, is 333 pages ling and costs $39 including handling.

SPICE, Lou Henry Hoover Building, Room 200, Stanford University, Stanford, California 94305-3219. Many outstanding teaching units about China and other countries have been developed by this international education project. Write for a catalog which describes teacher-tested units for all grade levels. Some are Demystifying the Chinese Language (originally published by SPICE), Traditional Chinese Celebrations: Continuity and Change in Taiwan, and Contemporary Family Life in Rural China.

142

SUPERINTENDENT OF PUBLIC INSTRUCTION, Office of
Multicultural and Equity Education, Old Capitol Building,
FG-11, Olympia, Washington 98504. This office publishes a
variety of teaching materials about Asia and Asian
Americans. <u>Letters from Chengdu</u>, an introduction to China
for elementary school students, is one of them. All are
free.

A
Curriculum Guide
for

5TH GRADE SOCIAL STUDIES

AMERICAN HERITAGE

MESA COUNTY VALLEY SCHOOL DISTRICT NO. 51
Department of Curriculum Services

July 1990

TABLE OF CONTENTS

Mesa County Valley School District No. 51
2115 Grand Avenue
Grand Junction, Colorado 81501

BOARD OF EDUCATION

Mrs. Debbie Johns, President . . . . District E
Mrs. Kathie Pinson, Vice President . . . . District C
Mr. John A. Achziger . . . . District A
Dr. W. Taft Moore . . . . District B
Mrs. Eula Boelke . . . . District D

SUPERINTENDENT OF SCHOOLS

Dr. Paul W. Rosier

DIVISION OF INSTRUCTIONAL SERVICES

Assistant Superintendent for Instructional Services
Mr. Merritt L. Vanderhoofven

Director of Secondary Education
Mr. Eldon D. Beard

Director of Elementary Education
Dr. A. Wayne Reeder

Director of Program Support Services
Mr. Tedd S. Brumbaugh

Director of Curriculum Services
Mr. Gary W. Hannah

Director of Pupil Personnel Services
Mr. Howard B. Littler

ACKNOWLEDGEMENTS

Mesa County Valley School District No. 51
wishes to especially acknowledge the professional input and
commitment of those who were instrumental in the writing of this

5th GRADE SOCIAL STUDIES INSTRUCTIONAL GUIDE.

Members of the Elementary Social Studies Curriculum Committee

Sheila Duke . . . . Columbus Elementary
Jean Gauley (Chair) . . . . **Lincoln Park Elementary**
Ila May Keithley . . . . Broadway Elementary
Mary Main . . . . Fruitvale Elementary
Tess Mullin . . . . Columbine Elementary
Dianna Pasqua . . . . Nisley Elementary
Bill Rudy . . . . Clifton Elementary
Mark Schmalz . . . . Lincoln Orchard Mesa Elementary

5th Grade Social Studies Pilot Teachers

Margie Bligh . . . . Shelledy Elementary
Paula Edson . . . . Columbine Elementary
Craig Fay . . . . Clifton Elementary
David Fricke . . . . Shelledy Elementary
Jean Gauley . . . . Lincoln Park Elementary
Norm Lindauer . . . . Fruitvale Elementary
Karen Marty . . . . Columbine Elementary
Dianna Pasqua . . . . Nisley Elementary
Mark Schmalz . . . . Lincoln Orchard Mesa Elementary

* * * * * * * * * * * *

Lydia Trujillo . . . . Coordinator of Dropout Prevention
Hawthorne Building

Kathleen Kain . . . . Curriculum Specialist
B.T.K. Staff Center

Rose Whaley, Typist . . . . Department of Curriculum Services

Social Studies: A Definition

Social studies is one of the broadest and perhaps one of the most difficult of the content areas to define. Social studies draws its content primarily from the disciplines of Anthropology, Economics, Geography, History, Political Science, Psychology, and the sciences and humanities. Social studies is a subject basic to and integrated throughout the K-12 curriculum. The aims of social studies are interrelated, none of which is developed wholly independent of the rest.

Social studies derives its goals from the nature of citizenship in our democratic society within a framework that links us to other nations and peoples of the world.

Life becomes defined by the decisions or policies that we make for our lives. It has been said that social studies is best defined as "the study of how citizens in a society make personal and public decisions on issues that affect their destiny." (Bragraw, Hartoonian 1988)

Social studies strives to help students answer these essential life questions:

o   How do people experience life and try to bring meaning to their lives?

o   How has and will human/social evolution change our conception of who we are?

o   How has shared membership in institutions defined our world view?

o   How do people in different societies and in different times and places organize for the production and consumption of economic goods and services?

o   How do human beings through their institutions, communities, and as individuals interact with the environment?

o   How do we develop and share beliefs and value systems?

o   How do we understand ourselves in time?

SOCIAL STUDIES MISSION STATEMENT

"I know of no safe depository of the ultimate powers of the society but with the people themselves; and if we think them not enlightened enough to exercise their control with a wholesome discretion, the remedy is not to take power from them, but to inform their discretion through instruction."

Thomas Jefferson (1820)

Our mission, as social studies teachers, is to prepare students for the world they will inherit. We know that the world will reflect increasing interdependence among nations, will be more complex, and will face a myriad of critical concerns. It is our endeavor to build a strong social studies program based on the areas of knowledge, skills, and awareness of ourselves and the world in which we live. Through these three areas, it is our aim to provide students with the opportunity to live and participate fully and responsibly in all the systems which affect their lives.

Recognizing the importance of learning as a lifetime endeavor, the social studies curriculum will provide the knowledge and content necessary for our students to have equal opportunity for success in this ever-changing world. This aim necessitates educating our students to become culturally, economically, ethically, geographically, historically, and sociopolitically literate.

Within the framework of knowledge, we believe that basic study skills, critical thinking, problem solving, decision making, and participation skills must be emphasized and integrated into all areas of the social studies curriculum. These skills will help students clarify their place in the world as products of the past, present, and future. Students must be able to think and reason in order to recognize that many areas of the social sciences are open to debate, revision, conflicting interpretations, and even acknowledgment of mistakes.

In addition to knowledge and skills, awareness of one's self and the world around us remains a central focus of the social studies curriculum. We must help our students recognize the dignity and worth of all peoples, including self; only then can there be any expectation that they can become self-sufficient, contributing members of society. We believe that through awareness our students will accept the obligations as well as the privileges involved in citizenship in our democracy. Furthermore, it is increasingly important to foster the awareness of cause and effect as integral to understanding human relationships in a world whose survival depends on the interdependence and cooperation of people and global systems.

We propose that a successful social studies program should reflect an awareness of the richness of diversity within the personal, social, and cultural experience of each learner. Central to this effort is the recognition of students' individual learning styles and developmental levels, as well as individual teaching styles and the use of quality instructional materials.

Ultimately, our social studies program must empower students and help them develop into enlightened citizens who can carry our nation into the future with dignity and wisdom.

Why Study the Social Sciences?

"*To the individual who can develop an understanding of his or her cultural heritage also goes the knowledge that they can begin to answer the question, 'Who am I?'*

"*Whether we call it 'roots,' 'tradition,' or 'heritage' we are concerned with history and history provides a way for human beings to perceive. . .a way to see with more sensitive eyes.*

"*When we see ourselves in the light of the past, we have a much greater chance of lighting our way into the future.*

"*Knowledge of our cultural heritage. . .is taking what is good and trying to extend it into the future. In this task, we become more than just passive learners of history. We become the active link between the past and the future. We become the doers of important work . . .the work of passing on 'the good.'*"

Dr. H. Michael Hartoonian

The committee would like to acknowledge Dr. Michael Hartoonian for his inspiration and guidance in this curriculum development. We thank Dr. Hartoonian for sharing many wonderful articles with us, and especially acknowledge his input on the importance of a participatory citizenship, and the development of an excellent, workable thinking skills model.

Most of all, the Social Studies Curriculum Committee would like to thank Dr. Hartoonian for reminding us of the importance of what we do as teachers and the fact that we should all consider the difference between information and knowledge. We must always remember the tension between "what is" and "what ought to be" and work towards wisdom, grace, quality, and love in our classrooms.

SOCIAL STUDIES CURRICULUM GOALS

I.   Government and Civic Values
The goal of Government and Civic Values is to instill in students a sense of civic responsibility.

The Social Studies Curriculum strives to develop:

o   an understanding of the need for government
o   an understanding and appreciation of our constitutional and national heritage
o   an understanding of comparative political and economic systems
o   an appreciation of the pluralistic and multicultural nature of American society

II.   Thinking and Processing
The goal of Thinking and Processing is to enable students to examine the validity and meaning of what they read, hear, think, and believe in a complex, information-based, technological society.

The Social Studies Curriculum strives to enable students to develop:

o   lifelong learning skills
o   study skills
o   critical and creative thinking skills
o   decision making and problem solving skills

A more detailed explanation of thinking skills follows on page 13, "Suggested Thinking Skills Model"

III.   Self-Awareness and Social Participation
The goal of Self-Awareness and Social Participation is to encourage students to develop a positive self-image and take an active part in the world around them.

The Social Studies Curriculum strives to:

o   enable students to recognize the dignity and worth of all people, including self
o   promote group interaction and leadership skills
o   develop the ability to identify and address human and environmental issues that require social action
o   encourage students to become thoughtful, self-sufficient, contributing citizens
o   enable students to understand their cultural heritage and history by encouraging them to look back into the past and ahead toward their own human potential

IV.   Cultural Understanding
The goal of Cultural Understanding is to foster an awareness of human relationships in a world whose survival depends on the interdependence and cooperation of all people.

The Social Studies Curriculum strives to:

o   enable students to understand the way people from diverse cultures perceive, think, and interact
o   foster an awareness of the commonalities, as well as the uniqueness, of world cultures
o   develop an understanding of the role that culture plays in economic and political world relations
o   develop in students an awareness of the historical and geographical influences on the continual development of a culture

5

The four categories of goals described on the previous page (Government and Civic Values, Thinking and Processing, Self-Awareness and Social Participation, and Cultural Understanding) are integrated with the areas of Knowledge, Skills, and Attitudes as depicted below:

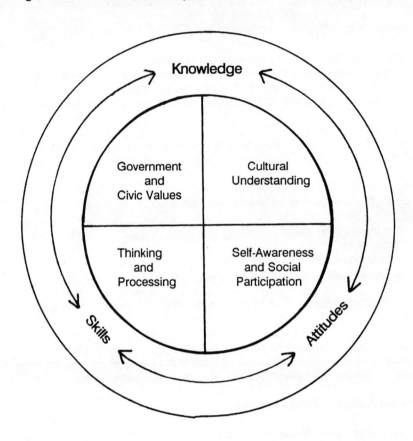

Knowledge   -   Knowledge is understanding the relationship between and among bits of information. This knowledge assumes the higher level of wisdom as it is applied to human dilemmas and dreams.

Information <———> Knowledge <———> Wisdom

Skills   -   Study skills, thinking skills, and participation skills are essential for effective citizenship and refer to finding, organizing, and making use of knowledge.

Attitudes   -   Attitudes depend upon the application of concepts, such as: Cooperation, Diversity, Equality, Freedom, Human Dignity, Justice, Privacy, Responsibility, and Truth.

SOCIAL STUDIES SKILLS

Skill development must be a part of all social studies teaching. It is important because it helps students become more efficient at acquiring and understanding social studies content, as well as helping them to learn, practice, and apply those skills and processes they need as citizens in school today, and will need as adult citizens tomorrow. Skills and content are interrelated. Students need skills to learn content, and they need to work with content to develop skills.

Skill development is neither so simple that the social studies teacher can take it for granted, nor so difficult that the teacher should avoid it. There are a few "complexities" that should be kept in mind as skill development is planned and conducted.

o   All of the skills listed are important to social studies but few, if any, are exclusive to the field.
o   Skill development should be coordinated with what is being done in other subject areas.
o   Even after a skill has been developed, a skill can be lost if it is not reinforced by continued use.
o   The different skills are interrelated; there must be a spiral development. All skills should be practiced in appropriate ways at all levels.
o   Skill and content are interrelated; just because students can use a skill to process simple or familiar content does not mean they will be able to apply it to new content without further teaching and practice.
o   Skill development must be continued until students not only know the skill and perform it well, but until they understand the conditions or situations in which it is, or is not, appropriate to use it.

As we thought about skill development, two major questions helped guide us:

o   What skills are necessary for students to do well in studying social studies?
o   What skills would students need as participating citizens in the years following high school?

In answering these questions, the committee divided skills into four major categories:

o   Locating Information
o   Evaluating Information
o   Using Time and Place
o   Analyzing Societal Skills

An outline with examples follows:

I. Locating Information
    A. Home Resources
        1. Using the yellow pages/telephone directory
        2. Using the dictionary
    B. Community resources
        1. Using the library (card catalog, Reader's Guide, etc.)
        2. Using an Atlas
        3. Using government/community agencies
    C. Multiple sources
        1. Maps
        2. Graphs
        3. Charts

II. Evaluating Information
   A. Evaluating sources
   B. Determining bias
   C. Distinguishing fact from opinion
   D. Identifying relevant and irrelevant information
   E. Determining cause and effect
   F. Detecting stereotypes
   G. Analyzing pictures
   H. Interpreting charts, graphs and maps
   I. Synthesizing information
   J. Drawing conclusions - making inferences
   K. Organizing ideas in writing/taking useful notes

III. Using Time and Place Skills
   A. Developing a sense of chronology
      1. Constructing a time line
   B. Using time schedules
      1. Reading a bus schedule
   C. Using local geography
      1. Using maps (constructing, interpreting, evaluating)
   D. Using American history
   E. Using World Area Studies
   F. Spatial relationships
   G. Drawing inferences from maps

IV. Societal Skills
   A. Defining social problems
   B. Identifying value statements
   C. Identifying values in conflict
   D. Recognizing implicit values
   E. Identifying the consequences of actions
   F. Seeing other's point of view
   G. Making judgments
   H. Problem solving
   I. Decision making
   J. Working effectively in a group

Skill Development Procedures

Because skills are both important and interrelated, the school and teacher should have a systematic plan for their development. Systematic development involves:

- o Diagnosis
- o Teaching
- o Practice
- o Reinforcement
- o Remediation, as needed
- o Application
- o With assessment at every step

Teachers should determine at the beginning of each year/semester the proficiency level of students in the various skill areas.

The following diagram suggests an example for skill development.

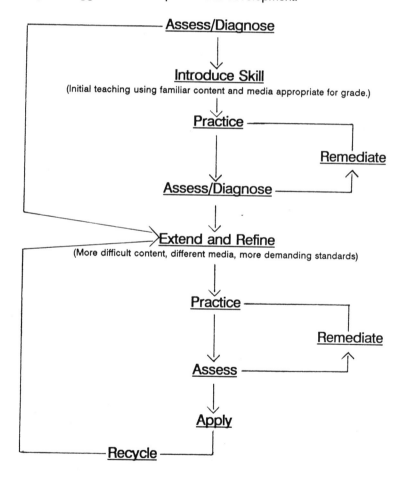

Adapted from information from New York State *Social Studies: Participation in Government; Tentative Syllabus Guide*, and *Land of Promise*, Scott, Foresman, Teacher's Resource Book.

Suggested Thinking Skills Model
and Accompanying Rationale

One of the most important goals of this curriculum is to develop thinking and processing skills. These skills should enable students to examine the validity and meaning of what they read, hear, think, and believe in a more complex, information-based, technological society.

The curriculum committee feels strongly that a thinking skills model is crucial not only to enhance the new social studies curriculum, but should be incorporated throughout the other content areas. With the ever-expanding knowledge base and the increasing interdependence of peoples of the world, it becomes obvious that we must, as teachers, stress the skills of critical and creative thinking to prepare students to be participating, enlightened citizens who can wisely make decisions and propose policies for the public good.

> "In social studies, as in other fields of inquiry, there are several basic interrelated components of critical study involved in the construction and use of knowledge. They constitute the necessary elements in thinking about personal and social questions, and present a model for higher order or reflective thinking. These components are identified here as 1) comprehension or conceptualization, 2) causality, 3) validity of explanation, and 4) creative extension."
>
> *Dr. Michael Hartoonian (1988)*

(Diagrams depicting these four interrelated components follow on page 14.)

In order for this model to be successful, the teacher must keep in mind the following:

o   The components of this model are interrelated and can be accessed at any level as long as all four levels are included.

o   It is crucial to create a safe environment where students are respected, where there is a conscious effort to develop standards of ethics (justice) and aesthetics (craft, quality, excellence) and where the development of meaning in the personal lives of its members is a top priority.

o   You must consider beliefs and perceptions before you can teach thinking skills. Consider what "stories" our students come to us with and more importantly, consider the "stories" we want our students to come away from our classrooms with, and get from us as teachers.

o   Because of the nature of thinking skills, the teacher must realize that there will not always be clear cut answers to the questions generated. In fact, ambiguity and a certain level of frustration may occur.

Figure 1 - The Model

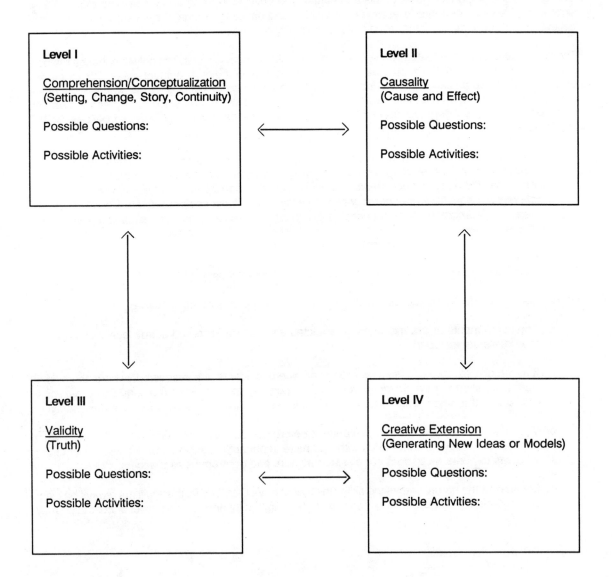

Figure 2 - The Model with Related Skills

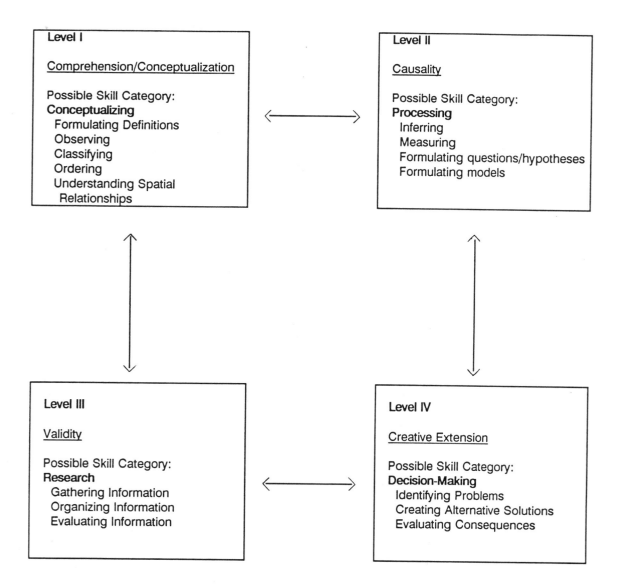

SOCIAL STUDIES SCOPE AND SEQUENCE THEMES

Introduction

The Social Studies Scope and Sequence provide a framework for describing the social studies program for Mesa County Valley School District No. 51. The term scope refers to the range of substantive content, values, skills, and/or learner experiences to be included in our social studies education. The scope is based upon seven major themes that logically extend from the Social Studies Goals. These themes appear in each grade level, although different themes may be emphasized in various grade levels or courses depending on their focus. The seven themes are <u>History</u>, <u>Geography</u>, <u>Economics</u>, <u>Government</u>, <u>Citizenship</u>, <u>Global Perspective</u>, and <u>Self-awareness</u>. Sequence refers to the ordering of courses to be taught as well as the examination of course content in a logical order.

History

Human beings without an understanding of their past are not equipped to deal with the present or the future. No society can function without a knowledge of its heritage - where it came from, how it got there, what traditions, ideals, dreams, successes, and failures have helped to shape it. Instruction in history is basic to social studies education.

Areas of emphasis in this theme are:

- o Ideals of Our Heritage
- o Relating the Past to the Present
- o Exploration, Settlement, and Expansion
- o Individuals, Groups, and Events That Have Shaped History
- o Peoples, Groups, Societies, and Nations Change Through Time

Geography

Geography helps students to understand their world and how human beings interact with it. Human activities are profoundly affected by the natural environment. The unique perspectives and skills gained from studying the five fundamental geographic themes clarify knowledge about the earth and its people.

The five geographic themes are:

1) Location
   - o Absolute
   - o Relative
2) Place
   - o Physical
   - o Human
   - o Observed
3) Relationships Within Places: Humans and Environments
   - o Cultural
   - o Physical
4) Movement
   - o Relationships Between and Among Places
5) Regions
   - o Types of Regions
   - o Uses of Regions

For a more detailed explanation of the 5 Themes of Geography see page 21.

15

Economics

Economics is the study of how people make choices in the world of limited resources. To satisfy virtually unlimited wants, people learn to turn resources into goods and services. They also learn to depend on each other in their pursuit of the things they want. Students must learn that often something must be given up in order to obtain something else that is more desired. This means the ability to make personal decisions and evaluate the decisions of others. As students are introduced to different societies, they learn that countries have adopted different ways of making the economics choices they face as a result of scarcity. They learn to appreciate our free enterprise system, and become aware of their economic opportunities and obligations. They gain fundamental understandings about supply and demand, consumerism, and competition in the marketplace.

Areas of emphasis in this theme are:

- o Scarcity
- o Opportunity Cost
- o Production
- o Consumerism
- o Interdependence
- o Economic Systems and Institutions

Government

Social participation, civic responsibility, and an understanding of our government are crucial to the success of a <u>democratic society</u>. Students need to see how governments in other societies are structured, and to compare those governments with our political system. The ongoing interest in and investigation of current events, as they relate to government and political action, are also important to effective participation in our society.

Areas of emphasis in this theme are:

- o The Need for Government
- o The Development of Our United States Government (Historical Documents)
- o Comparative Governments
- o Current Political Events and Issues

Citizenship

The goals of civic education should be to impart knowledge of the political system, and how it really and ideally works. Citizenship also stresses the development of the skills of participation in civic life, improvement of civic competence, commitment to values compatible with the principles which underlie democratic institutions, and the capacity to analyze the consequences of these values. It is very important, as well, to build in students their positive self-esteem so that all individuals feel that their participation in civic life can make a difference. Students must realize that citizenship permeates their life roles as members of a family, classroom, school, community, state, nation, and world.

Areas of emphasis in this theme are:

- o Rights and Responsibilities
- o Knowledge of Issues
- o Law-Related Education
- o Critical Thinking/Decision Making
- o Active Participation
- o Community Service

16

Global Perspective

Global Perspective emphasizes the need for students to achieve an understanding of the variety of people who live in the world. This theme was developed on the premise that the world has become increasingly complex and interdependent, and that citizens of the United States must respond to the many problems and issues in the world today.

Global Perspective is an expanded view of citizenship education, in that one of its goals is to assist students in determining their individual and collective world roles and responsibilities.

Areas of emphasis in this theme are:

- o Appreciating Cultural Diversity
- o Developing Effective Relationships With Others
- o Understanding the World as an Interdependent System
- o Understanding Prevailing World Conditions, the Process of Change, and Emerging Trends

Self-Awareness

Awareness of one's self and the world around us is a central focus of the Social Studies Curriculum. We must help our students recognize the dignity and worth of all peoples, including self. Only then can they become self-sufficient, contributing members of society.

Areas of emphasis in this theme are:

- o The Individual Can Make a Difference in Dealing with Issues that Require Social Action
- o Being Comfortable with One's Self Allows for Openness and Acceptance of Others and Their Uniqueness
- o The Development of Group Interaction and Leadership Potential
- o Providing Hope for the Future and Allowing Students to Feel a Part of Society

DESCRIPTION OF THE FIVE BASIC THEMES IN GEOGRAPHY

Geography is an integrating discipline which seeks to understand places in the world. To do so requires both knowledge of the human/cultural and physical environments. The concepts which explain life at a place, and that are fundamental to geography, are applicable to all social studies disciplines. Geography helps explain historical events, scientific processes, spatial organization, cultural development, political processes, and spatial relationships.

The first task in geography is to locate places, describing and explaining their physical and cultural characteristics. Geographic inquiry continues by exploring the relationships that develop as people respond to and shape their physical and cultural environment. Geography permits people to compare, contrast, and comprehend regions on a local, national, and global scale.

Five geographic themes provide a conceptual framework for organizing geography curriculum.

LOCATION: Position on the Earth's Surface

Location answers the basic question: "Where?" Absolute locations are precise points on the earth's surface which are determined by using a mathematical grid system such as latitude and longitude. Relative location, understanding locations and their characteristics, is a key aspect of understanding interdependence on local, regional, national, and global scales.

PLACE: Physical and Cultural Characteristics

Every place on the earth has special features that distinguish it from other places. The physical characteristics of a place include its geology, topography, climate, soil, and vegetation. Cultural characteristics include such factors as population composition, economic activity, religious beliefs, languages, and political organization.

HUMAN-ENVIRONMENT INTERACTIONS: Changing the Face of the Earth

All places on earth have advantages and disadvantages for human settlement. The natural environment poses certain constraints which affect the kinds of human activity that can be undertaken within a place. The ways in which people interact with their environment, by modifying it or by adapting to it, reveal much more about their cultural values, economic needs, political circumstances, and technological abilities.

MOVEMENT: Humans Interacting on the Earth

People everywhere interact. They travel from place to place, they communicate with each other, and they depend upon other people in distant places for products, ideas, and information. The most visible evidence of global interdependence and global interaction is the transportation and communication networks that link virtually every part of the world.

REGIONS: How They Form and Change

Regions are areas defined by certain unifying characteristics. Some regions are defined by a single physical or human or cultural characteristic (e.g., soil, population, language). Other regions represent the complex interplay of many different features. Regions can be of any size and they likely will change with time. Regions divide the world into manageable units for study.

GRADE 5

AMERICAN HERITAGE

INTRODUCTION

The Grade 5 Social Studies program focuses on our American heritage by studying the land, its people, and the dynamics of change.

A chronological view of our history will be the structure used to study key historical periods in our heritage as outlined:

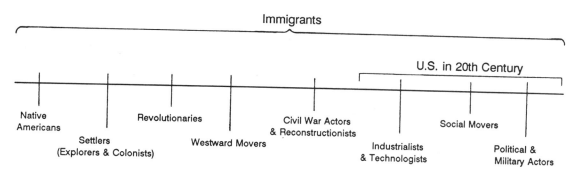

The study of each historical period should be integrated with Reading and Language Arts by using biographies, historical fiction, journals and diaries, and historical documents. Extension activities should be integrated with other subject areas whenever appropriate.

Our goal is that students leave grade 5 with an understanding of and a personal connection to our common American heritage in hopes that these serve as a catalyst for their curiosity to learn more about our history. Through the study of the various aspects of American Heritage, students will develop an appreciation of the pluralism of the United States as a microcosm of the world.

The important factor to note is that this curriculum departs from a survey approach to United States history.

The study of some key peoples or groups of people in each historical period, and the impact their decisions have had on our past, present, and future, will be emphasized. Incorporating higher level thinking skills is crucial to the success of the program and the goals we all hold for our future citizens of the 21st century.

The scope of our K-12 Social Studies Curriculum is based on seven major themes that are expected to be integrated at grade 5, where appropriate. These themes include History, Geography, Economics, Government, Citizenship, Global Perspective, and Self-Awareness.

A variety of instructional materials and lessons are provided to support this approach to teaching American Heritage.

SCOPE AND SEQUENCE

Topics/Concept	Skills	Attitudes
History		
Ideals of our heritage	Reading, interpreting and making time lines	Appreciation of some historical figures as heroes
We can relate our past to our present	Developing a sense of chronology	Appreciation for our freedoms
Individuals, groups, and events have shaped our history	Gathering information from a variety of sources	Appreciation for different perspectives
	Interpreting cause and effect	
	Identifying contributions of individuals, groups and events in our history	
	Identifying differences in points of view	
Exploration, settlement, expansion, and modernization of the United States	Interpreting historical maps	
	Interpreting graphs	
	Recognizing settlement patterns	
Geography		
The United States, and places within the United States, can be identified using relative terms and absolute reference systems	Using latitude and longitude to locate places	Recognition of ways and systems in organizing and identifying geographic information
	Identifying time zones	
Places within the United States have physical and human characteristics	Interpreting maps to identify physical characteristics of a place	
	Making comparisons from maps	
Historically, people within the area of the United States have adapted to and altered the environment	Analyzing effects of humans adaptation of our environment	Appreciation of the relationships between man and environment in American history
	Identifying physical features and landforms	
	Evaluating human and scientific forces that change the earth (erosion, water, wind, bulldozers, etc.)	
	Locating areas of environmental concern	
Patterns of movement involving people, goods and ideas can be identified in U.S. History		
The United States can be divided into historical and geographic regions according to common characteristics. These regions have impacted the development of the U.S.	Defining types and uses of regions	

23

Topics/Concept	Skills	Attitudes

Economics

Scarcity: Some goods and services in the U.S. are scarce because some resources are scarce (e.g. land, energy)	Interpret economic charts and graphs Defining supply and demand	Recognition of the economic resources in the U.S.
Opportunity Cost: Historically, the U.S. has made decisions concerning use of its resources which have involved both costs and benefits	Analyzing cause and effect	Obligation to effectively utilize our nation's available resources
Consumerism: Historically, Americans have become increasing specialized in the production of its goods and services	Comparing economic choices	Appreciation of the difficulty and responsibility of making informed choices that effect our nation
Exchange, Money, Interdependence: The U.S. economy has developed a monetary system to facilitate exchange and communication in the market place here and abroad	Analyzing the free enterprise system for its pros and cons Evaluating the role of currency in trade	
Economic Systems and Institutions: The U.S. utilizes the free enterprise system which has encouraged Americans to tap their resources and develop innovative uses for those resources	Identifying key elements in the free enterprise system	

Government

Organization and functions of U.S. government	Identifying the structure and functions of the branches of government	
United States has a democratic form of government	Explaining the democratic process	Loyalty to our country
Development of our government and historical documents	Identifying key documents in U.S. history and explaining their purpose Using democratic methods in making group decisions Comparing and contrasting different forms of government (e.g. capitalist, communist, monarchy, republic)	Recognition of our strengths and problems in the U.S.

Topics/Concept	Skills	Attitudes
Citizenship		
United States citizens have important rights and responsibilities	Identifying the role of the citizen in a democracy	Willingness to accept responsibilities as well as rights of a U.S. citizen
U.S. laws are made for the public good	Identifying the reasons for a given law in terms of the public good	Concern and tolerance for all citizens' rights
U.S. citizens have a knowledge of current issues	Determining fact from opinion	
	Making inferences and drawing conclusions	
	Evaluating relevance of information	
	Demonstrating responsibility	
	Identifying a problem and proposing a plan of action	
	Recognizing propaganda techniques	
	Identifying and utilizing community resources	
Service project	Analyzing a poll and voting returns	Obligation to participate in service project for the good of our nation
	Conducting community surveys	
Global Perspective		
Cultural Diversity: Different cultural groups have shaped American history (e.g. Native Americans, Hispanics, and other immigrant groups)	Identifying and interpreting cultural and societal differences and similarities	Appreciation of the contributions made by various groups in our country's history
	Detecting stereotypes	
	Seeing others points of view	
Conflict Resolution: Conflict and choices for resolution have affected our American history (e.g. British-American relationship before Revolutionary War)	Identify cause and effect relationships	
	Defining individual roles in conflict resolution	
Process of Change: Change is natural and affects American heritage	Identifying agents of change	Obligation and loyalty as a participating U.S. citizen
Prevailing World Conditions: Trends around the world have affected our history (e.g. European influence on World War II)	Identifying and analyzing trends and future needs	Realization of importance of having a global perspective on American actions
Interdependence: The United States is impacted by and impacts the actions of other nations	Identifying and defining the parts and process of systems	Concern for our world as an increasingly interrelated and interdependent system
Our country is part of a global community	Explaining the effects of interdependence	

Topics/Concept	Skills	Attitudes
Self-Awareness		
I am an integral part of a larger societal group (U.S.A.)	Cooperating in groups	Awareness of one's responsibilities to self and others
Personal heritage is an integral part of who I am	Identifying one's own personal strengths and weaknesses Developing respect for self Recognizing individual relationship with personal heritage	Appreciation of the development of one's potential throughout his/her life

LEARNING OUTCOMES

Learning outcomes are relatively specific statements which identify the major learnings that a student should be able to know or do at the end of a unit of study. These summary statements describe the learning outcomes for the eight historical periods which provide in-depth focus for the study of American Heritage.

K=Knowledge   S=Skill   A=Attitude

At the end of these units, the student will be able to:

Native Americans

Explain the geographical and cultural origin of Native Americans. **(K)**

Appreciate the relationships between man and his environment. **(A)**

Explorers and Settlers

Describe and compare the settlements of Colonial America and the reasons for these settlements. **(S)**

Construct, interpret and evaluate maps and charts relating to the exploration and settlement of early America. **(S)**

Appreciate the cultural and religious diversity of the settlers. **(A)**

Revolutionaries

Identify and explain how individuals, groups, and events have shaped our history. **(K)**

Describe the formation and democratic process of our American government. **(K)**

Identify conflict and choices for resolution that have affected our American heritage. **(K)**

Recognize the responsibilities, as well as rights of being a U.S. citizen. **(A)**

Westward Movers

Analyze territorial acquisitions involving people, goods, and ideas in U.S. history. **(S)**

Recognize economic and other reasons for the westward movement. **(S)**

Appreciate the diversity of the heroes of the westward movement. **(A)**

Civil War Actors and Reconstructionists

Recognize this historical era as a time of survival for our democracy. **(K)**

Identify and define the economic and geographic reasons for the civil war and reconstruction. **(S)**

Identify differences in points of view. **(S)**

Recognize the need for concern and tolerance for all people's rights. **(A)**

Industrialists and Technologists

Recognize the causes of and the people who had an impact on the Industrial Revolution. **(K)**

Explain the impact that industrial growth made on our history. **(S)**

Examine the possible impact the technological revolution will have on the future of our nation. **(S)**

Social Movers

Identify 20th century people who made important contributions to our heritage. **(K)**

Be aware of one's responsibilities to self and others. **(A)**

Political and Military Actors

Recognize the strengths and problems in the United States and its relationships with other nations. **(K)**

Understand our world as an increasingly interrelated and interdependent system. **(K)**

Immigrants

Explain who, why, and how people came/come to our country. **(S)**

Examine the impact that forced migation of blacks has had on our heritage. **(S)**

Appreciate the richness of our cultural diversity. **(A)**

COMMUNITY SERVICE PROJECT

Understanding the responsibilities as well as rights of being a citizen of the United States is often too abstract a concept for 5th graders. Some still struggle with personal responsibilities toward each other, in the family, school, neighborhood, community, and state.

The Social Studies Committee is recommending a service project at each grade level that is appropriate to the Social Studies focus at that level. (For example, first graders focus on school and neighborhood, and might do a neighborhood or school beautification project.)

Our hope is that this project be planned and implemented by the students with minimal direction from parents and teachers.

Some suggestions for fifth grade projects focused on our country would include:

-- Keeping track of current disasters, and offering aid (helping with the oil spill cleanup by sending cotton rags to Alaska in Spring '89).

-- Pen pal project with a Native Indian tribe school and helping with one of their projects.

-- Letters to United States congresspersons about current issues affecting our country.

-- National Park cleanup (Colorado National Monument would qualify here).

We believe these projects will support our endeavor to educate enlightened and sensitive citizens for the 21st century.

NATIVE AMERICANS UNIT

Unit Outcomes: At the end of this unit the student will be able to:
- o Explain the geographical and cultural origin of Native Americans.
- o Examine the relationships between man and his environment.

Unit Outline	Activities/Resources	Extension/Integrated Activity

I. Understanding Culture*
  A. Attributes
    1. Religion
    2. Education
    3. Language
    4. Family
    5. Government
    6. Economic system
	Lesson: Meeting Our Needs	*Gateways to Science*: 5
		  Unit 3: "Social Insects" p. 33
		Game: "Rafa-Rafa"
		  (B.T.K. Professional Library)
		Video Letters from Japan
		  (in Japan trunk at B.T.K.)
		Lesson: I Need, I Want**

B. Student's own culture	Lesson: Getting To Know Me	"Here's Looking At You 2000" - Lesson #1

C. Eskimo - Apply attributes
  to this group
	Lesson: Eskimo Culture
	Cobblestone Magazine, "The
	  Eskimos of Alaska"
		Film: *Alaskan Eskimo* (29 min.)
		Activities from *Think, Inc.*
		Reproduction: "Tlingit Bear"
		  from *Art-In-Action*
		Film: *Great Deserts of the
		  World: Arctic* (20m)
		Film: *Matthew Aliuk: Eskimo in
		  Two Worlds*
		Reproduction: "Face Masks"
		  from *Art-In-Action*

D. Iroquois - Apply
  attributes to this
  group
	Lesson: Iroquois Culture	Auditory Tape: "The Great
		  Peace: An Oral Tradition As
		  Historical Evidence"
		  (in trunk)

E. Comparing Iroquois to
  Eskimo
F. Cultural conflicts
	Silver Burdett text, pp. 50-53
	An American Indian Perspective,
	  p. 9
		The Iroquois, by Barbara
		  Graymont
		*Inquiring About American
		  History*. Holt Databank,
		  pp. 38-54 "The Iroquois"
		Lesson: Nature of Conflict**
		Film or Book: *Sneeches*,
		  by Dr. Seuss
		Supplementary Conflict
		  Lessons**

* Understanding culture should be integrated throughout the year by applying the cultural attributes to all groups studied.

31

Unit Outline	Activities/Resources	Extension/Integrated Activity

II. Origin and Migration
  A. Land Bridge Theory
  B. Existence before last ice age
  C. "Original home" belief
	An American Indian Perspective, pp. 4-6
	Silver Burdett text, pp. 46-50
	Lesson: Origin and Migration of Native Americans
		Film: *American Indian Yesterday Today*

III. Adaptation and Attitude Toward Environment
  A. Geographic location of various tribes
  B. How each tribe adapted
  C. Application of environmental adaptation to today's issues (e.g. water conservation, air pollution, etc.)
	An American Indian Perspective, pp. 1-3
	Silver Burdett text, pp. 46-49
	American History Through Maps, pp. 4-5
	Lesson: Chief Seattle
	
	Begin *The Sign of the Beaver* novel unit
		Lesson: Mother Earth...Friend or Foe**
		Morning Star, Black Sun: Northern Cheyenne and America's Energy Crisis, by B. Ashabranner
		Gateways to Science: 5 Unit 12: "Conserving Water" p. 179
		Lesson: Keeping Score**
		Auditory tape: *Sign of the Beaver* (B.T.K. Professional Library)
		Keepers of The Earth: Native American Stories and Environmental Activities for Children, by Michael J. Caduto and Joseph Bruchac

IV. Legends of Native Americans
  A. Importance of oral history
  B. Respect for cultural beliefs
  C. Learning of culture
	Lesson: Legends of Native Americans	Film: *Arrows To The Sun*
		Explorations, pp. 372-381 - "Heroine of Kapiti"
		Lesson: How A Legend Was Made**
		Interact Unit: *Honor* (B.T.K.)

** Lessons found in Supplementary Notebook

Lesson: Meeting Our Needs

Knowledge of what culture is, is crucial to any understanding or appreciation of the diversity of peoples, detection and acceptance of others' point of view, and appreciation for contributions of all groups to our heritage.

Culture cannot be understood without knowing the difference between needs and wants. All humans have certain needs in common. Those needs are met through institutions created by cultures. It is important to know that the institutions look different in different cultures <u>and</u> change throughout the culture's history.

These institutions can be considered a culture's attributes. They include religion, education, language, family, government, and economic system.

<u>Objectives:</u> Students will be able to:

1. Describe the difference between needs and wants.
2. Name institutions all cultures create to meet their needs.
3. Describe changes in attributes of culture and predict how they will change in the future.
4. Draw and explain a Venn diagram.
5. Draw and use a line graph.

<u>Time Required:</u> Four class periods

<u>Materials Needed:</u>

- Culture Box - page 35 (copy for each student or large display chart)
- Description of Attributes - page 36

<u>Procedure:</u>

Day 1
1. Lead class discussion with following questions:
    a. What are needs?
    b. What is the difference between needs and wants?
    c. Are all peoples' needs the same?
    d. How have human needs changed over time?
2. Class makes a list of <u>human needs</u> and puts them in order from most important to least important.
3. Class adds <u>human wants</u> to the list of needs.
4. Draw and describe a Venn diagram (perhaps using hair and eye color in the class as the example).
5. Draw Venn diagram and students classify needs, wants, and other which overlap from previous list.
6. If time, have students make a collage of needs and wants from the Venn diagram.

Day 2
1. Lead discussion about cultural attributes using the following questions:
    a. How do people meet their needs?
    b. How have people changed the ways they meet their needs?
2. Display chart of "Culture Box." Brief discussion of these attributes as cross-cultural and description of what each attribute means.
3. Give statistics on numbers of working women in 1960 and 1989. (If not available, suffice it to say that it has changed drastically.) Students brainstorm in cooperative groups stating reasons for institutional change and the effects of these changes.
4. Students brainstorm what the family will be like when the students are adults.

33

Procedure (continued)

Day 3
1. Lead discussion:
   a. How can we find out what others think their needs are, locally and statewide?
   b. Do men and women have different needs?
2. Review a lesson on graphs (whatever kind which students need more practice).
3. Students conduct a poll of the student population, neighborhood population, or parent population to generate a prioritized list of each person's top ten needs. (This may have to be an after-school assignment.)

Day 4
1. With results from poll, class (cooperative groups) can graph the results.
2. Class discussion of results.
3. Each student (or cooperative group) write a story describing the world where one of the human needs studied no longer exists. What would the world look like under these circumstances?

Debriefing:

How do you think conflict might arise because of misunderstanding of needs and wants?

Evaluation:

Teacher observation of class participation.
Venn diagrams
Graphs
Stories

Culture Box

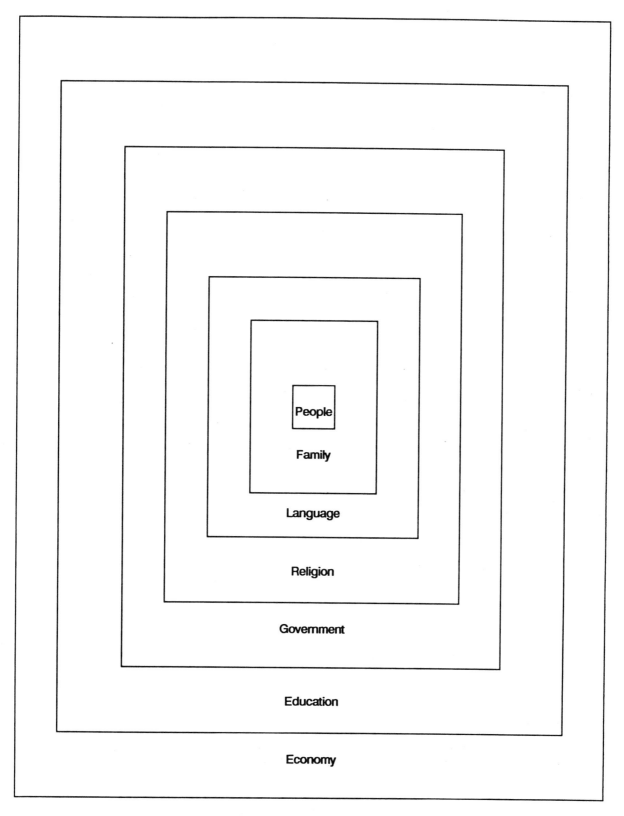

Descriptions of Attributes

Family:

The primary group I belong to. The family meets the biological needs of an individual (food, clothing, shelter, love). The family also teaches values to the individual. Not all family make-ups are the same. Rituals, values.

Language:

The way individuals communicate with each other. There is non-verbal as well as verbal communication.

Education:

The way societies prepare their people for their role as citizens. Educational systems change and develop according to society's needs.

Religion:

Religion consists of three parts: 1) The thing or person worshiped, 2) standard of conduct, and 3) rituals. Religion can unite people into a community from which they derive emotional support and helps fulfill their need for others.

Government:

The political institutions, laws, and customs through which people are directed and/or controlled. Who makes rules and regulations? How those people are selected?

Economic System:

The way a group produces, distributes, and consumes goods and services.

Lesson: Getting To Know Me

Children need to understand their own culture and reason for doing things before they can understand or appreciate a different culture.

Objectives: Students will be able to:

1. Describe cultural attributes (from Worksheet #1 - Culture Box chart).
2. Apply cultural attributes (from previous lesson) to their own culture.
3. Write a letter in correct form. (Language Arts)

Time Required: 1-2 class periods.

Materials Needed: None

Procedure:

1. Demonstrate correct form in writing a letter.
2. Display or write a sample on board for students to refer to.
3. Review cultural attributes from previous lesson.
4. Choose one attribute (e.g., family) and makes a list of all the different family configurations of the students (one parent, extended, etc.).
5. Students write individual letters to pretend friends from another culture. In the letter, they tell what their culture is like using all of the cultural attributes.

Debriefing:

What do you think your foreign friend might find "strange" about your culture?
Are you more alike or different than other children you know?

Evaluation:

Written letter format.
Content of the letter.

Creative Extensions:

Play simulation "Rafa-Rafa."
Use video letter, "My School," from Japan trunk to compare the attributes of education in Japanese and American culture.

Lesson: Eskimo Culture

When teaching about American heritage, it is sometimes easy to neglect the native Americans from Alaska. This is usually due to its geographic location.

By using the Eskimo as a case study for understanding culture, teachers have an opportunity to study this unique geographic and cultural contribution to America's rich heritage.

It is important for students to realize that the culture of the Eskimo has changed with their history.

<u>Objectives:</u> Students will be able to:

1. Apply cultural attributes to the culture of the Eskimo.
2. Compare their own culture to that of the Eskimo and describe similarities and differences.
3. Predict how a culture might change when the needs of the people change and more technology is available.
4. Locate areas of the world where the Eskimo live.
5. Distinguish fact from opinion.

<u>Time Required:</u> Two classes

<u>Materials Needed:</u>

- *Cobblestone*, "The Eskimos of Alaska" - November 1985 (in trunk)
- Copies of pages 41-42, Background Information on Eskimos, for each student
- Library books about the Eskimo optional (list included in resource section in notebook)
- Atlas (optional)
- World map

<u>Procedure:</u>

1. Review attributes of culture.
2. Students read background information sheet or excerpts from available library books and *Cobblestone Magazine.*
3. Instruct or review the skill of distinguishing fact from opinion. (Explanation in *Explorations* Teacher's Guide, p. 508.)
4. Students make a list of 10 facts about the Eskimo people. Across from each fact, they are to state an opinion.
5. Students share their facts and opinions with each other and must support their opinions.
6. Using the attributes "Culture Box" framework, class (together with the teacher) describes the culture of the Eskimo at the present time.
7. Using a world map, students locate the geographic location of the Eskimo and discuss the area in terms of the climate and all of its ramifications.
8. Compare our culture to that of the Eskimo and similarities and differences.

Debriefing:

How might the culture of the Eskimo change if their was a drastic warming trend in that region of the world?
Compare the population and land area of Alaska with that of California. Hypothesize why there is such a difference.

Evaluation:

Lists of facts and opinions.
Eskimo worksheet.
Eskimo quiz.
Teacher evaluation of group discussions.
Map test on location of Eskimo.

Creative Extensions:

Art activity on soap carving.
Make up a legend that might be written 500 years from now about how technology has changed the life of the Eskimo.
Film: *Matthew Aliuk: Eskimo in Two Worlds*
Film: *Alaska Eskimo*

Background Material on Eskimos

Two groups of people live on the land that stretches from Russia to Greenland across Alaska and Canada. They call themselves Inupiat and Yupiks ("the real people"). We call them Eskimos.

Eskimos are the only people who live year round in the Arctic regions of our planet. Some inhabit Greenland; some dwell up near Melville Bay. Other Eskimos live on the Atlantic coast of North America. There are tribes on the islands between North America and Greenland. The Mackenzies are in northwest Canada and the Yupiks are in northeastern Siberia.

There are many theories about the original homeland of the Eskimos. These include:

1. Land bridge from Siberia to Alaska made it possible for the Eskimos to have left Asia 6,000 years ago and migrated through northern Alaska and Canada.
2. The Eskimos were driven up from the lakes of northern Canada toward the Arctic Ocean by American Indian tribes.

The polar climate is harsh. Eskimos live near salt or fresh water. They hunt and fish for food. However, in southern Greenland, Eskimos can harvest wheat and rice. Eskimos have learned they can waste nothing. For example, all of an animal they kill is eaten by the people or their dogs. Bones and teeth of the animal are made into tools. Some fat is melted into oil. Skins are made into clothes, boat coverings, or tents. The women sew clothes from furs and skins. They are so skillful using sinew thread that seams are watertight.

Eskimos live in ice igloos (temporarily) and stone and peat winter houses which are also called igloos. In summer they may dwell in a tent made of skins. Tar paper shacks are also used for shelter. Prosperous families may live in wooden homes or high-rise apartments in more densely populated areas of Alaska.

In the Eskimo family where survival is the prime goal, chores are very difficult. A man's primary duty is to hunt. The women sew the clothing and care for the home and children. Eskimo families are often extended to include three generations. They must learn to live harmoniously in close quarters. Children tend to be pampered, although they have definite chores to prepare them for a demanding life as adults. There is still great respect between young and old.

Before Europeans and Americans had contact with them, the Eskimos were not accustomed to trading. They gave a "gift" to someone who gave to them. This was considered a "thank-you." It is considered very rude to brag about material possessions, and it is their custom to purposely downgrade their own possessions.

Background Information on Eskimos - Page 2

The Eskimos embrace no specific organized religion. They believe in the presence of evil spirits, and ancestral spirits which can protect against these spirits. Shamans are advisors on the appeasement of the spirits. Eskimo religion is concerned mostly with survival. Gods are appealed to for good hunting, curing the sick, and good weather. Religious leaders beat small drums, sing and dance when appealing to the gods. Ceremonies include magical tricks. Christian missionaries have converted many Eskimos but their religion is still carried on even for entertainment only.

Crime is rare in the Arctic. The Eskimos believe that good behavior is necessary for survival. Also, the Eskimo belief is that property belongs to everyone; not just an individual. Crimes are dealt with by ridiculing the criminal. In the event of a serious crime, the punishment was usually death. The sentence was carried out by a great hunter of the tribe.

The Eskimo language is the same throughout the world. It has something in common with some Indian dialects. Eskimo and Indian tongues are polysynthetic. That means they join words and word roots together to form complete thoughts. This is unlike English in which thoughts are expressed in sentences. The Eskimos had no written language until they had contact with Europeans.

Children are educated in survival skills by their parents and grandparents. Today they attend modern schools for their education.

Refer to *U.S. and Its Neighbors*, pages 412, 422, and 430 for more background.

Worksheet - Eskimo Culture   NAME _____

1. What are two possible ways that Eskimos arrived in the Arctic regions in which they live today?

   _____

   _____

2. Eskimos hunt and fish for food. Name six other ways they use parts of the animals they kill:

   1. _____   4. _____

   2. _____   5. _____

   3. _____   6. _____

3. Name five ways that Eskimo family life differs from family life that we are used to:

   <u>Eskimo Family Life</u>   -   <u>Our Family Life</u>

   1. _____

   2. _____

   3. _____

   4. _____

   5. _____

4. Describe Eskimo religion.

   _____

   _____

5. How do Eskimos deal with crime?

   _____

   _____

6. What is the education of Eskimo children like?

   _____

   _____

7. If you suddenly found yourself living with an Eskimo family, what things would you like? What things would you find difficult? (Write on the back if you need more space.)

43

Eskimo Culture Quiz   NAME _____

1. Eskimos were mainly:
   a. hunters
   b. farmers
   c. gathers
   d. both b and c

6. The Eskimo language:
   a. has many different dialects
   b. uses many hand signals
   c. uses pictures
   d. is the same throughout the world

2. Eskimos probably first came to North America:
   a. from Asia
   b. from Europe
   c. across a land bridge
   d. both a and c

7. A common religious ceremony would:
   a. appeal to the gods for good hunting
   b. appeal to the gods for good weather
   c. appeal to the gods to cure the sick
   d. all of these

3. The polar climate is:
   a. rainy
   b. harsh
   c. mild
   d. both a and b

8. Eskimos depend upon:
   a. whales
   b. corn, beans and squash
   c. buffalo
   d. wild plants and berries

4. Today, Eskimo children:
   a. have no written language
   b. learn only survival skills
   c. attend modern schools
   d. do not go to school

9. Eskimo boats:
   a. are made from bark
   b. are made from skins
   c. are made from logs
   d. none of these

5. The Eskimo religion was concerned mostly with:
   a. survival
   b. power
   c. morality
   d. leaders

10. Eskimo shelter was:
    a. caves
    b. long houses
    c. igloos
    d. tepees

Lesson: Iroquois Culture

After students know the attributes or universals of culture, they need to apply those attributes to diverse cultures in order to understand and appreciate those cultures.* The Iroquois were chosen as a cultural example because they were one of the first tribes to be affected by the explorers and settlers. Also, their form of government was a model for our own.

<u>Objectives:</u> Students will be able to:

1. Apply cultural attributes to the culture of the Iroquois.
2. Make an outline about culture. (Reading)
3. Show, on a current United States map, where the Iroquois nation is located.

<u>Time Required:</u> 2 class periods

<u>Materials Needed:</u>

- Copy of pages 47-48, Background Material on Iroquois for each group
- Copy of page 49, United States map for each group
- Silver Burdett text, pp. 50-53
- Auditory tape, "The Great Peace - An Oral Tradition" (in trunk)

<u>Procedure:</u>

Day 1
1. Review attributes of culture.
2. Divide class into 6 research groups. Each group concentrates on one cultural attribute of the Iroquois and give them Background Material on Iroquois to read.
3. Student research groups find information about attribute assigned.
4. Each student research group finds the location of Iroquois on their map and is able to indicate location.

Day 2
1. Give instruction on making an outline (*Explorations* Teacher's Manual, pages 292-296.
2. Class makes one outline (on overhead, chart or board) on *Culture of Iroquois* using the six cultural attributes as sub-topics and information they researched.

*It is important to note that the attributes of this culture (and all cultures) manifest themselves differently depending on the time and needs of the people.

Debriefing:

From your research, how has the culture of the Iroquois changed since their early history?
How is the culture different from your own?

Evaluation:

Iroquois Culture Quiz
Evaluate group work and information gathered and its relevance to the specific attribute assigned to that group.
Group outline of *Culture of Iroquois.*
Group maps
Individual outlines on another topic.

Creative Extensions:

Art project depicting various attributes (e.g., make or draw masks fashioned after those the Iroquois used for their religious rituals).

Background Material on Iroquois

The Iroquois lived in five separate but related Indian nations in what is now New York state. Specifically, they were located south of Lake Ontario, along the Mohawk River and westward to the Finger Lakes and the Genesie River. It was a land full of trees, lakes, and rivers. It was a good environment for hunting and fishing. They were the Mohawks, Oneidas, Onondagas, Cayugas, and Senecas.

Warfare was a way of life for these Indians. They even made war upon each other. Consequently, warriors had incredible power and prestige.

The Iroquois people traditionally lived in long houses made of poles covered with bark. They were about 80 feet long and 18 feet wide. Each long house housed an extended family (including married children and their children). A large meeting room was located at one end of the long house.

To obtain food the men hunted and fished and the women were responsible for planting and harvesting corn, beans, and squash. Each family had its own field and each village had a collective field to grow food for festivals.

The Iroquois family was organized by clan. A clan was a group of relatives who traced their heritage to one woman. A person was born into the clan of his/her mother. Each clan had a certain bird or animal as its name or symbol. The head mothers picked the chiefs for their clan.

The five tribes had separate but similar languages. Their language was not written until the missionaries came and invented a system of writing the language. Since there was no written language, the Iroquois had to memorize their legends to pass down their traditions and rituals. Sometimes the legends were 75,000 words. This required a very intelligent tribe member to memorize. Wampum belts (with pictures from beads) were also used to tell stories.

Religion was a part of the Iroquois' daily life. Spiritual powers were all around the natural world and the people were always trying not to offend the spirits. Rituals and ceremonies were held to ward off evils. For example, the Green Corn Festival was held at harvest time to give thanks for their good fortune. Dreams were considered important communications from supernatural beings. Physical sickness was also related to evil spirits. Spiritual healers were very important.

In the early 1800's a new religion came about because of the dreams of a Seneca Indian named Handsome Lake. This "new" religion emphasized loyal, strong family relations, abstinence from alcohol, witchcraft and other "evils." It is now known as the "Long house Religion."

Background Material on Iroquois   Page 2

There was no formal education in a structured school until the Iroquois were impacted by white missionaries about 1800. Before that time, Indian children were taught by their parents and grandparents. They were taught survival skills, not reading and writing skills.

The government of the Iroquois was a model for our own. Benjamin Franklin wanted the 13 colonies to join together in a confederation in the same way that the five Iroquois tribes did. The five tribes joined together in a league or confederation. There were 50 leaders (called sachems) in the league. The sachems held a peace council each year. It is interesting that women could not be sachems, but they chose the sachems.

The Iroquois used bead wampum for money. But it was also used to record great events in history. Wampum was made from ground seashells that were polished. They then used a small hand drill to make a hole in the center.

United States Map

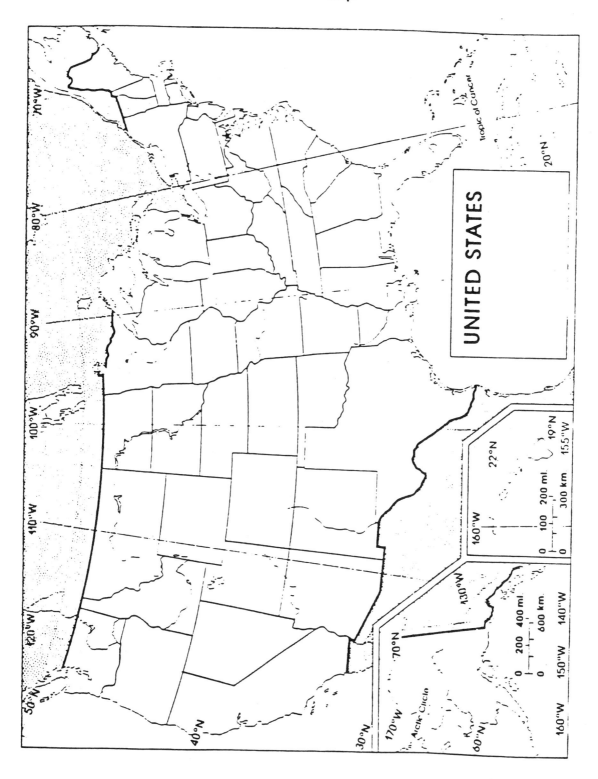

UNITED STATES

Iroquois Culture Quiz   NAME _____

1. The Iroquois depended upon:
   a. buffalo
   b. farming
   c. whales
   d. all of the above

2. The Iroquois:
   a. lived in tepees
   b. lived in igloos
   c. lived in long houses
   d. lived in adobe houses

3. False faces were:

   a. used for hunting
   b. used in curing the sick
   c. used in fighting
   d. used for trading

4. For the Iroquois, spirits were:
   a. unimportant
   b. everywhere
   c. only important on holidays
   d. entertaining

5. Wampum was:
   a. used as money
   b. used to tell stories
   c. used as clothing
   d. both a and b

6. Legends were important to the Iroquois:
   a. to entertain the children
   b. to tell of their history
   c. to worship their gods
   d. to prepare for ceremonies

7. In the Iroquois government:
   a. men were the chiefs
   b. women were the chiefs
   c. women picked the chiefs
   d. both a and c

8. Before the establishment of the
   League of Five Nations, the Iroquois:
   a. lived at peace with each other
   b. were always at war with each other
   c. had no system of government
   d. had no spoken language

9. The three sisters were:
   a. corn, beans and squash
   b. Mohawks, Oneidas, Senicas
   c. leaders of the tribe
   d. Iroquois priests

10. According to Iroquois legend,
    creation occurred when:
    a. Firedragon made man
    b. Muskrat held earth on his back
    c. Sky Woman fell from heaven
    d. both a and c

Lesson: Origin and Migration of Native Americans

This lesson is to introduce students to the land bridge theories and to inform students that many Native American tribal legends indicate that North America was their original home.

<u>Objectives:</u> Students will be able to:

1. Use a world map to trace the land bridge migration into the Americas.
2. Identify three theories of origin; land, land when covered with ice, and boats.
3. Label continents and oceans on a given outline map.

<u>Time Required:</u> One lesson of 40 minutes.

<u>Materials Needed:</u>

- *An American Indian Perspective*, pp. 4-5, project R.E.A.C.H.
- Silver Burdett text, pp. 46-50
- Origin and Migration of Native Americans, page 53
- Copies for each student of page 54, Origin and Migration of Native Americans Map
- (Optional) *The U.S. and Its Neighbors*, pp. 16-17, workbook
- *American History Through Maps*, page 3

<u>Procedure:</u>

1. Use the material on pp. 4-5 of *An American Indian Perspective* to begin a class discussion.
2. Use a wall map of the world to show students the location of the Bering Strait. Information from page 53 can be used at this time.
3. Students may read silently or orally text pages 46-50. Use the information for class discussion. Use additional information from page 53.
4. Use the map on text page 48 for students to locate Asia, North America, South America, Pacific Ocean, Bering Sea, and Bering Strait (not labeled on map).
5. Distribute copies of the world map. Have students trace the migration routes indicated on the map, color and label. (Workbook pages 15-17 may be assigned.)

<u>Debriefing:</u>

What is a strait?
What are three theories of migration?
Why is it tribes did not remain in one location?

<u>Evaluation:</u>

The accuracy of labeling the map may be used.

<u>Creative Extensions:</u>

Film: *American Indian: Yesterday and Today* (18 minutes)

Origin and Migration of Native Americans

It is believed that the first American Settlers were primitive Asiatic people. It is quite generally accepted by scientists that they came from Siberia to Alaska across the Bering Strait thousands of years ago. However, there are two theories about the Strait. Some scientists believe that it was a land bridge at the time of the migration. Others contend that it was frozen at the time of the crossings. A third group of scientists believe that the migration was accomplished by using boats. This group contends that the islands of Big Diomede and Little Diomede were used as stopping points for the long journey. These two islands shorten the trip from a distance of 60 miles to only 25.[1]

Until the Ice Age ended, about 9000 B.C., the Wisconsin Glacier covered most of North America for 70,000 years. The ice of the glacier reached a depth of two miles in places and it is estimated that the glacier contained about one-third of the earth's surface water. This resulted in a lower sea level which should have allowed the Bering Strait to be a land bridge for migrating from Siberia to Alaska.[2]

Some researchers contend that the culture of Eskimos seems to have come from inland. They believe that other Indian tribes caused the Eskimos to migrate from the northern lakes of Canada to the Arctic Ocean.[3]

---

[1] Felix, Sutton, <u>North American Indians</u>, p. 4.

[2] Jones, Jayne Clark, <u>The American Indian in America</u>, Vol. 1, pp. 11-12.

[3] Bringle, Mary, <u>Eskimos</u>, p. 6

Worksheet - Origin and Migration of Native Americans Map

Trace in red the routes followed by Native Americans from Asia to North and South America.

Label and color the following continents: Europe, Asia, North America, Africa, Australia, South America, Antarctica

Label and color the following oceans: Atlantic, Indian, Pacific

Label the Bering Strait

54

Lesson: Legends of Native Americans

This lesson will briefly touch upon the purposes of legends and introduce students to an Iroquois legend.

<u>Objectives:</u> Students will be able to:

1. List some reasons for Native American Legends.
2. Recognize importance of oral history, develop respect for cultural beliefs and learning of culture.
3. Compare methods of recording family history of the past (oral legends) to those currently used (video, photo, etc.)
4. Recognize skills required of a good listener. (Language)
5. Identify the character, setting, and plot of the legend. (Reading)
6. Identify the characteristics of a legend as a story told from one generation to another, a story that relates to the education, culture, or beliefs of a specific group. (Reading)

<u>Time Required:</u> One class of 40 minutes.

<u>Materials Needed:</u>

- The Iroquois Story of Creation, page 56
- (Optional) *Exploration*, Teacher's edition, pp. 465-466; Student text, pp. 372-381

<u>Procedure:</u>

1. Discuss with students that legends were used for the teaching of history and cultural beliefs of the tribe as well as education purposes. Written records were not available which made the legends as important as our newspapers and books. Listening skills were of great importance to the teller as well as the listener.   One who was listening was expected to understand double meanings and unexplained circumstances in the legend. Memory of detail was required in order to paint the story in the mind of the listener for future re-telling.
2. Read The Iroquois Story of Creation. Ask students to form pictures in their minds as you read.
3. Ask students to identify the characters, setting, and plot.
4. Some students may want to share the mental pictures they formed while listening to the legend.
5. Ask students if they have oral history to share from their family.
6. Discuss how methods have changed from the oral legends to those using video, camera, tape recorder, and the print media.
7. Have students make an illustration for the legend.
8. Have students write a legend for their family history. These legends could then be put on a tape for future reference.

<u>Debriefing:</u>

What are some reasons for the importance of legends?
How have methods changed for recording history?

<u>Evaluation:</u>

Teacher observation of class participation in discussion and completion of illustration.

<u>Creative Extensions:</u>

"The Heroine of Kapiti" from *Explorations* may be used as a legend example from another part of the world.
Film: *Arrow to the Sun* (12 minutes)

The Iroquois Story of Creation

Long before there were human beings, there were Sky People. They dwelled in the celestial world. In those days there was no sun. All light came from the large white blossoms on the celestial tree that stood in front of the Lodge of the Sky Chief. This Sky Chief had married a young wife. In time his wife, Sky Woman, began to show signs that she would soon bear a child.

There was a troublesome being, called Firedragon, in the Sky World. Firedragon was always spreading rumors. Now he whispered to Sky Chief that the child who was about to be born would not be his. In a fit of anger and jealousy, Sky Chief uprooted the great celestial tree in front of his lodge. He pushed his wife through the hole where the tree had once stood.

Sky Woman fell rapidly down toward the vast dark waters below. The birds, feeling sorry for her, flew underneath and gently supported her, breaking her fall and carrying her slowly downward. At the same time, the water animals hurried to make a place for her. Turtle said that he would support a world on his back.. The sea animals plunged down into the water looking for some earth. Muskrat succeeded and came up with a large mouthful of earth, which he placed on Turtle's back. The light from the blossoms of the fallen celestial tree shone through the hole where it had stood and became the sun. When Sky Woman landed, everything was in readiness for her, with grass and trees beginning to grow.

Sky Woman gave birth to a daughter. When this daughter grew to womanhood, she began to be with child. No one knows whether her husband was Turtle or West Wind, but she gave birth to two remarkable twin boys--one good and one evil. The Good Twin was born in the usual way, but the Evil Twin was in a hurry and pushed through his mother's side to be born. In doing so, he killed his mother.

Sky Woman buried her daughter, and plants miraculously began to grow from various parts of the daughter's body--a tobacco plant, a cornstalk, a bean bush, and a squash vine. This was the origin of all the plants that would be most important to the human beings who would come later.

The Good Twin and the Evil Twin quickly grew to manhood. As soon as they were grown, they proved true to their names. The Good Twin began creating all sorts of good things: plants, animals, medicinal herbs, rivers, and streams. The Evil Twin began to spoil his brother's work, putting rapids and boulders in the rivers, creating poisonous plants, thorns and briars, diseases, and monsters. The Good and Evil Twins fought against each other to see who would predominate in creation, but the Evil could never overcome the Good. Finally the Good Twin created human beings to enjoy all the good things he had made for them. And that is how it all began.

Indians of North America: The Iroquois by Barbara Graymont. Chelsea House Publishers, New York. 1988

Lesson: Chief Seattle

Native Americans feel very strongly about their interaction with the environment. Their lifestyle reflected their attitudes.

<u>Objectives:</u> Students will be able to:

1. Describe how many Native Americans view their environment.
2. Choose main idea of a speech. (Reading)

<u>Time Required:</u> One lesson of 50 minutes

<u>Materials Needed:</u>

- Letter from Chief Seattle and Indian proverb, page 58
- Silver Burdett textbook

<u>Procedure:</u>

1. Read and discuss page 58 - Letter from Chief Seattle and Indian proverb.
2. Students read pages 53-54 from text about the Sioux and their use of wildlife. Discuss how all parts of the buffalo were used.
3. Instruction on how to choose the main idea. (*Explorations* Teacher's Manual, pp. 66-69)
4. Review speech by Chief Seattle and discuss the main idea.
5. Students read page 195 (Two Views of the Land) from Silver Burdett text. They write or orally report the main idea of what they read.

<u>Debriefing:</u>

Why was the environment so important to the Native Americans?
Have Americans followed the example of the Native Americans use of wildlife?

<u>Evaluation:</u>

Reports of main idea reading.

<u>Creative Extension:</u>

Students could research in other books examples of Native Americans' interaction with their environment, and write a report, highlighting main ideas.
This theme is also threaded throughout *Sign of the Beaver* unit

Letter from Chief Seattle

"You must teach your children that the ground beneath their feet is the ashes of our grandfathers. So that they respect the land, tell your children that the earth is rich with the lives of our kin. Teach your children what we have taught our children -- that the earth is our mother. Whatever befalls the earth, befalls the sons of the earth. If men spit upon the ground they spit upon themselves.

"This we know. The earth does not belong to man; man belongs to the earth. This we know. All things are connected like the blood which unites one family. All things are connected.

"Whatever befalls the earth befalls the sons of the earth. Man did not weave the web of life; he is merely a strand in it. Whatever he does to the web, he does to himself."

Indian Proverb

"The frog does not drink up the pond in which it lives."

Name _____

Native Americans: Unit Evaluation

(6 pts)   1. Name six attributes of culture.

a._____   d._____

b._____   e._____

c._____   f._____

(36 pts)   2. Describe each attribute of culture.

(20 pts)   3. Describe the culture of the Eskimo using at least 4 of the cultural attributes.

Native Americans: Unit Evaluation - Page 2

(10 pts)

4. Explain the land bridge theory.

(12 pts)

5. What important contribution did the Iroquois Indians make to the United States of America?

(8 pts)

6. Name 2 reasons why legends were important in the Native American cultures.

(8 pts)

7. What caused conflicts between cultures? Recommend some solutions.

Novel Unit - Teacher's Guide to *The Sign of the Beaver*
by Elizabeth Speare

This guide was developed for teachers who have never used novels in the classroom for group study and need help getting started, or for teachers who may have used novels before and know how much time it takes to develop questions and activities for group work. The guide is divided into these sections:

1. Teacher's Introduction
2. Pre-reading Readiness Activities
3. Vocabulary Development Suggestions
4. Post-reading Follow-up Activities and Geography Tie-in

Please remember that, just like our basal, this guide included more than one might reasonably want to do. Tailor it to meet your needs and time frame.

Teacher's Introduction

Main Characters: Matt: age 12, white settler
        Attean: Indian boy of Penobscot tribe approaching teens
        Saknis: Attean's grandfather

Setting: Maine wilderness in the year 1769

Plot: Twelve-year-old Matt is left to guard his family's cabin and land in the Maine wilderness while his father goes back to Massachusetts to get his mother, sister, and new baby. Matt meets a boy from the neighboring Penobscot Indians, and through their experiences together, he matures into a self-reliant adult capable of making difficult decisions.

Basic Themes: Survival in the wilderness, personal growth, and "coming of age" of main character, Matt, and empathy for and trust in a person from another (and opposing) culture.

Pre-Reading Readiness

Activities

1. Use a current map of the Maine area to compare its present appearance with its probable appearance in the 1700's. Discuss flora, fauna, rivers, travel hazards, etc. of the two time periods.

2. Research the Indians of the northeast during this time period (the 1700's); investigate their clothing, housing, culture, lifestyles, beliefs, etc.

3. Create a small museum of "artifacts" made by students after research showing weapons, clothing, articles used in daily life, etc., of both settlers and Indians. Display.

4. Develop a time line showing world events surrounding the 1700's. What famous people were alive? What was the state of industry and technology? Medicine? Give students some concept of time period.

5. Four maps follow this novel unit for your use.

Vocabulary Development Suggestions

On the following pages are vocabualry development suggestions for Chapter 1-24. At the beginning of each chapter is a list of suggested vocabulary words. This list is only a suggestion. Gear it for your students and use as much or little as you like. Further suggestions for enhancing vocabulary:

1. Make a banner or poster to be hung in the room during the group study of the novel, listing words studied. This helps all of you keep track of vocabulary studied and can assist you, the teacher, when reviewing.

2. Develop a game to be played periodically to review words. It can be Vocabulary Charades, or Twenty Questions, or even a card game following the rules of Go Fish, Old Maid, etc., depending on the words you have selected and how they break into categories.

3. Choose, or have students choose, a passage from the story and type it on a primary typewriter, leaving out key words to make a "Cloze" type of assignment. Students must supply words that fit the context. They can go back and compare with the original when done.

4. Directions for Dictionary Master on page 79. Having the student take a guess at the meaning of the word in context gets him actively involved in thinking about that word's meaning. After looking the word up in the dictionary, he can compare his idea to the true definition. This is not an exercise to be graded right or wrong, but one that students can bring to a group to be shared and discussed. To extend the activity, have students use words in a sentence of their own, demonstrating understanding. Copy the "Dictionary Work" sheet, one or two for each chapter, and fill in the words you wish to emphasize for each chapter.

Adapted from a unit written by Alison Lindsey.

Dictionary Work

Name_____

Find the word from the chapter listed below. Write the exact sentence the way it appears in your novel. Then define the word in your own way using the context to help you guess its meaning. Finally, locate the word in the dictionary and write its definition. If there is more than one meaning for the word, choose the one that seems closest to the author's meaning.

Title of Novel: _____

Chapter Name or Number: _____

Word: _____ Page No. ____

Sentence from the story: _____

_____

_____

My Guess: _____

_____

Dictionary Definition: _____

_____

_____

Word: _____ Page No. ____

Sentence from the story: _____

_____

_____

My Guess: _____

_____

Dictionary Definition: _____

_____

_____

SOURCE LIST
FOR IDEAS AND MATERIALS

by Kent Freeland
Professor of Education
Morehead State University, Morehead, Kentucky

and

Charles E. Holt, Jr.
Professor of History
Morehead State University, Morehead, Kentucky

THE era of the isolated classroom teacher has passed. Today the social studies teachers in rural or urban schools, large or small schools, poor or wealthy districts, have available to them resources that would have been unthought of just a decade or two before.

The purpose of this chapter is to introduce today's K-12 social studies teacher to some of the resources that will enhance instruction. From traditional written material to video and computer software, and including interactive CD materials, today's teacher has a multitude of resources. In addition, social studies teachers may apply for summer programs, international educational opportunities, or other competitive programs. Teachers may also involve their students in many local, state, and national activities.

The arrangement of chapter 9 divides the items into seven categories. The first six correspond to the major social sciences: anthropology, economics, geography, history, political science, and sociology. The seventh category, "interdisci-plinary," covers the entries that apply to two or more of the social sciences. Once you have read this chapter, you will have some ideas on places to write to or telephone. Be aggressive and take advantage of the resources listed on the following pages.

Anthropology

AMIDEAST is a private, nonprofit organization promoting understanding and cooperation between Americans and the people of the Middle East and North Africa through education, information, and development programs.
AMIDEAST
1100 17th Street, N.W.
Washington, DC 20036-4601

AWAIR is an organization that distributes a free newsletter describing the curriculum resources and teacher services offered on the Arab world and Islamic resources.

250 / *Source List for Ideas and Materials*

AWAIR
1400 Shattuck Avenue, Suite 9
Berkeley, CA 94709

The Crow Canyon Archeological Center provides experiential education programs for students in grades 4-12, as well as a summer high school field school, a teacher's workshop, and other adult programs.

Crow Canyon Archeological Center
23390 County Road K
Cortez, CO 81321
(303) 565-8975

The Peace Corps seeks ways to actively involve people in the United States with projects that are carried out in foreign countries by Peace Corps workers. Students can raise money and then exchange letters, tapes, essays, and artifacts with the Peace Corps Partners overseas.

Peace Corps Partnership Program
1990 K Street, N.W.
Washington, DC 20526
(800) 424-8580 or (202) 606-3406

Faces is a publication which introduces young readers to the lifestyles, beliefs, and customs found throughout the world. Published in cooperation with the American Museum of Natural History, this magazine allows students in grades 4-9 to learn about multicultural studies.

Cobblestone Publishing, Inc.
30 Grove Street
Peterborough, NH 03458
(603) 924-7209

The Stanford Program on International and Cross-Cultural Education (SPICE) has developed interactive teaching materials for grades K-12. For a catalog describing the 75 units which this organization has developed, contact:

SPICE
Littlefield Center, Room 14
300 Lasuen Street
Stanford University
Stanford, CA 94305-5013
(415) 723-1114

The Archaeological Assistance Divison of the U.S. National Park Service has established the LEAP Clearinghouse (Listing of Education in Archaeological Programs). LEAP includes summary information about public education efforts carried out as part of federal agencies' or other organizations' archaeological projects. The AAD also has compiled for teachers information about archaeology (e.g., titles of magazines, videotapes, simulations, and programs around the country).

Archaeological Assistance Divison
National Park Service
P.O. Box 37127
Washington, DC 20013-7127
(202) 343-6843

Culture kits with artifacts from around the world are available. When used in the classroom, these kits are designed to increase multicultural literacy, critical thinking, and writing skills.

Ethnic Arts & Facts
P.O. Box 20550
Oakland, CA 94620
(415) 469-0451

Teaching guides, class activities, and primary sources are available on China, Japan, Korea, and Southeast Asia for grades K-12.

East Asian Curriculum Project
Columbia University
420 West 118th Street
New York, NY 10027

The Society for American Archaeology publishes a sheet entitled "Sources of Information on Archaeology." In the future it will be publishing a pamphlet called "Archaeology and You." Both of these center on public awareness of archaeology.

Society for American Archaeology
808 17th Street, N.W.
Washington, DC 20006
(202) 223-9774

The American Anthropological Association distributes flyers on such topics as "What is Anthropology?," "Evolution," and "Careers in Anthropology."

American Anthropological Association
1703 New Hampshire Avenue, N.W.
Washington, DC 20009
(202) 232-8800

Smithsonian's publication "Anthropology Notes" is available for teachers. The Smithsonian has an office of public outreach which distributes this very helpful bulletin for teachers who want to get information about teaching anthropological content in the classroom.

Smithsonian
900 Jefferson Drive
Washington, DC
(202) 357-1592

Economics

"Commodity Challenge" gives secondary students a practical learning experience applying the basic theories of economics. It uses the future market as a learning tool and systematically teaches supply, demand, and price discovery. Student projects are judged in this competition and awards are given.

Chicago Board of Trade
Education and Marketing Services
141 West Jackson Boulevard
Chicago, IL 60604-2994
(312) 435-7206

The Consumer's Resource Handbook is published by the United States Office of Consumer Affairs. The handbook includes two majors sections. The first covers how to be a smart consumer, while the second is a consumer assistance directory. It includes addresses for such agencies as Better Business Bureaus, State Banking Authorities, the Federal Information Center, selected federal agencies, and state utility commissions. The handbook also includes the addresses and telephone numbers of more than 750 companies.

The Consumer Information Catalog lists approximately 200 free or low-cost federal booklets with helpful information for consumers. It is a free quarterly publication that includes such topics as careers and education, the environment, and small businesses. For either or both of the above publications, contact:

Consumer Information Center
Pueblo, CO 81009
(719) 948-4000

Dollars & Sense is a monthly magazine which attempts to simplify economics so students can understand it more easily.

Dollars & Sense Magazine
Economic Affairs Bureau
One Summer Street
Somerville, MA 02143

Classroom materials are available from the World Bank. These include case studies, poster kits, maps, and videocassettes that teach about eco-nomic and social development in developing countries.

World Bank
Room T-8082
1818 H Street
Washington, DC 20433

The Foundation for Teaching Economics promotes economic education in grades 7-10 by developing instructional materials and conducting applied research.

Foundation for Teaching Economics
550 Kearny Street, Suite 1000
San Francisco, CA 94114

The Joint Council on Economic Education is an important resource for elementary and secondary materials and activities. The "Stock Market Game" is operated by individual states for middle grade and high school students. In addition, its National Awards Program for the Teaching of Economics is available to all elementary and secondary teachers.

Joint Council on Economic Education
432 Park Avenue South
New York, NY 10016
(212) 685-5489/5499

Junior Achievement provides encouragement for K-12 students with regard to economic education materials that feature hands-on learning, a one-semester high school curriculum, and at-risk programs for elementary and middle school grades.

Junior Achievement, Inc.
45 East Clubhouse Drive
Colorado Springs, CO 80906
(719) 636-2474

Procter & Gamble publishes materials for the middle or high school classroom. "Decisions about Product Safety," "Insights into Economics," "Perspectives," "How to Clean," "Food Preparation," "Personal Care," and "Environmental Education" are the titles available.

Procter & Gamble
Educational Services
P.O. Box 14009
Cincinnati, OH 45250
(513) 983-2029

The twelve Federal Reserve Banks and the Board of Governors of the Federal Reserve System have prepared 454 publications and other informational materials that can be used in elementary and secondary social studies classes. Topics include consumer protection, monetary policy, coins and currency, basic economics, and more. For a copy of this directory, contact:

Public Information Department
Federal Reserve Bank of New York
33 Liberty Street
New York, NY 10045
(212) 720-5000

Geography

The Geography Bee is an annual competition for students in grades 4-8. The purpose of the Bee is to encourage the teaching of geography as part of the curriculum. Questions in school, state, and national competition address the study of the earth and its inhabitants.

National Geographic Society
Geography Bee
Washington, DC 20036
(202) 857-7000

The National Geography Olympiad is sponsored by the National Council for Geographic Education. It is a competitive event for students in grades 2-9. The contest is held in the respective schools of participants.

National Social Studies Olympiad
P.O. Box 477
Hauppauge, NY 11788-0477
(516) 265-4792

Students can create a competition entry in one of three categories: (1) Managing the Environment in a Changing World, (2) The Geography of Travel and Trade, and (3) Geographic Patterns of Cultural Contact and Cultural Diversity. The competition is supported by a grant from American Express.

American Express Geography Competition
P.O. Box 13769
Atlanta, GA 30324-9842
(800) 395-GLOBE

The Worldwatch Institute is an independent, nonprofit research organization with a goal of helping to raise understanding of global environmental issues to the point where the public will support the policies needed to create an environmentally sustainable global economy. Its annual publication, *State of the World*, is a guide--avail-

able for purchase--to the world's resources and how they are being managed.

Worldwatch Institute
1776 Massachusetts Avenue, N.W.
Washington, DC 20036-1904
(202) 452-1999

The United States Postal Service Olympic Pen Pal Club is sponsoring a program whereby U.S. students (ages 6-18) are matched by computer with their peers in 14 foreign countries. A world map is included in the kit that is sent to participating students.

USPS Olympic Pen Pal Club
P.O. Box 9419
Gaithersburg, MD 20898-9419
(800) 552-3922

The International Geographical Congress sponsors a number of events for high school students. Field trips, symposia, short courses, and workshops are conducted in Washington, DC.

International Geographical Congress
1145 17th Street, N.W.
Washington, DC 20036
(202) 828-6688

History

National History Day is a competition held in the individual states. Students vie for scholarships and prizes. Teachers should work with state coordinators, or call the national headquarters.

National History Day
11201 Euclid Avenue
Cleveland, OH 44106
(216) 421-8803

Many teachers want their students to experience the tasks of historians. There is an organization which publishes books and information to assist in teaching and learning about history.

American Association for State and Local
  History
172 Second Avenue North, Suite 202
Nashville, TN 37201

Cobblestone is a history magazine for young people, grades 4-9. This publication presents people, events, and ideas that have shaped the American experience through the use of historic photographs and illustrations, activities, and contests, plus recommendations on books to read, places to visit, and videos to watch.

Cobblestone Publishing Co., Inc.
30 Grove Street
Peterborough, NH 03458
(603) 924-7209

The Concord Review seeks to publish the best essays being written by students of history. High school history teachers have their students submit their essays on any historical topic. The best essays are then published.

The Concord Review
P.O. Box 476
Canton, MA 02021

Calliope tries to infuse world history with reality for elementary and middle school students. This magazine for young people is published five times during the school year. It presents world history in the context of anthropology and archaeology.

Cobblestone Publishing Co., Inc.
30 Grove Street
Peterborough, NH 03458
(603) 924-7209

Each spring a conference on women's history is held in Massachusetts for elementary and high school teachers. The conference has a different focus each year.

The NETWORK, Inc.
300 Brookstone Square, Suite 900
Andover, MA 01810

March is National Women's History Month. The National Women's History Project is dedicated to continuing its year-round promotion of women's history in classrooms, communities, and workplaces. A K-12 resource catalog can be obtained by contacting

National Women's History Project
7738 Bell Road
Windsor, CA 95492-8518
(707) 838-6000

Nearly fifty teaching units for history teachers are available at low cost. They are based on primary sources and involve students in the practice of history. Additional services are available to teachers as well.

National Center for History in the Schools
University of California, Los Angeles
Moore Hall 231
405 Hillgard Avenue
Los Angeles, CA 90024-1521

The Organization of American Historians provides a number of services for history teachers. *The Magazine of History* is an excellent publication for teachers. The OAH also sponsors awards and prizes, lectures, and other outreach activities.

Organization of American Historians
112 North Bryan Street
Bloomington, IN 47408-4199
(812) 855-7311

The learning materials program of the Education Branch, National Archives, encourages teachers of upper elementary through secondary school students to use historical documents in the classroom through publications and teacher training programs. For information about the publications, AV resources, or workshops on U.S. history, contact:

Education Branch, NEE-E
National Archives
Washington, DC 20408
(202) 724-0454

Political Science

Each year, Mock Trial Competition is held in nearly all of the states. Judges and lawyers are encouraged to assist in the local competitions, which involve teams of students who argue actual or hypothetical court cases. Inquiries should be made to one's state coordinator.

The Center for Civic Education has a number of programs for students. For example, "We the People" teaches upper elementary, middle, and high school students the historical development and basic principles and values of our constitutional democracy. High school classes who complete the textbook course of study are eligible to enter the National Bicentennial Competition. The "Law in a Free Society" program, for students in grades K-12, is based on four concepts fundamental to understanding our constitutional democracy. For information about these and other programs, contact:

Center for Civic Education
5146 Douglas Fir Road
Calabasas, CA 91302
(800) 350-4223 or (818) 591-9321

Teachers can write to many agencies to obtain free information for classroom use. Names and addresses of state boards of tourism, U.S. embassies in other countries, foreign embassies in the

U.S., and other governmental agencies can be found in this reference book, found in many libraries:

World Chamber of Commerce Directory
P.O. Box 1029
Loveland, CO 80539
(303) 663-3231

The Foreign Policy Association is a private, nonprofit, nonpartisan organization dedicated to developing and disseminating international education programs and resources including publications, videotapes, and teacher activity books on foreign policy issues.

Foreign Policy Association/Ford Foundation
1726 M Street, N.W., Suite 800
Washington, DC 20036

"Presidential Classroom" is a program available to high school students. Students meet with the nation's leaders in Washington and see the U.S. government in action. Through a comprehensive curriculum of seminars, discussions, visits, and meetings, students gain an understanding of the political process and how national and international policy decisions are made.

Presidential Classroom for Young Americans
441 North Lee Street
Alexandria, VA 22314-2346
(800) 441-6533

The James Madison Fellowship Program is an opportunity for high school social studies teachers to compete for a fellowship. If selected, a teacher enrolls in part-time graduate study, in any accredited institution of higher education in the United States, leading to a master's degree. The intent of the program is to produce teachers who have an excellent understanding of the U.S. Constitution.

James Madison Memorial Fellowship Program
P.O. Box 6304
Princeton, NJ 08541-6304
(609) 951-6240

AT&T has developed a program which is described as a hands-on, newspaper/polling program that involves junior and senior high school students in the democratic process. A class receives copies of the *Voices that Count* newspaper and then participates in a poll, the results of which are phoned in to AT&T. Results are distributed nationally to the media and policymakers.

AT&T Voices that Count
P.O. Box 1697
Murray Hill Station
New York, NY 10156-0608
(212) 684-2484

Teachers can purchase high school teaching units from the Center for Foreign Policy Development. Sample titles are "The Arab-Israeli Conflict," "Facing a Disintegrating Soviet Union," and "The Role of the United States in a Changing World." For information about these and their newsletter, contact:

Choices for the 21st Century Education Project
Center for Foreign Policy Development
Brown University, Box 1948
Providence, RI 02912
(401) 863-3155

Center for Research & Development for Law-Related Education (CRADLE) is a clearinghouse for teacher-developed materials on law and citizenship. It collects and catalogs teacher-developed and -tested lesson plans and other classroom resource materials, and then makes them available to other K-12 teachers. CRADLE serves as a national repository of lesson plans on the Constitution, the Bill of Rights, and other law-related issues.

Center for Research & Development for
Law-Related Education (CRADLE)
Wake Forest University School of Law
P.O. Box 7206 Reynolda Station
Winston-Salem, NC 27109
(800) 437-1054 or (919) 759-5872

The Taft Institute sponsors a number of seminars for social studies teachers each summer. For minimal expense, teachers receive materials and housing; they participate in discussions; and they sometimes receive graduate credit in political science. These regional institutes focus on political participation issues. To find out if there is an institute in your area, contact:

Taft Institute
420 Lexington Avenue
New York, NY 10170
(212) 682-1530

Close Up is a nonpartisan, nonprofit educational foundation that provides interested citizens with a variety of programs and curricular resources designed to enhance their understanding of, and appreciation for, their role in the political process.

One of their efforts is the week-long high school program of seminars and on-site visits with members of Congress, executive branch experts, lobbyists, representatives of the media, and other Washington insiders.

Another program for high school students is the Citizen Bee, a competition designed to improve students' understanding of their American heritage.

The Close Up Program for New Americans offers 10th- and 11th-grade students who have recently immigrated to the United States an opportunity to acquire the knowledge, skills, and confidence needed to become active, informed citizens.

The Civic Achievement Award Program (CAAP) serves grades 5-8. Students learn the basics of U.S. history, government, geography, economics, culture, and current events; they complete a research project; and they identify and conduct a community service project.

Close Up Foundation
44 Canal Center Plaza
Alexandria, VA 22314
(703) 706-3300

The YMCA sponsors several programs for middle and high school students. The model legislature program and the model United Nations program are popular in many states. There are also statewide leadership conferences for students. To find out if your state participates in these programs, contact your state YMCA.

Sociology

The United States Holocaust Memorial Museum encourages and supports serious, thoughtful reflection on the Holocaust and its implications for our lives today. It has an educational outreach division. One of its projects is to sponsor a writing contest for students in grades 7-12.

U.S. Holocaust Memorial Council
Writing Contest
2000 L Street, N.W., Suite 588
Washington, DC 20036
(202) 653-9220

The RespecTeen "Speak for Yourself" curriculum program is offered to 7th- and 8th-grade social studies classes. In the final activity, each student selects and researches a youth-related issue, then writes and mails a letter on that issue to his or her U.S. Representative. Copies of the letters can be entered in the "Speak for Yourself" competition, where they will be reviewed and judged by a panel of educators; the winner attends a forum in our nation's capital.

RespecTeen
c/o Padilla Speer Beardsley, Inc.
224 Franklin Avenue West
Minneapolis, MN 55404
(800) 888-3829

This governmental agency provides data and teaching information about the population of the United States covering a period of many decades.

Bureau of the Census
Data User Service Division
Washington, DC 20233
(301) 763-4100

CARE has educational packages that focus on life in developing countries and tropical deforestation; these contain lesson plans and videotapes.

CARE
660 First Avenue
New York, NY 10016

StarServe, a nonprofit organization funded by Kraft General Foods Foundation and operated in partnership with United Way of America, offers free materials, resources, and technical assistance to help teachers and students plan and implement community service projects.

StarServe
P.O. Box 34567
Washington, DC 20043
(800) 888-8232

Zero Population Growth is an organization which publishes elementary, intermediate, and secondary materials to teach students about population dynamics and their social, political, and environmental effects in the United States and worldwide.

Zero Population Growth, Inc.
1400 Sixteenth Street, N.W.
Suite 320
Washington, DC 20036
(202) 332-2200

An opportunity is available for students to attack the problem of hunger throughout the world. Videotapes, action packets, guidelines on forming coalitions, publications, and ideas for projects are available by contacting:

U.S. National Committee for World Food Day
1001 22nd Street, N.W.
Washington, DC 20437
(202) 653-2404

Another group which addresses the problem of food shortages is The Hunger Project. It is a nonprofit organization dedicated to ending chronic hunger worldwide. It offers assistance in setting up school clubs and has created a list of project ideas students can do.
    The Hunger Project
    1388 Sutter Street
    San Francisco, CA 94109
    (415) 928-8799

Amnesty International works to protect the human rights of prisoners around the world. Groups exist around the country to write letters on behalf of prisoners, participate in long-term actions focusing on particular issues and/or countries, raise money for the organization, and so forth.
    Amnesty International USA
    53 West Jackson, Room 1162
    Chicago, IL 60604-3606
    (312) 427-2060

The Population Institute POPLINE explores, analyzes, and evaluates facts and public policies relating to the problems of world overpopulation, which are then published bimonthly in its newsletter, *POPLINE*.
    Population Institute
    110 Maryland Avenue, N.E.
    Washington, DC 20002
    (202) 544-3303

Interdisciplinary

The Institute of Peace is an independent, nonpartisan federal institution which aims to expand the body of knowledge about the nature of international peace, disseminate this knowledge to individuals involved in peacemaking, and help educate the American public and promote public discourse on issues of war and peace. It sponsors a National Peace Essay Contest for students in grades 9-12.
    The United States Institute of Peace
    National Peace Essay Contest
    P.O. Box 27720, Central Station
    Washington, DC 20038-7720
    (202) 457-1700

The American Field Service promotes intercultural learning through worldwide exchange programs for students, teachers, and families.
    American Field Service (AFS)
    313 East 43rd Street
    New York, NY 10017

Learning Enrichment produces and distributes free teaching materials underwritten by corporations, foundations, and countries.
    Learning Enrichment, Inc.
    50 Vanderbilt Avenue
    New York, NY 10017

A new program is available for early elementary students. It combines social studies and language arts with a whole language component. "Discovery" is for grades K-3, integrating map and globe skills, geography skills, reading skills, writing skills, speaking skills, listening skills, and thinking skills. The lessons in "Discovery" are also designed to be used with children's literature.
    George F. Cram Co., Inc.
    P.O. Box 426
    Indianapolis, IN 46206
    (800) 227-4199

Although *Cricket* is not a social studies magazine, it does have benefits for a social studies teacher. *Cricket* is for children aged preschool through thirteen. There are art, poetry, and story contests for students, as well as excellent fiction and nonfiction for them to read--much of it on topics related to social studies.
    Cricket
    Box 2672
    Boulder, CO 80321

Every year the National Endowment for the Humanities offers professional development opportunities for K-12 teachers. Seminars are held during the summer months on a variety of topics in the humanities. Each seminar provides teachers the chance to work under the direction of a distinguished teacher and active scholar.
    National Endowment for the Humanities
    Division of Education Programs, Room 302
    1100 Pennsylvania Avenue, N.W.
    Washington, DC 220506
    (202) 786-0282

Social Studies School Service publishes a catalog containing a wide spectrum of materials that can be purchased: posters, books, reproducible activities, simulations and games, computer sofware, laser discs, and videotapes.

Social Studies School Service
10200 Jefferson Boulevard
P.O. Box 802
Culver City, CA 90232-0802
(800) 421-4246 or (310) 839-2249

The American Newspaper Publishers Association Foundation (ANPA) offers a variety of materials for newspapers in the following major areas: The Newspaper in Education program (*New York Times*, *Wall Street Journal*, *Los Angeles Times*, *USA Today*, etc.), career education, support of the First Amendment, furthering work force diversity in the newspaper business, and promoting literacy.

ANPA Foundation
The Newspaper Center
Box 17407 Dulles Airport
Washington, DC 20041
(703) 648-1000

The Fulbright-Hays Seminars Abroad Program provides short-term study/travel opportunities for U.S. educators in the social sciences and the humanities.

Fulbright-Hays Seminars Abroad Program
Center for International Education
U.S. Department of Education
7th and D Streets, S.W.
Washington, DC 20202-5332
(202) 708-9493

Services are available for teachers who want to utilize television in the classroom for news events. Some of these include:

C-Span in the Classroom
400 North Capitol Street, N.W., Suite 650
Washington, DC 20001
(800) 523-7586 or (202) 737-3220

The Discovery Channel
7700 Wisconsin Avenue
Bethesda, MD 20814-3522

A number of weekly news magazines offer programs for middle school and high school students.

Time Education Programs
Communications Park, Box 8000
Mount Kisco, NY 10549
(800) 882-0852

U.S. News & World Report
Education Program
10 North Main Street, Suite 301
Yardley, PA 19067-9986
(800) 523-5948

Newsweek
P.O. Box 414
Livingston, NJ 07039-9965
(800) 526-2595

Knowledge Unlimited distributes a weekly filmstrip, "Newscurrents," for grades 3-12 to inform students about happenings around the world.

Knowledge Unlimited
Box 52
Madison, WI 53701
(408) 836-6660

Magazines are available for social studies teachers to further their professional development.

Teaching K-8
P.O. Box 54805
Boulder, CO 80323-4805
(800) 678-8793

Instructor
Scholastic Inc.
P.O. Box 53895
Boulder, CO 80323-3895
(800) 544-2917

Teacher
P.O. Box 2091
Marion, OH 43306-2191
(202) 364-4114

Social Education
National Council for the Social Studies
3501 Newark Street, N.W.
Washington, DC 20016-3167
(202) 966-7840

Social Studies & the Young Learner
School of Education
University of Missouri--St. Louis
8001 Natural Bridge Road
St. Louis, MO 63121-4499

The Social Studies
Heldref Publications
4000 Albemarle Street, NW
Washington, DC 20016

Learning
530 University Avenue
Palo Alto, CA 94301

Video Pals matches families, children, adults,
groups, and classrooms of students with each
other for the purposes of global understanding,
peace, friendship, and education. Classrooms
produce videotapes and exchange them with their
"video pal classroom" during the academic year.
    Video Pals
    630 North Tustin Avenue, Suite 165
    Orange, CA 92667
    (800) VID-PALS

The Center for Social Studies Education, with
help from Educators for Social Responsibility and
the Vietnam Veterans of America Foundation,
offers a teacher/veteran partnership program to
promote more and better teaching of the Vietnam
War and its lessons and legacies.
    Center for Social Studies Education
    3857 Willow Avenue
    Pittsburgh, PA 15234
    (412) 341-1967

Each summer a number of U.S. and Canadian
social studies educators are selected to visit Japan.
This program is offered to help educators learn
about contemporary Japanese society in order
that they might enhance the teaching of global
perspectives in U.S. and Canadian schools.
    Program Coordinator
    Keizai Koho Center Fellowships
    4332 Fern Valley Road
    Medford, OR 97504
    (503) 535-4882

NewsCurrents, the weekly current events discussion program for students in grades 3-12, has a
cartoon contest.
    NewsCurrents Editorial Cartoon Contest
    P.O. Box 52
    Madison, WI 53701-0052
    (800) 356-2303 or (608) 836-6660

A number of "classroom magazines" summarize
recent news in a readable manner:
    My Weekly Reader is published for grades K-6;
Currrent Events is published for grades 7 and 8.
For either, contact
    Bruce Seide Publications
    245 Long Hill Road
    Middleton, CT 06457

Scholastic News is for grades K-5, while *Junior
Scholastic* is for grades 6-8.
    Scholastic Inc.
    P.O. Box 644
    Lyndhurst, NJ 07071-9985

Magazines for Children, published by the Educational Press Association of America and the
International Reading Association, lists more
than 125 kids' periodicals. In addition to cost and
order information, the listings contain concise
annotations describing the magazines' content,
age ranges, goals, and philosophies.
    International Reading Association
    Order Department
    800 Barksdale Road
    P.O. Box 8139
    Newark, DE 19714-8139

Teachers can obtain free or inexpensive materials
simply by sending a request on school letterhead.
Filmstrips, brochures, kits, and other materials are
described in a directory which is available from:
    Educators Free Guide to Materials
    Educators Progressive Service
    Randolph, WI 53956

Educational Resources Information Center/
Clearinghouse for Social Studies/Social Science
Education (ERIC/ChESS) is a clearinghouse for
current published and unpublished materials such
as research, teaching guides, and units.
    ERIC/ChESS
    Indiana University
    2805 East 10th Street, Suite 120
    Bloomington, IN 47405
    (812) 335-3838

The Social Science Education Consortium is an
organization of social scientists and social studies
educators providing services to teachers. It
publishes many reports on social studies.
    Social Science Education Consortium
    3300 Mitchell Lane, Suite 240
    Boulder, CO 80301-2272

The Ag in the Classroom Program provides a bimonthly newsletter and information on projects to
help students understand the important role of
agriculture in the United States economy. There
are separate state offices. To find yours, contact:
    Ag in the Classroom
    Room 317-A, Administration Building
    U.S. Department of Agriculture
    Washington, DC 20250-2200

Sources of Information on United Nations Member States

Many foreign countries maintain embassies, consulates, or information services in the United States. Letters of inquiry can yield a large quantity of information from these offices, such as maps, information on tourist attractions, and statistical data about their countries.

Afghanistan
Embassy of the Republic of Afghanistan
2341 Wyoming Avenue, N.W.
Washington, DC 20008
(202) 234-3770
(send self-addressed stamped envelope)

Albania
Permanent Mission of the Republic of Albania to
  the United Nations
320 East 79th Street
New York, NY 10021
(212) 249-2059

Algeria
Embassy of Algeria
2118 Kalorama Road, N.W.
Washington, DC 20008
(202) 265-2800

Angola
Permanent Mission of the People's Republic of
  Angola to the United Nations
125 East 73rd Street
New York, NY 10021
(212) 861-5656

Antigua and Barbuda
Permanent Mission of Antigua and Barbuda to
  the United Nations
610 Fifth Avenue, Suite 311
New York, NY 10020
(212) 541-4117

Argentina
Consulate General of Argentina
Cultural Office
12 West 56th Street
New York, NY 10019
(212) 603-0400/43

Australia
Australian Information Services
c/o Australian Consulate General
630 Fifth Avenue, 4th Floor
New York, NY 10111
(212) 245-4000

Austria
Austrian Information Service
31 East 69th Street
New York, NY 10021
(212) 288-1727

Bahamas
Bahamas Consulate General
767 Third Avenue, 9th Floor
New York, NY 10017
(212) 421-6420

Bahrain
Permanent Mission of the State of Bahrain to the
  United Nations
Two United Nations Plaza
25th Floor
New York, NY 10017
(212) 223-6200

Bangladesh
Consulate General of Bangladesh
Attn: Mr. Hannan
821 United Nations Plaza
6th Floor
New York, NY 10017
(212) 599-6767

Barbados
Consulate General of Barbados
800 Second Avenue
18th Floor
New York, NY 10017
(212) 867-8431

Belarus (formerly Byelorussian Soviet Socialist
  Republic)
Permanent Mission of the Republic of Belarus to
  the United Nations
136 East 67th Street
New York, NY 10021
(212) 535-3420

Belgium
Belgium Consulate General
Culture Section
50 Rockefeller Plaza
Suite 1120
New York, NY 10020
(212) 586-5110

Belize
Embassy of Belize
2538 Massachusetts Avenue, N.W.
Washington, DC 20008
(202) 332-9638

Benin (formerly Dahomey)
Permanent Mission of Benin to the United
  Nations
4 East 73rd Street
New York, NY 10021
(212) 249-6014

Bhutan
Permanent Mission of the Kingdom of Bhutan to
  the United Nations
Two United Nations Plaza
27th Floor
New York, NY 10017
(212) 826-1919

Bolivia
Consulate General of Bolivia
211 East 43rd Street
Room 801
New York, NY 10017
(212) 687-0530

Botswana
Embassy of Botswana
3400 International Drive, N.W.
Suite 7M
Washington, DC 20008
(202) 244-4990

Brazil
Permanent Mission of Brazil to the United
  Nations
747 Third Avenue, 9th Floor
New York, NY 10017
(212) 832-6868

Brunei Darussalam
Permanent Mission of Brunei Darussalam to the
  United Nations
866 United Nations Plaza
Room 248
New York, NY 10017
(212) 838-1600

Bulgaria
Embassy of the Republic of Bulgaria
1621 22nd Street, N.W.
Washington, DC 20008
Attn: Public Relations
(202) 387-7969

Burkina Faso (formerly Upper Volta)
Embassy of Burkina Faso
2340 Massachusetts Avenue, N.W.
Washington, DC 20008
(202) 332-5577

Burundi
Permanent Mission of the Republic of Burundi to
  the United Nations
336 East 45th Street
12th Floor
New York, NY 10017
(212) 687-1180/1179/1209

Cambodia
Permanent Mission of Cambodia to the United
  Nations
820 Second Avenue
Suite 1500
New York, NY 10017
(212) 697-2009

Cameroon
Embassy of the Republic of Cameroon
2349 Massachusetts Avenue, N.W.
Washington, DC 20008
(202) 265-8790

Canada
Canadian Consul Library
Information Center
Consulate General of Canada
1251 Avenue of the Americas
New York, NY 10020-1175
(212) 768-2400

Cape Verde
Consulate General of Cape Verde
535 Boylston Street
2nd Floor
Boston, MA 02116
(617) 353-0014

Central African Republic
Permanent Mission of the Central African
 Republic to the United Nations
386 Park Avenue, Room 1614
New York, NY 10016
(212) 689-6195

Chad
Permanent Mission of the Republic of Chad to
 the United Nations
211 East 43rd Street
Suite 1703
New York, NY 10017
(212) 986-0980 or (212) 490-2072

Chile
Consulate General of Chile
866 United Nations Plaza
Room 302
New York, NY 10017
(212) 980-3707

China
Consulate General of China
Education Department
520 Twelfth Avenue
New York, NY 10036
(212) 330-7425

Colombia
Colombian Information Service
140 East 57th Street
4th Floor
New York, NY 10022
(212) 421-8300

Comoros
Permanent Mission of Comoros to the United
 Nations
336 East 45th Street
2nd Floor
New York, NY 10017
(212) 972-8010

Congo
Permanent Mission of the Republic of Congo to
 the United Nations
14 East 65th Street
New York, NY 10021
(212) 744-7840

Costa Rica
Consulate General of Costa Rica
80 Wall Street, Suite 718
New York, NY 10005
(212) 425-2620/1

Côte d'Ivoire
L'Ambassade de Côte d'Ivoire
2424 Massachusetts Avenue, N.W.
Washington, DC 20008
(202) 797-0300

Cuba
Center for Cuban Studies
124 West 23rd Street
New York, NY 10011
(212) 242-0559/1937

Cyprus
Consulate General of Cyprus
13 East 40th Street
New York, NY 10016
(212) 686-6016/7

Czechoslovakia
Permanent Mission of Czechoslovakia to the
 United Nations
1109-1111 Madison Avenue
New York, NY 10028
(212) 535-8814

Denmark
Royal Danish Consulate General
825 Third Avenue
New York, NY 10022
(212) 223-4545

Djibouti
Embassy of the Republic of Djibouti
1156 15th Street, N.W.
Suite 515
Washington, DC 20005
(202) 331-0270

Dominica
Permanent Mission of the Commonwealth of
  Dominica to the United Nations
820 Second Avenue, 9th Floor
New York, NY 10017
(212) 949-0853

Dominican Republic
Permanent Mission of the Dominican Republic to
  the United Nations
144 East 44th Street
4th Floor
New York, NY 10017
(212) 867-0833

Ecuador
Embassy of Ecuador
2535 15th Street, N.W.
Washington, DC 20009
(202) 234-7200

Egypt
Permanent Mission of Egypt to the United
  Nations
36 East 67th Street
New York, NY 10021
(212) 879-6300

El Salvador
Permanent Mission of El Salvador to the United
  Nations
46 Park Avenue
New York, NY 10016
(212) 679-1616/7

Equatorial Guinea
Permanent Mission of Equatorial Guinea to the
  United Nations
57 Magnolia Avenue
Mount Vernon, NY 10553

Estonia
Permanent Mission of Estonia to the United
  Nations
9 Rockefeller Plaza
Suite 1421
New York, NY 10020
(212) 247-1450

Ethiopia
Permanent Mission of Ethiopia to the United
  Nations
866 United Nations Plaza
Room 560
New York, NY 10017
(212) 421-1830

Fiji
Permanent Mission of Fiji to the United Nations
One United Nations Plaza
Room 560
New York, NY 10017
(212) 355-7316

Finland
Consulate General of Finland
380 Madison Avenue
New York, NY 10017
(212) 573-6007

France
French Cultural Service
Information Service
972 Fifth Avenue
New York, NY 10021
(212) 439-1400

Gabon
Embassy of the Republic of Gabon
2034 20th Street, N.W.
Washington, DC 20009
(202) 797-1000

Gambia
Permanent Mission of Gambia to the United
  Nations
820 Second Avenue, Suite 900C
New York, NY 10017
(212) 949-6640

Germany
German Information Center
950 Third Avenue, 24th Floor
New York, NY 10022
(212) 888-9840

Ghana
Permanent Mission of Ghana to the United
  Nations
19 East 47th Street
New York, NY 10017
(212) 832-1300

Greece
Greek Press and Information Office
601 Fifth Avenue, 3rd Floor
New York, NY 10017
(212) 751-8788

Grenada
Grenada Consulate
820 Second Avenue, Suite 900D
New York, NY 10017
(212) 599-0301

Guatemala
Consulate General of Guatemala
57 Park Avenue
New York, NY 10016
(212) 686-3837

Guinea
Embassy of the Republic of Guinea
2112 Leroy Plaza, N.W.
Washington, DC 20008
(202) 332-1936

Guinea-Bissau
Guinea-Bissau Embassy
918 16th Street, N.W.
Mezzanine Suite
Washington, DC 20006
(202) 872-4222

Guyana
Consulate General of the Republic of Guyana
866 United Nations Plaza
Room 304
New York, NY 10017
(212) 527-3215/6

Haiti
Consulate General of Haiti
60 East 42nd Street
13th Floor
New York, NY 10017
(212) 697-9767

Honduras
Embassy of Honduras
3007 Tilden Street, N.W.
POD-4M
Washington, DC 20008
(202) 966-9750

Hungary
Consulate General of the Republic of Hungary
223 West 52nd Street
New York, NY 10022
(212) 752-0661

Iceland
Consulate General of Iceland
370 Lexington Avenue
5th Floor
New York, NY 10017
(212) 686-4100

India
Indian Consulate General
Information Section
3 East 64th Street
New York, NY 10021
(212) 879-8048

Indonesia
Consulate General of Indonesia
5 East 68th Street
New York, NY 10021
(212) 879-0600

Iran
Interest Section of Iran
2209 Wisconsin Avenue, N.W.
Washington, DC 20007
(202) 965-4990

Iraq
Press Office
Iraqi Interest Section
1801 P Street, N.W.
Washington, DC 20036
(202) 483-7500

Ireland
Consulate General of Ireland
515 Madison Avenue
18th Floor
New York, NY 10022
(212) 319-2555

Israel
Consulate General of Israel
Information Office
800 Second Avenue
New York, NY 10017
(212) 351-5200

Italy
Italian Government Travel Office
630 Fifth Avenue
New York, NY 10111
(212) 245-4822

Jamaica
Consulate General of Jamaica
Information Service
866 Second Avenue, 9th Floor
New York, NY 10017
(212) 935-9000

Japan
Japan Information Center
Consulate General of Japan
299 Park Avenue, 16th Floor
New York, NY 10171-0025
(212) 371-8222

Jordan
Jordan Information Bureau
2319 Wyoming Avenue, N.W.
Washington, DC 20008
(202) 265-1606

Kenya
Embassy of Kenya
2249 R Street, N.W.
Washington, DC 20008
(202) 387-6101/2/3

Korea, Democratic People's Republic of
Permanent Mission of the Democratic People's
 Republic of Korea to the United Nations
225 East 86th Street
New York, NY 10028
(212) 722-3536/89

Korea, Republic of
Permanent Mission of the Republic of Korea to
 the United Nations
866 United Nations Plaza
Suite 300
New York, NY 10017
(212) 371-1280

Kuwait
Consulate General of Kuwait
321 East 44th Street
New York, NY 10017
(212) 973-4318

Laos
Embassy of the Lao People's Democratic
 Republic
2222 S Street, N.W.
Washington, DC 20008
(202) 332-6416

Latvia
Permanent Mission of Latvia to the United
 Nations
115 East 183rd Street
Bronx, NY 10453
(212) 933-4500

Lebanon
Embassy of Lebanon
2560 28th Street
Washington, DC 20008
(202) 939-6300

Lesotho
Permanent Mission of the Kingdom of Lesotho to
 the United Nations
204 East 39th Street
New York, NY 10016
(212) 661-1690/1/2/73

Liberia
Embassy of Liberia
Information Section
5305 Colorado Avenue, N.W.
Washington, DC 20011
(202) 291-0761

Libya
Permanent Mission of the Socialist People's
 Libyan Arab Jamahiriya to the United Nations
Press Section
309 East 48th Street
New York, NY 10017
(212) 752-5775

Liechtenstein
Permanent Mission of Liechtenstein to the
 United Nations
405 Lexington Avenue
Suite 4301
New York, NY 10174
(212) 599-0220

Lithuania
Permanent Mission of Lithuania to the United
 Nations
41 East 82nd Street
New York, NY 10024
(212) 877-4552

Luxembourg
Luxembourg National Tourist Office
801 Second Avenue
13th Floor
New York, NY 10017
(212) 370-9850

Madagascar
Embassy of Madagascar
Cultural Attaché
2374 Massachusetts Avenue, N.W.
Washington, DC 20008
(202) 265-5525

Malawi
Embassy of Malawi
2408 Massachusetts Avenue, N.W.
Washington, DC 20008
(202) 797-1007

Malaysia
Consulate General of Malaysia
140 East 45th Street
43rd Floor
New York, NY 10017
(212) 490-2722

Maldives
Permanent Mission of the Republic of Maldives
 to the United Nations
820 Second Avenue
Suite 800C
New York, NY 10017
(212) 599-6195

Mali
Permanent Mission of the Republic of Mali to the
 United Nations
111 East 69th Street
New York, NY 10021
(212) 737-4150
(send self-addressed stamped envelope)

Malta
Consulate of Malta
249 East 35th Street
New York, NY 10016
(212) 725-2345

Marshall Islands
Permanent Mission of the Republic of the
 Marshall Islands to the United Nations
1 Dag Hammarskjöld Plaza
7th Floor
New York, NY 10017-2289
(212) 702-4850

Mauritania
Embassy of the Islamic Republic of Mauritania
2129 Leroy Place, N.W.
Washington, DC 20008
(202) 232-5700

Mauritius
Permanent Mission of Mauritius to the United
 Nations
211 East 43rd Street
Room 1502
New York, NY 10017
(212) 949-0190

Mexico
Consulate General of Mexico
8 East 41st Street
New York, NY 10017
(212) 689-0456

Micronesia
Permanent Mission of the Federated States of
 Micronesia to the United Nations
820 Second Avenue, Suite 800A
New York, NY 10017
(212) 599-6192

Moldova
Permanent Mission of the Republic Moldova to
 the United Nations
573-577 Third Avenue
New York, NY 10016
(212) 682-3274 or (212) 818-1491/1376

Mongolia
Embassy of Mongolia
10201 Iron Gate Road
Potomac, MD 20854
(301) 983-1962

Morocco
Permanent Mission of Morocco to the United
 Nations
767 Third Avenue, 30th Floor
New York, NY 10017
(212) 421-1580/1/2/3

Mozambique
Permanent Mission of the People's Republic of
  Mozambique to the United Nations
70 East 79th Street
New York, NY 10021
(212) 517-4550

Myanmar (formerly Burma)
Embassy of Myanmar
2300 S Street, N.W.
Washington, DC 20008
(202) 332-9044

Namibia
Permanent Mission of the Republic of Namibia to
  the United Nations
135 East 36th Street
New York, NY 10016
(212) 685-2003

Nepal
Royal Nepalese Embassy
2131 Leroy Place, N.W.
Washington, DC 20008
(202) 667-4550

Netherlands
Netherlands Consulate General
One Rockefeller Plaza
11th Floor
New York, NY 10020
(212) 246-1429

New Zealand
Embassy of New Zealand
37 Observatory Circle, N.W.
Washington, DC 20008
(202) 328-4800

Nicaragua
Permanent Mission of Nicaragua to the United
  Nations
Information Officer
820 Second Avenue, Suite 801
New York, NY 10017
(212) 490-7997

Niger
Permanent Mission of the Niger to the United
  Nations
417 East 50th Street
New York, NY 10022
(212) 421-3260

Nigeria
Consulate General of Nigeria
Nigerian Information Services
575 Lexington Avenue
33rd Floor
New York, NY 10022
(212) 758-2634

Norway
Norwegian Information Service
825 Third Avenue, 38th Floor
New York, NY 10022
(212) 421-7333

Oman
Permanent Mission of Oman to the United
  Nations
866 United Nations Plaza, Suite 540
New York, NY 10017
(212) 355-3505/6/7

Pakistan
Permanent Mission of Pakistan to the United
  Nations
Press Attaché
8 East 65th Street
New York, NY 10021
(212) 879-8600

Panama
Consulate General of Panama
1212 Avenue of the Americas
10th Floor
New York, NY 10036
(212) 840-2450

Papua New Guinea
Permanent Mission of Papua New Guinea to the
  United Nations
866 United Nations Plaza, Suite 322
New York, NY 10017
(212) 832-0043

Paraguay
Consulate General of Paraguay
One World Trade Center
Suite 1947
New York, NY 10048
(212) 432-0733

Peru
Peru Tourist Office
1000 Brickell Avenue
Suite 600
Miami, FL 33131
(305) 374-1579

Philippines
Consulate General of the Philippines
Cultural Office
556 Fifth Avenue
New York, NY 10036
(212) 764-1330

Poland
Consulate General of the Republic of Poland
233 Madison Avenue
New York, NY 10016
(212) 889-8360/1/2/3

Portugal
Embassy of Portugal
2125 Kalorama Road, N.W.
Washington, DC 20008
Attn: Cultural Attaché
(202) 328-8610

Qatar
Permanent Mission of Qatar to the United
 Nations
747 Third Avenue, 22nd Floor
New York, NY 10017
(212) 486-9335

Romania
Romanian Library
200 East 38th Street
New York, NY 10016
(212) 687-0181

Russian Federation
Permanent Mission of the Russian Federation to
 the United Nations Public Relations Office
136 East 67th Street
New York, NY 10021
(212) 861-4900

Rwanda
Permanent Mission of the Rwandese Republic to
 the United Nations
124 East 39th Street
New York, NY 10016
(212) 696-0644/5/6

Saint Kitts and Nevis
Permanent Mission of Saint Kitts and Nevis to the
 United Nations
414 East 75th Street
5th Floor
New York, NY 10021
(212) 535-1234

Saint Lucia
Permanent Mission of Saint Lucia to the United
 Nations
820 Second Avenue, Suite 900
New York, NY 10017
(212) 697-9360/1

Saint Vincent and the Grenadines
Permanent Mission of Saint Vincent and the
 Grenadines to the United Nations
801 Second Avenue
21st Avenue
New York, NY 10017
(212) 687-4490

Samoa
Permanent Mission of the Independent State of
 Western Samoa to the United Nations
820 Second Avenue
Suite 800D
New York, NY 10017
(212) 599-6196/0/1/2

Sao Tome and Principe
Permanent Mission of Sao Tome and Principe to
 the United Nations
801 Second Avenue, Suite 603
New York, NY 10017
(212) 697-4211

Saudi Arabia
Royal Saudi Arabian Embassy
601 New Hampshire Avenue, N.W.
Washington, DC 20037
Attn: Information Office
(202) 342-3800

Senegal
Permanent Mission of the Republic of Senegal to
 the United Nations
238 East 68th Street
New York, NY 10021
(212) 517-9030/1/2

Seychelles
Permanent Mission of the Republic of Seychelles
 to the United Nations
820 Second Avenue, Suite 900F
New York, NY 10017
(212) 687-9766/7

Sierra Leone
Permanent Mission of Sierra Leone to the United
 Nations
245 East 49th Street
New York, NY 10017
(212) 688-1656

Singapore
Permanent Mission of Singapore to the United
 Nations
Two United Nations Plaza
25th Floor
New York, NY 10017
(212) 826-0840

Solomon Islands
Permanent Mission of the Solomon Islands to the
 United Nations
820 Second Avenue, Suite 800A
New York, NY 10017
(212) 599-6193

Somalia
Permanent Mission of the Somali Democratic
 Republic to the United Nations
425 East 61st Street, Suite 703
New York, NY 10021
(212) 688-9410/1/2

South Africa
South African Consulate General
333 East 38th Street, 9th Floor
New York, NY 10016
(212) 213-4880

Spain
Embassy of Spain
Information Office
2700 15th Street, N.W.
Washington, DC 20009
(202) 265-0190

Sri Lanka
Embassy of Sri Lanka
2148 Wyoming Avenue, N.W.
Washington, DC 20008
Attn: Information Service
(202) 483-4025

Sudan
Embassy of Sudan
2210 Massachusetts Avenue, N.W.
Washington, DC 20008
(202) 338-8565

Suriname
Consulate General of the Republic of Suriname
7235 N.W. 19th Street, Suite A
Miami, FL 33126
(305) 593-2163

Swaziland
Embassy of the Kingdom of Swaziland
3400 International Drive, Suite 3M
Washington, DC 20008
(202) 362-6683

Sweden
Swedish Information Service
885 Second Avenue, 45th Floor
New York, NY 10017
(212) 751-5900

Syria
Embassy of the Syrian Arab Republic
2215 Wyoming Avenue, N.W.
Washington, DC 20008
(202) 232-6313

Thailand
Tourism Authority of Thailand
5 World Trade Center, Suite 2449
New York, NY 10048
(212) 432-0433

Togo
Togo Embassy
2208 Massachusetts Avenue, N.W.
Washington, DC 20008
(202) 235-4212

Trinidad and Tobago
Trinidad and Tobago Consulate
Graybar Building, Room 333
420 Lexington Avenue
New York, NY 10170-0191
(212) 682-7272

Tunisia
Embassy of Tunisia
1515 Massachusetts Avenue, N.W.
Washington, DC 20005
(202) 862-1850

Turkey
Turkish Tourism and Information Office
821 United Nations Plaza, 4th Floor
New York, NY 10017
(212) 687-2194

Turkmenistan
Permanent Mission of Turkmenistan to the
 United Nations
136 East 67th Street
New York, NY 10021
(212) 861-4900
Fax: (212) 628-0252

Uganda
Permanent Mission of the Republic of Uganda to
 the United Nations
336 East 45th Street
New York, NY 10017
(212) 949-0110/1/2/3

Ukraine
Permanent Mission of Ukraine to the United
 Nations
Public Relations Office
136 East 67th Street
New York, NY 10021
(212) 535-3418

United Arab Emirates
Embassy of the United Arab Emirates
600 New Hampshire Avenue, N.W.
Suite 740
Washington, DC 20037
(202) 338-6500

United Kingdom
British Information Services
845 Third Avenue
New York, NY 10022
(212) 752-5747

United Republic of Tanzania
Embassy of United Republic of Tanzania
2139 R Street, N.W.
Washington, DC 20008
(202) 939-6125

United States of America
U.S. State Department
Public Inquiries
2201 C Street, N.W.
Washington, DC 20520
(202) 647-6575

Uruguay
Consulate General of Uruguay
747 Third Avenue, 21st Floor
New York, NY 10017
(212) 753-8191

Vanuatu (formerly New Hebrides)
Mission of Vanuatu to the United Nations
416 Convent Avenue
New York, NY 10031
(212) 926-3311

Venezuela
Venezuelan Consulate
7 East 51st Street
New York, NY 10022
(212) 826-1660

Vietnam, Socialist Republic of
Permanent Mission of the Socialist Republic of
 Vietnam to the United Nations
20 Waterside Plaza
New York, NY 10010
(212) 679-3779

Yemen
Embassy of the Republic of Yemen
Watergate 600, Suite 840
600 New Hampshire Avenue, N.W.
Washington, DC 20037
(202) 965-4760/81

Yugoslavia
Yugoslavian Press and Cultural Center
767 Third Avenue
18th Floor
New York, NY 10017
(212) 838-2306

Zaire
Embassy of the Republic of Zaire
1800 New Hampshire Avenue, N.W.
Washington, DC 20009
(202) 234-7690

Zambia
Zambia National Tourist Board
237 East 52nd Street
New York, NY 10022
(212) 758-1110

Zimbabwe (formerly Southern Rhodesia)
Zimbabwe Embassy
1608 New Hampshire Avenue, N.W.
Washington, DC 20009
(202) 332-7100

Sources of Information on Accredited Observer Non-Member States

Holy See
Apostolic Nunciator
3339 Massachusetts Avenue, N.W.
Washington, DC 20008
(202) 333-7121

Monaco
Consulate of Monaco
845 Third Avenue
19th Floor
New York, NY 10022
(212) 759-5227

San Marino
Consulate General of San Marino
2 East Saxwood Street
Deer Park, New York 11729
(516) 242-2212

Switzerland
Consulate General of Switzerland
665 Fifth Avenue
New York, NY 10022
(212) 758-2560

Sources of Information on Inter-Governmental and Other Observer Organizations

Asian-African Legal Consultative Committee
Office of the Permanent Observer for the Asian-African Legal Consultative Committee to the United Nations
404 East 66th Street, Apt. 12C
New York, NY 10021
(212) 734-7608

Commonwealth Secretariat
Office of the Commonwealth Secretariat at the United Nations
820 Second Avenue
Suite 800A
New York, NY 10017
(212) 599-6190

European Economic Community (Common Market)
Delegation of the Commission of the European Communities
3 Dag Hammarskjöld Plaza
305 East 47th Street
New York, NY 10017
(212) 371-3804

International Committee of the Red Cross
International Committee of the Red Cross
780 Third Avenue, Room 2802
New York, NY 10017
(212) 371-0770

League of Arab States (Arab League)
Office of the Permanent Observer of the League of Arab States to the United Nations
747 Third Avenue
35th Floor
New York, NY 10017
(212) 338-8700

Organization of African Unity (OAU)
Office of the Executive Secretary of the Organization of African Unity
346 East 50th Street
New York, NY 10022
(212) 319-5490

Organization of American States (OAS)
Pan-American Union
17th Street and Constitution Avenue, N.W.
Washington, DC 20006
(202) 458-3000

Organization of the Islamic Conference
Office of the Permanent Observer for the Organization of the Islamic Conference to the United Nations
130 East 40th Street, 5th Floor
New York, NY 10016
(212) 883-0140

Palestine
Office of the Permanent Observer of Palestine to the United Nations
115 East 65th Street
New York, NY 10021
(212) 288-8500

CHILDREN'S TRADE BOOKS: A GUIDE TO RESOURCES

by Christina B. Woll

Consultant for Library Services
Palacios, Texas

THE search for resources often poses a dilemma for the teacher or administrator working in curriculum development. The difficulty of identifying materials is compounded by an explosion in quantity of publishing for children. Fortunately, a variety of lists and bibliographies exists which aids in bringing about an appropriate match between materials and curriculum objectives. The pages which follow introduce and discuss some of the particularly helpful listings and bibliographies available.

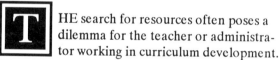

General Lists: Elementary

Children's Catalog

At the elementary school level, the H. W. Wilson *Children's Catalog* is a longtime, standard selection source used by teachers and librarians as a buying guide and all-around information source. Available in virtually all library media centers, *Children's Cat*, as it is familiarly known, lists more than 6,000 titles recommended for preschool through sixth grade use.

The 1991 edition has 1,346 pages, of which 746 are a Dewey Decimal-ordered listing of resources. Social science subjects appear primarily in sections with Dewey numbers in the 300s and

the 900s. The 900s also include biographies.

Program developers will find the combined author/title/subject index of Part 2 of *Children's Catalog* most valuable. Here it is possible to identify materials by subject and to pull together easily lists of related resources. As an example, a search of Part 2's index section for books about African Americans quickly shows that such materials are listed under the subject heading BLACKS and that the books about this subject are listed in the following quantities in the classified section (Part 1):

Bibliography	1
Poetry	9
Folklore	11
Biography	21
Fiction	78
Civil Rights	8

Checking the biographies mentioned under the subject heading BLACKS--BIOGRAPHY shows that the included biographies reflect publishing of the last two decades. Subjects are Benjamin Banneker, Paul Robeson, Frederick Douglass (2 books), Jesse Jackson, George Washington Carver, Jan Matzeliger, Daniel Hale Williams, Malcolm X, Matthew Henson, Amos Fortune,

Mary McLeod Bethune (2), Katherine Dunham, Paul Laurence Dunbar, Langston Hughes, Mahalia Jackson, and more.

Martin Luther King, Jr., leads in quantity of books, as he is the subject of seven biographies. Recommended biographies of King cover the standard materials available for young readers. Those listed in *Children's Catalog* include David A. Adler's *A Picture Book of Martin Luther King, Jr.* Published in 1989 by Holiday House, Adler's book is directed toward an early elementary audience and features moving watercolor illustrations by Robert Casilla.

For an older audience, *Children's Catalog* also lists *Martin Luther King, Jr.* by Jean Darby (Lerner, 1990), *The Life and Death of Martin Luther King, Jr.* by James Haskins (Lothrop, Lee & Shepard, 1977), and *Martin Luther King, Jr., and the Freedom Movement* by Lillie Patterson (Facts on File, 1989). Recommended for grades 4 and up are *Martin Luther King, Jr.* by Diane Patrick (Franklin Watts, 1990) and *Martin Luther King, Jr.; A Man to Remember* by Patricia C. McKissack (Childrens Press, 1984).

Most of the titles listed in *Children's Catalog* are in print and available for purchase from book wholesalers or publishers. A certain number of out-of-print "classics" also are included.

A new edition of *Children's Catalog* is brought out every five years. The large, bound volume is updated in the interim by annual paper supplements which are sent automatically to purchasers of the hardcover volume. Each supplement contains approximately 500 additional recommended books.

Titles are selected for inclusion in *Children's Catalog* by a committee of librarians. Introductory material in the sixteenth edition indicates that the committee's concerns or criteria were "interest; relevance; accuracy; currency, especially for nonfiction in social studies and the sciences; coverage of minorities and non-Western cultures; avoidance of stereotyping; and authenticity in retelling of folk literature" (p. v).

In addition to standard bibliographic information for each title included in *Children's Catalog*, suggested grade levels are given and an annotation is provided. Rather than using original annotations prepared by committee members or H. W. Wilson staff, most annotations are excerpted from various established publications that review children's trade books.

An examination of books listed in the high-appeal 910.4 section (which contains accounts of travel, seafaring life, and buried treasure) shows the following recommended titles and annotation sources:

Ballard, Robert D. 1988. *Exploring the Titanic.* Scholastic. Annotation source: *School Library Journal.*

Ballard, Robert D., with Rick Archbold. 1990. *The Lost Wreck of the Isis.* Scholastic. Annotation source: *Science and Children.*

Fine, John Christopher. 1986. *Sunken Ships & Treasure.* Atheneum. Annotation source: *School Library Journal.*

Gibbons, Gail. 1988. *Sunken Treasure.* HarperCollins Children's Books. Annotation source: *Horn Book.*

Hackwell, W. John. 1988. *Diving to the Past: Recovering Ancient Wrecks.* Charles Scribner's Sons. Annotation source: *Science and Children.*

Hidden Treasures of the Sea. 1988. National Geographic Society. Annotation source: unattributed.

Humble, Richard. 1990. *The Travels of Marco Polo.* Franklin Watts. Annotation source: *Booklist.*

Schwartz, Alvin. 1988. *Gold & Silver, Silver & Gold: Tales of Hidden Treasure.* Farrar, Straus and Giroux. Annotation source: *Booklist.*

Elementary School Library Collection: A Guide to Books and Other Media, Phase 1-2-3

Published every two years, *Elementary School Library Collection* (*ESLC*) is a comprehensive listing of recommended resources for the elementary grades. In contrast to *Children's Catalog,* which offers only books and periodicals, *ESLC* contains audio-visual items, CD-ROM, and software as well as print materials. The eighteenth edition contains 11,401 recommended titles. Publication date of the eighteenth edition was 1992; the publisher is Brodart. Lauren Lee edited the current edition.

Entries in *ESLC* are arranged in Dewey Decimal order. Each entry includes a critically descriptive annotation and a reading level based on Fry Formula for Estimating Readability (upper grades) or the Spache scale (grades 1 and 2).

Annotations in *ESLC* are written by the educators and librarians nationwide who constitute the publication's ten-person selection team. Each annotation gives a brief description of the book discussed, mentions special features, and may make recommendations for use. Annotations are 50-100 words in length. Sample annotations from page 398 (Dewey numbers 971.3-972) include the following:

Granfield, Linda. *All About Niagara Falls: Fascinating Facts, Dramatic Discoveries*. William Morrow and Co., 1988. Opens with a list of 20 things to do at Niagara Falls and follows with a wide-ranging collection of Falls-related miscellany. Contents include anecdotes, cartoons, jokes, historic tidbits, maps, and drawings. Browsers and trivia fans will fall for this one.

Hauserr, Rosmarie. *City Girl Who Went to the Sea*. Four Winds Press, 1990. Captures with sensitivity and warmth the routines and people of a fishing village in Newfoundland as seen by a girl visiting from New York City. Handsome black-and-white photographs and striking design are notable features. Good as a browser or as a trigger for creative writing projects.

Klondike Gold Rush. (Picture). Documentary Photo Aids, n.d. Provides 15 black-and-white study prints with captions which tell of the Klondike Gold Rush. Useful for display purposes as well as for individual study, the prints supply an additional dimension when used with Ray's *Gold! the Klondike Adventure* or Cooper's *Klondike Fever*.

Ray, Delia. *Gold! The Klondike Adventure*. Lodestar Books, 1989. Relives the Klondike adventure in an effective mesh of period photographs and well-written text. Valuable in its own right and as an important resource as the Klondike Gold Rush centenary approaches in 1996-1998.

Diaz del Castillo, Bernal. *Cortez and the Conquest of Mexico by the Spaniards in 1521; Being the Eye-Witness Narrative of Bernal Diaz del Castillo, Soldier of Fortune and Conquistador with Cortez in Mexico*. Linnet/Shoestring, 1988. Offers an abridged text of the famed narrative written by Bernal Diaz in 1572 and first published in 1632 in Spain. Reproductions of sixteenth-century Indian drawings accompany Diaz's report. An important basic source useful to advanced students and to teachers who wish to use brief portions in introducing Spanish impact on the New World.

A separate subject index makes *ESLC* a natural for curriculum developers. An examination of the subject index quickly activates ideas of variety in approaches and uses for resources. *ESLC* also provides access through title and author indexes.

Special appendices include listings of media for preschool children, books for beginning independent readers, and recommended titles in series. Sections related to professional resources and periodicals are also available.

Best Books for Children: Preschool through Grade 6

Now in its fourth edition and with a 1990 copyright date, *Best Books for Children* is part of a series of three similar titles published by R. R. Bowker. Editors of the publication are John T. Gillespie and Corrinne J. Naden.

Classed as a general bibliography, *Best Books for Children* offers review citations for all entries published after 1985, separate indexes by author, title, subject, and illustrator. It is designed to identify resources suitable for children ages 3 through 14 years.

Best Books for Children contains mention of more than 12,000 in-print titles published through the book's mid-1989 closing date. It offers very brief annotations. Most of the nonfiction books listed have received favorable reviews in two review sources such as *Booklist* and *School Library Journal*. The arrangement is by broad subject areas. Entries give title, grade level, illustrator, publisher, and price information.

Subject Guide to Children's Books in Print

This bibliographic source is an annual publication which lists by subject almost all of the children's books available at the time it was printed. The number of works mentioned is over 60,000. *Subject Guide* contains no evaluative statements regarding quality of items. It lists the good, the mediocre, and the weak with impartiality and supplies an awareness of the breadth of resources available for any subject K-12.

Subject Guide is a companion volume to *Children's Books in Print*. Both are part of R. R. Bowker's extensive family of bibliographies. A cousin in the Bowker group which is also of value to curriculum designers is *El-Hi Textbooks and Serials in Print*. This specialized reference work contains more than 40,000 entries in 21 basic subject categories. Texts, text series, workbooks, periodicals, tests, and other resources are included. Again, it is useful as an identifier rather than as an evaluative source.

It is important to note that Bowker offers on CD-ROM a package of 40 resources which includes those mentioned above. An early step for anyone preparing subject bibliographies should be a check of local libraries to determine availability of the Bowker bibliographic CD-ROM information service titled *Children's Reference Plus*.

General Lists: Secondary

Senior High School Library Catalog

With its fourteenth edition carrying a 1992 copyright date, the venerable *Senior High School Library Catalog* serves as a major source of information about basic books recommended for high school library media centers.

As with other books in the Standard Catalog Series published by H. W. Wilson, *Senior High School Library Catalog* is arranged with three parts: a classified section which is arranged in Dewey Decimal order, a combined author/title/subject listing, and a directory of publishers and distributors.

The hardcover editions of *Senior High School Library Catalog* normally list 4,500-5,000 titles. Most of the books listed are in print. A softcover supplement annually updates the main volume for four years following publication.

An area of particular value to those working in program design is that of subject headings for standard fiction titles. These indicators encourage the teacher to put together packages of resources to expand and extend student sense of place and time. For additional listing of fiction titles, programmers may wish to consult the subject index of Wilson's *Fiction Catalog*, a public library resource frequently used by high school librarians.

Best Books for Senior High Readers

A star in Bowker's *Best Books* trilogy, *Best Books for Senior High Readers* is copyrighted 1991 and contains a listing of nearly 11,000 recommended books. It is edited by John T. Gillespie. Arrangement is by broad subject areas such as literary forms, guidance and personal development, history and geography, physical and applied sciences, biography and true adventure, and more.

The section titled "History and Geography" has 80 subsections and recommends 1,231 books. An additional 498 titles are listed under the broad heading "Society and the Individual."

Entries in *Best Books for Senior High Readers* are short in the annotation category (less than 20 words) but more than adequate in provision of other information. Appropriate author, title/subtitle, grade level, publication date, binding information, review citation for post-1985 publications, and Dewey Decimal classification are given.

Selection of titles is fresh. An examination of the sample subject PRESIDENCY shows that nine books are suggested. Among them are Paul C. Boller's *Presidential Anecdotes* (Oxford, 1981),

Ann Grimes's *Running Mates: Image and Reality of the First Lady Role* (Morrow, 1990), and Paul Taylor's *See How They Run: Electing the President in an Age of Mediaocracy* (Knopf, 1990).

Best Books for Senior High Readers closes with author and title indexes and a helpful subject/grade level index.

Junior High School Library Catalog

An additional H. W. Wilson title, *Junior High School Library Catalog*, fits neatly between *Children's Catalog* and *Senior High School Library Catalog*. The junior high version, edited by Juliette Yaakov, indexes more than 3,300 nonfiction and fiction titles. Its arrangement is similar to the other two series members discussed: classified listing, author/title/subject index to the classified listing, and a directory of publishers.

Best Books for Junior High Readers

This volume lists materials for students in grades 7-9. Entries are similar to those in *Best Books for Senior High Readers* and are equally brief. Books which are included were published between 1985 and 1990 and received favorable reviews in at least two standard journals specializing in books for young readers. Editor is John T. Gillespie.

Specialized Lists: K-12

Our Family, Our Friends, Our World: An Annotated Guide to Significant Multicultural Books for Children and Teenagers

This gold mine of carefully written descriptions of more than 1,000 multicultural books lists titles published between 1970 and 1991. Copyright date for *Our Family, Our Friends, Our World* is 1992.

Books included reflect growing immigrant populations and increasing size of traditional minority groups in the United States and in countries abroad.

Although introductory material in many books is often bypassed in the reader's desire to move to the body of a text, a careful review of the introduction of *Our Family* is strongly recommended.

After establishing the need for such a book, author Lyn Miller-Lachmann discusses curricular changes which have given impetus to the search for multicultural materials. She then moves to an overview of the history of publishing of multicultural books. Here she travels from Helen Bannerman's 1929 work *Little Black Sambo* through the stereotypes that marked many decades of children's book publishing.

The author points out that the first wave of multicultural publishing came in the 1960s and 1970s, and that some small presses continued multicultural publishing during the 1980s. However, in the early 1980s, a retrenchment by many publishers began a decline in books by and about minorities. This slowdown continued until the end of the 1980s when a revitalization occurred.

Author Miller-Lachmann is knowledgeable, and her assessment of this area of publishing makes interesting reading.

The introduction of *Our Family* also carefully describes the scope of the bibliography. All books included were published in the United States or Canada. Bilingual books are included, but books that are written exclusively in a language other than English are not.

Titles which appear may or may not be in print. The bibliography is essentially inclusive but there is an emphasis on evaluating works deemed significant by contributors. All books listed have been published since 1970; however, some of the titles included are revisions of earlier publications. Series books (usually nonfiction "country books") are post-1985 releases. Emphasis is on giving readers a picture of the current situation of each group or region. Some folklore which is considered relevant to the contemporary situation of a group or a region is included.

The six-page discussion of the criteria used in selection of titles for inclusion in *Our Family* is a minicourse in evaluative considerations for multicultural books. Among criteria discussed are general accuracy, sensitivity to stereotypes, use of language, author's perspective, and currency of facts and interpretation. Other crucial yardsticks considered are the concept of audience, integration of cultural information, illustrations, and balance and multidimensionality.

Our Family has 18 chapters which vary from 18 to 68 pages in length. The page facing each chapter opening contains a map which displays with notable clarity the region of the world covered in upcoming pages.

Chapter subjects are The United States: African Americans; The United States: Asian Americans; The United States: Hispanic Americans; The United States: Native Americans; Canada; Mexico and the Caribbean; Central and South America; Great Britain and Ireland; Western Europe; Southern Europe; Eastern Europe and the Soviet Union; The Middle East and North Africa; Sub-Saharan Africa; South Africa; Southern and Central Asia; East Asia; Southeast Asia; and Australia, New Zealand, and the Pacific.

Each chapter is divided into four sections: Preschool-3, 4-6, 7-9, and 10-12. Chapters were developed by 21 subject specialists, many of whom are members of the cultural group of the area discussed. Each chapter carries the name of its author or authors.

Chapters in *Our Family* begin with a general introduction which gives an additional overview of publishing trends in the area with which the chapter deals. Though a history is not given, some facts, themes, and concepts are presented. Individual contributors also comment about special criteria which have been considered as materials have been selected and entries have been prepared.

Entries vary in length but typically are 100-200 words. Annotation quality is generally high and almost unfailingly perceptive. Entries within grade level groupings within each chapter are arranged alphabetically by author.

Appendix 1 in *Our Family* offers a list of additional professional resources for each of the 18 chapters. Some of the suggested materials are bibliographies; others are background-builders. Appendix 2 is a list of series in the areas of geography, biography, ethnic groups and immigration, current events, and fiction. Appendix 3 is a directory of publishers. Author, title/series, and subject indexes fill the final 105 pages of the 710-page book.

Our Family is a bibliography which curriculum developers working in the social sciences will find useful in many ways.

Plays for Children and Young Adults: An Evaluative Index and Guide

Program designers with access to *Plays for Children and Young Adults* will discover that this recent title offers possibilities for fresh approaches to alternative curriculum activities. Evaluative information for approximately 3,500 plays for students in grades K-12 is provided in this listing published in 1991 by Garland.

Authors and compilers of *Plays for Children and Young Adults* are Rashelle Karp and June H. Schlessinger. In addition to plays, the work includes choral readings, reader's theater, musicals, and skits.

Arrangement of *Plays for Children and Young Adults* is alphabetic by title. Audience grade level, evaluation (positive or negative as indicated by plus or minus), cast required, playing time, number of acts, setting, plot summary, and royalty information are given for each work listed.

Five indexes provide access to the main text by author, cast size, grade level, subject, and playing time. Items annotated in the main text appeared in collections or separately between 1975 and 1989.

American History for Children and Young Adults: An Annotated Bibliographic Index

This ambitious work by Vandelia VanMeter offers a list of recommended K-12 fiction and nonfiction trade books related to United States history. Most of the more than 2,900 books listed were published between 1980 and 1988. Bibliographic arrangement is by subject. *American History for Children and Young Adults* is available in book format as well as in IBM, Apple II, and Mac versions.

Stars, States and Historic Dates: Activities, Research and Readings in American History

Though primarily an activity book designed for teachers, *Stars, States and Historic Dates* earns a mention with its listing of readings. The extensive bibliography, which concludes the 90-page book, contains an annotated, graded listing of books supportive of American history studies. Authors of *Stars, States and Historic Dates* are Hilda K. Weisburg and Ruth Toor. Publisher is Library Learning Resources.

Magazines for Young People

Compiled by Bill Katz and Linda Sternberg Katz, *Magazines for Young People* examines and evaluates approximately 1,000 magazines suitable for young readers. Published in 1991 by R. R. Bowker, this resource has three major sections: children's magazines, young adult magazines, and professional education and library journals.

The children's magazines listing, periodicals for students in elementary or junior high school, describes 31 general publications and 77 subject-specific magazines. Among items of information included in each entry are date founded, frequency of publication, price, editor, order information, circulation, and an indication of inclusion of book reviews. An evaluative annotation discussing special features and journalistic quality accompanies each entry.

Subject categories of conspicuous interest to social studies educators are current events,

geography and travel, history, and social science; but, in actuality, titles from many subject areas included have strong social science potential. Closing the children's magazine portion of *Magazines for Young People* is a subsection which describes familiar classroom publications of the *Junior Scholastic* and *My Weekly Reader* variety.

The young adult (high school) section of *Magazines for Young People* follows a similar format to that found in the children's section as it evaluates 806 subject periodicals and 11 classroom publications. Annotations are of high quality, and the variety of materials discussed is intriguing.

The portion of *Magazines for Young People* which presents professional education and library publications annotates 199 journals.

Specialized Lists: Elementary

Literature-Based Social Studies: Children's Books to Enrich the Social Studies

In *Literature-Based Social Studies*, authors Mildred Knight Laughlin and Patricia Payne Kardaleff have put together a book of considerable interest to districtwide or building-level curriculum developers of resource-based instructional programs.

Using the 1989 report of the Curriculum Task Force of the National Commission on Social Studies in the Schools, the authors set about designing units and objectives, activities, and resource lists for grades K-1, 2-3, and 4-5.

Units in *Literature-Based Social Studies* are organized with similar formats. Each individual unit identifies objectives to be reached through use of recommended trade books. Anticipated behavioral outcomes are listed. Included in each unit are a bibliography, an introductory activity, and suggested follow-up activities.

The kindergarten/transition/first grade chapter offers nine units. Titles and content are traditional, as the topics used are myself, families, economics of family living, homes, children/families near and far, friendship, groups, transportation, and holidays.

The K-1 unit on friendship is accompanied by a 14-book bibliography. Each book listed has a brief annotation and an indication of specific unit objectives addressed by that book. Among the recommended readings for the unit are *We Are Best Friends* by Aliki (Greenwillow, 1982), *It's George* by Miriam Cohen (Greenwillow, 1988), *Through Grandpa's Eyes* by Patricia MacLachlan (Harper, 1980), and *Lizzie Howard* by Elizabeth

Winthrop (Lothrop, Lee & Shepard, 1986).

The second grade/third grade chapter offers units on Native American communities, pioneer communities, rural and small town living, urban living, being an American, world neighbors, and celebrations. Sample titles from the unit on rural and small town life include *The Best Town in the World* by Byrd Baylor (Charles Scribner's Sons, 1983), *In Coal Country* by Judith Hendershot (Knopf, 1987), and *Yonder* by Tony Johnston (Dial Books for Young Readers, 1988).

The fourth grade/fifth grade chapter is American history-based with units titled Early America; Becoming a Nation; American Frontier; The Civil War Era; America, Land of Change; and The United States Today and Tomorrow. Among the 14 titles accompanying the Civil War unit are *Turn Homeward, Hannalee* by Patricia Beatty (William Morrow, 1987), *Lincoln: A Photobiography* by Russell Freedman (Clarion Books, 1987), *The Battle of Gettysburg* by Neil Johnson (Four Winds Press, 1989), and *Behind Rebel Lines* by Seymour Reit (Harcourt Brace Jovanovich, 1988).

Objectives and activities in *Literature-Based Social Studies* acknowledge student development principles and shift from teacher-direction to self-direction as grade levels progress.

Adventures with Social Studies (through Literature)

Strong bibliographies accompanying lively ideas earn Sharron McElmeel's *Adventures with Social Studies* a place in this bibliographic discussion. Laced with recommended titles, each of the 10-page chapters can be developed as a resource-based unit for upper elementary students.

Among topics covered in *Adventures with Social Studies* are folklore, pioneers, multicultural themes, and a calendar of "history breaks." Appendixes include author addresses and a directory of publishers.

Integrating the Primary Curriculum: Social Studies and Children's Literature

Author team Meredith and Tom McGowan have developed several books which offer ideas for utilization of trade books in the curriculum. *Integrating the Primary Curriculum* is basically a "how to" book which uses 20 prize-winning children's books as the foundation for interdisciplinary activities for grades K-3.

Divided into 20 chapters, the McGowans' book uses a similar format throughout. For each book, discussion and/or ideas are presented on (1) relationship to social studies, (2) developing communication skills, (3) nurturing affective domain, (4) promoting thinking skills, (5) map and globe skills, and (6) practicing social interaction.

The appendix of *Integrating the Primary Curriculum* offers a bibliography of additional suitable books. Other titles of similar value by the McGowans are *Children, Literature and Social Studies: Activities for the Primary Grades* and *Telling America's Story: Teaching American History through Children's Literature*.

Social Studies through Children's Literature: An Integrated Approach

Part theory, part application, and part bibliography, *Social Studies through Children's Literature* attempts to help the reader develop interdisciplinary approaches using children's books. To achieve this goal, author Anthony D. Fredericks uses in-depth activities for 32 books as springboards for classroom learning.

Following the sequence of the traditional seven major areas of social studies (child/self, family, community/neighborhood, city/country, states/region, nation/country, and world), the book works through a variety of ideas, activities, and processes. Each chapter is identically structured: story summary, social studies topic areas, content-related words, curricular perspectives, critical-thinking questions, related books and references, and activities.

Chapter 10, "Nation and Country," is built around *Anno's U.S.A.* by Mitsumasa Anno (Philomel Books, 1983), *John Henry* by Ezra Jack Keats (Pantheon Books, 1965), *A Picture Book of Abraham Lincoln* by David A. Adler (Holiday House, 1989), *A Picture Book of Martin Luther King, Jr.* by Adler (Holiday House, 1989), *The Star-Spangled Banner* by Peter Spier (Doubleday, 1973), and *Those People in Washington* by David Flitner (Children's Press, 1973).

In the four-page section tied to *Anno's U.S.A.*, the author suggests 9 additional books and references and offers 16 student participation ideas which include recipes for blue corn bread and apple butter, a word game, and math, map, letter-writing, and music activities.

Appendices of *Social Studies Through Children's Literature* include additional annotated bibliographies of children's books, social studies activities books, and sources for children's literature in social studies.

Peoples of the American West:
Historical Perspectives through Children's Literature
Teachers and curriculum directors will find
Peoples of the American West by Mary Hurlburt
Cordier and Maria A. Perez-Stable a helpful aid
in finding books which provide a realistic understanding of the American West. It successfully
pinpoints 100 of the most useful fiction and
nonfiction books on the subject for elementary
students.

Three criteria were used in selection of titles
for inclusion in *Peoples of the American West*: (1)
realism of time, place, events, and character; (2)
literary qualities based on a good storyline; and
(3) availability of books. That care was taken in
preparation of the listing is evident, and recommended books are indeed standard titles usually
found in school library media centers or public
libraries.

Arrangement of *Peoples of the American West*
is thematic. Each entry is accompanied by a 150-
200-word synopsis. A reading difficulty assessment which indicates Fry, Flesch, Fog, and
Bormuth reading levels is included. Closing
paragraphs about each book discuss strengths and
suggest specific portions for curriculum activity.

A to Zoo: Subject Access
to Children's Picture Books

From its first publication in 1982 with 4,400 titles
to today's third edition which identifies almost
12,000 books, *A to Zoo*'s story has been one of
acceptance and steady growth. An important key
to its success is that it is the most extensive subject
guide available for picture books.

Written by Carolyn W. Lima and John A.
Lima, *A to Zoo* opens with an 11-page listing of
the 700 subjects used. The subject guide follows.
In the subject guide, books appear alphabetically
by author/title under appropriate subject headings. The number of books listed under specific
subjects varies widely; BEHAVIOR--LOSING THINGS
lists 57 books, but ROCKS is the subject of only 7
picture books.

The chapter or section of *A to Zoo* titled
"Bibliographic Guide" runs for 339 pages. Here
citations are arranged by author and give title,
illustrator, publisher, date, and the subject
headings under which the book is listed. The book
also offers a title index. The final section of *A to
Zoo* provides an illustrator index.

Beyond Picture Books: A Guide to First Readers

This selective, annotated bibliography, which
identifies 1,610 titles intended for early readers at
the first and second grade level, is a surefire
teacher-pleaser. Developed by Barbara Barstow
and Judith Riggle, *Beyond Picture Books* offers
good access to its contents through an annotated
listing which provides 25-word descriptions of
each book, a subject index, title and illustrator
indexes, series lists, and a readability index. Trade
books included in the readability index range
from 1.0 to 3.9 on the Spache scale. Most of the
books included are between 1.2 and 3.3.

In addition to identifying 1,600-plus first
readers, the authors have selected a special group
of 200 outstanding titles drawn from the total
bibliography. This list--fiction and nonfiction, old
and new--forms the opening section of *Beyond
Picture Books* and sets the stage for the quality of
work which follows.

Eyeopeners! How to Choose and Use Children's
Books about Real People, Places, and Things

In *Eyeopeners!*, author Beverly Kobrin provides an
idea book packed with bibliographies. More than
500 nonfiction titles appear, complete with
annotations and suggestions for use with elementary students.

Celebrations:
Read-Aloud Holiday and Theme Book Programs

Pleasing design and clever ideas are hallmarks of
this compilation of book programs by creative
author/storyteller Caroline Feller Bauer in
Celebrations.

Some of the holidays selected by Bauer are
far from traditional, but social studies practitioners will feel an affinity for Calendar Day, Saint
Patrick's Day, a seasonal celebration of spring, a
fresh Thanksgiving, Christmas, and Valentine's
Day. Each unit contains suggestions for development, prose and poetry selections, creative
activities, bulletin board ideas, and an annotated
bibliography of 50 or more trade books related in
some fashion to the theme.

Index to Collective Biographies for Young Readers

Now in its fourth edition, *Collective Biographies*
lists 9,773 people representing the contents of
1,129 standard collective biographies. Titles
selected for inclusion are those considered most
suitable for elementary and junior high school
readers, but occasionally a senior high school title
is listed.

The section of *Collective Biographies* which
will most interest curriculum planners is the

portion of the book which is titled "Subject Listing of Biographees." Here is the information which will assist in putting together thematic units: Individuals are identified by fields of activity and nationality. Entries are keyed to specific books of collective biography and provide assistance in locating information about often elusive historical figures.

Books to Help Children Cope with Separation and Loss: An Annotated Bibliography

This standard resource, compiled by Joanne E. Bernstein and Masha Kabakow Rudman, was published by R. R. Bowker in 1989. Listed as volume 3, the current volume of *Separation and Loss* serves as a supplement to volume 2, which was published in 1983. Volume 3 annotates more than 600 books useful in bibliotherapy. Grade levels covered are preschool through grade 10; however, most entries are books for elementary students. Arrangement is by category of loss. A strong subject index aids in identifying materials.

Notable Children's Trade Books in the Field of Social Studies

Notable Children's Trade Books is a prestigious listing of roughly 150 books published during the preceding year. It is available as a monograph and also appears annually (usually in the April/May issue) in *Social Education* magazine.

Development of the notable list is a project sponsored jointly by the National Council for the Social Studies and the Children's Book Council. Selection of fiction and nonfiction titles for inclusion is made by a committee of social studies and media professionals appointed by the National Council for the Social Studies.

Books chosen for the list (1) are written for children in grades K-8; (2) emphasize human relations; (3) represent a diversity of groups and are sensitive to a broad range of cultural experiences; (4) present an original theme or a fresh approach to a traditional topic; (5) are readable and of high literary quality; and (6) have a pleasing format and, when appropriate, illustrations that enrich the text.

Books are grouped broadly by topic. Reading levels are indicated as primary, intermediate, or advanced. Subject groupings used on the 1991 list include biography (16 books); contemporary concerns (9 books); environment, energy, and ecology (18); folktales (21); geography, peoples, and places (18); history, life, and culture in the Americas (27); U.S. history and government (13);

human relations (21); understanding oneself and others (14); and world history and culture (15).

Periodicals: Indexes

Three major indexes serve as subject guides to periodicals used by elementary and secondary students. They serve the curriculum planner by assisting in location of up-to-date information on current topics and as identification sources of reviews of materials for possible use.

Children's Magazine Guide

Children's Magazine Guide, an index to elementary level magazines, provides listings by subject of articles in more than 30 publications ranging from *Book Report* and *Boy's Life* to *Zillions* and *Zoobooks*. Frequency of publication is 10 issues per year. Subject headings are aligned with student interests and vocabulary. A second section of each issue of *Children's Magazine Guide* indexes seven professional journals often used by elementary teachers and media specialists.

Abridged Readers' Guide to Periodical Literature

Abridged Readers' Guide, an H. W. Wilson publication, is a smaller version of *Readers' Guide to Periodical Literature*. Better suited to junior and senior high school use than elementary, *Abridged Readers' Guide* indexes 60 journals of general interest.

Readers' Guide to Periodical Literature

Readers' Guide is the best-known of the periodical indexes used by students and the general public. Published since 1900 by H. W. Wilson Company, *Readers' Guide* is issued twice monthly, with quarterly and annual cumulations. It indexes more than 200 publications. Arrangement is alphabetic, with authors and subjects interfiled in a combined listing. A separate listing of book reviews is provided. *Readers' Guide* is available in printed format, online, or on CD-ROM.

Bibliography

Resource Books

Barstow, Barbara, and Judith Riggle. 1989. *Beyond Picture Books: A Guide to First Readers.* New Providence, NJ: R. R. Bowker.

Bauer, Caroline Feller. 1985. *Celebrations: Read-Aloud Holiday and Theme Book Programs.* New York: H. W. Wilson.

Bernstein, Joanne E., and Masha Kabakow Rudman. 1989. *Books to Help Children Cope with Separation and Loss: An Annotated Bibliography*. Vol. 3. New Providence, NJ: R. R. Bowker.

Best Books for Children: Preschool through Grade 6. 1990. 4th ed., ed. John T. Gillespie and Corrine J. Naden. New Providence, NJ: R. R. Bowker.

Best Books for Junior High Readers. 1991. Ed. John T. Gillespie. New Providence, NJ: R. R. Bowker.

Best Books for Senior High Readers. 1991. Ed. John T. Gillespie. New Providence, NJ: R. R. Bowker.

Children's Books in Print. Annual. New Providence, NJ: R. R. Bowker.

Children's Catalog. 1991. 16th ed., ed. Juliette Yaakov with the assistance of Anne Price. New York: H. W. Wilson.

Cordier, Mary Hurlburt, and Maria A. Perez-Stable. 1989. *Peoples of the American West: Historical Perspectives through Children's Literature*. Metuchen, NJ: Scarecrow Press.

El-Hi Textbooks and Serials in Print. Annual. New Providence, NJ: R. R. Bowker.

The Elementary School Library Collection: A Guide to Books and Other Media, Phase 1-2-3. 1992. 18th ed., ed. Lauren Lee with Gary D. Hoyle. Williamsport, PA: Brodart.

Fredericks, Anthony D. 1991. *Social Studies through Children's Literature: An Integrated Approach*. Englewood, CO: Teacher Ideas.

Index to Collective Biographies for Young Readers. 1988. 4th ed., ed. Karen Breen. New Providence, NJ: R. R. Bowker.

Junior High School Library Catalog. 1990. 6th ed., ed. Juliette Yaakov. New York: H. W. Wilson.

Karp, Rashelle, and June H. Schlessinger. 1991. *Plays for Children and Young Adults: An Evaluative Index and Guide*. New York: Garland.

Katz, Bill, and Linda Sternberg Katz. 1991. *Magazines for Young People*. 2d ed. New Providence, NJ: R. R. Bowker.

Kobrin, Beverly. 1988. *Eyeopeners! How to Choose and Use Children's Books about Real People, Places, and Things*. New York: Viking Penguin.

Laughlin, Mildred Knight, and Patricia Payne Kardeleff. 1991. *Literature-Based Social Studies: Children's Books and Activities to Enrich the Social Studies*. Phoenix: Oryx.

Lima, Carolyn W., and John A. Lima. 1989. *A to Zoo: Subject Access to Children's Picture Books*. 3d ed. New Providence, NJ: R. R. Bowker.

McElmeel, Sharron L. 1991. *Adventures with Social Studies (through Literature)*. Englewood, CO: Teacher Ideas.

McGowan, Tom, and Meredith McGowan. 1986. *Children, Literature and Social Studies: Activities for the Intermediate Grades*. Indianapolis: Special Literature Press.

———. 1988. *Integrating the Primary Curriculum: Social Studies and Children's Literature*. Indianapolis: Special Literature Press.

———. 1989. *Telling America's Story: Teaching American History through Children's Literature*. New Berlin, WI: Jenson.

Miller-Lachmann, Lyn. 1992. *Our Family, Our Friends, Our World: An Annotated Guide to Significant Multicultural Books for Children and Teenagers*. New Providence, NJ: R. R. Bowker.

Notable Children's Trade Books in the Field of Social Studies. Annual. Washington, DC: National Council for the Social Studies; New York: Children's Book Council.

Senior High School Library Catalog. 1987. 13th ed., ed. Ferne E. Hillegas and Juliette Yaakov. New York: H. W. Wilson.

Subject Guide to Children's Books in Print. Annual. New Providence, NJ: R. R. Bowker.

VanMeter, Vandelia. 1990. *American History for Children and Young Adults: An Annotated Bibliographic Index*. Englewood, CO: Libraries Unlimited.

Weisburg, Hilda K., and Ruth Toor. 1987. *Stars, States, and Historic Dates: Activities, Research and Readings in American History*. Berkeley Heights, NJ: Library Learning Resources.

Indexes

Abridged Readers' Guide to Periodical Literature. New York: H. W. Wilson.

Children's Magazine Guide. New Providence, NJ: R. R. Bowker.

Readers' Guide to Periodical Literature. New York: H. W. Wilson.

CURRICULUM MATERIAL PRODUCERS

THIS chapter provides information on publishers and producers of social studies curriculum materials, textbooks, supplementary materials, software, and other items. For some of the larger publishers, we have provided a listing of social studies series and book titles. For other companies, we provide a description of products. Much of the information in this chapter is based on the publishers' catalogues; for more details, you should contact the publishers and producers directly. The addresses and phone numbers given are for the offices that will supply catalogues and other promotion material; note that these phone numbers are not for the editorial offices.

Addison-Wesley Publishing Company
Jacob Way
Reading, MA 01867
800-447-2226

Civics

Civics: Participating in Our Democracy
Grades 7-11. Student and teacher's edition, teacher's resource binder, transparency package, testing software

Economics

Addison-Wesley Economics
Grades 10-12. Textbook, teacher's edition, teacher's resource book, software

Economics
Grade 12. Textbook, teacher's manuals, supplementary materials including "Economics in the News," software

Mini-Society: Experiencing Real-World Economics in the Elementary School Classroom

Our Economy: How It Works
Grades 7-10. Textbook, teacher's guide, workbook

Pursuing the Past
Grades 5-8. Student book, teacher's guide

Teaching Economics
Grades 9-12. Teacher's sourcebook

Understanding Economics: Overview for Teachers, Experiences for Students
Grades 4-8. Teacher's sourcebook

You and the Constitution
Grades 5-8. Student book, teacher's guide

Social Studies Resources/Multicultural Resources
Teacher's Sourcebooks, Student Workbooks
Grades 4-12. Includes "Seeds of Change," "National Security Series," and "Pathways to Pluralism"

Multicultural Sourcebooks
Grades K-12. Includes "Our People and Their Stories" and "Worldways: Bringing the World into the Classroom"

United States History

The United States and Its People
Grades 9-12. Textbook, teacher's edition,

teacher's resource package, transparency package, testing software

World History

World History: Traditions and New Directions
Grades 9-12. Textbook, teacher's edition, teacher's resource package, supplementary materials including software

American School Publishers

SRA School Group
P.O. Box 5380
Chicago, IL 60680-5380
1-800-843-8855

Multicultural Geography: Content Area Reading
Grades 4-9. Softcover texts, teacher's guides
(See also under SRA School Group)

Amsco School Publications, Inc.

315 Hudson Street
New York, NY 10013-1085
212-675-7000

Economics

Economics and You
Textbook, workbook, teacher's manual

Economics for Everybody
Textbook

Economics: Institutions and Analysis
Textbook, teacher's manual

Geography

Global Geography
Textbook, teacher's manual, activity book

Government

Basic Principles of American Government
Textbook

Government and You
Text, teacher's manual, unit tests

Government for Everybody
Textbook, teacher's manual, activities and tests

Regional Studies/State Histories

California through Five Centuries

India

Japan

Northwest Heritage
(Washington, Oregon, Idaho)

Social Studies/Psychology

Mastering Social Studies Skills
Textbook

Psychology: A Way to Grow
Textbook

United States History

American History
Textbook, review text

American Studies: A Conceptual Approach
Textbook

Americans All
Textbooks, workbook

Comprehensive United States History
Textbook, teacher's manual

Current Issues in American Democracy

Enjoying American History
Textbook, teacher's manual

Mastering American History Skills

U.S. History and Government

USA: The Unfolding Story of America
Textbook, teacher's guide, supplementary material

United States History, Review Text

World History

Enjoying World History
Softcover text

Global Studies: Civilizations of the Past and Present
Textbook, teacher's manual

Western Civilization
Textbook

World History
Textbook, review text

Book-Lab
P.O. Box 7316
500 74th Street
North Bergen, NJ 07047-1016
800-654-4081
201-861-6763

Instructional materials for language-delayed learners. Texts, workbooks, teacher's guides in U.S. history, geography, and government

Brown Roa Publishing Media
P.O. Box 539
Dubuque, IA 52001
800-338-5578

Grades 7-12. English curriculum units, lesson plans, student handouts, tests. Series include current issues, U.S. history, U.S. government, world history, economics, biography, basic skills, research

Cambridge Social Studies
P.O. Box 2153, Dept. SS2
Charleston, WV 25328-2153
800-468-4227

Video cassette series, books, teacher's resource books, charts, maps, globes, games. Topics include contemporary issues, environmental studies, U.S. history, native American studies, the U.S. Civil War, world history, geography, presidents and leaders, Vietnam Era, world wars I and II, ancient history, Persian Gulf crisis

Charlesbridge Publishing
85 Main Street
Watertown, MA 02172
800-225-3214
617-926-0329

Young Discovery Library
Grades 3-6. Pocket-sized encyclopedias

Cobblestone Publishing, Inc.
30 Grove Street
Peterborough, NH 03458
603-924-7209

Magazines in world history, U.S. history, and multicultural studies. Teacher's resource guides, activity books

Continental Press
520 East Bainbridge Street
Elizabethtown, PA 17022
800-233-0759

Communities around the World
Grades 3-5. Integrated global awareness units. Student text-workbooks, teacher's editions

Map Skills Series: Practical Applications
Grades 2-9. Student work-texts, teacher's guides

Map Skills: Programmed Instruction
Student work-text, teacher's guide

Creative Teaching Press
P.O. Box 6017
Cypress, CA 90630-0017
800-444-4CTP

Learning about the United States (series)
Grades K-8. Reference charts

Critical Thinking Press & Software
Midwest Publications
P.O. Box 448
Pacific Grove, CA 93950
800-458-4849

Grades K-12. Remedial, average, gifted, at risk. Activity books, resource books, software, tests

Curriculum Associates, Inc.
5 Esquire Road
N. Billerica, MA 01862-2589
800-225-0248
508-667-8000

Grades 2-adult ed. Student books, teacher's guides. Series titles include "The Classroom Traveler," "One People, One Flag," "One People, One Constitution," "The World We Share," and "Global Views"

Didax, Inc.
One Centennial Drive
Peabody, MA 01960
800-458-0024

Preschool, elementary, special needs. Maps, educational games, puzzles, books

The Dushkin Publishing Group, Inc.
Sluice Dock
Guilford, CT 06437-9989
800-243-6532

American National Government: Institutions, Policy, and Participation
Grades 11-12. Softcover text, teacher's resource guide, microcomputer test generator

Annual Editions (series)
Grades 11-12. Softcover text, teacher's resource guides. Topics include economics, history, American government, international studies, sociology/anthropology, psychology, legal studies, and geography/environment

Cultural Anthropology: Understanding Ourselves and Others
Grades 11-12. Softcover text, teacher's resource guide, microcomputer test generator

The Drama of Democracy: American Government and Politics
Grades 11-12. Text, teacher's resource guide, microcomputer test generator, student study guide

Global Studies (series)
Grades 11-12. Softcover texts, teacher's manuals. Includes "Africa," "China," "Japan and the Pacific Rim," "Middle East," "The Soviet Union and Eastern Europe," "Latin America," and "Western Europe"

International Politics on the World Stage
Grades 11-12. Softcover text, teacher's resource guide, microcomputer test generator

The Study of Economics: Principles, Concepts & Applications
Grades 11-12. Softcover text, teacher's resource guide, microcomputer test generator, full-color transparency set

Taking Sides (series)
Grades 11-12. Softcover texts, teacher's manuals. Topics include American history, political issues, world politics, mass media and society, social issues, crime and criminology, moral issues, and environmental education

ECS Learning System, Inc.
P.O. Box 791437
San Antonio, TX 78379-1437
800-68-TEACH

Grades pre-K-12. Softcover texts, workbooks, teacher's resources, maps, and games

EMC Publishing
300 York Avenue
St. Paul, MN 55101
800-328-1452

Decisions: Making Personal Economic Choices
Textbook, teacher's edition, teacher's resource binder, student workbook, software

Introduction to Economics
Textbook, teacher's edition, teacher's resource binder, student workbook, software

Software Programs
Series include "Working: Today and Tomorrow," "Banking," "Credit," "Budgeting," "Introduction to Economics," and "Decisions"

Enterprise for Education
1320-A Third Street, Suite 302
Santa Monica, CA 90401
310-394-9864

Grades 5-12. Curriculum-based energy and environmental program. Student booklet, teacher's guide, teacher's resource books, yearbook, workbooks

Entry Publishing, Inc.
P.O. Box 20277
New York, NY 10025
800-736-1405

Reading disabled, grades 5-adult. Softcover texts, workbooks, teacher's guides, software, maps

Fearon/Janus/Quercus

500 Harbor Boulevard
Belmont, CA 94002
800-877-4283

Special education/remedial programs. Textbooks, teacher's resource binders, activity books, teacher's guides

Glencoe/Macmillan/McGraw-Hill

P.O. Box 543
Blacklick, OH 43004-0543
800-334-7344

Civics/Government

Civics: Citizens in Action
Textbook, teacher's edition, teacher's resource book, supplementary materials including software

Civics: Responsibilities and Citizenship
Textbook, teacher's edition, teacher's resource binder, supplementary materials including software

Government in the United States
Textbook, teacher's edition, teacher's resource binder, supplementary materials including software

Merrill American Government: Principles and Practices
Textbook, teacher's edition, teacher resource package, supplementary materials including software

Economics

Basic Economic Principles
Textbook, teacher's edition, teacher's resource binder, supplementary materials

Consumer Education and Economics
Textbook, teacher's resource book, supplementary materials including software

Economics: Today and Tomorrow
Textbook, teacher's edition, teacher's resource binder, supplementary materials including software and video cassettes

Merrill Economics: Principles and Practices
Textbook, teacher's edition, teacher's resource book, supplementary materials including software

Scribner Economics
Textbook, teacher's edition, supplementary materials including software

Understanding Economics
Textbook, teacher's guide, activities resource book

Geography

Building Skills in Geography
Workbook, teacher's edition

Essentials of Geography
Text, teacher's guide

Glencoe World Geography
Textbook, teacher's edition, teacher's classroom resources, supplementary materials in software and video cassettes

Laidlaw World Geography
Textbook, teacher's edition, teacher's resource binder, software

McGraw-Hill World Geography
Textbook, teacher's edition, teacher's resource file

Merrill World Geography: People and Places
Textbook, teacher's edition, teacher's resource book, supplementary materials including software

Psychology

Understanding Psychology
Textbook, teacher's edition, teacher's resource binder

United States History

America Is
Textbook, teacher's edition, teacher's resource book package, supplementary materials including software

American Issues: A Documentary Reader
Textbook, teacher's guide

American Odyssey: The United States in the 20th Century
Textbook, teacher's edition, teacher's classroom resources, supplementary materials including software

The American Tradition: A History of the United States
Textbook, teacher's edition, teacher's resource book package, supplementary materials including software

Challenge of Freedom
Textbook, teacher's editions, teacher's resource binder, supplementary materials including software

History of a Free Nation
Textbook, teacher's edition, teacher's classroom resources, supplementary materials including software, and Spanish summaries and glossary

Legacy of Freedom
Textbooks, teacher's editions, teacher's resource binders, supplementary materials

The Living Constitution
Textbook, teacher's edition

Ohio: Geography, History, Government
Textbook, teacher's edition, workbook

Texas and Texans
Textbook, teacher's edition, teacher's resource binder, student activity book, supplementary materials including software

Two Centuries of Progress
Textbook, teacher's edition, teacher's resource binder, supplementary materials including software

United States History Enrichment series
Teacher's resource books. Includes "Map and Graph Skill Activities," "Reinforcing Social Studies Skills," "American Literary Heritage," and "American Portraits." U.S. history diagraph transparencies, U.S. history and art transparencies

World History

Global Insights: People and Cultures
Textbook, teacher's guide, teacher's resource book package

The Human Expression: World Regions and Cultures
Textbook, teacher's edition, teacher's resource binder

Human Heritage: A World History
Textbook, teacher's edition, teacher's resource book package, supplementary materials including software

Introduction to the Arab World Video with Guidebook

World History: The Human Experience
Textbook, teacher's edition, teacher's classroom resources, supplementary materials including software

World History Enrichment Series
Includes "Map Skills" and "Reinforcing Social Studies Skills"

Social Studies Enrichment

American History I and II Review Bank Software
Includes "Period of Exploration to Reconstruction" and "Post-Civil War America to Present"

Glencoe Social Studies Enrichment Series
Includes "Reinforcing Social Studies Skills" and "Writer's Guidebook." SAT practice tests, outline map resource book

National Issues Forums (series)
Booklets including "The Boundaries of Free Speech," "America's Role in The World," and "Energy Options"

Social Studies Videos
Includes "Modern Presidential Campaigns" and "Great Speeches"

Globe Book Company
Simon and Schuster
4350 Equity Drive
P.O. Box 2649
Columbus, Ohio 43216
800-848-9500

The African American Experience: A History
Texts, teacher resource manual with tests

Economics and the American Free Enterprise System
Textbook, teacher resource manual

Exploring American Citizenship
Textbook, teacher resource materials, workbook

Exploring American History
Textbook, teacher's edition, teacher's resource book, workbook

Exploring a Changing World
Textbook, teacher's resource book, supplementary materials

Exploring Latin America
Softcover text, teacher's manual

Exploring the Non-Western World
Textbook, teacher's resource book, supplementary materials including software

Exploring United States History
Grades 11-12. Textbook, teacher's resource book, supplementary materials

Exploring World History
Textbook, teacher's edition, teacher's resource book, supplementary materials including Spanish language supplement

Foundations in American History
Softcover text, teacher's manual

The Newcomers Series
Softcover texts, teacher's manuals. Includes "African Americans in U.S. History" and "Hispanics in U.S. History"

The Regional Studies Series
Softcover texts, teacher's manual. Includes "The Soviet Union," "China," "The Middle East," "Latin America," "Africa," "India-Pakistan-Bangladesh," "Japan-Korea-Taiwan," and "Southeast Asia"

The United States in the Making
Softcover text, teacher's manual

Unlocking Geography Skills and Concepts
Softcover text, teacher's manual

Unlocking Social Studies Skills
Softcover text, teacher's manual

Unlocking the Constitution and the Declaration of Independence
Softcover text, teacher's manual

World History for a Global Age
Softcover work-texts, teacher's resource manual

Graphic Learning
61 Mattatuck Heights Road
Waterbury, CT 06705
800-874-0029

Grades K-12. Integrated language arts/social studies programs. Student desk maps, activity pages, teacher's guides, workbooks, supplementary materials. Integrates geography, history, economics, politics, sociocultural concepts, map and globe skills, language/study skills, thinking skills

Greenhaven Press, Inc.
P.O. Box 289009
San Diego, CA 92198-0009
800-231-5163

America's Wars (series)
Softcover texts

Greenhaven World History Program (series)
Grades 5-9. Softcover texts, test-discussion activities. Topics include history makers, great revolutions, enduring issues, great civilizations, political and social movements

Opposing Viewpoints (series)
Grades 5-12. Books, pamphlets, teacher's guides. Topics include area studies, criminal justice, foreign policy, government and economics, social issues, great mysteries

World Disasters (series)
Softcover texts

Hammond Education Catalog
515 Valley Street
Maplewood, New Jersey 07040
800-526-4935

Grades K-12. School atlases and supplementary materials, maps, charts, books, blackline masters, transparencies

Harcourt Brace Jovanovich, Inc.
School Department
6277 Sea Harbor Drive
Orlando, FL 32821-9989
800-CALL-HBJ

HBJ Social Studies
Grades K-6. Textbooks, teacher's editions, teacher resource banks, supplementary materials including software, state books

D. C. Heath and Company
School Division
125 Spring Street
Lexington, MA 02173
800-235-3565

Civics/Government

American Foreign Policy: A History
High school (advanced placement). Softcover texts

American Government: Institutions and Policies
High school (advanced placement). Textbook, teacher's guide, supplementary materials including software

An American Government Reader
Textbook, teacher's edition

Social Studies

Heath Social Studies
Grades K-7. Textbooks, teacher's editions, teacher resource packages, supplementary materials including software. Includes "Exploring My World," "Exploring Our Country," "Exploring World Communities," "State Studies," and "Exploring Canada and Latin America"

United States History

The American Pageant: A History of the Republic
High school (advanced placement). Textbook, guidebooks, teacher's resource guide, supplementary materials including software

The American People: A History
Middle/junior high school. Textbook, teacher's edition, teacher's resource binder, supplementary materials including software

The American Spirit: United States History as Seen by Contemporaries
High school (advanced placement). Textbooks

Conflict and Consensus in American History
High school (advanced placement). Softcover text

The Enduring Vision: A History of the American People
High school (advanced placement). Textbook, teacher's guide, supplementary materials including software

The Great Republic
High school (advanced placement). Textbook, teacher's guide, supplementary materials including software

Major Problems in American History (series)
High school (advanced placement). Softcover readers. Includes "Major Problems in American Women's History," "Major Problems in the History of the Vietnam War," "Major Problems in the History of the American South," and "Major Problems in American Foreign Policy"

Problems in American Civilization (series)
High school (advanced placement). Softcover readers. Includes "The Abolitionists: Means, Ends, and Motivations," "The Causes of the American Civil War," "The Causes of the American Revolution," and "The Origins of the Cold War"

The Ways We Lived: Essays and Documents in American Social History
High school (advanced placement). Textbook

World History/World Cultures

Exploring Canada and Latin America
Middle/junior high school. Textbook, teacher's edition, teacher resource package, supplementary materials including software

Exploring Our World, Past and Present
Middle/junior high school. Textbook, teacher's edition, teacher resource package, supplementary materials including software

1492: Discovery, Invasion, Encounter: Sources and Interpretations
High school (advanced placement). Textbook

Heath World Geography
Junior/senior high school. Textbook, teacher's edition, teacher's resource binder, supplementary materials including software

The Humanities: Cultural Roots and Continuities
High school (advanced placement). Softcover texts, teacher's guide, test item file

Problems in European Civilization (series)
High school (advanced placement). Softcover readers. Includes "The End of the Roman Empire: Decline or Transformation?," "The Greatness of Louis XIV," "The Holocaust," and "The Industrial Revolution in Britain: Triumph or Disaster?"

The Western Tradition
High school (advanced placement). Textbooks

World History: Perspectives on the Past (series)
High school. Textbooks, teacher's editions, teacher resource package, supplementary materials including software, Spanish resources

Holt, Rinehart and Winston
6277 Sea Harbor Drive
Orlando, FL 32821-9989
800-225-5425

Anthropology

Anthropology
High school (advanced placement). Text, teacher's manual, study guide, test bank software

Civics/Government

American Civics
Grades 7-12. Textbook, teacher's edition, teacher's resource binder, workbook, test generator software

We the People
Grades 7-12. Textbook, teacher's edition, teacher's resource binder, supplementary materials including test generator software

Economics

Economics
High school (advanced placement). Textbooks, teacher's manuals, supplementary materials including test bank software

Economics: Free Enterprise in Action
Grades 7-12. Textbook, teacher's edition, teacher's resource package, supplementary materials including audio cassettes, test bank software

Economics: Principles and Policy
High school (advanced placement). Textbooks, study guide, teacher's manual, supplementary materials including test banks software

Geography

Essentials of Physical Geography
High school (advanced placement). Text, teacher's manual, supplementary materials including test generator software

Geography Video Programs
Grades 7-12. Video cassettes, discussion guides, worksheets, glossaries. Includes "Religions of the World" and "Mapmaking Today"

World Geography: The Earth and Its People
Grades 7-12. Textbook, teacher's edition, teacher's resource bank, supplementary materials including test generator software

World Geography Today
Grades 7-12. Textbook, teacher's edition, teacher's resource binder, supplementary materials including test generator software, video cassettes

Sociology

Introduction to Sociology
High school (advanced placement). Text, teacher's manual, study guide test bank, computerized test bank, overhead transparencies, software

Sociology in a Changing World
High school (advanced placement). Text with workbook kit, teacher's manual, supplementary materials including test bank software

Sociology: The Study of Human Relationships
Grades 7-12. Textbook, teacher's manual and resource guide, workbook, tests

United States History

An American History Primer
High school (advanced placement). Softcover text

The Constitution: Foundation of Our Freedom
Grades 7-12. Textbook, teacher's edition

The Constitution: Past, Present, and Future
Grades 7-12. Student edition, answer key

Eyewitnesses and Others: Readings in American History
Grades 7-12. Textbook, teacher's manual

50 American Biographies
Grades 7-12. Textbook, teacher's manual

The National Experience (series)
High school (advanced placement). Text, supplementary materials

Our Land, Our Time
Grades 7-12. Textbook, teacher's edition, teacher resource organizer, supplementary materials including test generator software

The Story of America
Grades 7-12. Textbooks, teacher's edition, teacher's resource binder, supplementary materials including audio cassettes (English and Spanish), test generator software, video cassettes

Triumph of the American Nation
Grades 7-12. Textbook, teacher's edition, teacher's resource package, supplementary materials

United States History
Grades 7-12 (remedial). Textbook, teacher's edition, teacher's resource binder, supplementary materials including test generator software

United States History Resource Materials
Transparency packages, software, instructional materials

World History/World Cultures

Arts and Ideas
High school (advanced placement). Text, teacher's manual, musical cassettes, computer test bank, slide set

Culture and Values
High school (advanced placement). Softbound text, teacher's manual, computer test bank, musical cassette, slide set

The Mainstream of Civilization
High school (advanced placement). Text, supplementary materials

Readings in World History
Grades 7-12. Student edition, answer key

World History
Grades 7-12. Textbook, teacher's manual, teacher's resource binder, supplementary materials

World History: People and Nations
Grades 7-12. Textbook, teacher's edition, teacher's resource bank, supplementary materials including test generator software

Houghton Mifflin
Department J
One Beacon Street
Boston, MA 02108-9971
800-323-5663

Civics/Government

American Politics: Classics and Contemporary Readings
High school (advanced placement). Softcover texts, teacher's resource manual, supplementary materials

The Challenge of Democracy
High school (advanced placement). Textbooks, teacher's manual, supplementary materials

Government in America
Grades 11-12. Textbooks, teacher's edition, student workbook, teacher's resources, supplementary materials including test generator software, video cassette series

Vital Issues of the Constitution
Grades 10-12. Softcover texts, teacher's guide

Economics

Economics
High school (advanced placement). Softcover texts, teacher's resource manual, supplementary materials

Geography

Geography
Grades 7-10. Textbooks, teacher's edition, teacher's resource book, student activity book, supplementary materials

Social Studies (General)

Houghton Mifflin Social Studies K-8 (series)
Textbooks, teacher's editions, Spanish editions, student text, supplementary materials including trade book sets

The National Proficiency Survey Series
Test booklets, answer sheets, technical manual, administrator's summary

United States History

America: The Glorious Republic
Grades 9-12. Textbooks, teacher's annotated edition, teacher's resource binder, student workbook, supplementary materials including test generator software

America's Story
Grades 7-9. Textbooks, teacher's edition, teacher's resource binder, student workbook, supplementary materials

Discovering the American Past: A Look at Evidence
High school (advanced placement). Softcover texts, teacher's manual, supplementary materials

Great Cases of the Supreme Court
Grades 7-9. Softcover texts, teacher's guide

History of the United States
Grades 9-12. Textbooks, teacher's edition, teacher's resource file, student workbook, supplementary materials including software

History of the United States Volume 1: Beginnings to 1877
Grades 7-9. Textbook, teacher's edition, teacher's resource file, supplementary materials including test generator software

History of the United States Volume 2: Civil War to the Present
Grades 9-12. Textbook, teacher's editions, teacher's resource file, supplementary materials including test generator software

A More Perfect Union
Grade 8. Textbook, teacher's edition, supplementary materials

A People and a Nation: A History of the United States
High school (advanced placement). Complete and brief textbooks, teacher's resource manual, supplementary materials

Voices of America: Readings in American History
Grades 9-12. Softcover text

World History

Across the Centuries
Grades 7-9. Textbook, teacher's edition, teacher's resources, supplementary materials

Discovering the Western Past: A Look at the Evidence
High school (advanced placement). Softcover texts, supplementary materials

A History of Western Society (series)
High school (advanced placement). Softcover texts, supplementary materials

History of the World
Grades 9-12. Textbook, teacher's edition, teacher's resources, supplementary materials including test generator and lesson plan software

A History of World Societies (series)
High school (advanced placement). Softcover texts, supplementary materials

A Messsage of Ancient Days
Grades 6-9. Textbook, Spanish student edition, teacher's edition, teacher's resources, supplementary materials

Sources of the Western Tradition
High school (advanced placement). Softcover texts, supplementary materials

World Regional Studies (series)
Grades 9-12. Softcover texts, teacher's guides

Interact
Box 997-H92
Lakeside, CA 92040
800-359-0961

Grades K-12. Simulation programs. Student guides, teacher's guides, supplementary materials. Topics include geography, U.S. history, world history, government, economics, psychology, ecology

Kendall/Hunt Publishing Company
2460 Kerper Boulevard
P.O. Box 539
Dubuque, IA 52004-0539
800-258-5622

National Issues Forums (series)
Student booklets, teacher's guides, audio and video cassettes. Includes "America's Role in the

World: New Risks, New Realities," "Freedom of Speech: Where to Draw the Line," and "Immigration: What We Promised, Where to Draw the Line"

Learning Connections Publishers, Inc.
3450 Penrose Place, Suite 110
Boulder, CO 80301
800-347-9559

Grades 5-12. Supplemental texts, source books, activity books, reproducible masters for U.S. history, world geography, world history, government/civics, advanced placement

LEGO Dacta
555 Taylor Road
Enfield, CT 06082
800-527-8339

Grades pre-K-2. Manipulatives, curriculum support materials. Scope and sequence includes cognitive development; transportation; animals and the environment; homes, family, and neighborhoods; problem solving and whole language; themes and project work

Grades 3-12. Technic sets for simple machines through technic control sets for robotics, physics, and artificial intelligence, integrating science, mathematics, social studies, and technology curriculum

Longman Publishing Group
10 Bank Street
White Plains, NY 10606
800-447-2226

Ancient History Softcover Texts
Titles include "The Ancient World," "History Begins," "View From the Forum," "View From Olympus," "Aspects of Greek Life," "Aspects of Roman Life," "Roman Rulers and Rebels," "Legend, Myth and History in the Old Testament," "Old Bones," "Imperial China," "History Inquiries," and "A Map History of the Ancient World"

The Ancient World
Grades 6-8. Softcover text, student workbook

The Early Modern Age
Grades 9-11. Textbook

Economics: Our American Economy
High school. Textbook, teacher's guide, test generator software

European History Softcover Texts
Titles include "Habsburg and Bourbon Europe" and "An Illustrated History of Modern Europe"

Geography Softcover Texts
Titles include "Global Environment," "Themes in Geographic Development," "Our Wonderful World," and "The Collins-Longman Atlas"

Global Studies Series
Softcover texts. Includes "Japan: Tradition and Change," "Latin America: Tradition and Change," "China: Tradition and Change," and "India: Its Culture and People"

Investing and Trading
Supplementary economics text

Longman 20th Century History Series
High school. Softcover texts. Includes "Stalin and the Soviet Union," "Roads to War," "The End of Old Europe," "Weimar Germany," and "Italy and Mussolini"

Longman World History Program
Textbooks, teacher's handbooks, supplementary materials

The Middle Ages
Grades 7-10. Softcover text, student workbook

The Modern World Since 1870
Softcover text, teacher's guide, sourcebook

Then and There Series
Supplementary history books, teacher's guide. Series topics include the ancient world, the medieval world, European history, the Elizabethan world

Twentieth Century History Softcover Texts
Titles include "America's Intervention in Vietnam," "The Arab-Israeli Conflict," "South Africa," "Twentieth Century History," "The Great Powers," "The Contemporary World: Conflict or Co-operation?" "The Rise of Modern China," "The USA as a World Power," and "After Hiroshima"

United States History Softcover Texts
Titles include "The United States Since 1945," "American West 1840-1895," "Black Civil Rights in the U.S.A., 1954-1970," and "An Illustrated History of America"

Wall Street: How It Works
Supplementary economics text

World History Softcover Texts
Titles include "Threads of Time," "History Begins," "Makers and Milestones of the Middle Ages," and "Men and Women of the Renaissance 1300-1600"

Macmillan/McGraw-Hill

School Division
220 East Danieldale Road
De Soto, Texas 75115-9990
800-442-9685

The World around Us Activity Program (series)
Grades K-2. Big books, project books, social studies anthology, teacher's editions, supplementary materials including audio cassettes

El Mundo que nos rodea programa de actividades (series)
Grades K-2. Spanish program. Big books, project books, social studies anthology, teacher's editions, supplementary materials including audio cassettes

The World around Us (series)
Grades K-7. Textbooks, teacher's editions, supplementary materials including software

The World around Us: State Studies Program (series)
Textbooks, teacher's editions, supplementary materials

World Atlas for Primary Students
Grades K-2. Text

World Atlas for Intermediate Students
Grades 3-7. Text

Integrating Catholic Heritage (series)
Grades K-7. Supplementary texts

Our Constitution and What It Means
Grades 5-8. Textbook

McDonald Publishing Company

10667 Midwest Industrial Boulevard
St. Louis, MO 63132
800-722-8080

Grades 4-9. Teaching poster sets, activity sheets, teacher's guides, reproducible and duplicating books for history, geography, government

McDougal, Littell & Company
P.O. Box 8000
St. Charles, IL 60174
800-225-3809

The American People (series)
Grades 7 and above. Textbooks, teacher's editions, teacher's resource binders, supplementary materials

The Americans
Grades 7 and above. Textbook, teacher's edition, supplementary materials including software

Daily Geography (series)
Grades 2-11. Five-minute workouts. Available in Spanish. Teacher's manuals

Earth's Geography and Environment
Grades 7-9. Textbook, teacher's edition, teacher's resource book

Links across Time and Place
Grade 9 and above. Textbook, teacher's edition, supplementary materials including test generator software

McDougal, Littell Economics
Grades 9 and above. Textbook, teacher's edition, teacher's resource binder, supplementary materials including test generator software

Peoples and Cultures (series)
Grades 9-12. Softcover texts, teacher's manuals

A Proud Nation
Grades 7-8. Textbook, teacher's edition, teacher's resource binder, supplementary materials

Study Guide for the United States Constitution
Grades 7 and above. Student workbook

Merrill
SRA School Group
P.O. Box 5380
Chicago, IL 60680-5380
800-621-0476

Grades 6-12. Workbooks in American history, historical novels. (See also under SRA School Group for supplementary programs; see under Glencoe/Macmillan/McGraw-Hill for grades 6-12 texts; see under Macmillan/McGraw-Hill for grades K-8 texts.)

Milliken Publishing Company
1100 Research Boulevard
P.O. Box 21579
St. Louis, MO 63132-0579
800-643-0008

Pre-K-8. Duplicating masters, blackline reproducibles, transparency/reproducible books

Modern Curriculum Press
13900 Prospect Road
Cleveland, OH 44136
800-321-3106

Atlas of the World
Grades 4-8. Atlas, teacher's edition

Elementary Social Studies (series)
Grades 3-6. Basal texts, teacher's editions, workbooks. Includes "The Earth: Regions and Peoples," "The United States: People and Leaders," "Homelands of the World: Resources and Cultures," and "Civilizations of the Past: Peoples and Cultures"

Learning About America (series)
Grades 4-6. Thematic units include "Our Nation's Constitution," "Economics," "Our Nation's Government," "Elections in the United States," and "America's Holidays"

Map Adventures
Grades 3-6. Interactive fiction books, teacher's handbook, desk maps, supplementary materials

Maps, Charts, and Graphs (series)
Grades 1-8. Softcover texts, teacher's guide, transparencies

Multicultural Celebrations (series)
Student editions, teacher's resource book, posters, audio cassettes

Ohio--The Heart of It All
Grades 3-8. Textbook, teacher's guide

Quest for America (series)
Grades 4-6. Softcover texts, teacher's guide, activity cards

Social Studies Concepts
Grades 3-6. Supplementary readers in economics, government, exploration, industrialization

Young Explorers in Social Studies
Grades K-4. Story books, big books, teaching companions

The Peoples Publishing Group

P.O. Box 70
365 West Passaic Street
Rochelle Park, NJ 07662
800-822-1080

Texts for the student-at-risk. Topics include U.S. geography, economics, government, civics and citizenship, content area writing, ethnic studies, law education, the Constitution

Prentice Hall

School Division of Simon & Schuster
Englewood Cliffs, NJ 07632-9940
800-848-9500

Civics/Government

Civics: Government and Citizenship
Grades 7-12. Textbook, teacher's guide and resource book, transparencies, CNN VideoLink

Constitution Study Guide
Grades 7-12. Textbook, teacher's manual

Government in Action Transparencies
Grades 7-12. Complete teaching package

Magruder's American Government, 1991
Grades 9-12. Textbook, teacher's edition, teacher's resource book, supplementary materials including software, CNN VideoLink

Magruder's American Government, 1992
Grades 9-12. Textbook, teacher's edition, supplementary materials including software, CNN VideoLink

Elective/Advanced Placement

Anthropology
Grades 11-12. Textbook, study guide, test item file

Countries and Concepts: An Introduction to Comparative Politics
Grades 11-12. Textbook, teacher's edition, test item file

The Economic Problem
Grades 11-12. Textbook, study guide, test item file

Government by the People (series)
Grades 11-12. Includes basic edition, national edition, national/state/local edition, study guides, test item file

A History of Civilization
Grades 11-12. Textbook, study guide, teacher's manual, test item file

A History of the Human Community
Grades 11-12. Textbook, study guide, teacher's resource manual

In Our Times: America since World War II
Grades 10-12. Softcover text

Psychology: An Introduction
Grades 11-12. Textbook, study guide, test item file

Social Problems
Grades 11-12. Textbook, study guide, teacher's edition, test item file

The United States
Grades 10-12. Textbook, study guides, teacher's manual, test item file

Geography

Prentice Hall World Geography
Textbook, teacher's edition, teacher's resource file, supplementary materials including atlases, software, video cassettes, CNN VideoLink

Social Sciences/Social Studies

Follett Social Studies (series)
Grades 5-7. Textbooks, teacher's editions, supplementary materials. Includes "Our United States," "Latin America and Canada," "Our World Today," and "People, Time and Change"

Introduction to the Social Sciences
Grades 6-12. Textbook, teacher's guide and resource book

Social Studies Classroom Resources
Transparencies, American history enrichment support file, constitution study guide, supplemental readings, software, student atlases, map books

Sociology/Psychology

Psychology: Exploring Behavior
Grades 9-12. Textbook, teacher's guide, student handbook

Sociology: Understanding Society
Grades 9-12. Textbook, teacher's resource book, overhead transparencies

United States History

America's Heritage
Grades 9-12. Textbook, teacher's resource book, supplementary materials

American History Enrichment Support File
Grades 7-12. Primary Source readings, literature excerpts, songs, art, simulation activities, great

debate readings, biographical sketches

American History Transparencies
Grades 7-12. Complete teaching package

American Journey: The Quest for Liberty
Grades 7-11. Textbooks, teacher's editions,
supplementary materials including software,
audio cassettes, video cassettes, CNN VideoLink

The American Nation
Grades 7-9. Textbook, teacher's edition, supplementary materials including software, video
cassettes, CNN VideoLink

American Spirit: A History of American People
Grades 7-12. Textbook, teacher's resource book,
supplementary materials

A History of the United States
Grades 9-12. Textbook, teacher's edition, supplementary materials including software, video
cassettes, CNN VideoLink

A History of the United States since 1861
Grades 9-12. Textbook, teacher's edition,
teacher's resource book, supplementary materials
including software, video cassettes

*Perspectives: Readings on American History in the
20th Century*
Grades 9-12. Textbook, teacher's guide

State Histories/State Supplements

The United States: A History of the Republic
Grades 9-12. Textbook, teacher's edition,
teacher's resource book, supplementary materials
including software, video cassettes, CNN
VideoLink

Voices of Freedom: Sources in American History
Grades 7-12. Textbook

World History/World Cultures

The Pageant of World History
Grades 7-12. Textbook, teacher's edition,
teacher's resource book, supplementary materials
including software, video cassettes, CNN
VideoLink

World Cultures
Textbook, teacher's resource file, supplementary
materials

World History: Patterns of Civilization
Grades 9-12. Textbook, teacher's edition,
teacher's resource book, supplementary materials
including software, video cassettes, CNN
VideoLink

World History Transparencies
Grades 7-12. Complete teaching package

Phoenix Learning Resources
468 Park Avenue South
New York, NY 10016
800-221-1274

Map Skills Series
Grades 3-12. Student workbooks, teacher's
editions

Sadlier-Oxford
11 Park Place
New York, NY 10007
800-221-5175

Mastering American History
Grades 9-12. Textbook

Psychology for You
Grades 9-12. Textbook, teacher's guide

Understanding American Government and Politics
Grades 9-12. Textbook, teacher's guide

The Young American Citizen
Grades 7-9. Textbook, teacher's guide

Scholastic, Inc.
P.O. Box 7501
Jefferson City, MO 65105
800-325-6149

*African American History: Four Centuries of Black
Life*
Grades 7-12. Textbook, teacher's resource
manual, student timeline folder, classroom
libraries

*American Adventures: People Making History
(series)*
Grades 7-10. Textbooks, teacher's editions,
teacher's resource package, supplementary
materials including filmstrips, classroom library

American Citizenship (series)
Grades 7-12. Softcover texts, teaching guides,
supplementary materials including filmstrips.
Includes "Foundations of Our Government,"
"The Presidency, Congress and the Supreme
Court," "State and Local Government," and
"Politics & People"

Living Law (series)
Grades 7-12. Softcover texts, teaching guides, print-master sets. Includes "Criminal Justice" and "Civil Justice"

Map Skills (series)
Grades 1-6. Student work-texts, teacher's editions

Point of View : The Scholastic History Processor
Grades 5-12. Software, activity books. Includes "An Overview of United States History" and "The Civil War and Reconstruction"

Real Life Program
Grades 7-12. Student work-texts, teacher's editions, transparencies, ESL teaching guide, audio cassettes. Includes "Real Life Citizenship," "Real Life Employment," and "Real Life Consumer Economics"

Scholastic Economics
Grades 9-12. Text, teacher's edition, teacher's resource package, supplementary materials including software, Spanish summaries

Scholastic Sociology: The Search for Social Patterns
Grades 7-12. Textbook, teacher's resource manual, teacher's resource binder

Scholastic Update Magazine
Grades 8-12. Biweekly issues, teacher's guide

Scholastic World Cultures Text Series
Grades 7-12. Softcover texts, teaching guides, print masters. Includes "The Pacific Rim," "Mexico," "Latin America," "China," "Japan," "Southeast Asia," "The Indian Subcontinent," "The Middle East," "Western Europe," "Great Britain," "Canada," and "Africa"

Scholastic World Geography
Grades 7-10. Textbook, teacher's edition, teacher's resource binder, supplementary materials including test bank software

Scholastic World History Program (series)
Grades 7-10. Softcover texts, teacher's resource manuals, filmstrips. Includes "The Ancient World," "Early Civilization in Asia, Africa, and the Americas," "The Age of Europe," and "The Modern World"

Scholastic's Social Studies Skills (series)
Teaching guides, transparencies, masters. Includes "World Maps," "U.S. Maps," "Graphs," "Reference and Research," "Critical Thinking," "Charts," "Making Decisions," and "Time and Sequence"

Social Studies Resources
Filmstrips, magazines, readings, plays, transparencies

Social Studies Supplements
Includes "American Adventures: Historical Cartoons," "American Adventures: History Plays," "Economics Charts, Tables, and Graphs Transparencies," and "Readings for Economics"

Success with Maps (series)
Grades 1-6. Student work-texts, teacher's editions

Update: A History of the United States since 1945
Grades 8-12. Softcover text, teacher's resource manual

Scott, Foresman & Co.
1900 East Lake Avenue
Glenview, IL 60025
800-554-4411

Civics/Government

American Government
High school (advanced placement, honors). Textbook

American Government: Readings and Cases
High school (advanced placement, honors). Softcover text

Civics for Americans
Grades 7-9. Textbook, teacher's edition, supplementary materials

Comparative Politics Today: A World View
High school (advanced placement, honors). Textbook

Consent of the Governed
Grades 10-12. Textbook, teacher's edition, teacher's resource book, supplementary materials

The Constitution
Grades 7-12. Softcover text, teacher's handbook

Government in America: People, Politics, and Policy
High school (advanced placement, honors). Textbook

Introduction to Comparative Government
High school (advanced placement, honors). Textbook

Economics

Economics Today
High school (advanced placement, honors).

Textbook, teacher's manual, supplementary materials

Invitation to Economics
Grades 10-12. Textbook, teacher's editions, teacher's resource book, supplementary materials including software

Geography

People on Earth: A World Geography
Grades 7-8. Textbook, teacher's edition, supplementary materials

ScottForesman World Geography
Grades 9-12. Textbook, teacher's edition, teacher's resource book, supplementary materials including software

Supplementary Resources
Atlases, geography coloring book

Psychology/Sociology

Invitation to Psychology
Grades 9-12. Textbook, teacher's guide, teacher's resource book, overhead transparencies

Psychology
High school (advanced placement, honors). Textbook

Sociology: A Brief Introduction
High school (advanced placement, honors). Softcover text

United States History

America: Past and Present
High school (advanced placement, honors). Textbook

America: The People and the Dream
Student edition, teacher's edition, teacher's resource file, supplementary materials including laser videodisc, software

The American Nation: A History of the United States
High school (advanced placement, honors). Textbook, teacher's manual

The American People: Creating a Nation and a Society
High school (advanced placement, honors). Textbook

American Voices: A History of the United States
Grades 9-12. Textbook, teacher's edition, teacher's resource file, supplementary materials including software, laser videodisc

Law in American History
Grades 7-12. Softcover text, teacher's edition

Life and Liberty
Grades 9-12. Textbook, teacher's handbook, workbook, tests

Reading American History
Grades 7-12. Softcover text, teacher's edition

ScottForesman Social Studies (series)
Grades K-7. Textbooks, teacher's editions, teacher's resource files, Spanish language edition, supplementary materials including software

ScottForesman Social Studies Learning Systems
Grades 1-2. Hands-on materials, visual aids including laser videodisc packages, teacher's guides, maps, games, activity masters

World History

Civilization in the West
High school (advanced placement, honors). Softcover text

Civilization: Past and Present
High school (advanced placement, honors). Textbook, supplementary materials

Civilizations of the World: The Human Adventure
High school (advanced placement, honors). Textbook

History and Life
Grades 9-12. Textbook, teacher's edition, teacher's resource file, supplementary materials including software

Living World History
Grades 9-12. Textbook, teacher's edition, teacher's resource file, supplementary materials

Practicing World History Skills
Grades 9-12. Text-workbook, teacher's edition

Silver Burdett & Ginn

4350 Equity Drive
P.O. Box 2649
Columbus, OH 43216
800-848-9500

Multimedia Resources
Social studies literature libraries, citizenship and American values video library, CNN VideoLink

People in Time and Place (series)
Grades 1-junior high school. Textbooks, teacher's editions, teacher support systems, supplementary materials

People in Time and Place Activity Program
Grades K-2. Primary activity kits, poster book package

Silver Burdett & Ginn Estudios Sociales (series)
Grades 1-5. Textbooks, bilingual teacher's editions, teacher's resource files, supplementary materials including sound filmstrips

State Studies (series)
Textbooks, teacher's editions, teacher's resource files, supplementary materials

World Geography
Grades middle/junior high school. Textbook, teacher's edition, teacher support system, supplementary materials

South-Western Publishing Co.
5101 Madison Road
Cincinnati, OH 45227
800-543-7972

Consumer Economics
Textbook, teacher's manual, supplementary materials including test-generating software

Consumer Law
Text-workbook, teacher's manual

Criminal Law
Text-workbook, teacher's manual

Economic Experiences
Text-workbook, teacher's manual

Economics of Work
Softcover text, teacher's manual

Economics--Principles and Applications
Textbook, teacher's manual, study guide, test package

Economics: The Free Enterprise System
Textbook, teacher's edition, teacher's resource guide, supplementary materials including test generating software

Economics: The Science of Cost, Benefit, and Choice
Textbook, workbook, teacher's edition, teacher's resource package, supplementary materials including test generating software, audio cassettes

The Economy of New York State
Softcover text, teacher's manual

The Economy of Texas
Text-workbook, teacher's manual

Family Law
Text-workbook, teacher's manual

Introduction to Law
Text-workbook, teacher's manual

Law for Business
Textbook, workbook, achievement tests, video cassette

Letter of the Law
Quarterly newsletter

Student Rights and Responsibilities
Text-workbook, teacher's manual

Supplementary Cases in Everyday Law
Text-workbook, teacher's edition

Technology at Work
Textbook, teacher's manual, supplementary materials

Technology for Tomorrow
Textbook, teacher's manual, supplementary materials

Tort-Law
Text-workbook, teacher's manual

Whose Debt Is It Anyway?
Video cassette, teacher's supplement

The World of Economics
Text-workbook, teacher's manual, software

You and the Law
Textbook, workbook, teacher's manual, test-generating software

SRA School Group
American School Publishers
Barnell Loft-Merrill-SRA
P.O. Box 5380
Chicago, IL 60680-5380
800-843-8855

Grades 4-10. Supplementary programs for map and globe skills, American history, geography. Student workbooks, teacher's handbooks, historical novels, software

Steck-Vaughn Company
P.O. Box 26015
Austin, TX 78755
1-800-531-5015

American Government: Freedom, Rights, and Responsibilities

Grades 11-12, reading levels 4-5 (students with limited reading skills). Student work-texts, teacher's guide

America's Story
Grades 5-10, reading levels 2-3 (secondary students with limited English skills). Student text, teacher's guides, Spanish edition

Economics: Concepts and Applications
Grades 11-12, reading levels 4-5. Student work-text, teacher's guide

Geography Skills Series
Grades 3-8, reading levels 3-6. Student work-texts, teacher's guides

Portrait of America (series)
Grades K-12, reading level 4. Resource books on the 50 states and territories

Resource Materials
Classroom libraries, state and local histories

*Steck-Vaughn Maps * Globes * Graphs (series)*
Grades 1-6. Student work-texts, teacher's editions

Steck-Vaughn Social Studies (series)
Grades 1-6, reading levels 1-4. Softcover texts, teacher's editions

Student's Illustrated Activity Atlas
Grades 3-6, reading levels 3-5

Voices (series)
Grades 5-8. Softcover texts, teacher's editions. Includes U.S. history, world history, world geography

World Geography and You
Grades 5-10, readings levels 2-3. Student work-texts, teacher's editions

World History and You
Grades 5-10, reading level 4. Student work-texts, teacher's guides

Teacher Ideas Press
Libraries Unlimited, Inc.
P.O. Box 3988
Englewood, CO 80155-3988
800-237-6124

Teacher's resource books, puzzlers, software graphics programs

Wadsworth School Group
10 Davis Drive
Belmont, CA 94002-3098
800-831-6996

College textbooks and software appropriate for use by college-bound, honors, or advanced placement students in anthropology/archaeology, sociology, psychology, American history, world history/history of civilization, economics, government/political science, state government, criminal justice/law, international politics and relations, current issues, ethics

Weekly Reader Corporation
3000 Cindel Drive
P.O. Box 8037
Delran, NJ 08075

Weekly Reader Skills Books (series)
Grades K-9. Workbooks, duplicating masters, maps, games, posters. Topics include U.S. history, geography, the 1992 elections, Christopher Columbus

Zaner-Bloser
1459 King Avenue
P.O. Box 16764
Columbus, OH 43216-6764

Kits, games, story books on self-esteem, problem solving, values, conservation, cultural studies, economics

Zephyr Press
3316 North Chapel Avenue
P.O. Box 13448-E
Tucson, AZ 85732-3448
800-350-0851

Grades K-12. Activity books, teacher's sourcebooks, self-directed learning packets

STATEWIDE TEXTBOOK ADOPTION

THERE are twenty-two states that have statewide adoption of textbooks and other instructional materials: Alabama, Arizona, Arkansas, California, Florida, Georgia, Idaho, Indiana, Kentucky, Louisiana, Mississippi, Nevada, New Mexico, North Carolina, Oklahoma, Oregon, South Carolina, Tennessee, Texas, Utah, Virginia, and West Virginia.

The policies and procedures for textbook adoption are similar in all twenty-two states, with some minor variations.

Textbook Advisory Committee

In general, the state board of education is responsible for developing guidelines and criteria for the review and selection of textbooks and for appointing members to a textbook advisory committee. However, in a few states, the appointment of committee members is the responsibility of the governor or of the Commissioner of Education.

The textbook advisory committee is usually composed of educators, lay citizens, and parents, and can have from nine to twenty-seven appointees, depending upon the state. Membership is weighted, however, toward individuals who are educators: elementary and secondary teachers in the subject areas in which textbooks are to be adopted, instructors of teacher education and curriculum from local universities and colleges, school administrators, and school board members. Lay citizens, in order to sit on the committee, should be interested in and conversant with educational issues. An effort is made to select appointees who reflect the diversity of their states' population, and therefore decisions about

appointments are often made with the purpose of having a wide representation of ethnic backgrounds and geographical residence within the state.

Adoption Process

The textbook and instructional materials adoption process takes approximately twelve months.

Once the textbook advisory committee is formed, the members conduct an organizational meeting to formulate policy on such issues as adoption subjects and categories; standards for textbook evaluation, allocation of time for publisher presentations, and location of regional sites for such; sampling directions for publishers; and publisher contact. The committee may appoint subcommittees--made up of curriculum and/or subject specialists--to assist them in developing criteria for evaluating instructional materials.

After these procedural matters are agreed upon, the committee issues an official textbook call or "invitation to submit" to the textbook publishers. This document provides the publisher with adoption information and subject area criteria, which can either be the curriculum framework or essential skills list. Those publishers interested in having their materials considered for adoption submit their intention to bid, which shows the prices at which the publishers will agree to sell their material during the adoption period. Publishers usually bid current wholesale prices or lowest existing contract prices at which textbooks or other instructional materials are being sold elsewhere in the country.

If their bid has been accepted by the committee, the publishers submit sample copies of their textbooks for examination. The committee then hears presentations by the publishers. This meeting allows the publisher to present the texts submitted for adoption and to answer any questions the committee may have on the material. After publisher presentations, the textbooks are displayed in designated areas throughout the state for general public viewing. The committee then holds public hearings (usually two) which provide citizens with the opportunity to give an opinion on the textbooks offered for adoption. After much discussion and evaluation, the committee makes a recommendations for textbook adoption to the state board of education.

When the board of education approves the committee's recommendations, it negotiates the contract with the chosen publishers and disseminates the list of instructional materials to the school districts. The school districts will then make their textbook selections from this list. A few states also allow their school districts to use materials for the classroom that are not on the adoption list.

Textbook and Instructional Materials

There are two categories of instructional materials: basal and supplementary. Basal, or basic, materials address the goals, objectives, and content identified for a particular subject. Supplementary materials, used in conjunction with the basic text, enhance the teaching of the subject.

Instructional materials may include all or some of the following: hardcover books, softcover books, kits, workbooks, dictionaries, maps and atlases, electronic/computer programs, films, filmstrips, and other audiovisual materials.

The textbook adoption period generally runs from 4 to 6 years (California, the exception, has an 8-year contract period for K-8 only). The grade levels for adoption are usually K-12, with the following subject areas: English/language arts, social studies, foreign languages, English as a second language (ESL), science, mathematics, fine arts, applied arts.

Textbooks and instructional materials are ultimately judged by how well they reflect the state curriculum framework and/or essential skills objectives. Materials are rated on the following criteria: organization, accuracy, and currency of subject content; correlation with grade level requirements for the subject; adaptability for students with different abilities, backgrounds, and experiences; types of teacher aids provided; author's background and training; physical features; and cost.

In addition, some states have social content requirements that textbooks have to meet. For instance, textbooks should be objective in content and impartial in interpretation of the subject, and should not include "offensive" language or illustrations. American values (e.g., democracy, the work ethic, free enterprise), culture, traditions, and government should be presented in a positive manner. Respect for the individual's rights, and for the cultural and racial diversity of American society, can also be addressed in the text. Finally, some states declare that textbooks should not condone civil disorder, lawlessness, or "deviance."

Kraus thanks the personnel we contacted at the state departments of education, for their help in providing the states' textbook adoption lists.

List of Textbooks

Following is a compilation of the textbooks and instructional materials approved by the 22 states that have statewide textbook adoption. This listing is based on the relevant publications submitted to Kraus by the textbook division of the respective departments of educations.

The list is alphabetized by state; under each state, the materials are organized by subject (e.g., English, handwriting, reading, literature, etc.). Note that the categories are those used by each state, and therefore they are not always consistent from state to state. In some cases, supplemental material is also noted. For each textbook (and supplemental publication), the title, grade level, publisher, and copyright date are provided, as well as the termination year of the textbook's adoption period.

Alabama

Social Studies, General, Elementary
Latin America and Canada: Grade 6
Allyn, 1986 (Termination Year: 1993)

A History of Alabama--An Elementary Course:
Grade 4
Clairmont, 1987 (Termination Year: 1993)

Ourselves and Others: Grades K-1
Graphic, 1984 (Termination Year: 1993)

Our Homes and School: Grade 1
Graphic, 1986 (Termination Year: 1993)

Our Neighborhoods and Groups: Grade 2
Graphic, 1986 (Termination Year: 1993)

HBJ Social Studies: Grades K-5
Harcourt Brace Jovanovich, 1986 (Termination Year: 1993)

Holt Social Studies: Grades K-5
Harcourt Brace Jovanovich, 1986 (Termination Year: 1993)

Heath Social Studies: Grades 1-6
D. C. Heath, 1987 (Termination Year: 1993)

Macmillan Social Studies: Grades K-6
Macmillan, 1987 (Termination Year: 1993)

Laidlaw Social Studies Series: Grades K-6
Macmillan, 1985 (Termination Year: 1993)

Our Nation, Our World: Grades 1-5
Macmillan, 1986 (Termination Year: 1993)

Primary Social Studies Skills: Grades 1-3
Nystrom, 1984 (Termination Year: 1993)

Scott, Foresman Social Studies: Grades K-6
Scott, Foresman, 1983, 1986 (Termination Year: 1993)

Silver Burdett and Ginn Social Studies: Grades 1-5
Silver Burdett and Ginn, 1986 (Termination Year: 1993)

Canada and Latin America: Grade 4
Silver Burdett and Ginn, 1985 (Termination Year: 1993)

Our Alabama: Grade 4
Southern, 1980 (Termination Year: 1993)

Know Your Alabama: Grade 4
Viewpoint, 1986 (Termination Year: 1993)

Supplementary Material, Social Studies, General, Elementary
Follett Student Atlas: Grades 6-12
Allyn, 1986 (Termination Year: 1993)

The World of the Southern Indians: Grades 4-9
Beechwood, 1983 (Termination Year: 1993)

Basic Map Skills: Grades 1-3
Hammond, 1984 (Termination Year: 1993)

Understanding Maps: Grade 4
Hammond, 1985 (Termination Year: 1993)

American History through Maps: Grade 5
Hammond, 1984 (Termination Year: 1993)

World History through Maps: Grade 6
Hammond, 1984 (Termination Year: 1993)

Classroom Atlas: Grades K-7
D. C. Heath, 1987 (Termination Year: 1993)

The Governors of Alabama: Grades 4-12
Pelican, 1975 (Termination Year: 1993)

Alabama History: Grade 4
Silver Burdett and Ginn, 1987 (Termination Year: 1993)

Social Studies, Grades 7-8
The World: Past and Present: Grade 7
Harcourt Brace Jovanovich, 1986 (Termination Year: 1993)

The World Today: Grade 7
D. C. Heath, 1987 (Termination Year: 1993)

Nations of the World: Grade 7
Macmillan, 1987 (Termination Year: 1993)

Eastern Hemisphere: Europe, Asia, Africa and Oceania: Grade 7
Scott, Foresman, 1986 (Termination Year: 1993)

The Eastern Hemisphere: America's Origins: Grade 7
Silver Burdett and Ginn, 1987 (Termination Year: 1993)

Europe, Africa, Asia, and Australia: Grade 7
Silver Burdett and Ginn, 1986 (Termination Year: 1993)

Spirit of Liberty: An American History: Grade 8
Addison-Wesley, 1987 (Termination Year: 1993)

Civics: Government and Citizenship: Grades 7-9
Allyn, 1986 (Termination Year: 1993)

The Challenge of Freedom: Grade 8
Glencoe, 1986 (Termination Year: 1993)

Civics: Citizens in Action: Grade 8
Glencoe, 1986 (Termination Year: 1993)

We the People: Grade 8
Holt, Rinehart and Winston, 1983 (Termination Year: 1993)

American Civics: Grade 8
Holt, Rinehart and Winston, 1987 (Termination Year: 1993)

American History: Grade 8
Holt, Rinehart and Winston, 1986 (Termination Year: 1993)

The American People: A History: Grade 8
D. C. Heath, 1986 (Termination Year: 1993)

Land of Liberty: Grades 7-8
Holt, Rinehart and Winston, 1985 (Termination Year: 1993)

This Is America's Story: Grade 8
Houghton Mifflin, 1986 (Termination Year: 1993)

This Great Nation: Grade 8
Houghton Mifflin, 1985 (Termination Year: 1993)

History of the American Nation: Grade 8
Macmillan, 1987 (Termination Year: 1993)

A Proud Nation: Grade 8
McDougal, Littell, 1985 (Termination Year: 1993)

The American Nation: Grade 8
Prentice Hall, 1986 (Termination Year: 1993)

America! America!: Grade 8
Scott, Foresman, 1987 (Termination Year: 1993)

Civics for Americans: Grade 8
Scott, Foresman, 1986 (Termination Year: 1993)

One Flag, One Land: Grade 8
Silver Burdett and Ginn, 1985 (Termination Year: 1993)

Civics and Law for Alabama Schools: Grade 8
Viewpoint, 1981 (Termination Year: 1993)

Supplementary Material, Social Studies, Grades 7-8
Intermediate World Atlas: Grades 7-8
Hammond, 1984 (Termination Year: 1993)

Essential Map Skills: Grades 7-12
Hammond, 1985 (Termination Year: 1993)

Whole Earth Atlas: Grades 7-12
Hammond, 1984 (Termination Year: 1993)

Citation World Atlas: Grades 7-12
Hammond, 1984 (Termination Year: 1993)

Hammond World Atlas: Grades 7-12
Hammond, 1984 (Termination Year: 1993)

Law in American History: Grade 8
Scott, Foresman, 1983 (Termination Year: 1993)

Street Law: Grade 8
West, 1986 (Termination Year: 1993)

Excel in Civics: Grade 8
West, 1985 (Termination Year: 1993)

Sports and Law: Grade 8
West, 1984 (Termination Year: 1993)

Juvenile Problems and Law: Grade 8
West, 1980 (Termination Year: 1993)

Courts and Trials: Grade 8
West, 1980 (Termination Year: 1993)

Young Consumers: Grade 8
West, 1980 (Termination Year: 1993)

Law Making: Grade 8
West, 1980 (Termination Year: 1993)

Alabama History

A History of Alabama--A Secondary Course: Grade 9
Clairmont, 1987 (Termination Year: 1993)

Alabama Then and Now: Grade 9
Southern, 1986 (Termination Year: 1993)

Alabama's History: Past and Present: Grade 9
Southern, 1980 (Termination Year: 1993)

The Story of Alabama: Grade 9
Viewpoint, 1986 (Termination Year: 1993)

Alabama History for Schools: Grade 9
Viewpoint, 1981 (Termination Year: 1993)

World Geography

World Geography: Grade 9
Allyn, 1986 (Termination Year: 1993)

World Geography: Grade 9
Glencoe, 1984, 1985 (Termination Year: 1993)

Exploring a Changing World: Grade 9
Globe, 1984 (Termination Year: 1993)

World Geography: Grade 9
D. C. Heath, 1987 (Termination Year: 1993)

World Geography Today: Grades 9-12
Holt, Rinehart and Winston, 1985 (Termination Year: 1993)

Steck-Vaughn World Geography: Grade 9
Scholastic, 1983 (Termination Year: 1993)

People on Earth, a World Geography: Grade 9
Scott, Foresman, 1986 (Termination Year: 1993)

A World View: Grade 9
Silver Burdett and Ginn, 1985 (Termination Year: 1993)

Supplementary Material, World Geography
Comparative World Atlas: Grades 9-12
Hammond, 1985 (Termination Year: 1993)

World Atlas for Students: Grades 9-12
Hammond, 1985 (Termination Year: 1993)

Historical Atlas of the World: Grades 9-12
Hammond, 1984 (Termination Year: 1993)

Secondary Atlas: Grade 9
D. C. Heath, 1987 (Termination Year: 1993)

World History

The Pageant of World History: Grades 9-10
Allyn, 1986 (Termination Year: 1993)

Achievements through the Ages: Grade 10
Glencoe, 1985 (Termination Year: 1993)

The Human Experience: A World History: Grade 10
Glencoe, 1985 (Termination Year: 1993)

World History: Grade 10
Holt, Rinehart and Winston, 1984 (Termination Year: 1993)

People and Nations: A World History: Grade 10
Holt, Rinehart and Winston, 1987 (Termination Year: 1993)

World History: A Story of Progress: Grade 10
Holt, Rinehart and Winston, 1987 (Termination Year: 1993)

A History of the World: Grade 10
Houghton Mifflin, 1985 (Termination Year: 1993)

World History: Patterns of Civilization: Grades 9-10
Prentice, 1986 (Termination Year: 1993)

History and Life: Grades 10-12
Scott, Foresman, 1987 (Termination Year: 1993)

United States History
Addison-Wesley United States History: Grade 11
Addison-Wesley, 1986 (Termination Year: 1993)

America's Heritage: Grade 11
Allyn, 1986 (Termination Year: 1993)

A History of the United States: Grade 11
Allyn, 1986 (Termination Year: 1993)

Our Land, Our Time: Grade 11
Holt, Rinehart and Winston, 1985 (Termination Year: 1993)

Triumph of the American Nation: Grade 11
Holt, Rinehart and Winston, 1986 (Termination Year: 1993)

Legacy of Freedom, A History of the United States:
Grade 11
Glencoe, 1986 (Termination Year: 1993)

Heritage of Freedom: Grade 11
Glencoe, 1985 (Termination Year: 1993)

The American Tradition: A History of the United States: Grade 11
Glencoe, 1986 (Termination Year: 1993)

Exploring United States History: Grade 11
Globe, 1986 (Termination Year: 1993)

The American Pageant: A History of the Republic:
Grade 11
D. C. Heath, 1983 (Termination Year: 1993)

History of the American People: Grades 9-12
Holt, Rinehart and Winston, 1986 (Termination Year: 1993)

America: The Glorious Republic: Grade 11
Houghton Mifflin, 1985 (Termination Year: 1993)

The Americans: Grade 11
McDougal, Littell, 1985 (Termination Year: 1993)

The United States: A History of the Republic: Grade 11
Prentice Hall, 1986 (Termination Year: 1993)

American Adventures: Grade 11
Scholastic, 1987 (Termination Year: 1993)

Land of Promise: Grade 11
Scott, Foresman, 1987 (Termination Year: 1993)

Supplementary Material, United States History
United States History Atlas: Grades 9-12
Hammond, 1984 (Termination Year: 1993)

United States Government
Magruder's American Government: Grades 11-12
Allyn, 1987 (Termination Year: 1993)

Government in the United States: Grade 12
Glencoe, 1987 (Termination Year: 1993)

American Government: Principles and Practices:
Grade 12
Glencoe, 1987 (Termination Year: 1993)

We Are One: Grade 12
Holt, Rinehart and Winston, 1987 (Termination Year: 1993)

American Government: The Republic in Action:
Grade 12
Holt, Rinehart and Winston, 1987 (Termination Year: 1993)

Consent of the Governed: Grade 12
Scott, Foresman, 1987 (Termination Year: 1993)

**Supplementary Materials,
United States Government**
Communism Today: Grade 12
Southern, 1980 (Termination Year: 1993)

Economics and Consumer Economics
Essentials of Economics and Free Enterprise:
Grades 9-12
Addison-Wesley, 1987 (Termination Year: 1993)

Economics Today and Tomorrow: Grade 12
Glencoe, 1984 (Termination Year: 1993)

Understanding Economics: Grade 12
Glencoe, 1986 (Termination Year: 1993)

Economics: Principles and Practices: Grade 12
Glencoe, 1983 (Termination Year: 1993)

The American Economic System--Free Enterprise:
Grade 12
Glencoe, 1987 (Termination Year: 1993)

McDougal, Littell Economics: Grade 12
McDougal, Littell, 1986 (Termination Year: 1993)

Invitation to Economics: Grades 10-12
Scott, Foresman, 1985 (Termination Year: 1993)

Economics: The Science of Cost, Benefit, and Choice: Grades 9-12
South-Western, 1984 (Termination Year: 1993)

Economics: Principles and Applications: Grades 10-12
South-Western, 1984 (Termination Year: 1993)

Free Enterprise Today: Grades 10-12
South-Western, 1985 (Termination Year: 1993)

Consumer Economics: Grades 9-12
South-Western, 1983 (Termination Year: 1993)

Psychology

Psychology: Its Principles and Applications: Grades 9-12
Holt, Rinehart and Winston, 1984 (Termination Year: 1993)

Psychology: Exploring Behavior: Grades 10-12
Prentice Hall, 1985 (Termination Year: 1993)

Invitation to Psychology: Grades 10-12
Scott, Foresman, 1985 (Termination Year: 1993)

Sociology

Sociology: The Study of Human Relationships: Grades 9-12
Holt, Rinehart and Winston, 1982 (Termination Year: 1993)

Sociology: Understanding Society: Grades 10-12
Prentice Hall, 1984 (Termination Year: 1993)

Arizona

Social Studies

Scott, Foresman Social Studies: Grades K-7
Scott, Foresman, 1988, 1991 (Termination Date: 1996)

Silver Burdett & Ginn Social Studies: Grades 1-6
Silver Burdett & Ginn, 1990 (Termination Date: 1996)

The World around Us: Grades K-6
Macmillan/McGraw-Hill, 1990 (Termination Date: 1996)

Heath Social Studies: Grades K-7
D. C. Heath, 1989 (Termination Date: 1996)

HBJ Social Studies: Grades K-6
Harcourt Brace Jovanovich, 1988 (Termination Date: 1996)

American History Arizona Studies: Grades 4-6
Cloud Associates/Publishing, 1986-90 (Termination Date: 1996)

Arizona History: Grade 4
Macmillan/McGraw-Hill, 1990 (Termination Date: 1996)

American History

The American Nation: Grades 7-8
Prentice Hall, 1990 (Termination Date: 1996)

American Spirit: Grades 7-8
Prentice Hall, 1990 (Termination Date: 1996)

One Flag, One Land: Grades 7-8
Silver Burdett & Ginn, 1990 (Termination Date: 1996)

American History: Grades 7-8
Harcourt Brace Jovanovich, 1986 (Termination Date: 1996)

America Is: Grades 7-8
Glencoe/McGraw-Hill, 1987 (Termination Date: 1996)

Addison-Wesley Spirit of Liberty: Grades 7-8
Addison-Wesley, 1987 (Termination Date: 1996)

Challenge of Freedom: Grades 7-8
Glencoe, 1990 (Termination Date: 1996)

U.S. History: Grades 7-8
Holt, Rinehart and Winston, 1988 (Termination Date: 1996)

America's Story: Grades 7-8
Houghton Mifflin, 1990 (Termination Date: 1996)

America! America!: Grades 7-8
Scott, Foresman, 1987 (Termination Date: 1996)

The Constitution: Grades 7-8
Scott, Foresman, 1985 (Termination Date: 1996)

Reading American History: Grades 7-8
Scott, Foresman, 1987 (Termination Date: 1996)

World History

World History: Grades 7-8
Holt, Rinehart and Winston, 1990 (Termination Date: 1996)

Arizona History

Arizona Pathways: Grades 7-8
Cloud Associates/Publishing, 1989 (Termination Date: 1996)

Arizona: Its Place in the United States: Grades 7-8
Peregrine Smith Books, Gibb Smith, 1989 (Termination Date: 1996)

Arizona Government: Grades 7-8
Peregrine Smith Books, Gibb Smith, 1989 (Termination Date: 1996)

Arizona Government
Arizona: Government and Citizenship: Grades 7-8
Cloud Associates/Publishing, 1990 (Termination Date: 1996)

Arizona: Constitution and Government: Grades 7-8
Cloud Associates/Publishing, 1987 (Termination Date: 1996)

Arizona Civics
Arizona: Government and Citizenship: Grades 7-8
Cloud Associates/Publishing, 1990 (Termination Date: 1996)

Arizona: Constitution and Government: Grades 7-8
Cloud Associates/Publishing, 1987 (Termination Date: 1996)

Arizona Government: Grades 7-8
Peregrine Smith Books, Gibb Smith, 1989 (Termination Date: 1996)

Civics
American Civics: Grades 7-8
Harcourt Brace Jovanovich, 1987 (Termination Date: 1996)

We the People: Grades 7-8
Holt, Rinehart and Winston, 1989 (Termination Date: 1996)

Government and Citizenship: Grades 7-8
Prentice Hall, 1990 (Termination Date: 1996)

Constitution and Study Guide: Grades 7-8
Prentice Hall, 1989 (Termination Date: 1996)

American Citizenship: Grades 7-8
Scholastic, 1989 (Termination Date: 1996)

Civics for Americans: Grades 7-8
Scott, Foresman, 1986 (Termination Date: 1996)

The Constitution: Grades 7-8
Scholastic, 1985 (Termination Date: 1996)

World Geography
Glencoe World Geography '89: Grades 7-8
Glencoe/McGraw-Hill, 1989 (Termination Date: 1996)

The Earth and Its People: Grades 7-8
Harcourt Brace Jovanovich, 1989 (Termination Date: 1996)

World Geography Today: Grades 7-8
Holt, Rinehart and Winston, 1989 (Termination Date: 1996)

Scholastic World Geography: Grades 7-8
Scholastic, 1989 (Termination Date: 1996)

A World View: Grades 7-8
Silver Burdett & Ginn, 1990 (Termination Date: 1996)

Social Studies--Supplemental
Government and You: Grades 11-12
Amsco School Publications, 1987 (Termination Date: 1996)

Mastering American History Skills: Grades 7-11
Amsco School Publications, 1987 (Termination Date: 1996)

Mastering Social Studies Skills: Grades 9-12
Amsco School Publications, 1987 (Termination Date: 1996)

Our Country: Grades K-2
Carroll Publishing, 1972 (Termination Date: 1996)

World around Us: Grades K-2
Carroll Publishing, 1972 (Termination Date: 1996)

Arizona: Grade 4
Gibbs Smith, 1989 (Termination Date: 1996)

Exploring American History: Grades 7-8
Globe Book, 1991 (Termination Date: 1996)

Ourselves and Others: Grade K
Graphic Learning, 1986 (Termination Date: 1996)

Our Homes and Schools: Grade 1
Graphic Learning, 1986 (Termination Date: 1996)

Our Neighborhoods and Groups: Grade 2
Graphic Learning, 1986 (Termination Date: 1996)

Our Community and Others: Grade 3
Graphic Learning, 1986 (Termination Date: 1996)

Our Country: Its Land and People: Grades 4-6
Graphic Learning, 1986 (Termination Date: 1996)

Our Nation: Its Past and Present: Grades 5-11
Graphic Learning, 1986 (Termination Date: 1996)

Our World: Its Land and People: Grades 6-12
Graphic Learning, 1986 (Termination Date: 1996)

United States Studies: Grades 5-11
Graphic Learning, 1988 (Termination Date: 1996)

World Studies: Grades 5-12
Graphic Learning, 1988 (Termination Date: 1996)

State Studies Program: Grades 4-12
Graphic Learning, 1983 (Termination Date: 1996)

Reading and Writing in U.S. History: Grades 4-12
Graphic Learning, 1988 (Termination Date: 1996)

Reading and Writing in World Cultures: Grades 4-12
Graphic Learning, 1989 (Termination Date: 1996)

Study Guide for U.S. Constitution: Grades 7-12
McDougal, Littell, 1987 (Termination Date: 1996)

Economics and the Free Enterprise System: Grades 6-12
Media Materials, 1989 (Termination Date: 1996)

The Citizen Series: Grades 6-12
Media Materials, 1986 (Termination Date: 1996)

Learning about Our United States: Grades 6-12
Media Materials, 1988-89 (Termination Date: 1996)

World Geography: Grades 6-12
Media Materials, 1989 (Termination Date: 1996)

Our Nation's History: Grades 6-12
Media Materials, 1992 (Termination Date: 1996)

United States Government: Grades 6-12
Media Materials, 1987 (Termination Date: 1996)

Reading in the Content Area Social Studies Series: Grades 6-12
Media Materials, 1989 (Termination Date: 1996)

World Geography: Grades 6-12
Media Materials, 1989 (Termination Date: 1996)

Civilizations of the Past: Grades 3-6
Modern Curriculum Press, 1981 (Termination Date: 1996)

Learning about America: Grades 4-6
Modern Curriculum Press, 1986 (Termination Date: 1996)

Quest for America, Thematic Units: Grades 4-6
Modern Curriculum Press, 1989 (Termination Date: 1996)

Quest for America, Treasure Chest: Grades 4-6
Modern Curriculum Press, 1989 (Termination Date: 1996)

Atlas of the World: Grades 4-8
Modern Curriculum Press, 1986 (Termination Date: 1996)

See How It's Made: Grades K-6
Modern Curriculum Press, 1983 (Termination Date: 1996)

Beginning to Read Set: Grades 1-3
Modern Curriculum Press, 1975-88 (Termination Date: 1996)

Interaction Talk Abouts: Grades K-3
Rigby Education, 1986-88 (Termination Date: 1996)

Living in America: Grades 6-10
Steck-Vaughn, 1985 (Termination Date: 1996)

Champions of Change: Grades 5-9
Steck-Vaughn, 1989 (Termination Date: 1996)

The Great Series: Grades 6-12
Steck-Vaughn, 1991 (Termination Date: 1996)

World Geography and You: Grades 5-10
Steck-Vaughn, 1991 (Termination Date: 1996)

Moments in American History: Grades 4-10
Steck-Vaughn, 1989 (Termination Date: 1996)

World History and You: Grades 5-10
Steck-Vaughn, 1990 (Termination Date: 1996)

America's Story: Grades 5-10
Steck-Vaughn, 1990 (Termination Date: 1996)

Amnesty: A Real-Life Approach: Grades 9-12
Steck-Vaughn, 1990 (Termination Date: 1996)

Arkansas

Social Studies, Elementary
Heath Social Studies: Grades 1-6
D. C. Heath, 1991 (Termination Date: 1996)

Houghton Mifflin Social Studies: Grades 1-6
Houghton Mifflin, 1991 (Termination Date: 1996)

Social Studies: The World Around Us: Grades 1-6
Macmillan/McGraw-Hill, 1991 (Termination Date: 1996)

Supplemental Social Studies, Elementary
U.S./World Discovery Combination Map: Grades 1-6
George F. Cram, 1989 (Termination Date: 1996)

Political Maps (set of 9): Grades 1-6
George F. Cram, 1989 (Termination Date: 1996)

Growth of America Map: Grades 1-6
George F. Cram, 1989 (Termination Date: 1996)

U.S./World Discovery Desk Maps set: Grades 1-6
George F. Cram, 1990 (Termination Date: 1996)

Complete Discovery Desk Map Program: Grades 1-6
George F. Cram, 1990 (Termination Date: 1996)

American History through Maps: Grade 5
Hammond, 1984 (Termination Date: 1996)

Intermediate United States Atlas: Grade 5
Hammond, 1984 (Termination Date: 1996)

Intermediate World Atlas: Grade 6
Hammond, 1984 (Termination Date: 1996)

Heath Social Studies: Exploring Canada and Latin America: Grade 6
D. C. Heath, 1991 (Termination Date: 1996)

Maps, Charts and Graphs Series: Grades 1-6
Modern Curriculum Press, 1989 (Termination Date: 1996)

Learning about America Series: Grades 4-6
Modern Curriculum Press, 1986 (Termination Date: 1996)

Quest for America Series: Grades 4-6
Modern Curriculum Press, 1989 (Termination Date: 1996)

U.S./World Maps Readiness Combination: Grades 1-3
Nystrom, 1989/90 (Termination Date: 1996)

Primary Social Studies Skills Complete Program: Grades 1-3
Nystrom, 1989 (Termination Date: 1996)

United States Hands-on Geography Kit: Grades 4-6
Nystrom, 1984 (Termination Date: 1996)

World Hands-on Geography Kit: Grades 4-6
Nystrom, 1984 (Termination Date: 1996)

U.S./World Pictorial Relief Map Combination: Grades 4-6
Nystrom, 1989 (Termination Date: 1996)

U.S./Robinson World Sculptural Relief Map Combination: Grades 4-6
Nystrom, 1990 (Termination Date: 1996)

Simplified Political U.S./Alaska/World Maps: Grades 1-6
Rand McNally, 1989 (Termination Date: 1996)

U.S./Alaska/Beginner's Political World Maps: Grades 1-2
Rand McNally, 1989 (Termination Date: 1996)

Level III U.S./Alaska/World Combination Maps: Grades 4-6
Rand McNally, 1989 (Termination Date: 1996)

Level III Map Set (U.S., South America, North America, World, Europe, Asia, Africa): Grades 4-6
Rand McNally, 1989 (Termination Date: 1996)

Set of (8) American History Maps--From Settlement to Civil War: Grade 5
Rand McNally, 1989 (Termination Date: 1996)

United States and World Floor Activity Map: Grades 1-3
Rand McNally, 1989 (Termination Date: 1996)

Essential Skills in Social Studies: Grades 1-3
Rand McNally, 1989 (Termination Date: 1996)

Quick Reference World Atlas: Grades 4-6
Rand McNally, 1986 (Termination Date: 1996)

United States Map Activity Program: Grades 4-6
Rand McNally, 1989 (Termination Date: 1996)

World Map Activity Program: Grades 4-6
Rand McNally, 1989 (Termination Date: 1996)

Using the Atlas Program: Grades 4-6
Rand McNally, 1986 (Termination Date: 1996)

Geographical Terms Program: Grades 4-6
Rand McNally, 1989 (Termination Date: 1996)

Arkansas History
Arkansas Copymasters: Grade 4
D. C. Heath, 1991 (Termination Date: 1996)

Arkansas History: Grades 4-5
Houghton Mifflin, 1991 (Termination Date: 1996)

Arkansas History: Grade 5
Macmillan/McGraw-Hill, 1991 (Termination
Date: 1996)

Arkansas State Wall Map: Grades 4-6
Nystrom, 1990 (Termination Date: 1996)

Political Arkansas State Wall Map: Grades 1-6
Rand McNally, 1989 (Termination Date: 1996)

Arkansas Heritage: Grade 5
Rose Publishing Company, 1986 (Termination
Date: 1996)

Adventure Tales of Arkansas: Grades 4-6
Signal Media, 1986 (Termination Date: 1996)

Arkansas State Map: Grades 7-12
George F. Cram Co., 1989 (Termination Date:
1995)

Hearne Brothers Arkansas State Wall Map: Grades
7-12
Rand McNally, 1989 (Termination Date: 1995)

History of Arkansas: Grade 8
Rose Publishing Co., 1987 (Termination Date:
1995)

Researching Arkansas History: Grades 7-9
Rose Publishing Co., 1979 (Termination Date:
1995)

History of Arkansas: Grades 10-12
Rose Publishing Co., 1987 (Termination Date:
1995)

The Atlas of Arkansas: Grades 7-12
University of Arkansas, 1989 (Termination Date:
1995)

The History of Arkansas: Grades 7-12
University of Arkansas, 1991 (Termination Date:
1995)

Government in Arkansas: Grades 7-12
League of Women Voters of Arkansas, 1989
(Termination Date: 1995)

Authentic Voices: Grades 7-12
UCA Press, 1986 (Termination Date: 1995)

Arkansas Voices: Grades 7-12
UCA Press, 1989 (Termination Date: 1995)

The Civil War Quadrennium: Grades 7-12
UCA Press, 1985 (Termination Date: 1995)

Supplemental, Arkansas History
America the Beautiful--Arkansas: Grades 1-6
Childrens Press, 1989(Termination Date: 1996)

American History
American History and National Security: Grades 9-
12
Addison-Wesley, 1989 (Termination Date: 1995)

USA: The Unfolding Story of America: Grades 9-12
Amsco, 1987 (Termination Date: 1995)

Challenge of Freedom: Grades 7-8
Glencoe/McGraw-Hill, 1990 (Termination Date:
1995)

Two Centuries of Progress: Grades 7-8
Glencoe/McGraw-Hill, 1991 (Termination Date:
1995)

Exploring American History: Grade 8
Globe, 1991 (Termination Date: 1995)

African-Americans in U.S. History: Grades 7-12
Globe, 1989 (Termination Date: 1995)

Hispanics in U.S. History: Grades 7-12
Globe, 1989 (Termination Date: 1995)

United States History: Grades 7-8
Holt, Rinehart and Winston, 1988 (Termination Date: 1995)

The Story of America: Grades 7-12
Holt, Rinehart and Winston, 1991 (Termination Date: 1995)

Our Land, Our Time, A History of the United States: Grades 9-12
Holt, Rinehart and Winston, 1991 (Termination Date: 1995)

The Constitution: Past, Present, and Future: Grades 7-12
Holt, Rinehart and Winston, 1991 (Termination Date: 1995)

The Constitution: Foundation of Our Freedom: Grades 7-12
Holt, Rinehart and Winston, 1991 (Termination Date: 1995)

Voices of America: Grades 7-12
Holt, Rinehart and Winston, 1991 (Termination Date: 1995)

Eyewitnesses and Others: Readings in American History: Grades 7-12
Holt, Rinehart and Winston, 1991 (Termination Date: 1995)

The Story of America Video Library: Grades 7-12
Holt, Rinehart and Winston, 1991 (Termination Date: 1995)

A More Perfect Union: Grade 8
Houghton Mifflin, 1991 (Termination Date: 1995)

America's Story: Grade 8
Houghton Mifflin, 1990 (Termination Date: 1995)

Great Cases of the Supreme Court: Grades 7-9
Houghton Mifflin, 1989 (Termination Date: 1995)

History of the United States: Grades 9-12
Houghton Mifflin, 1991 (Termination Date: 1995)

America: The Glorious Republic: Grades 9-12
Houghton Mifflin, 1990 (Termination Date: 1995)

The Americans: Grades 9-12
McDougal, Littell and Company, 1991 (Termination Date: 1995)

The American People: A History to 1877: Grades 9-12
McDougal, Littell and Company, 1989 (Termination Date: 1995)

The American People: A History from 1877: Grades 9-12
McDougal, Littell and Company, 1989 (Termination Date: 1995)

Our Nation's History: Grades 7-12
Media Materials, 1989 (Termination Date: 1995)

The American Nation: Grade 8
Prentice Hall, 1991 (Termination Date: 1995)

A History of the Republic: Grade 8
Prentice Hall, 1990 (Termination Date: 1995)

The United States: A History of the Republic: Grades 9-12
Prentice Hall, 1990 (Termination Date: 1995)

A History of the United States: Grades 9-12
Prentice Hall, 1990 (Termination Date: 1995)

A History of the United States since 1861: Grades 9-12
Prentice Hall, 1990 (Termination Date: 1995)

American Spirit: Grades 9-12
Prentice Hall, 1990 (Termination Date: 1995)

Land of Promise: Grades 8-12
Scott, Foresman, 1986 (Termination Date: 1995)

America: The People and the Dream: Grade 8
Scott, Foresman, 1991 (Termination Date: 1995)

National Treasures: Grades 9-12
Scott, Foresman, 1987 (Termination Date: 1995)

Concepts of Social Studies
Mastering Social Studies Skills: Grades 7-12
Amsco, 1989 (Termination Date: 1995)

Introduction to the Social Sciences: Grades 9-12
Prentice Hall, 1991 (Termination Date: 1995)

Economics
Economics and National Security: Grades 9-12
Addison-Wesley, 1989 (Termination Date: 1995)

Economics: Grades 10-12
Addison-Wesley, 1988 (Termination Date: 1995)

Introduction to Economics: Grades 7-12
EMC, 1991 (Termination Date: 1995)

Economics Today and Tomorrow: Grades 9-12
Glencoe/McGraw-Hill, 1991 (Termination Date: 1995)

Economics: Free Enterprise in Action: Grades 9-12
Holt, Rinehart and Winston, 1988 (Termination Date: 1995)

McDougal, Littell Economics: Grades 9-12
McDougal, Littell, 1991 (Termination Date: 1995)

Economics: Principles and Practices: Grades 10-12
Merrill, 1988 (Termination Date: 1995)

Invitation to Economics: Grades 9-12
Scott, Foresman, 1988 (Termination Date: 1995)

The Science of Cost, Benefit, and Choice: Grades 10-12
South-Western, 1988 (Termination Date: 1995)

Economics and Making Decisions: Grades 9-12
West, 1988 (Termination Date: 1995)

Global Studies
Global Geography: Grades 9-12
Amsco, 1986 (Termination Date: 1995)

The Regional Studies Series: Grades 9-12
Globe, 1987 (Termination Date: 1995)

Peoples and Cultures Series: Grades 9-12
McDougal, Littell, 1989 (Termination Date: 1995)

Survey of World Cultures: Grades 7-12
Media Materials, 1990 (Termination Date: 1995)

Global Insights: People and Cultures: Grades 8-12
Merrill, 1987 (Termination Date: 1995)

Government and Civics
American Government and National Security: Grades 9-12
Addison-Wesley, 1989 (Termination Date: 1995)

National Security Series Booklets: Grades 9-12
Addison-Wesley, 1989 (Termination Date: 1995)

Civics: Grades 9-12
Addison-Wesley, 1991 (Termination Date: 1995)

Government for Everybody: Grades 9-12
Amsco School Publications, 1990 (Termination Date: 1995)

Government in the United States: Grades 9-12
Glencoe/McGraw-Hill, 1990 (Termination Date: 1995)

The Living Constitution: Grades 9-12
Glencoe/McGraw-Hill, 1991 (Termination Date: 1995)

Exploring American Citizenship: Grades 7-9
Globe, 1988 (Termination Date: 1995)

American Civics: Grades 7-12
Holt, Rinehart and Winston, 1987 (Termination Date: 1995)

We the People: Grades 9-12
Holt, Rinehart and Winston, 1989 (Termination Date: 1995)

Government in America: Grade 12
Houghton Mifflin, 1991 (Termination Date: 1995)

Vital Issues of the Constitution: Grades 10-12
Houghton Mifflin, 1989 (Termination Date: 1995)

United States Government: Grades 7-12
Media Materials, 1987 (Termination Date: 1995)

Civics: Citizens in Action: Grades 8-12
Merrill, 1990 (Termination Date: 1995)

American Government Principles and Practices: Grades 10-12
Merrill, 1991 (Termination Date: 1995)

Magruder's American Government: Grades 9-12
Prentice Hall, 1990 (Termination Date: 1995)

Civics: Government and Citizenship: Grades 9-12
Prentice Hall, 1990 (Termination Date: 1995)

Civics for Americans: Grades 7-9
Scott, Foresman, 1991 (Termination Date: 1995)

American Government and Politics Today: Grades 9-12
West, 1989 (Termination Date: 1995)

Street Law: A Course in Practical Law: Grades 9-12
West, 1990 (Termination Date: 1995)

The Bill of Rights and You: Grades 7-9
West, 1990 (Termination Date: 1995)

Teens, Crime and the Community: Grades 7-12
West, 1988 (Termination Date: 1995)

Juvenile Responsibility and Law: Grades 7-9
West, 1990 (Termination Date: 1995)

Newspapers

Arkansas Democrat: Grades 7-12
Arkansas Democrat (Termination Date: 1995)

The Living Textbook--Arkansas Gazette: Grades 7-12
Arkansas Gazette(Termination Date: 1995)

Psychology

Human Relations and Work Adjustment: Grades 7-12
EMC, 1989 (Termination Date: 1995)

Working at Human Relations: Grades 7-12
EMC, 1991 (Termination Date: 1995)

Understanding Psychology: Grades 10-12
Glencoe/McGraw-Hill, 1986 (Termination Date: 1995)

Psychology: Its Principles and Applications: Grades 9-12
Holt, Rinehart and Winston, 1989 (Termination Date: 1995)

Invitation to Psychology: Grades 9-12
Scott, Foresman, 1989 (Termination Date: 1995)

Psychology and You: Grades 9-12
West, 1990 (Termination Date: 1995)

Sociology

Sociology: The Study of Human Relationships: Grades 9-12
Holt, Rinehart and Winston, 1990 (Termination Date: 1995)

Sociology: Understanding Society: Grades 9-12
Prentice Hall, 1990 (Termination Date: 1995)

World Geography and Cultures

World Geography and National Security: Grades 9-12
Addison-Wesley, 1989 (Termination Date: 1995)

Glencoe World Geography: Grades 9-12
Glencoe/McGraw-Hill, 1989 (Termination Date: 1995)

Building Skills in Geography: Grades 9-12
Glencoe/McGraw-Hill, 1990 (Termination Date: 1995)

Exploring a Changing World: Grade 7
Globe, 1988 (Termination Date: 1995)

Unlocking Geography Skills and Concepts: Grades 7-12
Globe, 1988 (Termination Date: 1995)

Heath World Geography: Grades 10-12
D. C. Heath, 1989 (Termination Date: 1995)

World Geography Today: Grades 7-12
Holt, Rinehart and Winston, 1989 (Termination Date: 1995)

Earth's Geography and Environment: Grades 7-12
McDougal, Littell, 1991 (Termination Date: 1995)

The World Around Us: Grade 7
Macmillan/McGraw-Hill, 1991 (Termination Date: 1995)

World Geography: People and Places: Grades 7-10
Merrill, 1989 (Termination Date: 1995)

People on Earth: Grades 7-8
Scott, Foresman, 1988 (Termination Date: 1995)

Europe and the Soviet Union: Grade 7
Scott, Foresman, 1991 (Termination Date: 1995)

Latin America and Canada: Grade 7
Scott, Foresman, 1991 (Termination Date: 1995)

World Geography: Grades 9-12
Scott, Foresman, 1989 (Termination Date: 1995)

Geography: Our Changing World: Grades 9-12
West, 1990 (Termination Date: 1995)

World History

World History: Grades 9-12
Addison-Wesley, 1989 (Termination Date: 1995)

World History and National Security: Grades 9-12
Addison-Wesley, 1989 (Termination Date: 1995)

Exploring World History: Grades 8-10
Globe, 1990 (Termination Date: 1995)

World History: Perspectives on the Past: Grades 9-12
D. C. Heath, 1990 (Termination Date: 1995)

Religions of the World Video Package: Grades 7-12
Holt, Rinehart and Winston, 1989 (Termination Date: 1995)

World History: Grades 7-12
Houghton Mifflin, 1990 (Termination Date: 1995)

Links across Time and Place: A World History: Grades 9-12
McDougal, Littell, 1990 (Termination Date: 1995)

Experiencing World History: Grades 7-12
Media Materials, 1990 (Termination Date: 1995)

Human Heritage: A World History: Grades 7-10
Merrill, 1989 (Termination Date: 1995)

The Human Experience: A World History: Grades 9-12
Merrill, 1990 (Termination Date: 1995)

World History: Patterns of Civilization: Grades 9-12
Prentice Hall, 1990 (Termination Date: 1995)

The Pageant of World History: Grades 9-12
Prentice Hall, 1990 (Termination Date: 1995)

History and Life: Grades 9-12
Scott, Foresman, 1990 (Termination Date: 1995)

Supplemental Social Studies

American History Maps (set of 19): Grades 7-12
George F. Cram, 1989 (Termination Date: 1995)

Modern World History Maps (set of 19): Grades 7-12
George F. Cram, 1989 (Termination Date: 1995)

Ancient World History Maps (set of 19): Grades 7-12
George F. Cram, 1989 (Termination Date: 1995)

African American History Map: Grades 7-12
George F. Cram, 1989 (Termination Date: 1995)

American Heritage History Map: Grades 7-12
George F. Cram, 1989 (Termination Date: 1995)

Indian Heritage History Map: Grades 7-12
George F. Cram, 1989 (Termination Date: 1995)

Physical Political Maps (set of 8): Grades 7-12
George F. Cram, 1989 (Termination Date: 1995)

U.S./Western Hemisphere and World/Eastern Hemisphere Desk Maps: Grades 7-12
George F. Cram, 1989 (Termination Date: 1995)

Readings in American History: Grade 7
Educational Activities, 1987, 1989 (Termination Date: 1995)

Colonial Merchant: Grades 7-12
Educational Activities, 1988 (Termination Date: 1995)

What Do They Do in Quadadougou?: Grades 7-12
Educational Activities, 1989 (Termination Date: 1995)

Creating the U.S. Constitution: Grades 7-12
Educational Activities, 1987 (Termination Date: 1995)

The Constitution and the Government of the U.S: Grades 7-12
Educational Activities, 1987 (Termination Date: 1995)

Learning about Geography, Maps and Globes: Grade 7
Educational Activities, 1988 (Termination Date: 1995)

Atlas of the Eastern Hemisphere: Grades 7-12
Hammond, 1990 (Termination Date: 1995)

Atlas of the Western Hemisphere: Grades 7-12
Hammond, 1990 (Termination Date: 1995)

World Atlas for Students: Grades 7-12
Hammond, 1990 (Termination Date: 1995)

Essential Map Skills: Grades 7-12
Hammond, 1985 (Termination Date: 1995)

Comparative World Atlas: Grades 7-12
Hammond, 1989 (Termination Date: 1995)

Historical Atlas of the World: Grades 10-12
Hammond, 1989 (Termination Date: 1995)

World History through Maps: Grades 7-12
Hammond, 1984 (Termination Date: 1995)

United States History Atlas: Grades 10-12
Hammond, 1989 (Termination Date: 1995)

Physical World Atlas: Grades 7-12
Hammond, 1988 (Termination Date: 1995)

Crime: What We Fear, What Can Be Done: Grades 9-12
Kendall Hunt, 1987 (Termination Date: 1995)

Immigration: What We Promised, Where to Draw the Line: Grades 9-12
Kendall Hunt, 1987 (Termination Date: 1995)

The Farm Crisis: Who's in Trouble, How to Respond: Grades 9-12
Kendall Hunt, 1987 (Termination Date: 1995)

The Superpowers: Nuclear Weapons and National Security: Grades 9-12
Kendall Hunt, 1987 (Termination Date: 1995)

The Trade Gap: Regaining the Competitive Edge: Grades 9-12
Kendall Hunt, 1987 (Termination Date: 1995)

Freedom of Speech: Where to Draw the Line: Grades 9-12
Kendall Hunt, 1987 (Termination Date: 1995)

The Public Debt: Breaking the Habit of Deficit Spending: Grades 9-12
Kendall Hunt, 1988 (Termination Date: 1995)

Health Care for the Elderly: Moral Dilemmas, Mortal Choices: Grades 9-12
Kendall Hunt, 1988 (Termination Date: 1995)

The Day Care Dilemma: Who Should Be Responsible for the Children?: Grades 9-12
Kendall Hunt, 1989 (Termination Date: 1995)

The Drug Crisis: Public Strategies for Breaking the Habit: Grades 9-12
Kendall Hunt, 1989 (Termination Date: 1995)

The Environment at Risk: Responding to Growing Dangers: Grades 9-12
Kendall Hunt, 1989 (Termination Date: 1995)

Coping with AIDS: The Public Response to the Epidemic: Grades 9-12
Kendall Hunt, 1988 (Termination Date: 1995)

Maps, Charts and Graphs Series: Grades 7-8
Modern Curriculum Press, Inc., 1990 (Termination Date: 1995)

Geo-Themes Program with 30 Atlases: Grades 7-12
Nystrom, 1990 (Termination Date: 1995)

Mapping American History Combination Program: Grades 7-12
Nystrom, 1986 (Termination Date: 1995)

Mapping World History Program: Grades 7-12
Nystrom, 1986 (Termination Date: 1995)

Arkansas Basic Skillbook: U.S. History: Grade 8
Rainbow Educational Concepts, 1989 (Termination Date: 1995)

Visual Relief 12" Globe: Grades 7-12
Rand McNally, 1989 (Termination Date: 1995)

Advanced Physical/Political 16" Globe, Geosphere, Space Age, and Disc-base Mounting: Grades 7-12
Rand McNally, 1989 (Termination Date: 1995)

Visual Relief United States/Alaska/World Map Combination: Grades 7-12
Rand McNally, 1989 (Termination Date: 1995)

Visual Relief Regional Series Set: Grades 7-12
Rand McNally, 1989 (Termination Date: 1995)

Advanced Physical/Political Continental Maps: North America, South America, Europe, Asia, Africa: Grades 7-12
Rand McNally, 1989 (Termination Date: 1995)

Complete American Studies Series: Grades 7-12
Rand McNally, 1989 (Termination Date: 1995)

Complete World History Series: Grades 7-12
Rand McNally, 1989 (Termination Date: 1995)

Hearne Brothers Living Constitution Map: Grades 7-12
Rand McNally, 1987 (Termination Date: 1995)

Living Constitution Study Guide: Grades 7-12
Rand McNally, 1987 (Termination Date: 1995)

Hearne Brothers American History Wall Map:
Grades 7-12
Rand McNally, 1982 (Termination Date: 1995)

North America Map Activity Program: Grades 7-12
Rand McNally, 1989 (Termination Date: 1995)

South America Map Activity Program: Grades 7-12
Rand McNally, 1989 (Termination Date: 1995)

Europe Map Activity Program: Grades 7-12
Rand McNally, 1989 (Termination Date: 1995)

Asia Map Activity Program: Grades 7-12
Rand McNally, 1989 (Termination Date: 1995)

Africa Map Activity Program: Grades 7-12
Rand McNally, 1989 (Termination Date: 1995)

Eastern Hemisphere Map Activity Program: Grades
7-12
Rand McNally, 1989 (Termination Date: 1995)

Western Hemisphere Map Activity Program: Grades
7-12
Rand McNally, 1989 (Termination Date: 1995)

Goode's World Atlas: Grades 7-12
Rand McNally, 1989 (Termination Date: 1995)

Historical Atlas of the World: Grades 7-12
Rand McNally, 1965 (Termination Date: 1995)

Atlas of American History: Grades 7-12
Rand McNally, 1990 (Termination Date: 1995)

World Atlas of Nations: Grades 7-12
Rand McNally, 1989 (Termination Date: 1995)

California

The Story of America: Beginnings to 1914: Grade 8
Holt, Rinehart and Winston, 1986, 1990, 1991
(Termination Year: 1999)

Houghton Mifflin Social Studies: Grades K-8
Houghton Mifflin, 1991 (Termination Year: 1999)

Florida

Florida Studies

Florida: Grade 4
Holt, Rinehart and Winston, 1986 (Termination
Year: 1993)

Florida's State History: Grade 4
Silver Burdett and Ginn (Schoolhouse Press),
1987 (Termination Year: 1993)

Florida Yesterday and Today: Grade 4
Silver Burdett and Ginn, 1987 (Termination Year:
1993)

A Panorama of Florida II: Grades 6-8
Walsworth, 1988 (Termination Year: 1995)

General Social Studies

HBJ Social Studies: Grades K-6
Harcourt Brace Jovanovich, 1985 (Termination
Year: 1993)

Heath Social Studies: Grades K-8
D. C. Heath, 1987 (Termination Year: 1993)

Holt Social Studies: Grades K-6
Holt, Rinehart and Winston, 1986 (Termination
Year: 1993)

The Laidlaw Social Studies Series: Grades K-6
Macmillan/McGraw-Hill, 1985 (Termination
Year: 1993)

Macmillan Social Studies: Grades K-7
Macmillan/McGraw-Hill, 1987 (Termination
Year: 1993)

Our Nation, Our World: Grades K-6
Macmillan/McGraw-Hill, 1986 (Termination
Year: 1993)

Scott, Foresman Social Studies Program: Grades K-
7
Scott, Foresman, 1986 (Termination Year: 1993)

Ginn Social Studies Program: Grades K-6
Silver Burdett and Ginn (Schoolhouse Press),
1987 (Termination Year: 1993)

The World and Its People: Grades K-6
Silver Burdett and Ginn, 1984 (Termination Year:
1993)

Introduction to the Social Studies: Grades 9-12
Allyn & Bacon, 1985 (Termination Year: 1993)

U.S. History

Exploring American History: Grades 6-8
Globe, 1986 (Termination Year: 1992)

America's Heritage: Grades 6-8
Prentice Hall (Allyn & Bacon), 1986 (Termination Year: 1992)

America! America!: Grades 6-8
Scott, Foresman, 1985 (Termination Year: 1992)

American Adventures: Grades 6-8
Scholastic, 1987 (Termination Year: 1992)

America Is: Grades 6-8
Glencoe (Merrill), 1992 (Termination Year: 1992)

The Challenge of Freedom: Grades 6-8
Glencoe (Laidlaw), 1986 (Termination Year: 1992)

America: Its People and Values: Grades 6-8
Harcourt Brace Jovanovich, 1985 (Termination Year: 1992)

The American People: Grades 6-8
D. C. Heath, 1986 (Termination Year: 1992)

Land of Liberty: Grades 6-8
Holt, Rinehart and Winston, 1985 (Termination Year: 1992)

A Proud Nation: Grades 6-8
McDougal, Littell, 1985 (Termination Year: 1992)

History of the American Nation: Grades 6-8
Macmillan, 1984 (Termination Year: 1992)

The American Nation: Grades 6-8
Prentice Hall, 1986 (Termination Year: 1992)

One Flag, One Land: Grades 6-8
Silver Burdett and Ginn, 1985 (Termination Year: 1992)

American History: Grades 6-8
Harcourt Brace Jovanovich, 1986 (Termination Year: 1992)

American Spirit: Grades 6-8
Prentice Hall (Silver Burdett and Ginn), 1985 (Termination Year: 1992)

Life and Liberty: Grades 9-12
Scott, Foresman, 1984 (Termination Year: 1992)

Addison-Wesley United States History: Grades 9-12
Addison-Wesley, 1986 (Termination Year: 1992)

Legacy of Freedom, A History of the United States: Grades 9-12
Glencoe (Laidlaw), 1986 (Termination Year: 1992)

The American Tradition: A History of the United States: Grades 9-12
Glencoe (Merrill), 1984 (Termination Year: 1992)

Triumph of the American Nation: Grades 9-12
Harcourt Brace Jovanovich, 1986 (Termination Year: 1992)

Our Land, Our Time: Grades 9-12
Holt, 1992 (Termination Year: 1992)

History of the American People: Grades 9-12
Holt, Rinehart and Winston, 1986 (Termination Year: 1992)

America: The Glorious Republic: Grades 9-12
Houghton Mifflin, 1985 (Termination Year: 1992)

The Americans: Grades 9-12
McDougal, Littell, 1987 (Termination Year: 1992)

The American Pageant: Grades 9-12
Heath, 1983 (Termination Year: 1992)

A History of the United States: Grades 9-12
Prentice Hall, 1986 (Termination Year: 1992)

Land of Promise: Grades 9-12
Scott, Foresman, 1983 (Termination Year: 1992

World History

The World Yesterday and Today: Grades 6-8
Silver Burdett and Ginn, 1988 (Termination Year: 1995)

World History: A Basic Approach: Grades 9-12
Holt, 1984 (Termination Year: 1992)

The Pageant of World History: Grades 9-12
Prentice Hall, 1986 (Termination Year: 1992)

History and Life: The World and Its People: Grades 9-12
Scott, Foresman, 1984 (Termination Year: 1992)

Achievements through the Ages: Grades 9-12
Glencoe (Laidlaw), 1985 (Termination Year: 1992)

The Human Experience: A World History: Grades 9-12
Glencoe (Merrill), 1985 (Termination Year: 1992)

The Human Expression: Grades 9-12
Glencoe, 1985 (Termination Year: 1992)

People and Nations: A World History: Grades 9-12
Harcourt Brace Jovanovich, 1983 (Termination Year: 1992)

People and Our World: A Study of World History: Grades 9-12
Holt, Rinehart and Winston, 1984 (Termination Year: 1992)

World History: Patterns of Civilization: Grades 9-12
Prentice Hall, 1986 (Termination Year: 1992)

A History of the World: Grades 9-12
Houghton Mifflin, 1985 (Termination Year: 1992)

Economics
Introduction to Economics: Grade 9
Addison-Wesley, 1984 (Termination Year: 1993)

Free Enterprise Today: Grades 9-12
South-Western, 1985 (Termination Year: 1993)

Essentials of Economics and Free Enterprise: Grades 10-12
Addison-Wesley, 1987 (Termination Year: 1993)

Economics: Institutions and Analysis: Grades 11-12
Amsco School Publications, 1985 (Termination Year: 1993)

Economics: Principles and Practices: Grades 9-12
Glencoe (Merrill), 1983 (Termination Year: 1993)

Scribner Economics: Grades 9-12
Glencoe, 1988 (Termination Year: 1993)

Understanding Economics: Grades 10-12
Glencoe (Random House), 1986 (Termination Year: 1993)

The American Economy: Analysis, Issues, Principles: Grades 11-12
Houghton Mifflin, 1986 (Termination Year: 1993)

McDougal, Littell Economics: Grades 9-12
McDougal, Littell, 1986 (Termination Year: 1993)

Invitation to Economics: Grades 9-12
Scott, Foresman, 1985 (Termination Year: 1993)

Economics: The Science of Cost, Benefit, and Choice: Grades 10-12
South-Western, 1984 (Termination Year: 1993)

Geography
Exploring a Changing World: Grades 6-8
Globe, 1984 (Termination Year: 1992)

Geography: Grades 6-8
Houghton Mifflin, 1985 (Termination Year: 1992)

World Neighbors: Grades 6-8
Macmillan, 1985 (Termination Year: 1992)

A World View: Grades 6-8
Silver Burdett and Ginn, 1985 (Termination Year: 1992)

World Geography: Peoples and Places: Grades 6-8
Glencoe (Merrill), 1984 (Termination Year: 1992)

World Geography: Grades 9-12
D. C. Heath, 1983 (Termination Year: 1992)

World Geography: Grades 9-12
Glencoe, 1985 (Termination Year: 1992)

World Geography Today: Grades 9-12
Holt, Rinehart and Winston, 1985 (Termination Year: 1992)

Political Science
Civics: Citizens in Action: Grades 6-8
Glencoe (Merrill), 1986 (Termination Year: 1992)

Civics: Citizens and Society: Grades 6-8
McGraw-Hill/School Division, 1983 (Termination Year: 1992)

Teens, Crime and the Community: Grades 7-9
West, 1987 (Termination Year: 1995)

Magruder's American Government: Grades 10-12
Allyn & Bacon, 1987 (Termination Year: 1993)

American Government: Principles and Practices:
Grades 9-12
Glencoe (Merrill), 1987 (Termination Year: 1993)

Government in the United States: Grades 9-12
Glencoe, 1987 (Termination Year: 1993)

American Government: The Republic in Action:
Grades 11-12
Harcourt Brace Jovanovich, 1986 (Termination
Year: 1993)

We Are One: Grades 11-12
Holt, 1987 (Termination Year: 1993)

Consent of the Governed: Grades 9-12
Scott, Foresman, 1987 (Termination Year: 1993)

American Civics: Grades 9-12
Harcourt Brace Jovanovich, 1983 (Termination
Year: 1992)

Civics: Government and Citizenship: Grades 9-12
Prentice Hall, 1986 (Termination Year: 1992)

Civics for Americans: Grades 9-12
Scott, Foresman, 1986 (Termination Year: 1992)

Living Law Series: Grades 9-12
Scholastic, 1988 (Termination Year: 1995)

Street Law: A Course in Practical Law (with
Florida Supplement): Grades 9-12
West, 1986 (Termination Year: 1995)

Psychology
Understanding Psychology: Grades 9-12
American School Publishers, 1986 (Termination
Year: 1995)

Psychology: Its Principles and Applications: Grades
9-12
Harcourt Brace Jovanovich, 1989 (Termination
Year: 1995)

Invitation to Psychology: Grades 9-12
Scott, Foresman, 1989 (Termination Year: 1995)

Sociology
Sociology: Understanding Society: Grades 10-12
Prentice Hall, 1989 (Termination Year: 1995)

Sociology: The Search for Social Patterns: Grades
9-12
Scholastic, 1989 (Termination Year: 1995)

Georgia

Social Studies, General
Our State: Georgia: Grade 4
Graphic Learning, 1992 (Termination Year: 1996)

HBJ Social Studies: Grades K-6
Harcourt Brace Jovanovich, 1991 (Termination
Year: 1996)

Heath Social Studies: Grades K-6
D. C. Heath, 1991 (Termination Year: 1996)

Houghton Mifflin Social Studies: K-5
Houghton Mifflin, 1991 (Termination Year: 1996)

Adventures in Georgia: Grade 4
Linton Day, 1989 (Termination Year: 1996)

The World Around Us: Grades K-7
Macmillan/McGraw-Hill, 1990-91 (Termination
Year: 1996)

Scott, Foresman Social Studies: Grades 6-7
Scott, Foresman, 1991 (Termination Year: 1996)

People in Time and Place: Grades K-7
Silver Burdett and Ginn, 1991 (Termination Year:
1996)

Georgia Studies
A History of Georgia: Grade 8
Clairmont, 1992 (Termination Year: 1996)

The Georgia Studies Book: Grades 8
The Institute of Government of the University of
Georgia, 1991 (Termination Year: 1996)

Government in Georgia: Grades 8-12
The Institute of Government of the University of
Georgia, 1991 (Termination Year: 1996)

Georgia in American Society II: Grade 8
Linton Day, 1991 (Termination Year: 1996)

Georgia Studies: Grade 8
Viewpoint, 1991 (Termination Year: 1996)

Fourth Star: Georgia in American History: Grade 8
Walsworth, 1992 (Termination Year: 1996)

Anthropology
Anthropology: Grades 10-12
Prentice Hall, 1990 (Termination Year: 1996)

Current Issues

Current Issues: Critical Issues Confronting the Nation and the World: Grades 9-12
Close Up Foundation, 1991 (Termination Year: 1996)

Economics

Economics for Everybody: Grades 9-12
Amsco, 1992 (Termination Year: 1996)

The Study of Economics: Principles, Concepts and Applications: Grades 11-12
Dushkin, 1991 (Termination Year: 1996)

Introduction to Economics: Grades 9-12
EMC, 1991 (Termination Year: 1996)

Basic Economic Principles: Grades 9-12
Glencoe, 1989 (Termination Year: 1996)

Economics: Today and Tomorrow: Grades 9-12
Glencoe, 1991 (Termination Year: 1996)

Understanding Economics: Grades 9-12
Glencoe, 1991 (Termination Year: 1996)

Scholastic Economics: Grades 9-12
Scholastic, 1991 (Termination Year: 1996)

Invitation to Economics: Grades 9-12
Scott, Foresman, 1988 (Termination Year: 1996)

Economics: Our American Economy: Grades 9-12
Addison-Wesley, 1990 (Termination Year: 1996)

The Economic Problem: Grades 9-12
Prentice Hall, 1990 (Termination Year: 1996)

Dollars and Sense: Grades 9-12
Scott, Foresman, 1991 (Termination Year: 1996)

Economics Today: Grades 9-12
Scott, Foresman, 1991 (Termination Year: 1996)

Ethnic Studies

African American History: Four Centuries of Black Life: Grades 7-12
Scholastic, 1990 (Termination Year: 1996)

Government/Citizenship Education

Civics: Grade 9
Addison-Wesley, 1991 (Termination Year: 1996)

Government for Everybody: Grades 9-12
AMSCO, 1992 (Termination Year: 1996)

The Drama of Democracy: Grades 11-12
Dushkin, 1990 (Termination Year: 1996)

Civics: Responsibilities and Citizenship: Grades 8-12
Glencoe, 1992 (Termination Year: 1996)

Civics: Citizens in Action: Grades 8-12
Glencoe, 1990 (Termination Year: 1996)

Government in the United States: Grades 9-12
Glencoe, 1990 (Termination Year: 1996)

American Government: Principles and Practices: Grades 9-12
Glencoe, 1991 (Termination Year: 1996)

We the People: Grades 9-12
Holt, Rinehart and Winston, 1989 (Termination Year: 1996)

American Civics: Grades 9-12
Holt, Rinehart and Winston, 1992 (Termination Year: 1996)

Government in America: Grades 9-12
Houghton Mifflin, 1992 (Termination Year: 1996)

An Introduction to Law in Georgia: Grades 9-12
The Institute of Government of the University of Georgia, 1991 (Termination Year: 1996)

Government in Georgia: Grades 9-12
The Institute of Government of the University of Georgia, 1991 (Termination Year: 1996)

Civics: Government and Citizenship: Grades 9-12
Prentice Hall, 1990 (Termination Year: 1996)

Magruder's American Government: Grades 9-12
Prentice Hall, 1991 (Termination Year: 1996)

Civics for Americans: Grades 9-12
Scott, Foresman, 1991 (Termination Year: 1996)

Street Law: A Course in Practical Law: Grades 9-12
West, 1990 (Termination Year: 1996)

Government by the People: Grades 9-12
Prentice Hall, 1990 (Termination Year: 1996)

American Government: Readings and Cases:
Grades 9-12
Scott, Foresman, 1990 (Termination Year: 1996)

Government in America: Grades 9-12
Scott, Foresman, 1991 (Termination Year: 1996)

Exploring American Citizenship: Grades 6-12
Globe, 1992 (Termination Year: 1996)

United States Government: Grades 9-12
Media Materials, 1992 (Termination Year: 1996)

Psychology
Understanding Psychology: Grades 9-12
Glencoe, 1992 (Termination Year: 1996)

Psychology: Its Principles and Applications: Grades
9-12
Holt, Rinehart and Winston, 1989 (Termination
Year: 1996)

Psychology: An Introduction: Grades 10-12
Prentice Hall, 1990 (Termination Year: 1996)

Invitation to Psychology: Grades 9-12
Scott, Foresman, 1989 (Termination Year: 1996)

Psychology: Grades 9-12
Scott, Foresman, 1990 (Termination Year: 1996)

Psychology and You: Grades 9-12
West, 1990 (Termination Year: 1996)

Sociology
Sociology: The Study of Human Relationships:
Grades 9-12
Holt, Rinehart and Winston, 1990 (Termination
Year: 1996)

Sociology: Understanding Society: Grades 9-12
Prentice Hall, 1990 (Termination Year: 1996)

United States History
History of a Free Nation: Grades 10-12
Glencoe, 1992 (Termination Year: 1996)

*American Odyssey: The United States in the
Twentieth Century:* Grades 10-12
Glencoe, 1992 (Termination Year: 1996)

Challenge of Freedom: Grades 8-12
Glencoe, 1990 (Termination Year: 1996)

Exploring American History: Grades 9-12
Globe, 1991 (Termination Year: 1996)

Our Land, Our Time: Grades 9-12
Holt, Rinehart and Winston, 1991 (Termination
Year: 1996)

The Story of America: Grades 9-12
Holt, Rinehart and Winston, 1991 (Termination
Year: 1996)

United States History: Grades 9-12
Holt, Rinehart and Winston, 1991 (Termination
Year: 1996)

History of the United States: Grades 9-12
Houghton Mifflin, 1991 (Termination Year: 1996)

The Americans: Grades 9-12
McDougal, Littell, 1992 (Termination Year: 1996)

A History of the United States: Grades 9-12
Prentice Hall, 1992 (Termination Year: 1996)

The United States: A History of the Republic:
Grades 9-12
Prentice Hall, 1990 (Termination Year: 1996)

The American Nation: Grades 9-12
Prentice Hall, 1991 (Termination Year: 1996)

American Voices: A History of the United States:
Grade 11
Scott, Foresman, 1992 (Termination Year: 1996)

The American Nation: Grades 11-12
Scott, Foresman, 1991 (Termination Year: 1996)

America: Past and Present: Grades 11-12
Scott, Foresman, 1991 (Termination Year: 1996)

America: The People and the Dream: Grades 7-12
Scott, Foresman, 1991 (Termination Year: 1996)

Our Nation's History: Grades 9-12
Media Materials, 1992 (Termination Year: 1996)

*The Enduring Vision: A History of the American
People:* Grades 11-12
D. C. Heath, 1990 (Termination Year: 1996)

The American Pageant: A History of the Republic:
Grades 11-12
D. C. Heath, 1991 (Termination Year: 1996)

World Geography

Glencoe World Geography: A Physical and Cultural Approach: Grades 9-12
Glencoe, 1992 (Termination Year: 1996)

World Geography Today: Grades 9-12
Holt, Rinehart and Winston, 1992 (Termination Year: 1996)

Prentice Hall World Geography: Grades 7-10
Prentice Hall, 1992 (Termination Year: 1996)

Scholastic World Geography: Grades 9-12
Scholastic, 1989 (Termination Year: 1996)

Scott, Foresman World Geography: Grades 9-12
Scott, Foresman, 1989 (Termination Year: 1996)

Geography: Our Changing World: Grades 9-12
West, 1990 (Termination Year: 1996)

Exploring A Changing World: Grades 6-12
Globe, 1988 (Termination Year: 1996)

World History

Addison-Wesley World History: Grades 9-12
Addison-Wesley, 1991 (Termination Year: 1996)

The Human Expression: World Regions and Cultures: Grades 9-12
Glencoe, 1992 (Termination Year: 1996)

World History: The Human Experience: Grades 9-12
Glencoe, 1992 (Termination Year: 1996)

World History: Perspectives on the Past: Grades 9-12
D. C. Heath, 1992 (Termination Year: 1996)

World History: People and Nations: Grades 9-12
Holt, Rinehart and Winston, 1990 (Termination Year: 1996)

History of the World: Grades 9-12
Houghton Mifflin, 1992 (Termination Year: 1996)

The Pageant of World History: Grades 9-12
Prentice Hall, 1990 (Termination Year: 1996)

World History: Patterns of Civilization: Grades 9-12
Prentice Hall, 1990 (Termination Year: 1996)

History and Life: The World and Its People: Grades 9-12
Scott, Foresman, 1990 (Termination Year: 1996)

Civilizations in the West: Grades 9-12
Scott, Foresman, 1991 (Termination Year: 1996)

Civilizations of the World: Grades 9-12
Scott, Foresman, 1990 (Termination Year: 1996)

Exploring World History: Grades 9-12
Globe, 1990 (Termination Year: 1996)

World History: Grades 9-12
Holt, Rinehart and Winston, 1990 (Termination Year: 1996)

Experiencing World History: Grades 9-12
Media Materials, 1991 (Termination Year: 1996)

Atlases and Map Skills

Basic Map Skills: Grade 4
Hammond, 1991 (Termination Year: 1996)

American History Through Maps: Grades 5-6
Hammond, 1984 (Termination Year: 1996)

World History Through Maps: Grades 6-7
Hammond, 1991 (Termination Year: 1996)

Atlas of the Eastern Hemisphere: Grades 7-8
Hammond, 1990 (Termination Year: 1996)

Atlas of the Western Hemisphere: Grades 7-8
Hammond, 1990 (Termination Year: 1996)

Intermediate United States Atlas: Grades 7-8
Hammond, 1990 (Termination Year: 1996)

Intermediate World Atlas: Grades 7-8
Hammond, 1991 (Termination Year: 1996)

Citation World Atlas: Grades 7-12
Hammond, 1991 (Termination Year: 1996)

Comparative World Atlas: Grades 7-12
Hammond, 1990 (Termination Year: 1996)

Historical Atlas of the World: Grades 7-12
Hammond, 1990 (Termination Year: 1996)

United States History Atlas: Grades 7-12
Hammond, 1989 (Termination Year: 1996)

Essential Map Skills: Grades 7-12
Hammond, 1985 (Termination Year: 1996)

World Atlas for Students: Grades 7-12
Hammond, 1991 (Termination Year: 1996)

Nystrom World Atlas, No. 9A90: Grades 4-5/10-12
Nystrom, 1990 (Termination Year: 1996)

Nystrom Geo-Themes Program, No. 9A900: Grades 6-7
Nystrom, 1990 (Termination Year: 1996)

Early Learning Skills Program, No. 2ELS100: Grade K
Nystrom, 1990 (Termination Year: 1996)

Primary Social Studies Skills (Classroom Kits): Grades 1-12
Nystrom, 1986, 1989 (Termination Year: 1996)

Classroom Atlas: Grades 4-9
Rand McNally, 1992 (Termination Year: 1996)

Atlas of American History: Grades 5-11
Rand McNally, 1991 (Termination Year: 1996)

Quick Reference World Atlas: Grades 5-12
Rand McNally, 1992 (Termination Year: 1996)

Historical Atlas of the World: Grades 6-12
Rand McNally, 1991 (Termination Year: 1996)

Goode's World Atlas (1991 revision): Grades 9-12
Rand McNally, 1990 (Termination Year: 1996)

Essential Skills in Social Studies: Grades K-3
Rand McNally, 1989 (Termination Year: 1996)

Map Activity Program: Grades 5-10
Rand McNally, 1989, 1991 (Termination Year: 1996)

Mastering Social Studies Skills: Grades 8-10
Amsco, 1992 (Termination Year: 1996)

Discovery Series Map Skills Kits: Grades K-3
George F. Cram, 1989-91 (Termination Year: 1996)

Idaho

Elementary Social Studies
Elementary/Junior High--Basic
The Pageant of World History: Grades 7-12
Allyn & Bacon/Prentice Hall, 1986 (Termination Date: 1992)

World Geography: Grades 7-12
Allyn & Bacon/Prentice Hall, 1986 (Termination Date: 1992)

Our Economy: How It Works: Grades 7-12
Addison-Wesley, 1988 (Termination Date: 1992)

Spirit of Liberty: Grades 7-9
Addison-Wesley, 1987 (Termination Date: 1992)

America Is: Grades 7-10
Merrill, 1985 (Termination Date: 1992)

Human Heritage: A World History: Grades 7-12
Merrill, 1989 (Termination Date: 1992)

Global Insights: People and Cultures: Grades 8-12
Merrill, 1987 (Termination Date: 1992)

United States History-vol. 1: Grades 7-9
Merrill, 1986 (Termination Date: 1992)

World Geography: People and Places: Grades 7-12
Merrill, 1989 (Termination Date: 1992)

The Challenge of Freedom: Grades 7-9
Glencoe/Macmillan/McGraw-Hill, 1990 (Termination Date: 1992)

Laidlaw World Geography: Grades 7-12
Glencoe/Macmillan/McGraw-Hill, Laidlaw, 1987 (Termination Date: 1992)

Exploring the Non-Western World: Grades 7-12
Globe, 1988 (Termination Date: 1992)

Exploring a Changing World: Grades 7-12
Globe, 1988 (Termination Date: 1992)

World History for a Global Age, Books 1 and 2: Grades 7-9
Globe, 1988 (Termination Date: 1992)

America: Its People & Values: Grades 7-9
Harcourt Brace Jovanovich, 1985 (Termination
Date: 1992)

American History: Grades 7-12
Harcourt Brace Jovanovich, 1986 (Termination
Date: 1992)

HBJ Social Studies: Grades K-6
Harcourt Brace Jovanovich, 1988 (Termination
Date: 1992)

World Geography: Grades 7-12
Harcourt Brace Jovanovich, 1989 (Termination
Date: 1992)

Sociology: The Study of Human Relations: Grades
7-12
Harcourt Brace Jovanovich, 1990 (Termination
Date: 1992)

The American People: Grade 8
D. C. Heath, 1986 (Termination Date: 1992)

Heath Social Studies: Grades K-7
D. C. Heath, 1989 (Termination Date: 1992)

Heath World Geography: Grades 7-12
D. C. Heath, 1989 (Termination Date: 1992)

This Is America's Story: Grades 7-9
Houghton Mifflin, 1988 (Termination Date: 1992)

Geography: Grades 7-10
Houghton Mifflin, 1985 (Termination Date: 1992)

Holt Social Studies: Grades K-6
Holt, Rinehart and Winston/Harcourt Brace
Jovanovich, 1986 (Termination Date: 1992)

United States History: Grades 7-9
Holt, Rinehart and Winston/Harcourt Brace
Jovanovich, 1988 (Termination Date: 1992)

World Geography Today: Grades 7-9
Holt, Rinehart and Winston/Harcourt Brace
Jovanovich, 1985 (Termination Date: 1992)

History of the American Nation: Grade 8
Macmillan, 1987 (Termination Date: 1992)

Macmillan Social Studies: Grades K-7
Macmillan, 1987 (Termination Date: 1992)

The World around Us: Grades K-6
Macmillan/McGraw Hill, 1990 (Termination
Date: 1992)

Our Nation, Our World: Grades K-8
McGraw-Hill, 1988 (Termination Date: 1992)

A Proud Nation: Grades 7-8
McDougal, Littell, 1985 (Termination Date: 1992)

The American People: A History to 1877: Grades 7-
8
McDougal, Littell, 1985 (Termination Date: 1992)

The American Nation: Grades 7-9
Prentice Hall, 1986 (Termination Date: 1992)

A History of the Republic: Grades 7-10
Prentice Hall, 1986 (Termination Date: 1992)

The World and Its People--My World and Me:
Grade K
Silver Burdett and Ginn, 1984 (Termination Date:
1992)

Silver Burdett & Ginn Social Studies: Grades 1-8
Silver Burdett and Ginn, 1988 (Termination Date:
1992)

One Flag, One Land: Grade 8
Silver Burdett and Ginn, 1988 (Termination Date:
1992)

Sociology: Grades 7-12
Scholastic, 1987 (Termination Date: 1992)

World Geography: Grades 7-10
Scholastic, 1987 (Termination Date: 1992)

America! America!: Grades 7-9
Scott, Foresman, 1987 (Termination Date: 1992)

People on Earth: A World Geography: Grades 7-8
Scott, Foresman, 1988 (Termination Date: 1992)

Scott, Foresman Social Studies: Grades 1-7
Scott, Foresman, 1988 (Termination Date: 1992)

Scott, Foresman Social Studies: Grades 6-7
Scott, Foresman, 1990 (Termination Date: 1992)

Supplemental

Introduction to the Social Sciences: Grades 6-12
Allyn & Bacon/Prentice Hall, 1985 (Termination
Date: 1992)

Follet Student Atlas: Grades 4-12
Allyn & Bacon/Prentice Hall, 1986 (Termination
Date: 1992)

Skills for Understanding Maps and Globes: Grades
4-7
Allyn & Bacon/Prentice Hall, 1986 (Termination
Date: 1992)

The Pacific Northwest: Past, Present and Future:
Grades 8-12
Directed Media, 1986 (Termination Date: 1992)

American Foreign Policy: Grades Sec.
Greenhaven Press, 1987 (Termination Date:
1992)

Central America: Grades Sec.
Greenhaven Press, 1985 (Termination Date:
1992)

Nuclear War: Grades Sec.
Greenhaven Press, 1985 (Termination Date:
1992)

Problems of Africa: Grades Sec.
Greenhaven Press, 1986 (Termination Date:
1992)

The Environmental Crisis: Grades 9-12
Greenhaven Press, 1986 (Termination Date:
1992)

Visions and Values: Grades K-8
Harcourt Brace Jovanovich, 1987 (Termination
Date: 1992)

American Civics: Grades 7-9
Harcourt Brace Jovanovich, 1987 (Termination
Date: 1992)

The Constitution: Foundation of Our Freedom:
Grades 7-12
Harcourt Brace Jovanovich, 1990 (Termination
Date: 1992)

Great Cases of the Supreme Court: Grades 7-12
Houghton Mifflin, 1989 (Termination Date: 1992)

Vital Issues of the Constitution: Grades 7-12
Houghton Mifflin, 1989 (Termination Date: 1992)

Wildlife of Idaho Coloring Book, vol. 1: Grades K-6
Idaho Youth Ranch, 1985 (Termination Date:
1992)

Recreation in Idaho Coloring Book, vol. 2: Grades
K-6
Idaho Youth Ranch, 1985 (Termination Date:
1992)

Idaho: A Tribute to Its History Coloring Book, vol.
3: Grades 4-6
Idaho Youth Ranch, 1985 (Termination Date:
1992)

Our Constitution and What It Means: Grades 5-12
McGraw-Hill, 1987 (Termination Date: 1992)

*McDougal, Littell Study Guide for the U.S. Consti-
tution:* Grades 7+
McDougal, Littell, 1987 (Termination Date: 1992)

Honor Our Flag through Knowledge: Grades 4-8
Otha McGill, 1983 (Termination Date: 1992)

The Constitution: Yesterday, Today and Tomorrow:
Grades 6-9
Scholastic, 1987 (Termination Date: 1992)

Criminal Justice & Civil Justice: Grades 7-12
Scholastic, 1984 (Termination Date: 1992)

Success with Maps, Series A--F: Grades 1-6
Scholastic, 1985 (Termination Date: 1992)

World Cultures Series: Grades 7-12
Scholastic, 1986 (Termination Date: 1992)

World History: Grades 7-12
Scholastic, 1987 (Termination Date: 1992)

Scott, Foresman World Atlas: Grades 7-12
Scott, Foresman, 1988 (Termination Date: 1992)

The Constitution: Grades 7-12
Scott, Foresman, 1985 (Termination Date: 1992)

Reading American History: Grades 7-12
Scott, Foresman, 1987 (Termination Date: 1992)

SRA Social Studies Series: Grades 4-12
Science Research Associates, 1985 (Termination Date: 1992)

Your World of Facts: Grades 3-6
Science Research Associates, 1984 (Termination Date: 1992)

Illustrated Dictionary of Physical Geography: Grades 3-6
Walsworth, 1987 (Termination Date: 1992)

Northwest History--Supplemental

Beyond The Rockies: A Narrative History of Idaho: Grade 4
Alpha Omega, 1985 (Termination Date: 1992)

West to the Pacific: The Story of the Lewis & Clark Expedition: Grades 4-8
Alpha Omega, 1989 (Termination Date: 1992)

The Pacific Northwest: Past, Present and Future: Grades 8-12
Directed Media, 1986 (Termination Date: 1992)

Idaho Ag in the Classroom: Grade 4
Idaho Ag in The Classroom, 1988 (Termination Date: 1992)

State and Local Government: Grades 7-12
University of Idaho Press, 1984 (Termination Date: 1992)

The Story of Idaho: Grade 4
University of Idaho Press, 1990 (Termination Date: 1992)

Horizons of Idaho: Grade 4
Walsworth, 1988 (Termination Date: 1992)

A Panorama of Idaho: Grade 8
Walsworth, 1988 (Termination Date: 1992)

Idaho, Magnificent Wilderness: Grades 7-12
Westcliffe, 1989 (Termination Date: 1992)

Atlases/Maps--Supplemental

Skills for Understanding Maps and Globes: Grades 4-7
Allyn & Bacon/Prentice Hall, 1986 (Termination Date: 1992)

Basic Map Skills: Grades Elem.
Hammond, 1984 (Termination Date: 1992)

Understanding Maps: Grades Elem.
Hammond, 1985 (Termination Date: 1992)

American History through Maps: Grades Elem.
Hammond, 1984 (Termination Date: 1992)

Intermediate U.S. Atlas: Grades Elem.
Hammond, 1984 (Termination Date: 1992)

World Atlas for Students: Grades Elem.
Hammond, 1984 (Termination Date: 1992)

Essential Map Skills: Grades Elem.
Hammond, 1985 (Termination Date: 1992)

Comparative World Atlas: Grades Elem.
Hammond, 1985 (Termination Date: 1992)

Historical Atlas of the World: Grades Elem.
Hammond, 1984 (Termination Date: 1992)

U.S. History Atlas: Grades Elem.
Hammond, 1984 (Termination Date: 1992)

U.S. Atlas: Grades Elem.
Hammond, 1984 (Termination Date: 1992)

World Atlas: Grades Elem.
Hammond, 1987 (Termination Date: 1992)

Times Concise Atlas of World History: Grades Elem.
Hammond, 1982 (Termination Date: 1992)

Success with Maps, Series A-F: Grades 1-6
Scholastic, 1988 (Termination Date: 1992)

World History
Secondary--Basic

Exploring World Cultures: Grades 9-12
Allyn & Bacon/Prentice Hall, 1986 (Termination Date: 1992)

The Pageant of World History: Grades 7-12
Allyn & Bacon/Prentice Hall, 1986 (Termination Date: 1992)

Our Common Heritage: A World History: Grades 9-12
Allyn & Bacon/Prentice Hall, 1984 (Termination Date 1992)

Human Heritage: A World History: Grades 7-10
Merrill, 1985 (Termination Date: 1992)

Global Insights: People and Cultures: Grades 8-12
Merrill, 1987 (Termination Date 1992)

The Human Experience: Grades 10-12
Merrill, 1990 (Termination Date: 1992)

The Human Experience: Grades 9-12
Merrill, 1985 (Termination Date: 1992)

Achievements through the Ages: Grades 8-9
Glencoe/Macmillan/McGraw-Hill, 1985 (Termination Date: 1992)

Exploring World History: Grades 9-12
Globe, 1987 (Termination Date: 1992)

World History: People & Nations: Grades 9-12
Harcourt Brace Jovanovich, 1987 (Termination Date: 1992)

People and Nations: A World History: Grades 9-12
Harcourt Brace Jovanovich, 1987 (Termination Date: 1992)

Heath World History: Perspectives on the Past: Grades 9-12
D. C. Heath, 1988 (Termination Date: 1992)

A History of the World: Grades 10-12
Houghton Mifflin, 1990 (Termination Date: 1992)

A History of the World: Grades 9-12
Houghton Mifflin, 1988 (Termination Date: 1992)

World History: A Story of Progress: Grades 9-12
Holt, Rinehart & Winston/Harcourt Brace Jovanovich, 1987 (Termination Date: 1992)

A World History: Links across Time and Place: Grades 9+
McDougal, Littell, 1988 (Termination Date: 1992)

Peoples and Cultures Series: Grades 9-12
McDougal, Littell, 1988 (Termination Date: 1992)

World History: Patterns of Civilization: Grades 9-12
Prentice Hall, 1988 (Termination Date: 1992)

History and Life: The World and Its People: Grades 9-12
Scott, Foresman, 1990 (Termination Date: 1992)

World History
Secondary--Supplemental
World Cultures Series: Grades 7-12
Scholastic, 1985, 1986 (Termination Date: 1992)

World History: Grades 7-12
Scholastic, 1987 (Termination Date: 1992)

Practicing World History Skills: Grades 9-12
Scott, Foresman, 1987 (Termination Date: 1992)

U.S. History
Secondary--Basic
U.S. History: Grades 9-12
Addison-Wesley, 1986 (Termination Date: 1992)

U.S. History to 1877: Grades 9-12
Addison-Wesley, 1987 (Termination Date: 1992)

U.S. History from 1865: Grades 9-12
Addison-Wesley, 1987 (Termination Date: 1992)

A History of the United States: Grades 9-12
Allyn & Bacon/Prentice Hall, 1986 (Termination Date: 1992)

A History of the U.S. since 1861: Grades 9-12
Allyn & Bacon/Prentice Hall, 1986 (Termination Date: 1992)

America's Heritage: Grades 9-12
Allyn & Bacon/Prentice Hall, 1986 (Termination Date: 1992)

United States History--vol. 2: Grades 10-12
Merrill, 1986 (Termination Date: 1992)

The American Tradition: A History of the U.S.: Grades 10-12
Merrill, 1986 (Termination Date: 1992)

America Is: Grades 7-10
Merrill, 1985 (Termination Date: 1992)

Legacy of Freedom: Grades 10-12
Glencoe/Macmillan/McGraw-Hill, 1986 (Termination Date: 1992)

Legacy of Freedom: Grades 9-10
Glencoe/Macmillan/McGraw-Hill, 1986 (Termination Date: 1992)

American History: Grades 7-12
Harcourt Brace Jovanovich, 1986 (Termination Date: 1992)

Triumph of the American Nation: 9-12
Harcourt Brace Jovanovich, 1990 (Termination Date: 1992)

The American Pageant: Grades 11-12
D. C. Heath, 1987 (Termination Date: 1992)

America: The Glorious Republic: Grades 9-12
Houghton Mifflin, 1988 (Termination Date: 1992)

A History of the American People: Grades 9-12
Holt, Rinehart and Winston/Harcourt Brace Jovanovich, 1986 (Termination Date: 1992)

Our Land, Our Time: Grades 9-12
Holt, Rinehart and Winston/Coronado, 1986 (Termination Date: 1992)

We Are One: Grade 9-12
Holt, Rinehart and Winston/Coronado, 1987 (Termination Date: 1992)

The American People: Grades 9+
McDougal, Littell, 1986 (Termination Date: 1992)

The Americans: Grades 9+
McDougal, Littell, 1988 (Termination Date: 1992)

The United States: A History of the Republic: Grades 9-12
Prentice Hall, 1988 (Termination Date: 1992)

A History of the Republic: Grades 7-10, 9-12
Prentice Hall, 1986 (Termination Date: 1992)

American History: A Survey: Grades 10-12
Random House, 1987 (Termination Date: 1992)

Land of Promise: Grades 9-12
Scott, Foresman, 1986 (Termination Date: 1992)

Land of Promise--A History of the U.S.: Grades 9-12
Scott, Foresman, 1987 (Termination Date: 1992)

Life & Liberty: Grades 9-12
Scott, Foresman, 1987 (Termination Date: 1992)

U.S. History
Secondary--Supplemental

Taking Sides: Clashing Views on Controversial Issues in American History: Grades Sec.
Dushkin, n.d. (Termination Date: 1992)

Annual Editions: American History: Grade 11
Dushkin, 1987 (Termination Date: 1992)

The HBJ Historian: Grades 9-12
Harcourt Brace Jovanovich, 1986 (Termination Date: 1992)

U.S. History Test Bank: Grades 9-12
Harcourt Brace Jovanovich, 1986 (Termination Date: 1992)

The Constitution: Foundation of Our Freedom: Grades 7-12
Harcourt Brace Jovanovich, 1990 (Termination Date: 1992)

Great Cases of the Supreme Court: Grades 7-12
Houghton Mifflin, 1989 (Termination Date: 1992)

Vital Issues of the Constitution: Grades 7-12
Houghton Mifflin, 1989 (Termination Date: 1992)

McDougal Littell Study Guide for the U.S. Constitution: Grades 7+
McDougal, Littell, 1987 (Termination Date: 1992)

Update, History of the U.S. since 1945: Grades 9-12
Scholastic, 1987 (Termination Date: 1992)

American Government
Secondary Basic

Macgruder's American Government: Grades 9-12
Allyn & Bacon/Prentice Hall, 1989 (Termination Date: 1992)

American Government: Principles and Practices: Grades 9-12
Merrill, 1987 (Termination Date: 1992)

American Government: The Republic in Action: Grades 9-12
Harcourt Brace Jovanovich, 1986 (Termination Date: 1992)

American Government: Institutions and Policies: Grades 11-12
D. C. Heath, 1986 (Termination Date: 1992)

Government in America: Grades Sec.
Houghton Mifflin, 1988 (Termination Date: 1992)

Consent of The Governed--A Study of American Government: Grades 9-12
Scott, Foresman, 1988 (Termination Date: 1992)

Government in the U.S.: Grades 9-12
Scribner, 1987 (Termination Date: 1992)

American Government
Secondary--Supplemental
Annual Editions: American Government: Grade 12
Dushkin, 1987 (Termination Date: 1992)

Taking Sides: Clashing Views on Controversial Political Issues: Grade 12
Dushkin, 1987 (Termination Date: 1992)

American Government Test Bank: Grades 9-12
Harcourt Brace Jovanovich, 1986 (Termination Date: 1992)

Our Constitution and What It Means: Grades 5-12
McGraw-Hill, 1987 (Termination Date: 1992)

The Constitution: Yesterday, Today and Tomorrow: Grades 6-9
Scholastic, 1987 (Termination Date: 1992)

The Constitution: Grades 7-12
Scott, Foresman, 1985 (Termination Date: 1992)

Totalitarianism: Adversary of Democracy: Grades 9-12
Walsworth, 1986 (Termination Date: 1992)

Teaching the Constitution: A Collection of Lessons: 1987 Grades 7-12
Walsworth, 1986 (Termination Date: 1992)

Northwest History
Secondary--Basic
State and Local Government: Grades 7-12
University of Idaho Press, 1984 (Termination Date: 1992)

Northwest History
Secondary--Supplemental
The Pacific Northwest: Past, Present and Future: Grades 8-12
Directed Media, 1986 (Termination Date: 1992)

A Panorama of Idaho: Grade 8
Walsworth, 1988 (Termination Date: 1992)

Geography
Secondary--Basic
World Geography: Grades 7-12
Allyn & Bacon/Prentice Hall, 1986 (Termination Date: 1992)

World Geography: People and Places: Grades 10-12
Merrill, 1989 (Termination Date: 1992)

Laidlaw World Geography: Grades 7-12
Glencoe/Macmillan/McGraw-Hill, Laidlaw, 1987 (Termination Date: 1992)

Glencoe World Geography: Grades 10-12
Glencoe/Macmillan/McGraw-Hill, 1989 (Termination Date: 1992)

Exploring the Non-Western World: Grades 7-12
Globe, 1988 (Termination Date: 1992)

Exploring a Changing World: Grades 7-12
Globe, 1988 (Termination Date: 1992)

World Geography: Grades 7-12
Harcourt Brace Jovanovich, 1989 (Termination Date: 1992)

World Geography Today: Grades 9-12
Harcourt Brace Jovanovich, 1989 (Termination Date: 1992)

Heath World Geography: Grades 9-12
D. C. Heath, 1989 (Termination Date: 1992)

Geography: Grades 7-10
Houghton Mifflin, 1985 (Termination Date: 1992)

McGraw-Hill World Geography: Grades 9-10
McGraw-Hill, 1989 (Termination Date: 1992)

World Geography: Grades 9+
McDougal, Littell, 1986 (Termination Date: 1992)

World Geography: Grades 7-10
Scholastic, 1987 (Termination Date: 1992)

Scott, Foresman World Geography: Grades 9-12
Scott, Foresman, 1989 (Termination Date: 1992)

Geography
Secondary--Supplemental
Follett Student Atlas: Grades 4-12
Allyn & Bacon/Prentice Hall, 1986 (Termination Date: 1992)

Regional Studies Series: Grades 9-12
Globe, 1987 (Termination Date: 1992)

Scott, Foresman World Atlas: Grades 7-12
Scott, Foresman, 1988 (Termination Date: 1992)

Psychology
Secondary--Basic
Psychology: A Concise Introduction: Grades 11-12
Dushkin, 1987 (Termination Date: 1992)

Psychology: Its Principles and Applications: Grades 9-12
Harcourt Brace Jovanovich, 1984 (Termination Date: 1992)

Psychology: Grades 9-12
Harcourt Brace Jovanovich, 1989 (Termination Date: 1992)

Psychology: Grades 9-12
Holt, Rinehart and Winston/Harcourt Brace Jovanovich, 1986 (Termination Date: 1992)

Psychology: Exploring Behavior: Grades 9-12
Random House, 1985 (Termination Date: 1992)

Understanding Psychology: Grades 10-12
Random House, 1986 (Termination Date: 1992)

Invitation to Psychology: Grades 9-12
Scott, Foresman, 1989 (Termination Date: 1992)

Psychology
Secondary--Supplemental
Taking Sides: Clashing Views on Controversial Psychological Issues: Grades 11-12
Dushkin, 1986 (Termination Date: 1992)

Annual Editions: Psychology: Grades 11-12
Dushkin, 1987 (Termination Date: 1992)

Sociology
Secondary Basic
Sociology: The Study of Human Relations: Grades 7-12
Harcourt Brace Jovanovich, 1990 (Termination Date: 1992)

Sociology: Understanding Society: Grades 9-12
Prentice Hall, 1984 (Termination Date: 1992)

Sociology
Secondary--Supplemental
Taking Sides: Clashing Views on Controversial Social Issues: Grades 11-12
Dushkin, 1986 (Termination Date: 1992)

Annual Editions: Sociology: Grades 11-12
Dushkin, 1987 (Termination Date: 1992)

Law-Related Education
Secondary--Supplemental
Understanding the Law: Grades 9+
McDougal, Littell, 1983 (Termination Date: 1992)

Criminal Justice & Civil Justice: Grades 7-12
Scholastic, 1984 (Termination Date: 1992)

Street Law: A Course in Practical Law: Grades Sec.
West, 1986 (Termination Date: 1992)

Economics
Secondary--Basic
Economics: Grades 11-12
Addison-Wesley, 1988 (Termination Date: 1992)

Our Economy: How It Works: Grades 7-10
Addison-Wesley, 1988 (Termination Date: 1992)

Economics: Principles and Practices: Grades 9-12
Merrill, 1987 (Termination Date: 1992)

The Study of Economics: Principles, Concepts and Applications: Grade 12
Dushkin, 1987 (Termination Date: 1992)

The American Economic System--Free Enterprise: Grades 9-12
Glencoe/Macmillan/McGraw-Hill, Laidlaw, 1987 (Termination Date: 1992)

Economics: Free Enterprise in Action: Grades 9-12
Harcourt Brace Jovanovich, 1988 (Termination Date: 1992)

Economics for Decision Making: Grades 10-12
D. C. Heath, 1988 (Termination Date: 1992)

Applied Economics: Grades 10-12
Junior Achievement, 1987 (Termination Date: 1992)

McDougal, Littell Economics: Grades 9+
McDougal, Littell, 1988 (Termination Date: 1992)

Scribner Economics: Grades 9-12
Scribner, 1988 (Termination Date: 1992)

Invitation to Economics: Grades 10-12
Scott, Foresman, 1988 (Termination Date: 1992)

Economics: The Science of Cost, Benefit and Choice: Grades 9-12
South-Western, 1988 (Termination Date: 1992)

Skills for Consumer Success: Grades 10-12
South-Western, 1987 (Termination Date: 1992)

Skills for Consumer Success, Susan Thompson Tests: Grades 10-12
South-Western, 1987 (Termination Date: 1992)

The World of Economics: Grades Sec.
South-Western, 1988 (Termination Date: 1992)

Economics: The Free Enterprise System: Grades Sec.
South-Western, 1988 (Termination Date: 1992)

Economics
Secondary--Supplemental
Decisions--Making Personal Economic Choices: Grades Sec.
EMC, 1985 (Termination Date: 1992)

Economics and the American Free Enterprise System: Grades 9-12
Globe, 1988 (Termination Date: 1992)

Economics in America: Grades 9-12
Greenhaven Press, 1996 (Termination Date: 1992)

Indiana

Social Studies
HBJ Social Studies: Grades 1-5
Harcourt Brace Jovanovich, 1991 (Termination Date: 1997)

Heath Social Studies: Grades 1-5
D. C. Heath, 1991 (Termination Date: 1997)

Houghton Mifflin Social Studies: Grades 1-5
Houghton Mifflin, 1991 (Termination Date: 1997)

Primary Social Studies Skills: Grades 1-2
Nystrom, 1989 (Termination Date: 1997)

People in Time and Place: Grades 1-7
Silver Burdett and Ginn, 1991 (Termination Date: 1997)

Global Studies, Western and Eastern Cultures
Human Heritage: A World History: Grade 6
Glencoe, 1989 (Termination Date: 1997)

HBJ Social Studies: Grade 6
Harcourt Brace Jovanovich, 1991 (Termination Date: 1997)

Exploring Our World Past and Present: Grades 6-7
D. C. Heath, 1991 (Termination Date: 1997)

A Message of Ancient Days: Grade 6
Houghton Mifflin, 1991 (Termination Date: 1997)

World: Past and Present: Grade 6
Macmillan, 1991 (Termination Date: 1997)

Scott, Foresman Social Studies: Grades 6-7
Scott, Foresman, 1991 (Termination Date: 1997)

People in Time and Place: Grades 6-7
Silver Burdett and Ginn, 1991 (Termination Date: 1997)

World Geography: Grade 7
Silver Burdett and Ginn, 1991 (Termination Date: 1997)

World Geography: People and Places: Grade 7
Glencoe, 1989 (Termination Date: 1997)

Exploring the Non-Western World: Grade 7
Globe, 1988 (Termination Date: 1997)

World Geography Today: Grade 7
Holt, Rinehart and Winston, 1989 (Termination Date: 1997)

Across the Centuries: Grade 7
Houghton Mifflin, 1991 (Termination Date: 1997)

The World around Us: Grade 7
Macmillan, 1991 (Termination Date: 1997)

United States History
Challenge of Freedom: Grade 8
Glencoe, 1990 (Termination Date: 1997)

Two Centuries of Progress: Grade 8
Glencoe, 1991 (Termination Date: 1997)

Exploring American History: Grade 8
Globe, 1991 (Termination Date: 1997)

The Story of America: Grade 8
Holt, Rinehart and Winston, 1991 (Termination Date: 1997)

The Story of America, Beginnings to 1914: Grade 8
Holt, Rinehart and Winston, 1991 (Termination Date: 1997)

A More Perfect Union: Grade 8
Houghton Mifflin, 1991 (Termination Date: 1997)

America's Story: Grade 8
Houghton Mifflin, 1990 (Termination Date: 1997)

The American People: A History to 1877: Grade 8
McDougal, Littell, 1989 (Termination Date: 1997)

The American Nation: Grade 8
Prentice Hall, 1991 (Termination Date: 1997)

A History of the Republic, to 1877: Grade 8
Prentice Hall, 1990 (Termination Date: 1997)

American Adventures: People Making History: Grade 8
Scholastic, 1991 (Termination Date: 1997)

America: People and the Dream: Grade 8
Scott, Foresman, 1991 (Termination Date: 1997)

One Flag, One Land: Grade 8
Silver Burdett and Ginn, 1990 (Termination Date: 1997)

Triumph of the American Nation: Grades 9-12
Holt, Rinehart and Winston, 1986 (Termination Date: 1997)

Our Land, Our Time: Grades 9-12
Holt, Rinehart and Winston, 1991 (Termination Date: 1997)

United States History: Grades 9-12
Holt, Rinehart and Winston, 1988 (Termination Date: 1997)

History of the United States: Grades 9-12
Houghton Mifflin, 1991 (Termination Date: 1997)

The American People: A History from 1877: Grades 9-12
McDougal, Littell, 1989 (Termination Date: 1997)

The Americans: Grades 9-12
McDougal, Littell, 1991 (Termination Date: 1997)

The United States: A History of the Republic: Grades 9-12
Prentice Hall, 1990 (Termination Date: 1997)

A History of the Republic from 1877: Grades 9-12
Prentice Hall, 1990 (Termination Date: 1997)

A History of the United States: Grades 9-12
Prentice Hall, 1990 (Termination Date: 1997)

A History of the United States since 1861: Grades 9-12
Prentice Hall, 1990 (Termination Date: 1997)

United States Government

Government for Everybody: Grades 9-12
Amsco, 1990 (Termination Date: 1997)

American Government: Principles/Practices: Grades 9-12
Glencoe, 1991 (Termination Date: 1997)

Government in the United States: Grades 9-12
Glencoe, 1990 (Termination Date: 1997)

Exploring American Citizenship: Grades 9-12
Globe, 1988 (Termination Date: 1997)

We the People: Grades 9-12
Holt, Rinehart and Winston, 1989 (Termination Date: 1997)

Government in America: Grades 9-12
Houghton Mifflin, 1991 (Termination Date: 1997)

Magruder's American Government: Grades 9-12
Prentice Hall, 1990 (Termination Date: 1997)

Citizenship/Civics

Civics: Grades 9-12
Addison-Wesley, 1991 (Termination Date: 1997)

Civics: Citizens in Action: Grades 9-12
Glencoe, 1990 (Termination Date: 1997)

Civics: Government and Citizenship: Grades 9-12
Prentice Hall, 1990 (Termination Date: 1997)

Civics for Americans: Grades 9-12
Scott, Foresman, 1991 (Termination Date: 1997)

Economics

Addison-Wesley Economics: Grades 9-12
Addison-Wesley, 1988 (Termination Date: 1997)

Economics: Institutions and Analysis: Grades 9-12
Amsco, 1985 (Termination Date: 1997)

Introduction to Economics: Grades 9-12
EMC, 1991 (Termination Date: 1997)

Economics: Principles and Practices: Grades 9-12
Glencoe, 1988 (Termination Date: 1997)

Economics: Today and Tomorrow: Grades 9-12
Glencoe, 1991 (Termination Date: 1997)

Basic Economic Principles: Grades 9-12
Glencoe, 1989 (Termination Date: 1997)

Economics for Decision Making: Grades 9-12
D. C. Heath, 1988 (Termination Date: 1997)

Economics: Free Enterprise in Action: Grades 9-12
Holt, Rinehart and Winston, 1988 (Termination Date: 1997)

McDougal, Littell Economics: Grades 9-12
McDougal, Littell, 1991 (Termination Date: 1997)

Scholastic Economics: Grades 9-12
Scholastic, 1991 (Termination Date: 1997)

Invitation to Economics: Grades 9-12
Scott, Foresman, 1988 (Termination Date: 1997)

Economics: Science of Cost: Grades 9-12
South-Western, 1988 (Termination Date: 1997)

Economics and Making Decisions: Grades 9-12
West, 1988 (Termination Date: 1997)

Psychology

Understanding Psychology: Grades 9-12
Glencoe, 1986 (Termination Date: 1997)

Psychology: Its Principles and Applications: Grades 9-12
Holt, Rinehart and Winston, 1989 (Termination Date: 1997)

Psychology: An Introduction: Grades 9-12
Prentice Hall, 1990 (Termination Date: 1997)

Invitation to Psychology: Grades 9-12
Scott, Foresman, 1989 (Termination Date: 1997)

Psychology and You: Grades 9-12
West, 1990 (Termination Date: 1997)

Sociology

Sociology: The Study of Human Relationship: Grades 9-12
Holt, Rinehart and Winston, 1990 (Termination Date: 1997)

Sociology: Understanding Society: Grades 9-12
Prentice Hall, 1990 (Termination Date: 1997)

Sociology: The Search for Social Patterns: Grades 9-12
Scholastic, 1989 (Termination Date: 1997)

World Geography

Global Geography: Grades 9-12
Amsco, 1986 (Termination Date: 1997)

World Geography: Physical/Cultural Approach: Grades 9-12
Glencoe, 1989 (Termination Date: 1997)

Heath World Geography: Grades 9-12
D. C. Heath, 1989 (Termination Date: 1997)

World Geography Today: Grades 9-12
Holt, Rinehart and Winston, 1989 (Termination Date: 1997)

World Geography: The Earth and Its People: Grades 9-12
Holt, Rinehart and Winston, 1989 (Termination Date: 1997)

Human Geography: People, Places and Cultures: Grades 9-12
Prentice Hall, 1989 (Termination Date: 1997)

Scholastic World Geography: Grades 9-12
Scholastic, 1989 (Termination Date: 1997)

Scott, Foresman World Geography: Grades 9-12
Scott, Foresman 1989 (Termination Date: 1997)

Geography: Our Changing World: Grades 9-12
West, 1990 (Termination Date: 1997)

World History/Civilization

Addison-Wesley World History: Grades 9-12
Addison-Wesley, 1991 (Termination Date: 1997)

The Human Experience: A World History: Grades 9-12
Glencoe, 1990 (Termination Date: 1997)

Exploring World History: Grades 9-12
Globe, 1990 (Termination Date: 1997)

World History: Perspectives on the Past: Grades 9-12
D. C. Heath, 1990 (Termination Date: 1997)

World History: Grades 9-12
Holt, Rinehart and Winston, 1990 (Termination Date: 1997)

World History: People and Nations: Grades 9-12
Holt, Rinehart and Winston, 1990 (Termination Date: 1997)

History of the World: Grades 9-12
Houghton Mifflin, 1990 (Termination Date: 1997)

Links Across Time and Place: Grades 9-12
McDougal, Littell, 1990 (Termination Date: 1997)

World History: Patterns of Civilization: Grades 9-12
Prentice Hall, 1990 (Termination Date: 1997)

The Pageant of World History: Grades 9-12
Prentice Hall, 1990 (Termination Date: 1997)

History and Life: Grades 9-12
Scott, Foresman, 1990 (Termination Date: 1997)

Living World History: Grades 9-12
Scott, Foresman, 1990 (Termination Date: 1997)

Kentucky

Elementary Social Studies

HBJ Social Studies: Grades K-6
Harcourt Brace Jovanovich, 1985 (Termination Date: 1993)

Frontier Kentucky: Grade 4
Kentucky Images, 1985 (Termination Date: 1993)

Kentucky: Story of Proud Heritage: Grade 5
Kentucky Images, 1987 (Termination Date: 1993)

Heath Social Studies: Grades 1-7
D. C. Heath, 1987 (Termination Date: 1993)

Holt Social Studies: Grades 1-6
Holt, Rinehart and Winston, 1986 (Termination Date: 1993)

Laidlaw Social Studies: Grades K-6
Laidlaw, 1985 (Termination Date: 1993)

Macmillan Social Studies: Grades 1-7
Macmillan, 1987 (Termination Date: 1993)

Scott, Foresman Social Studies: Grades K-7
Scott, Foresman, 1986 (Termination Date: 1993)

The World and Its People: Grades 1-5, 7
Silver Burdett and Ginn, 1986 (Termination Date: 1993)

Ginn Social Studies: America's Origins: Grades 1-7
School House, 1987 (Termination Date: 1993)

Addison-Wesley U.S. History to 1877: Grade 8
Addison Wesley, 1986 (Termination Date: 1993)

America: Glorious Republic, vol. 1: Grade 8
Houghton Mifflin, 1986 (Termination Date: 1993)

Legacy of Freedom, vol. 1: Grade 8
Laidlaw, 1986 (Termination Date: 1993)

History of the American Nation, vol. 1: Grade 8
Macmillan, 1986 (Termination Date: 1993)

Human Heritage: A World History: Grade 7
Merrill, 1985 (Termination Date: 1993)

United States History, vol. 1: Grade 8
Merrill, 1986 (Termination Date: 1993)

A History of the Republic: vol. 1: Grade 8
Prentice Hall, 1986 (Termination Date: 1993)

Land of Promise, vol. 1: Grade 8
Scott, Foresman, 1986 (Termination Date: 1993)

A World View: Grade 6
Silver Burdett and Ginn, 1985 (Termination Date: 1993)

One Flag, One Land, vol. 1: Grade 8
Silver Burdett and Ginn, 1986 (Termination Date: 1993)

The American People: History to 1877: Grade 8
McDougal, Littell, 1986 (Termination Date: 1993)

World History: Grade 7
Coronado, 1984 (Termination Date: 1993)

Our Land, Our Time: History of the U.S. from 1865:
Grade 8
Coronado, 1986 (Termination Date: 1993)

Kentucky Studies
Geography of Kentucky: Grades 9-12
Kentucky Images, 1987 (Termination Date: 1993)

Law and Justice
American Civics: Grades 9-12
Harcourt Brace Jovanovich, 1987 (Termination
Date: 1993)

Civics: Citizens in Action: Grades 9-12
Merrill, 1986 (Termination Date: 1993)

We the People: Grades 9-12
Coronado, 1983 (Termination Date: 1993)

Street Law: Course in Practical Law: Grades 9-12
West, 1986 (Termination Date: 1993)

Geography
World Geography: Grades 9-12
Allyn & Bacon, 1986 (Termination Date: 1993)

Exploring a Changing World: Grade 9
Globe, 1984 (Termination Date: 1993)

Heath World Geography: Grades 9-12
D. C. Heath, 1987 (Termination Date: 1993)

World Geography Today: Grades 9-12
Holt, Rinehart and Winston, 1985 (Termination
Date: 1993)

Geography: Grades 9-12
Houghton Mifflin, 1985 (Termination Date: 1993)

Laidlaw World Geography: Grades 9-12
Laidlaw, 1987 (Termination Date: 1993)

World Geography: People and Places: Grades 9-12
Merrill, 1984 (Termination Date: 1993)

People on Earth: A World Geography: Grades 9-12
Scott, Foresman, 1986 (Termination Date: 1993)

World Geography: Grades 9-12
Scribner, 1985 (Termination Date: 1993)

World Geography: Grades 9-12
McDougal, Littell, 1986 (Termination Date: 1993)

World Civilization
The Pageant of World History: Grades 9-12
Allyn & Bacon, 1986 (Termination Date: 1993)

Exploring World History: Grade 10
Globe, 1987 (Termination Date: 1993)

People & Nations: World History: Grades 9-12
Harcourt Brace Jovanovich, 1987 (Termination
Date: 1993)

World History: Story of Progress: Grades 9-12
Holt, Rinehart and Winston, 1987 (Termination
Date: 1993)

A History of the World: Grades 9-12
Houghton Mifflin, 1985 (Termination Date: 1993)

Achievements through the Ages: Grades 9-12
Laidlaw, 1985 (Termination Date: 1993)

The Human Experience: A World History: Grades
9-12
Merrill, 1985 (Termination Date: 1993)

World History: Patterns of Civilization: Grades 9-12
Prentice Hall, 1986 (Termination Date: 1993)

History and Life: Grades 9-12
Scott, Foresman, 1987 (Termination Date: 1993)

The Human Expression: Grades 9-12
Scribner, 1985 (Termination Date: 1993)

U.S. History
Addison-Wesley U.S. History from 1865: Grades 9-
12
Addison Wesley, 1986 (Termination Date: 1993)

History of the U.S. since 1861: Grades 9-12
Allyn & Bacon, 1986 (Termination Date: 1993)

Triumph of the American Nation: 1865-Present, vol.
2: Grades 9-12
Harcourt Brace Jovanovich, 1986 (Termination
Date: 1993)

Legacy of Freedom, vol. 2: Grades 9-12
Laidlaw, 1986 (Termination Date: 1993)

History of the American Nation, vol. 2: Grades 9-12
Macmillan, 1986 (Termination Date: 1993)

United States History, vol. 2: Grades 9-12
Merrill, 1986 (Termination Date: 1993)

A History of the Republic, vol. 2: Grades 9-12
Prentice Hall, 1986 (Termination Date: 1993)

Land of Promise, vol. 2: Grades 9-12
Scott, Foresman, 1986 (Termination Date: 1993)

One Flag, One Land, vol. 2: Grades 9-12
Silver Burdett and Ginn, 1986 (Termination Date: 1993)

Our Land, Our Time: History of the U.S. to 1877:
Grades 9-12
Coronado, 1986 (Termination Date: 1993)

Basic Economics
Essentials of Economics and Free Enterprise:
Grades 9-12
Addison-Wesley, 1987 (Termination Date: 1993)

*Economics and the American Free Enterprise
System:* Grades 9-12
Globe, 1983 (Termination Date: 1993)

The American Economy: Analysis: Grades 9-12
Houghton Mifflin, 1986 (Termination Date: 1993)

Economics: Principles & Practices: Grades 9-12
Merrill, 1983 (Termination Date: 1993)

Invitation to Economics: Grades 9-12
Scott, Foresman, 1985 (Termination Date: 1993)

Understanding Economics: Grades 9-12
Random House, 1986 (Termination Date: 1993)

Economics: Principles & Application: Grades 9-12
South-Western, 1985 (Termination Date: 1993)

Economics Today and Tomorrow: Grades 9-12
Scribner, 1984 (Termination Date: 1993)

McDougal, Littell Economics: Grades 9-12
McDougal, Littell, 1986 (Termination Date: 1993)

Decisions: Making Personal Economic Choices:
Grades 9-12
EMC, 1995 (Termination Date: 1993)

Psychology
Psychology: Principles & Applications: Grades 9-12
Harcourt Brace Jovanovich, 1984 (Termination
Date: 1993)

Psychology: Exploring Behavior: Grades 9-12
Prentice Hall, 1985 (Termination Date: 1993)

Invitation to Psychology: Grades 9-12
Scott, Foresman, 1985 (Termination Date: 1993)

Understanding Psychology: Grades 9-12
Random House, 1986 (Termination Date: 1993)

Political Science
Magruder's American Government: Grades 9-12
Allyn & Bacon, 1987 (Termination Date: 1993)

American Government: The Republic in Action:
Grades 9-12
Harcourt Brace Jovanovich, 1986 (Termination
Date: 1993)

American Government: Principles & Practice:
Grades 9-12
Merrill, 1987 (Termination Date: 1993)

Consent of the Governed: Grades 9-12
Scott, Foresman, 1987 (Termination Date: 1993)

Government in the United States: Grades 9-12
Scribner, 1987 (Termination Date: 1993)

American Government: We Are One: Grades 9-12
Coronado, 1987 (Termination Date: 1993)

Sociology
Sociology: Study of Human Relations: Grades 9-12
Harcourt Brace Jovanovich, 1982 (Termination
Date: 1993)

Sociology: Understanding Society: Grades 9-12
Prentice Hall, 1984 (Termination Date: 1993)

Special Education: Functional Social Studies I
America's Heritage: Grades 9-10
Allyn & Bacon, 1986 (Termination Date: 1993)

Special Education: Functional Social Studies II
Introduction to the Social Sciences: Grades 10-11
Allyn & Bacon, 1985 (Termination Date: 1993)

Life and Liberty--American History: Grades 10-11
Scott, Foresman, 1987 (Termination Date: 1993)

History of United States, Books 3-4: Grades 10-11
Entry, 1982 (Termination Date: 1993)

Special Education: Functional Social Studies III
Civics for Americans: Grades 11-12
Scott, Foresman, 1986 (Termination Date: 1993)

American Adventures: Grades 11-12
Steck-Vaughn, 1987 (Termination Date: 1993)

Our Government in Action: Grades 11-12
Janus, 1986 (Termination Date: 1993)

American Government--How It Works, Book 1:
Grades 11-12
Entry, 1984 (Termination Date: 1993)

We the People of the United States: Grades 11-12
Entry, 1984 (Termination Date: 1993)

Louisiana

Social Studies
HBJ Social Studies: Grades K-6
Harcourt Brace Jovanovich, 1991 (Termination Date: 1999)

Heath Social Studies: Grades K-6
D. C. Heath, 1991 (Termination Date: 1999)

The World around Us: Grades K-6
Macmillan, 1991 (Termination Date: 1999)

People in Time and Place: Grades K-6
Silver Burdett and Ginn, 1991 (Termination Date: 1999)

African American Studies
Black History Facts and Activity Book: Grades K-4
ABC Educational Services, 1990 (Termination Date: 1999)

Our Multiethnic Heritage: Grades 2-8
Childrens Press, 1990 (Termination Date: 1999)

The African American Experience: A History:
Grades 7-12
Globe, 1992 (Termination Date: 1999)

African-American Literature: Grades 9-12
Holt, Rinehart and Winston, 1992 (Termination Date: 1999)

American Government
Government for Everybody: Grades 9-12
Amsco, 1992 (Termination Date: 1999)

Government in the United States: Grades 10-12
Glencoe, 1990 (Termination Date: 1999)

Magruder's American Government: Grades 11-12
Prentice Hall, 1991 (Termination Date: 1999)

Consent of the Governed: Grades 7-12
Scott, Foresman, 1988 (Termination Date: 1999)

American History
History of a Free Nation: Grades 10-12
Glencoe, 1992 (Termination Date: 1999)

The Story of America: Grades 9-12
Holt, Rinehart and Winston, 1991 (Termination Date: 1999)

History of the United States: Grades 9-12
Houghton Mifflin, 1991 (Termination Date: 1999)

The Americans: A History: Grades 9-12
McDougal, Littell, 1992 (Termination Date: 1999)

A History of the United States: Grades 10-11
Prentice Hall, 1992 (Termination Date: 1999)

The United States: A History of the Republic:
Grades 10-11
Prentice Hall, 1990 (Termination Date: 1999)

American Voices, A History of the United States:
Grades 9-12
Scott, Foresman, 1992 (Termination Date: 1999)

American Studies
Comprehensive United States History: Grade 7
Amsco, 1986 (Termination Date: 1999)

Challenge of Freedom: Grade 7
Glencoe, 1990 (Termination Date: 1999)

Two Centuries of Progress: Grade 7
Glencoe, 1991 (Termination Date: 1999)

Exploring American History: Grade 7
Globe, 1991 (Termination Date: 1999)

America's Story: Grade 7-9
Houghton Mifflin, 1990 (Termination Date: 1999)

The American Nation: Grade 7
Prentice Hall, 1991 (Termination Date: 1999)

America, the People and the Dream: Grade 7
Scott, Foresman, 1991 (Termination Date: 1999)

Civics
Civics: Grades 7-12
Addison-Wesley, 1991 (Termination Date: 1999)

American Government: Principles and Practices:
Grades 10-12
Glencoe, 1991 (Termination Date: 1999)

Civics: Citizens in Action: Grade 9
Glencoe, 1990 (Termination Date: 1999)

Civics: Responsibilities and Citizenship: Grade 9
Glencoe, 1992 (Termination Date: 1999)

Exploring American Citizenship: Grades 9-12
Globe, 1992 (Termination Date: 1999)

American Civics: Grades 9-12
Holt, Rinehart and Winston, 1992 (Termination
Date: 1999)

Civics: Government and Citizenship: Grade 9
Prentice Hall, 1990 (Termination Date: 1999)

Civics for Americans: Grades 7-12
Scott, Foresman, 1991 (Termination Date: 1999)

Economics
Economics: Institution and Analysis: Grades 10-12
Amsco, 1991 (Termination Date: 1999)

Economics: Principles and Practices: Grades 10-12
Glencoe, 1988 (Termination Date: 1999)

Introduction to Economics: Grades 10-12
EMC, 1991 (Termination Date: 1999)

The Economic Problem: Grades 10-12
Prentice Hall, 1990 (Termination Date: 1999)

Invitation to Economics: Grades 10-12
Scott, Foresman, 1988 (Termination Date: 1999)

Free Enterprise
Economics for Everybody: Grades 9-12
Amsco, 1992 (Termination Date: 1999)

Economics: Today and Tomorrow: Grades 10-12
Glencoe, 1991 (Termination Date: 1999)

Basic Economic Principles: Grades 10-12
Glencoe, 1989 (Termination Date: 1999)

Decisions: Making Personal Economic Choices:
Grades 9-12
EMC, 1992 (Termination Date: 1999)

Economics: Free Enterprises in Action: Grades 9-12
Holt, Rinehart and Winston, 1988 (Termination
Date: 1999)

Economics: Grades 9-12
McDougal, Littell, 1991 (Termination Date: 1999)

Economics: Grades 9-12
Scholastic (Termination Date: 1999)

Economics: The Free Enterprise System: Grades 9-
12
South-Western, 1988 (Termination Date: 1999)

Louisiana Studies
America the Beautiful: Grade 8
Chldrens Press, 1988 (Termination Date: 1999)

Louisiana: The Pelican State: Grade 8
Louisiana State University Press, 1985 (Termination Date: 1999)

Louisiana: Its Land and People: Grade 8
Louisiana State University Press, 1985 (Termination Date: 1999)

Louisiana: The Land and Its People: Grade 8
Pelican, 1986 (Termination Date: 1999)

Louisiana: A Study in Diversity: Grade 8
Steck-Vaughn, 1992 (Termination Date: 1999)

Psychology
Understanding Psychology: Grades 10-12
Glencoe, 1992 (Termination Date: 1999)

Psychology: Its Principles and Applications: Grades 9-12
Holt, Rinehart and Winston, 1989 (Termination Date: 1999)

Psychology: Grades 11-12
Prentice Hall, 1990 (Termination Date: 1999)

Invitation to Psychology: Grades 7-12
Scott, Foresman, 1989 (Termination Date: 1999)

Psychology and You: Grades 9-12
West, (Termination Date: 1999)

Sociology
Sociology: The Study of Human Relationships: Grades 9-12
Holt, Rinehart and Winston, 1990 (Termination Date: 1999)

Sociology: Understanding Society: Grades 11-12
Prentice Hall, 1990 (Termination Date: 1999)

Western Civilization
Living World History: Grades 9-12
Scott, Foresman, 1990 (Termination Date: 1999)

World Geography
Global Geography: Grades 10-12
Amsco, 1986 (Termination Date: 1999)

World Geography: Grades 10-12
Glencoe, 1992 (Termination Date: 1999)

Exploring A Changing World: Grades 9-12
Globe, 1988 (Termination Date: 1999)

World Geography Today: Grades 9-12
Holt, Rinehart and Winston, 1992 (Termination Date: 1999)

World Geography: Grades 9-11
Prentice Hall, 1992 (Termination Date: 1999)

World Geography: Grades 9-12
Scholastic (Termination Date: 1999)

Scott, Foresman World Geography: Grades 7-12
Scott, Foresman, 1989 (Termination Date: 1999)

Geography: Our Changing World: Grades 9-12
West, 1990 (Termination Date: 1999)

Addison-Wesley World History: Grades 9-12
Addison-Wesley, 1991 (Termination Date: 1999)

World History: The Human Experience: Grades 10-12
Glencoe, 1992 (Termination Date: 1999)

Exploring World History: Grades 9-12
Globe, 1990 (Termination Date: 1999)

World History: People and Nations: Grades 9-12
Holt, Rinehart and Winston, 1990 (Termination Date: 1999)

Perspectives on the Past: Grades 9-12
D. C. Heath, 1992 (Termination Date: 1999)

History of the World: Grades 9-12
Houghton Mifflin, 1992 (Termination Date: 1999)

World History: Patterns of Civilization: Grades 10-11
Prentice Hall, 1991 (Termination Date: 1999)

The Pageant of World History: Grades 10-11
Prentice Hall, 1990 (Termination Date: 1999)

History and Life: Grades 9-12
Scott, Foresman, 1990 (Termination Date: 1999)

Social Studies: Special Education, Gifted and Talented
The American Nation: Grades 9-12
Scott, Foresman, 1991 (Termination Date: 1999)

Voices: Grades 5-8
Steck-Vaughn, 1991 (Termination Date: 1999)

Social Studies: Special Education, Honors
A History of the United States: Grades 10-12
Brandywine Press, 1991 (Termination Date: 1999)

Government by the People: Grades 10-12
Prentice Hall, 1988, 1990-91 (Termination Date: 1999)

Louisiana Trivia Challenge: Grades 8-12
Radco, 1985 (Termination Date: 1999)

The American People: Grades 9-12
Scott, Foresman, 1990 (Termination Date: 1999)

Economics Today: Grades 9-12
Scott, Foresman, 1991 (Termination Date: 1999)

Government in America: People, Politics, and Policy: Grades 9-12
Scott, Foresman, 1991 (Termination Date: 1999)

Civilization in the West: Grades 9-12
Scott, Foresman, 1991 (Termination Date: 1999)

Psychology: Grades 9-12
Scott, Foresman, 1991 (Termination Date: 1999)

Social Studies: Special Education, Regular

Mastering Social Studies: Grades 10-12
Amsco, 1992 (Termination Date: 1999)

Mastering American History Skills: Grades 10-12
Amsco, 1989 (Termination Date: 1999)

World History: Grades 10-12
Amsco, 1990 (Termination Date: 1999)

Government and You: Grades 10-12
Amsco, 1990 (Termination Date: 1999)

Basic Principles of American Government: Grades 10-12
Amsco, 1992 (Termination Date: 1999)

Economics and You: Grades 10-12
Amsco, 1991 (Termination Date: 1999)

American History: Grades 10-12
Amsco, 1989 (Termination Date: 1999)

Current Issues in American Democracy: Grades 10-12
Amsco, 1992 (Termination Date: 1999)

World Geography: People and Places: Grades 9-12
Glencoe, 1989 (Termination Date: 1999)

Building Skills in Geography: Grades 9-12
Glencoe, 1990 (Termination Date: 1999)

Fearon's United States History: Grades 7-12
Fearon/Janus, 1990 (Termination Date: 1999)

Quercus American History Series: Grades 6-12
Fearon/Janus, 1989 (Termination Date: 1999)

Quercus Biographies from American History Series: Grades 6-12
Fearon/Janus, 1987 (Termination Date: 1999)

Meet the States: Grades 5-12
Fearon/Janus, 1990 (Termination Date: 1999)

Quercus Nation Builders Biographies Series: Grades 7-12
Fearon/Janus, 1990 (Termination Date: 1999)

Our Century Magazines: Grades 7-12
Fearon/Janus (Termination Date: 1999)

Janus United States: Grades 7-12
Fearon/Janus, 1988 (Termination Date: 1999)

Fearon's American Government: Grades 7-12
Fearon/Janus, 1990 (Termination Date: 1999)

Quercus Government and Civics Series: Grades 6-12
Fearon/Janus, 1989 (Termination Date: 1999)

Janus World History: Grades 7-12
Fearon/Janus, 1990 (Termination Date: 1999)

Fearon's World History: Grades 7-12
Fearon/Janus, 1990 (Termination Date: 1999)

Quercus World History Series: Grades 6-12
Fearon/Janus, 1989 (Termination Date: 1999)

Geography: Key Concepts and Basic Skills: Grades 7-12
Fearon/Janus, 1989 (Termination Date: 1999)

Fearon's Economics: Grades 7-12
Fearon/Janus, 1991 (Termination Date: 1999)

Quercus Economics Series: Grades 7-12
Fearon/Janus, 1989 (Termination Date: 1999)

World History: Grades 7-12
Fearon/Janus, 1990 (Termination Date: 1999)

Our Nation's History: Grades 6-12
Media Materials, 1992 (Termination Date: 1999)

Experiencing World History: Grades 6-12
Media Materials, 1991 (Termination Date: 1999)

U.S. Government: Grades 6-12
Media Materials, 1992 (Termination Date: 1999)

A Survey of World Culture Series: Grades 6-12
Media Materials, 1990 (Termination Date: 1999)

Learning about Our United States Series: Grades 6-12
Media Materials, 1988, 1990 (Termination Date: 1999)

First Map: Grades K-1
Nystrom, 1991 (Termination Date: 1999)

Geography Skills Program: Grades Elem.
Nystrom, 1991 (Termination Date: 1999)

Globe Skills Program: Grades Elem.
Nystrom, 1991 (Termination Date: 1999)

Steck-Vaughn Social Studies: Grades 1-6
Steck-Vaughn, 1991 (Termination Date: 1999)

Strategies for Success: Social Studies: Grades 4-8
Steck-Vaughn, 1989 (Termination Date: 1999)

World Geography and You: Grades 5-10
Steck-Vaughn, 1991, 1987 (Termination Date: 1999)

World History and You: Grades 5-10
Steck-Vaughn, 1990 (Termination Date: 1999)

America's Story: Grades 5-10
Steck-Vaughn, 1990, 1987 (Termination Date: 1999)

Steck-Vaughn Maps-Globes-Graphs: Grades 1-6
Steck-Vaughn, 1989 (Termination Date: 1999)

Becoming an Informed Citizen: Grades 6-8
Steck-Vaughn, 1990 (Termination Date: 1999)

My Country--the U.S.A.: Grades 6-8
Steck-Vaughn (Termination Date: 1999)

Amnesty: A Real-Life Approach: Grades 9-12
Steck-Vaughn (Termination Date: 1999)

Steck-Vaughn GED: Social Studies: Grades 9-12
Steck-Vaughn, 1991 (Termination Date: 1999)

GED Exercise Book Series: Social Studies: Grades 9-12
Steck-Vaughn, 1990 (Termination Date: 1999)

Economics: Concepts and Applications: Grades 7-8
Steck-Vaughn (Termination Date: 1999)

American Government: Freedom, Rights, and Responsibilities: Grades 7-8
Steck-Vaughn (Termination Date: 1999)

Mississippi

Social Studies (Average to Accelerated)
HBJ Social Studies: Grades 1-6
Harcourt Brace Jovanovich, 1985 (Termination Date: 1992)

Heath Social Studies: Grades 1-6
D. C. Heath, 1987 (Termination Date: 1992)

Macmillan Social Studies: Grades 1-6
Macmillan, 1987 (Termination Date: 1992)

Our Nation, Our World: Grades 1-6
Webster Div. McGraw-Hill, 1986 (Termination Date: 1992)

Scott, Foresman Social Studies: Grades 1-6
Scott, Foresman, 1986 (Termination Date: 1992)

The World and Its People: Grades 1-6
Silver Burdett and Ginn, 1985-86 (Termination Date: 1992)

General Social Studies
Introduction to the Social Sciences: Grades 9-12
Harcourt Brace Jovanovich, 1985 (Termination Date: 1992)

Mississippi History
Mississippi Life: Past and Present: Grade 7
Magnolia, 1987 (Termination Date: 1992)

Mississippi History through Four Centuries: Grade 7
Walthall, 1987 (Termination Date: 1992)

World Cultures
People, Time and Change: Grade 7
Allyn & Bacon, 1986 (Termination Date: 1992)

The World Today: Grade 7
D. C. Heath, 1987 (Termination Date: 1992)

Living in the World: Grade 7
Macmillan/Scribner/Laidlaw, 1985 (Termination Date: 1992)

Nations of the World: Grade 7
Macmillan, 1987 (Termination Date: 1992)

Our World: Lands and Cultures: Grade 7
Scott, Foresman, 1986 (Termination Date: 1992)

U.S. History

Our Land, Our Time: A History of the United States to 1877: Grade 8
Coronado, 1986 (Termination Date: 1992)

Our Land, Our Time: A History of the United States from 1865: Grades 9-12
Coronado, 1986-87 (Termination Date: 1992)

Our Land, Our Time: A History of the United States: Grades 9-12
Coronado, 1986-87 (Termination Date: 1992)

Triumph of the American Nation, vol. 1: Grade 8
Harcourt Brace Jovanovich, 1986 (Termination Date: 1992)

Triumph of the American Nation, vol. 2: Grades 9-12
Harcourt Brace Jovanovich, 1986 (Termination Date: 1992)

Triumph of the American Nation: Grades 9-12
Harcourt Brace Jovanovich, 1986 (Termination Date: 1992)

America: Its People and Values: Grade 8
Harcourt Brace Jovanovich, 1985 (Termination Date: 1992)

A Proud Nation: Grade 8
McDougal, Littell, 1985 (Termination Date: 1992)

A History of the Republic, vol. 1: Grade 8
Prentice Hall, 1986 (Termination Date: 1992)

A History of the Republic, vol. 2: Grades 9-12
Prentice Hall, 1986 (Termination Date: 1992)

The United States: A History of the Republic: Grades 9-12
Prentice Hall, 1986 (Termination Date: 1992)

The American Nation: Grade 8
Prentice Hall, 1986 (Termination Date: 1992)

Exploring American History: Grade 8
Globe, 1986 (Termination Date: 1992)

One Flag, One Land, vol. 1: Grade 8
Silver Burdett and Ginn, 1986 (Termination Date: 1992)

Life and Liberty: Grades 9-12
Scott, Foresman, 1987 (Termination Date: 1992)

Advanced Placement U.S. History

The American Pageant: Grades 9-12
D. C. Heath, 1983 (Termination Date: 1992)

World History

People and Nations: A World History: Grades 9-12
Harcourt Brace Jovanovich, 1987 (Termination Date: 1992)

World History: A Story of Progress: Grades 9-12
Holt, Rinehart and Winston, 1987 (Termination Date: 1992)

A History of the World: Grades 9-12
Houghton Mifflin, 1985 (Termination Date: 1992)

Achievements through the Ages: Grades 9-12
Glencoe/Laidlaw, 1985 (Termination Date: 1992)

The Human Experience: A World History: Grades 9-12
Glencoe/Merrrill, 1985 (Termination Date: 1992)

History and Life: The World and Its People: Grades 9-12
Scott, Foresman, 1987 (Termination Date: 1992)

The Pageant of World History: Grades 9-21
Allyn & Bacon, 1986 (Termination Date: 1992)

Advanced Placement World History

History of the Modern World: Grades 9-12
Random House, 1984 (Termination Date: 1992)

Ancient and Medieval History

The Human Venture, vol. 1: Grades 9-12
Prentice Hall, 1986 (Termination Date: 1992)

Mainstreams of Civilization: Grades 9-12
Glencoe/Scribner, 1983 (Termination Date: 1992)

U.S. Government

Magruder's American Government: Grades 9-12
Allyn & Bacon, 1987 (Termination Date: 1992)

We Are One: Grades 9-12
Coronado, 1987 (Termination Date: 1992)

American Government: The Republic in Action: Grades 9-12
Harcourt Brace Jovanovich, 1986 (Termination Date: 1992)

American Government: Principles and Practices: Grades 9-12
Gencoe/Merrill, 1987 (Termination Date: 1992)

Consent of the Governed: Grades 9-12
Scott, Foresman, 1987 (Termination Date: 1992)

Government in the U.S.: Grades 9-12
Glencoe/Merrill, 1987 (Termination Date: 1992)

Civics for Americans: Grades 9-12
Scott, Foresman, 1986 (Termination Date: 1992)

Advanced Placement U.S. Government
Government by the People: Grades 9-12
Prentice Hall, 1985 (Termination Date: 1992)

Mississippi: State and Local Government
Civics and Law for Mississippi: Grades 9-12
Magnolia, 1987 (Termination Date: 1992)

Law-Related Education
Law in American History: Grades 9-12
Scott, Foresman, 1983 (Termination Date: 1992)

American Law: Grades 9-12
South-Western, 1988 (Termination Date: 1992)

Street Law: A Course in Practical Law: Grades 9-12
West, 1986 (Termination Date: 1992)

Economics
The American Economic System: Free Enterprise: Grades 9-12
Glencoe/Laidlaw, 1987 (Termination Date: 1992)

McDougal, Littell Economics: Grades 9-12
McDougal, Littell, 1986 (Termination Date: 1992)

Economics: Principles and Practices: Grades 9-12
Glencoe/Merrrill, 1983 (Termination Date: 1992)

Invitation to Economics: Grades 9-12
Scott, Foresman, 1985 (Termination Date: 1992)

Economics Today and Tomorrow, Enterprise: Grades 9-12
Glencoe/Scribner, 1984 (Termination Date: 1992)

Psychology
Psychology: Its Principles and Applications: Grades 9-12
Harcourt Brace Jovanovich, 1984 (Termination Date: 1992)

Psychology: Exploring Behavior: Grades 9-12
Prentice Hall, 1985 (Termination Date: 1992)

Understanding Psychology: Grades 9-12
Random House, 1986 (Termination Date: 1992)

Invitation to Psychology: Grades 9-21
Scott, Foresman, 1985 (Termination Date: 1992)

Sociology
Sociology: The Study of Human Relationships: Grades 9-12
Harcourt Brace Jovanovich, 1982 (Termination Date: 1992)

Sociology: Understanding Society: Grades 9-12
Prentice Hall, 1984 (Termination Date: 1992)

Geography
World Geography: Grades 9-12
D. C. Heath, 1987 (Termination Date: 1992)

World Geography Today: Grades 9-12
Holt, Rinehart and Winston, 1985 (Termination Date: 1992)

Laidlaw World Geography: A Physical and Cultural Approach: Grades 9-12
Glencoe/Laidlaw, 1987 (Termination Date: 1992)

World Geography: Grades 9-12
McDougal, Littell, 1986 (Termination Date: 1992)

A World View: Grades 9-12
Silver Burdett and Ginn, 1985 (Termination Date: 1992)

Global Studies
Exploring World Cultures: Grades 9-12
Allyn & Bacon, 1986 (Termination Date: 1992)

Nevada

General Social Studies
Scott, Foresman Social Studies: Grades K-7
Scott, Foresman, 1988 (Termination Date: 1994)

HBJ Social Studies: Grades 1-6
Harcourt Brace Jovanovich, 1988 (Termination Date: 1992)

Silver Burdett and Ginn Social Studies: Grades K-8
Silver Burdett and Ginn, 1988, 1991 (Termination Date: 1992)

People in Time and Place: Grade 4
Silver Burdett and Ginn, 1991 (Termination Date: 1996)

HBJ Social Studies: Grades K-6
Harcourt Brace Jovanovich, 1991 (Termination Date: 1996)

Houghton Mifflin Social Studies: Grades 1-7
Houghton Mifflin, 1991 (Termination Date: 1996)

The World around Us: Grades K-6
Macmillan, 1990 (Termination Date: 1994)

American History

American Nation: Grade 8
Prentice Hall, 1990 (Termination Date: 1994)

American Adventures: Grade 7
Scholastic, 1987 (Termination Date: 1992)

United States History: Grades 10-12
Addison-Wesley, 1986 (Termination Date: 1994)

The American People: Creating a Nation and Society: Grade 11
Harper and Row, 1989 (Termination Date: 1994)

A History of the United States: Grade 11
Prentice Hall, 1990 (Termination Date: 1994)

United States History, Presidential History: Grades 10-12
Addison-Wesley, 1986 (Termination Date: 1993)

The American Pageant: A History of the Republic: Grades 10-12
D. C. Heath, 1987 (Termination Date: 1993)

History of the American People: Grades 10-12
Holt, Rinehart and Winston, 1986 (Termination Date: 1993)

America Is: Grades 7-8
Merrill, 1987 (Termination Date: 1993)

Land of Promise: A History of the United States: Grades 10-12
Scott, Foresman, 1987 (Termination Date: 1993)

History of the American Nation, vols. 1 & 2: Grades 7-8
Macmillan, 1987 (Termination Date: 1992)

The Challenge of Democracy: Grades 10-12
Houghton Mifflin, 1989 (Termination Date: 1995)

The Challenge of Freedom: Grade 8
Macmillan, 1986 (Termination Date: 1994)

America's Heritage: Grades 9-12
Ginn, 1986 (Termination Date: 1994)

Exploring U.S. History: Grades 9-12
Globe, 1986 (Termination Date: 1994)

U.S. History: The Story of America: Grades 9-12
Holt, Rinehart and Winston, 1991 (Termination Date: 1995)

The United States: A History of the Republic: Grades 9-12
Prentice Hall, 1990 (Termination Date: 1995)

The Americans: A History: Grades 9-12
McDougal, Littell, 1991 (Termination Date: 1995)

These United States: Questions of Our Past: Grades 10-12
Prentice Hall, 1989 (Termination Date: 1995)

The Enduring Vision: A History of the American People: Grades 9-12
D. C. Heath, 1990 (Termination Date: 1995)

A People and A Nation (A History of the United States): Grade 11
Houghton Mifflin, 1990 (Termination Date: 1995)

The Story of America: Grade 8
Harcourt Brace Jovanovich, 1991 (Termination Date: 1995)

One Flag, One Land, vol. 2: Grade 8
Silver Burdett and Ginn, 1990 (Termination Date: 1996)

America: The People and the Dream: Grades 6-8
Scott, Foresman, 1991 (Termination Date: 1996)

American Journey: The Quest for Liberty since 1865: Grades 9-10
Prentice Hall, 1992 (Termination Date: 1996)

American Adventures: People Making History: Grades 7-10
Scholastic, 1991 (Termination Date: 1996)

Our Country: Grade 5
Silver Burdett and Ginn, 1991 (Termination Date: 1996)

State History
Nevada: A History of Changes: Grade 8
Dangberg Foundation, 1987 (Termination Date: 1993)

World History
A World View: Grade 7
Silver Burdett and Ginn, 1990 (Termination Date: 1993)

World History, A Pattern of Civilization: Grades 9-12
Prentice Hall, 1990 (Termination Date: 1994)

World History: Perspectives on the Past: Grade 10
D. C. Heath, 1990 (Termination Date: 1993)

People and Nations: A World History: Grades 9-12
Harcourt Brace Jovanovich, 1990 (Termination Date: 1993)

A World History: Links across Time and Place: Grades 9-12
McDougal, Littell, 1988 (Termination Date: 1993)

Human Heritage: A World History: Grades 6-7
Merrill, 1989 (Termination Date: 1993)

Civilization: Past and Present: Grades 9-12
Scott, Foresman, 1987 (Termination Date: 1993)

Exploring World History: Grade 9
Globe, 1990 (Termination Date: 1995)

World History: Patterns of Civilization: Grades 9-12
Prentice Hall, 1990, 1991 (Termination Date: 1995)

Pageant of World History: Grades 7-12
Prentice Hall, 1990, 1991 (Termination Date: 1995)

World History: Perspectives on the Past: Grade 10
D. C. Heath, 1990 (Termination Date: 1995)

World History: Traditions and New Directions: Grades 9-12
Addison-Wesley, 1991 (Termination Date: 1995)

The Human Experience: A World History: Grades 9-12
Glencoe, 1990 (Termination Date: 1995)

The Western Heritage: Grade 12
Macmillan, 1987 (Termination Date: 1993)

Civics
Civics: Government and Citizenship: Grades 8-12
Prentice Hall, 1990 (Termination Date: 1993)

American Government
Magruder's American Government: Grades 9-12
Prentice Hall, 1990 (Termination Date: 1995)

American Government: Grades 9-12
Harper Row (Prentice Hall), 1988 (Termination Date: 1993)

Government in America: Grade 12
Houghton Mifflin, 1990 (Termination Date: 1993)

Government in the United States: Grade 12
Glencoe, 1990 (Termination Date: 1995)

Government by the People: Grade 12
Prentice Hall, 1990 (Termination Date: 1995)

American Government: Institution and Policies: Grade 12
D. C. Heath, 1989 (Termination Date: 1995)

Law
Living Law Program: Grade 7
Scholastic, 1988 (Termination Date: 1994)

Anthropology
Anthropology: Grades 10-12
Prentice Hall, 1988 (Termination Date: 1994)

Anthropology: The Explanation of Human Diversity: Grades 10-12
Random House, 1987 (Termination Date: 1993)

Economics
Scribner Economics: Grades 10-12
Glencoe, 1988 (Termination Date: 1994)

Geography

Geography: Grades 7-12
Houghton Mifflin, 1985 (Termination Date: 1994)

World Geography: Grade 7
McGraw-Hill, 1989 (Termination Date: 1994)

World Geography: Grades 11-12
Glencoe, 1990 (Termination Date: 1994)

World Geography: Grades 9-12
Prentice Hall, 1986 (Termination Date: 1994)

Laidlaw World Geography: Grades 7-12
Glencoe, 1987 (Termination Date: 1992)

World Geography: Grade 8
Scholastic, 1988 (Termination Date: 1992)

World Geography: The Earth and Its People: Grade 7
Harcourt Brace Jovanovich, 1991 (Termination Date: 1993)

World Geography: Grade 7
Silver Burdett and Ginn, 1991 (Termination Date: 1996)

Scott, Foresman World Geography: Grades 6-8
Scott, Foresman, 1989 (Termination Date: 1996)

World Geography: The Earth and Its People: Grades 7-12
Holt, Rinehart and Winston, 1989 (Termination Date: 1996)

Prentice Hall World Geography: Grades 9-12
Prentice Hall, 1992 (Termination Date: 1996)

Psychology

Psychology: Its Principles and Applications: Grades 9-12
Harcourt Brace Jovanovich, 1984 (Termination Date: 1993)

Psychology: Exploring Human Behavior: Grades 9-12
Prentice Hall, 1989 (Termination Date: 1993)

Sociology

Sociology: Understanding Society: Grades 9-12
Prentice Hall, 1989 (Termination Date: 1994)

Sociology: The Study of Human Relationships: Grades 9-12
Harcourt Brace Jovanovich, 1982 (Termination Date: 1993)

Scholastic Sociology: Grades 9-12
Scholastic, 1989 (Termination Date: 1993)

New Mexico

Ancient History
Mythology: Grades 9-12
Perma-Bound, 1969 (Termination Date: 1998)

Greek Gods: Grades 6-9
Perma-Bound, 1966 (Termination Date: 1998)

Book of Greek Myths: Grades 4-7
Perma-Bound, 1962 (Termination Date: 1998)

Social Studies (Area Studies)

Steck-Vaughn Voices: Grades 5-8
Steck-Vaughn, 1991 (Termination Date: 1998)

Construccion del Templo Mayar de Mexico: Grades 6-9
Perma-Bound, 1988 (Termination Date: 1998)

Springboard to Social Studies: Grades 5-8
Educational Activities, 1987 (Termination Date: 1998)

Civics
One People, One Flag: Grades 3-4
Curriculum Associates, 1990 (Termination Date: 1998)

Civics: Grades 9-12
Glencoe/McGraw-Hill, 1992 (Termination Date: 1998)

Unlocking the Constitution/Declaration of Independence: Grades 6-12
Globe, 1985 (Termination Date: 1998)

Exploring American Citizenship: Grades 6-12
Globe, 1992 (Termination Date: 1998)

American Civics: Grades 7-9
Holt, Rinehart and Winston, 1992 (Termination Date: 1998)

Civics: Grades 7-12
Prentice Hall, 1990 (Termination Date: 1998)

Civics for Americans: Grades 7-12
Scott, Foresman, 1983-91 (Termination Date:
1998)

Civics: Grades 8-12
Addison-Wesley, 1991 (Termination Date: 1998)

Consumer Education
Mi Cocina: Grades 9-12
DDL, 1990 (Termination Date: 1998)

Decisions: Making Personal Economic Choices:
Grades 9-12
EMC, 1992 (Termination Date: 1998)

Consumers and the Law: Grades 7-12
Educational Activities, 1987 (Termination Date:
1998)

Fearon's Practical Mathematics: Grades 7-12
Fearon/Janus/Quercus, 1990 (Termination Date:
1998)

Budgeting & Spending Skills, 1-2: Grades 7-12
Fearon/Janus/Quercus, 1988 (Termination Date:
1998)

Economics
Economics: Today and Tomorrow: Grades 9-12
Glencoe/McGraw-Hill, 1991 (Termination Date:
1998)

Understanding Economics: Grades 9-12
Glencoe/McGraw-Hill, 1991 (Termination Date:
1998)

Basic Economic Principles: Grades 9-12
Glencoe/McGraw-Hill, 1989 (Termination Date:
1998)

Economics: Principles & Practices: Grades 9-12
Glencoe/McGraw-Hill, 1988 (Termination Date:
1998)

Introduction to Economics: Grades 9-12
EMC, 1991 (Termination Date: 1998)

*Economics and the American Free Enterprise
System:* Grades 9-12
Globe, 1988 (Termination Date: 1998)

Economics: Free Enterprise/Action: Grades 9-12
Holt, Rinehart and Winston, 1988 (Termination
Date: 1998)

Economics Today: Grades 9-12
Scott, Foresman, 1991 (Termination Date: 1998)

Economics of Work: Grades 9-12
South-Western, 1988 (Termination Date: 1998)

Economics: The Science of Cost, Benefit & Choice:
Grades 9-12
South-Western, 1988 (Termination Date: 1998)

The World of Economics: Grades 9-12
South-Western, 1988 (Termination Date: 1998)

Consumer Economics: Grades 9-12
South-Western, 1988 (Termination Date: 1998)

Economic Experiences: Grades 9-12
South-Western, 1990 (Termination Date: 1998)

International Trade Studies: Import/Export Pro:
Grades 9-12
South-Western, 1992 (Termination Date: 1998)

Longman: Economics: Our American Economy:
Grades 9-12
Addison-Wesley, 1990 (Termination Date: 1998)

McDougal, Littell Economics: Grades 9-12
McDougal, Littell, 1991 (Termination Date: 1998)

Bonds, Preferred Stocks, & the Money Market:
Grades 8-12
Perma-Bound, 1988 (Termination Date: 1998)

Investing and Trading: Grades 8-12
Perma-Bound, 1988 (Termination Date: 1998)

Wall Street--How It Works: Grades 8-12
Perma-Bound, 1988 (Termination Date: 1998)

What Is a Share of Stock?: Grades 8-12
Perma-Bound, 1988 (Termination Date: 1998)

Economics and You: Grades 9-12
Amsco, 1991 (Termination Date: 1998)

Economics: Institutions and Analysis: Grades 9-12
Amsco, 1991 (Termination Date: 1998)

Economics for Everybody: Grades 7-12
Amsco, 1991 (Termination Date: 1998)

Quercus Economics 1-2: Grades 7-12
Fearon/Janus/Quercus, 1989 (Termination Date:
1998)

Elementary Social Studies

American Biographies: Grades 2-6
Econo-Clad, 1985 (Termination Date: 1998)

Social Studies Set: Grades K-9
Econo-Clad, 1990 (Termination Date: 1998)

Young Explorers, Social Studies: Grades 1-3
Modern Curriculum Press, 1990 (Termination
Date: 1998)

People in Time and Place: Grades K-7
Silver Burdett and Ginn, 1991 (Termination Date:
1998)

Bookline: Grades 1-6
Scholastic, 1991 (Termination Date: 1998)

HBJ Social Studies: Grades 1-6
Harcourt Brace Jovanovich, 1991 (Termination
Date: 1998)

Heath Social Studies: Grades K-7
D. C. Heath, 1991 (Termination Date: 1998)

The World around Us: Grade K-6
Macmillan/McGraw-Hill, 1990-91 (Termination
Date: 1998)

The World, Past and Present: Grade 6
Macmillan/McGraw-Hill, 1991 (Termination
Date: 1998)

Latin America and Canada: Grade 6
Macmillan/McGraw-Hill, 1991 (Termination
Date: 1998)

Basic Map Skills, English & Spanish: Grade 4
Hammond, 1991 (Termination Date: 1998)

World History through Maps: Grades 6-7
Hammond, 1984 (Termination Date: 1998)

American History through Maps: Grade 5
Hammond, 1984 (Termination Date: 1998)

Scott, Foresman Social Studies: Grades 6-7
Scott, Foresman, 1990-91 (Termination Date:
1998)

Steck-Vaughn Social Studies: Grades 1-6
Steck-Vaughn, 1991 (Termination Date: 1998)

El Algodon: Grades 1-3
Perma-Bound, 1987 (Termination Date: 1998)

Las Mariposas: Grades K-3
Perma-Bound, 1988 (Termination Date: 1998)

Tres Colorantes Prehispanicos: Grades 3-5
Perma-Bound, 1985 (Termination Date: 1998)

Un Dia en el Desierto: Grades 3-6
Perma-Bound, 1987 (Termination Date: 1998)

El Valle de la Niebla: Grades 1-4
Perma-Bound, 1987 (Termination Date: 1998)

Cuatro Elementos: Grades K-3
Perma-Bound, 1983-85 (Termination Date: 1998)

Cuatro Estaciones: Grades K-3
Perma-Bound, 1983-84 (Termination Date: 1998)

El Clima y Sus Cambios: Grades K-3
Perma-Bound, 1989 (Termination Date: 1998)

Criptas de Kaua y Otras Leyendas de America:
Grades 4-7
Perma-Bound, 1986 (Termination Date: 1998)

Decendientes de Sol y Otras Leyendas de America:
Grades 4-7
Perma-Bound, 1986 (Termination Date: 1998)

Let's Discover Series: Grades K-3
Perma-Bound, 1986 (Termination Date: 1998)

Constitutional Convention: Grades 4-7
Perma-Bound, 1985 (Termination Date: 1998)

Shh! We're Writing the Constitution: Grades 4-7
Perma-Bound, 1987 (Termination Date: 1998)

Children of the Wild West: Grades 4-7
Perma-Bound, 1983 (Termination Date: 1998)

Ciudad: Grades K-3
Perma-Bound, 1986 (Termination Date: 1998)

El Azucar: Grades 2-5
Perma-Bound, 1985 (Termination Date: 1998)

Campo y la Ciudad: Grades 1-3
Perma-Bound, 1989 (Termination Date: 1998)

Indian Chiefs: Grades 4-7
Perma-Bound, 1987 (Termination Date: 1998)

Incredible Journey of Lewis & Clark: Grades 4-7
Perma-Bound, 1987 (Termination Date: 1998)

Journey through History: Grades 2-4
Perma-Bound, 1988 (Termination Date: 1998)

La Lana: Grades 1-3
Perma-Bound, 1983 (Termination Date: 1998)

Martin Luther King, Jr.: Grades 4-7
Perma-Bound, 1989 (Termination Date: 1998)

Dinosaurs Walked Here and Other Stories: Grades 4-7
Perma-Bound, 1987 (Termination Date: 1998)

Leyendas Populares Españolas: Grades 4-7
Perma-Bound, 1985 (Termination Date: 1998)

Our Independence and the Constitution: Grades 4-7
Perma-Bound, 1950 (Termination Date: 1998)

Tierra: Grades 4-7
Perma-Bound, 1987 (Termination Date: 1998)

Going to School in 1876: Grades 4-7
Perma-Bound, 1984 (Termination Date: 1998)

¿Por Que?: Grades K-3
Perma-Bound, 1987 (Termination Date: 1998)

¿Que?: Grades K-3
Perma-Bound, 1987 (Termination Date: 1998)

Susanna of the Alamo: A True Story: Grades 2-5
Perma-Bound, 1986 (Termination Date: 1998)

Family Pictures: Grades 4-7
Perma-Bound, 1989 (Termination Date: 1998)

El Barro: Grades 1-3
Perma-Bound, 1983 (Termination Date: 1998)

Birth of a Nation: Grades 4-7
Perma-Bound, 1989 (Termination Date: 1998)

El Camion: Grades K-3
Perma-Bound, 1987 (Termination Date: 1998)

La Casa de la Ciudad: Grades 1-3
Perma-Bound, 1987 (Termination Date: 1998)

El Comercio: Grades 1-4
Perma-Bound, 1987 (Termination Date: 1998)

Cuando No Voy a la Escuela: Grades K-3
Perma-Bound, 1987 (Termination Date: 1998)

Cuentos de Sal y Sol: Grades K-3
Perma-Bound, 1984 (Termination Date: 1998)

Fuego: Grades 2-5
Perma-Bound, 1985 (Termination Date: 1998)

Leyendas de la Antiqua America: Grades 4-8
Perma-Bound, 1981 (Termination Date: 1998)

Viaje Atravez Series: Grades 2-4
Perma-Bound, 1988 (Termination Date: 1998)

And then What Happened, Paul Revere?: Grades 3-6
Perma-Bound, 1973 (Termination Date: 1998)

Developing Skills with Globes: Grades 4-6
Nystrom, 1989 (Termination Date: 1998)

Geography

Geografia Humana y Economica: Grades 9-12
DDL, 1987 (Termination Date: 1998)

Geografia Historia: Grades 7-12
DDL, 1987 (Termination Date: 1998)

Geografia 3: Grades 6-12
DDL, 1988 (Termination Date: 1998)

Espacio y Sociedad 8 Geografia Universal: Grades 7-12
DDL, 1988 (Termination Date: 1998)

All about the U.S.A.: Grades 4-9
Encyclopaedia Britannica, 1987 (Termination Date: 1998)

The Development of Transportation: Grades 4-12
Encyclopaedia Britannica, 1989 (Termination Date: 1998)

Global View Series: Grades 5-6
Curriculum Associates, 1991 (Termination Date: 1998)

East African Safari: Grades 3-8
Look and See, 1989 (Termination Date: 1998)

The Indian Way: Learning to Communicate with Mother Earth: Grades 4-6
John Muir, 1990 (Termination Date: 1998)

The Kids' Environment Book: What's Awry and Why: Grades 6-9
John Muir, 1991 (Termination Date: 1998)

Rads, Ergs, and Cheeseburgers: Kids Guide to Energy and the Environment: Grades 4-6
John Muir, 1991 (Termination Date: 1998)

Glencoe World Geography: Grades 9-12
Glencoe/McGraw-Hill, 1992 (Termination Date: 1998)

World Geography: People and Places: Grades 7-9
Glencoe/McGraw-Hill, 1989 (Termination Date: 1998)

People in Time and Place: Grades 6-7
Silver Burdett and Ginn, 1992 (Termination Date: 1998)

Exploring Latin America: Grades 6-12
Globe, 1988 (Termination Date: 1998)

Exploring a Changing World: Grades 6-9
Globe, 1988 (Termination Date: 1998)

Exploring the Non-Western World: Grades 6-9
Globe, 1988 (Termination Date: 1998)

Unlocking Social Studies Skills: Grades 6-12
Globe, 1992 (Termination Date: 1998)

Unlocking Geography Skills: Grades 6-12
Globe, 1992 (Termination Date: 1998)

World Geography Today: Grades 9-12
Holt, Rinehart and Winston, 1992 (Termination Date: 1998)

Essential Map Skills: Grades 7-12
Hammond, 1986 (Termination Date: 1998)

Prentice Hall World Geography: Grades 7-12
Prentice Hall, 1992 (Termination Date: 1998)

Scott, Foresman World Geography: Grades 7-12
Scott, Foresman, 1989 (Termination Date: 1998)

Maps, Globes, Graphs: Grades 1-6
Steck-Vaughn, 1989 (Termination Date: 1998)

Mastering Social Studies Skills: Grades 7-9
Amsco, 1992 (Termination Date: 1998)

Reading Maps, Globes, Charts, Graphs: Grades 4-6
Educational Activities, 1982 (Termination Date: 1998)

Geography: Key Concepts and Basic Skills: Grades 6-12
Fearon/Janus/Quercus, 1989 (Termination Date: 1998)

Geography: Our Changing World: Grades 9-12
West, 1990 (Termination Date: 1998)

Government
Government in the United States: Grades 9-12
Glencoe/McGraw-Hill, 1990 (Termination Date: 1998)

American Government: Principles and Practices: Grades 9-12
Glencoe/McGraw-Hill, 1991 (Termination Date: 1998)

We the People: Grades 9-12
Holt, Rinehart and Winston, 1989 (Termination Date: 1998)

Magruder's American Government: Grades 9-12
Prentice Hall, 1991 (Termination Date: 1998)

Vital Issues of the Constitution: Grades 10-12
Houghton Mifflin, 1989 (Termination Date: 1998)

Government in America: Grades 11-12
Houghton Mifflin, 1992 (Termination Date: 1998)

Introduction to Comparative Government: Grades 9-12
Scott, Foresman, 1990 (Termination Date: 1998)

Government for Everybody: Grades 9-12
Amsco, 1992 (Termination Date: 1998)

Our Government in Action: Grades 7-12
Fearon/Janus/Quercus, 1986 (Termination Date: 1998)

Government & Civics Series: Grades 6-12
Fearon/Janus/Quercus, 1989 (Termination Date: 1998)

Humanities

Introduccion a la Filosofia: Grades 9-12
DDL, 1989 (Termination Date: 1998)

Problemas Morales de Existencia Humana: Grades 9-12
DDL, 1990 (Termination Date: 1998)

Mundo y Sociedad, 7-8: Grades 7-12
DDL, 1985 (Termination Date: 1998)

Filosofia 2: Grades 9-12
DDL, 1981 (Termination Date: 1998)

Crucible: Grades 9-12
Perma-Bound, 1954 (Termination Date: 1998)

Law-Related Education

Teens, Crime and the Community: Grades 7-12
West, 1988 (Termination Date: 1998)

Street Law: A Course in Practical Law: Grades 9-12
West, 1990 (Termination Date: 1998)

New Mexico History and Culture

Hispanic Biographies: Grades 2-7
Econo-Clad, 1990 (Termination Date: 1998)

New Mexico History and Culture: Grades K-8
Econo-Clad, 1984 (Termination Date: 1998)

Indian Perspectives in New Mexico History: Grades 6-12
New Mexico Indian Education, 1991 (Termination Date: 1998)

A History of New Mexico: Grade 7
University of New Mexico Press, 1991 (Termination Date: 1998)

New Mexico!: Grades 4-7
University of New Mexico Press, 1991 (Termination Date: 1998)

Psychology

Understanding Psychology: Grades 9-12
Glencoe/McGraw-Hill, 1992 (Termination Date: 1998)

Psychology: Its Principles and Applications: Grades 9-12
Holt, Rinehart and Winston, 1989 (Termination Date: 1998)

Psychology: Grades 9-12
Scott, Foresman, 1990 (Termination Date: 1998)

Psychology and You: Grades 9-12
West, 1990 (Termination Date: 1998)

Sociology

Sociology: The Study of Human Relationships: Grades 9-12
Holt, Rinehart and Winston, 1990 (Termination Date: 1998)

Sociology: Understanding Society: Grades 9-12
Prentice Hall, 1990 (Termination Date: 1998)

U.S. History

U.S. History--Secondary--Fiction: Grades 5-12
Econo-Clad, 1990 (Termination Date: 1998)

U.S. History--Secondary--Non-Fiction: Grades 4-12
Econo-Clad, 1989 (Termination Date: 1998)

Annals of America: Grades 4-12
Encyclopaedia Britannica, 1976 (Termination Date: 1998)

Our Nation's History: Grades 8-12
Media Materials, 1991 (Termination Date: 1998)

Two Centuries of Progress: Grades 7-9
Glencoe/McGraw-Hill, 1991 (Termination Date: 1998)

Challenge of Freedom: Grades 7-9
Glencoe/McGraw-Hill, 1990 (Termination Date: 1998)

History of a Free Nation: Grades 9-12
Glencoe/McGraw-Hill, 1992 (Termination Date: 1998)

American Odyssey: U.S. Government in the 20th Century: Grades 9-12
Glencoe/McGraw-Hill, 1992 (Termination Date: 1998)

Exploring American History: Grades 6-9
Globe, 1991 (Termination Date: 1998)

Hispanics in U.S. History, vols. 1 & 2: Grades 6-12
Globe, 1989 (Termination Date: 1998)

African Americans in U.S. History, vols. 1 & 2:
Grades 6-12
Globe, 1989 (Termination Date: 1998)

Our Land, Our Time: Grades 9-12
Holt, Rinehart and Winston, 1991 (Termination
Date: 1998)

The Story of America: Grades 7-12
Holt, Rinehart and Winston, 1991 (Termination
Date: 1998)

Eyewitness/Others, vols. 1 & 2: Grades 7-12
Holt, Rinehart and Winston, 1991 (Termination
Date: 1998)

The Constitution: Past, Present, Future: Grades 7-
12
Holt, Rinehart and Winston, 1991 (Termination
Date: 1998)

The Constitution: Foundation of Freedom: Grades
7-12
Holt, Rinehart and Winston, 1990 (Termination
Date: 1998)

The American Nation: Grades 7-9
Prentice Hall, 1991 (Termination Date: 1998)

A History of the United States: Grades 9-12
Prentice Hall, 1991 (Termination Date: 1998)

American Journey: Quest for Liberty: Grades 7-12
Prentice Hall, 1992 (Termination Date: 1998)

The U.S.: A History of the Republic: Grades 9-12
Prentice Hall, 1990 (Termination Date: 1998)

Great Cases of the Supreme Court: Grades 7-9
Houghton Mifflin, 1989 (Termination Date: 1998)

America's Story: Grades 7-9
Houghton Mifflin, 1990 (Termination Date: 1998)

History of the United States: Grades 9-12
Houghton Mifflin, 1991-92 (Termination Date:
1998)

American History Bookshelf: Grades 6-8
Houghton Mifflin, 1990 (Termination Date: 1998)

The American Nation: Grades 9-12
Scott, Foresman, 1991 (Termination Date: 1998)

American Voices, A History of the U.S.: Grades 9-
12
Scott, Foresman, 1992 (Termination Date: 1998)

America: The People and the Dream: Grade 8
Scott, Foresman, 1991 (Termination Date: 1998)

The Americans: Grades 9-12
McDougal, Littell, 1991 (Termination Date: 1998)

Cornerstones of Freedom: Grades 2-6
Childrens Press, 1965-91 (Termination Date:
1998)

America the Beautiful: Grades 4-12
Childrens Press, 1987-91 (Termination Date:
1998)

American History Series: Grades 6-12
Fearon/Janus/Quercus, 1989 (Termination Date:
1998)

The History of the United States, vols. 1 & 2:
Grades 4-12
Book-Lab, 1987-89 (Termination Date: 1998)

World History
Historia de America y Mapas: Grades 9-12
DDL, 1984 (Termination Date: 1998)

Historiar 3: Grades 6-12
DDL, 1985 (Termination Date: 1998)

Experiencing World History: Grades 8-12
Media Materials, 1991 (Termination Date: 1998)

World History: The Human Experience: Grades 9-
12
Glencoe/McGraw-Hill, 1992 (Termination Date:
1998)

The Human Heritage: A World History: Grades 7-9
Glencoe/McGraw-Hill, 1989 (Termination Date:
1998)

World History: Perspectives on the Past: Grades 9-
12
D. C. Heath, 1992 (Termination Date: 1998)

World History: Grades 9-12
Holt, Rinehart and Winston, 1990 (Termination
Date: 1998)

World History: People and Nations: Grades 9-12
Holt, Rinehart and Winston, 1990 (Termination Date: 1998)

Readings in World History: Grades 9-12
Holt, Rinehart and Winston, 1990 (Termination Date: 1998)

The Pageant of World History: Grades 7-12
Prentice Hall, 1990 (Termination Date: 1998)

World History: Patterns of Civilization: Grades 9-12
Prentice Hall, 1990 (Termination Date: 1998)

World Regional Studies: Grades 9-12
Houghton Mifflin, 1990-91 (Termination Date: 1998)

History of the World: Grades 9-12
Houghton Mifflin, 1992 (Termination Date: 1998)

Civilization Past and Present: Grades 9-12
Scott, Foresman, 1987 (Termination Date: 1998)

History and Life: Grades 9-12
Scott, Foresman, 1990 (Termination Date: 1998)

Living World History: Grades 9-12
Scott, Foresman, 1990 (Termination Date: 1998)

The Essential Ideas: Grades 9-12
Addison-Wesley. 1991 (Termination Date: 1998)

World History: Grades 9-12
Addison-Wesley, 1991 (Termination Date: 1998)

Enchantment of the World: Grades 5-9
Childrens Press, 1982-91 (Termination Date: 1998)

Janus World History: Grades 6-12
Fearon/Janus/Quercus, 1990 (Termination Date: 1998)

Galileo: Grades 6-12
Fearon/Janus/Quercus, 1989 (Termination Date: 1998)

Quercus World History: Grades 6-12
Fearon/Janus/Quercus, 1989 (Termination Date: 1998)

Cleopatra: Grades 6-12
Fearon/Janus/Quercus, 1989 (Termination Date: 1998)

Soul Force: The Life of Mahatma Gandhi: Grades 6-12
Fearon/Janus/Quercus, 1989 (Termination Date: 1998)

World Cultures
Leyendas de Cultura Universal: Grades 7-12
DDL, 1987 (Termination Date: 1998)

A Survey of World Cultures: Grades 8-12
Media Materials, 1990 (Termination Date: 1998)

Human Expression: World Regions and Cultures: Grades 9-12
Glencoe/McGraw-Hill, 1992 (Termination Date: 1998)

Global Insights: People and Cultures: Grades 9-12
Glencoe/McGraw-Hill, 1987 (Termination Date: 1998)

Folklore: A Multi-Cultural Treasury: Grades 1-6
Modern Curriculum, 1990 (Termination Date: 1998)

People in Time and Places--World Cultures: Grades 6-7
Silver Burdett and Ginn, 1991 (Termination Date: 1998)

Global Studies: Grades 7-12
Amsco, 1988 (Termination Date: 1998)

Atlases
Historical Markers in New Mexico: Grades 5-12
Ancient City, 1990 (Termination Date: 1998)

Atlas of United States History: Grades 7-12:
Hammond, 1989 (Termination Date: 1998)

Historical Atlas of the World: Grades 7-12
Hammond, 1990 (Termination Date: 1998)

Atlas of the Bible Lands: Grades 7-12:
Hammond, 1990 (Termination Date: 1998)

Past Worlds: Times Atlas of Archaeology: Grades 7-12
Hammond, 1989 (Termination Date: 1998)

Times Atlas of World History: Grades 7-12
Hammond, 1984 (Termination Date: 1998)

World Atlas for Students: Grades 7-12
Hammond, 1991 (Termination Date: 1998)

Ambassador World Atlas: Grades 7-12:
Hammond, 1991(Termination Date: 1998)

Citation World Atlas: Grades 7-12:
Hammond, 1991 (Termination Date: 1998)

Comparative World Atlas: Grades 7-12
Hammond, 1990 (Termination Date: 1998)

Gold Medallion World Atlas: Grades 7-12
Hammond, 1991 (Termination Date: 1998)

Intermediate United States Atlas: Grade 8
Hammond, 1990 (Termination Date: 1998)

Intermediate World Atlas: Grades 7-8
Hammond, 1990 (Termination Date: 1998)

Atlas of American History: Grades 7-12
Rand McNally, 1991 (Termination Date: 1998)

Classroom Atlas: Grades 4-12
Rand McNally, 1986 (Termination Date: 1998)

Goode's World Atlas: Grades 4-12
Rand McNally, 1986 (Termination Date: 1998)

Historical Atlas of the World: Grades 7-12
Rand McNally, 1991 (Termination Date: 1998)

The New International Atlas: Ungraded
Rand McNally, 1991 (Termination Date: 1998)

North Carolina

Social Studies, General
HBJ Social Studies: Grades 1-5
Harcourt Brace Jovanovich, 1988 (Termination Date: 1993)

Scott, Foresman Social Studies: Grades 1-6
Scott, Foresman, 1988 (Termination Date: 1993)

Silver Burdett and Ginn Social Studies: Grades 1-4
Silver Burdett and Ginn, 1988 (Termination Date: 1993)

North Carolina: Grade 4
McGraw-Hill, 1988 (Termination Date: 1993)

North Carolina: Land and People: Grade 4
Scott, Foresman, 1988 (Termination Date: 1993)

North Carolina: Our People, Places and Past: Grade 4
Carolina, 1987 (Termination Date: 1993)

North Carolina: The Land and Its People: Grade 4
Silver Burdett and Ginn, 1988 (Termination Date: 1993)

US: Our Nation and Neighbors: Grade 5
McGraw-Hill, 1988 (Termination Date: 1993)

Exploring the Non-Western World: Grade 7
Globe, 1988 (Termination Date: 1993)

The World Past to Present: Grade 7
D. C. Heath, 1987 (Termination Date: 1993)

North Carolina: The History of an American State: Grade 8
Prentice Hall, 1988 (Termination Date: 1993)

North Carolina: The Story of a Special Kind of Place: Grade 8
Workman, 1987 (Termination Date: 1993)

World Geography
Scholastic World Geography: Grades 9-12
Scholastic, 1989 (Termination Date: 1993)

Heath World Geography: Grades 9-12
D. C. Heath, 1987 (Termination Date: 1993)

World Geography--People and Places: Grades 9-12
Glencoe, 1984 (Termination Date: 1993)

World Geography Today: Grades 9-12
Holt, Rinehart and Winston, 1985 (Termination Date: 1993)

United States History
American Adventures: Grades 9-12
Scholastic, 1987 (Termination Date: 1993)

American History: Grades 9-12
Harcourt Brace Jovanovich, 1986 (Termination Date: 1993)

The American Nation: Grades 9-12
Prentice Hall, 1986 (Termination Date: 1993)

United States History: Grades 9-12
Holt, Rinehart and Winston, 1988 (Termination Date: 1993)

Land of Promise: A History: Grades 9-12
Scott, Foresman, 1987 (Termination Date: 1993)

Our Land, Our Time: Grades 9-12
Holt, Rinehart and Winston, 1987 (Termination Date: 1993)

The Americans: Grades 9-12
McDougal, Littell, 1988 (Termination Date: 1993)

Triumph of the American Nation: Grades 9-12
Harcourt Brace Jovanovich, 1986 (Termination Date: 1993)

The United States: A History of the Republic:
Grades 9-12
Prentice Hall, 1988 (Termination Date: 1993)

The American Pageant: Grades 9-12
D. C. Heath, 1987 (Termination Date: 1993)

The United States: Grades 9-12
Prentice Hall, 1987 (Termination Date: 1993)

Economic, Legal, and Political Systems

Civil Justice: Grades 9-12
Scholastic, 1988 (Termination Date: 1993)

Criminal Justice: Grades 9-12
Scholastic, 1988 (Termination Date: 1993)

Economics: It's Your Business: Grades 9-12
New Readers, 1986 (Termination Date: 1993)

Government Today: Grades 9-12
New Readers, 1988 (Termination Date: 1993)

Our Government in Action: Grades 9-12
Janus, 1986 (Termination Date: 1993)

American Civics: Grades 9-12
Harcourt Brace Jovanovich, 1987 (Termination Date: 1993)

Civics: Citizens in Action: Grades 9-12
Glencoe, 1986 (Termination Date: 1993)

Civics for Americans: Grades 9-12
Scott, Foresman, 1986 (Termination Date: 1993)

Civics: Government and Citizenship: Grades 9-12
Prentice Hall, 1986 (Termination Date: 1993)

McDougal, Littell Economics: Grades 9-12
McDougal, Littell, 1988 (Termination Date: 1993)

Scribner Economics: Grades 9-12
Glencoe, 1988 (Termination Date: 1993)

World History

Exploring World History: Grades 9-12
Globe, 1987 (Termination Date: 1993)

The Pageant of World History: Grades 9-12
Prentice Hall, 1986 (Termination Date: 1993)

Scholastic World History Program: Grades 9-12
Scholastic, 1987 (Termination Date: 1993)

A History of the World: Grades 9-12
Houghton Mifflin, 1988 (Termination Date: 1993)

People and Nations: Grades 9-12
Harcourt Brace Jovanovich, 1987 (Termination Date: 1993)

World History: Patterns of Civilization: Grades 9-12
Prentice Hall, 1988 (Termination Date: 1993)

A History of Civilization: Grades 9-12
Prentice Hall, 1988 (Termination Date: 1993)

A World History: Grades 9-12
Addison-Wesley, 1988 (Termination Date: 1993)

Sociology

Sociology: The Study of Human Relationships:
Grades 9-12
Harcourt Brace Jovanovich, 1982 (Termination Date: 1993)

Sociology: Understanding Society: Grades 9-12
Prentice Hall, 1989 (Termination Date: 1993)

Economics

Economics for Decision Making: Grades 9-12
D. C. Heath, 1988 (Termination Date: 1993)

Economics: Principles and Practices: Grades 9-12
Glencoe, 1988 (Termination Date: 1993)

Understanding Economics: Grades 9-12
Random, 1986 (Termination Date: 1993)

Law and Justice

Street Law: Grades 9-12
West, 1986 (Termination Date: 1993)

Government

American Government: The Republic in Action:
Grades 9-12
Harcourt Brace Jovanovich, 1986 (Termination
Date: 1993)

American Government: Principles and Practices:
Grades 9-12
Glencoe, 1987 (Termination Date: 1993)

Magruder's American Government: Grades 9-12
Prentice Hall, 1988 (Termination Date: 1993)

Psychology

Invitation to Psychology: Grades 9-12
Scott, Foresman, 1985 (Termination Date: 1993)

Psychology: Its Principles and Applications: Grades
9-12
Harcourt Brace Jovanovich, 1984 (Termination
Date: 1993)

Oklahoma

Social Studies

The World around Us: Grades K-6
Macmillan, 1990 (Termination Date: 1995)

Heath Social Studies: Grades 1-6
D. C. Heath, 1987-89 (Termination Date: 1995)

Scott, Foresman Social Studies: Grades K-8
Scott, Foresman, 1988 (Termination Date: 1995)

HBJ Social Studies: Grades K-6
Harcourt Brace Jovanovich, 1988 (Termination
Date: 1995)

Silver Burdett and Ginn Social Studies: Grades K-6
Silver Burdett and Ginn, 1988-90 (Termination
Date: 1995)

Ready, Set, Go! Activity Pack: Grade K
Silver Burdett and Ginn, 1989 (Termination Date:
1995)

Maps, Globes, Graphs: Grades 1-6
Steck-Vaughn, 1989 (Termination Date: 1995)

Basic Map Skills: Grades 1-3
Hammond, 1984 (Termination Date: 1995)

Maps, Charts and Graphs: Grades 2-6
Modern Curriculum Press, 1989-90 (Termination
Date: 1995)

Understanding Maps: Grades 3-4
Hammond, 1985 (Termination Date: 1995)

The World, Past & Present: Grade 6
Macmillan, 1991 (Termination Date: 1995)

Scott, Foresman Social Science: Eastern Hemisphere: Grade 6
Scott, Foresman, 1990 (Termination Date: 1995)

Macmillan Social Studies: Grades 7-8
Macmillan, 1987 (Termination Date: 1995)

Human Heritage: A World History: Grades 7-8
Merrill, 1989 (Termination Date: 1995)

Introduction to the Social Sciences: Grades 7-8
Prentice Hall, 1991 (Termination Date: 1995)

World History through Maps: Grades 7-8
Hammond, 1984 (Termination Date: 1995)

Civics

Civics: Citizens in Action: Grades 7-8
Merrill, 1990 (Termination Date: 1995)

Civics for Americans: Grades 7-8
Scott, Foresman, 1986 (Termination Date: 1995)

American Civics: Grades 7-8
Harcourt Brace Jovanovich, 1987 (Termination
Date: 1995)

Civics: Government & Citizenship: Grades 7-8
Prentice Hall, 1990 (Termination Date: 1995)

We the People: Grades 7-8
Holt, Rinehart and Winston, 1989 (Termination
Date: 1995)

Exploring American Citizenship: Grades 7-8
Globe, 1988 (Termination Date: 1995)

Civics: The United States & Oklahoma: Grades 7-8
Walsworth, 1989 (Termination Date: 1995)

Economics

McDougal, Littell Economics: Grades 9-12
McDougal, Littell, 1988 (Termination Date: 1995)

Economics: Principles & Practices: Grades 9-12
Merrill, 1988 (Termination Date: 1995)

Economics for Consumers: Grades 9-12
Houghton Mifflin, 1989 (Termination Date: 1995)

Invitation to Economics: Grades 9-12
Scott, Foresman, 1988 (Termination Date: 1995)

Economics: Free Enterprise in Action: Grades 9-12
Harcourt Brace Jovanovich, 1988 (Termination Date: 1995)

Economics: The Science of Cost, Benefit and Choice: Grades 9-12
Southwestern, 1988 (Termination Date: 1995)

Economics and the American Free Enterprise System: Grades 9-12
Globe, 1988 (Termination Date: 1995)

Scribner Economics: Grades 9-12
Glencoe/McGraw-Hill, 1988 (Termination Date: 1995)

Addison-Wesley Economics: Grades 9-12
Addison-Wesley, 1988 (Termination Date: 1995)

Economics & Making Decisions: Grades 9-12
West, 1988 (Termination Date: 1995)

Geography

Macmillan Social Studies--World Neighbors: Grades 7-8
Macmillan, 1987 (Termination Date: 1995)

World Regions: Grades 7-8
Macmillan, 1991 (Termination Date: 1995)

World Geography: Grades 7-8
D. C. Heath, 1989 (Termination Date: 1995)

World Geography: People & Places: Grades 7-8
Merrill, 1989 (Termination Date: 1995)

McGraw-Hill World Geography: Grades 7-8
McGraw-Hill, 1989 (Termination Date: 1995)

People on Earth: A World Geography: Grades 7-8
Scott, Foresman, 1988 (Termination Date: 1995)

A World View: Grades 7-8
Silver Burdett and Ginn, 1990 (Termination Date: 1995)

Exploring the Non-Western World: Grades 7-8
Globe, 1988 (Termination Date: 1995)

Exploring a Changing World: Grades 7-8
Globe, 1988 (Termination Date: 1995

World Geography: The Earth and Its People: Grades 9-12
Harcourt Brace Jovanovich, 1989 (Termination Date: 1995)

Scott, Foresman World Geography: Grades 9-12
Scott, Foresman, 1989 (Termination Date: 1995)

World Geography Today: Grades 9-12
Holt, Rinehart and Winston, 1989 (Termination Date: 1995)

Glencoe World Geography: Grades 9-12
Glencoe/McGraw-Hill, 1989 (Termination Date: 1995)

Geography: Our Changing World: Grades 9-12
West, 1990 (Termination Date: 1995)

Essential Map Skills: Grades 9-12
Hammond, 1985 (Termination Date: 1995)

World Atlas for Students: Grades 9-12
Hammond, 1986 (Termination Date: 1995)

Comparative World Atlas: Grades 9-12
Hammond, 1989 (Termination Date: 1995)

Hammond World Atlas: Grades 9-12
Hammond, 1988 (Termination Date: 1995)

Prentice Hall World Geography: Grades 9-12
Prentice Hall, 1993 (Termination Date: 1995)

Government

American Government: Principles & Practices: Grades 9-12
Merrill, 1987 (Termination Date: 1995)

Government in America: Grades 9-12
Houghton Mifflin, 1991 (Termination Date: 1995)

Consent of the Governed: Grades 9-12
Scott, Foresman, 1988 (Termination Date: 1995)

American Government: The Republic in Action:
Grades 9-12
Harcourt Brace Jovanovich, 1986 (Termination
Date: 1995)

Magruder's American Government: Grades 9-12
Prentice Hall, 1991 (Termination Date: 1995)

Government by the People: National/State/Local:
Grades 9-12
Prentice Hall, 1990 (Termination Date: 1995)

Government in the United States: Grades 9-12
Glencoe/McGraw-Hill, 1990 (Termination Date:
1995)

Perspectives: Grades 9-12
Close Up Foundation, 1987 (Termination Date:
1995)

American Government & Politics Today: Grades 9-
12
West, 1989 (Termination Date: 1995)

Problems of Democracy
Great Cases of the Supreme Court: Grades 9-12
Houghton Mifflin, 1989 (Termination Date: 1995)

Vital Issues of the Constitution: Grades 9-12
Houghton Mifflin, 1989 (Termination Date: 1995)

Oklahoma History
Oklahoma!: Grades 9-12
Thunderbird Books, 1987 (Termination Date:
1995)

Oklahoma Heritage: Grades 9-12
Holt/Calhoun/Clark/Quaid, 1989 (Termination
Date: 1995)

The History of Oklahoma: Grades 9-12
University of Oklahoma Press, 1984 (Termination
Date: 1995)

The Oklahoma Story: Grades 9-12
University of Oklahoma Press, 1978 (Termination
Date: 1995)

Historical Atlas of Oklahoma: Grades 9-12
University of Oklahoma Press, 1986 (Termination
Date: 1995)

Historical Atlas of Oklahoma: Grades 9-12
University of Oklahoma Press, 1986 (Termination
Date: 1995)

Oklahoma! A History of Five Centuries: Grades 9-
12
University of Oklahoma Press, 1981 (Termination
Date: 1995)

A Panorama of Oklahoma: Grades 9-12
Walsworth, 1989 (Termination Date: 1995)

U.S. History
A Proud Nation: Grades 7-8
McDougal, Littell, 1989 (Termination Date: 1995)

America's Story: Grades 7-8
Houghton Mifflin, 1990 (Termination Date: 1995)

America! America!: Grades 7-8
Scott, Foresman, 1987 (Termination Date: 1995)

American History: Grades 7-8
Harcourt Brace Jovanovich, 1986 (Termination
Date: 1995)

The American Nation: Grades 7-8
Prentice Hall, 1990 (Termination Date: 1995)

American Spirit: Grades 7-8
Prentice Hall, 1990 (Termination Date: 1995)

One Flag, One Land: Grades 7-8
Silver Burdett and Ginn, 1990 (Termination Date:
1995)

United States History: Grades 7-8
Holt, Rinehart and Winston, 1988 (Termination
Date: 1995)

Challenge of Freedom: Grades 7-8
Glencoe/McGraw-Hill, 1990 (Termination Date:
1995)

Addison-Wesley Spirit of Liberty: Grades 7-8
Addison-Wesley, 1987 (Termination Date: 1995)

The Americans: Grades 9-12
McDougal, Littell, 1988 (Termination Date: 1995)

America, the Glorious Republic: Grades 9-12
Houghton Mifflin, 1990 (Termination Date: 1995)

Land of Promise: Grades 9-12
Scott, Foresman, 1986-87 (Termination Date:
1995)

America: Past and Present: Grades 9-12
Scott, Foresman, 1987 (Termination Date: 1995)

Triumph of the American Nation: Grades 9-12
Harcourt Brace Jovanovich, 1986-90 (Termination Date: 1995)

A History of the United States: Grades 9-12
Prentice Hall, 1990 (Termination Date: 1995)

A History of the United States Since 1861: Grades 9-12
Prentice Hall, 1990 (Termination Date: 1995)

The United States: A History of the Republic: Grades 9-12
Prentice Hall, 1990 (Termination Date: 1995)

Our Land, Our Time: Grades 9-12
Holt, Rinehart and Winston, 1987 (Termination Date: 1995)

Our Nation's History: Grades 9-12
Media Materials, 1989 (Termination Date: 1995)

Black History
Champions of Change: Famous Black Americans: Grades 9-12
Steck-Vaughn, 1989 (Termination Date: 1995)

Journey toward Hope: A History of Blacks in Oklahoma: Grades 9-12
University of Oklahoma Press, 1982 (Termination Date: 1995)

African Americans in U.S. History: Grades 9-12
Globe Book, 1989 (Termination Date: 1995)

World History
World History: Perspectives on the Past: Grades 9-12
D. C. Heath, 1990 (Termination Date: 1995)

The Human Experience: A World History: Grades 9-12
Merrill, 1990 (Termination Date: 1995)

History of the World: Grades 9-12
Houghton Mifflin, 1990 (Termination Date: 1995)

History & Life: Grades 9-12
Scott, Foresman, 1990 (Termination Date: 1995)

Living World History: Grades 9-12
Scott, Foresman, 1990 (Termination Date: 1995)

World History: People & Nations: Grades 9-12
Harcourt Brace Jovanovich, 1990 (Termination Date: 1995)

World History: Patterns of Civilization: Grades 9-12
Prentice Hall, 1990 (Termination Date: 1995)

The Pageant of World History: Grades 9-12
Prentice Hall, 1990 (Termination Date: 1995)

World History: Grades 9-12
Holt, Rinehart and Winston, 1990 (Termination Date: 1995)

Addison-Wesley World History: Grades 9-12
Addison-Wesley, 1989 (Termination Date: 1995)

Psychology
Invitation to Psychology: Grades 9-12
Scott, Foresman, 1989 (Termination Date: 1995)

Psychology: Its Principles & Applications: Grades 9-12
Harcourt Brace Jovanovich, 1989 (Termination Date: 1995)

Psychology: An Introduction: Grades 9-12
Prentice Hall, 1990 (Termination Date: 1995)

Psychology: Principles & Applications: Grades 9-12
Prentice Hall, 1989 (Termination Date: 1995)

Psychology and You: Grades 9-12
West, 1990 (Termination Date: 1995)

Sociology
Sociology: The Study of Human Relationships: Grades 9-12
Harcourt Brace Jovanovich, 1990 (Termination Date: 1995)

Sociology: Understanding Society: Grades 9-12
Prentice Hall, 1990 (Termination Date: 1995)

Sociology: Grades 9-12
Prentice Hall, 1989 (Termination Date: 1995)

Social Problems: Grades 9-12
Prentice Hall, 1989 (Termination Date: 1995)

Oregon

Social Studies

HBJ Social Studies: Grades K-2
Harcourt Brace Jovanovich, 1991 (Termination Date: 1997)

Heath Social Studies: Grades K-2
D. C. Heath, 1991 (Termination Date: 1997)

Houghton Mifflin Social Studies: Grades K-2
Houghton Mifflin, 1991 (Termination Date: 1997)

The World around Us Activity Program: Grades K-2
Macmillan/McGraw Hill, 1991 (Termination Date: 1997)

HBJ Social Studies: Grades 3-6
Harcourt Brace Jovanovich, 1991 (Termination Date: 1997)

Houghton Mifflin Social Studies: Grades 3-6
Houghton Mifflin, 1991 (Termination Date: 1997)

The World around Us: Grades 3-6
Macmillan/McGraw-Hill, 1991 (Termination Date: 1997)

World Geography

World Geography: People and Places: Grades 6-8
Glencoe/Macmillan/McGraw-Hill, 1989 (Termination Date: 1997)

Heath World Geography: Grades 6-8
D. C. Heath, 1989 (Termination Date: 1997)

Earth's Geography and Environment: Grades 6-8
McDougal, Littell, 1991 (Termination Date: 1997)

The World around Us Series: World Regions: Grades 6-8
Macmillan/McGraw-Hill, 1991 (Termination Date: 1997)

People on Earth: A World Geography: Grades 6-8
Scott, Foresman, 1988 (Termination Date: 1997)

Glencoe World Geography: Grades 9-12
Glencoe/Macmillan/McGraw-Hill, 1989 (Termination Date: 1997)

World Geography: The Earth and Its People: Grades 9-12
Holt, Rinehart and Winston/Harcourt Brace Jovanovich, 1989 (Termination Date: 1997)

World Geography Today: Grades 9-12
Holt, Rinehart and Winston/Harcourt Brace Jovanovich, 1989 (Termination Date: 1997)

Foresman World Geography: Grades 9-12
Scott, Foresman, 1989 (Termination Date: 1997)

Geography: Our Changing World: Grades 9-12
West, 1990 (Termination Date: 1997)

World History

The World: Past and Present: Grades 6-8
Harcourt Brace Jovanovich, 1991 (Termination Date: 1997)

Heath Social Studies: Exploring Our World, Past and Present: Grades 6-8
D. C. Heath, 1991 (Termination Date: 1997)

Houghton Mifflin Social Studies: Grades 6-8
Houghton Mifflin, 1991 (Termination Date: 1997)

The World around Us: Grades 6-8
Macmillan/McGraw-Hill, 1991 (Termination Date: 1997)

Addison-Wesley World History: Grades 9-12
Addison-Wesley, 1991 (Termination Date: 1997)

World History: Perspectives on the Past: Grades 9-12
D. C. Heath, 1990 (Termination Date: 1997)

World History: People and Nations: Grades 9-12
Holt, Rinehart and Winston/Harcourt Brace Jovanovich, 1990 (Termination Date: 1997)

A History of the World: Grades 9-12
Houghton Mifflin, 1990 (Termination Date: 1997)

Links across Time and Place: A World History: Grades 9-12
McDougal, Littell, 1990 (Termination Date: 1997)

The Pageant of World History: Grades 9-12
Prentice Hall, 1990 (Termination Date: 1997)

World History: Patterns of Civilization: Grades 9-12
Prentice Hall, 1990 (Termination Date: 1997)

History and Life: Grades 9-12
Scott, Foresman, 1990 (Termination Date: 1997)

U.S. History

The Story of America: Grades 6-8
Holt, Rinehart and Winston/Harcourt Brace
Jovanovich, 1991 (Termination Date: 1997)

*Houghton Mifflin Social Studies: A More Perfect
Union:* Grades 6-8
Houghton Mifflin, 1991 (Termination Date: 1997)

America's Story: Grades 6-8
Houghton Mifflin, 1990 (Termination Date: 1997)

The American Nation: Grades 6-8
Prentice Hall, 1991 (Termination Date: 1997)

American Adventures: People Making History:
Grades 6-8
Scholastic, 1991 (Termination Date: 1997)

America: The People and the Dream: Grades 6-8
Scott, Foresman, 1991 (Termination Date: 1997)

Our Land, Our Time: Grades 9-12
Holt, Rinehart and Winston/Harcourt Brace
Jovanovich, 1991 (Termination Date: 1997)

History of the United States: Grades 9-12
Houghton Mifflin, 1991 (Termination Date: 1997)

The Americans: Grades 9-12
McDougal, Littell, 1991 (Termination Date: 1997)

The United States: A History of the Republic:
Grades 9-12
Prentice Hall, 1990 (Termination Date: 1997)

A History of the Republic, Vol. 2: Grades 9-12
Prentice Hall, 1990 (Termination Date: 1997)

A History of the United States: Grades 9-12
Prentice Hall, 1990 (Termination Date: 1997)

A History of the United States since 1861: Grades 9-
12
Prentice Hall, 1990 (Termination Date: 1997)

Government

Civics: Grades 9-12
Addison-Wesley, 1991 (Termination Date: 1997)

American Government: Principles and Practices:
Grades 9-12
Glencoe/Macmillan/McGraw-Hill, 1991 (Termination Date: 1997)

Government in the United States: Grades 9-12
Glencoe/Macmillan/McGraw-Hill, 1990 (Termination Date: 1997)

Government in America: Grades 9-12
Houghton Mifflin, 1991 (Termination Date: 1997)

Magruder's American Government: Grades 9-12
Prentice Hall, 1990, 1991 (Termination Date: 1997)

Consent of the Governed: Grades 9-12
Scott, Foresman, 1988 (Termination Date: 1997)

Economics

Addison-Wesley Economics: Grades 9-12
Addison-Wesley, 1988 (Termination Date: 1997)

Economics: Today and Tomorrow: Grades 9-12
Glencoe/Macmillan/McGraw-Hill, 1991 (Termination Date: 1997)

Basic Economic Principles: Grades 9-12
Glencoe/Macmillan/McGraw-Hill, 1989 (Termination Date: 1997)

Economics: Principles and Practices: Grades 9-12
Glencoe/Macmillan/McGraw-Hill, 1988 (Termination Date: 1997)

Economics: Free Enterprise in Action: Grades 9-12
Holt, Rinehart and Winston/Harcourt Brace
Jovanovich, 1988 (Termination Date: 1997)

McDougal, Littell Economics: Grades 9-12
McDougal, Littell, 1991 (Termination Date: 1997)

Scholastic Economics: Grades 9-12
Scott, Foresman, 1991 (Termination Date: 1997)

Invitation to Economics: Grades 9-12
Scott, Foresman, 1988 (Termination Date: 1997)

*Economics: The Science of Cost, Benefit, and
Choice:* Grades 9-12
South-Western, 1988 (Termination Date: 1997)

South Carolina

Social Studies
HBJ Social Studies: Grades 1-6
Harcourt Brace Jovanovich, 1985 (Termination Date: 1991)

Heath Social Studies: Grades 1-6
D. C. Heath, 1987 (Termination Date: 1991)

Holt Social Studies: Grades 1-6
Holt, Rinehart and Winston, 1986 (Termination Date: 1991)

Ginn Social Studies: Grades 1-6
Schoolhouse Press, 1987 (Termination Date: 1991)

The World and Its People: Grades 1-6
Silver Burdett and Ginn, 1986 (Termination Date: 1991)

Civics
Addison-Wesley Civics: Participating in Our Democracy: Grades 9-12
Addison-Wesley, 1991 (Termination Date: 1995)

Civics: Citizens in Action: Grades 9-12
Merrill--Macmillan/McGraw-Hill, 1990 (Termination Date: 1995)

Civics: Government and Citizenship: Grades 9-12
Prentice Hall, 1990 (Termination Date: 1995)

Civics for Americans: Grades 9-12
Scott, Foresman, 1991 (Termination Date: 1995)

Economics
Longman's Economics: Our American Economy: Grades 10-12
Addison-Wesley, 1990 (Termination Date: 1995)

Introduction to Economics: Grades 10-12
EMC, 1991 (Termination Date: 1995)

Economics Today and Tomorrow: Grades 10-12
Glencoe/McGraw-Hill, 1991 (Termination Date: 1995)

Economics: Grades 10-12
Fearon, 1989 (Termination Date: 1995)

McDougal, Littell Economics: Grades 10-12
McDougal, Littell, 1991 (Termination Date: 1995)

Economics: Principles and Practices: Grades 10-12
Merrill--McGraw-Hill, 1988 (Termination Date: 1995)

Scholastic Economics: Grades 10-12
Scholastic, 1991 (Termination Date: 1995)

Geography
Laidlaw World Geography: A Physical and Cultural Approach: Grade 7
Glencoe, 1987 (Termination Date: 1992)

Exploring a Changing World: Grade 7
Globe, 1988 (Termination Date: 1992)

Intermediate World Atlas: Grade 9-12
Hammond, 1984 (Termination Date: 1994)

Intermediate United States Atlas: Grades 9-12
Hammond, 1984 (Termination Date: 1994)

Essential Map Skills: Grades 9-12
Hammond, 1985 (Termination Date: 1994)

World Atlas for Students: Grades 9-12
Hammond, 1985-86 (Termination Date: 1994)

Comparative World Atlas: Grades 9-12
Hammond, 1985-89 (Termination Date: 1994)

Physical World Atlas: Grades 9-12
Hammond, 1987 (Termination Date: 1994)

Discovery World Atlas: Grades 9-12
Hammond, 1988 (Termination Date: 1994)

Nova World Atlas: Grades 9-12
Hammond, 1988 (Termination Date: 1994)

World Atlas: Grade 9-12
Hammond, 1985-88 (Termination Date: 1994)

Gemini United States Atlas: Grades 9-12
Hammond, 1988 (Termination Date: 1994)

Historical Atlas of the World: Grades 9-12
Hammond, 1987 (Termination Date: 1994)

United States History Atlas: Grades 9-12
Hammond, 1989 (Termination Date: 1994)

American History through Maps: Grades 9-12
Hammond, 1984 (Termination Date: 1994)

World History through Maps: Grades 9-12
Hammond, 1984 (Termination Date: 1994)

Citation World Atlas: Grades 9-12
Hammond, 1988 (Termination Date: 1994)

Times Concise Atlas of World History: Grades 9-12
Hammond, 1982 (Termination Date: 1994)

Macmillan Social Studies: World Neighbors: Grade 7
Macmillan, 1987 (Termination Date: 1992)

People on Earth: A World Geography: Grade 7
Scott, Foresman, 1988 (Termination Date: 1992)

A World View: Grade 7
Silver Burdett and Ginn, 1988 (Termination Date: 1992)

World Geography: The Earth and Its People: Grades 9-12
Harcourt Brace Jovanovich, 1989 (Termination Date: 1994)

Heath World Geography: Grades 9-12
D. C. Heath, 1989 (Termination Date: 1994)

World Geography Today: Grades 9-12
Holt, Rinehart and Winston, 1989 (Termination Date: 1994)

World Geography: Learning about Our World: Grades 9-12
Media Materials, 1988 (Termination Date: 1994)

Geography of the United States: Learning about Our United States: Grades 9-12
Media Materials, 1988 (Termination Date: 1994)

World Geography: People and Places: Grades 9-12
Merrill, 1989 (Termination Date: 1994)

Scholastic World Geography: Grades 9-12
Scholastic, 1989 (Termination Date: 1994)

U.S. Government
Government for Everybody: Grades 10-12
Amsco, 1990 (Termination Date: 1995)

We the People: Grades 10-12
Holt, Rinehart and Winston, 1989 (Termination Date: 1995)

Government in America: Grades 10-12
Houghton Mifflin, 1991 (Termination Date: 1995)

Government by the People: National, State, Local Version Bill of Rights: Grades 10-12
Prentice Hall, 1990 (Termination Date: 1995)

Magruder's American Government: Grades 10-12
Prentice Hall, 1990 (Termination Date: 1995)

U.S. History
Our Land, Our Time P/E: Grade 11
Coronado, 1985 (Termination Date: 1990)

America's Heritage: Grade 11
Ginn, 1986 (Termination Date: 1990)

Triumph of the American Nation: Grade 11
Harcourt Brace Jovanovich, 1986 (Termination Date: 1990)

The American Pageant: Grade 11
D. C. Heath, 1983 (Termination Date: 1990)

America: The Glorious Republic: Grade 11
Houghton Mifflin, 1985 (Termination Date: 1990)

Life and Liberty: Grade 11
Scott, Foresman, 1984 (Termination Date: 1990)

World History
Exploring World History: Grades 9-12
Globe, 1990 (Termination Date: 1995)

World History: Perspectives on the Past: Grades 9-12
D. C. Heath, 1990 (Termination Date: 1995)

Links across Time and Place: A World History: Grades 9-12
McDougal, Littell, 1990 (Termination Date: 1995)

World History: Patterns of Civilization: Grades 9-12
Prentice Hall, 1990 (Termination Date: 1995)

History and Life: Grades 9-12
Scott, Foresman, 1990 (Termination Date: 1995)

Law-Related Education
Street Law: A Course in Practical Law: Grades 9-10
West, 1990 (Termination Date: 1994)

Psychology

Psychology: Its Principles and Applications: Grades 11-12
Harcourt Brace Jovanovich, 1989 (Termination Date: 1994)

Understanding Psychology: Grades 11-12
McGraw-Hill, 1986 (Termination Date: 1994)

Invitation to Psychology: Grades 11-12
Scott, Foresman, 1989 (Termination Date: 1994)

Psychology and You: Grades 11-12
West, 1990 (Termination Date: 1994)

Sociology

Sociology: The Study of Human Relationships: Grades 10-12
Harcourt Brace Jovanovich, 1990 (Termination Date: 1994)

Sociology: Understanding Society: Grades 10-12
Prentice Hall, 1990 (Termination Date: 1994)

Scholastic Sociology: The Search for Social Patterns: Grades 10-12
Scholastic, 1989 (Termination Date: 1994)

South Carolina Social Studies

At Home in South Carolina: Grade 3
Sandlapper, 1991 (Termination Date: 1995)

Horizons of South Carolina: Grade 3
Walsworth, 1991 (Termination Date: 1995)

South Carolina History

The History of South Carolina in the Building of the Nation: Grade 8
Alester G. Furman, 1991 (Termination Date: 1995)

South Carolina: One of the Fifty States: Grade 8
Sandlapper, 1991 (Termination Date: 1995)

Western Civilization

The Modern World: 16th Century to Present: Grades 9-12
Addison-Wesley, 1988 (Termination Date: 1995)

A History of Civilization: Prehistory to the Present: Grades 11-12
Prentice Hall, 1988 (Termination Date: 1995)

Tennessee

Integrated Social Studies
Supplementary

Basic Map Skills, Books A-C: Grades 1-3
Hammond, 1984 (Termination Year: 1996)

Map Skills Readiness Book: Grade 3
Hammond, 1980 (Termination Year: 1996)

Understanding Maps: Grade 4
Hammond, 1984 (Termination Year: 1996)

American History through Maps: Grades 4-5
Hammond, 1984 (Termination Year: 1996)

World History through Maps: Grades 5-6
Hammond, 1984 (Termination Year: 1996)

HBJ Social Studies: Grades 1-6
Harcourt Brace Jovanovich/HRW, 1988 (Termination Year: 1996)

Heath Social Studies: Grades 1-6
D. C. Heath, 1989 (Termination Year: 1996)

The World around Us: Grades 1-6
Macmillan, 1990 (Termination Year: 1996)

Scott Foresman Social Studies Learning Systems: Grades 1-7
Scott, Foresman, 1989 (Termination Year: 1996)

Silver Burdett and Ginn Social Studies: Grades 1-6
Silver Burdett and Ginn, 1990 (Termination Year: 1996)

Geography
Glencoe World Geography: Grades 7-8
Glencoe, 1989 (Termination Year: 1996)

Supplementary
Intermediate U.S. Atlas: Grades 7-8
Hammond, 1984 (Termination Year: 1996)

Intermediate World Atlas: Grades 7-8
Hammond, 1984 (Termination Year: 1996)

Reading Skills for American History and Geography: Grades 7-8
Hammond, 1981 (Termination Year: 1996)

Reading Skills for World History and Geography: Grades 7-8
Hammond, 1981 (Termination Year: 1996)

The World Today: Grade 7
D. C. Heath, 1989 (Termination Year: 1996)

Geography: Grade 7
Houghton-Mifflin Company, 1985 (Termination Year: 1996)

World Geography: People and Places: Grade 7
Merrill (Glencoe), 1989 (Termination Year: 1996)

People on Earth: A World Geography: Grade 7
Scott, Foresman, 1988 (Termination Year: 1996)

A World View: Grade 7
Silver Burdett and Ginn, 1990 (Termination Year: 1996)

Tennessee History
A History of Tennessee: Grade 7
Clairmont, n.d. (Termination Year: 1996)

Dynamic Tennessee: Land, History and Government: Grades 7-8
Steck-Vaughn, 1990 (Termination Year: 1996)

A Panorama of Tennessee II: Grades 7-8
Walsworth, 1990 (Termination Year: 1996)

Horizons of Tennessee: Grade 7
Walsworth, 1990 (Termination Year: 1996)

American History
Spirit of Liberty: Grades 7-9
Addison-Wesley, 1987 (Termination Year: 1996)

Challenge of Freedom: Grades 7-8
Glencoe, 1990 (Termination Year: 1996)

Experiencing American History: Grade 8
Globe, 1986 (Termination Year: 1996)

America's Story: Grade 8
Houghton-Mifflin, 1990 (Termination Year: 1996)

Great Cases of the Supreme Court: Grade 8
(Supplementary)
Houghton-Mifflin, 1989 (Termination Year: 1996)

American History: Grade 8
Harcourt Brace Jovanovich/HRW, 1986 (Termination Year: 1996)

U.S. History: Grade 8
Harcourt Brace Jovanovich/HRW, 1988 (Termination Year: 1996)

A Proud Nation: Grade 8
McDougal, Littell, 1989 (Termination Year: 1996)

America Is: Grade 8
Merrill (Glencoe), 1987 (Termination Year: 1996)

American Spirit: Grade 8
Prentice Hall, 1990 (Termination Year: 1996)

The American Nation: Grade 8
Prentice Hall, 1989 (Termination Year: 1996)

One Flag, One Land: Grade 8
Silver Burdett and Ginn, 1990 (Termination Year: 1996)

Civics
American Civics: Grades 9-10
Harcourt Brace Jovanovich/HRW, 1987 (Termination Year: 1996)

Civics: Citizens in Action: Grades 9-12
Merrill (Glencoe), 1990 (Termination Year: 1996)

Civics: Government and Citizenship: Grades 9-12
Prentice Hall, 1990 (Termination Year: 1996)

Civics for Americans: Grades 9-12
Scott, Foresman, 1986 (Termination Year: 1996)

Civics: The United States and Tennessee: Grades 9-12
Walsworth, 1990 (Termination Year: 1996)

Contemporary Issues
Supplementary
Participation in Government Course Implementation Guide: Grades 11-12
Kendall/Hunt, 1988 (Termination Year: 1996)

The Public Debt: Breaking the Habit of Deficit Spending: Grades 11-12
Kendall/Hunt, 1988 (Termination Year: 1996)

Health Care for the Elderly: Moral Dilemmas, Mortal Choices: Grades 11-12
Kendall/Hunt, 1988 (Termination Year: 1996)

Coping with Aids: The Public Response to the Epidemic: Grades 11-12
Kendall/Hunt, 1988 (Termination Year: 1996)

The Superpowers: Nuclear Weapons and National Security: Grades 11-12
Kendall/Hunt, 1988 (Termination Year: 1996)

The Trade Gap: Regaining the Competitive Edge: Grades 11-12
Kendall/Hunt, 1987 (Termination Year: 1996)

Freedom of Speech: Where to Draw the Line: Grades 11-12
Kendall/Hunt, 1987 (Termination Year: 1996)

Crime: What We Fear, What Can Be Done: Grades 11-12
Kendall/Hunt, 1987 (Termination Year: 1996)

Immigration: What We Promised, Where to Draw the Line: Grades 11-12
Kendall/Hunt, 1987 (Termination Year: 1996)

The Farm Crisis: Who's in Trouble, How to Respond: Grades 11-12
Kendall/Hunt, 1987 (Termination Year: 1996)

Economics

Addison-Wesley Economics: Grades 10-12
Addison-Wesley, 1988 (Termination Year: 1996)

Scribner Economics: Grades 9-12
Glencoe, 1988 (Termination Year: 1996)

Basic Economic Principles: Grades 9-12
Glencoe, 1989 (Termination Year: 1996)

Economics and the American Free Enterprise System: Grades 9-12
Globe, 1988 (Termination Year: 1996)

Economics: Free Enterprise in Action: Grades 9-12
Harcourt Brace Jovanovich/HRW, 1988 (Termination Year: 1996)

The American Economy: Analysis, Issues, Principles: Grades 9-12
Houghton-Mifflin, 1986 (Termination Year: 1996)

Economics for Consumers, Alternative Level--Low: Grades 9-12
Houghton-Mifflin (Glencoe), 1989 (Termination Year: 1996)

McDougal, Littell Economics: Grades 9-12
McDougal, Littell, 1988 (Termination Year: 1996)

Economics: Principles and Practices: Grades 10-12
Merrill (Glencoe), 1988 (Termination Year: 1996)

Economics: Its Your Business: Grades 9-12
New Readers Press, 1986, Supplementary (Termination Year: 1996)

Invitation to Economics: Grades 9-12
Scott, Foresman, 1988 (Termination Year: 1996)

Economics: The Science of Cost, Benefit and Choice: Grades 9-12
South-Western, 1988 (Termination Year: 1996)

The World of Economics: Grades 9-12
South-Western, 1988, Supplementary (Termination Year: 1996)

Economics and Making Decisions: Grades 9-12
West, 1988 (Termination Year: 1996)

Psychology

Understanding Psychology: Grades 10-12
Glencoe, 1986 (Termination Year: 1996)

Psychology: Its Principles and Applications: Grades 9-12
Harcourt Brace Jovanovich/HRW, 1989 (Termination Year: 1996)

Invitation to Psychology: Grades 9-12
Scott, Foresman, 1989 (Termination Year: 1996)

Psychology and You: Grades 9-12
West, 1990 (Termination Year: 1996)

Sociology

Sociology: The Study of Human Relationships: Grades 9-12
Harcourt Brace Jovanovich/HRW, 1990 (Termination Year: 1996)

Sociology: Understanding Society: Grades 9-12
Prentice Hall, 1990 (Termination Year: 1996)

Scholastic Sociology: The Search for Social Patterns: Grades 9-12
Scholastic, n.d. (Termination Year: 1996)

U.S. Government

Government in the U.S.: Grades 9-12
Glencoe, 1990 (Termination Year: 1996)

Understanding American Government: Grades 11-12
Glencoe, 1988 (Termination Year: 1996)

Experiencing American Citizenship: Grades 9-10
Globe, 1988 (Termination Year: 1996)

American Government: The Republic in Action: Grades 9-12
Harcourt Brace Jovanovich/HRW, 1986 (Termination Year: 1996)

We the People: Grades 9-12
Harcourt Brace Jovanovich/HRW, 1989 (Termination Year: 1996)

Government in America: Grades 9-12
Houghton-Mifflin, 1990 (Termination Year: 1996)

Vital Issues of the Constitution: Grades 9-12
Houghton-Mifflin, 1989 (Termination Year: 1996)

United States Government: Grades 9-12
Media Materials, 1987 (Termination Year: 1996)

American Government: Principles and Practices: Grades 10-12
Merrill (Glencoe), 1987 (Termination Year: 1996)

MaGruder's American Government: Grades 9-12
Prentice Hall, 1990 (Termination Year: 1996)

Government by the People National/State/Local: Grades 10-12
Prentice Hall (Simon and Schuster), 1990 (Termination Year: 1996)

Consent of the Governed: A Study of American Government: Grades 9-12
Scott, Foresman, 1988 (Termination Year: 1996)

The Constitution: Grades 7-12
Scott, Foresman, 1991 (Supplementary) (Termination Year: 1996)

American Government and Politics Today: Grades 9-12
West, 1989 (Termination Year: 1996)

U.S. History
Addison-Wesley U.S. History: Grades 9-12
Addison-Wesley, 1986 (Termination Year: 1996)

Exploring U.S. History: Grades 11-12
Globe, 1986 (Termination Year: 1996)

U.S. History Atlas: Grades 7-12
Hammond, 1989, Supplementary (Termination Year: 1996)

The American Pageant: Grades 11-12
D. C. Heath, 1987 (Termination Year: 1996)

Our Land, Our Time: Grades 11-12
Harcourt Brace Jovanovich/HRW, 1987 (Termination Year: 1996)

Triumph of the American Nation: Grades 11-12
Harcourt Brace Jovanovich/HRW, 1990/1986 (Termination Year: 1996)

America: The Glorious Republic: Grades 11-12
Houghton-Mifflin, 1990 (Termination Year: 1996)

The Americans: Grades 11-12
McDougal, Littell, 1988 (Termination Year: 1996)

A History of the U.S.: Grades 11-12
Prentice Hall, 1990 (Termination Year: 1996)

The United States: A History of the Republic: Grades 11-12
Prentice Hall, 1990 (Termination Year: 1996)

The United States: Grades 11-12
Prentice Hall (Simon and Schuster), 1987 (Termination Year: 1996)

Land of Promise: A History of the United States: Grades 11-12
Scott, Foresman, 1987 (Termination Year: 1996)

Life and Liberty: Grades 11-12
Scott, Foresman, 1987 (Termination Year: 1996)

Reading American History: Grades 7-12
Scott, Foresman, 1987, Supplementary (Termination Year: 1996)

World Geography
McGraw-Hill World Geography: Grades 9-12
Glencoe, 1989 (Termination Year: 1996)

Exploring a Changing World: Grades 9-12
Glencoe, 1988 (Termination Year: 1996)

World Atlas for Students: Grades 7-12
Hammond, 1984, Supplementary (Termination
Year: 1996)

Comparative World Atlas: Grades 7-12
Hammond, 1989, Supplementary (Termination
Year: 1996)

Essential Map Skills: Grades 7-12
Hammond, 1985, Supplementary (Termination
Year: 1996)

Heath World Geography: Grades 9-12
D. C. Heath, 1989 (Termination Year: 1996)

World Geography: The Earth and Its People:
Grades 9-12
Harcourt Brace Jovanovich/HRW, 1989 (Termi-
nation Year: 1996)

World Geography Today: Grades 9-12
Harcourt Brace Jovanovich/HRW, 1989 (Termination Year: 1996)

Scott Foresman World Geography: Grades 9-12
Scott, Foresman, 1989 (Termination Year: 1996)

Scott Foresman World Atlas: Grades 7-12
Scott, Foresman, 1988, Supplementary (Termination Year: 1996)

Geography: Our Changing World: Grades 9-12
West, 1990 (Termination Year: 1996)

World History
Addison-Wesley World History: Grades 9-12
Addison-Wesley, 1989 (Termination Year: 1996)

Exploring World History: Grades 9-12
Globe, 1990 (Termination Year: 1996)

Historical Atlas of World: Grades 7-12
Hammond, 1989, Supplementary (Termination
Year: 1996)

World History, Perspectives on the Past: Grades 9-
12
D. C. Heath, 1990 (Termination Year: 1996)

History of the World: Grades 9-12
Houghton-Mifflin, 1990 (Termination Year:
1996)

World History: Grades 9-12
Harcourt Brace Jovanovich/HRW, 1990 (Termination Year: 1996)

World History: People and Nations: Grades 9-12
Harcourt Brace Jovanovich/HRW, 1990 (Termination Year: 1996)

Links across Time and Place: A World History:
Grades 9-12
McDougal, Littell, 1990 (Termination Year: 1996)

The Human Experience: A World History: Grades
9-12
Merrill (Glencoe), 1990 (Termination Year: 1996)

Human Heritage: A World History: Grades 9-12
Merrill (Glencoe), 1989 (Termination Year: 1996)

World History: Patterns of Civilization: Grades 9-12
Prentice Hall, 1990 (Termination Year: 1996)

Pageant of World History: Grades 9-12
Prentice Hall, 1990 (Termination Year: 1996)

A History of Civilization: Grades 9-12
Prentice Hall (Simon and Schuster), 1988 (Termination Year: 1996)

History and Life: The World and Its People: Grades
9-12
Scott, Foresman, 1990 (Termination Year: 1996)

Living World History: Grades 9-12
Scott, Foresman, 1990 (Termination Year: 1996)

Practicing World History Skills: Grades 9-12
Scott, Foresman, 1991, Supplementary (Termination Year: 1996)

Texas

Social Studies Learning Systems
HBJ Social Studies: Grades 1-6 (also in Spanish
edition)
Harcourt Brace Jovanovich, 1988 (Termination
Year: 1994)

Heath Social Studies: Grades 1-6 (also in Spanish
edition)
D. C. Heath, 1988 (Termination Year: 1994)

The United States Past to Present: Grade 5 (also in
Spanish edition)
D. C. Heath, 1988 (Termination Year: 1994)

Primary Social Studies: Grades 1-2 (also in Spanish edition)
Nystrom, 1988 (Termination Year: 1994)

Scott, Foresman Social Studies: Grades 1-6 (also in Spanish edition)
Scott, Foresman, 1988 (Termination Year: 1994)

Silver Burdett and Ginn Social Studies: Grades 1-6 (also in Spanish edition)
Silver Burdett and Ginn, 1988 (Termination Year: 1994)

Our Nation, Our World: Grades 5-6 (also in Spanish edition)
Macmillan/McGraw-Hill (Termination Year: 1994)

Texas History and Geography

Texas and Texans: Grades 7
Glencoe/McGraw-Hill, 1987 (Termination Year: 1993)

Texas: Land and People: Grade 7
Hendrick-Long, 1987 (Termination Year: 1993)

Texas, Our Texas (Learned and Tested): Grade 7
Holt, Rinehart and Winston, 1987 (Termination Year: 1993)

U.S. History

America: The Glorious Republic, Vols. 1-2: Grades 8-12
Houghton Mifflin, 1986 (Termination Year: 1992)

Land of Promise, Vols. 1-2: Grades 8-12
Scott, Foresman, 1986 (Termination Year: 1992)

The American People: A History to 1877: Grade 8
McDougal, Littell, 1986 (Termination Year: 1992)

HBJ The American Nation: Grades 8-12
Harcourt Brace Jovanovich, 1986 (Termination Year: 1992)

A History of the Republic: The United States to 1877: Grade 8
Prentice Hall, 1986 (Termination Year: 1992)

A History of the United States since 1861: Grades 9-12
Prentice Hall, 1986 (Termination Year: 1992)

Our Land, Our Time: A History of the U.S. from 1865: Grades 9-12
Coronado, 1986 (Termination Year: 1992)

World History Studies

Addison-Wesley World History: Grades 9-12
Addison-Wesley, 1990 (Termination Year: 1996)

World History: People and Nations: Grades 9-12
Harcourt Brace Jovanovich, 1990 (Termination Year: 1996)

World History: Perspectives on the Past: Grades 9-12
D. C. Heath, 1990 (Termination Year: 1996)

A History of the World: Grades 9-12
Houghton Mifflin, 1990 (Termination Year: 1996)

Links across Time and Place: A World History: Grades 9-12
McDougal, Littell, 1990 (Termination Year: 1996)

World History: Patterns of Civilization: Grades 9-12
Prentice Hall, 1990 (Termination Year: 1996)

The Pageant of World History: Grades 9-12
Prentice Hall, 1990 (Termination Year: 1996)

History and Life: Grades 9-12
Scott, Foresman, 1990 (Termination Year: 1996)

World Geography

Glencoe World Geography: Grades 9-12
Glencoe/McGraw-Hill, 1989 (Termination Year: 1996)

World Geography: The Earth and Its People: Grades 9-12
Harcourt Brace Jovanovich, 1989 (Termination Year: 1995)

Heath World Geography: Grades 9-12
D. C. Heath, 1989 (Termination Year: 1995)

World Geography Today: Grades 9-12
Holt, Rinehart and Winston, 1989 (Termination Year: 1995)

World Geography: Grades 9-12
Glencoe/McGraw-Hill, 1989 (Termination Year: 1995)

Merrill World Geography: People and Places:
Grades 9-12
Glencoe/McGraw-Hill, 1989 (Termination Year:
1995)

World Geography: Grades 9-12
Scholastic, 1989 (Termination Year: 1995)

Scott, Foresman World Geography: Grades 9-12
Scott, Foresman, 1989 (Termination Year: 1995)

U.S. Government
American Government (Merrill): Grades 9-12
Glencoe/McGraw-Hill, 1987 (Termination Year:
1993)

Consent of the Governed: Grades 9-12
Scott, Foresman, 1987 (Termination Year: 1993)

American Government: Grades 9-12
Harcourt Brace Jovanovich, 1986 (Termination
Year: 1993)

Government (Scribner): Grades 9-12
Glencoe/McGraw-Hill, 1987 (Termination Year:
1993)

American Government (Allyn): Grades 9-12
Prentice Hall, 1987 (Termination Year: 1993)

Economics
Economics and Free Enterprise: Grades 9-12
Addison-Wesley, 1988 (Termination Year: 1993)

Economics Free Enterprise in Action: Grades 9-12
Harcourt Brace Jovanovich, 1988 (Termination
Year: 1993)

Economics for Decision Making: Grades 9-12
D. C. Heath, 1988 (Termination Year: 1993)

Economics: Principles and Practices (Merrill):
Grades 9-12
Glencoe/McGraw-Hill, 1988 (Termination Year:
1993)

Invitation to Economics: Grades 9-12
Scott, Foresman, 1988 (Termination Year: 1993)

Economics: The Free Enterprise System: Grades 9-
12
South-Western, 1988 (Termination Year: 1993)

Psychology
Psychology: Its Principles and Applications: Grades
9-12
Harcourt Brace Jovanovich, 1989 (Termination
Year: 1995)

Invitation to Psychology: Grades 9-12
Scott, Foresman, 1989 (Termination Year: 1995)

Sociology
Sociology: Understanding Society: Grades 9-12
Prentice Hall, 1989 (Termination Year: 1995)

Sociology: The Search for Social Patterns: Grades
9-12
Scholastic, 1989 (Termination Year: 1995)

Utah

Utah did not provide a list.

Virginia

Elementary Social Studies (Except Grade 4)
HBJ Series: Grades 1-6
Harcourt Brace Jovanovich, 1991 (Termination
Date: 1993)

Heath Social Studies: Grades 1-6
D. C. Heath, 1991 (Termination Date: 1993)

The World around Us: Grades 1-6
Macmillan/McGraw-Hill, 1991 (Termination
Date: 1993)

Scott, Foresman Social Studies: Grades 1-6
Scott, Foresman, 1991 (Termination Date: 1993)

People in Time and Place: Grades 1-6
Silver Burdett and Ginn, 1991 (Termination Date:
1993)

Citizenship Studies
Civics: Participation in Our Democracy: Grade 8
Addison-Wesley, 1991 (Termination Date: 1993)

Exploring American Citizenship: Grade 8
Globe, 1988 (Termination Date: 1993)

We the People: Citizens and Their Government:
Grade 8 Holt, Rinehart and Winston/Harcourt
Brace Jovanovich, 1989 (Termination Date: 1993)

Civics: Citizens in Action: Grade 8
Glencoe/Macmillan/McGraw-Hill, 1990 (Termination Date: 1993)

Civics: Government and Citizenship: Grade 8
Prentice Hall, (Termination Date: 1993)

Civics for Americans: Grade 8
Scott, Foresman, 1991 (Termination Date: 1993)

World Geography

Glencoe World Geography: A Physical and Cultural Approach: Grade 9
Glencoe/Macmillan/McGraw-Hill, 1989 (Termination Date: 1993)

Exploring a Changing World: Grade 9
Globe, 1988 (Termination Date: 1993)

Heath World Geography: Grade 9
D. C. Heath, 1989 (Termination Date: 1993)

World Geography: The Earth and Its People: Grade 9
Holt, Rinehart & Winston/Harcourt Brace Jovanovich, 1989 (Termination Date: 1993)

World Geography Today: Grade 9
Holt, Rinehart & Winston/Harcourt Brace Jovanovich, 1989 (Termination Date: 1993)

World Geography: People and Places: Grade 9
Glencoe/Macmillan/McGraw-Hill, 1989 (Termination Date: 1993)

Scholastic World Geography: Grade 9
Scholastic, 1989 (Termination Date: 1993)

Scott, Foresman World Geography: Grade 9
Scott, Foresman, 1989 (Termination Date: 1993)

People on Earth: A World Geography: Grade 9
Scott, Foresman, 1988 (Termination Date: 1993)

A World View: Grade 9
Silver Burdett and Ginn, 1990 (Termination Date: 1993)

World History

World History: Traditions and New Directions: Grade 10
Addison-Wesley, 1991 (Termination Date: 1993)

World History: Perspectives on the Past: Grade 10
D. C. Heath, 1990 (Termination Date: 1993)

World History: People and Nations: Grade 10
Holt, Rinehart and Winston/Harcourt Brace Jovanovich, 1990 (Termination Date: 1993)

History of the World: Grade 10
Houghton Mifflin, 1990 (Termination Date: 1993)

Links across Time and Place: Grade 10
McDougal, Littell, 1990 (Termination Date: 1993)

The Human Experience: A World History: Grade 10
Glencoe/Macmillan/McGraw-Hill, 1990 (Termination Date: 1993)

Human Heritage: A World History: Grade 10
Glencoe/Macmillan/McGraw-Hill, 1989 (Termination Date: 1993)

History: Patterns of Civilization: Grade 10
Prentice Hall, 1990 (Termination Date: 1993)

The Pageant of World History: Grade 10
Prentice Hall, 1990 (Termination Date: 1993)

History and Life: Grade 10
Scott, Foresman, 1990 (Termination Date: 1993)

Living World History: Grade 10
Scott, Foresman, 1990 (Termination Date: 1993)

Virginia and U.S. Government

Government in the United States: Grade 12
Glencoe/Macmillan/McGraw-Hill, 1990 (Termination Date: 1993)

Government in America: Grade 12
Houghton Mifflin, 1991 (Termination Date: 1993)

American Government: Principles and Practices: Grade 12
Glencoe/Macmillan/McGraw-Hill, 1991 (Termination Date: 1993)

Government by the People: Grade 12
Prentice Hall, 1990 (Termination Date: 1993)

Magruder's American Government: Grade 12
Prentice Hall, 1991 (Termination Date: 1993)

Consent of the Governed: Grade 12
Scott, Foresman, 1988 (Termination Date: 1993)

Economics

Addison-Wesley Economics: Grades 10-12
Addison-Wesley, 1988 (Termination Date: 1993)

Introduction to Economics: Grades 9-12
EMC, 1988 (Termination Date: 1993)

Basic Economic Principles: Grades 9-12
Glencoe/Macmillan/McGraw-Hill, 1989 (Termination Date: 1993)

Economics Today and Tomorrow: Grades 9-12
Glencoe/Macmillan/McGraw-Hill, 1991 (Termination Date: 1993)

Economics: Free Enterprises in Action: Grades 9-12
Holt, Rinehart and Winston/Harcourt Brace Jovanovich, 1988 (Termination Date: 1993)

McDougal, Littell Economics: Grades 9-12
McDougal, Littell, 1991 (Termination Date: 1993)

Economics: Principles and Practices: Grades Sec.
Glencoe/Macmillan/McGraw-Hill, 1988 (Termination Date: 1993)

Basic Economics: Grades 9-12
Scott, Foresman, 1989 (Termination Date: 1993)

Invitation to Economics: Grades 9-12
Scott, Foresman, 1988 (Termination Date: 1993)

Economics and Making Decisions: Grades 9-12
West, 1988 (Termination Date: 1993)

Sociology
Sociology: The Study of Human Relationships: Grades 9-12
Holt, Rinehart and Winston/Harcourt Brace Jovanovich, 1990 (Termination Date: 1993)

Sociology: Understanding Society: Grades 9-12
Prentice Hall, 1989 (Termination Date: 1993)

Sociology: The Search for Social Patterns: Grades 9-12
Scholastic, 1989 (Termination Date: 1993)

United States History (Grade 7)
Challenge of Freedom: Grade 7
Glencoe/Macmillan/McGraw-Hill, 1990 (Termination Date: 1993)

Exploring American History: Grade 7
Globe, 1991 (Termination Date: 1993)

America's Story: Grade 7
Houghton Mifflin, 1990 (Termination Date: 1993)

The American Nation: Grade 7
Prentice Hall, 1991 (Termination Date: 1993)

American Spirit: A History of the American People: Grade 7
Prentice Hall, 1990 (Termination Date: 1993)

America: The People and the Dream: Grade 7
Scott, Foresman, 1991 (Termination Date: 1993)

One Flag, One Land: Grade 7
Globe, 1990 (Termination Date: 1993)

United States History
American Pageant: A History of the Republic: Grade 11
D. C. Heath, 1991 (Termination Date: 1993)

Enduring Vision: A History of the American People: Grade 11
D. C. Heath, 1990 (Termination Date: 1993)

Our Land, Our Time: A History of the United States: Grade 11
Holt, Rinehart and Winston/Harcourt Brace Jovanovich, 1991 (Termination Date: 1993)

History of the United States: Grade 11
Houghton Mifflin, 1991 (Termination Date: 1993)

The Americans: Grade 11
McDougal, Littell, 1991 (Termination Date: 1993)

A History of the United States: Grade 11
Prentice Hall, 1990 (Termination Date: 1993)

The United States: A History of the Republic: Grade 11
Prentice Hall, 1990 (Termination Date: 1993)

Land of Promise: A History of the United States: Grade 11
Scott, Foresman, 1987 (Termination Date: 1993)

Life and Liberty: An American History: Grade 11
Scott, Foresman, 1987 (Termination Date: 1993)

Virginia Studies
Heath Social Studies--Exploring Virginia: Grade 4
D. C. Heath, 1991 (Termination Date: 1993)

The World around Us--Virginia: Grade 4
Macmillan/McGraw-Hill, 1991 (Termination Date: 1993)

Virginia History & Government: 1850 to the Present: Grade 4
Silver Burdett and Ginn, 1991 (Termination Date: 1993)

People in Time and Place--Virginia History and Geography: Grade 4
Silver Burdett and Ginn, 1991 (Termination Date: 1993)

Supplementary Materials

"By the Good People of Virginia . . . " Our Commonwealth's Government: Grade 12
Virginia Chamber of Commerce, 1991 (Termination Date: 1993)

West Virginia

Heath Social Studies: Grades K-6/7
D. C. Heath, 1991 (Termination Date: 1997)

Exploring the Non-Western World: Grade 7
Globe, 1988 (Termination Date: 1997)

HBJ Social Studies: Grades K-6
Harcourt Brace Jovanovich, 1991 (Termination Date: 1997)

Hougton Mifflin Social Studies: Grades K-5
Holt, Rinehart and Winston/Harcourt Brace Jovanovich, 1991 (Termination Date: 1997)

The World around Us: Grades K-7
Macmillan/McGraw-Hill, 1991 (Termination Date: 1997)

People in Time and Place: Grades K-7
Silver Burdett and Ginn, 1991 (Termination Date: 1997)

West Virginia Studies

Horizons of West Virginia: Grade 4
Walsworth, 1991 (Termination Date: 1997)

West Virginia: Our State: Grade 4
West Virginia Historical Education Foundation, 1990 (Termination Date: 1997)

Foundations of Democracy

Civics: Grade 8
Addison-Wesley, 1991 (Termination Date: 1997)

Civics: Citizens in Action: Grade 8
Glencoe/Macmillan/McGraw-Hill, 1990 (Termination Date: 1997)

Exploring American Citizenship: Grade 8
Globe, 1988 (Termination Date: 1997)

West Virginia Studies

Panorama of West Virginia: Grade 8
Walsworth, 1991 (Termination Date: 1997)

The 35th Star: Grade 8
Walsworth, 1991 (Termination Date: 1997)

West Virginia: Our Land--Our People: Grade 8
West Virginia Historical Education Foundation, 1990 (Termination Date: 1997)

Social Studies 9-12

Addison-Wesley World History: Grade 9
Addison-Wesley, 1991 (Termination Date: 1997)

World History: Perspectives on the Past: Grades 9-10
D. C. Heath, 1990 (Termination Date: 1997)

The American Pageant: A History of the Republic: Grade 10 (High Ability)
D. C. Heath, 1987 (Termination Date: 1997)

The Enduring Vision: A History of the American People: Grade 11 (High Ability)
D. C. Heath, 1990 (Termination Date: 1997)

The Human Experience: A World History: Grades 9-11
Glencoe/Macmillan/McGraw-Hill, 1990 (Termination Date: 1997)

American Odyssey: The United States in the 20th Century: Grade 11
Glencoe/Macmillan/McGraw-Hill, 1991 (Termination Date: 1997)

Human Heritage: A World History: Grades 9-10 (Low Ability)
Glencoe/Macmillan/McGraw-Hill, 1989 (Termination Date: 1997)

Two Centuries of Progress: Grade 10 (Low Ability)
Glencoe/Macmillan/McGraw-Hill, 1991 (Termination Date: 1997)

Exploring American History: Grades 10-11
Globe, 1991 (Termination Date: 1997)

Exploring World History: Grade 9 (Low Ability)
Globe, 1990 (Termination Date: 1997)

World History: People and Nations: Grades 9-10
Holt, Rinehart and Winston/Harcourt Brace
Jovanovich, 1990 (Termination Date: 1997)

Our Land, Our Time: Grade 10
Holt, Rinehart and Winston/Harcourt Brace
Jovanovich, 1991 (Termination Date: 1997)

The Story of America: Beginning to 1914: Grade 11
Holt, Rinehart and Winston/Harcourt Brace
Jovanovich, 1991 (Termination Date: 1997)

World History: Grade 9 (Low Ability)
Holt, Rinehart and Winston/Harcourt Brace
Jovanovich, 1990 (Termination Date: 1997)

History of the World: Grades 9-10
Houghton Mifflin, 1990 (Termination Date: 1997)

History of the United States: Grade 11
Houghton Mifflin, 1991 (Termination Date: 1997)

America's Story: Grades 10-11 (Low Ability)
Houghton Mifflin, 1990 (Termination Date: 1997)

Links across Time and Place: Grade 9
McDougal, Littell, 1990 (Termination Date: 1997)

The Americans: Grade 11
McDougal, Littell, 1991 (Termination Date: 1997)

The Pageant of World History: Grade 9
Prentice Hall, 1990 (Termination Date: 1997)

The United States: A History of the Republic: Grade 10
Prentice Hall, 1990 (Termination Date: 1997)

A History of the Republic, Vol. 1: Grade 10
Prentice Hall, 1990 (Termination Date: 1997)

A History of the United States since 1861: Grade 11
Prentice Hall, 1990 (Termination Date: 1997)

History and Life: Grade 9
Scott, Foresman, 1990 (Termination Date: 1997)

America: The People and the Dream: Grades 10-11
Scott, Foresman, 1991 (Termination Date: 1997)

INDEX TO REVIEWS
OF EDUCATIONAL MATERIALS

THIS index cites reviews of recently published materials for use in social studies classes, including curriculum guides, lesson plans, project books, software programs, videos, and filmstrips. The citations cover reviews from the past two years (up to March 1992), and they reflect a search of educational journals, magazines, and newsletters that would include reviews of social studies materials. The journals chosen are those that are available in teacher college libraries, in other college and university collections, and in many public libraries. They also include the major publications sent to members of the appropriate educational organizations. The review for each item can be found under the following listings:

· the title of the item
· the author(s)
· the publisher or producer/distributor
· school level (elementary, middle school, or high school)
· subject (a broad subject arrangement is used)
· special medium (for "Software packages" and "Films/videos")

ABC-Clio (publishers)
  Geography: A Resource Book for Secondary Schools, by David A. Hill and Regina McCormic (Santa Barbara, CA: ABC-Clio, 1989). Reviewed in: *Journal of Geography* 89, no. 2 (Mar./Apr. 1990): 87

Al Qassar, Ayad
  Arab World Notebook: Secondary School Level, by Ayad Al Qassar and Audrey Shabbas (Berkeley: Najda, 1989). Reviewed in: *Social Education* 56, no 1 (Jan. 1992): 73

Alarion (publishers)
  American Art and Architecture, video (Boulder: Alarion, 1990). Reviewed in: *Curriculum Review* 30, no. 5 (Jan. 1991): 31

American Art and Architecture
  video (Boulder: Alarion, 1990). Reviewed in: *Curriculum Review* 30, no. 5 (Jan. 1991): 31

American Adventures: True Stories from America's Past
  by Morrie Greenberg (Northridge, CA: Brooke-Richards, 1991). Reviewed in: *Curriculum Review* 31, no. 1 (Sept. 1991): 31

American history

American Adventures: True Stories from America's Past, by Morrie Greenberg (Northridge, CA: Brooke-Richards, 1991). Reviewed in: *Curriculum Review* 31, no. 1 (Sept. 1991): 31

Counterrevolution: US Foreign Policy, by Edward Boorstein and Regula Boorstein (New York: International Publications, 1990). Reviewed in: *Social Education* 56, no. 2 (Feb. 1992): 133

Landmark Decisions of the United States Supreme Court, ed. by Steve Gilbert and Maureen Harrison (Beverly Hills: Excellent Books, 1991). Reviewed in: *Curriculum Review* 30, no. 6 (Feb. 1991): 28

Poverty in America: What Do We Do about It?, by Bertha Davis (New York: Franklin Watts, 1991). Reviewed in: *Curriculum Review* 31, no. 2 (Oct. 1991): 31

The Press and Presidency, filmstrip (Madison: Knowledge Unlimited, 1991). Reviewed in: *Media and Methods* 28, no. 4 (Mar./Apr. 1992): 48

Religion in American History: What to Teach and How, by Charles C. Haynes (Alexandria, VA: Association for Supervision and Curriculum Development, 1990). Reviewed in: *Curriculum Review* 30, no. 5 (Jan. 1991): 33

Turning Points in American History, by various authors (Englewood Cliffs, NJ: Silver Burdett). Reviewed in: *Curriculum Review* 31, no. 7 (Mar. 1992): 28-9

Arab World Notebook: Secondary School Level by Ayad Al Qassar and Audrey Shabbas (Berkeley: Najda, 1989). Reviewed in: *Social Education* 56, no 1 (Jan. 1992): 73

Art

American Art and Architecture, video (Boulder: Alarion, 1990). Reviewed in: *Curriculum Review* 30, no. 5 (Jan. 1991): 31

Asia

Tibet: Where Continents Collide Part 1, film (Cheshire, CT: EarthVision, 1989). Reviewed in: *Journal of Geographical Education* 38, no. 2 (Mar. 1990): 71

Association for Supervision and Curriculum Development

Renewing the Social Studies Curriculum, by Walter C. Parker (Alexandria, VA: Association for Supervision and Curriculum Development, 1991). Reviewed in: *Curriculum Review* 31, no. 7 (Mar. 1992): 30

Religion in American History: What to Teach and How, by Charles C. Haynes (Alexandria, VA: Association for Supervision and Curriculum Development, 1990). Reviewed in: *Curriculum Review* 30, no. 5 (Jan. 1991): 33

Beacon Films

History in the Making, video/film (Evanston: Beacon Films, n.d.). Reviewed in: *Media and Methods* 28, no. 2 (Nov./Dec. 1991): 50

Black, Peggy Tubbs

Social Studies Readers Theater for Children: Scripts and Script Development, by Peggy Tubbs Black, Mildred Knight Laughlin, and Margery Kirby Loberg (Englewood, CO: Teacher Ideas, 1990). Reviewed in: *Curriculum Review* 31, no. 7 (Mar. 1992): 29

Boorstein, Edward and Regula

Counterrevolution: US Foreign Policy, by Edward Boorstein and Regula Boorstein (New York: International Publications, 1990). Reviewed in: *Social Education* 56, no. 2 (Feb. 1992): 133

Broderbund (publishers)

Galleons of Glory: The Secret Voyage of Magellan, software (San Rafael, CA: Broderbund, 1990). Reviewed in: *Instructor* 101, no. 3 (Oct. 1991): 63

Brooke-Richards (publishers)

American Adventures: True Stories from America's Past, by Morrie Greenberg (Northridge, CA: Brooke-Richards, 1991). Reviewed in: *Curriculum Review* 31, no. 1 (Sept. 1991): 31

Bushbuck Charms, Viking Ships, & Dodo Eggs software (Tempe, AZ: PC Globe, 1990). Reviewed in: *Technology & Learning* 12, no. 1 (Sept. 1991): 11

Cambridge Career Products
The United Nations: It's More than You Think, video (Charleston, WV: Cambridge Career Products, 1991). Reviewed in: *Media and Methods* 28, no. 4 (Mar./Apr. 1992): 57

China
Tibet: Where Continents Collide Part 1, film (Cheshire, CT: EarthVision, 1989). Reviewed in: *Journal of Geographical Education* 38, no. 2 (Mar. 1990): 71

Columbus, Christopher
Columbus: His Enterprise--Exploding the Myth, by Hans Koning (New York: Monthly Review, 1982). Reviewed in: *The Social Studies* 83, no. 1 (Jan./Feb. 1992): 40

The Discovery of the Americas, by Betsy Maestro and Giulio Maestro (New York: Lothrop, Lee & Shepard, 1991). Reviewed in: *Reading Horizons* 32, no. 1 (Oct. 1991): 79

Where Do You Think You're Going, Christopher Columbus?, by Jean Fritz, film/video (Weston, CT: Weston Woods, 1991). Reviewed in: *Media Methods* 28, no. 40 (Mar./Apr. 1992): 48

Columbus: His Enterprise--Exploding the Myth by Hans Koning (New York: Monthly Review, 1982). Reviewed in: *The Social Studies* 83, no. 1 (Jan./Feb. 1992): 40

Coronet/MTI (publishers)
Soviet Union: Socialist City, video disc (Deerfield, IL: Coronet/MTI, 1990). Reviewed in: *Media and Methods* 28, no. 1 (Sept./Oct. 1991): 90

Counterrevolution: US Foreign Policy by Edward Boorstein and Regula Boorstein (New York: International Publications, 1990). Reviewed in: *Social Education* 56, no. 2 (Feb. 1992): 133

Current events
Headline Harry and the Great Paper Race, software (Torrance, CA: Davidson and Assoc., 1992). Reviewed in: *Technology & Learning* 12, no. 3 (Nov./Dec. 1991): 6, 8

Here and Now, film/video (Lincoln: Great Plains National, 1991). Reviewed in: *Media Methods* 28, no. 4 (Mar./Apr. 1992): 48

History in the Making, video/film (Evanston: Beacon Films, n.d.). Reviewed in: *Media and Methods* 28, no. 2 (Nov./Dec. 1991): 50

Lines in the Sand, video/film (New York: Griffin-Wirth Associates, n.d.). Reviewed in: *Media and Methods* 28, no. 4 (Mar./Apr. 1992): 57

Curriculum renewal
Renewing the Social Studies Curriculum, by Walter C. Parker (Alexandria, VA: Association for Supervision and Curriculum Development, 1991). Reviewed in: *Curriculum Review* 31, no. 7 (Mar. 1992): 30

Davidson and Associates (publishers)
Headline Harry and the Great Paper Race, software (Torrance, CA: Davidson and Associates, 1992). Reviewed in: *Technology & Learning* 12, no. 3 (Nov./Dec. 1991): 6, 8

Davis, Bertha
Poverty in America: What Do We Do about It?, by Bertha Davis (New York: Franklin Watts, 1991). Reviewed in: *Curriculum Review* 31, no. 2 (Oct. 1991): 31

Dawnwood (publishers)
History's Trickiest Questions, by Paul Kuttner (New York: Dawnwood, 1990). Reviewed in: *Curriculum Review* 30, no. 7 (Mar. 1991): 31

Discover the World
software (Dimondale, MI: Hartley Courseware, 1986). Reviewed in: *Instructor* 101, no. 3 (Oct. 1991): 63

The Discovery of the Americas
by Betsy Maestro and Giulio Maestro (New York: Lothrop, Lee & Shepard, 1991). Reviewed in: *Reading Horizons* 32, no. 1 (Oct. 1991): 79

Earthalert
software (Seattle: Mike2, n.d.). Reviewed in: *Journal of Geography* 91, no. 1 (Jan./Feb. 1992): 47-48

Earthscope Series
film (Washington, DC: Global View Productions, 1991). Reviewed in: *Journal of Environmental Education* 22, no. 4 (Summer 1991): 41

EarthVision (publishers)
Tibet: Where Continents Collide Part 1, film (Cheshire, CT: EarthVision, 1989). Reviewed in: *Journal of Geographical Education* 38, no. 2 (Mar. 1990): 71

Economics
Poverty in America: What Do We Do about It?, by Bertha Davis (New York: Franklin Watts, 1991). Reviewed in: *Curriculum Review* 31, no. 2 (Oct. 1991): 31

Educational Insights (publishers)
Geo-Safari, software (Dominguez Hills, CA: Educational Insights, n.d.). Reviewed in: *Journal of Geography* 91, no. 1 (Jan./Feb. 1992): 49

Elementary materials
The Discovery of the Americas, by Betsy Maestro and Giulio Maestro (New York: Lothrop, Lee & Shepard, 1991). Reviewed in: *Reading Horizons* 32, no. 1 (Oct. 1991): 79

Geo-Safari, software (Dominguez Hills, CA: Educational Insights, n.d.). Reviewed in: *Journal of Geography* 91, no. 1 (Jan./Feb. 1992): 49

Nations of the World, software (Coral Gables, FL: Robert R. De Torres, 1986). Reviewed in: *Journal of Geography* 90, no. 4 (July/Aug. 1991): 195

Renewing the Social Studies Curriculum, by Walter C. Parker (Alexandria, VA: Association for Supervision and Curriculum Development, 1991). Reviewed in: *Curriculum Review* 31, no. 7 (Mar. 1992): 30

Energy: The Key to Our Future
filmstrip (Niles, IL: United Learning, 1991). Reviewed in: *Media Methods* 28, no. 4 (Mar./ Apr. 1992): 48-49

Environmental studies
Earthalert, software (Seattle: Mike2, n.d.). Reviewed in: *Journal of Geography* 91, no. 1 (Jan./Feb. 1992): 47-48

Earthscope Series, film (Washington, DC: Global View Productions, 1991). Reviewed in: *Journal of Environmental Education* 22, no. 4 (Summer 1991): 41

Energy: The Key to Our Future, filmstrip (Niles, IL: United Learning, 1991). Reviewed in: *Media Methods* 28, no. 4 (Mar./Apr. 1992): 48-49

European history
Soviet Union: Socialist City, video disc (Deerfield, IL: Coronet/MTI, 1990). Reviewed in: *Media and Methods* 28, no. 1 (Sept./Oct. 1991): 90

Excellent Books (publishers)
Landmark Decisions of the United States Supreme Court, ed. by Steve Gilbert and Maureen Harrison (Beverly Hills: Excellent Books, 1991). Reviewed in: *Curriculum Review* 30, no. 6 (Feb. 1991): 28

Exploration
Columbus: His Enterprise--Exploding the Myth, by Hans Koning (New York: Monthly Review, 1982). Reviewed in: *The Social Studies* 83, no. 1 (Jan./Feb. 1992): 40

The Discovery of the Americas, by Betsy Maestro and Giulio Maestro (New York: Lothrop, Lee & Shepard, 1991). Reviewed in: *Reading Horizons* 32, no. 1 (Oct. 1991): 79

Where Do You Think You're Going, Christopher Columbus?, by Jean Fritz, film/video (Weston, CT: Weston Woods, 1991). Reviewed in: *Media Methods* 28, no. 40 (Mar./Apr. 1992): 48

Filmmaking
History in the Making, video/film (Evanston: Beacon Films, n.d.). Reviewed in: *Media and Methods* 28, no. 2 (Nov./Dec. 1991): 50

Films/videos
American Art and Architecture, video (Boulder: Alarion, 1990). Reviewed in: *Curriculum Review* 30, no. 5 (Jan. 1991): 31

Earthscope Series, film (Washington, DC: Global View Productions, 1991). Reviewed in: *Journal of Environmental Education* 22, no. 4 (Summer 1991): 41

Energy: The Key to Our Future, filmstrip (Niles, IL: United Learning, 1991). Reviewed in: *Media Methods* 28, no. 4 (Mar./Apr. 1992): 48-49

Films/videos *(cont'd)*
Here and Now, film/video (Lincoln: Great Plains National, 1991). Reviewed in: *Media Methods* 28, no. 4 (Mar./Apr. 1992): 48

History in the Making, video/film (Evanston: Beacon Films, n.d.). Reviewed in: *Media and Methods* 28, no. 2 (Nov./Dec. 1991): 50

Lines in the Sand, video/film (New York: Griffin-Wirth Associates, n.d.). Reviewed in: *Media and Methods* 28, no. 4 (Mar./Apr. 1992): 57

The Press and Presidency, filmstrip (Madison: Knowledge Unlimited, 1991). Reviewed in: *Media and Methods* 28, no. 4 (Mar./Apr. 1992): 48

Regions of the World: An Overview, filmstrip. Reviewed in: *Media and Methods* 28 no. 4 (Mar./Apr. 1992): 58

Soviet Union: Socialist City, video disc (Deerfield, IL: Coronet/MTI, 1990). Reviewed in: *Media and Methods* 28, no. 1 (Sept./Oct. 1991): 90

Tibet: Where Continents Collide Part 1, film (Cheshire, CT: EarthVision, 1989). Reviewed in: *Journal of Geographical Education* 38, no. 2 (Mar. 1990): 71

The United Nations: It's More than You Think, video (Charleston, WV: Cambridge Career Products, 1991). Reviewed in: *Media and Methods* 28, no. 4 (Mar./Apr. 1992): 57

Where Do You Think You're Going, Christopher Columbus?, by Jean Fritz, film/video (Weston, CT: Weston Woods, 1991). Reviewed in: *Media Methods* 28, no. 40 (Mar./Apr. 1992): 48

Franklin Watts (publishers)
Poverty in America: What Do We Do about It?, by Bertha Davis (New York: Franklin Watts, 1991). Reviewed in: *Curriculum Review* 31, no. 2 (Oct. 1991): 31

Fritz, Jean
Where Do You Think You're Going, Christopher Columbus?, by Jean Fritz, film/video (Weston, CT: Weston Woods, 1991). Reviewed in: *Media Methods* 28, no. 40 (Mar./Apr. 1992): 48

Galleons of Glory: The Secret Voyage of Magellan software (San Rafael, CA: Broderbund, 1990). Reviewed in: *Instructor* 101, no. 3 (Oct. 1991): 63

Geography
Bushbuck Charms, Viking Ships, & Dodo Eggs, software (Tempe, AZ: PC Globe, 1990). Reviewed in: *Technology & Learning* 12, no. 1 (Sept. 1991): 11

Earthalert, software (Seattle: Mike2, n.d.). Reviewed in: *Journal of Geography* 91, no. 1 (Jan./Feb. 1992): 47-48

Earthscope Series, film (Washington, DC: Global View Productions, 1991). Reviewed in: *Journal of Environmental Education* 22, no. 4 (Summer 1991): 41

Galleons of Glory: The Secret Voyage of Magellan, software (San Rafael, CA: Broderbund, 1990). Reviewed in: *Instructor* 101, no. 3 (Oct. 1991): 63

Geography: A Resource Book for Secondary Schools, by David A. Hill and Regina McCormic (Santa Barbara, CA: ABC-Clio, 1989). Reviewed in: *Journal of Geography* 89, no. 2 (Mar./Apr. 1990): 87

Geo-Safari, software (Dominguez Hills, CA: Educational Insights, n.d.). Reviewed in: *Journal of Geography* 91, no. 1 (Jan./Feb. 1992): 49

MacGlobe, software (Tempe, AZ: PC Globe, 1991). Reviewed in: *Journal of Geography* 91, no. 1 (Jan./Feb. 1992): 47

PCUSA, software (Tempe, AZ: PC Globe, 1990). Reviewed in: *Journal of Geographical Education* 38, no. 4 (Sept. 1990): 371

USA Geograph, software (St. Paul: MECC, 1989). Reviewed in: *Journal of Geography* 89, no. 4 (July/Aug. 1989): 184

Regions of the World: An Overview, filmstrip. Reviewed in: *Media and Methods* 28 no. 4 (Mar./Apr. 1992): 58

Geography *(cont'd)*
> *Tibet: Where Continents Collide Part 1,* film (Cheshire, CT: EarthVision, 1989). Reviewed in: *Journal of Geographical Education* 38, no. 2 (Mar. 1990): 71

Geography: A Resource Book for Secondary Schools
> by David A. Hill and Regina McCormic (Santa Barbara, CA: ABC-Clio, 1989). Reviewed in: *Journal of Geography* 89, no. 2 (Mar./Apr. 1990): 87

Geo-Safari
> software (Dominguez Hills, CA: Educational Insights, n.d.). Reviewed in: *Journal of Geography* 91, no. 1 (Jan./Feb. 1992): 49

Gilbert, Steve, ed.
> *Landmark Decisions of the United States Supreme Court,* ed. by Steve Gilbert and Maureen Harrison (Beverly Hills: Excellent Books, 1991). Reviewed in: *Curriculum Review* 30, no. 6 (Feb. 1991): 28

Global View Productions (publishers)
> *Earthscope Series,* film (Washington, DC: Global View Productions, 1991). Reviewed in: *Journal of Environmental Education* 22, no. 4 (Summer 1991): 41

Great Plains National (publishers)
> *Here and Now,* film/video (Lincoln: Great Plains National, 1991). Reviewed in: *Media Methods* 28, no. 4 (Mar./Apr. 1992): 48

Greenberg, Morrie
> *American Adventures: True Stories from America's Past,* by Morrie Greenberg (Northridge, CA: Brooke-Richards, 1991). Reviewed in: *Curriculum Review* 31, no. 1 (Sept. 1991): 31

Griffin-Wirth Associates
> *Lines in the Sand,* video/film (New York: Griffin-Wirth Associates, n.d.). Reviewed in: *Media and Methods* 28, no. 4 (Mar./Apr. 1992): 57

Harrison, Maureen, ed.
> *Landmark Decisions of the United States Supreme Court,* ed. by Steve Gilbert and Maureen Harrison (Beverly Hills: Excellent Books, 1991). Reviewed in: *Curriculum Review* 30, no. 6 (Feb. 1991): 28

Hartley Courseware
> *Discover the World,* software (Dimondale, MI: Hartley Courseware, 1986). Reviewed in: *Instructor* 101, no. 3 (Oct. 1991): 63

Haynes, Charles C.
> *Religion in American History: What to Teach and How,* by Charles C. Haynes (Alexandria, VA: Association for Supervision and Curriculum Development, 1990). Reviewed in: *Curriculum Review* 30, no. 5 (Jan. 1991): 33

Headline Harry and the Great Paper Race
> software (Torrance, CA: Davidson and Assoc., 1992). Reviewed in: *Technology & Learning* 12, no. 3 (Nov./Dec. 1991): 6, 8

Here and Now
> film/video (Lincoln: Great Plains National, 1991). Reviewed in: *Media Methods* 28, no. 4 (Mar./Apr. 1992): 48

High school materials
> *American Art and Architecture,* video (Boulder: Alarion, 1990). Reviewed in: *Curriculum Review* 30, no. 5 (Jan. 1991): 31

> *American Adventures: True Stories from America's Past,* by Morrie Greenberg (Northridge, CA: Brooke-Richards, 1991). Reviewed in: *Curriculum Review* 31, no. 1 (Sept. 1991): 31

> *Arab World Notebook: Secondary School Level,* by Ayad Al Qassar and Audrey Shabbas (Berkley: Najda, 1989). Reviewed in: *Social Education* 56, no 1 (Jan. 1992): 73

> *Bushbuck Charms, Viking Ships, & Dodo Eggs,* software (Tempe, AZ: PC Globe, 1990). Reviewed in: *Technology & Learning* 12, no. 1 (Sept. 1991): 11

> *Counterrevolution: US Foreign Policy,* by Edward Boorstein and Regula Boorstein (New York: International Publications, 1990). Reviewed in: *Social Education* 56, no. 2 (Feb. 1992): 133

> *Discover the World,* software (Dimondale, MI: Hartley Courseware, 1986). Reviewed in: *Instructor* 101, no. 3 (Oct. 1991): 63

High school materials *(cont'd)*

Earthalert, software (Seattle: Mike2, n.d.). Reviewed in: *Journal of Geography* 91, no. 1 (Jan./Feb. 1992): 47-48

Earthscope Series, film (Washington, DC: Global View Productions, 1991). Reviewed in: *Journal of Environmental Education* 22, no. 4 (Summer 1991): 41

Energy: The Key to Our Future, filmstrip (Niles, IL: United Learning, 1991). Reviewed in: *Media Methods* 28, no. 4 (Mar./Apr. 1992): 48-49

Galleons of Glory: The Secret Voyage of Magellan, software (San Rafael, CA: Broderbund, 1990). Reviewed in: *Instructor* 101, no. 3 (Oct. 1991): 63

Geo-Safari, software (Dominguez Hills, CA: Educational Insights, n.d.). Reviewed in: *Journal of Geography* 91, no. 1 (Jan./Feb. 1992): 49

Geography: A Resource Book for Secondary Schools, by David A. Hill and Regina McCormic (Santa Barbara, CA: ABC Clio, 1989). Reviewed in: *Journal of Geography* 89, no. 2 (Mar./Apr. 1990): 87

Headline Harry and the Great Paper Race, software (Torrance, CA: Davidson and Assoc., 1992). Reviewed in: *Technology & Learning* 12, no. 3 (Nov./Dec. 1991): 6, 8

Here and Now, film/video (Lincoln: Great Plains National, 1991). Reviewed in: *Media Methods* 28, no. 4 (Mar./Apr. 1992): 48

History in the Making, video/film (Evanston: Beacon Films, n.d.). Reviewed in: *Media and Methods* 28, no. 2 (Nov./Dec. 1991): 50

History's Trickiest Questions, by Paul Kuttner (New York: Dawnwood, 1990). Reviewed in: *Curriculum Review* 30, no. 7 (Mar. 1991): 31

Landmark Decisions of the United States Supreme Court, ed. by Steve Gilbert and Maureen Harrison (Beverly Hills: Excellent Books, 1991). Reviewed in: *Curriculum Review* 30, no. 6 (Feb. 1991): 28

Lines in the Sand, video/film (New York: Griffin-Wirth Associates, n.d.). Reviewed in: *Media and Methods* 28, no. 4 (Mar./Apr. 1992): 57

MacGlobe, software (Tempe, AZ: PC Globe, 1991). Reviewed in: *Journal of Geography* 91, no. 1 (Jan./Feb. 1992): 47

PCUSA, software (Tempe, AZ: PC Globe, 1990). Reviewed in: *Journal of Geographical Education* 38, no. 4 (Sept. 1990): 371

Poverty in America: What Do We Do about It?, by Bertha Davis (New York: Franklin Watts, 1991). Reviewed in: *Curriculum Review* 31, no. 2 (Oct. 1991): 31

The Press and Presidency, filmstrip (Madison: Knowledge Unlimited, 1991). Reviewed in: *Media and Methods* 28, no. 4 (Mar./Apr. 1992): 48

Regions of the World: An Overview, filmstrip. Reviewed in: *Media and Methods* 28 no. 4 (Mar./Apr. 1992): 58

Religion in American History: What to Teach and How, by Charles C. Haynes (Alexandria, VA: Association for Supervision and Curriculum Development, 1990). Reviewed in: *Curriculum Review* 30, no. 5 (Jan. 1991): 33

Renewing the Social Studies Curriculum, by Walter C. Parker (Alexandria, VA: Association for Supervision and Curriculum Development, 1991). Reviewed in: *Curriculum Review* 31, no. 7 (Mar. 1992): 30

Social Studies Readers Theater for Children: Scripts and Script Development, by Peggy Tubbs Black, Mildred Knight Laughlin, and Margery Kirby Loberg (Englewood, CO: Teacher Ideas, 1990). Reviewed in: *Curriculum Review* 31, no. 7 (Mar. 1992): 29

Soviet Union: Socialist City, video disc (Deerfield, IL: Coronet/MTI, 1990). Reviewed in: *Media and Methods* 28, no. 1 (Sept./Oct. 1991): 90

Tibet: Where Continents Collide Part 1, film (Cheshire, CT: EarthVision, 1989). Reviewed in: *Journal of Geographical Education* 38, no. 2 (Mar. 1990): 71

High school materials *(cont'd)*
   The United Nations: It's More than You Think,
   video (Charleston, WV: Cambridge Career
   Products, 1991). Reviewed in: *Media and
   Methods* 28, no. 4 (Mar./Apr. 1992): 57

   USA Geograph, software (St. Paul: MECC,
   1989). Reviewed in: *Journal of Geography* 89,
   no. 4 (July/Aug. 1989): 184

Hill, David A.
   *Geography: A Resource Book for Secondary
   Schools,* by David A. Hill and Regina
   McCormic (Santa Barbara, CA: ABC-Clio,
   1989). Reviewed in: *Journal of Geography* 89,
   no. 2 (Mar./Apr. 1990): 87

History in the Making
   video/film (Evanston: Beacon Films, n.d.).
   Reviewed in: *Media and Methods* 28, no. 2
   (Nov./Dec. 1991): 50

History's Trickiest Questions
   by Paul Kuttner (New York: Dawnwood, 1990).
   Reviewed in: *Curriculum Review* 30, no. 7 (Mar.
   1991): 31

Homeless
   Poverty in America: What Do We Do about It?,
   by Bertha Davis (New York: Franklin Watts,
   1991). Reviewed in: *Curriculum Review* 31, no.
   2 (Oct. 1991): 31

International affairs
   Counterrevolution: US Foreign Policy, by
   Edward Boorstein and Regula Boorstein (New
   York: International Publications, 1990).
   Reviewed in: *Social Education* 56, no. 2 (Feb.
   1992): 133

   The United Nations: It's More than You Think,
   video (Charleston, WV: Cambridge Career
   Products, 1991). Reviewed in: *Media and
   Methods* 28, no. 4 (Mar./Apr. 1992): 57

International Publishers
   Counterrevolution: US Foreign Policy, by
   Edward Boorstein and Regula Boorstein (New
   York: International Publishers, 1990). Re-
   viewed in: *Social Education* 56, no. 2 (Feb.
   1992): 133

International studies
   Discover the World, software (Dimondale, MI:
   Hartley Courseware, 1986). Reviewed in:
   Instructor 101, no. 3 (Oct.

   Nations of the World, software (Coral Gables,
   FL: Robert R. De Torres, 1986). Reviewed in:
   Journal of Geography 90, no. 4 (July/Aug. 1991):
   195

Journalism
   Headline Harry and the Great Paper Race,
   software (Torrance, CA: Davidson and Assoc.,
   1992). Reviewed in: *Technology & Learning* 12,
   no. 3 (Nov./Dec. 1991): 6, 8

   The Press and Presidency, filmstrip (Madison:
   Knowledge Unlimited, 1991). Reviewed in:
   Media and Methods 28, no. 4 (Mar./Apr. 1992):
   48

Knowledge Unlimited (publishers)
   The Press and Presidency, filmstrip (Madison:
   Knowledge Unlimited, 1991). Reviewed in:
   Media and Methods 28, no. 4 (Mar./Apr. 1992):
   48

Koning, Hans
   Columbus: His Enterprise--Exploding the Myth,
   by Hans Koning (New York: Monthly Review,
   1982). Reviewed in: *The Social Studies* 83, no. 1
   (Jan./Feb. 1992): 40

Kuttner, Paul
   History's Trickiest Questions, by Paul Kuttner
   (New York: Dawnwood, 1990). Reviewed in:
   Curriculum Review 30, no. 7 (Mar. 1991): 31

*Landmark Decisions of the United States Supreme
Court*
   ed. by Steve Gilbert and Maureen Harrison
   (Beverly Hills: Excellent Books, 1991). Reviewed in: *Curriculum Review* 30, no. 6 (Feb.
   1991): 28

Laughlin, Mildred Knight
   *Social Studies Readers Theater for Children:
   Scripts and Script Development,* by Peggy Tubbs
   Black, Mildred Knight Laughlin, and Margery
   Kirby Loberg (Englewood, CO: Teacher Ideas,
   1990). Reviewed in: *Curriculum Review* 31, no.
   7 (Mar. 1992): 29

Legal history
Landmark Decisions of the United States Supreme Court, ed. by Steve Gilbert and Maureen Harrison (Beverly Hills: Excellent Books, 1991). Reviewed in: *Curriculum Review* 30, no. 6 (Feb. 1991): 28

Lines in the Sand
video/film (New York: Griffin-Wirth Associates, n.d.). Reviewed in: *Media and Methods* 28, no. 4 (Mar./Apr. 1992): 57

Loberg, Margery Kirby
Social Studies Readers Theater for Children: Scripts and Script Development, by Peggy Tubbs Black, Mildred Knight Laughlin, and Margery Kirby Loberg (Englewood, CO: Teacher Ideas, 1990). Reviewed in: *Curriculum Review* 31, no. 7 (Mar. 1992): 29

Lothrop, Lee & Shepard (publishers)
The Discovery of the Americas, by Betsy Maestro and Giulio Maestro (New York: Lothrop, Lee & Shepard, 1991). Reviewed in: *Reading Horizons* 32, no. 1 (Oct. 1991): 79

MacGlobe
software (Tempe, AZ: PC Globe, 1991). Reviewed in: *Journal of Geography* 91, no. 1 (Jan./Feb. 1992): 47

Maestro, Betsy and Giulio
The Discovery of the Americas, by Betsy Maestro and Giulio Maestro (New York: Lothrop, Lee & Shepard, 1991). Reviewed in: *Reading Horizons* 32, no. 1 (Oct. 1991): 79

McCormic, Regina
Geography: A Resource Book for Secondary Schools, by David A. Hill and Regina McCormic (Santa Barbara, CA: ABC-Clio, 1989). Reviewed in: *Journal of Geography* 89, no. 2 (Mar./Apr. 1990): 87

Maps
Discover the World, software (Dimondale, MI: Hartley Courseware, 1986). Reviewed in: *Instructor* 101, no. 3 (Oct. 1991): 63

Geo-Safari, software (Dominguez Hills, CA: Educational Insights, n.d.). Reviewed in: *Journal of Geography* 91, no. 1 (Jan./Feb. 1992): 49

MacGlobe, software (Tempe, AZ: PC Globe, 1991). Reviewed in: *Journal of Geography* 91, no. 1 (Jan./Feb. 1992): 47

PCUSA, software (Tempe, AZ: PC Globe, 1990). Reviewed in: *Journal of Geographical Education* 38, no. 4 (Sept. 1990): 371

USA Geograph, software (St. Paul: MECC, 1989). Reviewed in: *Journal of Geography* 89, no. 4 (July/Aug. 1989): 184

MECC (publishers)
USA Geograph, software (St. Paul: MECC, 1989). Reviewed in: *Journal of Geography* 89, no. 4 (July/Aug. 1989): 184

Middle school materials
American Adventures: True Stories from America's Past, by Morrie Greenberg (Northridge, CA: Brooke-Richards, 1991). Reviewed in: *Curriculum Review* 31, no. 1 (Sept. 1991): 31

Columbus: His Enterprise--Exploding the Myth, by Hans Koning (New York: Monthly Review, 1982). Reviewed in: *The Social Studies* 83, no. 1 (Jan./Feb. 1992): 40

Discover the World, software (Dimondale, MI: Hartley Courseware, 1986). Reviewed in: *Instructor* 101, no. 3 (Oct. 1991): 63

Earthalert, software (Seattle: Mike2, n.d.). Reviewed in: *Journal of Geography* 91, no. 1 (Jan./Feb. 1992): 47-48

Earthscope Series, film (Washington, DC: Global View Productions, 1991). Reviewed in: *Journal of Environmental Education* 22, no. 4 (Summer 1991): 41

Energy: The Key to Our Future, filmstrip (Niles, IL: United Learning, 1991). Reviewed in: *Media Methods* 28, no. 4 (Mar./Apr. 1992): 48-49

Galleons of Glory: The Secret Voyage of Magellan, software (San Rafael, CA: Broderbund, 1990). Reviewed in: *Instructor* 101, no. 3 (Oct. 1991): 63

Middle school materials *(cont'd)*
  Geo-Safari, software (Dominguez Hills, CA: Educational Insights, n.d.). Reviewed in: *Journal of Geography* 91, no. 1 (Jan./Feb. 1992): 49

  Headline Harry and the Great Paper Race, software (Torrance, CA: Davidson and Assoc., 1992). Reviewed in: *Technology & Learning* 12, no. 3 (Nov./Dec. 1991): 6, 8

  Here and Now, film/video (Lincoln: Great Plains National, 1991). Reviewed in: *Media Methods* 28, no. 4 (Mar./Apr. 1992): 48

  History in the Making, video/film (Evanston: Beacon Films, n.d.). Reviewed in: *Media and Methods* 28, no. 2 (Nov./Dec. 1991): 50

  Nations of the World, software (Coral Gables, FL: Robert R. De Torres, 1986). Reviewed in: *Journal of Geography* 90, no. 4 (July/Aug. 1991): 195

  The Press and Presidency, filmstrip (Madison: Knowledge Unlimited, 1991). Reviewed in: *Media and Methods* 28, no. 4 (Mar./Apr. 1992): 48

  Regions of the World: An Overview, filmstrip. Reviewed in: *Media and Methods* 28 no. 4 (Mar./Apr. 1992): 58

  Renewing the Social Studies Curriculum, by Walter C. Parker (Alexandria, VA: Association for Supervision and Curriculum Development, 1991). Reviewed in: *Curriculum Review* 31, no. 7 (Mar. 1992): 30

  Social Studies Readers Theater for Children: Scripts and Script Development, by Peggy Tubbs Black, Mildred Knight Laughlin, and Margery Kirby Loberg (Englewood, CO: Teacher Ideas, 1990). Reviewed in: *Curriculum Review* 31, no. 7 (Mar. 1992): 29

  Turning Points in American History, by various authors (Englewood Cliffs, NJ: Silver Burdett). Reviewed in: *Curriculum Review* 31, no. 7 (Mar. 1992): 28-9

  The United Nations: It's More than You Think, video (Charleston, WV: Cambridge Career Products, 1991). Reviewed in: *Media and Methods* 28, no. 4 (Mar./Apr. 1992): 57

  USA Geograph, software (St. Paul: MECC, 1989). Reviewed in: *Journal of Geography* 89, no. 4 (July/Aug. 1989): 184

  Where Do You Think You're Going, Christopher Columbus?, by Jean Fritz, film/video (Weston, CT: Weston Woods, 1991). Reviewed in: *Media Methods* 28, no. 40 (Mar./Apr. 1992): 48

Mike2 (publishers)
  Earthalert, software (Seattle: Mike2, n.d.). Reviewed in: *Journal of Geography* 91, no. 1 (Jan./Feb. 1992): 47-48

Monthly Review (publishers)
  Columbus: His Enterprise--Exploding the Myth, by Hans Koning (New York: Monthly Review, 1982). Reviewed in: *The Social Studies* 83, no. 1 (Jan./Feb. 1992): 40

Multicultural education
  Arab World Notebook: Secondary School Level, by Ayad Al Qassar and Audrey Shabbas (Berkeley: Najda, 1989). Reviewed in: *Social Education* 56, no 1 (Jan. 1992): 73

  Nations of the World, software (Coral Gables, FL: Robert R. De Torres, 1986). Reviewed in: *Journal of Geography* 90, no. 4 (July/Aug. 1991): 195

  Regions of the World: An Overview, filmstrip. Reviewed in: *Media and Methods* 28 no. 4 (Mar./Apr. 1992): 58

Najda (publishers)
  Arab World Notebook: Secondary School Level, by Ayad Al Qassar and Audrey Shabbas (Berkeley: Najda, 1989). Reviewed in: *Social Education* 56, no 1 (Jan. 1992): 73

Nations of the World
  software (Coral Gables, FL: Robert R. De Torres, 1986). Reviewed in: *Journal of Geography* 90, no. 4 (July/Aug. 1991): 195

PCUSA
  software (Tempe, AZ: PC Globe, 1990). Reviewed in: *Journal of Geographical Education* 38, no. 4 (Sept. 1990): 371

Parker, Walter C.
Renewing the Social Studies Curriculum, by Walter C. Parker (Alexandria, VA: Association for Supervision and Curriculum Development, 1991). Reviewed in: *Curriculum Review* 31, no. 7 (Mar. 1992): 30

PC Globe (publishers)
Bushbuck Charms, Viking Ships, & Dodo Eggs, software (Tempe, AZ: PC Globe, 1990). Reviewed in: *Technology & Learning* 12, no. 1 (Sept. 1991): 11

MacGlobe, software (Tempe, AZ: PC Globe, 1991). Reviewed in: *Journal of Geography* 91, no. 1 (Jan./Feb. 1992): 47

PCUSA, software (Tempe, AZ: PC Globe, 1990). Reviewed in: *Journal of Geographical Education* 38, no. 4 (Sept. 1990): 371

Politics
The Press and Presidency, filmstrip (Madison: Knowledge Unlimited, 1991). Reviewed in: *Media and Methods* 28, no. 4 (Mar./Apr. 1992): 48

Poverty in America: What Do We Do about It? by Bertha Davis (New York: Franklin Watts, 1991). Reviewed in: *Curriculum Review* 31, no. 2 (Oct. 1991): 31

The Press and Presidency
filmstrip (Madison: Knowledge Unlimited, 1991). Reviewed in: *Media and Methods* 28, no. 4 (Mar./Apr. 1992): 48

Quincenntenial (Columbus)
Columbus: His Enterprise--Exploding the Myth, by Hans Koning (New York: Monthly Review, 1982). Reviewed in: *The Social Studies* 83, no. 1 (Jan./Feb. 1992): 40

The Discovery of the Americas, by Betsy Maestro and Giulio Maestro (New York: Lothrop, Lee & Shepard, 1991). Reviewed in: *Reading Horizons* 32, no. 1 (Oct. 1991): 79

Where Do You Think You're Going, Christopher Columbus?, by Jean Fritz, film/video (Weston, CT: Weston Woods, 1991). Reviewed in: *Media Methods* 28, no. 40 (Mar./Apr. 1992): 48

Reading skills
Social Studies Readers Theater for Children: Scripts and Script Development, by Peggy Tubbs Black, Mildred Knight Laughlin, and Margery Kirby Loberg (Englewood, CO: Teacher Ideas, 1990). Reviewed in: *Curriculum Review* 31, no. 7 (Mar. 1992): 29

Regions of the World: An Overview
filmstrip. Reviewed in: *Media and Methods* 28 no. 4 (Mar./Apr. 1992): 58

Religion in American History: What to Teach and How
by Charles C. Haynes (Alexandria, VA: Association for Supervision and Curriculum Development, 1990). Reviewed in: *Curriculum Review* 30, no. 5 (Jan. 1991): 33

Renewing the Social Studies Curriculum
by Walter C. Parker (Alexandria, VA: Association for Supervision and Curriculum Development, 1991). Reviewed in: *Curriculum Review* 31, no. 7 (Mar. 1992): 30

Robert R. De Torres (publishers)
Nations of the World, software (Coral Gables, FL: Robert R. De Torres, 1986). Reviewed in: *Journal of Geography* 90, no. 4 (July/Aug. 1991): 195

Russia
Soviet Union: Socialist City, video disc (Deerfield, IL: Coronet/MTI, 1990). Reviewed in: *Media and Methods* 28, no. 1 (Sept./Oct. 1991): 90

Shabbas, Audrey
Arab World Notebook: Secondary School Level, by Ayad Al Qassar and Audrey Shabbas (Berkeley: Najda, 1989). Reviewed in: *Social Education* 56, no 1 (Jan. 1992): 73

Silver Burdett (publishers)
Turning Points in American History, by various authors (Englewood Cliffs, NJ: Silver Burdett). Reviewed in: *Curriculum Review* 31, no. 7 (Mar. 1992): 28-9

Social action
Poverty in America: What Do We Do about It?, by Bertha Davis (New York: Franklin Watts, 1991). Reviewed in: *Curriculum Review* 31, no. 2 (Oct. 1991): 31

Social Studies Readers Theater for Children: Scripts and Script Development
by Peggy Tubbs Black, Mildred Knight Laughlin, and Margery Kirby Loberg (Englewood, CO: Teacher Ideas, 1990). Reviewed in: *Curriculum Review* 31, no. 7 (Mar. 1992): 29

Software packages
Bushbuck Charms, Viking Ships, & Dodo Eggs, software (Tempe, AZ: PC Globe, 1990). Reviewed in: *Technology & Learning* 12, no. 1 (Sept. 1991): 11

Discover the World, software (Dimondale, MI: Hartley Courseware, 1986). Reviewed in: *Instructor* 101, no. 3 (Oct. 1991): 63

Earthalert, software (Seattle: Mike2, n.d.). Reviewed in: *Journal of Geography* 91, no. 1 (Jan./Feb. 1992): 47-48

Galleons of Glory: The Secret Voyage of Magellan, software (San Rafael, CA: Broderbund, 1990). Reviewed in: *Instructor* 101, no. 3 (Oct. 1991): 63

Geo-Safari, software (Dominguez Hills, CA: Educational Insights, n.d.). Reviewed in: *Journal of Geography* 91, no. 1 (Jan./Feb. 1992): 49

Headline Harry and the Great Paper Race, software (Torrance, CA: Davidson and Assoc., 1992). Reviewed in: *Technology & Learning* 12, no. 3 (Nov./Dec. 1991): 6, 8

MacGlobe, software (Tempe, AZ: PC Globe, 1991). Reviewed in: *Journal of Geography* 91, no. 1 (Jan./Feb. 1992): 47

Nations of the World, software (Coral Gables, FL: Robert R. De Torres, 1986). Reviewed in: *Journal of Geography* 90, no. 4 (July/Aug. 1991): 195

PCUSA, software (Tempe, AZ: PC Globe, 1990). Reviewed in: *Journal of Geographical Education* 38, no. 4 (Sept. 1990): 371

USA Geograph, software (St. Paul: MECC, 1989). Reviewed in: *Journal of Geography* 89, no. 4 (July/Aug. 1989): 184

Soviet Union: Socialist City
video disc (Deerfield, IL: Coronet/MTI, 1990). Reviewed in: *Media and Methods* 28, no. 1 (Sept./Oct. 1991): 90

Supreme Court (U.S.)
Landmark Decisions of the United States Supreme Court, ed. by Steve Gilbert and Maureen Harrison (Beverly Hills: Excellent Books, 1991). Reviewed in: *Curriculum Review* 30, no. 6 (Feb. 1991): 28

Teacher Ideas Press
Social Studies Readers Theater for Children: Scripts and Script Development, by Peggy Tubbs Black, Mildred Knight Laughlin, and Margery Kirby Loberg (Englewood, CO: Teacher Ideas Press, 1990). Reviewed in: *Curriculum Review* 31, no. 7 (Mar. 1992): 29

Theater
Social Studies Readers Theater for Children: Scripts and Script Development, by Peggy Tubbs Black, Mildred Knight Laughlin, and Margery Kirby Loberg (Englewood, CO: Teacher Ideas, 1990). Reviewed in: *Curriculum Review* 31, no. 7 (Mar. 1992): 29

Tibet: Where Continents Collide Part 1
film (Cheshire, CT: EarthVision, 1989). Reviewed in: *Journal of Geographical Education* 38, no. 2 (Mar. 1990): 71

Turning Points in American History (series) by various authors (Englewood Cliffs, NJ: Silver Burdett). Reviewed in: *Curriculum Review* 31, no. 7 (Mar. 1992): 28-9

United Learning (publishers)
Energy: The Key to Our Future, filmstrip (Niles, IL: United Learning, 1991). Reviewed in: *Media Methods* 28, no. 4 (Mar./Apr. 1992): 48-49

The United Nations: It's More than You Think
video (Charleston, WV: Cambridge Career Products, 1991). Reviewed in: *Media and Methods* 28, no. 4 (Mar./Apr. 1992): 57

U.S. foreign policy
Counterrevolution: US Foreign Policy, by Edward Boorstein and Regula Boorstein (New York: International Publications, 1990). Reviewed in: *Social Education* 56, no. 2 (Feb. 1992): 133

U.S. Presidents
The Press and Presidency, filmstrip (Madison: Knowledge Unlimited, 1991). Reviewed in: *Media and Methods* 28, no. 4 (Mar./Apr. 1992): 48

USA Geograph
software (St. Paul: MECC, 1989). Reviewed in: *Journal of Geography* 89, no. 4 (July/Aug. 1989): 184

Videos. *See* Films/videos

Weston Woods (publishers)
Where Do You Think You're Going, Christopher Columbus?, by Jean Fritz, film/video (Weston, CT: Weston Woods, 1991). Reviewed in: *Media Methods* 28, no. 40 (Mar./Apr. 1992): 48

Where Do You Think You're Going, Christopher Columbus?
by Jean Fritz, film/video (Weston, CT: Weston Woods, 1991). Reviewed in: *Media Methods* 28, no. 40 (Mar./Apr. 1992): 48

World cultures
Regions of the World: An Overview, filmstrip. Reviewed in: *Media and Methods* 28 no. 4 (Mar./Apr. 1992): 58

World history
History's Trickiest Questions, by Paul Kuttner (New York: Dawnwood, 1990). Reviewed in: *Curriculum Review* 30, no. 7 (Mar. 1991): 31

Nations of the World, software (Coral Gables, FL: Robert R. De Torres, 1986). Reviewed in: *Journal of Geography* 90, no. 4 (July/Aug. 1991): 195

Soviet Union: Socialist City, video disc (Deerfield, IL: Coronet/MTI, 1990). Reviewed in: *Media and Methods* 28, no. 1 (Sept./Oct. 1991): 90

KRAUS CURRICULUM
DEVELOPMENT LIBRARY CUSTOMERS

T HE following list shows the current subscribers to the Kraus Curriculum Development Library (KCDL), Kraus's annual program of curriculum guides on microfiche. Customers marked with an asterisk (*) do not currently have standing orders to KCDL, but do have recent editions of the program. This information is provided for readers who want to use KCDL for models of curriculum in particular subject areas or grade levels.

Alabama

Auburn University
Ralph Brown Draughton Library/Serials
Mell Street
Auburn University, AL 36849

Jacksonville State University
Houston Cole Library/Serials
Jacksonville, AL 36265

University of Alabama at Birmingham
Mervyn H. Sterne Library
University Station
Birmingham, AL 35294

*University of Alabama at Tuscaloosa
University Libraries
204 Capstone Drive
Tuscaloosa, AL 35487-0266

Alaska

*University of Alaska--Anchorage
Library
3211 Providence Drive
Anchorage, AK 99508

Arizona

Arizona State University, Phoenix
Fletcher Library/Journals
West Campus
4701 West Thunderbird Road
Phoenix, AZ 85069-7100

Arizona State University, Tempe
Library/Serials
Tempe, AZ 85287-0106

Northern Arizona University
University Library
Flagstaff, AZ 86011

University of Arizona
Library/Serials
Tucson, AZ 85721

Arkansas

Arkansas State University
Dean B. Ellis Library
State University, AR 72467

Southern Arkansas University
The Curriculum Center
SAU Box 1389
Magnolia, AR 71753

University of Central Arkansas
The Center for Teaching & Human Development
Box H, Room 104
Conway, AR 72032

California

California Polytechnic State University
Library/Serials
San Luis Obispo, CA 93407

California State Polytechnic University
Library/Serials
3801 West Temple Avenue
Pomona, CA 91768

California State University at Chico
Meriam Library
Chico, CA 95929-0295

*California State University, Dominguez Hills
Library
800 East Victoria Street
Carson, CA 90747

California State University at Fresno
Henry Madden Library/Curriculum Department
Fresno, CA 93740

California State University at Fresno/College of
the Sequoia Center
5241 North Maple, Mail Stop 106
Fresno, CA 93740

California State University at Fullerton
Library Serials BIC
Fullerton, CA 92634

*California State University at Long Beach
Library/Serials Department
1250 Bellflower Boulevard
Long Beach, CA 90840

*California State University at Sacramento
Library
2000 Jed Smith Drive
Sacramento, CA 95819

California State University, Stanislaus
Library
801 West Monte Vista Avenue
Turlock, CA 95380

*La Sierra University
Library
Riverside, CA 92515

Los Angeles County Education Center
Professional Reference Center
9300 East Imperial Highway
Downey, CA 90242

National University Library
4007 Camino del Rio South
San Diego, CA 92108

San Diego County Office of Education
Research and Reference Center
6401 Linda Vista Road
San Diego, CA 92111-7399

San Diego State University
Library/Serials
San Diego, CA 92182-0511

*San Francisco State University
J. Paul Leonard Library
1630 Holloway Avenue
San Francisco, CA 94132

San Jose State University
Clark Library, Media Department
San Jose, CA 95192-0028

*University of California at Santa Cruz
Library
Santa Cruz, CA 95064

Colorado

Adams State College
Library
Alamosa, CO 81102

University of Northern Colorado
Michener Library
Greeley, CO 80639

Connecticut

*Central Connecticut State University
Burritt Library
1615 Stanley Street
New Britain, CT 06050

District of Columbia

*United States Department of Education/OERI
Room 101
555 New Jersey Avenue, N.W., C.P.
Washington, DC 20202-5731

*University of the District of Columbia
Learning Resource Center
11100 Harvard Street, N.W.
Washington, DC 20009

Florida

*Florida Atlantic University
Library/Serials
Boca Raton, FL 33431-0992

Florida International University
Library/Serials
Bay Vista Campus
North Miami, FL 33181

Florida International University
Library/Serials
University Park
Miami, FL 33199

Marion County School Board
Professional Library
406 S.E. Alvarez Avenue
Ocala, FL 32671-2285

*University of Central Florida
Library
Orlando, FL 32816-0666

University of Florida
Smathers Library/Serials
Gainesville, FL 32611-2047

*University of North Florida
Library
4567 St. John's Bluff Road South
Jacksonville, FL 32216

*University of South Florida
Library/University Media Center
4202 Fowler Avenue
Tampa, FL 33620

University of West Florida
John C. Pace Library/Serials
11000 University Parkway
Pensacola, FL 32514

Georgia

*Albany State College
Margaret Rood Hazard Library
Albany, GA 31705

Atlanta University Center in Georgia
Robert W. Woodruff Library
111 James P. Brawley Drive
Atlanta, GA 30314

*Columbus College
Library
Algonquin Drive
Columbus, GA 31993

Kennesaw College
TRAC
3455 Frey Drive
Kennesaw, GA 30144

University of Georgia
Main Library
Athens, GA 30602

Guam

*University of Guam
Curriculum Resources Center
College of Education
UOG Station
Mangilao, GU 96923

Idaho

*Boise State University
Curriculum Resource Center
1910 University Drive
Boise, ID 83725

Illinois

Community Consolidated School District 15
Educational Service Center
505 South Quentin Road
Palatine, IL 60067

Illinois State University
Milner Library/Periodicals
Normal, IL 61761

Loyola University
Instructional Materials Library
Lewis Towers Library
820 North Michigan Avenue
Chicago, Illinois 60611

National-Louis University
Library/Technical Services
2840 North Sheridan Road
Evanston, IL 60201

Northeastern Illinois University
Library/Serials
5500 North St. Louis Avenue
Chicago, IL 60625

*Northern Illinois University
Founders Memorial Library
DeKalb, IL 60115

Southern Illinois University
Lovejoy Library/Periodicals
Edwardsville, IL 62026

*University of Illinois at Chicago
Library/Serials
Box 8198
Chicago, IL 60680

University of Illinois at Urbana-Champaign
246 Library
1408 West Gregory Drive
Urbana, IL 61801

Indiana

Indiana State University
Cunningham Memorial Library
Terre Haute, IN 47809

Indiana University
Library/Serials
Bloomington, IN 47405-1801

Kentucky

Cumberland College
Instructional Media Library
Williamsburg, KY 40769

*Jefferson County Public Schools
The Greens Professional Development Academy
4425 Preston Highway
Louisville, KY 40213

Maine

University of Maine
Raymond H. Fogler Library/Serials
Orono, ME 04469

Maryland

*Bowie State University
Library
Jericho Park Road
Bowie, MD 20715

Western Maryland College
Hoover Library
2 College Hill
Westminster, MD 21157

Massachusetts

*Barnstable Public Schools
230 South Street
Hyannis, MA 02601

Boston College
Educational Resource Center
Campion Hall G13
Chestnut Hill, MA 02167

Framingham State College
Curriculum Library
Henry Whittemore Library
Box 2000
Framingham, MA 01701

Harvard University
School of Education
Monroe C. Gutman Library
6 Appian Way
Cambridge, MA 02138

*Lesley College
Library
30 Mellen Street
Cambridge, MA 02138

*Salem State College
Professional Studies Resource Center
Library
Lafayette Street
Salem, MA 01970

Tufts University
Wessell Library
Medford, MA 02155-5816

*University of Lowell
O'Leary Library
Wilder Street
Lowell, MA 01854

*Worcester State College
Learning Resource Center
486 Chandler Street
Worcester, MA 01602

Michigan

*Grand Valley State University
Library
Allendale, MI 49401

*Wayne County Regional Educational Services
Agency
Technical Services
5454 Venoy
Wayne, MI 48184

Wayne State University
Purdy Library
Detroit, MI 48202

*Western Michigan University
Dwight B. Waldo Library
Kalamazoo, MI 49008

Minnesota

Mankato State University
Memorial Library
Educational Resource Center
Mankato, MN 56002-8400

Moorhead State University
Library
Moorhead, MN 56563

University of Minnesota
170 Wilson Library/Serials
309 19th Avenue South
Minneapolis, MN 55455

Winona State University
Maxwell Library/Curriculum Laboratory
Sanborn and Johnson Streets
Winona, MN 55987

Mississippi

Mississippi State University
Mitchell Memorial Library
Mississippi State, MS 39762

University of Southern Mississippi
Cook Memorial Library/Serials
Box 5053
Hattiesburg, MS 39406-5053

Missouri

Central Missouri State University
Ward Edwards Library
Warrensburg, MO 64093-5020

Missouri Southern State College
George A. Spiva Library
3950 Newman Road
Joplin, MO 64801-1595

Northeast Missouri State University
Pickler Library/Serials
Kirksville, MO 63501

Southwest Baptist University
ESTEP Library
Bolivar, MO 65613-2496

Southwest Missouri State University
#175 Library
Springfield, MO 65804-0095

*University of Missouri at Kansas City
Instructional Materials Center
School of Education
5100 Rockhill Road
Kansas City, MO 64110-2499

University of Missouri at St. Louis
Library
St. Louis, MO 63121

Webster University
Library
470 East Lockwood Avenue
St. Louis, MO 63119-3194

Nebraska

Chadron State College
Library
10th and Main Streets
Chadron, NE 69337

University of Nebraska
University Libraries
Lincoln, NE 68588

University of Nebraska at Kearney
Calvin T. Ryan Library/Serials
Kearney, NE 68849-0700

University of Nebraska at Omaha
Education Technology Center/Instructional
   Material
Kayser Hall, Room 522
Omaha, NE 68182-0169

Nevada

*University of Nevada, Las Vegas
Materials Center--101 Education
Las Vegas, NV 89154

*University of Nevada, Reno
Library (322)
Reno, NV 89557-0044

New Hampshire

Plymouth State College
Herbert H. Lamson Library
Plymouth, NH 03264

New Jersey

Caldwell College
Library
9 Ryerson Avenue
Caldwell, NJ 07006

Georgian Court College
Farley Memorial Library
Lakewood, NJ 08701

Jersey City State College
Forrest A. Irwin Library
2039 Kennedy Boulevard
Jersey City, NJ 07305

*Kean College of New Jersey
Library
Union, NJ 07083

Paterson Board of Education
Media Center
823 East 28th Street
Paterson, NJ 07513

*Rutgers University
Alexander Library/Serials
New Brunswick, NJ 08903

St. Peter's College
George F. Johnson Library
Kennedy Boulevard
Jersey City, NJ 07306

Trenton State College
West Library
Pennington Road CN4700
Trenton, NJ 08650-4700

William Paterson College
Library
300 Pompton Road
Wayne, NJ 07470

New Mexico

University of New Mexico
General Library/Serials
Albuquerque, NM 87131

New York

*BOCES-REPIC
Carle Place Center Concourse
234 Glen Cove Road
Carle Place, NY 11514

*Canisius College
Curriculum Materials Center
Library
2001 Main Street
Buffalo, NY 14208

Fordham University
Duane Library
Bronx, NY 10458

Hofstra University
Library
1000 Hempstead Turnpike
Hempstead, NY 11550

*Hunter College
Library
695 Park Avenue
New York, NY 10021

*Lehman College
Library/Serials
Bedford Park Boulevard West
Bronx, NY 10468

*New York University
Bobst Library
70 Washington Square South
New York, NY 10012

*Niagara University
Library/Serials
Niagara, NY 14109

Queens College
Benjamin Rosenthal Library
Flushing, NY 11367

St. John's University
Library
Grand Central and Utopia Parkways
Jamaica, NY 11439

State University of New York at Albany
University Library/Serials
1400 Washington Avenue
Albany, NY 12222

State University of New York, College at Buffalo
E. H. Butler Library
1300 Elmwood Avenue
Buffalo, NY 14222

State University of New York, College at
Cortland
Teaching Materials Center
Cortland, NY 13045

State University of New York, College at
Oneonta
James M. Milne Library
Oneonta, NY 13820

Teachers College of Columbia University
Milbank Memorial Library/Serials
525 West 120th Street
New York, NY 10027

North Carolina

*Appalachian State University
Instructional Materials Center
Belk Library
Boone, NC 28608

Charlotte-Mecklenburg Schools
Curriculum Resource Center
Staff Development Center
428 West Boulevard
Charlotte, NC 28203

*East Carolina University
Joyner Library
Greenville, NC 27858-4353

North Carolina A&T State University
F. D. Bluford Library
Greeensboro, NC 27411

North Carolina State University
D. H. Hill Library
Box 7111
Raleigh, NC 27695-7111

University of North Carolina at Chapel Hill
Davis Library/Serials
Campus Box 3938
Chapel Hill, NC 27599-3938

University of North Carolina at Charlotte
Atkins Library
UNCC Station
Charlotte, NC 28223

University of North Carolina at Wilmington
William M. Randall Library
601 South College Road
Wilmington, NC 28403-3297

Ohio

Bowling Green State University
Curriculum Center
Jerome Library
Bowling Green, OH 43403-0177

Miami University
Library
Oxford, OH 45056

*Ohio State University
2009 Millikin Road
Columbus, OH 43210

University of Akron
Bierce Library/Serials
Akron, OH 44325

*University of Rio Grande
Davis Library
Rio Grande, OH 45674

*Wright State University
Educational Resource Center
Dayton, OH 45435

Oklahoma

Southwestern Oklahoma State University
Al Harris Library
809 North Custer Street
Weatherford, OK 73096

*University of Tulsa
McFarlin Library
600 South College
Tulsa, OK 74104

Oregon

Oregon State University
Kerr Library/Serials
Corvallis, OR 97331-4503

Portland State University
Library/Serials
Portland, OR 97207

University of Oregon
Knight Library/Serials
Eugene, OR 97403

Pennsylvania

*Bucks County Intermediate Unit #22
705 Shady Retreat Road
Doylestown, PA 18901

*Cheyney University
Library
Cheyney, PA 19319

East Stroudsburg University of Pennsylvania
Library
East Stroudsburg, PA 18301

Holy Family College
Grant and Frankford Avenues
Philadelphia, PA 19114

*Indiana University of Pennsylvania
Media Resource Department
Stapleton Library
Indiana, PA 15705

Kutztown University
Curriculum Materials Center
Rohrbach Library
Kutztown, PA 19530

La Salle College
Instructional Materials Center
The Connelly Library
Olney Avenue at 20th Street
Philadelphia, PA 19141

Lock Haven University of Pennsylvania
Library
Lock Haven, PA 17745

*Millersville University
Ganser Library
Millersville, PA 17551-0302

*Pennsylvania State University
Pattee Library/Serials
University Park, PA 16802

*Shippensburg University of Pennsylvania
Ezra Lehman Library
Shippensburg, PA 17257-2299

*Slippery Rock University
Bailey Library
Instructional Materials Center
Slippery Rock, PA 16057

University of Pittsburgh
Hillman Library/Serials
Pittsburgh, PA 15260

West Chester University
Francis H. Green Library
West Chester, PA 19383

Rhode Island

Rhode Island College
Curriculum Resources Center
600 Mt. Pleasant Avenue
Providence, RI 02908

South Dakota

Northern State University
Williams Library
Aberdeen, SD 57401

University of South Dakota
I. D. Weeks Library
414 East Clark
Vermillion, SD 57069

Tennessee

Tennessee Technological University
Library
Cookeville, TN 38505

Trevecca Nazarene College
Curriculum Library
Mackey Library
333 Murfreesboro Road
Nashville, TN 37210-2877

*University of Tennessee at Chattanooga
Library/Serials
Chattanooga, TN 37403

*University of Tennessee at Martin
Instructional Improvement
Gooch Hall--Room 217
Martin, TN 38238

*Vanderbilt University
Curriculum Laboratory
Peabody Library
Peabody Campus, Magnolia Circle
Nashville, TN 37203-5601

Texas

Baylor University
School of Education
Waco, TX 76798-7314

East Texas State University
Curriculum Library
Commerce, TX 75429

*East Texas State University
Library
Texarkana, TX 75501

*Houston Baptist University
Moody Library
7502 Fondren Road
Houston, TX 77074

*Incarnate Word College
Library
4301 Broadway
San Antonio, TX 78209

*Southern Methodist University
Fondren Library
Dallas, TX 75275-0135

Stephen F. Austin State University
Library/Serials
Box 13055 SFA Station
Nacogdoches, TX 75962

Texas A&M University
Library/Serials
College Station, TX 77843-5000

*Texas Tech University
Library
Lubbock, TX 79409

Texas Woman's University
Library
Box 23715 TWU Station
Denton, TX 76204

University of Houston--University Park
University of Houston Library
Central Serial
4800 Calhoun
Houston, TX 77004

University of North Texas
Library
Denton, TX 76203

University of Texas at Austin
General Libraries/Serials
Austin, TX 78713-7330

University of Texas at El Paso
Library
El Paso, TX 79968-0582

Utah

Utah State University
Educational Resources Center
College of Education
Logan, UT 84322-2845

Vermont

University of Vermont
Guy W. Bailey Library/Serials
Burlington, VT 05405

Virginia

Longwood College
Dabney Lancaster Library
Farmville, VA 23909-1897

*Regent University
Library
Virginia Beach, VA 23464-9877

University of Virginia
Alderman Library
Serials/Periodicals
Charlottesville, VA 22901

Washington

Central Washington University
Library/Serials
Ellensburg, WA 98926

University of Puget Sound
Collins Library
Tacoma, WA 98416

University of Washington
Library/Serials
Seattle, WA 98195

Washington State University
Library
Pullman, WA 99164-5610

Western Washington University
Wilson Library
Bellingham, WA 98225

Wisconsin

University of Wisconsin--Eau Claire
Instructional Media Center
Eau Claire, WI 54702-4004

University of Wisconsin--Madison
Instructional Materials Center
225 North Mills
Madison, WI 53706

University of Wisconsin--Oshkosh
F. R. Polk Library
Oshkosh, WI 54901

University of Wisconsin--Platteville
Library
One University Plaza
Platteville, WI 53818-3099

University of Wisconsin--Whitewater
Learning Resources
Whitewater, WI 53190

Wyoming

*University of Wyoming
Coe Library
15th and Lewis
Laramie, WY 82071

AUSTRALIA

Griffith University
Library
Mount Gravatt Campus
Nathan, Queensland 4111

CANADA

*The Ontario Institute for Studies in Education
Library
252 Bloor Street West
Toronto, Ontario M5S 1V6

*University of New Brunswick
Harriet Irving Library/Serials
Fredericton, New Brunswick E3B 5H5

University of Regina
Library/Serials
Regina, Saskatchewan S4S 0A2

University of Saskatchewan
Library
Saskatoon, Saskatchewan S7N 0W0

University of Windsor
Leddy Library/Serials
Windsor, Ontario N9B 3P4

*Vancouver School Board
Teachers' Professional Library
123 East 6th Avenue
Vancouver, British Columbia V5T 1J6

HONG KONG

*The Chinese University of Hong Kong
University Library
Shatin, N.T.

THE NETHERLANDS

National Institute for Curriculum Development
(Stichting voor de Leerplanontwikkeling)
7500 CA Enschede

INDEX